SMITHSONIAN INSTITUTION
BUREAU OF AMERICAN ETHNOLOGY
BULLETIN 78

HANDBOOK

OF THE

INDIANS OF CALIFORNIA

BY

A. L. KROEBER

VOLUME II

WASHINGTON
GOVERNMENT PRINTING OFFICE
1925

Reprinted 1972
Scholarly Press, Inc., 22929 Industrial Drive East
St. Clair Shores, Michigan 48080

Library of Congress Catalog Card Number: 75-108501
ISBN 0-403-00369-5

CHAPTER 35.

THE YOKUTS: THE CONCRETE BASIS OF LIFE.

DRESS AND BODILY HABITS.

Clothing sufficed only for the very limits of decency, as we see them. Men wrapped a deerskin, *sep*, around the loins, or went naked. Old men in particular were wont to go without even this covering. Boys and little girls also were nude; but from the time of puberty on women wore a two-piece fringed skirt of the usual Californian type, the hind part larger. With the Yaudanchi, both portions were made of willow bark, as among the Mohave. The Chukchansi made the back piece of buckskin, the front of pounded masses of a long grass called *chulochul*. The well-known rabbit-fur blanket protected against cold and rain on occasion, and was excellent to sleep in. Moccasins of deer and elk skin were worn only as there was special need. Rude sandals of bear fur have been reported as worn in winter.

Women's hair was worn long, but for men the custom was more variable. Both sexes were wont to gather it under a string when at work. In mourning, men burned their hair off to the neck, women, for a near relative, close to the head. A glowing stick was used, and the Chukchansi controlled the singeing with a natural comb of *tumu*, which has close-set parallel branches.

Women, but not men, had their nose septum pierced for ornaments of bone.

Tattooing was more practiced in the north than in the south, and more extensively by women than by men. It ran in lines, zigzags, and rows of dots, chiefly down the chin and across from the corners of the mouth; the Mono style of marking the upper cheeks was not followed. The general type of women's face pattern tolerated infinite individual variety, as in the Yuki region; the Yurok and their neighbors clung strictly to a tribal style. Chukchansi women might be tattooed across breast, abdomen, arms, and legs also. The method followed was to rub charcoal dust into cuts made with flint or obsidian. Chukchansi face patterns are shown in Figures 45 *h–l*, 46 *m–o*.

Men frequently squatted rather than sat. For longer periods they sat on their heels, with toes turned together and hands on knees. The cross-legged position, the most common of all the world over, was not used, except perhaps on special occasions like gambling. Women stretched one leg out and folded the other back; or, at rest,

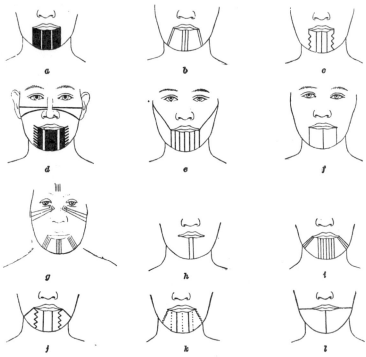

FIG. 45.—Women's tattoo. *a*, Yurok and northwestern tribes; *b, c*, San Francisco, probably Costanoan; *d*, Sinkyone; *e*, northwestern valley Maidu; *f*, northeastern and southern Maidu; *g*, Yuki; *h–l*, Chukchansi Yokuts. Compare the Wailaki, Yuki, Huchnom, and northern Pomo tattoos shown in Powers, Tribes of California, pages 116, 130, 140, 142, 144, 158.

drew the knees up and joined the hands in front of them. The Plains Indian woman's attitude, with both legs to one side, was not adopted. The habits of all the California Indians in these interesting matters are little known, but it is clear that custom and not inherited nature is the chief determinant. As at so many other points, nature seems at once to have furnished us a structure that permits a surprising variety of sustained positions, and to have deprived us of instincts favoring one rather than the other; so that culture has a clear opportunity to evolve the most diverse habits.

HOUSES.

The Yokuts built at least five kinds of dwellings.

1. Most distinctive was the mat-covered, gabled, communal *kawi* of the Tulamni, Hometwoli, Wowol, Chunut, and perhaps Tachi. The roof pitch was steep. Probably each family constructed its own portion, with door to front and back, closed at night with tule mats. Each household had its own space and fireplace, but there were no partitions, and one could look through from end to end.

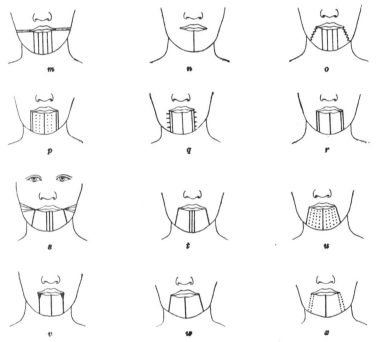

FIG. 46.—Women's and men's tattoo. Women: *m–o*, Chukchansi Yokuts; *p–u*, Mohave. Men: *v–x*, Mohave.

These houses sometimes ran to a size where they accommodated a little more than 10 families. A shade porch extended along the front. The tule stalks were sewn together with an eyed bone needle and string of tule fiber.

2. The Yauelmani and their neighbors of the southern plains off the lake approached this long structure in aligning their wedge-shaped tule houses or *dumlus*. but kept each contiguous family domicile separate.

3. The middle plains tribes, such as the Wechihit and Tachi, to-day build small tule houses of another type, elliptical or oblong

with rounded but vertical ends. There may be a ridgepole on two posts, with perhaps five poles planted along each side and bent over to the ridgepole. In this case the door is on one side of the front post. Or the ridgepole may be dispensed with and the poles bent all the way over or lashed together. The total length is only a dozen feet or so. The covering is of loose tule mats, each stalk wrapped to the next by a hitch in a single strand of string. Floor mats and bedding are sewn through. The Wechihit use a covering of tall *mohya* stems, reaching from the ground to the ridge, and held in place outside by several horizontal poles lashed to the framework. This type of house was called *te* or *chi*.

4. The Yaudanchi, though a hill tribe, built their principal winter houses or *te* of tule, of which a species called *shuyo* grows along streams to the very limit of the plains. This was a conical dwelling, and its most distinctive feature was a hoop at top to attach and at the same time separate the leaning poles of the framework, and leave a smoke hole. The tule mat covering was sewn as by the lake tribes. The houses were placed in rows.

A larger, ridged house, with two fireplaces and a door at each end, was also built by the Yaudanchi. In this a valley influence can scarcely be questioned.

When camping well up in the hills in summer, or traveling, the Yokuts built small structures, apparently conical, covered with brush or bark.

Among the northern hill tribes, such as the Chukchansi and Gashowu, the house is also conical with a ring at the top, but usually thatched. The floor is lowered perhaps a foot with the digging stick. The door faces south, the diameter is 12 to 15 feet, the height not quite as much. Allowing for the lack of tule, this is the same house as that of the Yaudanchi, but it is called *ho*, literally " live," " sit."

5. A bark house of similar type is called *samish*. Sometimes bark is first leaned against the framework as a partial covering, then brush thatch added, and the whole held fast by bands of pliable poles or withes tied around.

It is interesting that there is no reference anywhere to tule thatching. The thickness of this rush may make its sewing or binding into mats more practicable than bundling it into thatch. The Serrano and other southern Californians also built tule mat houses, but the Pomo employed tule thatch.

The *ch'iniu* or shade, a flat roof on posts, was used by all the Yokuts. It must have been almost indispensable in the intensely hot summers of the plains.

The sweat house, *mosh* or *mos*, is a true sudatory, oblong, dug down several feet, with a ridge log resting on two posts at the ends, and dirt covered. It was small, not over 15 feet in length, and in no sense a dance house or assembly chamber. Women never entered it. It was the regular sleeping place of the older men during the winter when they were at the home village. The door faced the creek, or south, and was sometimes sheltered by parallel windbreaks. Often on retiring, the inmates sang and sweated, perhaps in competition along the two sides, the fire being added to to make the opposite row cry out first that they had enough. Then came a plunge into the stream, and a return to dry and sleep. In the morning they ran shouting to the water again.

There is no house for dances and rituals. The rattlesnake "stepping," the mourning ceremony, and perhaps other rites were held in large roofless inclosures of brush, a sort of fence. This is the southern California form of ceremonial structure. North of the Yokuts it reaches to the Maidu as an adjunct of the mourning ceremony.

THE FOOD PROBLEM IN CALIFORNIA.

The California Indians are perhaps the most omnivorous group of tribes on the continent. The corn, salmon, buffalo, reindeer, or seal which formed the predominant staple in other regions, did indeed have a parallel in the acorn of California; but the parallel is striking rather than intrinsic.

To begin with, the oak is absent from many tracts. It does not grow in the higher mountains, in the desert, on most of the immediate coast; and it is at best rare in districts like the baked plains inhabited by the southern Yokuts valley tribes, a fact that may help to explain the permanent association and commingling of the majority of these tribes with their foothill neighbors. It is true that at worst it is rarely a far journey to an abundant growth of bearing acorns anywhere in California; but the availability of such supplies was greatly diminished by the habits of intense adherence to their limited soil followed by the great majority of divisions.

Then, where the acorn abounded, the practices both of collecting and of treating it led directly to the utilization also of other sources of nourishment. The farmer may and does hunt, or fish, or gather wild growths; but these activities, being of a different order, are a distraction from his regular pursuits, and an adjustment is necessary. Either the pursuit of wild foods becomes a subsidiary activity, indulged in intermittently as leisure affords, and from the motive of variety rather than need, or a sexual or seasonal division becomes established, which makes the same people in part, or for part of the year, farmers and in part hunters. An inclination of this sort is not wanting in many districts of California. The dry and hot summer makes an outdoor life in the hills, near the heads of the vanishing streams, a convenience and a pleasure which coincide almost exactly with the opportunity to hunt and to gather the various natural crops as they become available from month to month. The wet winter renders house life in the permanent settlement in a valley or on a river correspondingly attractive, and combines residence there with the easiest chance to fish the now enlarged streams on an extensive scale, or to pursue the swarms of arrived water fowl.

But this division was not momentous. The distances ranged over were minute. Fishing was not excluded among the hills. Deer, rabbits, and gophers could be hunted in the mild winter as well as in summer. And while acorns and other plant foods might be garnered each only over a brief season, it was an essential part of their use that much of their preparation as well as consumption should be spread through the cycle of the calendar.

Further, the food resources of California were bountiful in their variety rather than in their overwhelming abundance along special lines. If one supply failed, there were a hundred others to fall back upon. If a drought withered the corn shoots, if the buffalo unaccountably shifted, or the salmon failed to run, the very existence of peoples in other regions was shaken to its foundations. But the manifold distribution of available foods in California and the working out of corresponding means of reclaiming them prevented a failure of the acorn crop from producing similar effects. It might produce short rations and racking hunger, but scarcely starvation. It may be that it is chiefly our astounding ignorance of all the more intimate and basal phases of their lives that makes it seem as if downright mortal famine had been less often the portion of the Californian tribes than of those in most other regions of the continent. Yet, with all allowance for this potential factor of ignorance in our understanding, it does appear that such catastrophes were less deep and less regularly recurring. Both formulated and experiential tradition are nearly silent on actual famines, or refer to them with rationalizing abstraction. The only definite cases that have come to cognizance, other than for a few truly desert hordes whose slender subsistence permanently hung by a thread, are among the Mohave, an agricultural community in an oasis, and among the Indians of the lower Klamath, whose habits, in their primal dependence on the salmon, approximated those of the tribes of the coasts north of California.

The gathering of the acorn is like that of the pine nut; its leaching has led to the recognition of the serviceability of the buckeye once its poison is dissolved out; the grinding has stimulated the use of small hard seeds, which become edible only in pulverized form. The securing of plant foods in general is not separated by any gap of distinctive process from that of obtaining grasshoppers, caterpillars, maggots, snails, mollusks, crawfish, or turtles, which can be got in masses or are practically immobile: a woman's digging stick will procure worms as readily as bulbs. Again, it is only a step to the taking of minnows in brooks, of gophers, or lizards, or small birds: the simplest of snares, a long stick, a thrown stone even, suffice with patience, and a boy can help out his grandmother. The fish pot is not very different from the acorn receptacle, and weirs, traps, stiff nets, and other devices for capturing fish are made in the same technique of basketry as the beaters, carriers, and winnowers for seeds. Even hunting was but occasionally the open, outright affair we are likely to think. Ducks were snared and netted, rabbits driven into nets, even deer caught in nooses and with similar devices. There is nothing in all this like the difference between riding down buffalo and gathering wild rice, like the break from whale hunting to berry picking, from farming to stalking deer.

The California Indian, then, secured his variety of foods by techniques that were closely interrelated, or, where diverse, connected by innumerable transitions. Few of the processes involved high skill or long experience for their successful application; none entailed serious danger, material exposure, or even strenuous effort. A little modification, and each process was capable of successful employment on some other class of food objects. Thus the activities called upon were distinguished by patience, simplicity, and crude adaptability rather than by intense endeavor and accurate specialization; and their outcome tended to manifold distribution and approximate balance in place of high yields or concentration along particular but detached lines.

The human food production of aboriginal California will accordingly not be well understood until a really thorough study has been made of all the activities of this kind among at least one people. The substances and the means are both so numerous that a recapitulation of such data as are available is always only a random, scattering selection.

Observers have mentioned what appealed to their sense of novelty or ingenuity, what they happened to see at a given moment, or what their native informants were interested in. But we rarely know whether such and such a device is peculiar to a locality or widespread, and if the former, why; whether it was a sporadic means or one that was seriously depended on; and what analogous ones it replaced. Statements that this tribe used a salmon harpoon, another a scoop net, a third a seine, a fourth poison, and that another built weirs, give us in their totality some approximation to a picture of the set of activities that underlie fishing in California as a whole: but for each individual group the statement is of little significance, for it is likely that those who used the nets used the spear and poison also, but under distinctive conditions; and when they did not, the question is whether the lack of one device is due to a more productive specialization of another, or to natural circumstances which made the employment of this or that method from the common stock of knowledge impracticable for certain localities.

There is, however, one point where neither experience nor environment is a factor, and in which pure custom reigns supreme: the animals chosen for the list of those not eaten. Myth, magic, totemism, or other beliefs may be at the bottom; but every tribe has such an index, which is totally unconnected with its abilities, cultural or physical, to take food.

Among the Yokuts, one animal stands out as edible that everywhere in northern California is absolute taboo and deadly poison: the dog. The Yurok give as their formal reason for not drinking river water that a large stream might contain human foetuses or a dead dog. The Yokuts did not shrink from eating dogs.

Coyote flesh was generally avoided, whether from religious reverence or magical fear is not clear. Grizzly bear meat was also viewed askance. The bear might have devoured human flesh, which would be near to making its eater a cannibal. Besides, in all probability, there was a lurking suspicion that a grizzly might not be a real one, but a transformed bear doctor. The disposition of the animal showed itself in the muscular fibers bristling erect when the flesh was cut, the Yokuts say. Brown bears had fewer plays of the imagination directed upon them, but even their meat was sometimes avoided. Birds of prey and carrion from the eagle down to the crow were not eaten. Their flesh, of course, is far from palatable; but it is these very birds that are central in Yokuts totemism, and the rigid abstinence may have this religious motivation. All reptiles were unclean to the southern Yokuts, as to the Tübatulabal; but the northern tribes exercised a peculiar discrimination. The gopher snake, water snakes, and frogs were rejected, but lizards, turtles, and, what is strangest of all, the rattlesnake, were fit food to the Chukchansi. There is a likely alien influence in this, for the neighboring Miwok probably, and the Salinans to the west certainly, ate snakes, lizards, and even frogs. On the other hand, the southern Yokuts relished the skunk, which when smoked to death in its hole was without offensive odor; while to the Miwok and Salinans it was abomination.

YOKUTS PLANT FOODS AND THEIR PREPARATION.

The buckeye process, which was probably similar to usages elsewhere in the State, was the following: The nuts were broken with a stone and soaked in water for a day. Next, the kernels were crushed to powder with the pestle. The last step was the extraction of the poison, which was done in the acorn-leaching place by the creek. Each time the flour dried a stick was laid aside; the pourings were so timed that the tenth stick was taken as the sun was nearly setting. The woman then cooked the flourlike acorn mush, and it was usually consumed on the spot.

The digger pine nut was not only eaten whole and raw but often treated like small seeds, being winnowed in a scoop-shaped basket, pounded into flour, and cooked.

Acorn granaries were of Miwok and Maidu type. There is no record of their occurrence south of the Yokuts.

Small shallow cook pots of soft stone, perhaps steatite, though described as reddish, were used by the Chukchansi and no doubt irregularly by other tribes who had access to a suitable supply of material. They were dug out with quartz. *Kuyati* and *kulosun* grubs, and angleworms, were perhaps stewed in these vessels, or more likely fried in their own fat at the edge of the fire.

The paddle for stirring boiling acorn mush is not a Yokuts implement, the central Miwok being the most southerly group among whom it makes its regular appearance until southern California is reached. The Yokuts substitute a stick looped on itself, a less efficient stirrer but more serviceable for removing the cooking stones, and far more readily made. (Fig. 38.)

THE MORTAR.

The mortar was a pit in an outcrop of granite, used until the depth of the hole became inconvenient. A convenient exposure of bedrock near a village often contains dozens of holes in all stages of wear within a few yards. (Pl. 45.) Poles leaned together with brush thrown on made an arbor under which a group of women would work for hours, gossiping or singing. Their pestles were often left on the spot; they are rude, irregular, with little taper, and somewhat oval in cross section, even with one or two sides flat or concave; in fact, little more than longish river bowlders, somewhat shaped, partly by pecking with the edge of a flat cobble, and in part by continued usage.

On the alluvial plains portable mortars were necessary. The most common form of these among the Tachi was one of white oak. The flat-bottomed wooden block was little more than a foot high, half as much again in diameter. Except for a narrow rim, the whole upper surface was excavated a few inches, chiefly by fire; but the actual pounding was done in a smaller doubly sunk pit in the center. The pestle was the same as on bedrock. Even the hill Chukchansi knew the wooden mortar, which they called *kowish;* and the Choinimni used it. It is a type that has rarely been observed north of Tehachapi outside the San Joaquin Valley: there are attributions to the Konomihu and the Patwin. (Pl. 45.)

Loose mortars of stone were found and used on occasion by all the tribes, but the universal testimony is that they were not made. In fact, the Chukchansi declare their inability to do so, and attribute all stone mortar holes, in situ as well as portable, to the coyote, who employed an agency of manufacture that decency debars from mention.

It is reported that the Yokuts sometimes fastened a hopper of basketry to the edge of a stone mortar; but this practice is established only for the southern California tribes, and needs confirmation. There is no Yokuts mortar basket, and the few available specimens of the combination suggest that an American may have cut the bottom out of a cooking basket and asphalted it to the stone.

Small stone mortars were probably used for special purposes quite different from those usually assumed. A toothless woman, for instance, was likely to keep such a one for pounding up the whole gophers or ground squirrels that younger relatives might from time to time toss her. Others may have been used for tobacco or medicines.

THE TAKING OF GAME AND FISH.

One hears less of deer snaring among the Yokuts than in the north; but they knew the device. Only, instead of setting the loop in a runway so as to encircle the neck, they laid it in a small concealed pit and fastened the end to a log.

Deer stalking with a deer's head as a decoy was shared with all the tribes of the north and central parts of the State. The Yokuts add that they painted their arms and breasts white like a deer's underside, and aided their traveling on all fours by holding a stick in each hand. When an animal was approached from the leeward, these sticks were rubbed together to produce the sound of a buck scraping his antlers.

Elk were too large to be snared, and in the open plains impossible to approach within bow range. They were chiefly secured in long-distance surrounds and drives called *taduwush.*

Antelope were similarly hunted, the valley groups uniting for intertribal drives, in circles that must often have been many miles in diameter at the start. When the ring had narrowed down so that a shout could be heard across it, two warriors famous for dodging stepped forward from each tribe, and each shot one flint-tipped deer arrow from fully bent bow at his companion. Then these men, and they only, shot the crazed antelopes as they circled about within the human inclosure, or sometimes ran until they dropped from fear and exhaustion. Certain of the antelopes with peculiar horns were believed to sing as they ran, with ground owls sitting on their heads. These individuals were spared. The mimic warfare no doubt had magic intent; but the delegation of the shooting to select men served to keep the circle intact, which would certainly have broken under the excitement of every man aiming his arrow at his own quarry.

A safe though far from certain way of hunting bears was to shoot them on moonlight nights from a sort of nest constructed in a tree in their acorn feeding grounds.

When the geese traveled, inflammable brush was piled up, and when the birds were heard approaching on dark, still nights these were suddenly lit. The birds swooped down to the flare, and in their bewilderment were easily killed.

Pigeons were snared in the earliest morning from a comfortable brush booth with a grass window looking out on a leveled platform on which a live decoy was staked and bait scattered. The running noose was on a stick that was slowly shoved through the curtain until a bird stepped within. The victim was smothered with the knee, and the flock soon returned to feed. (Pl. 46.) The decoy was carried in a spindle-shaped cage.

The Yaudanchi capture of eagles was modeled on the principle of their pigeon taking. The hunter lay in a concealed hut of brush. He did not look at his quarry until it was caught, fearing that it flee his glance. Outside were placed a stuffed animal skin as bait and a live hawk as decoy. The trap was a noose fastened to a bent-over pole sprung from a trigger. Before the eagle was killed by being trod on, it was addressed: " Do not think I shall harm you. You will have a new body. Now turn your head to the north and lie flat! " Only men who knew this prayer and the necessary observances undertook to kill eagles.

Of the many ways of capturing fish, a few more unusual ways may be mentioned. Completely darkened booths were built, in which a man lay to spear the fish passing beneath. This device suggests the pigeon snaring and eagle taking arbor. Small fish could sometimes be taken with the scoop-shaped openwork baskets of the women. Poisons were two: ground buckeye nuts with earth stamped into them and crushed *nademe* leaves. Soon after these preparations were thrown into a small stream the fish began to float on the surface. The *t'unoi* net was fastened to a circular frame on a pole, held vertically, and raised. The more usual Californian net of this type is on a half hoop, and is used rather for scooping or horizontal lifting.

Salt may have been obtained at springs, but the reported cases are from the Pitkachi, whose "salt" stank; from the Chukchansi, who went to the plains to scrape a sort of alkali off the ground; and from the Yaudanchi, who, with other southern tribes, gathered a salty grass known as *alit* and beat it on stones to extract the juice; which was particularly favored with green clover.

THE BOW.

Common bows for small game were little more than a shaped stick; good bows were carefully smoothed of large mountain cedar wood and sinew backed. The commonest type, primarily for the hunt, was nearly as long as a man, of about two fingers' width and the thickness of one. The ends were recurved, probably through a curling back of the thickened sinew. Bows made specifically for fighting were shorter, broader, and flatter, and pinched in the middle. Except for being unpainted and probably not quite so extreme in form, this type appears to have been the same as the northern California one.

Mention of the right and left end of the bow makes it seem to have been held horizontally, or at least diagonally, as by most California tribes.

The arrow, *shikid* generically, had three forms among the Yaudanchi, known as *t'uyosh, djibaku,* and *wuk'ud.* The war arrow had no foreshaft, but a rather long wooden point, notched. It measured from the finger tip nearly to the opposite shoulder or a trifle more than the possible pull of the bow. The Mohave also fought with arrows lacking flint tips. The ordinary hunting arrow had a long sharpened foreshaft, but no real head. The deer arrow had foreshaft and flint head, but the foreshaft was socketed without glue or tie, so that the main shaft would disengage after hitting.

The prevailing arrow straightener among the Yokuts is the southern California form: a well-shaped rectangular block of soft stone, often rounded or ridged on top, and invariably with a polished transverse groove. (Pl. 49, *c.*) This implement is undoubtedly associated with the employment of cane for arrows: the Yokuts are known to have used this plant, though not exclusively. The joints were warmed in the groove and bent by hand or on the ridge after the stone had been heated; the groove was also used for smoothing. The holed straightener of wood or horn for wooden shafts, as employed all over northern California, has not been reported from the Yokuts.

The sling was used only by boys, but the hill tribes report the Mono to have employed it in war. In the high Sierra it might often be more effective than an arrow.

BOATS.

Boats of bundled tule must have been in use among nearly all the valley tribes. On the tumbling streams in the hills these heavy rafts would have been utterly unmanageable. The northernmost Yokuts, below the Miwok of the hills, must have employed these craft constantly in their broad, sluggish streams and multitudinous still sloughs. They remained longest in service on Tulare Lake. Reconstructed models reveal only a cigar-shaped aggregation of bundles of rush, but the best specimens of old days may have approximated real boats in having raised edges. It can scarcely be presumed that the tule stalks could be bundled or beaten together so tight as to exclude the water; rather their lightness raised the whole mass so high that even the bottom of the hollow was above the water line, the gunwales serving only the convenience of preventing wave wash from entering and load or killed game from slipping overboard. Some of these lake boats carried three or four men in comfort, and could bear a small fire on an earth hearth. In maneuvering among the tules the entire vessel and occupants were often covered over with tules, forming a movable blind for the pursuit of waterfowl.

TEXTILES.

Yokuts baskets are distinguished by one special type, a coiled jar-like vessel with flat shoulder and constricted though sometimes re-flaring neck. The pattern is one or more bands in red and black, either diamonds or hexagons or alternate trapezoids. The shoulder was often ornamented with a horizontally projecting fringe of quail crests (Pl. 50), for which red worsted is a modern substitute. These " Tulare bottlenecks," as they have come to be known in the curiosity and antique trade, as well as the quail plume decoration, are not found among the Miwok on one side of the Yokuts nor among the true southern Californians on the other. The two-color pattern is also rare if not lacking among the tribes to the north and south, except among the Chumash. The western Mono, Tübatulabal, Koso, Kawaiisu, and Kitanemuk worked according to Yokuts type, but as they form a fringe of Shoshoneans they have probably derived the art from their lowland neighbors. Kawaiisu technique is, however, as fine as Yokuts. The Chumash also did beautiful work, but the shapes which they gave to their incurved baskets are perhaps less specialized. At least they lack the sharp shoulder and distinct neck which the Yokuts fancied; but their baskets are very small-mouthed.

Chemehuevi forms are rounder, while the farthest traceable affinity is the small spherical basket of the Luiseño and Cahuilla. It is therefore possible to set the focus of the constricted neck forms among the southern Yokuts or the Chumash. As between these two groups, general grade of culture favors the Chumash, while the Yokuts are more central in the distribution of the type. The northern Yokuts, on and near the San Joaquin, do a much poorer grade of work than their southerly kinsmen, as do the Mono. But the Tübatulabal approximate the Tulare-drainage Yokuts in fineness of execution.

The woman's basket cap was probably Yokuts. At least the southern Yokuts seem to have shared it with their southern and eastern Shoshonean neighbors. This hat was, however, worn only with a load on the back, not habitually. It is curious that the range of the southern California cap coincides with that of the carrying net; of the northern form, with the technique of exclusive twining.

The pattern scheme of Yokuts baskets varies from the prevailing horizontal banding of southern California to the diagonal, vertical, and broken effects of Miwok basketry—largely according to locality. Materials and technique are also intermediate. The sewing is close, as in the north; in the Shoshonean area to the south, wider spaced. The foundation is a bundle of *Epicampes* grass, as in southern California; the wrapping, however, is not *Juncus*, as there, but more woody materials: root fibers of sedge (*Carex* or *Cladium?*) for the ground color, *Pteridium* fern root for black, bark of *Cercis* or redbud for red.

Very flat trays were made in coiling. The banded decoration of these brings them nearer Cahuilla and Luiseño ware than Maidu, where radiating designs prevail in flat work. Miwok coiled trays have gone out of use, if they were ever made. Yokuts women employed the finest of their trays for dice throwing; but of course the type was also put to more lowly and daily service.

Twined baskets were more poorly made, but filled a greater variety of needs and perhaps outnumbered coiled pieces in the normal household. The carrying basket was loose enough in texture to be describable as openwork. The interstices were filled with a mucilaginous smear. The commonest of all receptacles is an oval or ovate tray, with a rounding bottom. The term "winnower" describes only one of its manifold uses. The seed beater was but such a tray, one end of which was continued to a handle. Another form of tray was rounded triangular, nearly flat, and wholly or partly in diagonal twining. This has almost certainly been borrowed by the Yokuts from the Shoshoneans on their east. The Tulare Lake tribes must once have possessed a considerable array of special ware in tule, both coiled and twined; but as it made no decorative endeavor it has passed away with the disintegration of the culture of these tribes almost without preservation. (Pl. 50.)

The Yaudanchi affirm that they knew the pitched water bottle of the desert and southern California; but no specimens have survived.

Large baskets were used by the men to ferry women and children across rivers, as by the Yuki. The Mohave employed pots for the same purpose.

Basket patterns had more or less aptly descriptive names, but these were ordinarily without symbolic or religious reference. Some of the names were adjectival, like "zigzag" and "crooked"; others denoted parts of animals, whole small animals, or familiar objects. The significance might be in the pattern as a whole or in the design element. (Fig. 47.) The number of names was not over a few dozen.

The pattern designations of the Yokuts, like most of the patterns, are generally confined to themselves or their immediate neighbors; but their range, character, and limitation of meaning are typical for all the California Indians, whatever their varieties of techniques, materials, and forms of basketry. Where

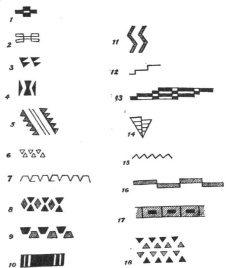

FIG. 47.—Yokuts basket designs. Yaudanchi: 1, 2, flies; 3, 4, deer foot; 5, arrow points; 6, 7, crooked; 8, 9, rattlesnake markings; 10, king snake markings; 11, water snake; 12, *chok*, wood-gathering crook; 13, tied in the middle. Chukchansi: 14, arrow point; 15, crooked; 16, millipede; 17, king snake markings; 18, rattlesnake markings.

the matter has been most fully inquired into, as among the Pomo, it is found that design names are often combined, or modified by standardized epithets, which allow of the accurate description of even a complex pattern. It is not unlikely that the Yokuts may prove to have followed a similar system.

The carrying net, *chutia*, into which either a conical basket or a less shapely load could be set, reappears with the Yokuts. It seems to have been of southern California type, light and with detachable supporting band or rope. Pack straps of braided string were also slung around the load and forehead.

The commonest string material was milkweed, *Asclepias*, called *shah* or *chaka*. The stems were collected in early winter, the bark or covering peeled off, and shredded by rubbing between the hands. The thin epidermis was then removed by drawing the mass of fibers over a stick. The fibers were not separately disentangled, but loosely rolled together as they adhered. Two of these rolls were then twisted tight, on themselves as well as on each other, by rolling on the thigh with the spit-into hand, the other hand holding and feeding the loose ends. The exact process of adding further material is not known; it consisted probably of rubbing together the ends of a mass of fibers, perhaps with some twist. String was two-ply. This is a practically universal rule for California. Except for a few ancient fragments, every piece of three-ply rope or twine in the State is of American provenience or obviously modern.

The other great string material of the bulk of the Californians, wild hemp, *Apocynum*, has not been reported from the Yokuts; but this is likely to be only an oversight. The inner bark of a large shrub called *hoh* was made by the Yokuts into rough rope for withes, pigeon cages, and similar bound articles.

CRADLES OF THE YOKUTS AND OTHER CALIFORNIANS.

The Yokuts cradle shows three types. The first is a flat rectangle or trapezoid of twined basketry with a curved hood. The hood is loosely or not at all attached to the top edge of the base, and is carried by a basketry hoop or side supports. (Pl. 40, *h, i, j*.) This type is found also among the western Mono, and, with some modification, among the eastern Mono. (Pl. 40, *k*.) The latter run the rods of their base across instead of lengthwise, and set a smaller and rounder hood on more snugly. The Miwok (Pl. 39, *a, c, d, e*) and western Mono (Pl. 40, *l*) sometimes use the base of the Yokuts, without the hood. The Washo cradle is substantially that of the Yokuts.

The second type is built up on half a dozen sticks lashed across a large wooden fork. A layer of string-twined tules is put over the sticks. (Pl. 40, *m*.)

The third form is a mat of twined tules, with loops at the edges to pull the lashings through. (Pl. 40, *g*.)

The hooded basketry cradle seems to predominate in the north, the forked stick type in the south, and the soft frameless tule form on Tulare Lake; but this distribution is not altogether certain, and it is possible that the age of the child, or the season of the year, may have been of influence.

The Maidu cradle is often made on a forked framework, and in summer carries a basketry hood. It differs, however, in carrying numerous light transverse rods, in having the ends of the fork united by a stick loop, and in often lacking the point of the fork. (Pl. 40, *n, o*.) None of the Yokuts cradles, clearly, is made for hanging, except perhaps by a strap. The Maidu cradle may be described as a combination of the Yokuts first and second types; among the latter people no such combination or transitional type has been found.

The southern California cradle, so far as known, has a ladderlike foundation of a few short sticks on two long ones. The two long rods are, however, joined at the top instead of at the bottom: that is, there is a loop at the top instead of a fork below. The hood is also a separate hoop of wickerwork. (Pl. 39, *b*.)

The cradle of northeastern California, northwestern California, and the Pomo region is, in spite of much local variation, uniformly of a different order. It is of basketry, not of sticks; it is hollow instead of flat; and a rounded bottom is an integral part of the structure, while the hood is clearly a subsidiary feature. This northern cradle is built essentially for sitting (Pl. 35); that of central and southern California only for lying.

The stiff cradles of central and southern California may be schematized as in Figure 48, *a–e* being types with a wooden frame,

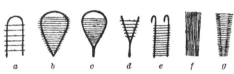

Fig. 48.—Cradle types of central and southern California. *a*, Diegueño, Mohave; *b, c*, Maidu; *d*, Yokuts, Kitanemuk; *e*, northern Miwok; *f*, Yokuts, Miwok, western Mono; *g*, eastern Mono. (Cf. Pls. 39, 40.)

f–g basketry forms. It will be seen that there is a complete transition from *a* to *d: b* differs superficially from *c* only in lacking the point of the latter. Structurally, however, the gap in the series comes between these two, *b* being only *a* with the ends of the frame rod joined, whereas *c* is *d*, namely, a natural fork at the bottom, with an added hoop. That form and consequent use may be of more importance than structural plan, so far as connections go, appears from the fact that *b* and *c* are the winter and summer types of the same people, the Maidu.

Even the stick and the basketry types shade into each other: *b* and *c*, whose transverse rods are close and slender, need only the substitution of a few courses of twining for their underlying hoop or fork frame to become *g*.

In Miwok basketry pieces of type *f*, like Plate 39, *e*, the strengthening hoop seems secondary, but may be a vestige of a former wooden foundation.

The hood is primarily associated with the basketry cradle, but again there are exceptions on both sides that make transitions. *B* and *d* are always hoodless, so far as known, and the hood of *a* is structurally separate. *C*, however, is hooded; on the other hand, *f* is found without a hood as well as with it.

Finally, the soft tule-mat cradle of the Tachi (Pl. 40, *g*) is the same in plan as Mono stiff basketry specimens like Plate 40, *l*, differing only in its pliability.

An aberrant type is *e*, so far reported only from the northerly Miwok. The frame is wooden, but distinctive in not being in a single plane. The two rods curl up from the base. This enables them to serve at once as hooks for hanging and as a hood frame. (Pl. 39, *f*.)

The historical interrelations of the several types can only become known through ampler material than is now available, both from within California and without. It is only possible to say that in spite of transitions the basketry and the wooden-frame types seem fundamental.

The former has its rods running longitudinally and is intra-Californian, or rather cis-Sierra, the northern sitting cradle linking with it in this feature of direction of the elements.

The wooden-frame cradle with cross rods is trans-Sierra, including southern California. On this interpretation the hill and mountain Maidu cradle has been shaped by Shoshonean influences from the Great Basin, and the Yokuts have been infiltrated to some extent by the same influences. On the other hand, the Shoshoneans within the Sierra Nevada, such as the western Mono, and presumably the Tübatulabal, follow the Californian method of construction at least as frequently as do the neighboring native stocks.

An interesting minor feature of Yokuts cradles is the expression of sex in the decoration. The Chukchansi put a band of parallel diagonal lines on a boy's hood, a zigzag on a girl's. A number of the Yokuts cradles from other localities show the same designs; several have the twining of the frame analogously disposed (Pl. 40, *h*, *i*, *j*). Diamonds may be the equivalent of the zigzag, in which case a genital connotation is possible. Eastern and western Mono hoods show patterns of the same kind (Pl. 40, *k*); the Washo denote sex in their hood ornamentation; the Miwok may therefore be guessed to follow the principle also; and the Mohave use distinct patterns for boys and girls in the braided bands with which the child is lashed to the frame, besides putting feathers only on a boy's hood. The device is therefore of some geographical extent, and may represent an eastern influence into California. It is of special appeal because of the rarity of symbolic expression in California outside of ritual; and even in ritual the symbolism is scant compared with the habits of the Southwest, the Plains, and the East.

While the same patterns probably occur over a large area with the same symbolism, the sex denotation itself is expressed in other ways also. Thus the Nutunutu boy's cradle is said to have the hood fastened only at the sides, the girl's at the top and the base also.

POTTERY.

The Yokuts practice one curious and hitherto undescribed art: that of pottery making. The precise distribution of this industry remains to be ascertained. The southern hill tribes made pots; the adjacent valley tribes appear to have; on the lake tribes there is no information; the Chukchansi and probably other northern tribes did not follow the art. Of adjacent Shoshoneans, the Tübatulabal made pots; some of the western Mono probably did. Outside of these groups there is no record whatever of the industry. It is not connected geographically with the pottery-making area of southern California, which does not come north of the San Bernardino Range, so far as known; and the territorial gap is paralleled by a thorough diversity of the ware.

The distinctive feature of this pottery is its excessive crudeness. It appears to have been made by a rough fitting together of pieces of clay, or a pressing out of a lump: there is no evidence of the coiling and smoothing method. It is doubtful whether the clay contains tempering. Glue, blood, or a sticky substance may have been introduced as binding material. The color is from light to dark gray. There is no slip, wash, or pattern, except now and then a rude incision obviously modeled on a basket pattern. The shapes are indefinitely varied, without approach to standardized forms. A row of the vessels looks as if produced by children or experimenters. (Pl. 51.)

Even the uses are not known. Most of the pots show evidences of employment in the fire. But their purposes must have been special, since the ordinary cooking of the Yokuts is as regularly performed in baskets as among other groups. Small vessels may have been intended for services that we can only suspect. Thus the Yaudanchi affirm that they formerly kept tobacco in hollowed clay balls.

Archaeology gives no information as to the age of the industry. There has been little collecting in the Yokuts area and no systematic exploration. The prehistoric clay cooking balls or sling shots of the stoneless Stockton plains, where the Yokuts Chulamni lived in the historic period, suggest a connection; but no vessels of the same material have ever been found with these. The Clear Lake Pomo sometimes make a minute receptacle by pressing a hole in a lump of clay; but they do not bake these little articles. Evidently there were some anticipations toward pottery making latent in parts of California; and the Yokuts carried these tentative steps a little further. But the inference of a stimulus, however indirect, coming through their immediate Shoshonean neighbors from the pottery-making Shoshoneans of the south or east can hardly be avoided; and therewith the interpretation of an ultimate southwestern origin of the art.

The pipe is small among the Yokuts. (Pl. 30, c, d.) A wooden pipe is found among the Chukchansi and Gashowu; the Yaudanchi and southern tribes normally used a bit of cane, which was carried in the pierced lobe of the ear. The northern Yokuts implement suggests the southern Californian stone pipe in size and shape, and the Mohave equivalent of clay. Outwardly it is similar to the abbreviated Miwok pipe, but the latter has a very short reed or stem inserted as a mouthpiece. Occasionally a pipe with enlarged bowl, of Pomo shape but very much smaller, is to be found among the northerly Yokuts. All the Yokuts declare that they did not use stone pipes; and the random finds of prehistoric material in their habitat include very few, if any, such implements.

The reason for the abortiveness of the Yokuts pipe is to be found in the fact that a common practice of all the tribes was to eat tobacco instead of smoking it. This custom is affirmed by the Chukchansi, Gashowu, Tachi, Wükchamni, Yaudanchi, and Yauelmani, and was therefore evidently universal. Garcés, in 1776, found a Serrano Shoshonean tribe bordering on the Yokuts, either the Kitanemuk or the Alliklik, following the same practice, to the serious discomfort of his unaccustomed Mohave companions. One method was to mix the leaves with fresh-water mussel shells that had been burned to lime. This procedure is of interest because it recurs in the northernmost part of the Pacific coast. A probably less usual plan was to drink a decoction of tobacco in water. In either event vomiting followed except for the long-hardened. The after effects of the emetic may have been pleasant. At any rate they were considered beneficial, and in some cases at least they were thought to impart supernatural efficiency. The Chukchansi speak of being able to detect wizards after eating tobacco.

Among the Yokuts the guessing or hand game becomes less important than among the tribes of northern California. Its place in the prime estimation of men is taken, as in parts of southern California, by the hoop and pole and the shinny game, though which of these two enjoyed preeminence it is hard to say—perhaps shinny.

This game, *katauwish*, was named from the shinny stick, *kated.* The ball was called *odot.* It was not shinny in our sense, played with one pall, but rather a form of the ball or stick race of the Southwest, each party propelling its knob of white oak with sticks instead of feet. The course, however, was short, within a definite field, the *katadwishchu;* and among the Chukchansi the ball had to be holed to win.

Chukchansi women played the same game with straighter sticks, and threw a hoop in place of striking the ball.

Another variant, though for men, was lacrosse, *ch'ityuish,* named after the racket, *ch'itei.* The "net" was nothing but a loop that half fitted the ball. This game was secondary to the *katduwish.*

In hoop and pole the throwing stick was called *payas,* the rolling buckskin-wound ring *tokoin,* and the carefully smoothed ground, often by the side of the sweat house, *i'n.* The game itself, *hochuwish,* was substantially that of the Mohave; it extended as far north as the Chukchansi.

In the *aikuich* the pole was thrown at a sliding billet, *t'ieh.* The same name is now applied to the Spanish "nine men's morris": the men are *aiek.*

A third form was the *haduwush,* in which darts were thrown at a mark hidden by a fence of brush.

There is no record of any Yokuts cup and ball game.

The guessing game was called *wehlawash* by the Chukchansi, *a'liwash* by the Yauelmani, *hi'uniwich* by the Yaudanchi. The former, like the northern Californians, used wooden pieces, or in a good set, bones; the latter, bits of cane slipped, as in southern California, over an endless string to prevent the deceit of interchange after the guess. The marked piece was called "man" and guessed for; the plain one was the "woman." The Yaudanchi shot out one finger if he meant the hand at which he pointed, but two to indicate the ignored side as containing the "man." When there were two pairs of players confronting each other, a single finger signified a guess at the hand indicated and at the partner's opposite hand; two fingers, the same hand of both players. These complications look like arbitrary elaborations; but like most such Californian devices, they spring from an intensive development of the spirit of the game. A gesture begun with one finger can be finished with two if the instant suffices for recognition of a trace of satisfaction in the opponent's countenance as he realizes an impending false guess. These attempts to provoke betrayal imply instantaneous shiftings of features and fingers and lightninglike decisions and reactions; and it is impossible to have seen a Californian Indian warmed to his work in this game when played for stakes—provided its aim and method are understood—and any longer justly to designate him mentally sluggish and emotionally apathetic, as is the wont. It is a game in which not sticks and luck but the tensest of wills, the keenest perceptions, and the supplest of muscular responses are matched; and only rarely are the faculties of a Caucasian left sufficiently undulled in adult age to compete other than disastrously against the Indian practiced in his specialty. Seen in this light, the contortions, gesticulations, noises, and excitement of the native are not the mere uncontrolledness of an overgrown child, but the outward reflexes of a powerfully surcharged intensity, and devices that at once stimulate the contestant's energy still further and aid him in dazzling and confusing his opponent. There is possibly no game in the world that, played sitting, has, with equal intrinsic simplicity, such competitive capacities.

The Yaudanchi shuffled under a blanket instead of behind the back or in bunches of hay. Among the Chukchansi only women used the blanket.

Chomwosh is the guessing or matching of hidden fingers. It is too little described to allow of a decision between the possibilities of native and Mediterranean origin.

Dice was the woman's game. There were two forms. *Huchuwish* was played with 8 *huech*, half shells of nut filled with pitch or asphalt and bits of sea shell, thrown from both hands on a basketry tray, *t'aiwan*. The far-away Chemehuevi play this much like the southern Yokuts, though with 6 instead of 8 pieces; it appears to be a game of Shoshonean origin. The Chukchansi keep the name, but use 6 split acorn kernels. Beyond them, the course of the game becomes uncertain. For the Miwok nothing is known, and the Maidu seem to lack all dice. The Yaudanchi played for 12 counters, and the scoring ran: 5 of 8 flat surfaces up, 2 counters; 2 up, 1; any other number, none. The Chukchansi won by taking 10 counters, and considered only the possible combinations of falls, irrespective of side. Six to none counted 4 points; 4 to 2 or 3 to 3, 1; 5 to 1, nothing. Such variations seem to occur in all Californian games, even between adjacent areas.

The second dice game, *tachnuwish*, was played with 6 (or 8) split sticks, *dalak*, of elderwood in the north, of cane in the south, burned with a pattern on the convex side and thrown on end on a skin.

There was a generic word, *goyuwinich*, for gambler. *Gwiunauzhid mak*, "let us gamble," the Yaudanchi would say.

AESTHETICS.

Apart from basket patterns, there was no trace of activity of graphic or plastic art in Yokuts life. The images in the mourning ceremony were symbols of the rudest kind. Anything like the tracing of a picture or shaping of a figure was foreign to the native mind. Even conventionalized symbols were lacking, for conventionalization is a standardization of some artistic impulse, and this impulse never manifested itself. The stiff figures of men and animals that occasionally appear on baskets are invariably due to American influence, among the Yokuts as well as among all other Californian groups. One can not have become imbued with a feeling for the decorative value of California basketry without resenting these childish introductions as fatal to the inherent aesthetic qualities of the work. Our tastes have been infinitely more cultivated than those of the native Californian; but in the few directions, or one direction, in which he had made an incipient progress in ornamentation, his habits had poise and restraint.

The ungraphic, unplastic, and unsymbolic character of native Californian civilization is complete to a degree that is almost inconceivable. It is only rarely that an Indian can be induced to draw in the sand the most schematic sketch of the rivers or mountains of his habitat. In southern California there are indeed some faint stirrings in the sand paintings, but only under a strong ritualistic motive; and the poverty and rudeness of these, compared with their Navaho and Pueblo prototypes, reveal the aridity of the artistic soil which this southwestern religio-aesthetic influence encountered in its invasion of California.

In all the remainder of the State even this trace is wanting. For once the deep cleavage between the northwest and the central south is effaced. The Yurok and Hupa culture may be a North Pacific coast civilization in nine-tenths of its essential impulses and goals; in representative art it is as Californian as that of the Maidu or Yokuts.

How far some beginnings of literary form have evolved in Yokuts traditions, in comparison with those of their neighbors, it would be difficult to state. The languages, the emotions, and the pleasures of the natives are everywhere known with too little intimacy for a judgment to be of value. Myths have been recorded primarily with reference to their episodic content, their religious associations, or their systematic coherence. Such as are available from the Yokuts evince a lower literary pitch, a less intensity of presentation, than those of northern and southern California at their best. But we do not know how far they are artistically representative; and what has already been said about the animal pantheon of these people suffices to reveal that the real merits of their folklore lie implicit in a background or setting of which the skeletonized translations that are available give to us but rudimentary hints.

Much the same must be said of music, only in a still stronger degree. Some differences of external form, or involved system, are apparent between the songs of various parts of California. But as long as no exact analysis has been rendered, and especially as long as no one has approached this music with any desire to enter into its essential spirit, comparisons between the aesthetic value of the inclinations and achievements of this and that tribe are empty.

Southern Yokuts men sometimes played the musical bow after settling themselves in bed; the Chukchansi in mourning the dead. These may be but two expressions of one employment. Modern forms of the instrument have a peg key for adjusting the tension, or are made on cornstalks. In old days a true shooting bow, or a separate instrument made on the model of a bow, was used. *Mawu,* or *mawuwi,* was its name. One end was held in the mouth, while the lone string was tapped, not plucked, with the nail of the index finger; the melody, audible to himself only, was produced by changes in the size of the resonance chamber formed by the player's oral cavity.

THE TYPE OF YOKUTS CIVILIZATION.

The affiliations of Yokuts civilization are nearly equal in all directions. To the north, their system of totemic moieties connects them with the Miwok while certain detailed elements of their culture, such as the Y-frame cradle and the magpie headdress, link them definitely with the Maidu. To the east their twined basketry has close relations as far as the remoter edge of the Great Basin. Toward the Shoshonean and Yuman south there are innumerable threads: the Jimson weed ritual, the arrow straightener, the carrying net, to mention only a few. Toward the west the decay of Salinan and Chumash culture makes exact comparison difficult, but what little is known of the former people evidences a strong Yokuts impress, while with-the nearer Chumash relations of trade were close and must have brought many approaches of custom in their train. It is difficult to say where the most numerous and most basic links stretch.

Equally impressive, however, are the features distinctive of the civilization of the Yokuts, or rather of the group composed of themselves and their smaller and less known Shoshonean neighbors on the immediate east and south. These specialties include the true tribal organization, the duality of chieftainship, the regulated functions of transvestites, the coordinated animal pantheon, the eagle-down skirt, the constricted coiled basket, a distinctive pottery, and the communal house, to mention only a few points.

It thus seems that the Yokuts were a nation of considerable individuality. It appears throughout California that the dwellers in the larger valleys, though they were the first to crumble at the touch of the Caucasian, elaborated a more complex culture than the hill tribes; and the Yokuts were a lowland people in a greater measure than any other stock in California.

But it is also evident that wherever the soil of history is really penetrated in California a rich variety of growths is found. If a little mountain group like the Yuki, placed between more highly civilized nations, has been able to evolve feature after feature of cultural distinctness, there is every reason to believe that the same would prove to be true of nearly all the California tribes, if only we really knew them; and a large, compact, and prosperous block of people like the Yokuts would be exceptional only in having carried the development of their originality somewhat farther than the majority.

It so happens that in the long stretch of land between the Maidu and the Luiseño no tribe has yet been exhaustively studied with any array of information. It is therefore inevitable that the present account of the Yokuts, the first rendered in any detail, scattered as that is, should reveal many novelties. But there is nothing to encourage the belief that if the Miwok, the Tübatulabal, the Serrano, or the Salinans had happened to be chosen, there would have been any notably less quantity of interesting peculiarities revealed; not to mention that for the Pomo and Chumash, little known as they are, we have every indication of a civilizational richness greater, if anything, than that evinced by the Yokuts.

In other words, the exact understanding of the Indian history of California still lies before us. Some foundations may have been laid for it in the present work. The outlines were sketched for all time 40 years ago by the masterly hand of Stephen Powers. But the real structure will be a gift of the future; and its materials can only be assembled by investigations far more intensive, as well as continuous, than those yet undertaken.

3625°—25——36

CHAPTER 36.

THE ESSELEN AND SALINANS.

The Esselen.

With this people, we are back in the Hokan family, with which, except for a long Shoshonean excursion, the remainder of this survey will be occupied.

Long reckoned as an independent stock, the Esselen were one of the least populous groups in California, exceedingly restricted in territory, the first to become entirely extinct, and in consequence are now as good as unknown, so far as specific information goes—a name rather than a people of whom anything can be said. There are preserved a few hundred words and phrases of their speech; some confused designations of places, and a few voyagers' comments, so generic in tone as to allow no inferences as to the distinctiveness of the group.

The only clue to their ultimate history is, as usual, afforded by language. On two sides the Esselen had the Penutian Costanoans as neighbors, on the third the Hokan Salinans; they faced the ocean on the fourth. Salinan speech, however, leans toward Chumash, its southern sister; and the obvious affinities of Esselen are toward Yuman, far to the south, and to Pomo, Yana, and other north Hokan languages, before which a broad belt of alien Penutian tongues intervenes. In short, Esselen is free from the peculiarities of Chumash and Salinan, and is a generalized Hokan language. It can not well, therefore, have originated in the same branch of the family as Salinan, and probably represents a separate wave or movement. Further than this, nothing can be said until the internal organization of the Hokan family shall have been better determined.

There is only one conjecture that may be alluded to. The smallness of the group is in marked contrast to the degree of its linguistic distinctness. It is therefore likely to be a remnant of a people that once ranged over a much larger territory. Now the Penutians of California were very plainly the people of the great interior valley. It is chiefly from the vicinity of San Francisco to Monterey that they impinged on the ocean. They have therefore presumably spread out along this stretch of coast, in which their Costanoan division was located in historic times and where it may be supposed to have taken shape as a group. This stretch is adjacent to the soil which the Esselen still held when they were discovered; and it seems reasonable to believe, accordingly, that the Esselen once owned at least part of this region to their north. This ancient extension might have connected them with the northern Hokans, particularly if the Pomo or some allied group formerly lived farther south.

The heart of Esselen territory at the time of discovery was the drainage of Carmel River, exclusive, however, of its lower reaches, where Costanoans were situated and the mission was established. The Esselen also held Sur River and the rocky coast for 25 miles from a little short of Point Sur to Point Lopez. At the great peak of Santa Lucia they met the Salinans. Nearly all of this territory is rolling or rugged, part of it sierra. The Esselen, like most small groups in California, were therefore distinct mountaineers. A thousand souls would be a very liberal estimate for their population. Five hundred seems nearer the mark.

Esselen, Eslen, Escelen, Ecselen, or Ensen, also Ecclemach, is used by all authorities of the Spanish period as a tribal name and commonly provided with the plural ending –es. It seems, however, to be the name of a village, after which, following Caucasian custom, the group was denominated. This is borne out by a reference to Eslanagan and Ecgeagan (also recorded as Ekheya) as on opposite sides of the Carmel River. The final –n itself is hardly likely to be of native Esselen origin. The word "Eslanagan" looks like a stem *Esla*, plus possibly the common Esselen noun suffix –*nah* or –*neh*, to which in turn the Costanoans added their –*n*. The Eslen or Ensen and Rumsien or Runsen seem to have been habitually distinguished as the two predominant groups at mission Carmelo, much in the sense in which we might distinguish Esselen and Costanoan. The names were easy and rhymed; and travelers came away and reported the two "tribes," sometimes as extending 20 leagues from Monterey. Data were scarce; and for nearly a century almost every book on California refers to the famous "Ensenes and Runsenes," as if they were great ethnic groups instead of villages. Huelel—that is, Welel—is mentioned once as the "language of the Esselenes" attached to mission Soledad.

The settlements cited in various authorities are: Ensen, at Buena Esperanza; Ekheya, in the mountains; Echilat, 12 miles southeast of mission Carmelo; Ichenta, at San Jose (this is certainly a Costanoan name, whoever inhabited the spot; compare the locative ending –*ta*); Xaseum, in the sierra; Pachhepes, near the last; and the following "clans or septs": Coyyo, Yampas, Fyules (*f* is an Esselen sound), Nennequi, Jappayon, Gilimis, Yanostas. These are all in the original orthography, which in most cases is Spanish.

Several terms in the preserved vocabularies may be of ethnographic interest. Thus, *pawi* or *lottos*, arrow (two kinds may have been used); *tuwano*, house;

tsila, kuʼuh, ishpashaʼa, shaka, various kinds of baskets; *ehepas,* rabbit-skin blanket; *shikili,* asphalt(?); *kaʼa,* tobacco; *makhalana,* salt; *lelima* a " favorite dance," possibly the *Loli* of the Kuksu system; *tumas-hachohpa,* night spirit; *kuchun,* arroyo; *aspasianah,* dry creek. The last two may be names of places rather than generic terms.

The Salinan Indians.

The Salinan Indians are one of those bodies of natives whom four generations of contact with civilization have practically extinguished. Some 40 remain, but among these the children do not speak the language, and even the oldest retain only fragmentary memories of the national customs of their great-grandfathers. Missionaries and explorers happen to have left only the scantiest notices of the group; and thus it is that posterity can form but a vague impression of their distinctive traits. Even a name for the tribe or for their language has not been recorded or remembered; so that they have come to be called from the Spanish and modern designation of the river which drains most of their territory.

TERRITORY.

The Salinan language extended from the headwaters of the Salinas, or perhaps only from the vicinity of the Santa Margarita divide, north to Santa Lucia Peak and an unknown point in the valley somewhere south of Soledad; and from the sea presumably to the main crest of the Coast Range. Much of this territory is rugged; nearly all of it is either rough or half barren. Along the steep harborless coast one dialect or division of the language, the extinct " Playano " or "beach " idiom, was spoken; in the mountains and valley the second or " principal." This in turn was divided into a northern and a southern subdialect, of both of which records have been made, and which are usually named after the missions of San Antonio and San Miguel.

The Salinan language is wholly unconnected with the neighboring Yokuts and Costanoan. It has remote affinity with Esselen, and a greater resemblance to Chumash. These three tongues constitute the central Californian representatives of the Hokan family.

NUMBERS.

Cabrillo in 1542 saw no natives on the Salinan coast, and Vizcaino 60 years later only a few on tule rafts. The true discoverers of the group were the members of the Portolá expedition of 1769. In the mountains between the future sites of San Luis Obispo and Monterey they saw, going and coming, 10 different towns whose population they estimated to range between 30 and 400 souls, with an aggregate of 1,200. As Chumash, Esselen, or Costancan villages were included, these figures shed little light on the numbers of the Salinan stock; but they are of interest in giving an average of over 100 people per town.

The records of the missions furnish an approximate Salinan census. San Antonio was founded in 1771, and reached a maximum population of 1,124—or 1,296—neophytes in 1805. San Miguel, established in 1797, had 1,076 converts at the end of 17 years. The sum, about 2,300 souls, includes some Yokuts—Tachi, Telamni, and perhaps other tribes—from the San Joaquin Valley; so that even if allowance is made for conjectural unreduced Salinan villages as late as 1814, the total aboriginal population of the family can not possibly be placed above 3,000; and 2,000 seems a safer estimate. The record of baptisms—not quite 7,000 at both missions up to 1834, during a period which on the average took in nearly three generations—would confirm the smaller rather than the larger figure.

SETTLEMENTS.

Of the 20 or so Salinan villages known other than as mere names, some can be placed on a map only with a question (Fig. 49). Ehmal, Lema, Ma'tihl'she, and Tsilakaka are entirely undetermined except for having been on the coast. Trolole has been located at points so widely separated as Santa Margarita and Cholame. Cholame, the most important town of the San Miguel division, is stated by some to have been situated at that mission, by others on Cholame Creek. As the Cholame land grant lies along this creek, and the Spaniards and Mexicans were rather precise in their application of native names, the latter vicinity seems more likely. But Estrella Creek, as the lower course of Cholame Creek is now designated on maps, flows into the Salinas near the mission; and as it is the general custom of the California Indians to name streams after the sites at their mouths, the name may in this way have been, correctly enough, carried upstream by the Spaniards. Conjecture, however, is all that is possible on such disputed points. The majority of Salinan towns of ascertained location lie on San Antonio and Nacimiento Rivers. In part this unevenness may be the fault of the preservation of knowledge; but it seems also to reflect the preponderating distribution. Even in the barren hills of the Cholame drainage there are known as many villages as in the long valley of the Salinas proper.

TYPE OF CIVILIZATION.

The Salinan Indians were completely omnivorous. Every obtainable variety of fish, reptiles, birds, and mammals, with the single exception of the skunk, and possibly the dog and coyote, was eaten. An incomplete list of their vegetable dietary contains six kinds of acorns, three of grasses, three of clover, six at least of berries, and two of pine nuts; besides wild oats, buckeye, sunflower, chia and sages, grapes, prickly pears, yucca, and Brodiaea bulbs. This wealth of plant foods is typical of aboriginal California.

Salinan industries and customs were largely influenced by those of the Yokuts, with whom they traded, visited, and communicated freely, whereas the Costanoans on the north were generally their bitter enemies, and the main body of the Chumash to the south were too far removed, and of too different an outlook, to hold much relation with them. Baskets were essentially Yokuts in material and technique. Women's hats and mortar hoppers of coiled basketry are

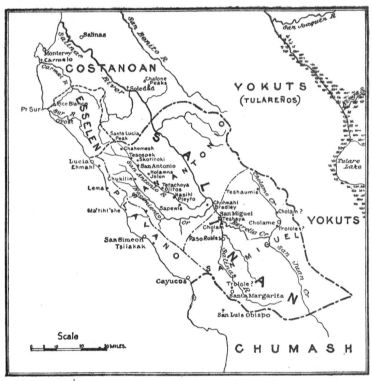

Fig. 49.—Salinan and Esselen territory and probable Salinan settlements.

reported. The former may have been introduced by the missionized Yokuts; the latter is a southern California type that seems out of place in Salinan territory. Roughly interlaced receptacles of willow for the storage of acorns also recall those of southern California. Grooved arrow straighteners, reed smoking pipes, the eating of tobacco mixed with lime, and the practice of cremation indicate Yokuts affiliations. The initiation of boys into manhood with a toloache drinking rite, whereas the advent of adolescence in girls was disposed of with less circumstance, also suggest Yokuts contact.

On the contrary, the few names of Salinan dances that are still remembered point to an origin of these ceremonies from the Patwin-Pomo-Maidu-Miwok cycle in the north. These dances are: the Kuksui, made by a feather-covered performer;.the Hiwei, by men; and the Lolei, by women. But their introduction may possibly have been due to commingling of nationalities at the Salinan missions.

Beliefs, again, were substantially those of the Tachi and other valley Yokuts. Certain medicine men were thought capable of bringing rain with amulets; others of turning themselves into grizzly bears. Souls inhabited a western island of the dead. Earth was brought up from primeval water, given shape as this world, and mankind fashioned from it, by a trio of animal creators, the eagle, coyote, and kingfisher.

Only two distinctive peculiarities are known of the rude civilization of the Salinan Indians. One is the use of the musical rasp, a notched stick rhythmically rubbed with another. The second is the remarkable report from mission sources that at San Miguel they lent each other shell money at 100 per cent interest per day! The rasp is a simple implement, easily invented even by a rude tribe, or perhaps learned by it from others who have allowed it to degenerate into a toy, or to go out of use altogether. Usury, however, is contrary to all the known customs of the California Indians, and the rate of increase seems incredible, especially as a temporary or emergency use for money is hard to conceive under aboriginal conditions. Still, a report as definite as this can hardly be without some foundation.

CHAPTER 37.

THE CHUMASH.

HISTORY AND TERRITORY.

Except for a brief and unsettled experience of Alarcon with the aggressive tribes of the lower Colorado a year or two before, the Chumash are the first Californian group discovered by Caucasians. Cabrillo in 1542–43 sailed back and forth among the islands, coasted the shore, had abundant and most friendly contact with the natives, lived on San Miguel, and died there.

Subsequent explorers and voyagers have left a number of casual observations on the Chumash, but none of the missionaries settled among them showed inclination to develop into a painstaking historian like Boscana; and when California was long enough American for ethnologists to survey it, the old life of the Chumash was a dimming memory. The result is that there exist more impressions than information. There is no group in the State that once held the importance of the Chumash concerning which we know so little.

The Spaniards were disposed to regard the Chumash as superior to the other tribes of California with whom they had acquaintance, and on the whole they seem to have been correct in this opinion. We know so little of the religion of the group that it is impossible to decide whether they attained to the comparative height of semi-abstruse symbolism that the Gabrielino and Luiseño displayed. In their industries, in the arts that accompany ease of life, possibly in the organization of society, they rather surpassed these Shoshoneans. The consequence is that Chumash culture presents the appearance of a higher development on the material, technological, and economic side than on the religious, but we can not be altogether certain that such a formulation would be reliable.

The Chumash are predominantly a coast people, and were more nearly maritime in their habits than any other Californian group. They held the three northern large islands of the Santa Barbara archipelago—Anacapa does not appear to have been inhabited permanently. They clustered thickly along the calm shore from Malibu Canyon westward to Point Concepcion, and from there extended northward along the more boisterous and chillier coast as far as Estero Bay. Inland, in general, they reached to the range that divides the direct ocean drainage from that of the great valley; except that in the west their frontier was the watershed between the Salinas and the Santa Maria and short coast streams; and in the east, some small fragments had spilled into part of the most southerly drainage of the San Joaquin-Kern system. The Carrizo plains are doubtful as between Chumash and Salinans, and may not have contained any permanent villages.

Marine life along the Chumash shores is exceptionally rich, the climate far famed, and every condition favored the unusual concentration of population among a people living directly upon nature. The land, however, is dry; the watercourses, though long, are small and rarely run permanently, and each successive mountain chain increases the aridity. Only some narrow stretches among the uplands of the western end of the Tehachapi range are more favorable. There was thus every occasion for the inlander to drift to the edge of the ocean, if he could, but small inducement for the coast people to go to the interior, except for occasional visits. The population in the districts away from the sea must have been comparatively light.

From Point Concepcion north the coast is exposed to westerly winds, fogs, and heavy surfs, and the inhabitants were noted by the Spaniards as less numerous and poorer than on the Channel of Santa Barbara.

Five missions—San Buenaventura, Santa Barbara, Santa Ynez, La Purisima Concepcion, and San Luis Obispo—were established among the Chumash. These being recruited almost wholly from the members of the stock, would argue a population of about 8,000 or 10,000; and this figure seems reasonable on the basis of the character of the land and sea. The Chumash accepted the Spaniards with unusual kindliness. But the subjection which the residence of the superior people entailed broke their spirit and produced a deep inward depression, which manifested itself in the alarming spread of the practice of abortion, and as late as 1824 fanned itself into a feeble and timid flame of insurrection at three of the missions. By the time of secularization, the population was heavily on the wane. The disorganized decade and a half that followed melted it even more rapidly, and when the American came there were scattered peons on ranchos, but no more Chumash nation. To-day there remain scarcely a dozen old men and women who still speak the language of their grandfathers, although the number of individuals admitting pure or partial Chumash blood is somewhat greater.

There was a dialect for each mission; at least one other on the islands; another in the mountain region where the Tehachapis meet the coast ranges; and possibly others. As to the limits of these, there is no information whatever. Some attempt has been made to estimate their boundaries on Plate 1. But it must be frankly confessed that the lines there drawn represent little but conjectures based on topography.

A rough classification of the known dialects is possible. That of San Luis Obispo, the most northwesterly, thrust into an angle between the Salinans and the sea, is the most divergent. Next in degree of specialization seems to be that of the islands. Santa Ynez and Santa Barbara are rather close, Ventura somewhat more different. San Emigdio appears to lean on Ventura.

When it comes to villages, information is abundant as regards names, but often less precise as to location and almost wholly wanting as to relations. Several hundred Chumash place names are on record, the majority referring to inhabited sites. Nearly 100 of these can be located with some approximation to accuracy on a map of the scale of Plate 48; and these undoubtedly include most of the important towns near the ocean. The interior is less satisfactorily represented.

The following may be added to the data contained in Plate 48:

The native name of San Luis Obispo was Tishlini. Pismo and Huasna appear to derive their designations from Chumash originals. Upop is mentioned as near Point Concepcion, Awawilashmu near the Cañada del Refugio, Alwatalam and Elhiman in the Goleta marsh; Shtekolo at the Cienega and Kulalama and Tenenam and Tokin near the mission at Santa Barbara; Skonon and Mismatuk in Arroyo Burro in the same neighborhood; Kinapuich', Mishtapalwa, Kachyoyukuch, Antap, and Honmoyanshu near Ventura; Mahalal at San Cayetano. Ho'ya or Huya has been recorded for San Miguel Island, Santa Catalina Island (which is Gabrielino), and a village on Santa Cruz. Another name for Santa Catalina is Himinakots, with which Cabrillo's Taquimine, "Spaniards," may possibly be connected.

Kamupau, Tashlipunau, Takuyo, and Lapau are Yokuts forms, but some of them may rest on Chumash originals. Takuyo, reflected in the modern name of Mount Tecuya, may be a locative of Tokya, the generic name which the Yokuts apply to the Chumash.

CABRILLO'S DISCOVERIES.

The report of Cabrillo's voyage mentions by name a considerable number of coast and island Chumash villages. As this list antedates by more than two centuries any similar record for other California Indians, its examination is of interest.

Beginning with Xucu, the Pueblo de las Canaos, sometimes placed at Santa Barbara or Ventura but more likely to have been at Rincon, the Cabrillo narrator names Xucu, Bis, Sopono, Alloc, Xabaagua, Xotococ, Potoltuc, Nacbuc, Quelqueme, Misinagua, Misesopano, Elquis, Coloc, Mugu, Xagua, Anacbuc, Partotac. Susuquey, Quanmu, Gua (or Quannegua), Asimu, Aguin, Casalic, Tucumu, Incpupu. The context implies that these extended westward not quite to Dos Pueblos. Subsequently Cabrillo speaks of the greater part of this coast, namely, the stretch from Las Canoas to Cicakut or Pueblo de Sardinas, identified with Goleta, as the province of Xucu, appearing to contrast it with the province of Xexu which reaches from Xexu or Xexo on the lee side of Point Concepcion to Dos Pueblos. From Sardinas to Point Concepcion he then names Ciucut (the "Capital," where an old woman reigned as "señora"), Anacot (or Anacoac), Maquinanoa, Paltatre, Anacoat, Olesino, Caacat (or Caacac), Paltocac, Tocane, Opia, Opistopia, Nocos, Yutum, Quiman, Micoma, Garomisopona.

It is clear from the misspelled repetitions in these lists, as well as their correspondences, that they cannot represent any consistent geographical order. Sopono, Misesopano, and Garomisopona; Potoltuc, Paltatre, Partocac, and Paltocac; Anacot, Anacoat, and probably Nacbuc and Anacbuc; Opia and Opistopia; Cicakut, Ciucut, and perhaps Caacat, are all duplicate references.

The identifications with villages mentioned in more recent sources point to the same conclusion. The more probable of these are:

Xucu: Shuku, at Rincon (not Ventura).
Alloc: Heliok, near Goleta.
Xabaagua: Shalawa, near Santa Barbara (b for 1?).
Quelqueme: Wene'me, at Hueneme (q for g?).
Elquis: Elhelel (?), near Santa Barbara.
Coloc: Kolok, at Carpinteria.
Mugu: Muwu, on Mugu lagoon.
Xagua: Shawa on Santa Cruz island, or for Xabaagua (?).
Susuquey: Shushuchi, between Refugio and Gaviota.
Quanmu: Kuyamu (?), at Dos Pueblos.
Casalic: Kasil (?), at Refugio.
Tucumu: Tuhmu'l, near Shushuchi.
Incpupu: Humkaka, on Point Concepcion.
Ciucut: Siuhtun or "Siuktu" in Santa Barbara.
Tocane: Perhaps a misreading of Tucumu, but Tukan, the name of San Miguel Island, may be intended.
Xexo: Shisholop, inside Point Concepcion.

It may be added that Paltocac is placed by a later authority near Goleta, presumably on native information.

The islands present more difficulty, since the expedition may have confounded or rediscovered them. Two of the three Cabrillo names for the islands can not be identified: Liquimuymu, San Miguel, and

Nicalque, Santa Rosa. The third is involved in doubt: Limu or Limun, Santa Cruz.

Liquimuymu is said to have had two towns: Zaco or Caco, which may be for Tukan (the island may well have been named after the principal settlement) ; and Nimollolo, which suggests Nimalala on Santa Cruz. Liquimuymu itself suggests the Santa Cruz village of L'aka'amu, or, as it has also been written in Spanish orthography, Lucuyumu.

On Nicalque three villages are named: Nichochi or Nicochi; Coycoy; and Caloco or Estocoloco ("este Coloco, this Coloco"?). None of these can be identified. Coloco may be another Kolok distinct from that at Carpinteria: compare Shisholop at both Point Concepcion and Ventura. Nicalque itself might possibly stand for either Nümkülkül or Niakla on Santa Rosa.

Limu is said to contain eight towns, and ten are then enumerated, whose names seem unusually corrupted: Miquesesquelua, Poele, Pisqueno, Pualnacatup, Patiquiu and Patiquilid (*sic*), Ninumu, Muoc, Pilidquay (*sic*), and Lilibeque. If these words are Chumash, the initial syllables in *P–* suggest a native article or demonstrative which has been erroneously included. Not one name of this list can be connected with any known Chumash settlement.

A previous mention of " San Lucas " has been interpreted as referring to Santa Rosa, but several of its six villages can be safely identified as on Santa Cruz: Maxul is Mashch'al; Xugua (compare the mainland list), Shawa; and Nimitopal, Nimalala. The others are Niquipos, Nitel, and Macamo. If we are willing to allow a considerable play to misprints, Nitel might be Swahül (Ni– for Su–), and Macamo, L'aka'amu (M for L). Hahas, one of the principal towns in later times, is not mentioned by Cabrillo. Even if some of these identifications with Santa Cruz settlements seem doubtful, it is significant that not one of the San Lucas villages bears any resemblance of name to the villages of Santa Rosa.

It follows, therefore, that " San Lucas," as the designation of a single island, is Santa Cruz, and not Santa Rosa. Limu or " San Salvador," for which an entirely different list of villages is given, accordingly would be not Santa Cruz but Santa Catalina, as indeed at least one authority has already asserted. There is the more warrant for this attribution, since the name Santa Catalina in the mouths of all Shoshoneans is Pimu, of which Limu is an easy misreading. Hence, too, the eight or ten unidentifiable village names on " Limu ": they would not agree with any known designations of Chumash villages because Santa Catalina is Gabrielino, that is, Shoshonean. It is true that the words do not ring Shoshonean. They are almost certainly not Gabrielino, which has " *r* " where more southerly cognate dialects have "*l.*" Various conjectures can be advanced on this point. Perhaps the simplest is that Chumash names were obtained for Shoshonean settlements.

It may be added that these reinterpretations are much more consonant with a reasonable course for Cabrillo's little vessels. The route formerly accepted is: San Pedro Harbor (San Miguel), then westward to Santa Cruz (San Salvador), back easterly to Santa Monica (Bahia de los Fumos or Fuegos), then west once more to Mugu, and then to Ventura (Xucu); with Catalina, which is in plain sight of San Pedro, unmentioned until later. The following chart is suggested instead: San Diego or Newport Bay (San Miguel); Santa Catalina; either San Pedro or Santa Monica (Los Fumos); Mugu; and Rincon (Las Canaos, native name Xucu). This gives a continuous course.

On the other hand, Limu reappears in later sources, and almost certainly as Santa Cruz. Father Tapis in 1805 wrote of two islands, whose position seemingly best fits that of Santa Cruz and Santa Rosa, as being called, respectively, Limú and Huima. The latter is clearly Wima'l, that is, Santa Rosa. It was said to contain seven settlements, which is the number located on it in Plate 48. Limú must therefore be Santa Cruz. Its 10 rancherias nearly reach the number on the map. The three principal, with populations of 124, 145, and 122 adults, respectively, were Cajatsá—that is, Hahas; Ashuagel; and Liam, the Liyam of the map.

This evidence seems almost inescapable; but its acceptance gives Cabrillo a confused route; makes his San Salvador (Limú) and San Lucas (Maxul, etc.) the same island; furnishes two entirely different lists of villages said by him to be on this island, one of them identifiable and the other wholly unidentifiable by more recent Chumash data; and makes the voyager silent on the inhabitants of Santa Catalina. These difficulties lend a certain seduction to the temptation somehow to regard Cabrillo's Limú as having been Pimu-Catalina; enough, perhaps, to justify the maintenance of some suspicions until further elucidation is forthcoming.

With "San Lucas" and possibly "San Salvador" shifted one island east from the accepted interpretation, it may be that the "Isla de la Posesion" or "Juan Rodriguez," where Cabrillo wintered and lies buried, was Santa Rosa instead of San Miguel. Since nothing certain can be made of the native names that seem to refer to either island, this problem is one for the geographer rather than the ethnologist.

Two things are clear that are of general interest to the historian of the natives of California. First, many place names have endured for centuries in California. And, second, on allowance for the accumulation of errors in successive recording by mariners, copying, and printing of meaningless terms, there is no evidence that the Chumash language has materially altered in more than 350 years.

INTERTRIBAL RELATIONS.

The Chumash knew the Salinans as At'ap-alkulul; the Yokuts or San Joaquin drainage Indians in general as Chminimolich or " northerners "; the Alliklik, their Shoshonean neighbors on the upper Santa Clara River, by that name; the Fernandeño, Gabrielino, and perhaps the groups beyond as At'ap-lili'ish. Most of these names in their full plural form carry a prefix *I*–.

All accounts unite in making the Chumash an unwarlike people, although intervillage feuds were common and the fighter who killed was accorded public esteem. A little war between Santa Barbara and Rincon, probably in Mission times, seems to be the chief one of which knowledge has been perpetuated.

SOCIAL INSTITUTIONS.

Notices of the status of the chief, *wot* or *wocha*, are brief and as conflicting as is customary when no intensive study has been made. One statement is to the effect that chiefs had no authority and were not obeyed. This is no doubt true if "authority" is taken in the strict legal sense which the word can possess among more advanced peoples. But, on the contrary, everything goes to show that the Chumash chief enjoyed influence and honor to a rather unusual degree. Cabrillo's reference to his "princess" indicates that rank was carefully regulated. In an anarchic society, leadership would have been in the hands of a man of natural capacity; a woman can attain to accorded preeminence only through definitely crystallized custom. It is also repeatedly stated that the chief received food and shell money from the people—no doubt for a return of some kind. It is specifically said that he was head among the rich men. Ordinarily, he alone had more than one wife. The chief summoned to ceremonies—the general Californian practice; and no doubt entertained the visitors. Refusal to attend was a cause of war. As the same is reported from the Juaneño, the fact can not be doubted. But it is likely that some motive other than resentment at slighted prestige was operative. Declination of an invitation may have been a formal imputation of witchcraft, or a notice that hostile magic had been practiced in revenge.

The Chumash, alone among their neighbors, buried the dead. The Salinans cremated; so did the Shoshoneans eastward; the Yokuts both buried and burned. Only the inhabitants of the three Shoshonean islands followed the Chumash practice. The custom must have been very ancient, since skeletons are as abundant in most of the Chumash area as they are rare in adjoining territory; and there is no clear record of calcined human bones.

The body was roped in flexed position. The prehistoric burials frequently show the same position, and sometimes contain fragments of heavy cord. One man alone carried the corpse and made the grave. This practice indicates belief in defilement. Those who assisted at a funeral were given shell money. The widow observed food restrictions for a year and wore the husband's hair on her head. The cemeteries seem to have been inside the villages, and were marked off with rows of stones or planks. For prominent men, masts bearing the possessions of the dead were erected, or tall boards bearing rude pictures. The mourners, it appears, danced around the cemetery, or perhaps about the family plot within it.

DWELLINGS.

According to all accounts, the Chumash house was large—up to 50 feet or more in diameter—and harbored a community of inmates; as many as 50 individuals by one report, 40 by another, three or four families according to a third. The structure was hemispherical, made by planting willows or other poles in a circle and bending and tying them together at the top. Other sticks extended across these, and to them was fastened a layer of tule mats, or sometimes, perhaps, thatch. There was no earth covering except for a few feet from the ground, the frame being too light to support a burden of soil.

The ordinary sweat house seems to have been small, but nothing is known of its construction. There was, however, also a large type of sweat house or ceremonial chamber, apparently dirt roofed, with steps leading up to the top, where the entrance was by ladder. This is clearly the Sacramento Valley dance house, whose appearance among the Chumash is rather remarkable in view of the fact that otherwise it was not built south of the Miwok, several hundred miles away. Such discontinuous croppings out are not rare in California; witness the distribution of totemic exogamy, of caps, and the acorn soup paddle. They indicate a greater group individuality than has generally been assumed or than appears on first acquaintance. It is extremely probable that of such now separated cultural elements many once extended over a large unbroken tract, from certain middle portions of which they were subsequently eliminated by the increasing activity of other factors of social life.

The Chumash are one of the California nations that knew true beds and made what might be called rooms inside their houses.

The beds were platforms raised from the ground, on which rush mats were spread. A rolled-up mat served as pillow. Other mats were hung about the bed, both for privacy and for warmth, it appears. The islanders, on the other hand, slept crowded and on the ground, according to Cabrillo.

CANOES.

The canoe, *tomol* or *tomolo*, was one of the glories of the Chumash. Their northern neighbors were entirely without; only toward Cape Mendocino were canoes again to be encountered; and these were of a quite different type. The Shoshoneans of the islands, of course, had boats; and in some measure the Chumash-Gabrielino form of canoe was employed southward at least as far as San Diego. But the Luiseño and Diegueño did not voyage habitually; and for local use, the rush balsa seems to have been commoner. The Chumash, however, were mariners; they took to their boats not only when necessity demanded, but daily, so far as weather permitted.

The canoe as generally described was made of separate planks lashed together and calked with the asphalt that abounds on the beach. Fragments from ancient sites tally exactly with the accounts. Whether the dugout form of boat was also made is not altogether certain, but seems not unlikely. The planked vessel has less strength; but the sea is generally remarkably calm in the Santa Barbara Channel, and landings would normally be made in sheltered coves. This type of boat is, of course, also lighter and swifter. It has sometimes been thought that the Chumash had recourse to planks because of lack of timber suitable for hollowing, especially on the islands. This explanation seems to be only indirectly true. Santa Cruz still bears tolerable pines, Santa Rosa was not wholly without trees, and on the mainland there were, of course, forests. But the rainfall is light in Chumash land, and trees of any size grow only on the mountains, in the most favorable cases several miles from the shore. There are no streams large enough to float a heavy log, and the carriage of one would have been extremely laborious at best, perhaps quite impracticable. A long board, however, was easily carried down a trail by a pair of men. The abundance of asphalt remedied any deficiencies of carpentering, so far as tightness to water went. Once the type was worked out and established, it might be given preference over the dugout even in the rarer cases where the latter was practicable.

The larger canoes must have had some sort of skeleton, or at least thwarts; but there are no clear reports as to such constructional elements. Neither do we know if the bow was pointed, as the speed attained would indicate, or blunt, as in the river boat of north-western California. One account mentions that the ends were high. Prehistoric stone models are sharp and raised at both ends, with a vertical drop in the gunwale aft of the stem and forward of the stern.

The canoes are described as holding from 2 or 3 to 12 people; one account even says 20. Another mentions 8 paddlers and 6 passengers. The length is said to have run to 8 or 10 varas, say 25 feet, with a 4-foot beam; but this size must have been exceptional. It is certain that double-bladed paddles were used; their employment has already been noted on San Francisco Bay and recurs among the Diegueño. This implement seems elsewhere in North America to be known only to the Eskimo. The ordinary one-bladed paddle may also have been in use by the Chumash.

The planking was split with wedges, which would be needed also for cemetery boards and probably for wooden dishes. The Chumash replaced the usual Californian antler wedge with one of whale rib. The adze is not known. Its blade must have been of shell, as with the Yurok, since flint chips too jaggedly to be of service for planing, and grained stone can not be rubbed down to a fine enough edge and retain strength. The handle may be conjectured to have been of wood, since no remains of stone or bone have been found that would answer the purpose.

WOODEN IMPLEMENTS.

Another device that is unique among the Chumash, at least so far as California is concerned, is the spear thrower. Our knowledge of this rests exclusively upon a single specimen brought to England by Vancouver. The record that it was obtained at Santa Barbara is not entirely free from suspicion, but seems authentic. It might be conjectured that the Chumash learned the implement from the Aleutians who were brought to some of the islands by Russian sea otter hunters during the latter part of the Mission period; but there is nothing in the specimen to suggest an Alaskan prototype, and Vancouver seems to have preceded the Russians. The shape is remarkable: a very short and rather thick board, nearly as broad as long, and appearing extraordinarily awkward for its purpose. It is, however, indubitably a spear thrower, with groove and point for the butt of the spear. While the circumstances surrounding this solitary example are such as to necessitate some reserve in the acceptance of the implement as native in Chumash culture, it seems sufficiently supported to be added to other instances as an illustration of the technical advancement which this people had reached.

A companion piece in the British Museum is a harpoon quite different from any other known Californian one. It has a rather heavy shaft of wood painted red. Into this is set a slenderer foreshaft, a device never reported from California except in arrows. The head is of bone, with a barb and a chert point. The line is attached to the head in typical Californian manner: lashed on with cord, over which gum or asphalt has been smeared. The weapon is meant for sea otters or seals, not for fish. It is to be hoped that these two remarkable pieces may soon have the remnants of doubt that still cling to them dissipated by a searching scrutiny. A determination of their wood promises to be particularly convincing.

Also unique is a sinew-backed bow in the British Museum; and of special interest because southern California generally used self-bows. This specimen is narrower and thicker than the Yurok bows obtained by Vancouver at Trinidad on the same voyage; and its wood is more yellowish than the northern yew. The attribution to Santa Barbara is therefore probably correct. The grip is thong wound, the cord of three-ply sinew.

Otherwise, the Chumash bow is unknown. The arrow is said sometimes to have been of cane. This report is confirmed by the presence in graves of the grooved arrow straightener of steatite that is the invariable concomitant of the cane arrow in the southern half of California. It is less common, however, than might be anticipated among a people who worked soapstone so freely as the Chumash. The inference results that the cane arrow was less typical than one with a wooden shaft.

Several early sources speak of neatly made dishes and bowls of wood, beautifully inlaid with haliotis; but not a single representative specimen has survived. The type appears to have been confined to the Chumash; though inlaying on a smaller scale was practiced by the southern Californians on their ceremonial batons, and the Yurok and their neighbors occasionally set bits of haliotis into a pipe.

BASKETRY.

Chumash basketry is substantially that of the Shoshoneans of southern California, which is described in detail in the chapter on the Cahuilla, plus some leanings toward the Yokuts and certain minor peculiarities. Perhaps the most important of these is the substitution of three rushes (*Juncus*) for a bundle of grass stems (*Epicampes rigens*) as the foundation of coiled ware. The grass is used both by the Southern Yokuts and the Shoshoneans. The Chumash employed it, but rarely. One or more of their rushes were apt to be split with each stitch: the awl was as likely to pass through as between the soft and hollow stems. Sumac (*Rhus trilobata*) was also coiled about the *Juncus* foundation. The prevailing surface, however, at least in decorative baskets, was of the rush. Typical coloration of such vessels was threefold: a buff background, often inclining to red or mottled, with black patterns outlined in yellow or white, all of these shades except the black appearing to have been obtained from the undyed rush itself. This three-color effect is Yokuts rather than southern Californian. (Pl. 52.)

There is also northern resemblance in the shape of baskets intended for gifts or offerings. The shape of these stands midway between the Yokuts bottleneck and the southern California globular basket. They are low, with mouth rather small in the perfectly flat top. Sometimes there is a small rim or neck, but this never rises to any distance. One or two preserved specimens are fitted with a lid, but there is no evidence that this is an aboriginal feature. The direction of the coil in these shouldered baskets is antisunwise, as they are viewed from above, and contrary to the direction in vessels of other shapes. Exactly the same holds for the Yokuts and Shoshonean small-mouthed baskets, which, in all three regions, were evidently held or pierced in reverse position during manufacture.

The best Chumash work is somewhat finer and smoother than that of the Shoshoneans of southern California. In part, the difference may be attributed to the preservation chiefly of exceptional show pieces, which contrast with the average effect of the much more numerous modern utilitarian Cahuilla and Luiseño specimens. But there was no doubt also an actual distinction, in which the southern Yokuts were aligned with the Chumash as against the Shoshoneans. This is what one should expect from the general types of civilization of the peoples. The Chumash at all points show themselves finished and loving artisans of exceptional mechanical skill. The Shoshoneans of the south were coarse handicraftmen, but mystic speculators and religious originators.

An ancient Chumash cap which fortune has preserved in a cave is also southern Yokuts rather than Luiseño in appearance. (Pl. 53.)

Coiled storage baskets, wider at the bottom than at the mouth, were made by the Chumash. (Pl. 54.) These may have been known also to the other tribes of the south, but, if so, they have gone out of use.

Openwork rush baskets, both deep and plate form, were practically identical with those of the Luiseño.

A basketry water bottle must have been of some importance, since a number of prehistoric specimens have come to light. (Pl. 53.) They are usually in simple twining reinforced here and there by courses of three-strand or diagonal twining, flat bottomed, and lined with asphalt, which was applied with hot pebbles. The water bottle of the Plateau Shoshoneans and of the desert tribes of Arizona, which penetrated eastern and southern California at least as far as the Tehachapi range, was in diagonal twining, pitched outside, and

usually pointed or rounded below. It is intended for hanging and
for travel; the Chumash form, to be set about the house. The material of the latter seems most commonly to have been *Juncus*, which
the asphalt stiffened for enduring wear.

The woven fur blanket, which in its characteristic California form
is made, as in the Southwest and Plateau, of strips of rabbit skin, was
·partly replaced among the Chumash by one of feathers. Narrow
pieces of bird skin were twisted with a cord to give them strength;
into these were woven shorter strands of plain strings. This is a
form of blanket that appears to have been known through a considerable part of California.

This type of feather blanket is described by the Maidu, and is only a variant
of the rabbit-fur robe. Two specimens preserved in museums, one from the
Chumash and the other from an unspecified group in California, have a different
structure. The former has a long continuous warp of two cords wrapped with
strips of quill, to which feather web adheres. A double woof of unfeathered
cords is twined in. The second piece also has a double warp, but the two
strands are twisted on each other and a bit of feather inserted at each turn.
The woof is inserted in close rows. This makes at least three techniques followed in the manufacture of these blankets.

INDUSTRY IN STONE.

The Chumash did not make the pottery of their southeastern neighbors, and did not acquire it in trade, although stray pieces may now
and then have drifted among them. References to their " pots " or
" ollas " are to steatite vessels, both open dishes and nearly globular
bowls, often large—up to 2 feet in diameter—and usually thin
walled. Some are shell inlaid and have not been subjected to setting
in the fire, but the service of ceremony or show which they rendered
is unknown. When a pot broke, its pieces were used as fry pans; at
least, many such have been found, fired and usually perforated in
one corner, to allow of being moved with a stick.

The Chumash used the metate; the bowlder mortar; the mortar
finished outside; and the pounding slab with basketry hopper. The
latter is attested by numerous circles of asphalt on ancient stones—
sometimes on mortar edges, too. Whether the relation of the several
types was one of use or period, or both, is not known, since no attention appears to have been given to stratigraphy in any of the
numerous excavations of Chumash sites. The deposits are sometimes
of considerable thickness, and once they are examined with reference
to their time sequences, light may be shed on the obscure history of
mortar and metate, which is discussed in connection with the Maidu
and other tribes.

One consideration may be added here. There are indications
that the true or squared metate is a utensil which spread north-

ward from southern Mexico, probably in more or less close association with agriculture. This is the implement with flat or cylindrically concave surface, over which an elongated stone was worked back and forth. In contrast with this is the grinding stone more prevalent in California: an irregular slab on which a roundish or short stone was rubbed with a rotary motion. This is a ruder device, effective enough for the occasional grinding of seeds, and sufficiently simple, both in its manufacture and manipulation, to form part of a very rudimentary culture. It would not answer the daily needs of a population practicing maize agriculture systematically. The question for California is whether the grinding slab may go back to an early period with the metate superadded later, or whether the former is to be regarded as the contemporary equivalent among a lowly civilized people of the more specialized metate. Almost every specimen shows at a glance how its surface has been worn; but no consistent distinction of the two types appears to have been attempted.

Small and large show mortars are not rare in Chumash graves. They are of fine sandstone, flat bottomed, the walls of uniform thickness, and polished outside as well as in. The rim is nicely squared, sometimes even concave, or asphalted and inset with shell beads. Such pieces would necessarily be far too valuable for ordinary use, and would certainly break promptly under wear. That they were made for the toloache ritual is possible, but unproved. They do confirm, however, the early remark that " the constancy, attention to trifles, and labor which they [the Channel Indians] employ in finishing these pieces, are well worthy of admiration; " a fitting characterization, also, of most other products of Chumash industrial art.

Large stone rings or perforated disks have been found in great numbers in Chumash territory. These were slipped over the women's digging sticks to give the stroke momentum. Elsewhere in California such weighting of the stick has not been reported, and since stones with sufficiently large perforations are rare, it seems that the Chumash were nearly unique in not contenting themselves with the simple sharpened shaft. Most of the stones are well rounded and some are beautifully polished in hard, compact material. They were evidently highly prized and illustrate once more the fondness of the Chumash for perfection in manual matters.

There has been some inclination to interpret these objects as warclub heads, net sinkers, and the like, but as native statements on the subject are perfectly clear and decisive, mere conjectures are baseless. It does not matter that now and then a carefully polished piece shows wear as if someone had hammered with it. A hasty woman may occasionally have laid hold of the first implement that came to hand, or young or thoughtless members of the family may have aroused her resentment by putting a carefully preserved treasure to rough and ruinous use in her absence. We do not conclude from coffee stains on a chair that the owner regarded it indiscriminately as a seat and a table, nor from its violently fractured condition that it was intended as a weapon of offense. The remains of primitive people must be judged in the same spirit.

The pipe, as recovered by excavations, is a stone tube, slightly convex in profile, and thinning considerably from bowl to mouth end. A short bone mouthpiece remains in many specimens and is likely to have been set in regularly. The length varies, but 5 inches would be not far from the average. Steatite is perhaps the commonest material, but by no means the only one; a rough-breaking brick-red stone occurs rather frequently. Now and then the pipe is bent near the middle at an angle of from 15° to 60°. This form allowed comparatively easy perforation of pieces more than a foot long, since boring could be carried on in four sections—at each end and in both directions from the elbow. the two latter holes being subsequently plugged.

Analogy with the practices of other California Indians makes it almost certain that the stone pipes of the Chumash were employed by shamans. Their comparative abundance suggests that they were also put to profaner use. But, on the other hand, it is scarcely probable that a man would smoke only when he had a stone implement. Pipes of wood or cane are likely to have been used but to have perished.

SHELLS AND MONEY.

The commonest fishhook among the Chumash and their neighbors to the southeast was of haliotis, nearly circular, and unbarbed. The point is turned so far in as to make it difficult to see how it could have bit; but hooks of similar shape are used in Polynesia and Japan for fish that swallow slowly. As tension is put on the line, the point penetrates the jaw and slides through to the attachment of the line.

Chumash money appears to have been the clam-shell disk bead currency that was the ordinary medium of all those parts of California that did not employ dentalia. In fact, it is likely that the Chumash furnished the bulk of the supply for the southern half of the State, as the Pomo did farther north. The usual south and central Californian method of measuring the strung beads on the circumference of the hand was in vogue. The available data on this system have been brought together in Table 6.

TABLE 6.—CALIFORNIA SHELL BEAD MONEY MEASURES.

	Salinan Antoniano.	Salinan Migueleño.	Central Yokuts.	Southern Yokuts.	Chumash.	Gabrielino.	Luiseño.
Tip of middle finger to crease of palm.	wosemah (½)[1]	tewi (½)					
Half of circumference palm and fingers.	"1-its-name" (1)	"1-its-name" (1)					
Circumference palm and fingers.	mawiya (2)	"2-its-name" (2)	chok[3]	chok	skomuya[2] (½)[3]		
One and a half times around.							[½ ponko.]
Twice around.		"4-its-name" (4)		hista[4]	stil[4] (1)[3]	ponko (1)[3]	ponko.
Circumference elbow and finger tips.		hamawi[5]		([6])			
Four times around palms and fingers.		"8-its-name" (8)					
Six times around.						sakayo (4)	

[1] The figures in parentheses give the equivalent in Spanish *reales* or American "bits." Compare *iskom*, two, *skumu*, four.

[2] Plus the length of the middle finger.

[3] Probably the same word.

[5] Reckoned as nearly equal to the "4-its-name."

[6] The measure from the tip of the middle finger "to" the elbow is mentioned as worth 2 *reales*.

The following conclusions may be drawn from this table:

(1) There was no unit of identical length of strung disks that obtained among all tribes that measured on the hand. One, one and a half, or two circumferences, with or without the length of the middle finger of the hand superadded, and the circuit of the forearm, were the basis of valuation among different groups.

(2) The Migueleño system has been renamed, and possibly altered, to fit the Spanish currency of reales and pesos.

(3) The native system was everywhere one of duplicating or quadruplicating units.

(4) The equivalations to silver money must be accepted with caution, because they may date from various periods, when native currency perhaps had reached different stages of depreciation. But it is rather clear that the Chumash, who probably furnished most of the supply, held their bead money in the lowest estimation. It was worth a third more among the Gabrielino and four times as much among the Salinans. With the southern Maidu, who are probably the farthest group to whom money from the Santa Barbara Channel penetrated, the system of measuring on the hand seems to have been no longer in use; but the values were extremely high. A yard would rate from $5 to $25 in American money; whereas the Chumash *stü* and Gabrielino *ponko*, of nearly the same length, were rated at only 12½ cents.

Chumash graves, as a rule, yield but little of this thick clam money. Small curved beads of olivella are far more abundant, and sometimes occur in great bulk. It may be that the Chumash buried these inferior strings with the dead and saved their genuine money to burn at a subsequent mourning commemoration.

Long tubular beads, sometimes of the columella of large univalves, others of the hinge of a large rock clam, are also found. These were prized like jewels from the Yokuts to the Diegueño—much as the magnesite cylinders in the north. Again the Chumash seem to have been the principal manufacturers.

STATUS OF CHUMASH CULTURE.

Practically every implement here mentioned as Chumash was known also to the inhabitants of the Shoshonean islands, and most of them to the mainlanders of the coast for some distance south, especially the Gabrielino. The archipelago must be considered a unit as regards material culture, irrespective of speech and origin of the natives. Santa Catalina remains, at any rate, show all the characteristics of Chumash civilization, perhaps even in their most perfect form. The Chumash coast, however, appears to have been much more closely linked with the Chumash islands, at least technologically, than the Shoshonean mainland with the Shoshonean islands; so that the prevailing impression of the culture as a distinctively Chumash one is substantially correct.

The steatite of the Chumash, so far as known, came from Santa Catalina, although ledges of this stone are reported in the Santa Ynez Mountains and near Arroyo Grande. But it can not be doubted that the island was the source of much of the supply. With it came certain curiously shaped objects—shovel-form, hooked, and the like, even carvings of finned whales, all very variable in size, and clearly serving no utility. They are less frequent in Chumash graves than on Santa Catalina, as might be expected. Since this island is the source of the Chungichnish religion, the most developed form of any cult based on the taking of the toloache plant, it might be suspected that this worship and the soapstone figures, whose import is obviously ritualistic, had traveled to the Chumash together. This may be; but there is no evidence in the scant extant knowledge that any of the specific phases of the Chungichnish religion, such as the sand painting, prevailed among the Chumash. They did use the Jimson weed; but for all that is known to the contrary, the associated cult may have been a generalized one such as flourished among the Yokuts.

It must be plainly stated, in fact, that our ignorance is almost complete on Chumash religion, on the side of ceremony as well as belief and tradition. The plummet-shaped charm stones were regarded magically and made much of. This fact points to central rather than southern California affinities in religion. Seeds, or perhaps meal ground from them, were used in offerings; but this is a custom of wide prevalence in California. Sticks hung with feathers were set up in their "adoratories." Such isolated scraps of information allow of no broader conclusions. Even the habits of the shaman are undescribed. The god *Achup* or *Chupu*, whose "worship" a missionary report of 1810 mentions as being uprooted among the Purisima natives, may or may not have had connection with the toloache cult. We can believe that the great mourning anniversary of the larger half of California was practiced; but we do not really know.

The curious ceremonial baton known to the Luiseño as *paviut* was certainly used by the Chumash, since prettily inlaid pieces, though lacking the inserted crystals, have been found. Again it would be hasty to draw the inference that the outright Chungichnish cult had reached the Chumash. Concrete religious elements often have a wider distribution, especially among primitive peoples, than organized religions, which, like all flowers, are temporary and superficial. It is difficult, to be sure, to picture the Chungichnish religion originating on Santa Catalina and spreading east and south to tribes of much inferior arts while leaving the nearer and more advanced Chumash on Santa Cruz and of Ventura untouched by its influence. An interpretation that avoids this mental obstacle is the conjecture that the Chumash and Gabrielino jointly worked out a well-developed religion based on toloache, of which we happen to know only the Gabrielino or Chungichnish phase because its spread was very recent and its influence affected tribes that have survived.

On the other hand, it is possible that the Chumash were really inferior to the speculating Shoshoneans in power of abstract formulation. Such differences in national spirit exist in California, as witness the Shoshonean Luiseño and Yuman Diegueño. The technological abilities of the Chumash do not by any means prove an equal superiority in other directions. And yet their excellence in material matters is so distinct that it is difficult for the ethnologist to picture them as mere secondary copyists in other respects.

CHAPTER 38.

THE WASHO.

AFFILIATIONS.

The Washo have been unduly neglected by students of the Indian. What little is on record concerning them makes it difficult to place them.

Their speech, which is rather easy to an English tongue and pleasant to the ear, is distinctive and very diverse from that of the Shoshonean Mono and Northern Paiute with whom they are in contact and association. Such investigation as has been made—and it has not gone very deep—points to the Washo language as being Hokan and therefore no longer to be regarded as an independent stock. Still the affiliation with other Hokan languages can not be close. The position of the Washo makes this comparative distinctness remarkable. For a detached and quasi-independent little group the Washo are on the wrong side of the Sierra. Diversity is the true Californian habit. The moment the Plateau is entered single dialects stretch for monotonous hundreds of miles, and the basic Shoshonean tongue continues without interruption across the Great Basin and even over the Rockies. Now the Washo are a Basin tribe. Their settlements were all on streams that flow eastward to be lost in the interior desert. Even as the artificial lines of statehood run they are as much a Nevadan as a Californian people. Their anomaly as a separate fragment is therefore in their location.

It is tempting to conjecture, accordingly, and especially on the basis of their probable Hokan kinship, that they are an ancient Californian tribe, which has gradually drifted, or been pressed, over the Sierra. But there are no concrete grounds other than speech to support such an assumption.

HABITAT.

The Washo territory is the upper and more fertile drainage of the Truckee and Carson Rivers—streams born in California mountains to perish in Nevada sinks. How far down they ranged on these two rivers has not been ascertained with accuracy. It seems to have been but a little below Reno and Carson City. Long Valley Creek, which drains northwestward into Honey Lake, a Californian stream, was also in their possession. West of the crest of the Sierra they had no settlements, but the Miwok acknowledged their hunting rights on the upper Stanislaus nearly as far down as the Calaveras Big Trees. They may have enjoyed similar privileges elsewhere. Where there are no winter villages, information is often conflicting: boundaries may have been in dispute, or amicably crossed. If the Washo hunted on the North Stanislaus they may have come down the Middle Fork also, or frequented the Calaveras, Cosumnes, or American. Sierra Valley has been assigned both to them and the northeastern Maidu. The deep snows prevented more than temporary occupation. Honey Lake, too, may have been more largely Washo than the map (Pl. 46) shows, or entirely forbidden to them.

Lake Tahoe is central to Washo territory, and was and is still resorted to in summer, but its shores are scarcely habitable in the season of snow.

The Washo call themselves Washiu or Wasiu. The names applied to them by their neighbors are unknown, except for northern Maidu Tsaisuma or Tsaisü. Northern Miwok Hisatok or Histoko means merely " easterners."

The Washo were at times in conflict with the adjacent Northern Paiute, whom they call Paleu, and by whom they are said to have been defeated about 1860.

NUMBERS.

There are the usual statements, some made as much as 50 years ago, about enormous decrease and degeneration or impending extinction; but actually the Washo seem to have suffered less diminution as a consequence of the invasion of our civilization than the vast majority of California Indians. Estimates of their population were: In 1859, 900; 1866, 500; 1892, 400; 1910, 300. The Federal census in this last year enumerated over 800, about one-third in California and two-thirds in Nevada, some three-fourths or more being full blood. As the Washo are distinctly separated from the " Paiutes " and the "California Diggers " in the local American consciousness, it is not likely that this figure involves any erroneous inclusions of consequence. Their lack of any reservation, and the semiadjustment of their life to civilized conditions, leading to a scattering habitation on the fringes of white settlements, have evidently caused a persistent underestimation of their numbers.

Their original strength may have been double what it is to-day: 1,500 or under seems a likely figure in view of the nature of their country, their solidarity, and their unity of speech.

CULTURE.

The customs of the Washo will undoubtedly prove interesting once they are known. Their habitat on the flank of the Sierra Nevada must have made them in the main Californians. But being over the crest of the range, they must have had something of an eastern outlook, and their associations with the Northern Paiute, who maintained direct affiliations with the tribes in the Rocky Mountains, and were apparently subject to at least some indirect influences from the Plains, can hardly but have given the civilization of the Washo some un-Californian color.

BASKETRY.

Their basketry, which is deservedly noted for excellent finish and refinement of decorative treatment, is of the central Californian order. with coiling predominating in fine ware (Pl. 55, *f*), whereas the adjacent Shoshoneans, like most of those of the Great Basin, incline to plain and diagonal twining. The nearest analogues are in Miwok work. Both single and triple rod foundations are employed. The shapes are simple; the designs are characterized by a lack of bulk that is typical also of Miwok patterns, as well as by a delicacy and slenderness of motive to which the Miwok do not attain. The direction of the coil is from left to right, as among the Miwok and Maidu; the edge has the herringbone finish of diagonally crossed sewing, where most California tribes, except sometimes the Miwok, simply wrap the last coil.

A twined and pitched water jar is no doubt due to Shoshonean influence. The conical carrying basket is either of plain-twined wide-spaced openwork of peeled stems, as in northwestern California, or unpeeled like the wood-carrying basket of the Pomo, or diagonally twined in openwork, or closely with a pattern. The nearer Californian tribes use chiefly a narrow mesh filled in by smearing over. Oval and triangular trays, elliptical seed beaters, and the like were of the types common to all the Sierra tribes and the nearer Shoshoneans; with the weave in plain or diagonal twining. The latter technique is in use also for cooking baskets. Three-strand twining is employed for starts and reenforcements.

The almost universal basket material is willow, with fern root (*Pteridium aquilininum*) for the black of patterns, and redbud (*Cercis occidentalis*) for red. The latter material was also used for warp and coiling foundation. It is said to have been imported from west of the Sierras.

Cradles are of the hooded basketry type described among the Yokuts. A band of diagonal bars or crosses—diagonals in two directions—is put on a boy's cradle, of rhombuses on a girl's. Occasionally the cradle and hood are covered with buckskin, as in the eastern Great Basin.

DRESS AND IMPLEMENTS.

Sinew-sewed deerskin clothes for women are mentioned, but may possibly have had the same recent and eastern source as the small sweat lodge. Their description as consisting of a separate waist and skirt sounds rather unaboriginal.

Rabbits were taken in nets of a 3-inch mesh, $1\frac{1}{2}$ or 2 feet wide, and as much as 300 feet in length. These were hung loosely on stakes or bushes. Sometimes two were set at an angle. When the animals were driven, they became entangled in the sagging net, and had their temples crushed by hunters that sprang out from concealment. All hunts organized on a large scale were under the direction of the chief of the rabbit hunt, *peleu-lewe-tiyeli*, whose position was hereditary.

The bow was sinew backed and had recurved ends. The arrow was foreshafted, the quiver of deerskin had the hair side turned in. This indicates the usual north and central Californian type of weapon.

Piñon nuts, *tagum*, usually ground and boiled, were a commoner food of the Washo than acorns, *malil*, although these could also be gathered in some tracts and were obtained by trade from the west. The mortar was a hole in a bowlder, used without basketry hopper; the pestle usually an unshaped cobble. The metate was called *demge*. The mush-stirring paddle was called *k'a'as;* the looped stick which was used for the same purpose Yokuts-fashion, *beleyu*.

BUILDINGS.

The house was of poles joined in an oval dome, thatched with mats of tule, much as among the adjacent Northern Paiute. In the mountains leaves or bark were used for covering. The winter house was a cone of slabs of bark, about 8 feet high in the middle and 12 feet in length, with a projecting entrance. It must have been very similar to the Maidu *hübo*.

The Plains Indian type of sweat lodge, a pole frame temporarily covered with skins or mats, just large enough to sit in, and heated by steam, was used instead of the earth-covered Californian sweat house, it is said. This form is likely to be a recent one, introduced with the horse, or possibly a reflex of a ghost-dance movement.

The dance or assembly house with roof of earth was known to the Washo, who call it *dayalimi;* but whether they built and used it, or had merely seen it in the west, is not clear.

RELIGION AND SOCIETY.

The adolescence dance for girls was practiced, perhaps in a Shoshonean guise, since neither the valley Maidu, the hill Miwok, nor the Yokuts make this dance in developed form.

Some form of mourning anniversary was held—"cry" is its English name in vogue—but all details are lacking.

The chief, *teubeyu*, succeeded in the male line. At marriage an exchange of gifts is said to have been optional. As among the Northern Paiute, there evidently was no bride purchase, even in form. The dead were cremated.

It is clear that some real information on the Washo is highly desirable.

CHAPTER 39.

THE SHOSHONEAN STOCK.

RELATION OF THE STOCK TO THE CALIFORNIAN AREA.

The Shoshonean stock is easily the largest in California, in present-day numbers as well as in territory. It occupied a third of the area of the State. It stretched in a solid belt from the northeastern corner nearly to the southwestern. True, the Washo break the continuity at one point within the State limits. But this is a gap only in a nominal sense, for the Shoshoneans of the north and those of the south of California are connected by a broad band of territory that sweeps over nearly the whole of Nevada.

In one sense, however, the Shoshoneans are an un-Californian people. Except for a highland strip in the south (see Figs. 34, 52), they have nowhere crossed the Sierra Nevada, and therefore failed to penetrate the great valley and mountain area which is the heart and bulk of California. More than half of their territory that we are here concerned with is in that essentially Shoshonean region, the Great Basin. The lines that legislation has seen fit to impose on the States include this tract in California, but nature had planned differently and her line of division between the fertile lands that face the ocean and the deserts that front nothing at all ran nearer the shore. It is this natural line that the Shoshoneans have observed in their history. And in this sense the bulk of them are un-Californian, although within California.

In the south, it is true, they have arrived at the ocean, and there some of the most populous divisions had their seats. But southern California is in many ways a physiographic and climatic area distinct from the bulk of the State. At Point Concepcion on the coast, and at Tehachapi Pass inland, the vegetation, the marine life, the temperature, and the humidity change. The alteration of the land is visible from a train window. The south is in some parts the most fertile as it is the balmiest portion of the State. But the tract to which those traits apply is restricted. It is confined to the immediate drainage into the ocean, and its limits are nowhere more than

574

50 or 60 miles from the surf. Even of this fortunate belt the Shoshoneans held only part: Hokan, Chumash, and Diegueño clung to more than half.

In any event, the coastal territories of the Shoshoneans were small in contrast with their inland desert range, even within the limits of political California, and, when their whole habitat is considered, insignificant. From north to south the Shoshonean diffusion in the State was 600 miles: their ocean frontage, a scant 100 miles. Of at least 20 known divisions established on the basis of dialect, only 5 bordered on the sea, and only 3 of these in any notable degree.

THE LARGER UTO-AZTEKAN FAMILY.

Reference has been to " Shoshoneans "; but actually this group is only part of a larger one, from which habit rather than conviction has to date withheld the universal recognition which is its due: the Uto-Aztekan family. This mass of allied tribes, which extended from Panama to Idaho and Montana (Fig. 50), is one of the great fundamental families of aboriginal America, of importance in the origins of civilization, politically predominant at the time of discovery, and numerically the strongest on the continent to-day. The association of our Shoshoneans of east and south California with this aggregate at the centers of native culture opens a far perspective. The lowly desert tribes and simple-minded folk of the southern coast are seen in a new light as kinsmen, however remote, of the famous Aztecs; and an unexpected glimpse of a vista of history opens up before the concrete fact that the sites of the cities of Los Angeles and Mexico were in the hands of peoples whose affinity is certain.

Of course, any recent connections are out of the question. It was the ancestors of the Mexican Nahua and the California Shoshoneans some thousands of years ago who were associated, not their modern representatives; and, as to the former association, no one knows where it occurred. No tribe that could by any legitimate stretch be called Aztec was ever in California, nor for that matter within the present confines of the United States. That the speech of India and that of Germany go back to a common root is a circumstance of the utmost historic import. But no sane mind would infer from the existence of an Indo-Germanic family that Germans were Hindus or Hindus Germans. It is only reasonable that we should accord the Indian a similar discrimination.

The Shoshonean group, however, forms a solid block within the Uto-Aztekan group. It is a well-marked subdivision, with a long and justly recognized unity of its own, though of a lower order. The speech affiliations of the Shoshoneans of California are all with the other Shoshoneans, and not with the Pima, Yaqui, Tarahumare, Cora, and other Mexican groups of the Uto-Aztekan family. Hence it can only aid proper understanding to treat the California tribes as Shoshoneans rather than as Uto-Aztekans. Their relations to Mexico, however ultimately important, are through the Shoshonean group as a whole.

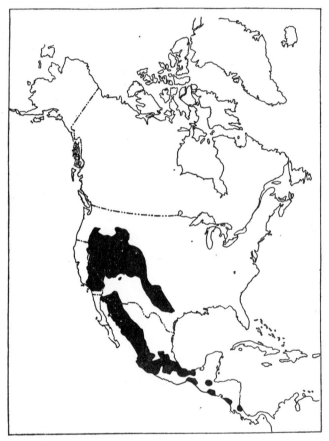

FIG. 50.—Uto-Aztecan family.

SHOSHONEAN BRANCHES AND DIVISIONS.

The Shoshonean group of languages is divided into four branches: the most extensive in the Great Basin or Plateau; the next in southern California; a third between these two on upper Kern River; and the fourth in the Pueblo area in Arizona. These are all about equally distinct from one another, except that the speech of the Hopi, the Pueblo tribe, who are territorially as well as culturally isolated from the others, is somewhat the most diverse. Two of the three other branches are subdivisible; and the organization of the whole body appears in the following scheme:

Groups in California.	Division.	Branch.
Northern Paiute	Mono-Bannock	
Eastern Mono		
Western Mono		
Koso (Panamint)	Shoshoni-Comanche	I. Plateau.
Chemehuevi	Ute-Chemehuevi	
Kawaiisu		
Tübatulabal		II. Kern River.
Kitanemuk	Serrano	
Alliklik		
Serrano		
Vanyume		
Fernandeño	Gabrielino	III. Southern California.
Gabrielino		
San Nicoleño		
Juaneño		
Luiseño		
Cupeño	Luiseño-Cahuilla	
Pass Cahuilla		
Mountain Cahuilla		
Desert Cahuilla		
	Hopi	IV. Pueblo.

The more intimate geography of these groups can be surveyed in Figure 51. The relative position and extent of the branches and divisions appear in Figure 52. The Shoshonean holdings in California will be seen to be but a small fraction of the entire territory of the stock. Yet seven of the eight divisions, or every one except Hopi, is represented within the borders of the State. The inclination to diversity of idiom which has followed us throughout our progress over California greets us once more.

As Figure 52 is regarded, the Shoshonean subdivisions appear as if raying in a semicircular fan from a point in south-central California, on or near Kern River. It is highly improbable that they have actually spread out thus. We must rather look upon the focus as the region where the condensation has been greatest, the tract where newcomers gradually agglomerated, not the hive from which the whole body swarmed.

SHOSHONEAN MOVEMENTS IN CALIFORNIA.

The languages of the southern California branch are sufficiently specialized to make it necessary to assume a considerable period for their development. This specialization could hardly have taken place without either isolation or alien contacts in a marginal loca-

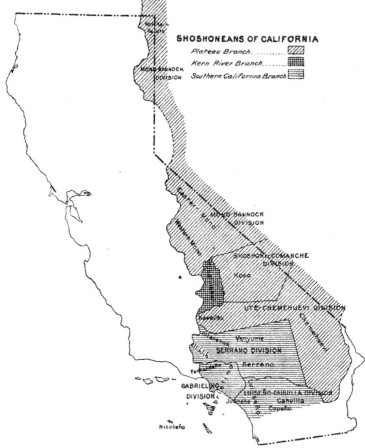

FIG. 51.— Shoshonean branches, divisions, and dialect groups in California.

tion, such as the branch is subject to now. Then, the ramifications of this branch imply a residence of some duration: there are three fully differentiated languages and a dozen dialects in southern California. How long it would take these to spring up it is impossible to say; but 1,000 years of location on the spot does not seem an excessive figure, and perhaps it would be conservative to allow 1,500 years since the Shoshoneans first began to reach the coast.   The languages of the Yuman and Chumash peoples, whom the Shoshoneans have apparently split apart in their ancient shoreward drift, are so extremely different from each other now that this period is certainly the minimum that can be assumed for their separation.

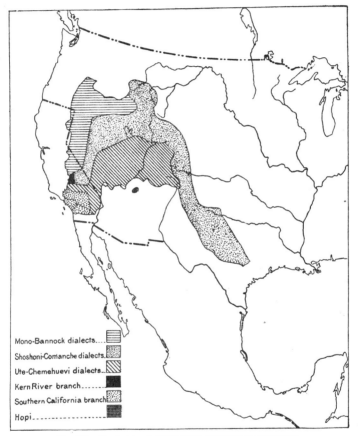

Mono-Bannock dialects....

Shoshoni-Comanche dialects.

Ute-Chemehuevi dialects.

Kern River branch.......

Southern California branch

Hopi................

FIG. 52.—Clustering of Shoshonean divisions in California.

The little Kern River branch, being equally distinctive, would seem to demand a nearly equal antiquity in the vicinity of its present seats.   This would involve a drift separate from the last, but a substantially simultaneous one.   It is possible that the Kern River group, being a much smaller one, and therefore much more susceptible to foreign influences, reached its high degree of specialization in a somewhat shorter time.

The languages of the Plateau branch in California represent a much more recent stratum. Those east of the Sierra are scarcely distinguishable from their congeners throughout the Great Basin. It is entirely conceivable that these tongues have been spoken in their present locations from time immemorial. Their territory is in the Great Basin; their speakers were actually part of the Plateau tribes; and there is no foreign element or anything else to indicate that they ever had any antecessors on the spot.

Two offshoots from them, however, have crossed the Sierra and entered the true Californian valley system: the Western Mono and the Kawaiisu, one north and the other south of the Kern River branch. Their speech, though somewhat changed from that of their respective neighbors and presumable ancestors to the east, is not greatly altered; certainly far less than that of the Kern River Tübatulabal. The Western Mono and Kawaiisu, then, are late comers. On the basis of reckoning which allows the Kern River and southern Californian branches 1,000 years in their present vicinity and 1,500 since their detachment from the main Shoshonean stock, 500 would be ample to account for the dialectic specialization of Mono and Kawaiisu. But we do not know. They may have been where they are now for a longer or a less period. Native tradition is silent; and civilized records go back barely a century.

At any rate, we can be positive that the Shoshoneans of California do not represent a single migration or drift, but rather a succession of local waves. The earliest and most important was that into southern California proper. Not much later, or perhaps synchronous but separate, was the entry of the Kern River division. Much the most recent was the movement of distinctive Plateau peoples to the west of the watershed.

CHAPTER 40.

THE PAIUTE, MONO, AND KOSO.

THE NORTHERN PAIUTE.

NOMENCLATURE.

The northeasternmost corner of California is held by a Shoshonean people who popularly are known by the blanket term "Paiute." People of the same speech and very similar customs occupy the adjacent parts of Nevada, in fact the whole northwestern third of that State; the majority of the eastern half of Oregon; roughly the southern half of Idaho; and they extend southward along the eastern border of California, except for the local interruption of the Washo, for 300 or 400 miles. In Nevada and Oregon they are called Paiutes; in central California sometimes by this term and sometimes Mono; in Idaho they are the Bannock. The form of speech over this vast stretch is, however, virtually identical: minor dialects may be numerous, but intelligibility prevails throughout. Mono-Bannock is perhaps the generic designation least open to confusion. Paviotso is the term of the Shoshoni proper for the Nevada members of the group, but, like Mono and Monachi, is too limited in its application to serve for the entire Mono-Bannock body without producing opportunity for error.

The unqualified term "Paiute" is unfortunate because it refers to two quite different peoples, both indeed Shoshonean, and Plateau Shoshonean at that, but of quite distinct divisions. The other Paiute are in southern Utah, southern Nevada, and southern California. Their affiliations are with the Ute and Chemehuevi, and their speech is divergent enough from that of their northern namesakes to be at first contact mainly unintelligible, at least as connected discourse.

As a matter of fact, the Mono-Bannock and Ute-Chemehuevi divisions seem nowhere to be even in contact, Shoshoni-Comanche tribes intervening from California to Colorado. The distinction between Southern Paiutes and Northern Paiutes will therefore be rigidly adhered to hereafter whenever the term is used at all. For the former term, Chemehuevi is a customary and convenient synonym in southern California. For the latter, "Mono" occupies a similar position in central California. Only the Northern Paiute in northern California have no alternative epithet. Paviotso originated in eastern Nevada, and is locally unknown in California. The northwestern Maidu call the Northern Paiute near them Monozi or Mona, which are evidently forms of Monachi and Mono. This very fact of its being a related name for a related people would make Monozi a desirable designation were it not that Mono has become so definitely identified with the central Californian Shoshoneans of the same division that its extension, even in slightly altered form, to a people several hundred miles distant would be certain to cause confusion. For our northeasterly Californians, then, the unwieldy designation "Northern Paiute" seems to remain as the only safe one.

The only other native ethnic name known for the Northern Paiute is Toloma, applied by the northeastern Maidu.

THE GREAT BASIN CULTURE.

These people should be described in connection with those of Nevada and Oregon, of whom they constitute a minute peripheral fraction. They can, in fact, not be described here because nothing of any significance is known of them, and little of moment of their main body to the east. Their country was un-Californian. What has been said before of Great Basin tribes that belong to California unnaturally and only through the courtesy of arbitrary political lines is particularly applicable here. The land is one of sagebrush and cedar, as what appears to be really a juniper is currently called. The acorn of California has vanished. The true pine nut takes its place only in a measure. The soil is desert, the mountains rocky, with timber in spots. Lakes are numerous, but they are evaporation pools, swampy sinks, or salt basins. Streams run only in the mountains, and flow nowhere. The outlook is wide of necessity, the population scant, travel and movement almost enforced. The Californian self-chaining to a short compass, with a dim gloom everywhere beyond, is impossible. But, to compensate, subsistence is slender and a constant makeshift. There may be leisure indeed, but it is an intermittent idleness, not the occupied and productive luxury of well-fed time. The imagination has little occasion for flight; or when the opportunity arises, there is but scant stimulus in the concrete basis of life.   Customs, therefore, remain rude.   They are too flexible to bear any ramifying elaboration.   Ritual, symbolism, and art attain little intensity, and monotonous simplicity takes the place of a rich growth.   Where an activity specializes, it develops in isolation, and fails to merge or expand into a broad scheme: eagle hunting, shamans' singing, mourning customs fix the attention, not an assemblage of the gods or a coordinated series of rites.

The very poverty of Nevadan native civilization endows it with an interest.   Its numberless little but crudely effective devices to struggle along under this burden, its occasional short plunges here or there, contain a wealth of significance.   But we can only glimpse this cultural story from bits of stray knowledge.   Its import and tenor can scarcely be mistaken; but the episodes that make the real tale have never been assembled.

We must leave the Northern Paiute of our northeasterly angle of California to some future historian of the bordering States.   That they had much in common with their Maidu and Achomawi neighbors in the detail of their existence can not be doubted.   But it is equally certain that in other respects they were true Basin people, members of a substantially homogeneous mass that extended eastward to the crest of the Rockies, and that in some measure, whether to a considerable or a subsidiary extent, was infiltrated with thoughts and practices whose hearth was in the Plains beyond.   Several traces of this remote influence have already been detected among the Achomawi.

THE TWO GHOST-DANCE WAVES.

It was a Northern Paiute, though one of Nevada, Jack Wilson or Wovoka, who in 1889 in his obscurity gave birth to the great ghost-dance movement; and before him his father, or another relative, about 1870, originated a similar wave, whose weaker antecedent stimulus carried it less far and scarcely impressed the American public.   In both cases the fringe of Northern Paiute whom we hold under consideration were involved with the main body of their kinsmen to the southeast, and passed the doctrine westward, the first time to the Modoc, the second to the Achomawi.   The later and greater agitation stopped there: the California Indian inside the Sierra had long since given up all hope and wish of the old life and adapted himself as best he might to the new civilization that engulfed him.   But in the early seventies less than 25 years had passed since the pre-American days of undisturbed and undiluted native existence.   The middle-aged Indian of northern California had spent his early years under its conditions: the idea of its renewal seemed not impossible; and its appeal to his imagination was stirring.   From Klamath Lake the tidings were carried to the Shasta; from them they spread to Karok,

Yurok, and Athabascan tribes. The doctrine, taking new forms, but keeping something of its kernel, worked its uneasy way about and somewhere was carried across and up the Sacramento Valley, until, among the Pomo and southern Wintun, it merged with the old religion, crystallized, and remains to-day a recognizable element in ceremonial.

TRIBAL DATA.

The band of Northern Paiute of Surprise Valley and on Upper, Middle. and Lower Alkali Lakes, south of Fort Bidwell, were the Kaivanungavidukw. To the north, around Warner Lake in Oregon, but ranging southward toward or to Fort Bidwell, were the Tuziyammo, also known as Ochoho's band. The Honey Lake group were the Waratika or Wadatika, the "wada-seed eaters." East of these, over the State line, the Smoke Creek region seems to have belonged to the Kuyui-dika or "sucker-eaters," the Pyramid Lake people or Winnemucca's band. (Pl. 37.)

The California limits of the Northern Paiute are not quite certain. The doubts that exist have been aired in the foregoing discussions of Achomawi, Atsugewi, and Maidu. The present population appears to be in the vicinity of 300. It probably never exceeded double this figure.

THE MONO.

DESIGNATIONS.

After the alien Washo have been passed in a southward journey along the eastern base of the Sierra Nevada, Mono-Bannock people are again encountered. They can now be named Monos with little fear of misunderstanding.

The word Mono means "monkey" in Spanish, but this signification, some guesses notwithstanding, can be eliminated from consideration of the origin of the term. So can a Yokuts folk etymology, which derives it from *monai, monoyi*, "flies," on the ground that the Mono scaled the cliffs of their high mountains as the insect walks up the wall of a house. Monachi is the Yokuts term for the people, corresponding to Miwok Mono-k, and to Maidu Monozi for the Northern Paiute. It is a meaningless name. The subtraction of the tribal suffix *chi* leaves a stem of which a Spaniard could hardly have made anything but Mono. Whether the Yokuts originated the word, or whether it comes from some Shoshonean or other source, is not known. The Mono call themselves only Nümü, which means no more than "persons."

Besides Monachi, the Yokuts call the western Mono Nuta'a (plural Nuchawayi), which, however, is only a directional term meaning "uplanders," and therefore generally easterners. That it is not a true ethnic term is clear from the fact that Garcés, in 1776, used the same name, in the form Noche for the southern foothill Yokuts themselves. Malda is a specific southern Yokuts term for the Kern River Shoshoneans, and perhaps for all members of the family.

The eastern Mono of Owens Valley are called by themselves or their kinsmen
Pitanakwat, which probably means "pine-nut-eaters," after a system of tribal
or band nomenclature that prevails over much of Nevada and the surrounding
Shoshonean regions. The Kern River Tübatulabal call the eastern Mono,
Yiwinanghal; the western Mono, Winanghatal.

EASTERN AND WESTERN MONO.

The bulk of Mono territory and population is still in the Great
Basin; but a branch is established in the high Sierra, at least in its
marginal, permanently habitable portion, from which they look
down on the foothill and valley Yokuts. The upper San Joaquin,
Kings, and Kaweah comprise this domain, in which all the pine
forest, and some stretches below it, are Mono. The dialect east and
west of the huge crest is not identical, but appears to be remarkably
similar considering that the two parts of the people have only their
backs in contact—if contact it be with one of the earth's greatest
walls between—and that their outlooks are opposite. The western,
cis-Sierra, truly Californian Mono can hardly, therefore, have come
into their present seats very long ago, as the historian reckons; and
they are certainly newer than their neighbors, the Tübatulabal of
Kern River, or the southern Californians of the same family. Both
the western and the eastern halves answer to the name Mono, and the
Yokuts call them both Monachi.

WESTERN MONO DIVISIONS.

The western Mono have several distinctive names applied to them
by the Yokuts. It is not clear whether the Mono themselves employ
these, or equivalents; nor whether, as the names might indicate, the
Mono have borrowed the tribal organization of the Yokuts, or the
latter merely attribute their own political unity to each Mono group
to which its habitat gives a topographic unity.

On the North Fork of the San Joaquin, close to the Chukchansi, Dalinchi, and
half-mythical Toltichi, as well as the uppermost of the southern Miwok on
Fresno River, was a Mono band that survives in some strength to-day, but for
which no "tribal" name is known.

South of the San Joaquin, on Big Sandy Creek, and toward if not on the
heads of Little and Big Dry Creeks, were the Posgisa or Poshgisha. Their
Yokuts neighbors were the Gashowu.

On a series of confluent streams—of which Big, Burr, and Sycamore Creeks
are the most important—entering Kings River above Mill Creek, were the
Holkoma. Towincheba has been given as a synonym and Kokoheba as the name
of a coordinate neighboring tribe, but both appear to be designations of Holkoma villages.

At the head of Mill Creek, a southern affluent of Kings River, and in the
pine ridges to the north, were the Wobonuch. Their Yokuts associates were
the Michahai, Chukaimina, and Entimbich. In regard to the latter there is
some confusion whether they are Yokuts or Mono.

On Limekiln and Eshom Creeks and the North Fork of Kaweah River were the Waksachi, whose Yokuts contacts were primarily with the Wükchamni.

On the Kaweah itself, especially on its south side, the Balwisha had their home. They, too, associated with the Wükchamni lower down on their own stream, but also with the Yaudanchi on the headwaters of Tule River, the next stream south.

This makes six named western Mono divisions, one each, roughly speaking, on each side of the three great streams that flow through their territory. Their more precise location appears on the Yokuts map (Pl. 47).

EASTERN MONO TERRITORY.

The eastern Mono inhabit a long, arid depression that lies along the base of the Sierra. Numerous small streams descend, even on this almost rainless side, from the snowy summits; and through most of the valley there flows one fair-sized longitudinal stream, the Owens River—the Jordan of California—and, like it, lost in a salt sea. The exact southward limits of the Mono have not been recorded, it appears. The line between them and the Koso, the next group beyond, has been drawn between Independence and Owens Lake; but it is possible that the shores of this sheet should have been assigned rather to the Mono.

Eastward and northward the Mono extend indefinitely across the diagonal line that gives the State of Nevada its characteristic contour. There appears to be no consequential change of dialect and no great modification of custom. On Owens River and around Mono Lake the people are sometimes called Mono and sometimes Paiute; in western Nevada they are only Paiutes; as the center of that State is approached, the Shoshoni name Paviotso begins to be applicable. To the Paiute of Pyramid Lake they are all, together with the bands far in Oregon, one people.

To the northwest, toward the Washo, the Mono boundary is formed by the watershed between Carson and Walker Rivers.

NUMBERS.

The Mono are to-day the most numerous body of Indians in California. The eastern Mono alone exceed, according to census returns, every group except the Maidu and Pomo; and at that both the latter are composite bodies, each including distinct languages, and are likely to have been more completely enumerated. The returns show 1,388 Mono in California. But as Mono and Inyo Counties, which are wholly eastern Mono except for a few Koso, are credited with nearly 1,200 Indians; and as the western Mono are about half as numerous as their eastern kinsmen, it is impossible to avoid the conclusion that the total for the combined group is above rather than below 1,500. Part of them have probably been classed under other names, such as Paiute, or reported without tribal designation.

This relatively high standing is, however, of recent date. A century ago the Mono were feeble in numbers compared with many other groups. The very inhospitability of their habitat, which then caused their population to be sparse, has prevented any considerable influx of Americans and has spared them much of the consequent incisive diminution that a full and sudden dose of our civilization always brings the Indian. They may retain in 1916 a full one-half of their numbers in 1816; the proportion among tribes situated as they are is in the vicinity of this fraction. A conservative estimate of their original number is 3,000 to 4,000; 5,000 or 6,000 a very liberal figure.

Much the same result is reached by comparison. If 50 Yokuts tribes totaled 15,000 to 20,000, the 6 western Mono divisions higher in the mountains may have aggregated 2,000 at best; and allowing double for the eastern division, we are still within the range of our estimate.

It is a subject for thought that a body of people that once stood to their neighbors as three or four to one should now be outranked by them one to three, merely because the former were a few miles more accessible to Caucasian contact.

CULTURE.

Mono civilization is little known, either as to customs or preserved implements. It is not even certain that they formed a group other than in speech and origin. There may have been a deep cultural cleft between the two halves, the western people being essentially Yokuts in practices and ideas, the eastern little else than Nevada Paviotso. Or they may really have been one people, whose western division had their civilization overlaid with a partial veneer of Yokuts customs. Information is practically lacking, for ethnologists have put little on record concerning either half of the group.

TOTEMIC GROUPING.

The western Mono, at least those on the San Joaquin and very likely those on other streams also, possessed one important central California institution that had not penetrated to their eastern brothers nor to any trans-Sierra people: the totemic moieties. But these moieties exhibit one feature that is neither Miwok nor Yokuts: they are not exogamous. Marriage is within or without the moiety. Descent is in the male line, and a group of animals is associated as "pets" or "dogs" with each moiety. These animals, at least the birds among them, were sometimes reared in captivity. When adult they were either despoiled of their feathers or released unharmed. The personal name is of Yokuts rather than Miwok type: it is inherited, and generally meaningless, not of totemic connotation. Chieftainship was dual as among the Yokuts, but the chief of the moiety represented by the eagle had precedence.

Besides being nonexogamous, the Mono moieties are peculiar in being definitely subdivided. The entire scheme is:

Moiety I, corresponding to Miwok "land" and Yokuts "downstream;" Yayanchi.
   Subdivisions: Dakats, Kunugechi.
   Totem animals: Eagle, crow, chicken hawk.
   The name Dakats suggests Kawaiisu *adagatsi*, "crow," and Yayanchi the *yayu* hawk, identified with the opposite moiety.
Moiety II, corresponding to Miwok "water" and Yokuts "upstream:" Pakwihu.
   Subdivisions: Tübahinagatu, Puza'ots or Pazo'odz.
   Totem animals: Buzzard, coyote, *yayu* hawk, bald eagle.
   Pakwihu is probably from *pakwi*, "fish"; Tübahinagatu perhaps from *tüba*, which seems to mean "pine nut" in certain Shoshonean dialects—compare "Tüba-tulabal"; Puza'ots recalls *oza'ots*, "magpie"—a bird of the opposite moiety among the Miwok—but the etymology seems more than venturesome. In fact, *oza'ots* may be nothing but a modified loan ward, the Yokuts *ochoch*.

The animal associations are the same as among the Miwok and Yokuts. The *yayu* may prove to be the Yokuts *limik*, the falcon, and as for the "bald eagle" on the buzzard or coyote side, this may be the "fish hawk" whom the Tachi put in the same division. But the Mono totemism is perhaps looser than that of their neighbors; it is said that a person may change his moiety.

OTHER NOTES.

The relationship terms of the San Joaquin Mono are, like those of the eastern Mono, of Great Basin type. Cross cousins are "brothers" or "sisters," not "parents" or "children" as among the Miwok and central Yokuts. This circumstance, coupled with the absence of exogamic regulations, makes it very probable that none of the Mono practiced cross-cousin marriage, a peculiar custom established among the Miwok.

The western Mono observed rather strictly the taboo between mother-in-law and son-in-law. If speech was necessary, these persons addressed each other in the plural, as if to dull the edge of personal communication by circumlocution. This device has already been noted among more northerly tribes. Some restraint or shame, though of a milder degree, was observed also toward the father-in-law; and—as among the Yana—between brother and sister. The eastern Mono knew nothing of these customs.

The rough Yokuts type of pottery seems to have been made by the western Mono but its precise range among them is unknown. Their basketry agreed with that of the Yokuts in forms, technique, and materials. A diagonally twined cap from the eastern Mono is shown in Plate 55, d.

The southern Yokuts report that the Mono cremated their dead; but it is not clear to what subdivision this statement refers. The eastern Mono about Bishop buried.

The mourning anniversary of south and central California was probably made by the western Mono. The eastern Mono burned considerable property over the graves of dead chiefs and possibly of other people, too; and saved their remaining belongings in order to destroy them a year later. This is an echo of the standard mourning anniversary.

The ritual number of the eastern Mono was four.

THE KOSO OR PANAMINT.

CONNECTIONS.

With the Koso (also called Kosho, Panamint, Shikaviyam, Sikaium, Shikaich, Kaich, Kwüts, Sosoni, and Shoshone) a new division of the Plateau Shoshoneans is entered—the Shoshoni-Comanche. This group, which keeps apart the Mono-Bannock and the Ute-Chemehuevi (Fig. 52), stretches in a tenuous band—of which the Koso form one end at the base of the Sierra Nevada—through the most desert part of California, across central and northeastern Nevada, thence across the region of the Utah-Idaho boundary into Wyoming, over the Continental Divide of the Rockies to the headwaters of the Platte; and, as if this were insufficient, one part, and the most famous, of the division, the Comanche, had pushed southeastward through Colorado far into Texas.

HABITAT AND POPULATION.

The territory of the westernmost member of this group, our Koso, who form as it were the head of a serpent that curves across the map for 1,500 miles, is one of the largest of any Californian people. It was also perhaps the most thinly populated, and one of the least defined. If there were boundaries, they are not known. To the west the crest of the Sierra has been assumed as the limit of the Koso toward the Tübatulabal. On the north were the eastern Mono of Owens River. Owens Lake, it seems, should go with the stream that it receives; and perhaps Koso territory only began east or south of the sheet; but the available data make the inhabitants of its shores

" Shoshones " and not " Paiutes." On the south the Kawaiisu and Chemehuevi ranged over a similarly barren habitat, and there is so little exact knowledge of ethnic relations that the map has had to be made almost at random. The boundaries in this desert were certainly not straight lines, but for the present there is no recourse but to draw them.

The fact is that this region was habitable only in spots, in oases, if we can so call a spring or a short trickle down a rocky canyon. Between these minute patches in or at the foot of mountains were wide stretches of stony ranges, equally barren valleys, and alkaline flats. All through California it is the inhabited sites that are significant in the life of the Indians, rather than the territories; and boundaries are of least consequence of all. In the unchanging desert this condition applies with tenfold force; but ignorance prevents a distributional description that would be adequate.

It is only known that at least four successive ranges, with the intervening valleys, were the portion of this people—the Coso, Argus, Panamint, and Funeral Mountains, with Coso, Panamint, and Death Valleys. Thirty years ago they actually lived at four spots in this area—on Cottonwood Creek, in the northwestern arm of Death Valley; south of Bennett Mills on the eastern side of the Panamint Mountains, in another canyon leading into Death Valley; near Hot Springs, at the mouth of Hall Creek into Panamint Valley; and northwest from these locations, on the west side of Saline Valley, near Hunter Creek at the foot of the Inyo Mountains.

It is not clear whether the terms " Coso " and " Panamint " were first used geographically or ethnically. The latter is the most common American designation of the group, and would be preferable to Koso except that, in the form Vanyume, it has also been applied to a Serrano group.

Koso population was of the meagerest. It is exceedingly doubtful whether the country would have supported as many as 500 souls; and there may have been fewer. In 1883 an estimate was 150; in 1891, less than 100; a recent one, between 100 and 150. The Koso are not sufficiently differentiated from adjoining groups in the popular American mind to make ordinary census figures worth much.

MANUFACTURES.

The Koso must have lived a very different life from the San Joaquin Valley tribes; but they share many implements with the Yokuts, through intercourse of both with the Tübatulabal; and it can not be doubted that ideas and practices were also carried back and forth.

The ceremonial skirt of strings of eagle down is one such evidence. Whether this traveled from west to east or the reverse, it is almost certain to have transported with it some religious associations. (Pl. 42.)

Flat feather bands are of the type of the yellow-hammer ornaments so characteristic of the whole cis-Sierra region, but their detailed form, as revealed in total length, inaccuracy of stringing, and proportion of feather to quill, allies them more particularly to the corresponding article of the Luiseño and other southern Californians. (Pl. 58.)

Baskets, again, are of Yokuts rather than southern affinities. The plate or shallow bowl, it is true, is coiled; but there is a conical carrying basket, and it is twined. The pitched water basket is indispensable to a potless desert people. The carrying cap was worn by women. It was coiled. The foundation for coiled ware is a bundle of *Epicampes* grass stems containing a single woody rod; the sewing is strands of willow, and black patterns are made with the horns of *Martynia* pods, or *Scirpus* bulrush roots soaked in ashes. For red, tree yucca root is used. Twined vessels are of strands of willow or sumac on shoots of the same. The patterns are also in *Martynia*, or if red, of tree yucca root.

FIG. 53. — Carrying net. Koso (Panamint) of Death Valley. (Cf. Fig. 59.)

The carrying net is of southern California type (Fig. 53), but without the convenient loops of the Cahuilla form (Fig. 59).

Earth-covered sweat houses were used regularly, at least by some men. They were large enough to stand up in. The soil was heaped over a layer of "arrowweed," *Pluchea sericea*. (Pl. 56.)

The bow is of juniper, short, and sinew-backed. The string is sinew, or *Apocynum*, wild hemp, the usual cordage material. The arrow is of willow, or of *Phragmites* cane; the latter has a long point of greasewood. The cane arrow is heated in the groove of a stone straightener of Yokuts-Cahuilla type, then seized in the teeth and the ends bent.

SUBSISTENCE.

The most important food in the oakless country was the Nevada pine nut, from *Pinus monophylla*. Seeds were gathered by beating as by the more favored Californian tribes. *Oryzopsis*, the desert sand grass, perhaps furnished the most abundant supply. Seeds of evening primroses, of *Ephedra*, and of the devil's pincushion cactus, were also available. Most of these were ground and then parched with coals in a shallow basket. The mesquite bean, *Prosopis*, was pounded in wooden mortars; the stalks of the common reed, *Phragmites*, were treated similarly and cakes of the flour toasted.

The "mescal" of the Southwest and southernmost California hardly penetrates the Koso country, but the tree yucca bud affords a substitute, which has the advantage of being edible after roasting on an open fire, whereas the agave butt or stalk requires prolonged steam cooking in an earth-covered pit.

Prickly pear joints, however, are treated by the Koso in this manner, and can then be kept indefinitely, or are sun dried and boiled when wanted. The thorns are first rubbed off.

The leaves and shoots of several varieties of crucifers are eaten.

In the fertile parts of California clover and other greens are mostly eaten raw, but the desert vegetation requires repeated boiling, washing, and squeezing to remove the bitter and perhaps deleterious salts.

Animal food is only occasionally obtainable. Rabbits, jack rabbits, rats, and lizards, with some birds, furnish the bulk. Mountain sheep take the place of deer as the chief big game. On the shores of Owens Lake countless grubs of a fly were scooped out of the shallow water and dried for food.

CHAPTER 41.

THE CHEMEHUEVI.

AFFILIATIONS.

With the Chemehuevi we encounter the third and last of the Shoshonean Plateau divisions, composed of this people, the Kawaiisu, the Southern or true Paiute, and the Ute, all speaking dialects of remarkable uniformity, considering the extent of territory covered by them.

In fact, the Chemehuevi are nothing but Southern Paiutes, and all their bands have at one time or another been designated as Paiutes, Payuchis, and the like.

Conversely, the term Chemehuevi has been applied to several more eastern bands, in Nevada and Arizona, on whom custom has now settled the name Paiute. The Mohave and other Yuman tribes follow this nomenclature consistently: Chemehuevi is their generic term for Paiute. Thus that remarkable pioneer Garcés, who in 1776 entered Shoshonean territory from the Mohave and with Mohave guides, speaks not only of the Chemegué and Chemeguaba—our Chemehuevi—but of the Chemegué Cuajála and Chemegué Sevinta, that is, the Paranüh Paiute of Muddy River in Nevada and the Shivwits Paiute of Shivwits Plateau in Arizona, the Kohoalcha and Sivvinta of the Mohave. In fact, the name Chemehuevi, whose etymology is uncertain, would seem to be of Mohave or at least Yuman origin.

At the same time, the appellation is a convenient one to distinguish the Southern Paiute of California from their brethren of Nevada, Arizona, and Utah; and it will be used here in this geographical rather than in any essential ethnic sense.

HABITAT.

The Chemehuevi are one of the very few Californian groups that have partly altered their location in the historic period, and that without pressure from the white man. Their shifts emanated in disturbances of the still more mobile and more compact Yuman tribes on whom they border.

Their old territory lay off the lower Colorado River westward. It commenced in the Kingston Range, south of Death Valley, where they met the Koso, and stretched southward through the Providence Mountains and other stony and sandy wastes, to about the boundary of Riverside and Imperial Counties. Roughly, this is the eastern half of the Mohave Desert. Somewhere along the middle of the southern half of this desert an ill-defined line must have run between the Chemehuevi and the Serrano divisions farther west. The oasis of Twenty-nine Palms was Serrano. So was the Mohave Desert to beyond Daggett, and probably to its sink. Somewhat nearer this sink, however, than to the Providence Mountains, Garcés found a Chemehuevi rancheria. North of the Serrano range, and south of that of the Koso, lies a stretch that if anything is more arid still than the neighboring ones—northwestern San Bernardino County. This seems to have formed a westward arm of Chemehuevi territory—if not permanently inhabited, at least visited and owned. True, there is no specific record of any of their bands being in this area, now or formerly. But it has not been claimed for either the Serrano or Koso; and to the west, where the region begins to rise toward the southern Sierra Nevada, it meets the land of the Kawaiisu, whose speech shows them to be a Chemehuevi offshoot. In the absence of knowledge the inherent probability would favor continuity of the territories of the two allied groups; and the Mohave speak of them as in contact. Intrinsically, it is of little import who exercised sovereignty in this tract: to all purposes it was empty. But it is extensive enough to loom large on the map, and in more favored regions three or four stocks like Esselen, Wiyot, Yurok, and Chimariko could be put into an equal area.

In 1776 there were no Chemehuevi on the Colorado River below Eldorado Canyon. The entire California frontage on this stream was in Yuman possession. Subsequently, however, the Mohave and Yuma drove the remnants of the Halchidhoma and Kohuana eastward; and the Chemehuevi, who were intimate with the victors, began to settle on the stream. According to the Mohave, they themselves brought the Chemehuevi to Cottonwood Island, where the two nations lived side by side, to Chemehuevi Valley, and to other points, At all events, when the Americans came, three-quarters of a century after the Spanish priest, they found the Chemehuevi on Cottonwood Island as well as in the valley that bears their name, and on both the Arizona and California sides, apparently.

About 1867 war broke out between the old friends. The Chemehuevi acquitted themselves well, according to the Mohave; but they must have been heavily outnumbered. At any rate, they fled from Mohave proximity to remoter spots in the desert. After a time they returned, and to-day there are even some individuals among the Mohave. A small group, however, remained at their asylum at Twenty-nine Palms, far to the southwest; and in recent years some members of this band have drifted still farther, across the San Bernardino range, to Cabezon in Cahuilla territory.

POPULATION.

The Chemehuevi area is the largest in California occupied by a people of uniform dialect; but it is also easily one of the most worthless, and was certainly among the two or three most thinly populated. A thousand inhabitants is a most liberal estimate.

The last Federal census reports 350 Chemehuevi in all, 260 of them in California. The decrease since aboriginal times has not been heavy in regions so empty and remote as this. A reduction by one-half or two-thirds is all that can be allowed; which would make the primitive population something between 500 and 800.

NAMES AND DIVISIONS.

The Chemehuevi and Southern Paiute name for themselves is only Niiwü, "people," corresponding to Mono and Northern Paiute Niimü. The Chemehuevi proper are sometimes called by their kinsmen: Tantawats or Tantüwach, "southerners," an appropriate enough term; and they accept the designation; but it has local, not tribal reference. The various Serrano groups call them Yuakayam. The Yuma are said to name them Mat-hatevach, "northerners," and the Pima: Ahalakat, "small bows." Tribes or local divisions that may fairly be included among the Chemehuevi are the following:

Mokwats, at the Kingston Mountains.

Yagats, at Amargosa.

Hokwaits, in Ivanpah Valley.

Tümpisagavatsits or Timpashauwagotsits, in the Providence Mountains.

Kauyaichits.

Moviats, on Cottonwood Island in the Colorado River.

Shivawach or Shivawats in the Chemehuevi Valley; it is not certain whether this is the name of a band or of a locality.

There must have been others farther west and south.

The Chemehuevi name their neighbors as follows: The Koso-Panamint, Kwiits or Panumits; the Serrano proper, Maringits; the Vanyume Serrano, Pitanta; the Kitanemuk Serrano, Nawiyat; the Kawaiisu, Hiniima or Hinienima; the Cahuilla, Kwitanemum; the Hopi, Mukwi or Mokwits. Yuman tribes are: the Mohave, Aiat; the Walapai, Huvarepats; the Havasupai, Pashaverats; for the Yuma there seems to be only the Mohave term "Kwichyana." The Yokuts were called Saiempive.

Place names are: Nüvant, Charleston Peak in Nevada, the most famous place in the mythology of both the Chemehuevi and the western bands of the Southern Paiute; Muvi, Eldorado Canyon (compare Moviats); Wianekat, Cottonwood Island; Pa'ash, Piute Springs, the Mohave Ahakuvilya, where there are petroglyphs; Toyagaba, near by; and Aipava, farther west on the trail to Mohave River.

WAR AND PEACE.

The international relations of the Chemehuevi were determined in general, and probably for a long time, by a series of interconnected amities and enmities that threw the tribes of southern California, southern Nevada, and western Arizona into two great alignments that ran counter to their origins as well as their mode of life. On one side were the Chemehuevi, Southern Paiute, Mohave, Yuma, Kamia, Yavapai, and Apache. These were generally friendly to the less enterprising and passive northern Serrano of the desert, and, so far as they knew them, to the Yokuts, the Tübatulabal, the Chumash, and perhaps the Gabrielino. On the other side were the Hopi; the Pima and most of the Papago; of Yuman tribes, the Havasupai, Walapai, Maricopa, Halchidhoma, Kohuana, Halyikwamai, Cocopa, Diegueño, and the Cuñeil or northernmost Baja Californians; of southern California Shoshoneans, the Serrano proper, the Cahuilla, and possibly the Luiseño. There was nothing like a confederation or even formal alliance among the tribes of either party. Rather, each had its enemies of long standing, and therefore joined hands with their foes, until an irregular but far-stretching and interlocking line-up worked itself out. Often tribes here grouped as on the same side had their temporary conflicts, or even a traditional hatred. But, on the whole, they divided as here indicated, as Garcés pictured the situation in the eighteenth century, as later reports of narrower outlook confirm, and as the recollections of the modern Mohave corroborate. Small, scattered, or timid tribes, like the Chemehuevi, the Hopi, the Havasupai, and the various Serrano divisions, were less involved in open war and more inclined to abiding suspicions and occasional conflicts, than aggressive, enterprising, or tenacious nations of numbers or solidarity such as the Apache, Pima, and Mohave; but their outward relations were largely predetermined by the general scheme.

This mere list of tribal friends and foes, especially when conceptualized on the map, lifts one with a bound out of the peasantlike, localized, and murkily dim world knowledge of the true Californians into a freer atmosphere of wide and bold horizons.

CULTURE.

The groundwork of Chemehuevi culture was the Shoshonean one of the Great Basin, of the participants in which they were a member physiographically as well as in speech and origin. This interior plateau civilization was largely composed of elements ultimately common to itself and the central Californian civilization. But specific Californian influences reached the Chemehuevi only to a limited extent. The civilization of the Pueblos also did not affect them directly. Their life was, however, strongly colored by contact with the quasi-Southwestern Yumans—in its material aspects more by the unsettled tribes, such as the Walapai; in religion especially by the Mohave.

ARTS.

Like the Southern Paiute, the Chemehuevi now and then farmed small patches where they could. In the main, they lived on what their bare habitat provided—game, rabbits, rats, lizards, perhaps other reptiles, seeds, mescal, and the like.

Also in imitation of the Mohave, they now and then, especially since settled along the river, ventured to bake a few pots. But such attempts were sporadic, and the Chemehuevi must in justice be classed as a tribe that made baskets and not pottery.

Their basketry suggests, in its coiling, the San Joaquin Valley and the ware of the Shoshoneans adjacent to this valley, as much as southern California. This is in part due to their presumably enforced use of woody willow or other fibers for the sewing, in place of the reedy *Juncus* of the Cahuilla and Luiseño; in part to their manufacture of vessels with constricted neck—not well definedly flat-shouldered as among the Yokuts, but of an approximating and rounded shape that is clearly due to the same influence. Their twined basketry is also foreign in spirit to that of southern California. Caps, triangular trays, and close-woven carrying baskets in diagonal twining, with an inclination to paint designs on instead of working them in, are pure Plateau types. (Pls. 59, 73, *a*.) The water basket was undoubtedly also used, but seems not to have been preserved.

The bow is distinctly shorter than the Mohave self-bow, with recurved ends. The back is painted, the middle wrapped, and the old game and fighting weapon was evidently sinew-backed, although no specimens seem to have survived. The arrow is at least sometimes of cane, foreshafted, and flint tipped with a small point. It differs entirely from the jointless *Pluchea* arrow of the Mohave, that lacks both foreshaft and stone head.

Women's dice were of gum-filled and shell-inlaid nut shells (Fig. 54), similar to those of the southern Yokuts.

Garcés found the Chemehuevi, at some springs in the desert west of Chemehuevi Valley, wearing "Apache" moccasins, skin shirts, perhaps of antelope or mountain sheep, and feathered caps. This is the dress of the nomadic Southwestern or Plateau Shoshonean tribes, and unconnected with that of the southern or central Californians or the Mohave, although the Serrano tell of having worn a similar costume.

The Mohave, however, declare the Chemehuevi men to have worn their hair in the peculiar style characteristic of themselves and the Yuma.

Houses need have been little else than shelters against the sun and wind. The sweat house has not been reported. Open-air storage baskets are also not mentioned; most of the Chemehuevi habitat would furnish more safe and dry rock crevices than food to keep in them.

BELIEFS.

The Chemehuevi origin myth is free from southern Californian or Southwestern suggestions. It does recall the central Californian account of the creation, but evidently only in so far as it rests upon a Plateau set of conceptions, and these in turn approximate those current in California. There is little that is common with the mythology of the Yokuts, the nearest of the central Californians.

Fig. 54.—Chemehuevi dice of filled shells.

The heroes are Coyote and his elder brother Puma—the Chemehuevi equivalent of the Wolf of the northern Plateau—who build a house on Charleston Peak while the world is still covered with water. When the earth has become dry through the instrumentality of an old woman in the west, Hawichyepam Maapuch, Coyote, failing to find men, marries a louse, from whose eggs spring many tribes. The Chemehuevi themselves, however, the Mohave, and other southerners come from Coyote's own voidings. They are taught to eat game by being given parts of a person, a human example of animal food. Puma is killed by eastern enemies, who, unwinding a powerful object that he has made, bring on the first and an unbroken night. Coyote mourns, but wishes daylight to burn his brother's belongings. He restores it when he shoots the yellow-hammer. After the completion of the funerary rites—the instituting ones for the world—Coyote recovers his brother's scalp from the foes who are dancing before it and escapes their pursuit.

Mohave traces are visible: the great sacred mountain, the building of an abode, the actionless but all-powerful old woman, the death of the older brother, the mourning for him. But they are elements which tinge rather than shape the story.

RITUAL.

Chemehuevi rituals have been influenced by the Mohave. They may have been equally affected by the religion of other peoples of the region, but these are too little known to estimate. The cremation of the property of the dead, and, no doubt, of added belongings, as a definite rite—especially notable because the body itself was buried and not cremated—extends, it is true, over a wide area. But the fact that the Kaibab Paiute, in the far-away tract where westernmost Arizona and Utah conjoin, possess a long series of mourning songs in the Mohave language, establishes probability that the nearer and intimate Chemehuevi also derived their funeral music, and with it no doubt a large part of the associated practices, from the same source.

Incidentally, the religious dominance of the Mohave over a vast region is clear. The Diegueño myths tell of the sacred Mohave Mountain Avikwame; some of their song cycles are Mohave in words as well as melody and name; and tribes so advanced, self-centered, and remote as the Zuñi perform dances that they attribute to the Mohave and whose songs are possibly derived from a Mohave stimulus.

The Chemehuevi sing four cycles—Salt, Deer, Mountain Sheep, and Shamans' or Doctoring—all of which, in effect, are sung by the Mohave also, though to these people they constitute only a small fraction of a much larger number of different kinds of singings. It seems that each of these song cycles refers to a story, which may or may not be related in the intermissions; and that this narrative is believed to have been dreamed—that is, actually experienced in a spirit condition—but that the presentation of the dream takes an essentially mythological form. Whether, as with the Mohave, dancing or other rudimentary ritual may accompany the singing—though only as a subsidiary feature, the songs remaining the kernel and essence of the complex—is not known as regards the Chemehuevi.

It is possible that these Chemehuevi-Mohave resemblances lie as much in an equivalation made by the Indians as in any similarity of the ceremonies themselves. When the Zuñi perform what they call the Mohave dance it is actually a purely Zuñi ritual in every particular, whatever its origin; but both tribes would nevertheless be likely to assert their corresponding rituals to be the same. It may be that analogous though slighter differences exist between Chemehuevi and Mohave ceremonies, which the native consciousness obliterates, and which therefore will become revealed only when the rites are concretely known in some detail. But this theoretical possibility is unlikely to amount to more than a partial qualification, so far as Chemehuevi similarities to the Mohave are concerned; for all the specific bits of knowledge that are available point to specific Mohave resemblances.

Thus, the Chemehuevi " dream " and tell and sing of the mountain Nüvant as the Mohave do of Avikwame. They see there Coyote and Puma and Yunakat, the personification of food. The shamans acquire their songs and powers from these or other mythological beings at Nüvant. A man "dreams," for instance, of the time when the earth was still wet from the primeval flood and without mountains, when the cane sprang up and Older Brother Puma instructed him in detail how to make each part of bow and arrow. This experience is the source of the "dreamer's" faculty to flake arrowheads. The assumptions, the implied concepts, the whole setting as well as many of the particulars in this instance, are characteristically Mohave.

CHAPTER 42.

THE KAWAIISU AND TÜBATULABAL.

The Kawaiisu.

NEIGHBORS.

An offshoot of no great antiquity, apparently, from the Chemehuevi, the Kawaiisu have become differentiated from the parent body as a result of a new setting. They lived in the Tehachapi Mountains, and therefore half across the watershed that separates the great valley of California from the undrained Great Basin. Behind them remained the westernmost of the Chemehuevi; and nominally the two bodies were in contiguity. Actually, however, the Chemehuevi tract in question was perhaps the least frequented of all the barren lands of that people; and the Kawaiisu had more to gain by clinging to the timbered and watered slopes of their mountains than by wandering among the rare vegetation and dry soda lakes of the desert. Intercourse between the two groups was therefore probably not specially active.

On the other side of the crest, however, the Kawaiisu were pressed close against a variety of neighbors. In the plains below them were the Yauelmani, and beyond them other Yokuts tribes. Relations with these seem to have been friendly, and intermarriages took place.

On both sides were Shoshoneans, but of quite distinct history and speech; to the north the Tübatulabal of Kern River, to the south the Serrano Kitanemuk; and a journey of less than a day led into Chumash territory.

It was inevitable, accordingly, that the Kawaiisu should be essentially Californian in culture, and that their speech should diverge from its original form. In all fundamentals it is pure Ute-Chemehuevi, but superficially, especially in its pronunciation, it is considerably changed. With such close and numerous alien associations as the Kawaiisu were subject to, this degree of alteration might be attained in a very few centuries, possibly in a few generations.

TERRITORY AND DESIGNATIONS.

Tehachapi Pass, a famous Agua Caliente or hot spring in the vicinity, Walker Basin, and probably some southern affluents of Kern River were in Kawaiisu possession. They owned also the eastward drier slope of the same mountains, and perhaps some of the desert beyond; but the limits of their extension in this direction are conjectural.

Tehachapi has its designation from a local name, which has been taken over by the Yokuts as Tahichpi-u. The hot springs were called Hihinkiava by the Kitanemuk; Tumoyo or Shatnau ilak by the Yokuts. Walker Basin, or probably the principal village in it, was Yutp or Yitpe. At or near Havilah were Wiwayuk and Anütap, Kitanemuk and Tübatulabal names of possibly the same locality; it may have belonged to the latter people or to the Kawaiisu, and certainly was near their boundary.

The origin of the name Kawaiisu is not known. The Yokuts call them thus, or by dialectic variants. The Tübatulabal say Kawishm. The Mohave designation, Kuvahya, may be from the same stem; Garcés, the discoverer of the Kawaiisu, writes it Cobaji, and says that the Yokuts call them Colteche. The Chemehuevi designate them Hiniima or Hinienima. The Kitanemuk and Vanyume Serrano call them Agutushyam, Agudutsyam, or Akutusyam. Their own name for themselves is merely Nuwu or Nuwuwu, "people"; it has also been written Newooah. Locally, Americans usually speak of them as the Tehachapi or Caliente Indians.

There were Kawaiisu or Chemehuevi at Victorville on the upper Mohave River some years ago who asserted that this was part of their ancient territory, and that they ranged from there west along the base of the Sierra Madre. Most of them were born in the vicinity of Tehachapi, but they comprised individuals from Sheep and Deadman Creeks, halfway, on the north side of the mountains, between the two railroad lines that cross the Mohave Desert. If these claims prove correct, a considerable part of the desert region that has been attributed to the Serrano must be assigned to the Kawaiisu instead.

The same little group asserted that the southern end of the Panamint Mountains—that is, the general range of which the Panamint Mountains of our maps are part—belonged to their own people, only the northern segments of the chain being "Shoshone" or Koso. They may, however, include with "their own people" the Chemehuevi.

There is in these statements a possible explanation of a puzzling vacillation in the use of the name Panamint. The people of what we call the Panamint Mountains are those here named the Koso, of Shoshoni-Comanche affiliations. The Mohave, and with them the explorer Garcés, apply the name, in the form Vanyume or Beñeme, to the Mohave Desert Serrano, who are Shoshoneans of quite a different branch. Garcés clearly recognizes them as speaking a southern Californian idiom. The Mohave, however, are not consistent, and sometimes place the Vanyume at Tehachapi or Tejon. If the Kawaiisu of Tehachapi, or a division of them, extended on the one hand to the upper Mohave River and on the other to the southern spurs of the Panamints, the application of the name Vanyume-Panamint to people as far separated as these two outlying localities begins to show some reason. This desert region is little known to the ethnologist and would prove a fascinating field for him, and this instance of apparent confusion as to the whole basis of ethnic conditions illustrates how urgently knowledge is needed.

For modern times the census, and for the older period even estimates, fail us in regard to the Kawaiisu. There seem to be nearly 150 of them; and the aboriginal population may have been 500.

SOCIETY.

The Kawaiisu lack the organization of society on a basis of totemic moieties which is so characteristic of the Miwok and most of the Yokuts. As the eastern Mono and even the Kern River people agree with them in doing without this dual plan, it is clear that the system is essentially a Californian one and, far from being in any sense a trait of life in the Great Basin, has scarcely succeeded in reaching the crest of the Sierra. Even traces of the moiety scheme are wanting with the Kawaiisu. Eagles and other birds are indeed kept in captivity; but they are without a personal or taboo relation to the owner, are not inherited, and in fact are released after having been plucked twice.

The mother-in-law taboo is another Yokuts institution that the Kawaiisu lack, no doubt under Plateau or southern California influence. Children are usually named after relatives. Kinship designations are full of reciprocal terms; an old woman will call her daughter's boy by the same word that he applies to her, plus a diminutive suffix. This is a habit widely spread among the Plateau Shoshoneans. Another device of much greater restriction geographically is the custom of altering a term of kinship or affinity when the connecting relative has died, as we might speak of an ex-son-in-law. The Tübatulabal and Yokuts share this practice with the Kawaiisu.

Chieftainship is said to be much less a matter of descent than among the Yokuts and to depend almost wholly and directly on the possession of wealth. If the son succeeded the father it was because he too had accumulated property rather than because of his parentage. As all a man's belongings were destroyed at his funeral the prospects of a chief's son being elevated to his father's place did not so greatly tower above those of other members of the community. In fact the Kawaiisu say outright that any rich man became a chief.

RELIGIOUS PRACTICES.

The inevitable mourning ceremony was practiced, but we know too little of it to relate it specifically to the type of rite prevalent among this or that group of people. As the use of crude representations of the dead occurs among nations to the north as well as to the south of Kawaiisu, the practice might be looked for among them, but it has not been reported. Property seems to have been de-

stroyed at the funeral itself rather than at the subsequent commemoration. This fact, if corroborated, indicates Chemehuevi and
Mohave influences rather than central Californian ones in this set
of customs.

On the other hand, a washing of the participants at the end of
the ceremony points northward; but the connection is weakened by
the fact that the Kawaiisu washed themselves, the Yokuts and
Miwok each other according to moiety affiliations. The commemorative rites are said to have been performed for several nights, a year
or two after a death. The impression given is that the ceremony
was made for one particular person of distinction by one of his close
relatives, who bore the cost of entertainment of visitors. This
suggests the Mohave practice of holding a commemorative rite only
for people of prominence. On the other hand, the difference from
the more communal form of anniversary generally reported from
central California is not so great as might appear. Thus among
the Yokuts, while everyone participated and mourned his dead of
the year, the initiative and direction of the affair, as well as the bulk
of the entertaining, rested upon one person, who undertook to make
the ceremony in honor of one of his relatives of rank or importance.
There is no mention of every mourner appearing with images of his
kin; and it is likely that this representation was confined to the one
deceased individual, or at most to the few persons for whom the chief
entrepreneur undertook the performance. Custom may well have
varied from tribe to tribe, in this point of the degree of association
of the commemorative ceremony respectively with individuals or the
community; but at bottom the divergences may have been differences
of emphasis more than absolute distinctions.

As Jimson weed is employed for religious purposes both by the
Yokuts and the southern Californians, the Kawaiisu might be expected to use it also; and they do. It is associated with puberty rites;
but, contrary to both Yokuts and Luiseño practice, seems to be
administered as regularly to girls as to boys. There are suggestions
of an approximation to shamanistic experiences, and of the initiate
standing in a definite relation to his vision for his adult life. One
girl, for instance, saw and was frightened by the grizzly bear while
under the influence of the drug. He did not address her; but thence-
forth she was forbidden bear meat.

As to Kawaiisu shamanism, nothing is on record, except that they
had powerful rain doctors. Thus, one member of the profession,
while lying on a summer's day with a wound in his neck—perhaps
received from an avenging relative of some one recently dead—
made a light rain to ease his pain and reduce the inflammation.

INDUSTRIES.

The manufactures and industries of the Kawaiisu are scarcely known. There is as yet no report that they made pottery of the San Joaquin Valley type. Their basketry is of Yokuts-Tübatulabal-Koso type rather than southern Californian, and excellently made. Their water bottle is in diagonal twining, round bottomed, and pitched. (Pl. 55, e.)

THE TÜBATULABAL.

ORIGIN AND MOVEMENTS.

With the Kawaiisu, the survey of the Plateau Shoshoneans in California is completed. We come now to an entirely distinct branch of the family—that of Kern River. There is only one people included in this divergent stem, the Tübatulabal. Looking downstream, they face the utterly alien Yokuts. On their left are the Kawaiisu, on their right the Mono, at their back the Koso. They are thus nearly surrounded by members of all three divisions of the great Plateau branch.

From what little knowledge is available, the speech of the Tübatulabal is, however, not more similar to the Plateau idioms than to the Shoshonean idioms of southern California. A long separate history is thus indicated for them; and it is hard to imagine a more favorable location for such continued aloofness than the one they now occupy—a clean-cut valley in a high mountain region; within the true California of nature and yet at its edge; outside the wide Shoshonean plateau but at the same time bordering upon it. Even the element of contact with totally strange peoples is given—a factor that would at once stimulate, accelerate, and tend to perpetuate novelties of speech formation, and thus lead to the condition of this little people ranking coordinate with much greater divisions, in the classification of the family to which they jointly appertain.

The situation of the Tübatulabal thus partly accounts for their distinctiveness, and renders it unnecessary to assume any extreme length of time for their separateness. On the other hand, their language is so thoroughly specialized as compared with that of their neighbors, the western Mono and the Kawaiisu, whose location with reference to topography and contact with aliens is similar, that it is clear that the Tübatulabal have lived where they are now, or in the immediate vicinity, for a period several times as long as these two groups of their kinsmen.

The Tübatulabal are the people upon whom in particular has been fostered the slander, or the undeserved reputation, of issuing in warlike mood from their highland fastness and raiding the sluggish,

peaceable Yokuts of the plains, dispossessing these, indeed, until
the southernmost Yokuts were almost separated from the main body
to the north. The story even goes on to picture how they would
have seized the entire Tulare Basin had they not become enervated
by malaria—somewhat as Greek and Latin civilization perished
before the same disease, according to a more recent and famous
fancy. Even the fact that the Tübatulabal were all found living in
the mountains when the white man came is explained: the same
scourge drove them back to the salubrious hills whence they had
emerged, and they utilized their conquests only for an annual or
occasional visit.

As a matter of fact, the visits took place; but they were the visits
of guests. The southern Yokuts tribes, both of the plains and of
the foothills, were generally quite thoroughly friendly, and joined
one another in their respective territories to such an extent, according to the season of the year, that it is almost impossible to assign
an exact habitat to any of them. The Tübatulabal, in spite of their
separateness of origin and speech, were also in the main on amicable
terms with these Yokuts tribes; and so came to join them in their
little migrations. Just as they came down to Bakersfield, to Kern
Lake, and to White River, probably even to Tejon and San Emigdio,
the Yokuts, as occasion warranted, ascended the Kern for miles to
fish, and to its forks, the center of the Tübatulabal home, to visit.

The entire little pseudo-history rests neither upon evidence nor
even native tradition, but is solely an imagination developed from
a knowledge of the facts that the Tübatulabal are Shoshonean and
that eastern tribes are often more aggressive than those of the Pacific
coast area.

Of course the amity between Yokuts and Tübatulabal suffered intermissions. But the Yokuts tribes fell out among each other also,
now and then; and the relations do not seem to have been different
in more than moderate measure.

GEOGRAPHY.

The land of the Tübatulabal was the region drained by Kern
River, down as far as a point about halfway between the forks
and Bakersfield. The exact spot has not been determined; it was
not far from the Paleuyami Yokuts settlements Shoko and Altau,
and a few miles above what the Yokuts call K'ono-ilkin, " water's
fall," a cascade, or perhaps a stretch of rapids that does not appear
on our maps but which served as a landmark to the natives.

The modern Tübatulabal settlements, and apparently the majority
of the old villages, were in the vicinity of the forks of Kern, both
above and below the junction, and apparently more largely on the

smaller South Kern. On the map the entire area tributary to both branches has been assigned to the Tübatulabal; but the upper reaches, which are little else than two great canyons among vast mountains, were assuredly uninhabited, and it is not even certain that the Tübatulabal laid exclusive claim to their hunting rights.

Substantially, this Kern River country is a rugged depression between the southern end of the main Sierra Nevada proper and a secondary parallel range. From this lower range to the west, Tule River, and Deer, White, and Poso Creeks flow westward, through Yokuts lands, directly into Tulare Lake. Kern River, however, is confined to a true southerly course until after it has worked its way around the end of the secondary range, when it sweeps westward, and finally almost northward, until lost in the tule swamps and lakes south of Tulare Lake. At least such was the condition until a generation ago: now the lake is nearly gone, and, except in times of flood, the volume of Kern River is dissipated in endless ditches and over irrigated stretches. The natural course of the stream is thus a great semicircle, open to the north: its upper half Tübatulabal, its lower Yokuts. Only at one point did the Tübatulabal leave their river. In the region of upper Deer Creek a small band seems to have had a home among the Yokuts. This group is referred to below as the Bankalachi.

Only a few names of places in Tübatulabal country can be located, and it is not known how many of these were villages. On the South Fork, Cheibü-pan was at Roberts, Tüsh-pan at Weldon. Yahaua-pan was at the forks; Piliwini-pan near Whiskey Flat or Kernville; Wokinapüi-pan farther up the main fork. Mount Whitney, "where all rivers begin," was called Otoavit. Owens Lake, on one side of the mountains, was Patsiwat, Bakersfield, on the other, Paluntanakama-pan.

The Yokuts called the village at the forks Pitnani-u; others, at Kernville, Tulonoya, at Keyes, Haukani-u; and at a hot spring above Vaughn, Tumoyo. The Tübatulabal territory is shown in most detail in the Yokuts map. (Pl. 47.)

The name Tübatulabal is Shoshonean and means "pine-nut eaters," but its dialectic source is not established. The Tübatulabal admit the designation, but also call themselves, or their speech, Pahkanapül. The Yokuts sometimes translate Tübatulabal into Wateknasi, from watak, "pine-nut"; but more frequently employ Pitanisha, from Pitnaniu, the central village. They also say Malda, but this term denotes any Shoshonean. Paligawonop and "Polokwynah" are unidentified names for the Tübatulabal.

They, in turn, name their neighbors as follows: Winanghatal, the western Mono of Kaweah River; Yiwinanghal, the eastern Mono or perhaps the Mono in general; Witanghatal, the Kitanemuk Serrano. These three names present the appearance of being directional terms. The Kawishm are the Kawaiisu, the Toloim the Bankalachi, the Amahaba the far-away Mohave. The Yokuts tribes in the valley along lower Kern River are the Molilabal; for the Yokuts in the foothills, somewhat distorted forms of their proper names are employed, as Witskamin, Paluyam, and Yokol, with perhaps an extension of these terms to wider groups. Thus the "Yokol" of the Tübatulabal seem to have included also the Gawia, Yaudanchi, and perhaps other tribes.

The Tübatulabal of to-day may aggregate 150. Perhaps the number is nearer 100. On the ancient population there are no data. A thousand seems as reasonable a guess as any other: at least it appears ample.

ARTS.

The Tübatulabal are one of the seemingly endless number of California tribes whose customs have never been described in any detail. Intercourse and intermarriage between them and the Yokuts were so frequent that they must have been strongly influenced by this much larger nation.

Their basketry is scarcely distinguishable from that of the southern Yokuts; it appears to average a little better in fineness. Tree yucca root replaced *Cercis* bark for red patterns. They made pottery of the same type as the Yokuts. Like these people, they ate tobacco mixed with lime. Their houses, or at least one form of dwellings, were covered with tule mats.

It is not certain that they had any form of sweat house: what may be remains of such have been reported. Balsas of bundled tules, with a keel, a slender prow, and a square stern, were made.

The dead were buried.

SOCIETY.

In their social life they stood more apart. The exogamous moieties of the Yokuts were not represented among them. There are possible traces of the totemic manifestations that accompany this dual organization. Young eagles were caught and reared. They were not killed, but were ultimately liberated. The plucking of their feathers seems to have been only a minor end of their captivity. Other birds, such as condors, crows, hawks, and geese, and even young coyotes, were kept as pets; in some cases inherited by the son from the father. In mythology the eagle is the chief, the coyote his antithesis; one has as associates a variety of birds, the other lizards, vermin, and trivial or noxious beasts.

In some matters Yokuts practices have failed to obtain a foothold, or a secure one, among the Kern River people. The parent-in-law taboos are not observed, or only by those individuals intimately associated with the Yokuts by intermarriage. This factor, incidentally, has introduced a number of Yokuts personal names among the Tübatulabal, who care very little whether an individual's appellation has any meaning as long as it is the name of an ancestor. The designation of kindred is almost identical with that of the Kawaiisu, and apparently of the Chemehuevi: the terms used are often quite different, but their significance is the same. The two groups thus think alike as regards relationship. A particular trait shared with the Yokuts is the custom of altering the kinship term when the connecting relative has died; but this has already been seen to be a Kawaiisu device, and the custom may well have had a Shoshonean origin and been borrowed by the Yokuts.

Chieftainship, on the other hand, resembles the Yokuts rather than the Kawaiisu institution. The prime requisite is to be the son of a *tiwimal* or chief; the approval of the community and the possession of wealth are also factors. The father selects the son who is to receive the dignity; if there is no male heir, a daughter succeeds. The feeling as regards descent must be strong, since the husband of a chieftainess is accorded no official authority, and the title passes to her son.

RELIGION. ·

Information fails as to whether the Tübatulabal practiced the southern Yokuts form of Jimson-weed ritual. They did have what the Yokuts seem to have lacked: a definite adolescence ceremony for girls. It is the old story: among the hill men this simple and personal observance stands out conspicuously, while in the more elaborate civilization of the lowlanders it is dwarfed or crowded aside.

The fact that the Tübatulabal are said in this ceremony to put their girls into a pit and cover them suggests an influence from southern California.

The mourning ceremony is called *Anangat*, is made primarily for a single person of prominence about two years after his death, and as among Maidu, Yokuts, and Luiseño, represents him by an image. Such a figure is made of bundled tules, and its sex denoted by bead necklaces and feathers, or an apron. The figure is burned at daybreak of the last night of the rites, together with baskets and other valuables.

So far we have substantially the same features as mark the ceremony among the other tribes mentioned. A trait that may be distinctive of the Tübatulabal is the fact that the mourner puts the observances in charge of visitors from other localities. This may be the substitute of an undivided people for the reciprocal division of function among a dually organized one; or the basic idea of the participation of nonmourners may be older and have been seized upon and fortified by those groups that were subsequently cleft into social moieties.

An invited chief had charge of the burning at the climax. His people gathered wood, tended the fire, burned the image, washed the faces of the mourners afterwards, and performed other services, for all of which they were paid.

THE BANKALACHI.

This small group was an offshoot from the Tübatulabal, that had crossed the divide from Kern River and settled among the Yokuts foothill tribes in the region where Deer Creek, White River, and Poso Creek head. Their speech was only slightly different from that of the Tübatulabal; but their associations were primarily with the Yokuts, and they probably followed the customs of the latter. Bankalachi (plural Bangeklachi) was their Yokuts name: the Tübatulabal called them Toloim. The majority of the little tribe are likely to have been bilingual; at any rate they were extensively intermarried with the Yaudanchi, Bokninuwad, Kumachisi, Paleuyami, and other Yokuts. Some of their blood flows in various of the Yokuts of to-day and something of their speech is not yet forgotten, but as a tribe they are extinct.

THE GIAMINA.

The Yokuts occasionally mention a supposed Shoshonean tribe, called Giamina by them, in the vicinity of the Bankalachi, probably on Poso Creek. It is extinct. A few words have been secured from the Yokuts. These are indubitably Shoshonean, but not of any known dialect nor wholly of affiliation with any one dialect group. It is impossible to decide whether this brief vocabulary is only the result of a distorted recollection by an individual Yokuts of a smattering acquaintance with Shoshonean; or a sort of jargon Shoshonean that prevailed among the Kumachisi or some other Yokuts tribe; or the vanishing trace of a distinctive Shoshonean language and group. The last alternative is by no means precluded; but it may never be proved or disproved. The existence of the name Giamina signifies little, for it may be a synonym. But it is an old appellation. Father Cabot in 1818 encountered the "Quiuamine" in the vicinity of the Yokuts Wowol (Bubal), Choinok, and Yauelmani ("Yulumne").

CHAPTER 43.

SERRANO DIVISIONS.

THE SERRANO GROUP.

The fourth and fifth Shoshonean tribes inside the Sierra, the Kitanemuk and the Alliklik, are in the same region of the head of the San Joaquin-Kern drainage as the preceding groups. With the Kitanemuk, however, an entirely new division of Shoshoneans is entered: the southern California branch of the stock.

The Kitanemuk and probably the Alliklik (the latter are extinct) belonged to a northern section of the southern Californians to which the generic appellation "Serrano" has been applied. This is an unfortunate name. Not only is there this Serrano group and the Serrano tribe proper within it, but the name means nothing but "mountaineers"—"those of the Sierras," to be exact. In fact, the Kitanemuk do not know themselves as Serranos, but extend the epithet to their neighbors the Kawaiisu, quite correctly in an etymological sense, since these people happen to live higher in the mountains than they. But an ethnological designation is necessary, however arbitrary. It is in the fertile portion of southern California that the term "Serrano" has acquired a definite ethnic meaning as the name of the people in the San Bernardino Mountains. Their dialect is close to that of the Vanyume and Kitanemuk; Alliklik speech was probably similar; and so "Serrano" is here used also in the wider sense as the name of the division.

THE KITANEMUK.

RANGE.

The Kitanemuk lived on upper Tejon and Paso Creeks, whose lower courses are lost in the Yokuts plains before reaching Kern River. They held also the streams on the rear side of the Tehachapi Mountains in the same vicinity and the small creeks draining the northern slope of the Liebre and Sawmill Range, with Antelope Valley and the westernmost end of the Mohave Desert. The extent of their territorial claims in this waste is not certain. The population perhaps resided more largely in the smaller San Joaquin part of the Kitanemuk area; the bulk of their territory was over the mountains in southern California.

A synonym of Kitanemuk is Kikitanum or Kikitamkar. All these words are perhaps from the stem *ki–*, "house." The Yokuts know the Kitanemuk as Mayaintalap, "large bows"; the Tübatulabal call them Witanghatal; the Chemehuevi, Nawiyat; the Mohave, Kuvahaivima—Garcés's "Cuabajai"— not to be confounded with Kuvahye, the Mohave designation of the Kawaiisu. The Americans are content to call them Tejon Indians, which would be satisfactory but for the fact that the former Tejon Reservation contained a little Babel of tribes. Most of the neighbors of the Kitanemuk to-day frequently refer to them as the Haminat. This is not a true designation but a nickname, a characteristic phrase of the language, meaning "what is it?"

It is necessary to distinguish between Tejon Creek, Tejon Rancho, and the old Tejon Reservation, all of which were in Kitanemuk territory, and Tejon Pass and the former Fort Tejon, which lie some distance to the west on the Cañada de las Uvas in Chumash habitat.

A few Serrano place names have been reported. Their present principal village, where Tejon Creek breaks out of the hills, is Nakwalki-ve, Yokuts Pusin-tinliu; Tejon ranch house on Paso Creek is Wuwopraha-ve, Yokuts Laikiu; below it lies Honewimats, Yokuts Tsuitsau; on Comanche Creek is Chivutpa-ve, Yokuts Sanchiu; Tehachapi Peak or a mountain near by is Mavin, perhaps Chapanau in Yokuts.

The Mohave or "Amahaba" of the Colorado River were known as "muy bravos" and were welcome guests among the Kitanemuk, penetrating even to the Yokuts, Alliklik, and perhaps Chumash. They came to visit and to trade. It is characteristic that the local tribes never attempted to reciprocate. Their range was not as confined as that of the northern Californians, but they still had no stomach for long journeys to remote places inhabited by strange people. The Mohave refer to the Tehachapi-Tejon region in their myths; it is not known and not likely that the Kitanemuk traveled as far as the sacred mountains of the Mohave even in imagination.

A curious and unexplained belief prevails among all the tribes in the Kitanemuk neighborhood, as well as among the Mohave, namely, that there is in this vicinity a tribe that in speech, and perhaps in customs too, is almost identical with the Mohave. Sometimes the Kitanemuk are specified, sometimes the Alliklik, or again ideas are vague. The Mohave themselves speak of the Kwiahta Hamakhava or "like Mohaves" as somewhere in this region; they may have meant the Alliklik. There is no known fragment of evidence in favor of this belief; but it must rest on a foundation of some sort, however distorted. Perhaps it is the presence of an Amahavit group among the Serrano, as mentioned below.

CUSTOMS.

Garcés in 1776 found the Kitanemuk living in a communal tule house, which differed from that of the lake Yokuts in being square. His brief description is best interpreted as referring to a series of individual family rooms surrounding a court that had entrances on two sides only, at each of which a sentinel—compare the Yokuts *winatum*—was posted at night. Each family had its door and fireplace. The framework of the structure was of poles; the rushes were attached in mats. The modern Yokuts deny that the Kitanemuk or any hill tribes built community houses, but Garcés's testimony is specific.

He mentions also the eating of tobacco. The leaves were brayed with a white stone (lime) and water in a small mortar, and the end of the pestle licked off. Even some of the natives swallowed the mess with difficulty. The avowed purpose of the practice was the relief of fatigue before sleep.

Seeds, possibly crushed to meal, were scattered in the fire and over sacred objects. The Pueblo sprinkling of corn meal is inevitably suggested.

The priest also tells of vessels, apparently of wood, with inlays of haliotis, "like the shellwork on the handles of the knives and all other manufactures that it is said there are on the Canal" of Santa Barbara—that is, among the Chumash. They trade much with the Canal, he adds, and suspects, though erroneously, that they may be the same nation. He had not himself been with the Chumash.

The Kitanemuk seem to have been at war at the time with the Alliklik, for Garcés mentions their killing a chief on the Santa Clara, and the Alliklik did not conduct him into Kitanemuk territory. Toward the Yokuts, also, there seems to have been no friendliness; he could not get a Quabajáy guide to the "Noches" because these were "bad"—except a Noche married among them.

The Yokuts of to-day declare that the Kitanemuk interred corpses. They danced differently from the Yokuts, and lacked the rattlesnake rite and the *Heshwash* doctor ceremony. They did have a memorial burning of property for the dead, when "clothing was stuffed" to represent them; and they practiced an initiation ritual with Jimson weed, which drug, or its drinking, they called *pa-manit*. The southern California deities to whom the Yokuts pray seem to have had their origin among the Serrano proper or, more likely, the Gabrielino; the Kitanemuk would in that case have been the transmitters.

Basketry (Pl. 55, c) seems to have been of the San Joaquin drainage type rather than southern Californian.

THE ALLIKLIK.

Bordering the Chumash, on the upper Santa Clara River, there lived a Shoshonean tribe that was probably of Serrano affinities, although the two or three words preserved of their speech allow of no very certain determination. They can not have been numerous. Taken to San Fernando or San Buenaventura missions, they dwindled rapidly, and the few survivors seem to have been so thrown in and intermarried with people of other speech that their own language became extinct in a couple of generations. In fact, there is nothing

known about them except that they held the river up from a point
between Sespe and Piru, most of Piru Creek, Castac Creek, and
probably Pastoria Creek across the mountains in San Joaquin Valley
drainage and adjacent to the Yokuts. The location of a few of the
spots where they lived is shown on the Chumash map. (Pl. 48.)
Alliklik, more properly I'alliklik in the plural, is the Ventureño
Chumash name.

The Vanyume.

The Vanyume are the Serrano of Mohave River. Dialectically
they stand nearer to the Kitanemuk than to the Serrano of the San
Bernardino Mountains; but all three idioms appear to be largely
interintelligible.

Except perhaps for a few individuals merged among other groups,
the Vanyume are extinct, and the limits of their territory remain
vaguely known. Garcés makes their habitat begin some few Spanish
leagues east of the sink of Mohave River, perhaps a third of the way
from it to the Providence Mountains; and Chemehuevi accounts
agree. From there up to Daggett or Barstow was undoubted Vanyume land. Beyond, there is conflict. The well-traveled Mohave
describe the Vanyume as extending to the head of the river. An
ancient survivor not long since attributed the upper course of the
stream to the brother tribe, the Serrano proper. Garcés, the first
white man in this region, who rode from the sink of the river to its
source, does not clear the problem, since he designates the Vanyume,
the Serrano, and evidently the Alliklik by a single epithet: Beñeme.
The point is of no vital importance because of the likeness of the
groups involved. Political affiliations may have conflicted with
linguistic ones. The Mohave and Chemehuevi were at times friendly
to the Vanyume, but hostile to the Serrano of the San Bernardino
Range; there could well have been a division of the Serrano proper
settled on upper Mohave River and allied with the Vanyume. The
whole relation of Serrano proper and Vanyume is far from clear.

It must also be remembered that there are some Kawaiisu claims
to a possession of Mohave River about where it emerges from the
mountains.

Vanyume is the Mohave name, whence Garcés's "Beñeme." The Chemehuevi
seem to call them Pitanta. The group has also been designated by the term
Mühineyam, but this appears to be not so much an ethnic designation as the
name of one of the local groups into which the Serrano proper were divided:
Mohiyanim. The word Vanyume seems to go back to the radical of our "Panamint," which in turn is a synonym for the Shoshoni-Comanche group called
Koso in this work.

The Vanyume population must have been very small. Garcés
mentions a village of 25 souls and a vacant settlement on the river

between Camp Cady and Daggett.   Then there was nothing until a short distance below Victorville he encountered a town of 40 people and a league beyond another where the chief resided.   These may have been Vanyume or Serrano proper.   In the mountains, but still on their north slope, the rancherias were larger: 70, 25, and 80.   These were probably Serrano proper.

The river carries water some distance from the mountains, and seepage beyond; but in much of its course it is only a thin line of occasional cottonwoods through an absolute desert.   The people must have been poor in the extreme.   At the lowest village Garcés found some bean and screw mesquite trees and grapevines; but the inhabitants had nothing but tule roots to eat.   They were naked, and a cold rain prevented their going hunting; but they possessed blankets of rabbit and otter fur.   Their snares were of wild hemp. At one of the upper villages there were small game and acorn porridge: and where the chief lived, welcome was extended by sprinkling acorn flour and small shells or beads.   The latter were strung in natural fathom lengths.

A punitive expedition against the Mohave in 1819 traversed Vanyume territory and names the following places and their distance in leagues from Cucamonga: Cajon de Amuscopiabit, 9; Guapiabit, 18; Topipabit, 38; Cacaumeat, 41; Sisuguina, 45; Angayaba, 60.   The first three names are in a Serrano dialect; the fourth seems to be; the fifth is doubtful; the sixth Chemehuevi. Their locations fall within the territories assigned respectively to the Vanyume and the Chemehuevi on the map.

THE SERRANO.

HABITAT.

The Serrano proper, or "mountaineers" of the Spaniards, are the last of the four bodies of people that have here been united, on account of their similarity of dialect, into a "Serrano division" of the Shoshonean stock.

Their territory was, first the long San Bernardino Range culminating in the peak of that name, and in Mount San Gorgonio, more than 11,000 feet high.   Next, they held a tract of unknown extent northward.   In the east this was pure desert, with an occasional water hole and two or three flowing springs.   In the west it was a region of timbered valleys between rugged mountains.   Such was the district of Bear Lake and Creek.   In the third place they occupied the San Gabriel Mountains or Sierra Madre west to Mount San Antonio.   This range is almost a continuation of the San Bernardino Range.   In addition, they probably owned a stretch of fertile lowland south of the Sierra Madre, from about Cucamonga east to above Mentone and halfway up San Timoteo Canyon.   This tract took in the San Bernardino Valley and probably just failed of reaching Riverside; but it has also been assigned to the Gabrielino, which would be a more natural division of topography, since it would leave the Serrano pure mountaineers.

There is another territory that may have been Serrano: the northern slope of the Sierra Madre for some 20 miles west of Mount San Antonio, the region of Sheep, Deadman, and Big and Little Rock Creeks. But this is uncertain. The Kawaiisu may have ranged here, in which case this Chemehuevi offshoot no doubt owned the whole western Mohave Desert also, and cut off the two western Serrano divisions, the Alliklik and Kitanemuk, from contact with the two eastern, the Vanyume and present true Serrano. In support of this view is a reference to the "Palonies—a subtribe of the Chemehuevi" as the northern neighbors of the Gabrielino.[1]

The best parts of the Serrano land are shown in the southern California map, Plate 57, which includes place names. Many of the latter no doubt originally denoted villages; but it is usually impossible to determine. The Indians of this region, Serrano, Gabrielino, and Luiseño, have long had relations to the old ranchos or land grants, by which chiefly the country was known and designated until the American began to dot it with towns. The Indians kept in use, and often still retain, native names for these grants. Some were the designations of the principal village on the grant, others of the particular spot on which the ranch headquarters were erected, still others of camp sites, or hills, or various natural features. The villages, however, are long since gone, or converted into reservations, and the Indians, with all their native terminology, think in terms of Spanish grants or American towns. Over much of southern California—the "Mission Indian" district—the opportunity to prepare an exact aboriginal village map passed away 50 years ago. The numerous little reservations of to-day do in the rough conserve the ancient ethnic and local distribution; but not under the old circumstances.

NAMES AND NUMBERS.

The most frequent name for the Serrano among their neighbors to-day is some derivative of Mara or Morongo. Thus, Luiseño: Marayam; Chemehuevi: Maringits; they call themselves Maringayam. These terms are derived from the name of one of the Serrano bands or groups discussed below, the Maringayam or "Morongo," formerly at Maringa, Big Morongo Creek, whence the designation of Morongo Reservation near Banning, on which Serrano are settled among Cahuilla. A similar word, Mara, is the native name of the oasis at Twenty-nine Palms.

[1] Recent inquiries by Mrs. Ruth Benedict, as yet unpublished, put Serrano groups in the canyons on the northern face of Mount San Jacinto, in territory assigned in Plates 1 and 57 to the Pass Cahuilla.

Tahtam has been given as the name of the Serrano for themselves: it means merely "people." Kauangachem is of unknown significance; Kaiviatam is only a translation into Indian of Spanish "Serrano."

The Mohave know the Serrano as Hanyuveche, the "Jenigueche" of Garcés.

The population must have been rather sparse; 1,500 seems an ample allowance in spite of the extent of the Serrano range. A part of the group may have kept out of the exterminating influence of the missions; yet few seem to survive. The census of 1910 reports something over 100.

SOCIAL SCHEME.

With the Serrano, the exogamous and totemic moieties of the Miwok and Yokuts reappear. Associated with them is a new feature, a series of bands or local subdivisions.

One moiety is called *Tukum*, "wild cats," after *tukut*, its chief totem. It has as other totems *tukuchu*, the puma or mountain lion, older brother of wild cat, and *kachawa*, the crow, his kinsman.

The other moiety is known as *Wahilyam*, "coyotes," and has as associate totems coyote's older brother *wanats*, the wolf or jaguar, and his kinsman *widukut*, the buzzard.

The word for "totem" is *nükrüg*, "my great-grandparent," or *nüngaka*. The creator established the institution. Moieties joke each other; members of the first are reputed lazy and dull, of the second swift and perhaps unreliable.

The bands offer more difficulty. Some are not assigned to either moiety in the available information. All of them are mentioned as localized within certain districts. Their recorded appellations are mostly either place names or words appearing to mean "people of such and such a place." For some districts a single band is mentioned, for other regions pairs of intermarrying bands.

In general, it would appear that the Serrano bands are not so much clans, as has been conjectured, as they are the equivalents of the "village communities" or political groups of northern and central California—what might be called tribes were they larger in numbers, set off by dialect, or possessed of names other than derivatives from one of the sites inhabited. Each of these Serrano groups or bands owned a creek and adjacent tract; its "village" or most permanent settlement usually lay where the stream emerges from the foothills. Each group was also normally or rigidly exogamous: and there was at least a strong tendency, if not a rule, for particular groups to intermarry. Each group or band was either Wild Cat or Coyote; but it appears that group and not moiety affiliation determined exogamy, since some of the regularly intermarrying bands are assigned to the same moiety.

The known groups, in west-east sequence along the southern edge of the San Bernardino Range, were the Wa'acham of San Bernardino, Redlands, and Yucaipa; the Tüpamukiyam (?) at Tümünamtu between El Casco and Beaumont; the Pavükuyam at Akavat near Beaumont; the Tamukuvayam of Pihatüpayam (*sic:* the name seems that of a group) at Banning Water Canyon; perhaps a group at Nahyu, Hathaway Canyon; one at Marki (Malki),

the present reservation near Banning; the Wakühiktam at Wakühi on Cabezon
Creek; the Palukiktam in Lyons Canyon; the Wanüpüpayam at the mouth of
Whitewater Canyon; three groups, the Maringayam, Mühiatnim (Mohiyanim),
and Atü'aviatam, more or less associated at Yamisevul on Mission Creek, Türka
on Little Morongo Creek, Maringa on Big Morongo Creek, Mukunpat on the
same stream to the north, and at Kupacham, the Pipes, across the mountains.
Of these, the second, eleventh, and twelfth were Wild Cat, the fifth and sixth
not known, the remainder Coyote.[2]

Other groups were the Tüchahüktam (Coyote moiety) of Tüchahü at Snow
Canyon or One Horse Spring at the foot of Mount San Jacinto, on the south
side of San Gorgonio Pass; the Coyote moiety people of Mara, Twenty-nine
Palms, northeast of Big Morongo Creek; the Yuhaviatam or Kuchaviatam of
Yuhaviat ("pine place") in or near Bear Valley, moiety unknown; the
Pauwiatum, Coyote; the people of Kupacha, Wild Cat; the people of Kayuwat,
Wild Cat (?)—these three in or north of the San Bernardino Mountains.
The Mawiatum are described as east of Kayuwat on Mohave River and the
people of Amahavit as east of these. Both of these would be Vanyume rather
than Serrano proper, by the classification here followed; and Amaha-vit
suggests Hamakhava, Mohave, and reminds of the rather close relations between
this people and some of the Vanyume. Some Serrano also list the Agutushyam
of the Tehachapi Mountains, that is, the Kawaiisu, as if they were one of their
own bands. This is in line with certain Kawaiisu claims, already mentioned,
to ownership of part of Mohave River and the northern foot of the Sierra
Madre.

Each group possessed a hereditary chief called *kika*. This word
is from a Shoshonean stem meaning "house" or "live." Associated
with each *kika* was a hereditary *paha'* or assistant chief with ceremonial functions. The Luiseño have the same official and call him
by the same name. Ceremonies were held in special houses built of
tules, not in an open inclosure as among the other southern Californians.

The moieties, at least as represented by the Maringayam and
Mühiatnim, partly divided and partly reciprocated religious functions. Each tended the dead of the other before cremation. The
Mühiatnim *paha'* named the children of both clans after their dead
ancestors. The Maringayam *kika* ordered ceremonies, and his people
built the tule house and acted as messengers. The Mühiatnim cooked
and served food to the Maringayam at ceremonies.

Acorns were fairly abundant in the western part of Serrano territory, but the eastern bands got their supply from the western ones,
or substituted other foods. Storage was in outdoor basketlike caches
raised on poles. Houses were covered with mats of tules, which are
said to grow along all the streams, even those that lose themselves in
the desert. The modern ceremonial house at Banning, apparently
kept up for a fragment of an annual mourning, is tule covered. A
sweat house that stood there until recently—it may have been built

---

[2] The list is incomplete and may be supplemented and corrected by the unpublished
Benedict data already referred to.

by a Pass Cahuilla, but was probably Serrano—was small, earth-covered, and had a center post (Pl. 60). Pottery was made by the Serrano, but rarely if ever decorated. No specimens have been preserved.

COSMOGONY.

The Serrano origin begins with Pakrokitat, from whose left shoulder was born his younger brother Kukitat. Pakrokitat created men. Kukitat wanted them to have eyes in the back and webbed feet, and quarreled constantly. It was he that caused death. Pakrokitat finally left him this earth, retiring to a world of his own, to which the hearts of the dead go after first visiting the three beautiful Panamam on the island Payait. This island and its goddesses were also made by Pakrokitat. Before the separation of the brothers, the human race, led by a white eagle, had come from its origin in the north to Mount San Gorgonio. After Pakrokitat's departure, men, under the influence of Kukitat, began to divide into nations, speak differently, and war on one another. They finally became tired of Kukitat and decided to kill him. The frog accomplished this end by hiding in the ocean and swallowing the god's excretions. Kukitat, feeling death approach, gave instructions for his cremation: but the suspected coyote, although sent away on a pretended errand, returned in time to squeeze through badger's legs in the circle of the mourners and make away with Kukitat's heart. This happened at Hatauva (compare Luiseño Tova, where Wiyot died) in Bear Valley. People continued to fight, until only one man survived of the Maringayam. His Kayuwat wife bore a posthumous boy, who was reared with his mother's people, but returned to his ancestral country, married two Mühiatnim sisters, and became the progenitor of the Maringayam or Serrano of today.

CHAPTER 44.

THE GABRIELINO.

THE FERNANDEÑO.

This group of people, more properly San Fernandeños, are named
from San Fernando, one of the two Franciscan missions in Los
Angeles County. At San Gabriel, the other establishment, were
the San Gabrielinos, more often known merely as Gabrielinos, popularly Gravielinos. In a larger sense, both people have been designated as the Gabrielino. Their idioms were distinguishable, but
not notably so; and if fuller knowledge were extant it might be
necessary to recognize half a dozen dialects instead of the two which
the presence of the missions has given the appearance of being
standard. The delimitation of Fernandeño and Gabrielino on the
map is mainly conjectural, and there is no known point in which the
two groups differed in customs. It will be best, therefore, to treat
them as a unit under the caption of the more prominent division.

THE GABRIELINO.

TERRITORY.

The wider Gabrielino group occupied Los Angeles County south
of the Sierra Madre, half of Orange County, and the islands of
Santa Catalina and San Clemente. The evidence is scant and somewhat conflicting as regards the latter; a divergent dialect, or even a
Luiseño one, may have been spoken there. The local culture on San
Clemente, however, was clearly connected with that of Santa Catalina, perhaps dependent upon it; and Catalina was pure Gabrielino
in speech.

On the west, the Gabrielino limits—here more exactly Fernandeño—against the Chumash were at the minor watershed through which the Santa Susanna tunnel has been bored; at the coast, between Malibu and Topanga Creeks. Eastward, toward the Serrano and Luiseño, the line probably passed from Mount San Antonio to the vicinity of Cucamonga, Mount Arlington, and Monument and Santiago Peaks; in other words, through western San Bernardino and Riverside Counties—although San Bernardino Valley has also been ascribed to the Gabrielino. Southward, Alisos Creek is cited as the boundary between Gabrielino and Juaneño.

Most of the ascertained place names of the Gabrielino are shown in Plate 57, whose limitations as regards the inclusion of true village sites have already been mentioned. Other places are these: Pimu or Pipimar, Santa Catalina Island: Kinki or Kinkipar, San Clemente Island; Aleupki-nga, Santa Anita; Pimoka-nga, Rancho de los Ybarras; Nakau-nga, Carpenter's; Chokish-nga, Jaboneria; Akura-nga, La Presa; Sona-nga, White's; Sisitkano-nga, Pear Orchard; Isantka-nga, Mision Vieja. Sua-nga near Long Beach is mentioned as the largest village.

Synonyms or dialectic variants of the Gabrielino names shown in Plate 57 are: Tuvasak for Siba; Iya for Wenot; Pashina for Pasino; Ongovi, Ungiivi for Engva; Chauvi and Unau for Chowi; Shua for Sua.

A language of "Kokomcar" and one of "Corbonamga" are mentioned as spoken by the neophytes at San Gabriel besides the "Sibanga"—Siba, the site of San Gabriel—and "Guiguitamcar" or Kikitanum, that is, Kitanemuk.

The Ventureño Chumash knew the Gabrielino, and perhaps all the Shoshoneans beyond, as Ataplili'ish (plural I'ataplili'ish).

GENERAL STATUS.

The Gabrielino held the great bulk of the most fertile lowland portion of southern California. They occupied also a stretch of pleasant and sheltered coast and the most favored one of the Santa Barbara Islands. They seem to have been the most advanced group south of Tehachapi, except perhaps the Chumash. They certainly were the wealthiest and most thoughtful of all the Shoshoneans of the State, and dominated these civilizationally wherever contacts occurred. Their influence spread even to alien peoples. They have melted away so completely that we know more of the fine facts of the culture of ruder tribes; but everything points to these very efflorescences having had their origin with the Gabrielino.

The Jimson weed or toloache ritual is a case in point. The religious use of this drug extends far eastward, and its ultimate source may prove to be Pueblo, like that of the sand painting that is associated with it in the region from the Gabrielino south. The definite cult, however, in which the plant is employed, the mythology with which it is brought into relation, the ritual actions and songs that constitute its body, were worked out primarily if not wholly by the Gabrielino. All southern accounts mention Santa Catalina and San

Clemente Islands as the seat of the source of this cult. Whether it was brought from there to the mainland Gabrielino, or whether these had long shared the ritual with their oceanic kinsmen, is not certain. At any rate, the ritual was carried to the Juaneño; from them to the Luiseño; and they in turn imparted it to the Cupeño and the northern or western Diegueño.

The last of this flow took place in historic time. It reached the interior Luiseño and the Diegueño from about 1790 to 1850. The very missions of the pious Franciscans stimulated the spread. They brought San Clemente Indians to San Luis Rey, and highland Luiseño to mingle with the coast Luiseño and islanders there. The Luiseño and Diegueño to-day sing nearly all their toloache songs in the Gabrielino language without concern at not understanding the words issuing from their mouths.

MYTHOLOGY.

Among the Juaneño and Luiseño the Jimson-weed cult is intimately associated with beliefs in a deity called Chingichnich or Chungichnish. This name has not been reported from the Gabrielino, but Kwawar occurs as a synonym of Chingichnich among the Juaneño and as the "creator" with the Gabrielino. Further, certain of the animals of the Luiseño worship, such as the raven and rattlesnake, reappear with religious significance among the Gabrielino. There can thus be little doubt that these people also acknowledged the divinity. The problem which we can not answer is whether they knew him under another name, or whether Chungichnish is itself a Gabrielino term which happens not to be mentioned in the scant sources of information upon this tribe. Pura, the Luiseño say, is what the Gabrielino called the deity; but the word looks suspiciously like the Luiseño term for shaman: *pula*.

On the other side, to the north, there are some traces of a pantheon of six or seven deities, in part female, more or less associated with the Jimson-weed cult, though whether primarily or not is uncertain. Among the southern Yokuts these divinities present the appearance of being of foreign origin, and this determination is corroborated by their entrance into wider phases of life with the Gabrielino: the names are not only those of gods, but titles of chieftainship. The information on this interesting little system of mythology is sadly fragmentary, but pieces together sufficiently to

·suggest some idea of the nature of the scheme. It is presented in the following table:

YOKUTS. In fixed order of Jimson-weed prayers.	YOKUTS. In fixed order of other prayers.	FERNANDEÑO. "Gods" in order of mention.	GABRIELINO.	SERRANO.
Tüüshiut....	Tüüshiut....	....	....	
Pamashiut..	Pamashiut....	....	....	
Yohahait....	Yohahait....	....	....	
	Echepat.....	5. Iuichepet..	....	
	Pitsuriut......	4. Pichurut...	....	
	Tsukit	3. Chukit....	Chukit (in myth, sister of 4 brothers).	Six stones at Nanamüyiat, Little Bear Valley, were "gods."
	Ukat (their sister).	1. Ukat.......	....	
		2. Tamur....	Tomar (title of oldest son of chief).	
		6. Manisar (wife of 5).	Manisar (title of oldest daughter of chief).	

FORMULA: 7 Yokuts (–t, prayers)–3 Yokuts (–t, Jimson weed)+2 Gabrielino (–r, chiefs)=6 Fernandeño (–t, –r, gods)=6 Serrano (?).

The Fernandeño list is from San Fernando in mission times, and might therefore go back to a Kitanemuk Serrano source. The Kitanemuk at any rate would have carried the religion to the Yokuts, who would not be praying to native gods under names that contain the sound r, which is lacking from their own language. How far the Chumash, Alliklik, Kawaiisu, and Vanyume shared in this complex is entirely undetermined.

It is observable that there is a distinction of function between the gods whose names end in –t and those whose names end in –r, and that this distinction coincides with tribal distribution.

South of the Gabrielino, this mythic-ritual-social six god system has not been reported. Whether it and the Chungichnish complex excluded each other or stood in relation remains to be ascertained by future investigations. But there is an approximation to the Gabrielino plan among the Juaneño, who possessed animal names as titles for their chiefs and chieftainesses; thus " coyote " and " ladybug." It is also possible that the Juaneño female mythological character Ikaiut is to be connected with Ukat.

The meanings of the deities' name are obscure. Manisar is very likely from mani-t, Jimson weed. Pitsuriut or Pichurut suggests Juaneño piuts or piuch, the breath of life. The names Tüüshiut and Yohahait, which have been reported only from the Yokuts, are translated by these people with some hesitation as " maker " and " crusher;" but these may be only folk etymologies of foreign terms, like their rendering of Ukat as " looker, seer." It is not impossible that Tüüshiut is connected with the tosaut or tushaut stone so important in Chumash ritual and Juaneño myth.

The creative mythology of the Gabrielino has been preserved only in the veriest scraps. The reputed creator of the world—he may or may not have been such to the Indians—was called Kwawar ("Qua-o-ar") by his sacred name, and "Y-yo-ha-riv-gnina" otherwise. Neither epithet yields to analysis. He fixed the earth on seven giants whose stirrings cause earthquakes. The first man was Tobohar, his mate Pabavit. Tobohar is from a widespread Shoshonean stem for "earth;" among the Gabrielino themselves *tobanga* means "the world." Perhaps Tobohar and Pabavit should be interchanged. Everywhere else in southern California the earth is the first mother.

Porpoises were believed to watch the world, circling around it to see that it was safe and in good order. The crow was thought to advise of the approach of strangers. This sounds much like beliefs associated with the Chungichnish cult. Still more significant in this direction is the report that a surpassingly wise "chief," before dying, told the people that he would become an eagle so that they might have his feathers for dances; and that consequently ceremonies were made to the eagle. This is surely the dying god of whom all the southern Californians know; perhaps even the very Wiyot of the Juaneño and Luiseño; and the ceremony must be their eagle killing mourning rite.

The origin of mankind was attributed, as by all the Shoshoneans of southern California, to the north, whence a great divinity, who still exists, led the people to their present seats. Perhaps this "capitan general" was the just-mentioned eagle, perhaps Wiyot or his equivalent.

Chukit, the virgin sister of four unnamed brothers, probably all members of the six-god pantheon, was married by the lightning flash, and gave birth to a wonderful boy who spoke when his navel string was cut.

Coyote raced with water, and ended exhausted and ashamed. Whether he entered also into less trivial traditions is not recorded.

The Pleiades are "seven" sisters—six seems a more likely native version—married to as many brothers, who, however, cheated them of the game they killed, until the women rose to the sky. The youngest alone had been good to his wife; he was allowed to follow them, and is now in the constellation Taurus.

A woman of Muhu-vit, married at Hahamo, lazy, gluttonous, and stingy, is said to have been fed with game stuffed with toads and vermin, and given urine to drink by her husband's people. Sick and with her hair fallen out, she returned to her parents, destroying her child on the way. Secretly she was nourished back to health by the old people, until her brother, finding hairs in his bathing pool, discovered her unrecognized presence, and threw her out. Ashamed, she started for the seashore, and drowned herself from a cliff.

Her father threw his gaming hoop in four directions; when it reached the sea, it rolled in, and he knew his daughter's fate. First he revenged himself on his own son, whom, in the form of the *Kuwot* bird, he carried off and destroyed. Then, taking the shape of an eagle, he allowed himself to be caught by the people of Hahamo; but when they touched him, pestilence spread from him, and killed every one except an old woman and two children.

An inconsequential appendix follows. The two children grow up and marry: then the woman maltreats the old grandmother, but is killed by her. The husband mourns his wife and follows her spirit to the land of the dead, where his experiences are like those of the Yokuts Orpheus. Like him, also, he brings his partner back, but loses her once more and irrevocably at the last moment.

The ethical inconsistency of this story is marked to our feelings. The heroine certainly is blameworthy, but those who rid themselves of her, even more so. Hardly is sympathy aroused for her when she dispels it by dashing out her child's brains. Then she becomes beautiful once more, and elicits interest through the disgraceful treatment accorded her by her brother. But this hardly seems sufficient cause for suicide. Her brother, too, committed the offense unwittingly; and his fatal punishment by his father comes to us as a shock. That the old chief should cruelly revenge himself by his magical powers on the foreigners who had first attempted his daughter's destruction seems natural enough; but the focus of interest is suddenly shifted from his means of vengeance to the successful escape from it of the old woman and her grandchildren. Then these, brother and sister as they are, marry. Now it is the old lady who is abused; but suddenly it is her granddaughter who is persecuted and finally slain; after which follows the episode in which the loving and grieving husband is the central character.

Nothing can be imagined farther from a plot according to the thoughts of a civilized people than this one; it appears to revel in acmes of purposeless contradictions. And yet, this trait is undoubtedly the accompaniment of an effect that, however obscure to us, was sought for; since it reappears in traditions, following an entirely different thread, told by the Luiseño and Diegueño, and is marked in the long tales of the Mohave. This deliberate or artistic incoherence, both as regards personages and plot, is thus a definite quality of the mythology of the southern Californian tribes. It has some partial resemblances in the Southwest, but scarcely any in central or northern California except in the loosely composite coyote tales. In central California we have the well-defined hero and villain of the normal folk tale of the world over; and however much the oppressed endure, there is never any doubt as to who is good and who wicked, and that before the end is reached the wicked will be properly punished. That in the southern California traditions this simple and almost universal scheme is departed from, is of course not due to absence of aesthetic feeling, but rather an evidence of subtle refinement of emotion, of decorative overelaboration of some literary quality, to such a degree that the ordinary rules of satisfaction in balance and moral proportion become inconsequential. The traits that shock us ethically and artistically were the very ones, we may be sure, that gave the keenest satisfaction to the craftsmen that told these tales and the accustomed public that delighted to listen to them.

Most likely, as among the Mohave, stories like this one are little else than a web that carries a rich embroidery of songs, which yield their own emotional stimulus, and at the same time endow the plot, when sensed through their medium, with a brilliant and profound luminousness that makes immaterial the presence or absence of everything else.

RITUAL.

Almost nothing specific is on record concerning the Gabrielino Jimson-weed cult, except that it is reported that the plant, called *manit*, was drunk mixed with salt water, in order to give strength, impenetrability to arrows, immunity from bear and snake bites, and fortune in the hunt. These very practical aims in no way indicate that the drinking was not also part of the sacred and esoteric ritual that we know to have been associated with it.

Among the Fernandeño a four-sided and roped-off ground painting was made, in the middle of which a man stood, holding twelve radiating strings, the ends of which were in the hands of as many assistants. When he shook the cords, the earth quaked, and whatever person he had in mind became sick. The setting of this rite is obscure. It suggests the Chumash use of charm stones more than any Luiseño ceremonial act; but the sand painting is Luiseño and not, so far as known, Chumash.

The mourning commemoration was held in the *yoba* enclosure. For eight days songs and perhaps dances were rehearsed outside. The ceremony itself endured another eight days.

On the first, the enclosure was erected or consecrated.

From the second to the seventh day men and boys danced inside the enclosure and women sat in a circle and sang. The dancers' faces, necks, arms, and thoraxes were painted; which makes it seem that their feather costume was the feather crown and skirt of the Luiseño and Juaneño. The songs related to the deceased, or perhaps to the god who first died; some were sung "to the destruction of his enemies." Each song or verse ended with a sort of growl. A pole with a feather streamer was erected at each of the four cardinal points.

On the eighth day the old women made ready more food than usual; about noon it was distributed. A deep hole was then dug and a fire kindled in it, whereupon the articles reserved at the time of death were committed to the flames. Baskets, shell money, and seeds were thrown to the spectators or out-of-town visitors. During the burning, one of the old men, reciting mystical words, kept stirring up the fire to insure the total destruction of the property. The hole was then filled with earth and well trodden down.

The end of this ceremony allies it with the Luiseño *yunish mata-kish*, made for a dead initiate. The rehearsing, the participation of boys, and the type of costume, all point to the existence of the kind of initiatory organization which the Juaneño and Luiseño possessed and in fact believed that they derived from the Gabrielino. The four poles suggest the one erected in the Luiseño *notush* mourning, to which, again, they attribute a Gabrielino origin. The cursing songs of hate are also southern. All that fails of mention is the image of the dead; and with the Kitanemuk on one side and the Luiseño on the other employing this, it is practically certain that the Gabrielino knew it.

It must be said once more that the frequent mention of the Juaneño and Luiseño in connections like the present one must not lead to an inference that the Gabrielino were in any sense dependent upon them. The influence was positively the other way. It merely happens that for the Juaneño a fuller account of the religion, and among the Luiseño the ceremonies themselves, have been preserved; so that the knowledge of the borrowed rites of the southerners must be drawn upon for an understanding of the recorded fragments of the older and probably more elaborate Gabrielino cult. Thus, something is known of the Luiseño *notush* and its *kutumit* pole; for the Gabrielino there is no record other than that at San Fernando a similar pole was called *kotumut*.

Several round stones, perforated, hafted on the ends of rather slender sticks, and feather decorated, have been discovered in a cave in Gabrielino territory. Such stones, which abound most among the Chumash, are ordinarily digging stick weights; but in this case the character of the handles precludes any employment as a tool. An unknown ritualistic use is therefore indicated.

That the Gabrielino word for " tobacco," *shuki*, is not from the usual southern Californian stem *piva*, but borrowed from Yokuts *shogon, sohon*, which has penetrated also into the Mono, Koso, and Tübatulabal dialects, suggests that the plant was perhaps more widely used, at least in religious connections, by the Yokuts, and that the neighboring Shoshoneans came under their influence in this matter.

The number most endowed with significance to the Gabrielino seems to have been four, or its double, eight. Six, seven, and ten are also referred to in connections that make probable a certain degree of sacredness or suggestive value; but five, which predominates among the Juaneño, has not been reported here.

SHAMANISM.

The removal of disease was by sucking blood and perhaps the disease object. Smoking, manipulation, and singing preceded. The words of the songs appear to have been descriptive of the practices applied, as among the Mohave. It may be conjectured that the doctor sang not so much of what he was doing as of what had been done to a god in the far past, or what he in a dream had seen a deity or animal perform.

Diseases were also treated by a variety of remedies. Jimsonweed was drunk for paralysis, debility, and stagnation. Whipping with nettles was resorted to in the same cases, as also for side pains. Eating red ants or letting the insects bite the skin, a favorite Yokuts remedy, were remedies for body pains. For local inflammations, blood was drawn. Tobacco, with or without an admixture of shell lime, was eaten for fever, strangury, wounds, stomach aches, and whenever vomiting was desired. Whether the old men habitually ate tobacco and lime, as was customary among the Kitanemuk and Yokuts, is not clear. Against rheumatism, blisters were burned with nettle or wild hemp furze and at once opened. Anise was for purging; *kayat*, "chuchupate," for headache; *thaïish*, *Echinocystis*, for inflammations, eye disease, suppressed periods, wounds, and urinary troubles; when boiled it was taken to produce sweating.

Medicine men were called *ahubsuvoirot*.

The bear doctor was a Gabrielino institution, although more than the naked fact is not known.

BUILDINGS.

The house was of tule mats on a framework of poles: size and shape have not been recorded. On the islands and in the hills thatch of other materials may sometimes have been used. Earth-covered dwellings have not been mentioned. The sweat house had a roof of soil; but it was small, and a true sudatory, heated by fire and smoke, of course, as in all California, and not by steam. The sweat house of the Serrano or Pass Cahuilla (Pl. 60) probably serves as a representative.

The place of assembly for any occasion not savoring too formally of ritual was presumably any large dwelling, such as the chief's, or the open brush shade. Religious gatherings took place in the open air ceremonial enclosure, the Juaneño *wankech*, Luiseño *wamkish*, Diegueño *himak*. The Gabrielino seem to have called it *yoba* ("yobare," "yobagnar") and to have built it circularly of willows inserted wicker fashion among stakes. It was consecrated for each ceremony. A similar structure, without sanctity, was used for rehearsals and the instruction of children. Each village had one *yoba*.

BASKETRY AND POTTERY.

Few if any baskets authentically assignable to the Gabrielino have been preserved. The type of the tribal ware was that common to all southern California and usually known as "Mission basketry"; it is described in the chapter on the Cahuilla. The pitched water bottle is specifically mentioned.

Pottery had come into use by the end of the mission period. But it is stated positively that clay was not worked in aboriginal days. Archeology confirms: no pottery has been found in ancient remains in the Gabrielino habitat.

STEATITE.

In the soapstone ledges of Santa Catalina the Gabrielino possessed the best available supply of this serviceable material in California; or at any rate the source most extensively utilized. The discoverers found them using stone vessels for cooking; and the condition of the island quarries, with half-finished pieces and tools still on the surface, is evidence that the industry was only interrupted after the importation of our civilization. From Santa Catalina the pots, and perhaps the raw material, were carried to the villages at Redondo and San Pedro and gradually distributed to the inland towns. The eastern Chumash may have got them from the people of Santa Monica and Topanga and from the Fernandeño. But the presence of steatite articles in fair abundance on Santa Cruz and the other northern channel islands suggests also a direct maritime dispersion to these Chumash, and from them to their kinsmen of the Santa Barbara coast. Inland the vessels penetrated at least sporadically as far as the Yokuts of Tulare Lake, if scant archeological records may be trusted. It is not sure that this entire area was served from Santa Catalina. But much of the supply evidently came from the island.

It is interesting that the steatite and the pottery areas of southern California substantially exclude each other. Gabrielino and Chumash were flooded with the one material, and did not touch clay. Juaneño, Luiseño, Cahuilla, Diegueño, Serrano, Mohave, and Yuma made pots; and it is only now and then that small or ornamental pieces of steatite were to be found among them.

When the soapstone pots broke, their pieces were bored at one corner to allow of the insertion of a stick to handle them by, and utilized as baking slabs or frying pans. Hundreds of such salvaged fragments have been found in old village sites. The occasional fine vessels of stone were not cook pots, but religious receptacles— possibly to drink toloache from. They are shell inlaid and untouched by fire. The shape, too, is that of an open bowl, not a jar. They have sometimes been taken for mortars, on account of their general form; but it is obvious that one blow with a pestle would have destroyed irreparably most of these delicately walled, polished, symmetrical, and ornamented objects of sandstone or waxlike steatite.

Most abundantly on Santa Catalina, but also on the coast immediately opposite, on the Chumash islands, and even on the Santa Barbara shore, a profusion of soapstone artifacts have been found. Besides recognizable ornaments and beads, there are several types whose evident lack of any utilitarian purpose has caused them to be generally classed as made with ceremonial intent. Besides peculiar objects of the shape of hooks, spades, and scoops, there are carvings of whales, which are of particular interest as one of the very few instances, in all aboriginal California, of anything like a representation. They are as simple as the stone is easy to work, but suggest a dorsally finned cetacean with considerable fidelity and no shadow of doubt. They may be plastic figures of the porpoises that guarded the Gabrielino world. The hooks and other shapes range from a fraction of an ounce to several pounds in weight, and pass through a transition of shapes which retain indeed a certain decorative or symbolic likeness that makes their unity of class certain, but are so variant in structural features as to dispel any possibility of each type having possessed a common utilitarian purpose. They served a religious purpose, then; and as their source corresponded with that ascribed by evidence and tradition alike to the Chungichnish cult—the balmy island of Santa Catalina—the conclusion is very hard to avoid that the worship and the art forms must have been associated. From this conviction we can argue, with somewhat less confidence, but yet with probability, that something of the same specific Chungichnish ritual and mythology traveled with the figures from Santa Catalina to the Chumash islanders and mainlanders. That the Chumash drank Jimson weed we know; the present reasoning establishes some likelihood that their cult of it was not a particular one.

TRADE AND MONEY.

For the islanders' journeys, canoes of the kind described by the discoverers, and known also from fragments in Chumash graves, were employed. The canoe may at times have been dug out from a log, but owing to the scarcity of suitable timber, especially on the islands, was usually built up out of planks, lashed and asphalted together. For lagoon navigation the rush balsa may also have been used.

Between the coast and interior trade was considerable. The shore people gave shell beads, dried fish, sea-otter furs, and soapstone vessels. They received deerskins, seeds, and perhaps acorns.

The standard currency was the disk bead, of clamshell, from one-half to three-quarters of an inch in diameter, and the thicker the better. The unit of measurement was the *ponko*. This reached from the base to the tip of the middle finger, thence around the outside of the hand past the wrist back to the point of the middle finger, and then once more not quite to the wrist. The length, about 30 inches, is half of the scant fathom reach of a man of small stature. The various local manners of this type of money measuring have been brought together in Table 6 in the chapter on the Chumash.

The next highest unit was four *ponko*, called a *sayako*. Two *sayako* were reckoned, in mission times, a Mexican *peso* or dollar; which made the *ponko* a *real*. This equivalation to the Spanish standard obtained also among the Chumash and Salinans, but the reckoning of values by doubling and quadrupling is probably native.

It is curious that the heavy clamshell beads are rare in ancient Gabrielino and Chumash graves, thin convex disks of *Olivella* being the common prehistoric type. These have also been found among the modern Luiseño and Cahuilla. The *Olivella* shell was known throughout central and northern California, but little esteemed; it ranked as beads rather than money. In the south it was more frequently ground into disks; but at that, it must have been secondary to the heavy clam bead, whose broad edge is susceptible of a much higher polish.

Both types are represented among the Southwestern tribes. The modern Zuñi bead is prevailingly of *Olivella*. The Pueblo, however, never distinguished as sharply between a mere necklace and currency as the Californian; he thought in terms of property rather than of standardized money.

FOOD.

When the Gabrielino first met the Spaniards they politely accepted every gift, but every scrap of food was held in such abhorrence as to be buried secretly. It was not that the natives feared deliberate poisoning, but they were evidently imbued with a strong conviction similar to that of the Mohave, who believed that every nation had its own peculiar food and that for one to partake of the characteristic nourishment of the other or to mingle with its women, or in fact associate in any prolonged contact, was bound in the very nature of things to bring sickness.

The native foods rejected are not known. They can not have been many, as dogs, coyotes, all birds whatsoever, and even rattlesnakes are mentioned as having been eaten. Whether the omission of the bear from the list of edible animals is significant or not must remain doubtful.

The Gabrielino are the first people of all those passed in review to use movable stone mortars to any great extent for the ordinary purpose of grinding acorns and plant foods, at least in historic time. The soil of northern California is studded with pot-shaped mortars, but the natives misunderstand their purpose or regard them as magical objects, and pound on slabs or in holes worn into natural surfaces of rock. In the central part of the State the portable mortar begins to appear, and the basket hopper, the accompaniment of the pounded slab, commences to go out of use, but the bedrock mortar hole remains the standard, at least for acorns. From the Gabrielino on, however, south to the Diegueño, east to the Mohave, and west, perhaps, to the Chumash, the stone mortar is not merely a buried relic from a remote prehistoric age but a utensil of everyday modern use. Some of these southern tribes cement a basket to the rim of the stone; the Chumash asphalt it also to slabs; but the mortar can often be used just as successfully, and sometimes perhaps more conveniently, without this extension. Perhaps this is why the hopper has not been reported from the Gabrielino. That they knew the device is nearly certain from their location between groups that employed it.

VARIOUS IMPLEMENTS.

The Gabrielino war club ranged from a straight heavy stick to a shorter form with a definitely marked cylindrical end—the southwestern type.

A curved flat stick, called *makana*, for throwing at rabbits and birds, is another southwestern type that pervades all southern California and seems to have come to the limit of its distribution among the Gabrielino. (Fig. 55.)

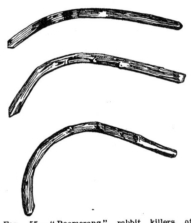

Rattles in the Spanish period were made of gourd or rawhide. These are almost certainly recent modifications of the old turtle-shell rattle still employed by the Luiseño and Diegueño, and, as a knee attachment, used from time immemorial by the Pueblo Indians. The modern Mohave rattle is a gourd; but it is not sure that this is native; in any event, the Mohave were an agricultural people, while the Gabrielino and other southern Californians were not.

Fig. 55.—" Boomerang " rabbit killers of southern California. From above downward, Cupeño, Luiseño, Mohave.

A wooden clapper rattle has been reported from the Gabrielino. This is the most southerly occurrence recorded for this universal north and central Californian implement. At that, the Gabrielino rattle is not a half-split stick, as elsewhere, but two boards bound and cemented together at one end.

Meat was cut with a splint of cane and not with a stone knife. Practicability or habit rather than any religious reason appears to have been the motive.

For arrow poison, gall was boiled down.

SOCIAL PRACTICES.

As in the whole of southern California, social institutions constitute the least known side of Gabrielino culture. Marriage was by purchase, but more was made of the wedding rite than of the payment; chiefs and prominent men often had several wives. All this is typical Juaneño procedure. The wife seems to have lived in the husband's village. It is said that he was at liberty to punish her at will for infidelity, even by death; but that the usual solution was to leave her to the seducer and appropriate the latter's spouse, with which practice no interference was tolerated. Deliberate incest was punished by shooting to death. There was a chief in each village. If any exercised wider influence, the fact has not been reported. To judge by Juaneño analogues, as well as the above-mentioned titles for the chieftain's children, the position conveyed much deference and respect. Each chief was known by the name of his town plus the suffix -*pik* or -*vik*. The rank was hereditary, apparently in the male line. It is said that the chief took no action against sorcerers, other than to leave punishment to the magical machinations of the medicine men of his own town. As an absolute negative, this statement may be doubted. It is likely to have been true under the outward restraints of mission life.

Captives taken in battle were tortured and killed.

The hair was at times plastered with clay for 24 hours, to impart gloss and keep it from splitting. The Mohave mix in a vegetable dye for this purpose; plain mud is applied by them to kill vermin.

The dead were burned by both Fernandeño and Gabrielino proper until the padres introduced interment. On Santa Catalina many skeletons have been found, but few if any evidences of cremation. Burial must therefore have been the prevalent manner on this island through most of its history. The mainland, on the other hand, is remarkably free of ancient human bones, except at immediate coast points opposite Santa Catalina, such as Topanga, Santa Monica, Redondo, and San Pedro. It seems, therefore, that an ancient difference of custom separated the islanders from the bulk of the Gabrielino on this point.

THE SAN NICOLEÑO.

San Nicolas, the farthest seaward of the Santa Barbara Islands, foggy and wind blown, harbored a tribe of which the last survivor died more than 60 years ago. Four badly spelled words are all that has been preserved of their speech. These suffice to prove it Shoshonean: they do not establish its dialectic relation. A divergent idiom may well have developed in the isolation of this sand-swept and

rocky island. It is stated that when the last survivor was brought
to Santa Barbara her speech was thoroughly unintelligible not only
to the Chumash of the vicinity but to the " Pepimaros " of Santa
Catalina (Pimu, Pipimar, the name of the island), of whom some
were sent for from Los Angeles.

The last handful of the natives, who are said to have suffered
previously in quarrels with Aleuts imported by Russian fur hunters,
and whose numbers had probably been diminished by drafts to the
missions, were taken to the mainland in 1835, soon after secularization. A woman who at the last moment missed her child was left
behind. Eighteen years later, when California was American, she
was discovered. Her romantic case aroused the greatest interest, and
she was given the best of treatment in her new home at Santa Barbara; but she died in a few months. More attention was bestowed
on her humble belongings than on the panoply of many a tribe; and
while the objects themselves seem all to have been scattered and
lost—the last traceable piece perished in the San Francisco fire of
1906—the descriptions, together with random but rather full recov-
eries from ancient village sites, enable a partial insight into the life
of this remote little group, the most westerly of all Uto-Aztekans.

Wood was scarce and small on the island. There was enough brush
for huts, but most dwellings were reared on a frame of whale ribs and
jaws, either covered with sea-lion hides or wattled with brush or
rushes. Bone implements were very numerous, and the use of several varieties is far from clear. The island may have afforded sufficient timber for plank canoes, or dugouts may have been burned from
drift logs. Steatite was imported from Santa Catalina, but is represented by small ornaments or charms rather than heavy bowls.
Whales must have been very abundant and frequently stranded;
there is nothing to indicate that they were hunted. Sea otters were
to be had in comparative profusion, and, to judge from the habits of
other tribes, their furs formed the most prized dress and the chief
export in a trade on which the San Nicoleño must have depended for
many necessities. Seals, water birds, fish, and mollusks were no
doubt the principal food; but roots were dug industriously. Baskets
are spoken of as of the type ordinary in southern California. They
were often asphalted, hot pebbles being employed to melt and spread
the lumps. Water baskets were in plain twining, as among the
Chumash; but the neck was long, much as in our wine bottles. The
lone woman wore a sort of gown of squares of bird skin sewn together; but this does not seem wholly aboriginal. The usual dress
may be conjectured to have been the scant costume of all California,
with capes or blankets of woven strips of bird skin added at need.

The cylinder-headed wooden war club was in use. The dead were buried, as by all the islanders, not cremated as on the Shoshonean mainland. Of religion we only know that there were weather invocations and hunting charms; whether the toloache cult or the image form of mourning anniversary had reached the island must remain in abeyance; and as to society, there is total ignorance.

Ghalas-at has been given as the name of the island. This is perhaps the native or the Chumash pronunciation of Gabrielino Haras-nga.

CHAPTER 45.

THE JUANEÑO.

EXTENSION.

The Juaneño Indians are so named after the mission of San Juan Capistrano in their territory. They were wedged in between the Gabrielino and the Luiseño; but their speech was a dialect of the latter language, not a transition between the two. Their land extended from the sea to the crest of the southern continuation of the Sierra Santa Ana. Southward, toward the Luiseño, the boundary ran between San Onofre and Las Pulgas; on the north, toward the Gabrielino, it is said to have followed Alisos Creek. The known settlements of the group are shown in Plate 57.

For Ahachmai, Akagchemem and Kwanisa-vit have also been given as dialectic variant or name of an associated site; for Pu-tuid-em, Niwiti.

The population may have been a thousand; the present survivors may be three or four.

Father Geronimo Boscana's " Chinigchinich," easily the most intensive and best written account of the customs and religion of any group of California Indians in the mission days, relates to San Juan Capistrano; and the pages that follow are almost wholly based on his careful statements. It has been generally assumed that this work referred to the Juaneño; but analysis of its native terms and designations of place leave a doubtful impression. A large part, possibly the bulk, of the information conveyed by the assiduous and sympathetic priest is certainly of Gabrielino origin. What is questionable is whether the lore was taken over by the Juaneño from the Gabrielino of their own accord and in premission times, as part of the Chungichnish cult or as the effect of still earlier streams of Gabrielino culture; or whether the father reported data from local Juaneños and imported Gabrielinos side by side without thinking it worth while for his purposes to specify the tribal differences. On the one hand, we know that the Gabrielino influence existed, for it prevails among the more distant Luiseño. On the other hand, the mission was but a very few miles from the Juaneño boundary, and southern Gabrielino converts must have become attached to the establishment in considerable numbers. The problem can not be answered with exactness: the only recourse is to present the information as a whole and preserve the mental caution called for by the circumstances.

MYTHOLOGY.

The Juaneño story of the creation has been preserved in two versions, one from the inhabitants of the interior, the other from the coast. The former is more similar to the Luiseño account.

According to this version, the first things in the universe were the sky and the earth, brother and sister. From their union were born, first, earth and sand, next, stone and flint, then trees, next herbs, after that animals, and finally Wiyot (Ouiot). From Wiyot were born men, or rather a first race of beings that preceded mankind. As they multiplied in number, the Earth, Wiyot's mother, grew southward, and the people followed. They used soil as food.

Wiyot was plotted against and poisoned. His mother prepared a remedy, but this was spilled and lost through the curiosity of the Coyote. After a sickness of some duration, Wiyot died, predicting his return. After some discussion his cremation was decided upon, but the people feared Coyote, and attempted to conduct the funeral in his absence. He appeared, however, and professing his affection for Wiyot, leaped upon the pyre, tore off a piece of flesh from the body, and swallowed it. Coyote had been the *eyake* or assistant chief to Wiyot.

After this, a new being appeared, who revealed himself as Chingichnich ("Chinigchinich"), with his habitation in the sky, or rather throughout the world. Chingichnich converted the first people into animals and plants, or into spirits having power over animals and plants, and caused them to scatter over the earth. In their place he made a new race, the present human species, out of earth, and taught them their laws and institutions, including the building of the *wankech* (*vanquech*) or ceremonial inclosure.

The coast Juaneño attributed the creation of the world, the sea, and animals and plants to "Night," Tukma or Tokuma ("Nocuma"). He fastened the earth by means of the smooth, black, hard rock called *tosaut*. The ocean at first was small and overcrowded with beings until a large fish brought the *tosaut*, the center of which was filled with gall. This being emptied into the water, it became salt and welled up until the ocean attained its present size. Tukma then created the first human being called Ehoni.

To two of Ehoni's descendants, Sirout ("handful of tobacco") and his wife Ikaiut ("above.") Wiyot was born as son, at Pubu-na, to the northwest of San Juan Capistrano, in Gabrielino territory. Wiyot ruled the people, but according to this story also was plotted against, and poisoned by means of the *tosaut* stone. He sickened, died, and was burned.

In this version also a new divinity appears after Wiyot's death, but under the name of Atahen, "man," who gave to certain of the people and their descendants the power to make rain, cause seeds to grow, and bring about the productivity of game animals.

Still later there was born at "Pubuna"—Pubu-nga, Los Alamitos, in Gabrielino territory—to Taku and Ausar, Wiamot ("Ouiamot"), who is said to have been Chingichnich. He announced that he had come from the stars, gave to the people the feather costume for dancing, instructed them in its use, thus constituting the order of *puplem* or initiated, and gave orders for the ceremonial inclosure to be built.

Wiamot or Chingichnich is also said to have become sick and to have announced that after his death he should ascend to the stars to watch the people; to punish by bears, rattlesnakes, famine, and sickness those who disobeyed his commandments; and to reward the faithful.

There is evidently some confusion in this story. Atahen, the second of the great leaders, is perhaps merely a synonym of either Wiyot, the first, or Chingichnich, the third. The appearance of Chingichnich under the name Wiamot, so similar to Wiyot, is also peculiar. Three other names of Chingichnich are given. He was called Tobet, which is the name of the ceremonial costume worn by those initiated into his cult; Saor, which denotes the uninitiated; and Kwawar, his appellation among the stars. The last name was in use among the Gabrielino also. The close association of myth and ritual at these points is evident. The use of the name of the dance costume for the deity himself, or vice versa, is a fusion parallel to that which has taken place in regard to the Kuksu in the religion of the Sacramento Valley.

The prominence of the *tosaut* stone in the creation myth of the coast Juaneño is partly cleared up by the fact that this word occurs among the entirely alien Chumash as the name of the charm stones used by medicine men, and probably in public ritual also. It follows that the intervening Gabrielino must have had similar sacred stones and given them the identical appellation. In fact it is not unlikely that the practice as well as the name, which is of undetermined etymology, are of Gabrielino origin. It is probably more than a coincidence that all indications of the *tosaut* cult come from coast points.

Tradition further told of a flood which submerged the whole earth except one mountain peak. This event is placed in the time of Chingichnich's appearance, subsequent to the death of Wiyot, and has parallels in Mohave belief. In general, the concept of primeval water is central Californian. In northwestern and in southern California the world is believed to have existed first, and the subsequent flood to have been temporary. Of all the southerners, only the Yuman tribes tend to begin their cosmology with the waters.

Another legend has been preserved which, although trivial and limited in its range, is of interest as evidencing the presence among these people of a migration tradition of the type characteristic of parts of southern California, but entirely without analogues in the central and northern portions of the State. It begins at Sehat, at Los Nietos, a Gabrielino village some 30 or more miles northwest of San Juan Capistrano. Here lived the Chief Oyaison, with his wife Sirorum. After the death of the latter, Oyaison escorted one of his three children, his daughter Korone, together with a portion of his people, southward to Niwiti, not far from San Juan Capistrano. Here, after the return of her father, Korone established a settlement which was named Pu-tuid-em after an enlargement of her abdomen or navel. She was enormously fat, and never married. The newcomers spread out into neighboring settlements and changed their speech from the original Gabrielino tongue which they had brought with them. Korone's body finally swelled up to such a degree, during her sleep, that it turned into a mound or small hill which remains to-day. The inhabitants of Pu-tuid-em then moved to Ahachmai or Akagchemem, a mile or two distant, at the spot where the mission was subsequently founded. They spent their first night in their new home huddled and piled together like a heap of insects, or other animated things, to which fact the name of this new and final settlement refers.

This is almost certainly a true Juaneño story, as shown by its location; but it is noteworthy that it begins in the land of the Gabrielino.

The general cast and tone of this tradition is similar to a number of Mohave legends, although the particular incidents differ throughout; and it obviously recalls the tribal and clan migration legends of the Pueblos, just as southwestern suggestions crop out in Juaneño cosmogony.

CULTS.

Juaneño ceremonies are primarily of two classes: initiatory or puberty rites, and mourning rituals. They were held in a sacred enclosure, and there appears to have been but one standard religious costume.

THE CEREMONIAL STRUCTURE.

The *wankech* or ceremonial chamber was an inclosure of brush, open to the sky, apparently with a subdivision or smaller inclosure. Near or in the latter place was placed the skin of a coyote, filled with feathers, horns, claws, and beaks, including particularly parts of the condor, and a number of arrows. This image or figure has no known parallels in California. It is said to have been the god Chingichnich. At any rate, it constituted an altar, in front of which was made a rude drawing or sand painting. Great respect was shown this sacred place. Conversation did not rise above a whisper, and the uninitiated were not even permitted to enter the outer inclosure.

It is specifically said that the altar in the *wankech* was an inviolable sanctuary, at which murderers, deposed chiefs, and all in fear of punishment found safe refuge. The practice is likely to have been actual, but the formulation of the idea of a recognized sanctuary seems un-Indian; there is nothing like it among any California tribe. It can hardly be doubted that the sanctity of the spot was great enough to prevent a killing or struggle. No matter what the provocation, punishment might be deferred until a more suitable occasion.

RITUAL DRESS.

The *tobet* or ceremonial costume comprised the *palet* ("*paelt*") skirt of eagle or condor feathers, reaching from the waist to the knees. On the head was fastened, by means of a cord of human hair, the *emech*, described as a pad or wig. Into this feathers were stuck, or an upright bunch of feathers called *eneat* was attached to it. The body was painted red and black, or sometimes white.

INITIATION CEREMONIES.

The Gabrielino Jimson-weed ceremonies were practiced by the Juaneño, who in turn helped to convey them to the Luiseño. As among the Luiseño, these were clearly initiation rites, and under the inspiration of the god Chingichnich. Young children were given the drug. From the fact that this is described as *pivat*, which is the native name for tobacco, it seems possible that a mixture of narcotic or stimulating plants was employed. In the visions caused by the drug the children expected to see an animal. In this they were instructed to place entire confidence, and it would defend them from all future dangers in war or otherwise. The animals mentioned are the coyote, the bear, the crow or raven, and the rattlesnake—all except the first specifically associated with Chingichnich among the Luiseño.

The suggestion of a personal guardian spirit in these beliefs must not be overestimated into their interpretation as a part of shamanism, since the protective animals were acquired not through involuntary dreams or individual seeking, but during a state of intoxication produced in a communal ritual.

The term *touch*, still translated by the Juaneño as "diablo," is mentioned by Father Boscana in connection with the Jimson-weed vision, but the context does not leave it entirely clear whether *touch* signified a form or apparition of Chingichnich, or was the generic name of the protecting animal. The Luiseño *towish* means "ghost."

There was another initiatory rite which is said to have been undergone by chieftains' sons and others of high rank who did not partake of the Jimson weed. But it is possible that the account may really refer to a subsequent and higher stage of the initiation, or perhaps to a second initiation leading to a higher degree. This is confirmed by the fact that this ceremony is mentioned as having been undergone by young men. These were painted black and red and wore feathers—a description given also of the initiated wearers of the *tobet*—were led in procession to the *wankech*, and placed at the side of the Chingichnich image or altar. Before them, then,

the older initiates made a sand painting—of an animal, it is said—
by which the novices fasted and refrained from drink for a period
of about three days.

As among the Luiseño, trials of endurance followed the general
drinking of the Jimson weed. The novices were blistered with fire,
whipped with nettles, and laid on ant hills. These ordeals hardened
them, and any who might fail to undergo them were looked upon
as unfortunate, feeble, and easily conquered in war.

About the same period of life the boys or young men were pro-
hibited certain foods, both meat and seeds. Some of these restrictions were maintained during manhood.

When boys were initiated—not into manhood, but into the use
of the *tobet* dance costume—they were one after another arrayed
in this, and danced with a turtle-shell rattle in their right hands.
If a boy became totally exhausted from the duration of the ceremony he was carried upon the shoulder of one of the older men,
who danced for him. At the conclusion a female relative danced
naked. It is not certain whether all young men underwent this
initiation, or only those who were of higher social status, or attained
a specially advanced religious rank. The nude dancing by women is
mentioned as having taken place on other occasions.

GIRLS' RITE.

Girls at their adolescence underwent a ceremony much like that
practiced by the Luiseño, except that no mention is made of a ground
painting. The girl was laid on branches of " estafiate " (*paksil*)
placed in a pit lined with stones that had been heated. The hole
is said to have resembled a grave in shape, a circumstance that is
paralleled in the Luiseño puberty rite for boys and appears to be
symbolic. Here the girl lay for several days fasting, while old
women with their faces painted sang, and young women at intervals
danced about her.

Girls were tattooed as part of their adolescent training shortly
before puberty, from the eyes or mouth down to the breast, and
on the arms. Agave charcoal was rubbed into bleeding punctures
made with a cactus spine.

MOURNING CEREMONIES.

The dead were cremated, usually within a few hours after their
decease. The pyre was lit by certain persons who derived their
office by descent, and were paid for the service like the Yokuts
tongochim. It is said that all but these personages withdrew from
the actual cremation, which was followed by several days of wailing
and singing. The words of the songs are stated to have related the

cause, location, progress, and completion of the disease that had resulted fatally. It is not probable that the illness of the departed
was thus described. Such reference to anything savoring of the
person of the dead would certainly have been extremely repugnant
to all other Californian tribes. The Luiseño on the same occasion
sing similar songs about the sickness and approaching death of
Wiyot; the Mohave have parallel practices; and it may therefore be
concluded that the burden of the Juaneño mourning also referred to
the fate of their dying god.

As in all parts of California and nearly all regions of America,
the hair was cut in sign of mourning, the length removed being pro-
portional to the proximity of kinship or degree of affection.

The hearts of those of the initiated whose flesh was eaten by the
takwe were thought to go to the sky and become stars. The hearts
or souls of all other persons went to an underground region called
tolmer (Luiseño *tolmal*), where they spent their existence at ease in
constant dancing and feasting.

The usual commemorative mourning ceremony was made for chiefs
and prominent persons, although Father Boscana has left no specific
account of it, and we do not therefore know whether, as seems probable, it included the burning of an image of the dead. It was, however, an exact anniversary, the precise condition of the moon at the
time of death being observed, and the rite held when the moon attained the same size in the month of the same name in the following
year.

Father Boscana describes a ceremony similar to the eagle-killing
rite of the Luiseño and Diegueño. Although he does not mention
it as a funerary observance, it can hardly have been anything else.
The bird employed he names *panes*, which has not been identified, but
from its description appears to have been the condor. It was carried
in procession to the *wankech*, placed upon a sort of altar, and danced
to by the initiated, while young women raced or ran about. Later
the bird was killed without the loss of any blood. The skin was
drawn off and preserved for making *palet* skirts, while the body was
interred within the *wankech*, while old women made offerings to it,
wept, and addressed it, after which dancing was resumed. This ceremony was definitely associated with Chingichnich. The very identical reincarnated *panes* was believed to be killed not only each year
but in every village.

The fire dance was another act which has southern analogues,
and is likely to have been introduced sometimes into mourning ceremonies. The dancers leaped into a large fire, which they trod until
every spark was extinguished.

On the death of one of the fully initiated a personage called either *ano*, " coyote," or *takwe*, " eater," cut off from the back or shoulder of the deceased a piece of flesh and devoured or appeared to consume it in the presence of the crowd. This character was much feared and was heavily paid for his act by contributions from the populace. The natives specifically connect the ceremony with their myth of the eating of part of Wiyot's body by the coyote.

Nothing like this astounding rite is known from any other region of California nor from any part of the Pacific coast, until the Hamatsa practices of British Columbia are reached, except for a mention that Pomo mourners now and then snatched and ate pieces of the dead.

SHAMANISM.

The source of power of the medicine man and his method of acquiring it are not known with exactness, either for the Juaneño or for the other Shoshoneans of southern California. Besides sucking, blowing was resorted to. The word for shaman is *pul*, which appears to be the unreduplicated singular of *puplem*, " the initiated." There would thus seem to have been a certain lack of differentiation between the shaman proper and the man who had been fully instructed in sacred tribal lore.

ORDINANCES AND BELIEFS.

The regulation that a hunter must not partake of his own game or fish was adhered to tenaciously. Infraction brought failure of luck and perhaps sickness. Often two men went out together, in order to exchange with each other what they caught. It would appear that this rule applied chiefly or only to young men. At any rate, there must have been limitations to its enforcement, since it is stated that sickness resulted only when the game was consumed secretly.

At the appearance of the new moon, old men danced, while the boys and youths raced. The words of the songs used on this occasion referred to the death and resurrection of the moon and were symbolic, although whether of a return to life of human beings in general, or only Wiyot, is not certain.

At eclipses every one shouted and made all possible noise to frighten away the monster thought to be devouring the sun or moon. It is probable that this custom was common to all the Indians in California.

Takwich or meteors were much feared. Young women fell upon the ground and covered their heads, fearing to become ugly or ill if looked upon by the spirit. Takwich or Takwish is prominent in the mythology of the Luiseño and Cahuilla and the name is presumably connected with *takwe*, the designation of the ceremonial eater of human flesh. The latter functionary has not been reported from the Luiseño or Cahuilla, but the traditions of these people consistently depict Takwish as a cannibal spirit.

Of immaterial essences, the *piuch* ("*piuts*") or breath was distinguished from the shun ("*pu-suni*") or heart. The former corresponded somewhat to our idea of life, the latter rather to the soul.

The ritualistic number of the Juaneño is not clear. Among the Luiseño, Gabrielino, and Diegueño there is also some variability and hesitance of formulation. Five seems to have been used with significance at least as often as any other number by the Juaneño.

The Gabrielino origin of a large share of Juaneño ritual and myth is clear, not only from the fact that both creation and migration traditions commence in Gabrielino territory, but especially from the names of religious import.

A considerable number of Juaneño ceremonial designations contain the sound "*r*," and very few contain "*l*." Now "*l*" is the Juaneño and Luiseño sound that corresponds to Gabrielino "*r*," especially at the end of words. "*R*" does occur in these two dialects, but is scarce and obviously a development from some other sound, since it appears only in the middle of native words. At least the majority of Juaneño terms containing "*r*" must therefore be from a Gabrielino source. Such are: *Saor, Kwawar, Sirout, Ausar, tolmer, Sirorum, Korone.* The only question that arises in this connection is the one already raised whether the larger part of the information extant concerning the Juaneño in the work of Father Boscana may not really relate to the southern Gabrielino themselves rather than to the Juaneño. Even if this possibility be answered affirmatively it indicates the cultural leadership of the Gabrielino; since although San Juan Capistrano lay not far distant from Gabrielino territory, it was nevertheless in Juaneño land, and for an observer to have slighted the natives in behalf of imported foreigners detached from their soil and with their institutions correspondingly weakened, conveys in itself a strong suggestion of the greater development of the latter.

CALENDAR.

The Juaneño calendar seems to have been unusually definite for California, and it is exceedingly regrettable that the account of it which has been preserved is not altogether clear. Ten months are named, and these are said to have been all that there were. The year was definitely divided by the solstices. The month or moon in which the solstice fell was somewhat longer than the others, after which there followed four regular lunations. If the number of these subsequent moons was really four and not five, then each of the solstitial months must have averaged somewhat over two moons in duration. Nothing like this attempt to combine a lunar and solar count has yet been reported from any other people in California. A similar plan is, however, the basis of the Pueblo calendar. We have here, therefore, one more of the many instances of the influence of the tribes of the Southwest upon those of southern California, and it can not be doubted that many others would be discovered if our knowledge were deeper. It is significant that these parallels to the southwest are most abundant in religion; but it is equally striking that they are detached ceremonial elements which ususally crop out in southern California in a quite different setting and organization.

The names of the " months," whose form suggests that they are in part of Gabrielino and in part of Juaneño or Luiseño origin, are the following:

A'apkomil (winter solstice).	Sintekar (summer solstice).
Peret.	Kukwat.
Yarmar.	Lalavaich.
Alasowil.	Awitskomel.
Tokoboaich.	A'awit.

SOCIAL RANKS.

Chieftainship was hereditary in the male line. In default of sons, the title remained in abeyance until a daughter gave birth to a son, a collateral relative meanwhile exercising the power of office. Neither the daughter nor her husband, it is expressly said, acted as chief. The chief was known as *Nu* and his lieutenant or assistant as *Eyake*. The wife of the former bore the title of *Korone*, and of the latter that of *Tepi*. *Eyake* occurs as the mythical name of the coyote; *Korone* as that of a traditional chieftainess who led a migration to San Juan Capistrano. Further, both *Korone* and *Tepi* are names of insects. Similar distinctive names, also appearing in mythology, are found connected with chieftainship among the Gabrielino. There it is the chief's son and daughter that are said to have borne the titles. Whether there was a real difference of detail between Gabrielino and Juaneño custom, or whether the discrepancy is one of report, is not certain.

In any event these names evidence a considerable development of the idea of rank, and according to all accounts chieftainship was invested with much prestige. This is confirmed by the fact that there was a specific ceremony for the installation of a new chief, who appeared in the *wankech* in the *tobet* costume, wearing also a feathered rod or slat bound to his forehead by a cord of human hair.

The authority of the chief is likely to have been less than his dignity, and his power less than his authority. He is said to have decided on war, to have led on the march, and to have made peace. He also announced through a crier or speaker the date of dances, though the fixing of the time of these was in the hands either of the older medicine men or those of high rank among the religiously initiated. The chief received irregular, voluntary contributions of food from the people. When a communal hunt or food-gathering trip was undertaken, it was under his direction, and the larger part of what was secured was turned over to him. In return, he fed the needy and entertained visitors. There seems even to have been some notion of his being responsible for the satisfaction of his village in time of scarcity, through his ability to fall back upon such accumulated stores. Most chiefs also had two or more wives, who seem to have been thought necessary for the acquisition, or at any rate the proper preparation, of the food he was expected to dispense. On ordinary occasions it is specifically stated that the chief was obliged to hunt for his own sustenance.

That the chief's ranking was considerable appears further from the fact that he was treated with the utmost deference, especially by the young; that it is stated, though probably with some exaggeration, that death was sometimes inflicted upon those of his younger people who had been disrespectful to him; and from the circumstance that war might be made upon another village because its chief had not returned adequate presents to the head of the home town. This last cause for fighting has been reported also from the Chumash, and may therefore be regarded as authentic, although actual occasions perhaps occurred only sporadically.

MARRIAGE AND BIRTH.

The bestowing of gifts upon the bride's family was customary. The amount of property, however, was small, and it was tendered when the marriage was first proposed rather than when it was consummated. It is evident that the idea of purchase as such was feeble, but that custom required the gift as a token.

It appears that the accepted suitor spent a certain period in his bride's house before marriage took place, hunting and working for his prospective parents-in-law. It would be rash to assume, from the vague reports that have been preserved, that this practice involved a trial of continence such as the Seri followed; but it is not impossible that this may have been the case. The wedding was a public affair, held under a shade in front of the bridegroom's house, with a prolonged feast and singing. The essential part of the marriage rite lay in the girl's being conducted to her husband, disrobed, and seated on the ground beside him. Small children and even infants were sometimes betrothed by their parents.

Children were named soon after birth, usually by a grandfather or grandmother, who bestowed upon it their own name, or that of another relative of the same sex.

The couvade was practiced for a period of half a month or more after birth. The father fasted from fish, meat, and tobacco, refused to gamble, work, or hunt, and did not leave the house if it was possible.

As nearly everywhere in California, considerable occasion was made of the removal of the remnants of the umbilical cord from the child. This was taken off by old women, in the presence of a gathering of relatives, and buried in a hole either within or outside of the house, after which dancing took place.

Habitual transvestites were called *kwit* by the Juaneño of the coast, *uluki* by the mountaineers. That they were deliberately " selected " in infancy, as stated, seems inconceivable; but it is extremely probable that under the lack of repression customary in Indian society against the involved inclination, the feminine tendencies sometimes revealed themselves in early youth and were readily recognized and encouraged to manifest themselves as natural. Such " women " were prized as robust workers, and often publicly married.

WAR.

The Juaneño " never waged war for conquest, but for revenge; and in many cases for some affront given to their ancestors, which had remained unavenged." Theft, a slight to a chief, the seizure of a woman, and perhaps also the conviction that witchcraft had been practiced, were causes. An assemblage of the initiated was held, over which the chief presided. Other villages were frequently asked to join in an attack. The women ground meal furnished by the chief, and accompanied the expedition, both as provision carriers and to gather up spent arrows. On the march the captain led the way, or delegated this position to another. No quarter was given, and any wounded who could be seized were at once decapitated. Women and children were kept as slaves and taken home without redemption.

As soon as possible the captured heads were scalped. The skin was dressed and preserved as a trophy on certain public occasions. These scalps were hung from a pole near the *wankech*. Strenuous efforts were made by the relatives of the slain to recover the scalps, heavy payment being resorted to if force failed.

CHAPTER 46.

THE LUISEÑO: ELEMENTS OF CIVILIZATION.

TERRITORY AND NUMBERS.

The Luiseño, named after the Mission San Luis Rey de Francia, occupied a somewhat irregular territory, considerably longer from north to south in the interior than on the coast and wholly west of the divide that extends south from Mount San Jacinto. To the northwest and north they had Juaneño, Gabrielino, and Serrano as neighbors; to the east the Cahuilla, and to the south the alien Diegueño of Yuman family. They were a hill rather than a mountain people, and scarcely anywhere reached the summit of the watershed.

The Luiseño lack a native tribal name. Designations like Payamkuchum, "westerners," were applied to the coast people by those of the interior, and perhaps by themselves in distinction from the more easterly Cahuilla and Cupeño. The Diegueño know them as Kohwai; the Colorado River tribes seem to include them with the Cahuilla; if the Cahuilla, Serrano, and Gabrielino have a designation for them it has not been recorded.

Names like Kechi and Kech-am or Hecham, sometimes cited, either mean merely "house, village," or are native designations for the vicinity of the mission.

Plate 57 shows some of the best identified places in Luiseño land. Most of these seem to have been villages, but with the concentration and subsequent dispersal of the population the old continuity of habitation was broken, and to-day most of the names refer to districts, principally the various Spanish land grants.

Place names additional to those listed on Plate 57 are: Topamai (Tapomai); Heish, Gheesh (Keish); Opila (Kwalam); Akipa, Hunalapa, Tutukwimai (near Kahpa); Washka (Woshha); Pa'auw, Wikyo (near Ta'i); Kome (Panakare); camp sites on Palomar Mountain: Wavam, Shoau, Shautushma, Malava, Wiya', Chakuli, Ashachakwo, Pahamuk, Pavla, Tokamai, Mokwonmai.

San Clemente Island, Kinki, may have been Luiseño or Gabrielino. Statements conflict. Culturally, it was certainly dependent on Santa Catalina, of which it formed, in native opinion, a sort of annex.

There are slight dialectic differences within the Luiseño range, especially between the extreme north and south, but on the whole the speech is remarkably uniform for so considerable a tract.

The ancient population is difficult to estimate: 3,000 seems rather a low figure, 4,000 a liberally allowed maximum. In 1856 the Indian Office reported over 2,500; in 1870, 1,300; in 1885, 1,150; but tribal discrimination is likely to have been inaccurate. To-day there are less than 500, according to the Federal census—an infinitely larger proportion of survivors than among the Gabrielino, but a distinctly smaller ratio than the Diegueño have succeeded in maintaining.

ETHNOBOTANY.

The following are the plants known to have been used for food by the Luiseño. It will be seen that seeds are the most numerous. Next in importance come plants whose foliage or shoots are eaten raw or boiled. In the third place are fruits and berries. Roots are of less consequence than other parts.

Seeds: *Artemisia dracunuloides, Layia glandulosa, Malacothrix californica, Helianthus annuus, Bigelovia parishii; Cucurbita foetidissima; Salvia carduacea, S. columbariae, Ramona stachyoides, R. polystachya;* Opuntia (several sp.) ; *Gilia staminea; Trifolium ciliolatum, T. tridentatum; Prunus ilicifolia; Lepidium nitidum; Calandrina caulescens; Chenopodium californicum; Avena fatua, Bromus maximus.* The seeds eaten by the California Indians are often spoken of as from grasses; but it appears that Compositæ and Labiatæ are drawn upon more than Gramineæ. Some varieties were employed as flavoring rather than foods.

With the seeds must be reckoned acorns, for which a grinding process is also required, though leaching replaces parching. In order of esteem, the acorns from these species are taken: *Quercus californica; agrifolia* (oily) ; *chrysolepis* (hard to grind) ; and *engelmanni, wizlizeni,* and *dumosa,* used only when the others fail. The Luiseño are still essentially an acorn people; the Cahuilla are not.

Stems and leaves, or parts of them, are sometimes cooked, sometimes eaten raw: *Carduus* sp., *Sonchus asper; Solanum douglasii; Ramona polystachya; Phacelia ramosissima; Philibertia heterophylla; Viola pedunculata; Sidalcea malvaeflora; Psoralea orbicularis, Lotus strigosus, Lupinus* sp., *Trifolium ciliolatum, T. gracilentum, T. microcephalum, T. tridentatum, T. obtusiflorum; Lepidium nitidum; Eschscholtzia californica; Portulaca oleracea, Calandrinia caulescens, Montia perfoliata; Chenopodium album; Scirpus* sp. ; *Yucca whipplei,* the source of baked "mescal," may also be included. Clovers are perhaps the most important in this group.

Pulpy fruits are small and not especially abundant in Luiseño habitat. Those eaten include *Sambuscus glauca;* Opuntia sp. ; *Arctostaphylos parryi; Vitis girdiana; Rhus trilobata; Rubus parviflorus, R. vitifolius, Prunus demissa, P. ilicifolia, Heteromeles arbutifolia; Mesembryanthemum aequilaterale; Yucca moharensis* (flowers boiled, pods roasted), *Y. whipplei* (flowers). Rosaceæ are the most numerous.

Of edible roots, the country affords *Orobanche tuberosa*, *Bloomeria aurea*, *Brodiaea capitata*, *Chlorogalum parviflorum*, and probably others, but the variety is not great.

All the California Indians used a considerable number of vegetal medicaments. Among the Luiseño, whose knowledge may be assumed typical, more than 20 species are known to have been employed. All these medicines appear to have been household remedies, whose use was not specifically associated with shamanistic practices.

Ambrosia artemisiaefolia, a species of *Adenostegia*, and one of *Malvastrum* were emetics. Wounds, ulcers, and sores were washed with an infusion of the leaves of *Baccharis douglasii*, the roots of *Psoralea macrostachya*, galls from *Quercus dumosa*, or *Woodwardia radicans* root decoction. *Echinocystis macrocarpa*, *Mirabilis californica*, and *Sisyrinchium bellum* roots served as purgatives. The flowers of *Sambucus glauca* were thought to cure women's diseases. The sap of *Solanum douglasii* berries was put on inflamed eyes. *Erythraea venusta* yielded a tea drunk in fever. *Croton californica* was reputed to produce abortion, and *Euphorbia polycarpa* to be of aid after a rattlesnake bite. *Ribes indecorum* or *malvaceum* was employed against toothache. Other medicinal plants, whose specific virtues have not been reported, are *Artemisia dracunuloides* and *heterophylla*, *Bigelovia parishii*, *Monardella lanceolata*, *Micromeria douglasii*, *Eriodictyon parryi* and *tomentosum* or *crassifolium*, *Deweya arguta*, *Cneoridium dumosum*, *Houttuynia californica*, *Rumex* sp., and *Pellœa ornithopus*.

A combined pharmaceutical and botanical study would be required to reveal what plants of therapeutic value grew in the territory but were not employed by the Luiseño. Such a determination, particularly if prosecuted to the point of an understanding of the motives which led to their neglect, would be extremely interesting.

Although knowledge is far from complete, a review of the plants used in technology may not be wasted.

Houses were thatched with *Pluchea borealis* or *Croton californicum;* near the coast, with tule, probably a species of *Scirpus*. These may be considered the typical materials; but it is scarcely open to doubt that others were also employed.

Bows were of willow, elder, ash, mountain ash, and an undetermined mountain shrub. Willow was perhaps the least esteemed but commonest for light hunting bows. Neither juniper nor cedar are mentioned. The bowstring was either of sinew or of any of the fiber cords.

The characteristic arrow was of cane, *Elymus condensatus*, with a foreshaft of greasewood, *Adenostoma fasciculatum*. This is the south central and southern Californian arrow with which the grooved straightener of soapstone is used, although different species may have replaced the above elsewhere. Inferior or smaller Luiseño arrows had the mainshaft of *Hetcrotheca grandifolia* or *Artemisia heterophylla*. These were straightened with the same implement. A totally distinct type of arrow, especially characteristic of the Yuman tribes of the Colorado River, was made by the Luiseño of *Pluchea borealis*. This was not foreshafted and presumably without stone point.

For string, the outer fibers of the two plants most commonly used in California, *Asclepias eriocarpa* (perhaps other species also) and *Apocynum cannabinum*, milkweed and Indian hemp, were of prime importance. The stinging nettle, *Urtica holosericea*, was also used, but less prized. *Yucca mohavensis* fiber was less employed by the Luiseño than that of *Agave deserti* by the Cahuilla, whose environment rendered them largely dependent on it.

The main or back petticoat of the women was made of the soft inner bark of either cottonwood or willow, as among the Mohave. The smaller front piece may sometimes have been constructed of the same material, but its standard form was a sheet of cords of the usual string materials.

Coiled baskets were made, as by all the Shoshoneans of southern California, on a foundation of *Epicampes rigens* grass stems, wrapped either with splints of sumac, *Rhus trilobata*, or with the stems of a species of rush, *Juncus*. The same rush was made into mats for wrapping ceremonial paraphernalia, while mats for household use were presumably of tule, where this could be obtained, although none such have been preserved. Twined baskets were apparently of another species of rush, *Juncus mertensianus*. These served for gathering food; as "sieves" or leachers; and, it is said, for cooking acorn meal. The latter type, which is entirely unknown except from description, must have been closely woven; the two former were openwork. (Pl. 73, *b*.) The seed beater was of sumac stems. The complete restriction of the entire art of basketry to three or four materials is significant; the attitude involved, characteristic of the California Indian generally. The Luiseño lacked the favorite hazel and redbud of the northern and central groups; but there was nothing to prevent them from employing conifer roots and willow shoots and splints.

The brush auxiliary to meal grinding was made, as in nearly all of California, of the bulb fibers of soap weed, *Chlorogalum pomeridianum*, but there is no mention of the plant for lather. Instead, the root of *Chenopodium californicum* and the ripe fruit of *Cucurbita foetidissima* served as soap.

Several woods appear to have been employed for drilling fire, but *Baccharis douglasii* was usual. Both hearth and drill were of the same material. Although such a practice is contrary to current theories among ourselves, which demand variant hardness in the two parts, it seems to have been frequent in California. The Yana and Maidu availed themselves of buckeye in this way.

The only known vegetal dye of importance was a yellow obtained by boiling the roots of *Psoralea macrostachya*. There may have been others. Blackberry juice was sometimes used to stain wooden objects. A red for rock paintings and perhaps other purposes consisted of scum from iron springs mixed with pine turpentine and oil from ground *Echinocystis macrocarpa* seeds. This mixture, which resisted weather admirably, suggests imitation of civilized technique, but the Luiseño declare that they never mixed their pigments with fat. The black of basket patterns was mineral; splints were boiled with mud and iron scum.

The juice of the berries of the black nightshade, *Solanum douglasii*, is said to have been used for tattooing. All other records for California refer to charcoal.

Gum came from pines, or more frequently from an exudation caused by a scale on the chamisal or greasewood, *Adenostoma fasciculatum*. Where it could be obtained, asphalt was probably used more than either.

The only plants known to have been employed ceremonially are tobacco, an undetermined species of *Nicotiana;* and the Jimson weed or toloache, *Datura meteloides*, mentioned in connection with so many Californian tribes.

ANIMAL FOOD.

The animals not eaten by the Luiseño included the dog, coyote, bear, tree squirrel, pigeon, dove, mud hen, eagle, buzzard, raven, lizards, frogs, and turtles. It is probably significant that snakes are not mentioned. Deer were shot, with or without decoy, or snared. A noose was laid in a runway, fastened to a bent sapling. Rabbits furnished a more regular supply of food. They were shot, knocked over with the curved stick called *wakut*, driven into long nets, or snared. Wood rats, ground squirrels, and mice were not disdained. They were sometimes taken in a deadfall of two stones held apart by a short stick stood on an acorn. Quails were shot, attracted at night by blazing cholla cactus and knocked down, or run down by boys in cold, rainy weather. Ducks were killed with the *wakut* or arrows: nets are not mentioned, and would not have been of service in the Luiseño country except on the lagoons at the entrance of streams into the sea.

Small game was broiled on coals; sometimes, too, venison and rabbits. The two latter were also cooked in an earth oven, whatever was not immediately eaten being crushed in a mortar—bones included in the case of rabbits—dried, and stored. The pounding of flesh is a habit common to most of the California Indians. Venison was sometimes boiled, though not often.

When grasshoppers were abundant in the wingless stage they were driven with branches into a pit, into which fire was then thrown.

The coast people fished from canoes or balsas with dip nets, seines, and lines of yucca fiber. The hook was of bone or cut from the central portions of haliotis shell where the grain twists. A harpoon was also used, no doubt of the customary type. Mollusks, of course, were important.

The mountain people had only a few trout and minnows, which they took by poisoning or with dip nets.

IMPLEMENTS.

The bow and arrow were of the usual southern Californian types: the one long, narrow, and unbacked, the other often of cane and generally foreshafted. Bow strings were of *Apocynum* or other cord materials, which in this case were sometimes three and four ply. Sinew bowstrings were regularly three ply, as among the Cahuilla and Mohave. The arrow hold is specifically described as the Mediterranean one; the primary release was employed only for unforeshafted or small arrows. The Mediterranean release has heretofore not been reported from North America except among the Eskimo.

Pottery and basketry need no description, being substantially identical with that of the Cahuilla.

The pipe, *hukapish*, was chiefly smoked lying down, presumably at bedtime. This is the favorite occasion for smoking among most California Indians. The pipe is described as most commonly of pottery, but shamans used ancient stone pipes in their practices.

Chisels, perhaps more accurately described as wedges, were of deer antler, driven by a stone. The present is the most southerly occurrence reported for this tool, which is the universal Californian substitute for the ax.

The Luiseño use the bedrock mortar of the northern tribes, and add a movable one. *Topal* and *arusut* are native names. The portable mortar was usually excavated in a large bowlder, that might weigh 200 pounds or more, and was evidently not intended to be carried away every time residence was shifted. A coiled basket hopper set on the stone is described as intended for new and shallow mortars, being discarded as the hollow deepens. If this is correct, the southern California mortar basket is a device to save labor in stone working. The northern California form, whose twining indicates an independent origin, is an outright substitute for the mortar, never being set on anything but a flat slab.

The toloache mortar, *tamyush*, was more symmetrical, often finely polished, and sometimes ornamented with exterior grooves. It was not used for profane purposes. Its pestle, too, was neatly shaped, instead of being merely a convenient bowlder. Paint mortars, also having religious association, were equally well finished, and were called "little tamyush," *tamya-mal*.

Some of the Luiseño profess that the metate is a Spanish importation, but their statements, which employ the name *ngohilish*, probably refer to the well-made three-legged article, introduced by the Mexicans and used by the Indians at the missions. This interpretation is confirmed by the designation of the muller, *po-ma*, "its hand," Spanish "mano." The crude grinding slab is undoubtedly native among all the tribes of southern California. The Luiseño name it *malal*, which is the same word as "metate," Aztec *metlatl*. It has been indicated above, in the chapter on the Maidu, that there is some evidence for believing the concept of the metate to have been introduced into California from Mexico. If this had happened after the Luiseño were in their present seats, they would not be designating the article by a word formed from an ancient common Uto-Aztekan stem. Nor, on the other hand, would they know the name if they had come as a metateless people into California after the metate was established there. It seems, therefore, that they always had the implement and brought it with them; in fact, it may possibly have been the Shoshonean drift of which the Luiseño were part that introduced the metate to California; but our uncertain chronologies of national migrations and archeology forbid such a hypothesis being taken very seriously.

Besides the balsa, the coast Luiseño knew the canoe, which they called *pauhit*, "yellow pine." The same name was given to boxes hollowed out of wood as receptacles for ceremonial feathers—another of the many cultural reminiscences of the Southwest. Incidentally, the name suggests that the canoe was a dugout, not a plank-built boat as among the Gabrielino and Chumash. It is said that canoe voyages were sometimes made to San Clemente Island.

DRESS.

Clothing was of the common type—nothing for men, a back and front apron for women, with yucca fiber sandals and caps on occasion. The cap was worn chiefly with loads. The Luiseño women of to-day do not habitually wear it; and it seems that this is the old fashion. A twined cap of *Juncus* is described besides the stiff coiled one that is still to be seen. The Diegueño knew both kinds also. As everywhere, there were two names among the Luiseño for the two pieces of skirt: *shehevish*, the larger, made of inner bark, and *pishkwut*, the front piece, of twine, and partly netted. Both sexes in cold weather wore long capes or robes of woven rabbit fur, deer-skins, or sea-otter furs. The latter were highly prized.

HOUSES.

The permanent houses of the Luiseño were earth covered and built over an excavation some 2 feet deep. As in the case of the Cahuilla, accounts vary between descriptions of a conical roof resting on a few logs leaned together, and of a less peaked top supported by one or two planted posts. The inference is that both constructions were employed, the latter especially for large dwellings. For less permanent residences, the ground might not be dug out, and the dirt covering was presumably also omitted. The earth was kept from dropping through the framework of the roof by a layer of cedar bark in the mountains, of stems in the lower belt, and of tule or sedges on the coast. There was a smoke hole in the middle of the roof, but entrance was by a door, which sometimes had a short tunnel built before it. Cooking was done outdoors when possible, on the central hearth when necessary. People slept with their feet toward this.

Except for its smaller size and lack of a roof entrance, this dwelling resembles the earth house of the Wintun, Maidu, and Miwok. No direct relationship may, however, be inferred until the steps of the connection have been ascertained. The intervening Yokuts and Gabrielino had no earth-covered lodges. The immediate linkage of the Luiseño is through the Cahuilla and Diegueño with the Mohave and Yuma structure; but the latter, which has several center posts and definite though low walls instead of an excavation, is a more advanced type. On the other hand, the conical form of the Luiseño earth lodge seems to have been rather similar to the Navaho *hogan*.

The sweat house was similar to the dwelling, except that it was smaller, elliptical, and had the door in one of the long sides. It rested on two forked posts connected by a ridge log. Men sweated in the evening, perhaps in the morning also, but did not regularly sleep in the sweat house. Perhaps it was too small an edifice to serve as a club. The heat was produced, as almost everywhere in California, directly by a wood fire.

The *wamkish* or "temple" or religious edifice was a mere round fence or *hotahish* of brush. The opening was usually to the north, although some accounts mention the east. On both sides were narrower openings for the dancers. The more esoteric actions were carried on toward the rear, if possible. Spectators looked in at the main entrance or saw what they could through and over the fence. No particular sanctity appears to have extended to the structure when not in use. Performers prepared and dressed in another but smaller circle, which stood some distance off on the side toward which the opening faced.

This unroofed ceremonial inclosure is found as far north as the Yokuts, and, for the mourning anniversary, even among the Maidu. It seems also to be distributed through the Shoshonean Plateau, and may have an ultimate connection with the Sun dance lodge of the Plains, although this, in turn, resembles the Missouri Valley earth lodge minus walls and covering, and may therefore be compared, in type if not in origin, with the Sacramento Valley ceremonial chamber and house. In California, however, the inclosure is, as its distribution shows, definitely associated with the mourning anniversary and the toloache religion. Both these religious cycles are quite undeveloped among the Colorado River tribes, especially the Mohave, and the inclosure is not known to them. It is therefore doubtful how closely the Navaho ceremonial inclosure may be historically connected with that of the southern Californians.

With the Mohave and Yuma, as with the Yokuts, the shade roof appears as a place for singing or religious exhibition, though apparently more as a convenience than with any attached idea of a definitely ritualistic structure. The shade was much used by the Luiseño and their neighbors in daily life, but not in ceremonial connections.

RELIGIOUS SCHEME.

On the side of its plan, the religious life of the Luiseño comprises two classes of ceremonies: initiations and mourning rites. These seem to be of distinct origin, but have come to be interrelated at several points. This interrelation appears to be due to their association with a relatively late form of the Jimson-weed cult, the form built around the deity Chungichnish or Changichnish, and carried to the Luiseño through the Juaneño, among whom it has already been mentioned, from its Gabrielino source, ascribed by tradition to Santa Catalina Island. Among the Luiseño this version of the Jimson-weed religion has touched the girls' adolescence rites, whose basis seems to be independent of it; and has colored the mourning observances, and even allowed these to react in some measure on itself. The god of this religion seems to be forced rather lamely into the cosmogony of the Gabrielino and Juaneño: what is said of him lacks the true mythological ring, the color of incident; the statements are abstract or rationalizing. Among the Luiseño he enters hardly if at all into narrative. The Diegueño, finally, though they have taken over most of the Luiseño practices, do not seem to know the god: at least his name has never been recorded among them, nor any synonym.

But with the Luiseño, Chungichnish is still the god who ordained the sacred practices, except the mourning ceremonies, which were instituted on the death of the more mythological divinity Wiyot; and he is also a living god, who watches and punishes. He is distinctly a Jehovah; and if it were not for the wholly native flavor of the ideas connected with the cult, and the absence of European symbols, it might be possible to think of missionary influence. At that, Christianity may well be the indirect stimulus at the root of the Chungichnish movement, since its spread into Luiseño territory went on at least in part, and may have occurred entirely, during the mission period.

This idea of a present and tremendously powerful god, dictating not only ritual but the conduct of daily life—a truly universal deity and not merely one of a class of spirits or animals—is certainly a remarkable phenomenon to have appeared natively among any American group north of Mexico.

It is clear that the Chungichnish cults are totally diverse from the elaborate rituals of the north that have been described as the *Kuksu* ceremonials, in spite of the fact that the central feature of both sets of practices is the initiation into a kind of esoteric society. The Sacramento Valley religion is conceptual only in spots; its cults as such, not any single idea permeated with some quality of grandeur, are its fundamental and subsuming element.

This conclusion of separate developments is borne out by the distribution of the two religions. They are separated by a tract of the magnitude of a third the length of California, in which indeed toloache is used in religion but Chungichnish and the symbols peculiar to him are unknown.

But before the initiation rites and then the mourning observances are described it is necessary to examine certain definite religious devices or forms, which have, it is true, become embodied in the Chungichnish cult, but seem to be neither an intrinsic nor an original part of it.

SONGS.

Luiseño ritual is complicated by the coexistence of two currents of expression. Until the relation of these is more exactly determined, the organization of the tribal religion will remain obscure at many points. On the one hand, there are ceremonies; on the other, songs. The more important ceremonies have each a set of its own songs. But there are series or kinds of songs that do not pertain specifically to any ceremony. These, as well as songs from other ceremonies, are freely introduced into almost any rite.

Thus, in the *Tauchanish*, there are sung in order the following: *Pi'mukvul*, *Temenganesh*, *Cham-towi*, *Kamalum*, *Kish*, *Anut*, *Nokwanish*, *Totawish*, *Monival*, *Nyachish*. In the *Wekenish*, the *Ashish* or *Wekenish* songs proper are followed by the *Cham-towi* set.

Songs forming part of a ceremony.

Totawish, name given the dancer in the *Morahash*.
Anut, "ant," from the initiatory ant ordeal.
Ashwut, "eagle," from the eagle killing.
Ashish, "first menses," from the *Wekenish* or adolescence ceremony.
Tauchanish, the memorial mourning rite with figures.
Shungamish, sung as the figures burn in the mourning ceremony.

Songs not belonging to specific ceremonies.

Pi'mukvul, "death."
Cham-towi, "our spirit," or *Kwinamish*, "root, origin."
Kamalum, "sons," referring to the first people.
Temenganesh, "season" (*teme-t* is "sun").
Nokwanish, sung for men dancing. First sung by the rabbit.
Tapa'sash, sung for men dancing.
Kish, "house."
Monival, "travel, tracks."
Nyachish, containing maledictions of foes.
Chatish, shamans' songs.
Numkish, shamans' songs to cause the growth of food.
Tuknish, the same in purpose, but distinct.

The "death" songs all refer to the death of Wiyot, and many are put in his mouth. Wiyot counsels the people before his departure,

or enumerates the months in which he may die. Others allude to
Wiyot's death through the frog, or the digging of the pit for his
funeral pyre.

" Our spirit " songs contain passages such as these:

" North, east, south, west, the hair lives." Hair is symbolic for spirit ; and
there is allusion to hair ropes at the four ends of the sand painting representing the world.

" North, the hair, the *wanawut*, lives tied, fastened. My origin lives there."
Presumably the other directions are also mentioned. The *wanawut* is the
sacred rope in the initiation rite.

" I thought (' hearted ') at the *hayish*-racing at the moon, I thought with
surprise at the moon." Death is connoted.

Another song refers to sky's heart as well as the *wanawut* and sand painting.

From songs of " Season ":

"All named *wanawut*."

" Hid the season in the water," an act of frog and earthworm.

" The ant has his speech,

" The butterfly has his *wamkish* inclosure,

" The chipmunk has his hollow log for acorn storage."

" I am doing something." The month Nemoyil, when the animals grow
fat, is mentioned or connoted.

" North the *uchanut* bears young,

" North the elk bears young,

" East the mountain sheep bears young,

" East the horned toad bears young,

" South the *awawut* bears young,

" South the *tamyasowut* bears young,

" West (the ocean) tosses.

" In the middle here the deer sheds its hair,

" The sky sheds its hair (changes color)." The reference is to the
month Pahopil.

" At Malmus rose the son Sun."

" See ye that San Gorgonio mountain." Cahuilla Valley, Kupa, Volcan,
Pine Mountain, and Malava on Palomar Mountain are also mentioned.

Part of a " Travel " song:

" Then I do not know the tracks,

" Then I err in the tracks."

A number of places are mentioned. apparently beginning with the spot near
San Gorgonio Mountain at which the ancient people could not pass through a
defile and their language became different. and proceeding southward to
Temecula.

An *Ashish* song beginning with the words: " I am adolescent "
seems to name a similar series of mountains: San Gorgonio, San
Jacinto, Kupa, Volcan, Cuyamaca, Cahuilla Valley, Pine Mountain,
Palomar.

The closing song of the same series begins near Bonsall, proceeds to Santa Margarita, and ends at Elsinore, where Swift and Kingbird were the first girls to be adolescent.

Another *Ashish* song refers to Deer's desire and failure to escape from death, which he found waiting at the north, east, south, and west. The same idea, but with Eagle as character, inspires a recitative in the Wiyot myth. Eagle goes from Temecula to mount San Gorgonio, Cuyamaca, Palomar, and returns to Temecula to die: the directional circuit agrees.

An "Ant" song:

"They did not wish to give their kill that they had." Puma, Jaguar (?), and Thunder Cloud seem to be referred to; Deer is their game.

A Toloache drinking song:

"*Tamyush* walked twisting." *Tamyush* is the sacred mortar from which the Jimson weed is drunk.

From shamans' *Chatish* songs:

"From my feet, from my hands, was drawn, was drawn."

"Something thundered from their feet, from their hands." This and the last refer to curative power.

"To me it comes, *Towut* comes, *Yawut* comes." *Towut* and *Yawut* are names for a fine dust or mist. This is evidently a weather shaman's song.

"Shot, shot, *towauya.*" This word is from the stem of *towish,* spirit. The reference is to killing by means of the shaman's stick.

It appears that nearly all the songs except those of a specific shamanistic character consist of mythological allusions. They may be said to float in a web of tradition. Those that are not mythological are directly descriptive of the ritual to which they pertain.

Further, the songs of different series are similar not only in character but in detailed content. The rising of constellations is mentioned in *Tauchanish,* Death, and Season songs. Long enumerations of places are frequent, whatever the connection; and these frequently begin or end at the same spot, such as Mount San Gorgonio or Temecula. *Ashish* and Ant songs both refer to Deer; Death and Season songs enumerate or allude to months. The indiscriminate prevalence of a certain ritualistic phraseology is thus obvious; and this must be admitted as being patterned in a fashion that can only be called highly decorative, in the sense that it is symbolic, abbreviated, and only conventionally representative.

This strong uniformity explains the frequent transfer of Luiseño songs from one ceremony to another.

All these traits recur in undiminished or exaggerated vigor in Mohave, Yuma, and Diegueño songs. As to their northward and westward distribution, enough is indicated by the statement that a large proportion of the songs sung by the Luiseño are in the Gabrielino language. Yokuts songs, on the other hand, as the examples quoted establish, lack all the peculiar traits of those of the south: they are more concretely picturesque, but are unmythological, ungeographical, and nearly lacking in astronomy and symbolism.

Precisely to what extent the Luiseño and Gabrielino songs of each kind constitute a series strung on a single plot can not yet be said. But is is clear that they approach closely to the song cycles of the Mohave and Yuma. On the coast, song and ceremony are two parallel developments, interconnected at innumerable points, yet essentially pursuing separate courses. In the Colorado Valley ritual has been nearly effaced, or has come to consist essentially of singing, with the choice of series dependent on the singer rather than the occasion. This allows the Mohave songs to be dreamed by the individual, in native theory, in place of being acquired by avowed tradition. The Mohave songs seem also to have reached a greater extremity of dependence on myth and wealth of geographic allusion; but, as might be anticipated from the greater poverty of ritual accompanying them, they are less permeated by metaphoric symbolism.

DANCES.

Much as songs of various kinds were introduced into the most diverse rituals, so the Luiseño had two or three standard dances which they performed on several occasions as part of their initiation as well as the mourning rites. It seems, therefore, that the dances, like the songs and in a measure the sand painting, were fixed elements upon which the ceremonies as larger wholes were built up.

The paucity of dances and abundance of song types among the Luiseño marks an approach to the method of religion of the Mohave and Yuma.

The commonest Luiseño dance to-day is the *Tatahuila*, which is always made by a single performer. *Tatahuila* is uniformly regarded by the Indians as a Spanish word. The Luiseño word is *Morahash*, which means " whirling for; " the dancer is called *totawish*, which may perhaps be regarded as a dialectic form of *tobet* (Spanish for *tow-et*), the name the Juaneño are said to have given the costume. The Diegueño say *Tapakwirp*. Besides the headdress, the principal apparel is a skirt of eagle feathers, which swing effectively in the very characteristic motion of the dance, a continued and very rapid whirling. The body was painted; probably as by the Diegueño, with horizontal white bands.

The fire dance, of which the native name is not known, served as a climax and was part of the magical stock in trade of the toloache initiates. A large fire was danced out, the performers approaching the edges, stamping the embers, falling back, rushing up once more, and sitting down to kick the blazing coals inward. The feet were bare and there seems to have been no treatment or mechanical preparation, but a certain amount of earth was pushed on the flames with the feet and when possible unobtrusively thrown on with the hands. As each dancer's attack lasted only a few seconds at a time, while he was in rapid motion, and the number of performers was great, it is probable that most of the blaze was extinguished by actual stamping. There is nothing astounding or cryptic about this exhibition, but it unquestionably was spectacular, and is described as impressive even to white people. No public fire dance is known anywhere to the north in California, and eastward it seems not to be encountered again until the Pueblos are reached.

Like the fire dance, the *Morahash* appears to have been in the hands of the toloache initiates, but both were certainly made as part of mourning rites.

The Diegueño add to these two dances a third, the *Hortloi*, which can probably be identified with the Luiseño *Tanish*, since the latter is described as the dance of the initiates or *pumal-um* in mass, which accords with the performance of the *Hortloi;* also because the songs of the latter are in the Gabrielino language. This Diegueño exhibition is the one that Americans have come to know as the " war dance," but it appears to have no reference whatever to war. The step is a forward jump with both feet, followed by a stride. To successive songs the dancers circle contraclockwise, stamp standing, and jump backward in line.

GROUND PAINTINGS.

With the Luiseño we encounter for the first time detailed references to a ritualistic device of the greatest interest, which is known to have been used also by the Juaneño, Gabrielino, and Fernandeño: the ground or sand painting. The Diegueño sand painting has also been recorded, and the Cupeño apparently used it. The Cahuilla and Chumash are in doubt. It is therefore rather clearly a development of the Shoshoneans of the coast region. It is connected with the Chungichnish form of the Jimson-weed cult, and about coterminous with it.

This sand painting of southern California is unquestionably connected with that of the Pueblos and Navahos. There can also be little doubt that it originated in the much more complex ceremonialism of these southwestern nations. But it is not a recent importation; and the history of its diffusion can only be appreciated properly with reference to the fact that not even a trace of the custom exists among the intervening tribes of the Colorado

River, nor apparently among the Pima. Like the Chungichnish religion with which it is associated, it is clear that the Californian sand painting rests upon old cultural materials common to the Southwest and southern California and probably evolved chiefly in the former region, but that its actual essential form is a purely local growth. This is not only indicated by its geographical distribution but confirmed by its subject matter, symbolism, and style, which reveal scarcely anything specifically southwestern.

The painting was made in the *wamkish* or ceremonial enclosure, the "temple" of older authors. The Luiseño brought it into the Jimsonweed initiation for boys; the *Yunish Matakish* or death rite for initiates; and the girls' adolescence ceremony. With the Diegueño the latter ceremony belongs to an old native stratum and has not been colored by Chungichnish influences as among the Luiseño. They therefore do not use the painting in this connection.

The Luiseño call the sand painting *torohaish* or *tarohaish*, or in ritualistic speech, following their usage of doubling terms, *eskanish tarohaish*.

Figure 56 shows all known restorations of Luiseño and Diegueño ground paintings. In spite of the variability, which may have been nearly as great in practice as in these reproductions, a distinct tribal style as well as a fundamental uniformity are apparent. This fact renders it highly probable that the lost paintings of the Juaneño and Gabrielino were similar in tenor but also distinctive in manner.

The elements in the Luiseño and Diegueño ground paintings shown in Figure 56 are as follows: 1, Milky way. 2, Night (or sky). 3, Root (of existence), *kwinamish*. 4, Our spirit or soul. 5, World. 6, Hands (arms) of the world. 7, Blood. 8, Rattlesnake. 9, Spider. 10, Raven. 11, Bear. 12, Puma. 13, Wolf.[1] 14, *Apmikat*. 15, "Breaker." 16, Stick, wood. 17, Coyote. 18–21, Black, gopher, garter, red racer snake. 22, Sun. 23–24, New and full moon. 25, Pleiades. 26, Orion. 27, Altair. 28–29, "Cross" and "Shooting" constellations. 30, Sea. 31, Mountains. 32, Hill of *hulwul* plant. 33, Boil, abscess. 34, Coronado Island. 35, Mountain of creation. 36, San Bernardino (Gorgonio?) Mountain. 37, Santa Catalina Island. 38, Four avenging animals. 39, Ceremonial baskets. 40, Toloache mortar and pestle. (The last two may be the actual objects rather than representations.) P, Pit in center. S, Spitting hole.

In all cases, it is clear that the essential subject of the depiction is the world. The Luiseño, however, are chiefly concerned with revealing its subtler manifestations—the mysterious encircling Milky Way, the all-encompassing night or sky—or its still more spiritual phases as expressed in a symbolism of human personality: the arms, the blood, our root or origin, the spirit. Within this frame are indicated—depicted would be an exaggerated word—the punishers sent by the invisible Chungichnish: the raven, rattlesnake, spider, bear, wolf,[1] mountain lion, and the cryptic *Apmikat* and "breaker."

---

[1] Or jaguar (?).

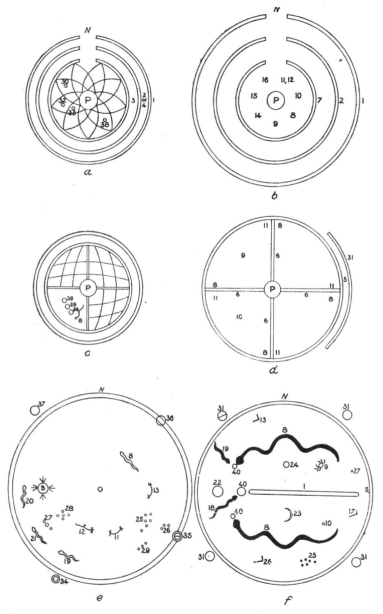

FIG. 56.—Southern California ground paintings (altars). *a–d*, Luiseño; *e–f*, Diegueño.

In the very center is the hole symbolical of death and of the burial of human ashes: called *tolmar* or *tolmal*, the abode of the dead; or the navel—of the universe.

To the Diegueño this abstruseness and mystic craving are foreign. They paint the world indeed; but it is the visible universe. The enclosing circle is merely the horizon or the edge of the earth. The figures within it are a downright map of the mundane surface and the celestial sphere. The Milky Way stretches across the middle as it bisects the heavens. On one side are the summer constellations Aquila and Cygnus, on the other Orion and the Pleiades of winter— each group identifiable by its form. The sun and moon are too conspicuously visible overhead to be omitted: so they are represented. To the Luiseño the luminaries mean nothing, because Chungichnish symbolism does not include them. The navel of death, again, is an idea, not a feature of land or sky—the Diegueño omits it. His mountains, too, are not vague harborers of the messengers and avengers of a cult, but actual named peaks; and the four in figure *e* stand in very nearly the relative geographical position, with Diegueño land as a center, that they occupy in the painting.

Having mapped his world, the Diegueño proceeds to fill it with living beings. These are not mere heaps of pigment to which an old man can point while naming dangerous animals in his sermon on the punishment of disobedience, but actual representations: excessively crude, it is true, even abbreviated to a few strokes, but still pictures. The spider can be distinguished from the snake, the snake from the wolf. This is not the case in any Luiseño painting. For good measure, as it were, perhaps because their drawing is easily effective, the Diegueño add to the dread rattlesnake (whose eyes are of haliotis and whose diamond-back pattern is carefully indicated) sketches of several harmless species, whose symbolic significance is unknown and probably slighter.

Among the Luiseño, two styles of painting are discernible, which appear to pertain respectively to the girls' adolescence rite and to the boys' initiation. The painting for the girls (*a* and probably *b*) has three concentric circles, open to the north; within, the several avengers are indicated in a more or less circular arrangement. The painting for the boys (*c, d*) perhaps lacks the gateway to the north, has only one or possibly two enclosing circles, and is quartered. The representations of the avengers seem to predominate in the western half. At the same time the network of interior lines in *a* and *c* is not very different, and may be intended for an identical pattern.

The diameter of the ground painting is described as being 2 to 3 feet for the girls' painting (*a*), and 4 (*c*), 12, 15, or 18 feet (*d, e, f*) for the boys. The materials include ashes and powdered soapstone for white; charcoal; reddish iron rust or scum; yellow may also have been used; and variously colored "sands" and "earths" are mentioned more vaguely. The harmless snakes in the Diegueño paintings were of "seeds."

There is some mention of cords of human hair leading from the Luiseño painting to sticks or canes planted in four little mounds on each of the cardinal sides: these tied the world and probably the human spirit also. It is not certain whether these objects were actual or only painted: the former seems more likely, since ropes that were pulled are mentioned of the Fernandeño ground painting.

CEREMONIAL OBJECTS.

The *pa'lut* was perhaps the most showy of Luiseño religious regalia. This was a net tied around the waist, from the lowest loops of which hung eagle or condor feathers. It was worn in the *morahash* dance, as part of what the Juaneño would call the *tobet* costume, and its free swishing added to the effect of the rapidly turning dancer. (Pls. 42, *c*; 61.)

Headdresses are simple, but the native recognition of types is not altogether clear. The commonest form was a bunch of owl or spotted hawk feathers, more or less slashed, and mounted on a stick. These appear to be called *cheyat*. They were worn in pairs, one at each side of the head, held by a band. The *hainit*, Juaneño *eneat*, apparently was a band or upright row of feathers encircling the head. The *apuma* is mentioned as an erect eagle feather headdress. Not one of these pieces was notably brilliant, large, or elaborate.

The *yukish* was an ancient headdress of human hair, held in place by a cord of the same material. Its form is not clear. It may have corresponded to the Juaneño *emech*. Hair was very sacred to the southern Californians, and the Luiseño used it with evident reference to the idea of human personality and employed the name *yula* as a constant metaphor for "spirit."

The yellow-hammer forehead band typical of central California is not found in most of the southern part of the State. The Luiseño, however, made *tuminut*, long bandoliers of dark feathers, less trimmed than in the central Californian ornament, but, like them, laid in opposite directions and sewn through. (Pl. 58.) Similar pieces have been found among the Koso and in an ancient cave cache in Gabrielino territory. The occasions on which they were worn are not known.

The *paviut* was a hand wand a foot and a half long, associated with the Chungichnish cult. It consisted of a board more or less pointed below, somewhat flaring at the upper end, where it was inlaid with haliotis, and tipped with a crystal or large flint.

The *elat* was also a board, a foot long, painted red, with snake rattles or the like attached, held upright by the feathered *cheyat* band against the forehead of the *pula* when he doctored, made rain, or juggled. The employment of this standardized piece of costume by the shaman is one of many links that closely ally him with the initiate or *pumal*.

Wooden "swords," that is, really, flexible wands, were swallowed either by the *pula* or the *pumal*, probably the former. This is a southwestern trick of which little is heard in central and northern California.

The rattle was a turtle shell on a stick, the openings wound with cord. Wild cherry pits made the sound. The deer-hoof rattle associated in northern California with the girls' adolescence ceremony was known to the Luiseño, but used only, it seems, in hunters' rites. Neither the clap stick nor the cocoon rattle of central California was employed.

The whistle of *huikish, Elymus* cane, stopped with asphalt, was blown by the men who sang and danced about the boys undergoing the ant ordeal. It was called *pahal*.

The bull-roarer, *momlahpish*, is a crude board, whirled as a summons to religious assembly and as a starting and stopping signal. Its size—from 1 foot to nearly 2—stamps it as an implement for outdoor use. (Pl. 44.)

Two traits characterize the religious regalia of the southern Californians as typified by the Luiseño.

First, they are simple and comparatively somber. Although of feathers, they lack the bright colors and showy forms that characterize the area of the Kuksu religion and of the northwestern open-air dances. There is not a trace of anything like a mask or a disguise of the performer. These qualities are a reflex of the toloache religion, which at least in its Luiseño form knew a god too lofty and pervading to be impersonated, but no nearer spirits other than animals. Hence while the initiates constituted a body that must unquestionably be considered as a sort of organization, they did without the masking which is so frequent an accompaniment of the esoteric society in aboriginal America. The comparative simplicity of dance costume is already observable among the Yokuts, the most northerly of the toloache-using tribes.

Second, the powerful psychic effect of the Jimson weed caused the cult based upon it to take on a specifically inward character. There are innumerable references to the human spirit, to the relation of life and death. What we should call the soul is constantly being symbolized or alluded to. The Maidu and Wintun have very little to say about the soul of man, but more about the spirits or minor gods that populate the world or helped to shape it. Thus their ritual is comparatively dramatic, representative, spectacular, its costuming diversified, picturesque, impressive; but both are symbolic in only minimum degree. The southerners thought of life as such, not of events. Their concepts must of needs be ritualized; yet as their abstractions were better expressible in the sand painting, in the *wanawut* representation of the grave, or in the burying of the dead *pumal's* badge than in any apparel of feathers and sticks, the costume, like their dance movements and cries, became wholly unrepresentative. It was worn because ancient tradition so ordained, not because it illustrated. Its form, therefore, crystallized largely along lines of simple convenience, and it came to matter little whether the regalia were diverse or the same for all occasions, as long as their conformity to custom indicated the sanctity of the occasion. The history of dance costume in southern California can accordingly not be traced from anything intrinsic to religious thought or feeling.

In general, then, ceremonial paraphernalia and dance actions stand apart from religious beliefs in southern California. Songs and ground paintings directly reflect concepts and myths, but run a course largely independent of ritualistic actions. Hence all four sets of elements are made use of in the scheme or organization of religion almost as if they were foreign matter.

ESOTERIC NAMES.

· The Luiseño consistently employ a distinctive device in their ritualistic designations. A double name, consisting of a pair of juxtaposed synonyms or approximate synonyms, is given to many ideas. So strong is this inclination that where two words are not available, as for animals, two of these are coupled as if they were one: compare "bear mountain-lion" in the little sermon quoted in the section headed Morality. The cosmogonies outlined also offer abundant illustrations. *Yunish matakish, eskanish tarohaish, wanal wanawut, antish tivihayish, kimal chehenish* are other examples; also the star names *piwish ahuta* and *ngoiwut chawochmush;* and *sivut paviut,* the crystal-tipped stick. There are indications of a similar habit among the Juaneño, as in the various names of *Chingichnich: Wiamot, Kwawar, Saor, Tobet,* and in the two terms *ano* and *takwe* applied to the ceremonial cannibal. Among the Luiseño even place names are usually coupled in myth or song: *Pawi Chawimai,* Cahuilla Valley, *Kupa Kawimal,* "Kupa little hill," *Ehva Temeku,* Temecula; two spots in the same vicinity appear to be treated as one.

CHAPTER 47.

THE LUISEÑO: ORGANIZATION OF CIVILIZATION.

THE TOLOACHE INITIATION.

The toloache ritual is the heart of the Chungichnish religion. In the main, it consists of a series of acts initiating boys, but there is also a feature that is rather uncommon in American Indian esoteric associations, a mourning observance for dead members. As is frequent, however, among primitive people, there is no formal ritual for adherents as such. The normal function of the society is to perpetuate itself rather than accomplish some clearly realized end.

The initial and most significant proceeding in the initiation, as the natives seem to see it, is the taking of the *Datura* drug. This act is called *pa'nish mani*, or *mani pa'ash*, or simply *mani*. As *pa–* means "to drink," *mani* appears to denote Jimson weed, which in fact is the meaning of the stem throughout the Shoshonean dialects of southern California. The Luiseño, it is true, call the plant itself *naktomush*. It is therefore probable either that *mani* has become with them a synonym of exclusively religious denotation or that *mani* means the principle or decoction.

The drinking takes place at night. All uninitiated boys are gathered and brought together. Small boys are sometimes carried in asleep. Any man who may have escaped initiation in his youth, or alien resident, is given the drug with the youngsters. A fire is lighted in the *wamkish*, and the people begin to gather there. The various *tamyush* or toloache mortars are dug from their hiding places, repainted, and set in the *wamkish*. Only the mortar actually to be used, together with a *tukmal* or flat basket, are brought to the small or preparatory enclosure which stands near the *wamkish*. It is in this smaller place, unlit and without audience of the uninitiated, that the toloache is drunk, and there the boys are taken. One of the *paha'*, ceremonial chiefs or managers, pounds the dried roots in the reserved mortar, to a sacred song or recitative, after which the potion is prepared with hot water. The usual way seems to have been to sift the powder from the basket back into the mortar and add the water, which was allowed to stand for a while. In other cases the hot water was poured over the basket, or the powder boiled in a pottery jar. The drinking itself, however, was from the mortar in which the plant was crushed, the boys kneeling before it. The manager held the forehead of each in turn, to pull it back when he had drunk enough. The drug was powerful, and the Luiseño tell of cases of fatal result.

Meanwhile one of the managers has gone three times to the large inclosure to notify the people there that *mani* is coming. Each boy, after the drinking, is taken in charge by a man who appears to direct and steady him. The procession to the *wamkish* seems to be performed crawling on hands and knees, by the men at least, each of whom utters the cry of an animal. Possibly this act takes place on later days of the ceremony. The mortar and baskets are believed to march along. There may have been a simple legerdemain to produce this effect. The party divides in two, each half making a three-quarter turn about the enclosure and entering by one of the side gates. They then march or stand the boys around the fire, apparently dancing the *tanish*. The youths soon begin to sway and reel and have to be supported under the armpits. Before long they fall and become entirely unconscious, and are then carried to the smaller enclosure, where they lie in complete stupefaction, watched only by a few men. The other adult members remain in the *wamkish*, dancing the *tanish* until morning. They seem to stand in a semicircle back of the fire, with a line of seated men singers facing them across it, and women, also singing, behind the men. Still farther back, outside the main entrance, stand the spectators.

The duration of complete narcosis is not quite certain. The Diegueño appear to reckon it one night, and speak of quantities of warm water being given the boys in the morning to remove the remaining effect of the drug. A Luiseño account speaks of two or three nights, and of a stupefaction of four being excessive. It is probable that the period was variable: there was no definite measure to the bulk of root used nor was accurate control possible of the quantity of liquid drunk by each novice; besides which, the boys were of different ages and their constitutional resistance to the drug must have varied individually. It may be added that the ceremony was not performed annually or at a fixed season, but every few years, as the old men might decide that there was a sufficient crop of fresh boys. Nor did anyone drink toloache twice.

The so-called intoxication is in any event the cardinal feature of the entire initiation, and therefore the heart of the cult. There is no doubt that its sacredness and supernatural basis lie to the native mind in the physiological effect of the drug. It produces visions or dreams as well as stupor; and what the boys see in their sleep becomes of lifelong intimate sanctity to them. This vision is usually an animal, and at least at times they learn from it a song which they keep as their own. It seems also that they will not kill any individual of the species. It is clear that the concept of the vision corresponds exactly with what among certain primitive tribes has been unfortunately denominated the "personal totem." It is certain that a special and individual relation of a supernatural kind is believed to exist forever after between the dreamer and the dream. The similarity to shamanism is also obvious; but it would be as misleading to name the Luiseño institution outright "shamanistic" or "totemic."

The duration of the ceremony is not clear, and may not have been fixed. A Luiseño account speaks of men from other villages dancing with the boys for four or five nights after the first one, painting and instructing them, and teaching them their songs. A Diegueño version is to the same effect, adding that each boy thus acquired a kind of proprietorship over certain alien songs in addition to those given him by his kinsmen; but this account makes the visitors come in only after six nights of dancing with the home people.

At any rate, a fast is observed by all the boys for about six days, complete at first, and relaxed later to a limited amount of acorn mush, but no meat or salt under any circumstances; and they dance—apparently the *tanish*—nightly and sleep during the day.

The first period is followed by a more temperate one of perhaps a month, and a third and still milder one of another month, during which the night dancing continues, but for briefer hours, and the novices are allowed all the acorn or sage-meal gruel they wish.

Even after this time has elapsed, the boys are forbidden meat for several months, and are then encouraged to refrain from it, or at least to eat it sparingly, for as much longer as possible. This commencement with the main act of the ceremony and gradual dying away of the ritualistic observances without definite end, instead of a climax, recurs also in the girl's initiation, and seems characteristic of Luiseño procedure.

Various other things are taught or half revealed to the boys, probably during the first intensive period of initiation. These include the fire dance, with its appearance of magic; the putting of feather headdresses into the flames and taking them out whole; the shooting of men; the cutting off of one's tongue; and the like. These tricks are at any rate performed; and while it is not likely that they are deliberately and wholly exposed to the youths at this time, they are no doubt carried out for them to know something about.

That some sort of progress in knowledge is made by the boys is likely from a Diegueño account of the boys instead of the men crawling to the *wamkish* on the second, third, and fourth days of the initiation.

A month or so after the toloache drinking, the boys dispose of the belts which they have heretofore worn on account of their hunger, and run a foot race back to the *wamkish.* At the end of the second month they are presented each with a feather headdress and a painted dance stick, which, though lacking the sacred crystal, is a sort of imitation of the *paviut.* After this the ground painting is made and then comes the final rite of the *wanawut.* A different account speaks of this being performed three days after the drinking, but all other informants agree that the *wanawut* act takes place after the period of fasting.

The ground painting is made in the *wamkish,* and has been described before.   As its meaning is explained, the boys are given an elaborate lecture, passages from which are quoted below in the section on Morality.   At the last, a lump of sage meal and salt is put in each boy's mouth, after having been touched against several parts of his body as in the girls' rite, and is spat by him into the central hole of the painting.   This is then erased by pushing the pigments into the hole, so that no uninitiated may see the figure.

THE WANAWUT.

Either the same day or the next, toward the end of the afternoon, the *wanawut* rite takes place.   Ceremonially this object is called *wanal wanawut* or *yula wanawut, wanal* being a seine or long net, *yula* hair or spirit.   The *wanawut* is a long mesh of milkweed or nettle twine, the size of a man, and having head, legs, arms, and perhaps a tail.   Its name is undoubtedly a derivative from *wanal;* its association with *yula* is probably only symbolic of spirituality, but may mean that the object was sometimes made of hair.   In the net are three flat stones, or according to another statement, four are set upon it.   The entire figure is laid in a trench, the feet apparently to the north: the Diegueño say east.

Each boy in turn now enters the trench, supported by the old man who has acted as his sponsor, and at a signal leaps from stone to stone.   Should he slip, it is an indication that he will die soon.   Very small boys are partially assisted by the old men.   When all have jumped, they help the old men push the earth into the trench, burying the figure.

The symbolism of this strange rite clearly refers to life and death. The trench represents the grave: the Luiseño cremated their corpses over a pit which was filled when the embers and bones had sunk in.

The figure is human. It is specifically said to denote the Milky Way—otherwise a symbol of the spirit or soul. There seems also to be present the idea that the spirit of the dead is to be tied, perhaps to the sky, at any rate away from earth; and the cordage of the object is probably significant in this regard. It is obvious that there existed a rich though perhaps but half-expressed symbolism in connection with the *wanawut*, of which only fragments are known to us.

When the *wanawut* is finally buried, the *tanish* is commenced for the last time and danced through the night, ending toward daybreak with the fire dance. There are some references to burning the *wamkish* about this time, or part of it for the whole. It may be conjectured that it is the brush enclosure that furnishes the fuel for the final fire dance. At any rate, this destruction of the sacred enclosure marks the termination of the collective acts of the initiation.

THE ANT ORDEAL.

The *Antish* (literally " anting," from *anut*, " red ant "), also called *Tivihayish*, was an ordeal for boys or young men, probably made within the toloache initiation, but perhaps held as a separate supplement. In the latter event, many features of the initiation were repeated, such as fasting, the foot race, and the ground painting. The rite itself was carried out with secrecy toward the public.

The boys were laid on ant hills, or put into a hole containing ants. More of the insects were shaken over them from baskets in which they had been gathered. The sting or bite of the large ant smarts intensely, and the ordeal was a severe one, and rather doubtfully ameliorated when at the conclusion the ants were whipped from the body with nettles.

There are special *anut* or *antish* songs, whose use, however, following Luiseño custom, is not restricted to this ceremony.

Ant bites were used medicinally as far away as the Yokuts, but an ant ceremony has not been reported from farther north than the Juaneño and probably did not extend beyond the Gabrielino at most. The animal is, however, very distinctive of southwestern ceremonialism. Many of the Pueblos have ant fraternities, and among probably all of them there exist esoteric rituals for curing sickness brought on by ants. These particular concepts are of course not Luiseño; but there can be little doubt that the southern California ordeal has at least received its impetus from the same source that caused the growth of the Pueblo ant ceremonies.

THE YUNISH MATAKISH.

The Yunish Matakish appears to be held as part of the mourning anniversary, but is a specific Chungichnish rite, of which the central feature is the burial, in the central hole of the ground painting, of the feather headdress and other cermonial paraphernalia which the dead man has had since initiation. The ritual seems to come on the last afternoon of the mourning, just preceding the night in which the images are burned. The painting is made in the *wamkish*, the sacred toloache mortars and baskets are set out, and the general aspect of events is similar to those which marked the entrance of the member into the religious life of his people years before.

His late companions have gathered at the small enclosure, and amid wailing by the spectators approach one by one toward the *wamkish*, imitating the deceased as well as they can. Finally, among the Diegueño, the whole membership crawls into the *wamkish*, each man painted with the footprint of the animal that he saw in his own toloache vision, and uttering its cry. It is very probable that the practice of the Luiseño is the same.

After the men are seated about the ground painting they grunt and blow, the feathers are placed in the central pit, and then the company buries them by pushing the painting into the hole.

The "grunting" is an element of all Luiseño ceremonies. It is a ritualistic sound, sometimes described as a groan or growl, ending in a marked expulsion of the breath, and accompanied by an exclamation *mwau* or *wiau*. It seems always to occur in threes and to have symbolic reference to the spirit or soul.

THE GIRLS' CEREMONY.

The *Wekenish* or girls' ceremony has as its central feature an act practiced by all the Shoshoneans of southern California: the "roasting."

The ceremony, according to established Luiseño practice, was called and financed by the home village, but its direction was in the hands of the ceremonial head of another village or "clan." Several girls of one "clan" were usually treated at once, only one, however, being at the actual physiological period indicated by the word *ash*. As it is said that they did not undergo the rite a second time, the number of performances of the ceremony in each locality can have been only a fraction as numerous as the arrivals at womanhood. Perhaps the wealthiest or most prominent men had the ritual made as their daughters reached the requisite period, while other parents availed themselves of the opportunity thus offered their younger girls to participate. Among small and poor hill tribes, having few public rituals to occupy them, the coming to age of each young woman may have furnished a welcome occasion for a general gathering. To relatively populous groups like those of southern California, with wider range of acquaintance and alliance and frequent festivals produced on a large scale, an equal attention accorded to every female member of the tribe would be likely to be monotonous, if not burdensome. Two alternatives are open: to maintain the ceremony as an important one but reduce its frequency by grouping the girls, or to minimize the significance of the rite, leaving it an affair for kinsmen and fellow residents rather than the larger community. The southern Californians followed the former plan: the Yurok and Hupa, and the Mohave, the latter.

The first step in the ceremony was to make the girls swallow balls of tobacco as an ordeal. Only those who did not vomit were considered virtuous. As the Indians say, this was a hard test.

The girls were then placed on their backs in a pit that had previously been lined with stones, heated, and then carpeted with tussock grass and sedge. Two warmed flat stones were put on the abdomen of each maiden. The girls lay as still as possible for three days. At night men and in the day women danced around the pit. Each girl had her head covered with an openwork basket to keep the flies off, the Luiseño say—perhaps to prevent undue and prejudicial movement. Northern Californians give as the reason for a similar veiling the balefulness of the young woman's glance at this time. Such ideas are, however, in the background if they enter the southern Californian's mind at all. It is an interesting case of an identical act having almost contrary import according to cultural attitude.

Scratching with the finger nails would be very bad. In former days the girls were therefore furnished with scratchers of haliotis.

The girls did not wholly fast, but refrained from meat, fish, and salt. Once every 24 hours they left the pit, which was then reheated.

When finally taken out the girls had their faces painted by the wife of the officiating chief. Bracelets and anklets of human hair and necklaces of *Echinocystis macrocarpa* were put upon them. They were now free to go about, but the food restrictions endured another month or several, and might be voluntarily prolonged for a year or two. Cold water was especially to be avoided.

At the end of the first month the sand painting is made, and its explanation is combined with a sermon by the ceremonial chief on the subject of good conduct in life and its rewards, as quoted below. Each girl then has her head, shoulders, arms, breast, and knees touched with a ball of sage meal and salt, whereupon this is put in her mouth. Leaning on hands and knees she spits this mess into the central hole of the painting. The painting itself is then shoved into the hole by the men seated about it, exactly as in the *yunish matakish* for dead initiates, and as the *wanawut* trench is filled in the boys' initiation.

The girls, accompanied by friends, thereupon run a race—another ceremonial device of which the Luiseño are fond. The chief's wife then again paints them. With the same paint she makes a large geometrical pattern upon a rock, or according to another account, the girls themselves do so. Their hair ornaments are deposited on the rock.

This face and rock painting is performed monthly three or four times. The last occasion marks the final act of the ceremony.

At some time in the period of the observances the girls are tattooed.

MOURNING CEREMONIES.

The impress of death is heavy on the mind of the California Indian. He thinks of it, speaks of it, tries to die where he has lived, saves property for years for his funeral, weeps unrestrainedly when the recollection of his dear ones makes him think of his own end. He wails for days for his kin, cuts his hair, and shudders at their mention, but lavishes his wealth in their memory. It is no wonder that he institutes public observances for them. In the north, indeed, these are scarcely developed; but from the Maidu south, the mourning anniversary has followed the course of our description with growing intensity. The Luiseño practiced at least half a dozen mourning ceremonies after the cremation of the body.

The relation of these is not altogether clear. The *Tuvish* appears to be first in order and simplest. This hinges about a ritualistic washing of the clothes of the deceased, as part of a night of singing, declaiming, and dancing in the ceremonial inclosure. Kin and fellow residents participate; the rite is for an individual. It is held soon after death, and its purpose is to banish the spirit from its familiar haunts.

The *Chuchamish* came next and ran a similar course. Here the clothing was burned and the dead instructed to depart to the sky.

The *Tauchanish* is the great public observance for the dead of the year, or several years, marked, as among many other tribes, by the exhibition and burning of images of the dead, rude figures of rushes, but often hung with valuable clothing and beads. The signal to start and stop the songs to which the images are carried is given with a bull-roarer. The rite is instituted and provided for by the chief, but conducted by the ceremonial leaders of invited clans or villages. The guests receive presents, and are privileged to despoil the images. This observance is not part of the Chungichnish cult, and is probably far older: in fact according to the Diegueño it was the first ceremony in the world; but, like almost everything in Luiseño religion, it has been affected by the Chungichnish worship.

The *Notush* was a local correlative of the *Tauchanish*, perhaps introduced from the Gabrielino to the northern Luiseño. It does not seem to have become established among the southern Luiseño in the mountains, but was brought to mission San Luis Rey probably in the time of the padres. It is described as a more elaborate and costly rite than the *Tauchanish*. The use of images is not mentioned. The characteristic feature was a tall painted pole representing the spirit of the dead person and called *kutumit*, Fernandeño *kotumut*, in Luiseño esoteric language *kimal chehenish*, that is, "little-house appearances." Each portion of the pole denoted a part of the body, but there seems to have been no attempt at actual representation. The top was painted white and bore a raven skin, called *levalwush*, "wide;" below this were baskets and other valuables, which apparently became the property of those who succeeded in climbing to them. Contests were a distinctive feature of the *Notush*, as the following "origin" tradition of the ritual reveals.

The first *Notush* ceremony was held between Pala and Temecula. Sea fog erected the great pole, and the uplanders of the east gathered to contend with the westerners of the coast. Squirrel alone climbed to the top, cut the string, and won the baskets for his mountain companions. *Mechish*, who crawls in the sea, carried off the great sack in which was all the gathered food, but this victory was in turn balanced by wide-mouthed Nighthawk, who was the only one able to devour the mass. Then the owl and a fish stared at each other; but at last the bird blinked and the west was victorious. The raven skin was hanging on the pole, the two sides were getting angry, and a fight portended. Thunder cloud roared, but failed to uproot Sea fog's house, but when Sea fog's wind blew, the mountain houses went down. They then raced to La Jolla in the mountains. Many became exhausted, but Eagle, Chickenhawk, and Raven now won for the east from Butterfly and Grasshopper. Another race was north to San Gorgonio Mountain, through the open country, and Antelope of the plains beat Deer of the mountains. A second match led through the rugged hills. and Deer earned his revenge. So they contested in the first *Notush*. The Yokuts have faintly reminiscent tales of contests between hill and valley people.

The *Ashwut maknash* or eagle killing was an anniversary held for chiefs—the Diegueño say for their dance leaders. Probably both accounts are correct for both tribes. Eagle and condor nests were personal and hereditary property. The young were taken from them and reared. In the ceremony, made at night in the *wamkish*, the eagle was danced with, and finally "shot" to death with a magic stick. Actually his heart was pressed in, but the trick was known only to the toloache initiates. The relatives of the dead man wailed and his successor gave away property to the invited performers. This arrangement pervades all Luiseño mourning rites: the home village issues the invitation and provides food and gifts, the guests perform the ceremony and receive the presents. The eagle's body was ritually burned or buried.

The *Yunish matakish* has already been described.

COSMOGONY.

The basis of the Luiseño origin tradition is a group of ideas that are widespread in southern California. But in the ritualistic cosmogony these appear in a very specialized shape. First, the concept of prime origins by birth, instead of a process of making, is more thoroughly worked out than by perhaps any other American tribe except possibly some of the Pueblos. Secondly, there is a remarkable attempt at abstract conceptualizing, which, though it falls short of success, leaves an impression of boldness and of a rude but vast grandeur of thought. The result is that the beginning of the Luiseño genesis reads far more, in spirit at least, like the opening of a Polynesian cosmogonic chant than like an American Indian tradition of the world origin.

It is a gratification to record this fact, and perhaps worth while remembering it, since it reveals the cultural worth that lies exposed but overlooked in the achievements of many an obscure tribe. The civilization of the California Indians was so nearly equally rudimentary that the temptation is great to regard it as a unitary if not a negligible datum. But we need only approach this civilization in a spirit free from haste, and it becomes apparent as endlessly diversified instead of monotonously homogeneous, flowering in the most unexpected places, and with all its childlikeness not devoid here and there of elements of subtlety and nobility. Few California tribes may have reached the attainments of the Luiseño; but each was possessed of its cultural individuality and endowed with potentialities that have now been cut off but which must continue to summon respect.

This is the story:

The first were *Kyuvish*, "vacant," and *Atahvish*, "empty," male and female, brother and sister. Successively, these called themselves and became *Omai*, "not alive," and *Yamai*, "not in existence"; *Whaikut Piwkut*, "white pale," the Milky Way, and *Harurai Chatutai*, "boring lowering"; *Tukomit*, "night," with the implication of "sky," and *Tamayowut*, "earth." She lay with her feet to the north; he sat by her right side; and she spoke: "I am stretched, I am extended. I shake, I resound. I am diminished, I am earthquake. I revolve, I roll. I disappear." Then he answered: "I am night, I am inverted (the arch of the heavens). I cover. I rise, I ascend. I devour, I drain (as death). I seize, I send away (the souls of men). I cut, I sever (life)."

These attributes were not yet; but they would be. The four double existences were not successive generations: they were transitions, manifestations of continuing beings.

Then as the brother took hold of her and questioned, she named each part of her body, until they were united. He assisted the births with the sacred *paviut* stick, and the following came forth singly or in pairs, ceremonial objects, religious acts, and avenging animals:

Hair (symbolical of the spirit) and *Nahut* (the mystic *wanawut* figure?)

Rush basket and throwing stick.

Paint of rust from springs and paint of pond scum.

Water and mud.

Rose and blackberry, which sting for Chungichnish.

Tussock grass and sedge, with which the sacred pits for girls were lined.

Salt grass (and grass?)

Bleeding and first periods.

These were human; and so were the next born, the mountains and rocks and things of wood now on the earth; and then followed the badger; Altair the buzzard; the feared meteor *Takwish;* the subterranean water monster *Chorwut; towish,* the spirit of man that survives the corpse; the black oak; "yellow-pine-canoe cottonwood" (a receptacle for feathers); *kimal chehenish,* the pole and offerings of the *Notush* mourning; the ash tree; the plant *isla;* the large brake fern; the black rattlesnake; the red rattlesnake; spider; tarantula hawk; raven; bear; sting ray; *tukmal,* the winnowing basket used in initiation; *shomkul papaiwish,* sea fish and urine for ceremonial sprinkling; *topal tamyush,* mortar and toloache mortar.

All these were the first people, touching one another in the obscurity, far in the north. They traveled to Darkening Dusk, where something high stopped them; then to Hill Climbing, the impassably narrow canyon; then to the lake at Elsinore; then to Temecula. There *Hainit Yunenkit* made the sun and the first people raised him in a net four times to the sky. There also Wiyot, bewitched by Frog, sickened and after long illness died. Under the direction of Kingbird, he was burned, but only after Coyote had stolen his heart. Kingbird announced his return: "Wiyot rises, Wiyot the moon," and all saw him in the west, soon to appear in the east. Eagle, knowing what was now in the world, went or sent his spirit north, east, south, west to escape, but finding *pi'mukvul,* death, everywhere, returned to Temecula, and, accepting his future fate of being danced with and killed, died. Deer, too, after a long evasion, resigned himself to death when he was told of the feathers that would wing the arrows sped after him. And last, Night, here at Temecula. divided the people, gave them the languages which they have now, and sent them to their fixed abodes.

Other versions, as among almost all tribes, vary indefinitely in minor content. The long list of sacred births in particular is never given alike. But the tenor of the conceptualizing is always the same; and every old man knows at least phases of this cosmogony, and is aware of their place and significance. We face, in short, more than the philosophizing of a gifted individual endeavoring to rise above the concrete and naive crudities of his age and land. The cultural creation of a nation lies before us.

Besides the migration legends embodied in the story of the origin of things, the Luiseño tell traditions that are primarily geographical.

Nahachish, "glutton, the disease consumption, old age, or male," a great man at Temecula, had the hook broken down on which he hung his abundance of food, and, starving, began to travel. Near Aguanga he was given gruel (which is light gray), so, saying "My stomach is *picha* (whitish)" he named the place Pichanga. On Palomar he was again fed, until his belly burned.

and he uttered "My stomach is nettle, *shakishla*," and the place became Shakishna. At Kayawahana he knelt and drank and left his footprints. Sovoyami he named because he was chilled, Pumai because he whistled, Yapichai for a feast witnessed, and Tomka because he was fed. Where he drank he called the place Pala, "water," and Pamai, "small water," and a muddy spot Yuhwamai. Below Pala, seeds were ground for him into meal too fine to handle, and he was poisoned. Perishing, he turned homeward, but died and became a rock just before he could arrive.

There are probably many other tales of this strange character—trivial or meaningless to us, surcharged with associations to the native.

THE SOUL.

The life or soul was called *shun*, Juaneño -*suni*, "heart." This was the part of the person believed to go to the stars.

The *towish*, Juaneño *touch*, was the ghost, and was applied both to a corpse and to the spirit detached from it. Its translation as "devil" is of course inaccurate, but yet not wholly of wrong implication, since a haunting ghost would work harm; otherwise it would not have been feared so vigorously and directed to depart. It is probable that it was the *towish* which went into the ground to what was known as *tolmar* or *tolmal*, which was also the name given to the symbolic pit in the center of the ground painting. As to the meaning of *tolmal*, compare the phrase *ha-tolmik*, translated as "inferno," but said literally to mean "he is gone."

Kwinamish, "root" or "origin," is much used to designate the spirit, apparently as such, or in the living, without the implication of death which attaches to *towish*.

Yula, "hair," has already been mentioned as a frequent symbolic designation of the spiritual.

The Juaneño *piuch* or "breath" should, on the analogy of *touch*-*towish*, appear in Luiseño as *piwish*. This word is actually found as a name of the Milky Way, particularly where this is coordinated, as in the ground painting, with the *towish* and *kwinamish*.

Huhlewish is said to have the significance of "religion" or "sacred matters."

Potish is a dream. The shamans are said to have their "dreams" tell them how to proceed with the treatment of a patient. Just what this may or may not imply as to a conception of a guardian spirit is not certain.

The word used in the sense of Algonkin *manitou*, Siouan *wakan*, Iroquois *orenda*, Yokuts *tipin*, and our "supernatural," is not known, except for one mention of *towauya*, evidently from the stem of *towish*.

Takwish, literally "eater" or "eating," denotes not so much a class of spirits as one particular monster or divinity that makes his home

on San Jacinto Mountain, carries off and devours human beings, and
appears usually as a low-flying meteor or ball of lightning, but also
in birdlike form or as a man in feathers. Sight of him portends
disaster and death. He also enters prominently into myth, but as
an independently acting being, unassociated either positively or
negatively with Wiyot or Chungichnish. His origin is thought to
have been in Diegueño land, where he is known as *Chaup*, and Poway
is mentioned as his birthplace. Part of his career was run among
the Luiseño, especially in association with Temecula, so often mentioned in song and story; and his final abode is the great peak San
Jacinto, where Cahuilla, Serrano, and Luiseño territory met. The
Luiseño leave the first part of his history to the Diegueño, but nar-
rate freely his later actions. There is a wideness of international
outlook in these relations that is characteristic of the southern Californians, but unheard of elsewhere in the State.

Wite, witiak, or *witiako* was a sort of greeting spoken when one
encountered a raven, the messenger of Chungichnish.

SHAMANISM.

None of the several investigators who have recorded information
on the Luiseño make very clear mention of a belief in the familiar
or guardian spirit. The same holds true of all other southern California tribes, whereas north of Tehachapi the guardian spirit is regularly and specifically referred to as the source of shamanistic power.
Knowledge for the south is admittedly imperfect; but the tenor of
the sources on the two regions is too uniformly distinct to allow of
any inference but that the attitude of the cultures differed. For the
Yuma and Mohave, indeed, it can be asserted positively that they did
not know this class of spirits. Now it is interesting that no mention
of personally owned spirits is made in any account of the several
Pueblo groups. Nor is there anything definite from the Navaho. As
to the Apache, there exists an extensive monograph on their medicine
men; and it is significant that while this describes numerous charms,
and discusses the practice of magic, it nowhere alludes in unmistakable manner to guardian spirits. For the Pima, statements as to
guardian spirits are also somewhat indefinite, whereas it is specifically stated that the most important shamans are those who receive
their ability from their fathers.

It may be concluded, therefore, that in the area which includes the
Southwest and southern California, the idea of the guardian spirit,
which is so basic in the conception of shamanism among the American Indians at large, is either lacking or very imperfectly developed.

Among the Pueblos the organized fraternities cure disease and
may likely have crowded not only the guardian spirit belief but

the shaman himself out of the culture. With the river Yumans, the shaman dreams indeed, but of an ancient divinity; and other men who do not practice medicine dream of him too, and quite similarly. For the Juaneño, Boscana reports that the toloache initiates had the animal or being visioned in their intoxication as protector through life. This is an undoubted approach to the guardian spirit idea. But the drug was drunk as part of a cult, initiation into which marked civic and religious maturity; it was not taken by individuals to acquire medical faculties. It seems, therefore, that the factors which have displaced the guardian spirit belief vary locally. The inference is that the concept, for some unknown reason, lacked vigor throughout the area, and that in consequence substitutes for it arose independently among several groups.

An alternative interpretation would be that the organizing of religion and intrusting of its exercise to official priests suppressed the guardian spirit type of individualistic shamanism among the Pueblos, and that this negative influence spread from this culturally most advanced group to other southwestern tribes as far as the Pacific, local groups of the tribes substituting diverse customs more or less of their own devising.

There is, it is true, one Luiseño statement to the effect that shamans dream of "a rock, a mountain, a person, or something similar" and receive songs from this object of their dream. But this reference is too vague to count for much. The mountain or person might be mythological, as among the Mohave; that is, an ancient bestowing divinity rather than a present and controllable spirit.

On the other hand, it is significant that of the three special classes of shamans known to all the Indians of central California, the bear doctors, rain doctors, and rattlesnake doctors, the latter are the only ones not known to the Luiseño and their neighbors.

The practices of the curing shamans are the conventional ones, in spite of the difference in conceptual attitude. They suck, blow tobacco smoke, spurt water or saliva over the patient, rub, or wave feathers over him. Sickness is considered to be largely the result of witchcraft—that is, of malevolent shamans—and counter-bewitchings and outright slayings were frequent. Sympathetic and perhaps imitative magic were liberally practiced in this connection; hair, nails, and blood carefully concealed. As in the remainder of California, except on the Colorado, disease was thought to be caused by the presence of a physical object in the body rather than by an affection of the soul. Thus sucking was the foremost reliance of the physician. True, there are monsters or water spirits, the *pavawut*, *koyul*, and *yuyungviwut*, that not only drown people but steal their souls and make them sick; but the immediate cause of the

illness in native opinion is perhaps the diet of frogs that the
yuyungviwut imposes upon his or her captive and enforced spouse.

The shaman, Spanish hechizero, is called *pula;* the toloache
initiate, *pumal.* The probable etymological connection of these two
words has already been commented on in the chapter on the Juaneño.

CALENDAR AND ASTRONOMY.

The Luiseño had more star names than most Californians. This
superiority may be connected with their belief that the dead turned
into stars. In all southern California constellations are named in
ritual, and particularly in song, much more frequently than in the
northern part of the State, and play a more important part even than
in the ceremonies of the Southwest. But where the Mohave and
Yuma sing over and over of Orion and the Pleiades, the Luiseño
appear to have had designations for all first-magnitude stars. The
known appellations are: *Hula'ch-um*, Orion's belt, and *Chehay-am*,
the Pleiades, usually mentioned together; *Nukulish*, Antares; *Nukulish po-ma*, "his hand," Arcturus; *Yungavish*, "buzzard," Altair;
Yungavish po-ma, Vega; *Yungavish po-cheya*, "his headdress," a
star near Altair; *Waunish*, Spica; *Ngoiwut chawochmush*, Fomal-
haut; *Tukmi iswut-um pom-shun*, "night wolves [1] their hearts," the
North Star, which does not move. The Pleiades were girls once, and
Aldebaran is their pursuer Coyote.

The only planet recognized was Venus, called *Eluchah*, "leavings,"
as of food over night.

The Milky Way, *piwish* or *ahuta*, had several esoteric designations, and was more than the mere ghosts' road of most Californians.
It was symbolically associated with the spirit of dead man, *towish*,
with the sacred cord *wanawut*—itself representative of life—and
probably with the mystic being *Whaikut Piwkut*, "white grayish,"
one of the preexistences of Night and Earth.

The Luiseño calendar has been preserved, but is not well understood. Eight periods are named. None of the terms has been translated; and their season and order are not certain. They are *Tasmoyil* (grass is green), *Tawut*, *Tausanal* (grass sere), *Tovakal*
(fallen leaves), *Novanut*, *Pahoyil*, *Nemoyil* (deer are fat), *Somoyil*.
Each has two divisions, the first designated by a diminutive form
with *alu'mal*, "lean," the second by the addition of *mokat*, "large."
Thus, *Tasmoi-mal alu'mal* and *Tasmoyil mokat*. The "lean" and
"large" evidently refer to the appearance of the moon. If we
add to eight lunar months two longer unnamed or overlooked periods
at the solstices, we have a calendar similar in plan to the peculiar

---

[1] There are no wolves in southern California; but *iswut* is from the stem of *isil*,
coyote. Possibly the word has come to denote the jaguar.

one described from the Juaneño. But a comparison of the names of the periods fails to reveal the least verbal resemblance; and the Luiseño names may have been seasonal without exact lunar correlation.

MORALITY.

A nation's ethical practices can best be judged by the foreigner; its code, by its own statements. We are fortunate in possessing extended addresses, recorded in the native dialect, of the kind that the Luiseño were wont to deliver to their boys and girls. The occasion was ritualistic, but it marked also the entry of the young people into manhood and womanhood, and much of what is enjoined is purely ethical with reference to daily life. The avengers are supernatural and determined by the prevailing cult, the punishment is concretely physical. One must respect his elders, listen to them, give them food freely, not eat meals secretly, refrain from anger, be cordial and polite to one's relatives-in-law. Then one will be stout, warm, and long haired, will grow old in good health and have children to whom to pass on counsel, be talked of when death comes, and have one's spirit go to the sky to live. The disobedient and heedless will be bitten by the rattlesnake or spider, they will vomit blood, swell up, go lame, fall into wasting cough: their eyes will granulate, their children be sickly. Fortune or misfortune hangs over every act. Virtue is far from being its own reward— it is the only path that leads to prosperity. Back of all hovers the unnamed figure of Chungichnish, whose messengers and instruments execute many of the punishments. But the afflictions are stated as inevitable facts: there is no allusion to the deity's will or pleasure, nor any outright reference to his anger. He is very far from being as personal as Yahweh; yet there is no concept of any law, nothing that we should call a principle, only an inexorable causality manifest in innumerable specific but endlessly varying instances. One does not reason about this sequence nor stop to bow before an omnipotent personality behind it. One merely adjusts himself to events as to the stress of nature, and takes measures for a wise arrangement of life instead of a series of troubles, in the same spirit as one might provide against storm and starvation. The Luiseño made efforts, indeed, to wrestle with the mysteries of the spiritual, but he attempted them through myth and religion; in his morality and aspect of life he is without exaltation, fatalistic, and a resigned materialist like most American Indians.

On the purely ethical side, one trait stands out which is also a general American rather than a tribal characteristic. There is no provision against theft, assault, rape, witchcraft, or murder, nor any mention of them. Such violent extremes are too obvious for condemnation, as incest was to the ancient Aryans. It is only with written codes that such horrid violations of the bases of morality seem to demand attention—not because they become more frequent, but because then silence concerning them would in the nature of things be an avowed condonation. The Indian, beyond taboos and cult observances, centers his attention on the trivial but unremitting factors of personal intercourse; affability, liberality, restraint of anger and jealousy, politeness. He, whom we are wont to regard as dark, reserved, and latent with cruelties and passions, sets up an open, even, unruffled, slow, and pleasant existence as his ideal. He preaches a code of manners rather than morals. He thinks of character, of its expression in the innumerable but little relations of daily life, not of right or wrong in our sense. It is significant that these words do not exist in his language. In California, at least, the Indian speaks only of " good " and " bad"; elsewhere he may add the terms " straight " and " crooked."

A part of the sermon addressed to boys over the sand painting:

See these, these are alive, this is bear-mountain lion; these are going to catch you if you are not good and do not respect your elder relatives and grown-up people. And if you do not believe, these are going to kill you; but if you do believe, everybody is going to see your goodness and you then will kill bear-mountain lion. And you will gain fame and be praised, and your name will be heard everywhere.

See this, this is the raven, who will shoot you with bow and arrow if you do not put out your winnowing basket. Harken, do not be a dissembler, do not be heedless, do not eat food of overnight (i. e., do not secretly eat food left after the last meal of the day). Also you will not get angry when you eat, nor must you be angry with your elder relations.

The earth hears you, the sky and wood mountain see you. If you will believe this you will grow old. And you will see your sons and daughters, and you will counsel them in this manner, when you reach your old age. And if when hunting you should kill a hare or rabbit or deer, and an old man should ask you for it, you will hand it to him at once. Do not be angry when you give it, and do not throw it to him. And when he goes home he will praise you, and you will kill many, and you will be able to shoot straight with the bow. . . .

When you die your spirit will rise to the sky and people will blow (three times) and will make rise your spirit. And everywhere it will be heard that you have died. And you will drink bitter medicine, and will vomit, and your inside will be clean, and illness will pass you by, and you will grow old, if you heed this speech. This is what the people of long ago used to talk, that they used to counsel their sons and daughters. In this manner you will counsel your sons and daughters. . . .

This is the breaker; this will kill you. Heed this speech and you will grow old. And they will say of you: He grew old because he heeded what he was told. And when you die you will be spoken of as those of the sky, like the stars. Those it is said were people, who went to the sky and escaped death. And like those will rise your soul (*towish*). . . .

The counsel to girls is similar:

See, these are alive; these will think well of you if you believe; and if you do not believe, they are going to kill you; if you are heedless, a dissembler, or stingy. You must not look sideways, must not receive a person in your house with anger; it is not proper. You will drink hot water when you menstruate, and when you are pregnant you will drink bitter medicine.

This will cause you to have your child quickly, as your inside will be clean. And you will roast yourself at the fire (after childbirth), and then your son or daughter will grow up quickly, and sickness will not approach you. But if you are heedless you will not bear your child quickly, and people will speak of your heedlessness.

Your elder relatives you must think well of; you will also welcome your daughters-in-law and your brothers-in-law when they arrive at your house. Pay heed to this speech, and at some future time you will go to their house, and they are going to welcome you politely at their house. Do not rob food of over-night; if you have a child it will make him costive; it is also going to make your stomach swell; your eyes are also going to granulate. Pay attention to this speech; do not eat venison or jack rabbit, or your eyes will granulate, and people will know by your eyes what you have done. And as your son or daughter will grow up, you will bathe in water, and your hair will grow long, and you will not feel cold, and you will be fat, if you bathe in water. And after the adolescence rite you will not scratch yourself with your hands; you will scratch yourself with a stick; your body will have pimples if you scratch yourself with your hands. Do not neglect to paint yourself, and people will see, and you will grow old, if you pay attention to this speech, and you will see your sons and daughters.

See these old men and women; these are those who paid attention to this counsel, which is of the grown-up people, and they have already reached old age. Do not forget this that I am telling you; pay heed to this speech, and when you are old like these old people, you will counsel your sons and daughters in like manner, and you will die old. And your spirit will rise northwards to the sky, like the stars, moon, and sun. Perhaps they will speak of you and will blow (three times) and (thereby) cause to rise your spirit and soul to the sky.

Sermons somewhat like those of the Luiseño were probably preached in other parts of California; but they have not been preserved. The harangues of the Wintun chiefs are somewhat similar, but vaguer in tenor, fuller of repetitions, and thoroughly tedious to us for their unceasing injunctions to do what the occasion of itself demands to be done. The Luiseño did not revel quite so untiringly in the obvious when they talked to the young people for their good.

SOCIETY.

Luiseño society presents a somewhat confused picture. Some of its subdivisions exercise religious functions; their relations to the soil have been disturbed by the invasion of Spaniard and American; and wasting of numbers has caused an irregular consolidation of groups.

The totemic moieties of the Serrano and of central California are lacking, except possibly on the northern border about Saboba. There are patrilinear family groups, and unions of these into ceremonial groups. Both bear nontotemic names, which are totally different in each locality.

The patrilinear family groups or "clans" are known as *tunglam*, "names," or *kamalum*, "sons, children," in distinction from the *kecham* ("houses"?), the larger territorial or national groups. People married into neither the father's nor the mother's "clan." This suggests that these clans consisted of actual kinsmen. Their number confirms this interpretation; some 80 are known, with part of Luiseño territory unaccounted for. On this basis the average "clan" would comprise only 25 or 30 souls, a number well within the limits of traceable blood. The total distinctness of the "clan" names in each district also argues for their being families of local origin.

The clan names are now borne by the Indians as if they were Spanish family names. They have a varied character. Many are verbal, some descriptive, some denote animals or objects, or occasionally places.

Thus, at Rincon, there are the *Omish*, "bloody," *Kalak*, "quickly," *Michah*, "rammed, stuffed," *Ngesikat*, "scrapers, grazers," *Shovenish*, "disagreeable," *Chevish*, "pulling apart," and *Kewewish*, "fox"; at Pauma the *Mahlanga*, "palm place," *Kengish*, "ground squirrel," *Shokchum*, "scratchers," *Chat*, "white owl," *Ayal*, "know(?)," and *Pauval*. It may be that some of these appellations are of nickname quality.

The religious groups or "parties" are known to the Luiseño as *not* or *nota* (plural *nonotum*), which is also the word for "chief." They are described as consisting of a chief, his "clan," members of other clans that are chief-less or greatly reduced, and individuals who have quarreled and broken with their proper "party." Their number is therefore less, their size greater, than that of the "clans." This may also have been true in ancient times. All ceremonies are in the hands of these "parties," each of which, however, generally performs the same rites as all the others. They might therefore be described as a series of parallel religious societies, resting on a clan basis, or more exactly, on consanguinity or personal affiliation with a chief who is at once head of a group of coresident kinsmen and a responsible undertaker of rituals. There is, however, no inherent relation between the social bodies and the ceremonies—nothing in any public rite that is peculiar to a social group. The families and parties built around them have merely been utilized as a means of executing ceremonies.

The present Rincon and former Kuka organizations are:-

Anoyum, "coyotes," so called on account of reputed greediness at gatherings; proper name, *Kengichum*, "ground squirrels." *Omish* clan or family; also *Tovik* and *Suvish* families, which formerly acted independently but now have no chiefs.

Ivangawish, "sitting apart," also a nickname; originally called *Nahyam,* from the ancestor of the *Kalak* family, *Nahmahkwis—nahat* means walking stick or cane.

Ehvayum or *Temekwiyum,* "Temeculas"—Ehva and Temeku' both denoting that place. *Ngesikat* family.

Sengyum, "gravels," or *Sereyum. Shovenish* family, said to have come from a gravelly place.

Navyam, "prickly pears," or *Siwakum. Siwak* family. Now extinct.

The *Michah, Chevish,* and *Kewewish* families adhere to the foregoing ceremonial groups.

At Pauma the three parties are the *Mahlangum, Sokchum,* and *Pauvalum,* all named after families. Pichanga, which is said once to have had 17 families, has two religious organizations, the *Seyingoish* and the *Kiungahoish,* the latter founded in 1915 and given the name of an extinct Temecula party.

Occasionally rites are said to be the property of particular organizations. Thus at Rincon, the *morahash* dance belongs to the Anoyum, the *tanish* to the Ivangawish. This condition seems to be a result of the dwindling of ceremonies, or their becoming identified, for a period and within a locality, with individuals of particular interest or ability. A division of function is clearly not the essential purpose of the "parties." The *morahash* is danced by the Luiseño of all districts, as well as by their neighbors, so that it can not be regarded as the specific rite characteristic of one local society. So far as such association exists, it must be due to a temporary or recent loss of this or that ceremony by other societies.

But the basic parallelism of the "parties" did not prevent certain songs, localized migration traditions, landmarks, and perhaps territorial claims, from being the property of particular families or societies. Such possessions seem eminently characteristic of "clans" or organizations centered on lines of descent. The public rituals were essentially communal or national, however completely their performances may have been entrusted to family societies.

It is clear that the chief was the fulcrum of Luiseño society. The religious group was called "a chief," the social group was "the children." A chief ordered ceremonies, his assistant, the *paha',* executed them. A chief-less family was nothing but a body of individuals, dependent for religious activity on personal affiliation with other groups: a family with a chief was *ipso facto* a religious society. It is conceivable that many of the surnames which the Luiseño now possess are the personal names of chiefs in authority when this European habit was adopted. The one thing that is wholly obscure is the relation of the chief to the territorial or political group. There can scarcely have been several family chiefs of equal standing at the head of such a group, and the families were so small that they could not have been the sole political units. Possibly there were always chief-less families, and in a large community the chief of a certain family may have been accorded primacy over his colleagues. The hereditary principle was strong. In default of male heirs, a woman sometimes succeeded, and a widow might exercise a sort of regency for her son. Nothing is on record concerning the chief's riches. This omission is in itself significant. It is not unlikely that the chief was kept in position to entertain and lead by contributions from his " children." If so, his office brought him wealth. It is clear that it was not his property that made him chief.

There was a definite installation of a new chief, a night rite called *unanisha noti*, held in the *wamkish*, with singing, dancing, eating, and no doubt long speeches.

Gifts or payments were expected by a bride's family, but a reputation for industry or ability in the hunt weighed for as much as the wealth formally tendered as basis to marriage. The usual Californian semicouvade was in force: fasting from meat and quiescence were enjoined on both parents for 20 to 40 days, on pain of the child's physical welfare. The umbilical cord was buried. Women withdrew each month from the house and slept and ate apart for a few days. Parent-in-law taboos seem unknown. Hunters ate no game of their own killing, on pain of losing their luck. A violation could be amended by public confession.

CHAPTER 48.

THE CUPEÑO AND CAHUILLA.

THE CUPEÑO.

TRIBAL RELATIONS.

The Cupeño are one of the smallest distinct groups in California. They state that they possessed only two permanent villages: Kupa—whence their Spanish name—near the famous hot springs of Warner's ranch, usually called merely Agua Caliente, a designation that has also been applied to the tribe; and Wilakal, in Luiseño Wolak, at San Ysidro. The Diegueño call the two sites Hakupin and Ephi. The entire territory controlled by the inhabitants of these two settlements is a mountainous district on the headwaters of the San Luis Rey, not over 10 miles by 5 in extent—a sort of Doris in an Indian Greece.

The Cupeño appear to have no name for themselves, other than Kupa-ngakitom, "Kupa-people," and perhaps Wilaka-ngakitom. Their language they call Panahil. The Diegueño call them Hekwach, which is a generic Yuman designation for the Cahuilla. The Cupeño name the Serrano Tamankamyam, the Cahuilla Tamikochem, the Diegueño Kíchamkochem, the Luiseño Kawikochem, perhaps all of them terms based on the cardinal directions.

The hot springs seem to have drawn the residence of various Indians for two or three generations, and some years ago the Cupeño were removed, with several other settlements, to Pala. Indian censuses, being more frequently based on location than on exact tribal discrimination, have therefore either ignored the Cupeño or exaggerated their strength. In 1910 there were not far from 200. Anciently, 500 must be set as their maximum.

It is above all their speech that warrants a separate recognition of the Cupeño. This is of the Luiseño-Cahuilla branch of Shoshonean, but more than a mere dialect of either of these tongues. Luiseño and Cahuilla have many words in common which in Cupeño are quite different. When Cupeño agrees with one and differs from the other, the resemblance is more frequently with Cahuilla. In accord with this fact is the Diegueño name of the tribe, which classes it with the Cahuilla. So small a body of people as the Cupeño could not, however, have developed so distinctive an idiom while in their recent intimate juxtaposition to two larger groups of the same origin. A former period of isolation, or of special contact with aliens, is indicated. We must infer, accordingly, that the Cupeño detached themselves from the still somewhat undifferentiated Luiseño-Cahuilla group at some former time, moved to their present abode, and later were overtaken by their more numerous kinsmen; or, that they represent a southerly advance guard which was crowded back into intimacy with its congeners by an expansion of the Diegueño. In either event, relations with the Diegueño appear to have been an important factor in Cupeño tribal history.

SOCIAL ORGANIZATION.

The Cupeño scheme of society is less disintegrated than the Luiseño, but appears also to have been modified in the past century. Its present form is this:

Moieties.	Clans.	Ceremonial groups.
1. *Istam* ("Coyotes")	1. *Nauwilot* ("body louse")	"Party" 1.
	2. *Changalangalish*	
	3. *Kauval*	
	4. *Po-tama-toligish* ("his tooth black")	"Party" 2.
2. *Tuktum* ("Wild cats")	5. *Aulingawish, Auliat* ("blood ——")	"Party" 3.
	6. *Sivimoat*	
	7. *Djutnika*	

The totem of the moiety is called *wala*, "great-great-grandparent," but there is no belief in descent from the totem animal. A sort of good-natured opposition is recognized between the moieties, whose members frequently taunt each other with being unsteady and slow witted, respectively. Mourning ceremonies are made by moieties, but the complementary moiety always participates. Throughout California the contact of the moiety scheme with religion was largely on the side of mourning rites. There is an association here which is undoubtedly of historical significance.

The nature of the " clans " is less clear. As there were several, and the Cupeño had only two villages, they can scarcely have been local bodies. Their appellations also do not seem to be based on place names. They are used as outright family names by the modern Indians; but this can hardly be old practice. The functions of the clans are said to have been chiefly religious. In recent years, as some of them dwindled in numbers, their members ceased their own ceremonies and affiliated themselves with other clans, most of the Cupeño say: in this way the "parties" became established. Others regard the "clans" as only synonymous designations of the religious "party" units. At any rate, the Cupeño designate both clan and party by the latter term in speaking English, and call them both *nout* in their own language. This word also means chief, and is found, as *nota* and *net*, among the Luiseño and Cahuilla. Each clan had its chief, it is said, and there were neither village nor moiety chiefs. At present there is a chief for each "party," besides a tribal political head chosen at the instigation of the whites. Each *nout* had a *paha* or ceremonial director, as among the Luiseño and Serrano; also a *kutvovosh*, who seems to have served as his speaker, messenger, fire tender, and assistant.

RELIGION.

The Cupeño call the toloache initiation *manit paninil*, "Jimson weed drinking." The director of this holds his post through inheritance, it is said, and is also known as *nout*. The *morahash* whirling dance was called *pukavihat*. The girls' adolescence rite, *aulinil* or *ülunika*, included the usual "roasting," and a ring dance in which the people were grouped by moieties. This ceremony is described as made by the girl's clan, but the statement may refer rather to her patrilinear kinsmen, who would generally constitute at least a considerable portion of a clan. *Piniwahat* is the singing of maledictions against "clan" enemies.

The mourning ceremonies are the *pisatuil*, *süshomnil*, and *nangawil*, apparently corresponding to the Luiseño *tuvish*, *chuchamish*, and *tauchanish*. The moieties constantly function in these. Each rite is made by the moiety to which the dead person belonged, and the other is invited. In all of them the guests sing during the early part of the night, the rite makers after midnight. In both the *süshomnil* and *nangawil* property is thrown away as well as burned, and this is seized and kept by members of the opposite moiety. The materials for the figures in the *nangawil* are prepared by the mourning moiety, and then assembled—for pay—by the invited one. This ceremony is said to last three days. The eagle killing ceremony is also in the hands of one moiety at a time, with the other present as guests. This organization by moieties must give the Cupeño mourning ceremonies a different color from those of the nonmoiety Luiseño, which in other respects they appear to resemble closely.

Cupeño mythology is closest to that of the Cahuilla, it would seem, and even perhaps more closely related to that of the Serrano than to that of the adjacent Luiseño. Tumayowit ("earth") and Mukat were the first deities and the creators or progenitors of everything in it. They led mankind southward to their approximate present seats. Either identified or associated with these two gods were Coyote and Wild Cat, who emerged from the halves of a primeval bag hanging in space. Mankind was already in existence, but in mud and darkness. Tumayowit and Mukat disagreed. The former wished death to be and finally descended to a lower world. Mukat caused people to quarrel, and was finally poisoned, by the wish of men, through Frog eating his voidings. Coyote was sent away on a pretext, but returned and seized Mukat's heart from the funeral pyre. The Cupeño were exterminated by their neighbors, only one baby boy, Hübüyak, escaping with his Diegueño mother. As he grew up, he rejoined his kinsmen of Coyote moiety and Kauval clan who had remained at Saboba (in historic Luiseño territory), returned to Kupa, slaughtered the destroyers of his people, and settled there with two Luiseño wives, to become the progenitor of the Cupeño of today. The Wild Cat moiety came to Kupa later.

Mukat is obviously the equivalent of Wiyot, but Tumayowit, the earth mother, appears here, as among the Cahuilla, as a man, if there is no error. This part of the myth suggests the Diegueño and Yuman belief in two first hostile brother gods.

THE CAHUILLA.

HISTORY AND HABITAT.

The Cahuilla, with 750 souls, are to-day one of the important tribes of California. Originally they may have numbered 2,500. They are Catholic and speak Spanish; but, although generally included among the Mission Indians, they were only to a slight extent brought under mission control in the first third of the nineteenth century. The western division may have been partially affiliated with the sub-mission at San Bernardino, and those from the vicinity of Cahuilla Valley, or some of them, appear to have been within the sphere of San Luis Rey or its station at Pala. After secularization, many of the Cahuilla entered into relations with the Spaniards on the grants in the fertile portion of southern California, either as seasonal visitors or more permanent peons. This brought them in some numbers into Serrano and Gabrielino territory and has led to the attribution of part of the habitat of the former people to the Cahuilla by some authorities. Of late years this westward movement from the desert and mountains has slackened. The Government has developed water and protected Indian rights, and the Cahuilla live regularly in their old homes—an instance of the enduring attachment of the California nations to their ancestral soil. There are fewer reservations than there once were villages; but they are rather fairly distributed through the same regions.

The name Cahuilla is in universal use, but its origin is obscure. Reid, our principal authority on the Gabrielino, says that the word means "masters"; but this has not been confirmed. Indians of all tribes regard the designation as of Spanish origin. The Yuman group about Ensenada Bay in Baja California, who are practically one people with the Diegueño, have sometimes been called Cahuillas; but whatever basis of local or official usage this appellation may have, it is unfortunate, since speech proves the Bajeños to have no connection at all with the American Cahuilla. There is also a Yokuts Kawia tribe, on Kaweah River, whose name, however, seems to be a coincidence. The Yokuts say Kā'wia or Gā'wia, while Cahuilla is of course Kawi'a. This is its universal pronunciation. The spellings Coahuilla and Coahuila, although the more frequent and established in government usage, are therefore erroneous; they would be pronounced Kwawia or Kwawila. The latter seems a mere confusion with the name of the Mexican State of Coahuila.

The Cahuilla are called Yuhikt-om or Kwimkuch-um ("easterners") by the Luiseño, Tamikoch-em by the Cupeño, Kitanemun-um by the Serrano proper, Kwitanem-um by the Chemehuevi, Hakwicha by the Mohave, and a dialectic equivalent of Hakwicha by the other Yuman groups that know them.

Cahuilla territory is somewhat irregular, but may be defined as the inland basin between the San Bernardino Range and the range extending southward from Mount San Jacinto; with a few spillings over into the headwaters of coast drainage. There are three natural topographical divisions.

The first comprises San Gorgonio Pass, lying nestled between the giant peaks of Mounts San Bernardino, San Gorgonio, and San Jacinto, all over 10,000 feet high. With this belongs Palms Springs Canyon, and the westward draining San Timoteo Canyon.[1] The elevation of the inhabited sites is between 1,500 and 2,500 feet. Serrano and Luiseño adjoin. The natives of this district, who are here

[1] This is in error. San Gorgonio Pass and San Timoteo Canyon were in Serrano possession, as set forth in the footnote appended to the section on the Serrano. Palm Springs Canyon thus remains as the focus of this Cahuilla group, and their boundary should be run northward or northeastward from Mount San Jacinto instead of forming the westward arm shown in Plates 1 and 57. The hill near White Water probably marked their limit against the Serrano and not against the Desert Cahuilla. The Serrano do not reckon the Palm Springs division as Cahuillas. They are said to call them Wanupiapayum and Tüpamukiyam; which, however, appear also as names of Serrano local groups.

designated as the Western or Pass Cahuilla, speak a somewhat different though intelligible dialect to the remainder of the group. Their range extended to Kawishmu, a hill a little east of White Water.

Southeastward is the Colorado Desert, partly below sea level, and forming an old arm of the Gulf of California. The southern end of this totally arid valley, occasionally watered by overflows from the great Colorado into New River—which looks on the map like an affluent but is really a spillway flowing in opposite direction from the main stream—was in the possession of the Kamia or other Yuman groups. The northern end, down to about Salton Sea, was Cahuilla. Most of this district is exceedingly fertile under irrigation, and has been partly reclaimed. In native times it appeared most forbiddingly desert. But its tremendous depression brought the ground waters near the surface, so that in many localities mesquite trees throve and the Cahuilla obtained water in comparatively shallow wells. The people here are the Kitanemun-um of the Serrano, our Desert Cahuilla.

The third division lived in the mountains south of San Jacinto Peak, chiefly in fairly watered canyons well up the less favored side of the range, overlooking the inland desert, as at Santa Rosa, Los Coyotes, and San Ygnacio. At one point these people were across the divide, in Pacific Ocean drainage. This is the district centering in the patch now known as "Coahuila Reservation"—though it harbors only a small minority of the entire group—on the head of the Santa Margarita. The elevation of these habitats is from 3,000 to 4,000 feet. The speech is said to be distinguishable from that of the desert; but the difference is insignificant, and the desert and mountain divisions might be grouped together.

Plate 57 shows a few important sites in part of the habitat of the Cahuilla. Other place names are: Kavinish, Indian Wells; Pal tewat, Indio; Pal seta, Cabezon; Temalwahish, La Mesa; Sokut Menyil, Martinez; Lawilvan or Sivel, Alamo; Tova, Agua Dulce; Wewutnowhu, Santa Rosa. San Ygnacio is both Pachawal and Sapela. Most of these seem to be old names of specific villages, but now refer to tracts or reservations. Other sites are mentioned in the list of clans under "Society" below.

PLANT FOODS.

The principal supplies of food drawn from plants by the Cahuilla are rather accurately known, and while somewhat more varied than usual owing to the range of the group from low desert to high and fairly watered mountains, may be considered typical of the Indians of the southern part of the State.

Oaks, of course, require reasonable precipitation and moderate elevation, so that they are available in quantities to only a part of the Cahuilla; but the acorns were utilized wherever obtainable and treated as by the other Californians. *Quercus lobata* was the species that the Cahuilla had most frequently accessible to them.

In the sunken desert, where the roots of the mesquite can in many places penetrate to ground water, the fruit of this tree was the staple food. Both the bean or honey and the screw mesquite (*Prosopis juliflora* and *pubescens*) were employed, the whole fruits being ground in wooden mortars. The former variety was the more important; the latter is sweeter.

Agaves and yuccas were less vital to the Cahuilla than to the mountain tribes of western Arizona and probably the Chemehuevi and Koso, but were made use of in the same way. The thick, short, succulent, sweet stalks were roasted in stone-lined and covered pits. The waxy flowers as well as the fruits of some species were eaten cooked.

Nearly every variety of cactus was made use of. Most generally the fruit was consumed, but the fleshy stalks or leaves of some species helped out when diet became scant, and sometimes buds or seeds are edible.

The native palm bears clusters of a small fruit which was not neglected.

Nearly every conifer, from pine to juniper, had its seeds eaten. The most important variety is the Nevada nut pine, *Pinus monophylla*, seeds of which were harvested by the Cahuilla in the same manner as by the Koso, the cones being roasted to extract the nuts.

Many plants furnished what is usually known by its Mexican name pinole—the Aztec original *pinolli* is significant of the wide distribution of the food habit—that is, seed flour. The most important kind was chia, *Salvia columbariae*, Cahuilla *pasal*. Other sages and a variety of plants were also made use of: *Atriplex lentiformus, Artemisia tridentata, Sisimbrium canescens, Lasthenia glabrata, Chenopodium fremontii*. These were all gathered with the seed beater (Fig. 57), parched or roasted with coals

FIG. 57.—Cahuilla seed beater.

shaken in a basket or pottery tray, and ground. The meal was eaten dry, boiled, or baked into heavy doughy cakes, according to species.

California is nowhere a berry country. The Cahuilla have available several varieties which are rather of the nature of small fruits. In some of these the seeds are perhaps of more food value than the flesh. Thus, in the wild plum, *Prunus*, Cahuilla *chamish*, Mexican *yslay*, the kernel of the pit is crushed, leached, and boiled like acorn flour. Manzanita, *Arctostaphylos*, is treated similarly. The berries of the elder, *Sambucus mexicana*, and of sumac, *Rhus trilobata*, are also dried. The influence of acorn-seed processes in the use of these food materials is evident. The arid to subarid climate of California produces fruits whose paucity of juicy pulp allows them to be made into meal; but a people unaccustomed to grinding would hardly have applied the process to varieties consumable otherwise.

Root parts of plants are of little service to the Cahuilla, whose dry habitat allows but a sparse growth of the lily-like bulb plants that are important farther north in the State. Flowers, on the other hand, are often thick and sappy.

Those of species of yucca, agave, sumac, and ocatilla (*Fouquiera spinosa*) are boiled, either fresh or after drying.

Altogether, more than 60 varieties of plants are known to have served the Cahuilla as food in one form or another, and the whole number may have been twice as great. It is obvious that a non-farming people living in a country of little game and limited fertility would be likely to leave no source of wild plant food idle which lay within their capacity to utilize. The value of ethnobotanical studies lies in a comprehension of the processes followed, and a determination of the manner in which these have positively and negatively affected methods of securing food. It is clear that a few well-developed processes were applied to the limits of applicability, rather than that the best possible method was independently devised for each product of nature. Thus grinding and drying stand out among the Cahuilla; the seed beater is more important than the digging stick. The true significance of the processes, of course, is clear only with the totality of the botanical environment in view. For this reason the plants and parts not utilized are as important to an interpretative understanding as those made use of; but on this side little information has been recorded.

MORTAR AND METATE.

The Cahuilla do not neatly square their metates, as the Mohave do, but use an irregularly rectangular or oval slab. Most specimens have only part of their surfaces worn, obviously by a circular motion. The rub stone sometimes is only a bowlder ground flat. Another form is dressed into an oval, and rather thin. This type could also be used for rotary grinding. In general, the implement is of the California type, as described in the chapters on the Maidu and Luiseño, and is more properly designated " grinding slab " than "metate."

But there are many " manos " that are as evenly squared as a brick, and even longer and narrower. These can be utilized only with a back and forth motion. Some metates, too, show that they have been rubbed with such a stone. Now the Cahuilla of to-day often grind wheat; and it is therefore a question whether this southwestern type of metate was frequent among them anciently, or whether its use has been stimulated by contact with Mexicans. The settlers from Mexico must have brought many metates of lava with them, or manufactured them after their arrival. Apparently the utensil was in daily service in every poorer Spanish Californian household for several generations; and from this source it penetrated, in its standard Mexican form with three legs, to the Indians. Occasional examples are still in use in Indian hands in central as well as southern California. Fragments have even been discovered in the surface layers of the San

Francisco Bay shell mounds and in graves on the Santa Barbara coast.

The southern California mortar is a block of stone hollowed out, when new, some 2 or 3 inches, but gradually wearing deeper. The hopper is by no means always employed. If present, it is always attached with asphalt or gum. Neither of the two central and northern types of mortar is known—the bedrock hole and the slab with loose, superposed hopper.

The pestle, as in central California, is frequently only a long cobble, sometimes slightly dressed at the grinding end or along one side (Fig. 58, b).

For mesquite beans and perhaps other foods, the desert Cahuilla use a deep wooden mortar sunk into the ground. This has its counterpart on the Colorado River; but the Cahuilla form appears to average a more extended section of log and deeper hole. A pestle of unusual

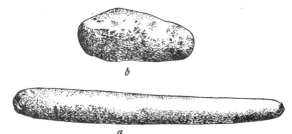

FIG. 58.—Cahuilla stone pestles for wooden (a) and for stone (b) mortar.

length, often 2 feet, is necessitated. To prevent undue weight, this must be made slender; and in turn, dressing is involved (Fig. 58, a). The pestle for the wooden mortar is therefore quite different from the much more roughly shaped form used on stone.

It is doubtful if the Cahuilla-Mohave wooden mortar is connected with that of the valley Wintun and Yokuts. One is used for mesquite, the other for acorns. The former has a deep, pointed pit; the other contains a broad bowl-shaped basin, in the center of which is a small shallow excavation in which all the actual pounding is done. The southern mortar of wood is perhaps a device to meet some particular quality of the mesquite bean; that of central California is clearly a substitute for a more general form in stone.

Somewhere in acornless southeastern California, probably from the Chemehuevi to the Eastern Mono, and in parts of Nevada, a very large and deep cone-shaped mortar of stone occurs, worked with a long and sharp but thick pestle of extraordinary weight. This seems to be connected with the wooden mortar of southern California.

The mountain Cahuilla, as well as the Luiseño and Diegueño, who have acorns but no mesquite, have not been observed to possess wooden mortars; and no pestle of wood has been reported from California except from the Mohave.

BASKETRY.

Cahuilla basketry is that of all the "Mission Indians" of southern California. Chumash ware alone was somewhat different, though clearly of the same type. It is a rather heavy but regular basketry, coiled on bundles of *Epicampes* grass stems, the wrapping being either sumac splints or *Juncus* rush. The varying shades of the latter produce a mottled effect, which is pleasing to most civilized people, though it is not certain that the natives sought it equally. But they obviously appreciated the lustrous texture of the rush,

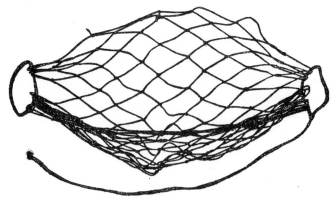

Fig. 59.—Cahuilla carrying net. (Cf. Fig. 53.)

which, as used for the groundwork, is normally buff in color, while red or brown lengths of stem serve for designs, and even olive and distinctly yellow shades can be obtained. Only black was produced by dyeing. The prevailing pattern arrangement is one of encircling bands.

The forms are as standardized and nearly as few as the materials. They are nearly flat plates; shallow flaring bowls; a large deeper basket; a small receptacle with slightly constricted mouth, the equivalent of the Chumash-Yokuts-Chemehuevi "bottle-neck," but without trace of a shoulder; and the woman's cap.

The large basket serves for storage and carriage. It differs fundamentally from the carrying basket of all central and northern California. It is close coiled instead of open twined; is flat bottomed instead of an inverted cone; and broader than deep. It is obviously not a form that originated for transport, but a receptacle or pot put secondarily to burden use. The explanation is found in the carrying net, which renders the precise shape of the contained basket of little moment.

The net has the form of a small hammock with a mesh of from 3 to 5 inches, the ends being gathered on heavy loops, which are joined by an adjustable rope passing across the cap-protected forehead (Fig. 59). Similar nets are found in central California to as far north as the Pomo without an accompanying alteration of the carrying basket from its conical form. The inference is that the central Californians employed the net only occasionally, the southern Shoshoneans regularly. All that is actually known of the use of the implement corroborates this conclusion. The net must therefore be regarded as of southern origin. It is a localized device: the adjacent Southwest reverts to the basket or employs the carrying frame; the Shoshonean Plateau appears to use the Californian cone basket.

It may be added that the Pomo carrying net has the headband woven in, so that the capacity can not be altered—a fact which indicates that it is designed only for certain specific usages.

The large, coiled, fairly deep storage and transport basket of the south may therefore be regarded as probably an original cooking vessel, and is certainly a form which elsewhere is used for cooking. It is not so used by the Cahuilla to-day, as indeed is not to be expected of a pottery making people. The history of the vessel can hardly be understood in full without more precise knowledge of the baskets in which the inland Gabrielino—who made no pots and were too remote from steatite to use it generally—did their cooking.

The same vessel undoubtedly served formerly, as it does to-day, for a general receptacle; but that it was not primarily a store basket is suggested by two circumstances. The first is that the ancient Chumash possessed a taller, larger, and distinctly bellied basket, similar to that of northwestern California in form, but coiled instead of twined. This was indubitably made for storing only. The second fact is that the Cahuilla (Pl. 60), the Mohave, and apparently the Luiseño also, make an outdoor granary. This is not set vertically and worked into posts, as among the Sierra tribes, but laid flat on the ground, on a rock, or on a scaffold. It is made of long stalks of wormwood, *Artemisia*, among the Cahuilla, or arrow weed, *Pluchea*, with the Mohave, and put together in bundles much on the plan of a bird's nest, without textile process. The Mohave and desert Cahuilla form is up to 6 feet in diameter, generally low, and without bottom. This type is mostly used to hold mesquite. The mountain Cahuilla make a smaller but taller form with bottom for their acorns. The entire device is obviously one that is serviceable only in an arid climate: there is no thatch or provision for cover except horizontally laid stalks that would not turn rain. This granary, together with the opportunities afforded by rock crevices in a dry country, make a true storage basket unnecessary in most of southern California. The large " mission " basket would be convenient to contain as much food as might be wanted about the house; it was not intended to hold provisions for the winter, nor was it serviceable for the purpose.

The small and more or less globular basket of the Cahuilla and their neighbors was no doubt sometimes useful as a deposit for awls and other little things; it must also have served particularly as a gift and as an offering in the mourning anniversary.

The basketry cap of southern California has the shape of a fairly tall frustum. Except for material and texture, it is identical with the Yokuts and Koso cap. This southern coiled form appears to have only a remote historical connection with the overlay-twined cap of northernmost California, which is low and more or less convex in profile, and whose range, toward the south at least, is exactly coterminous with that of the basket art that does not know coiling. The northern cap is worn habitually; southern women don theirs when they carry a load. The intervening tribes, such as Maidu, Miwok, and Pomo, use no headwear. A third type is represented in California among the Chemehuevi, and appears to be representative of the Shoshonean Plateau. This is diagonally twined, peaked, and sometimes has the design painted on. It seems that this form links the northern and southern California types geographically, rendering the distribution of the object continuous over an arc of territory. This arc and the Pacific Ocean inclose the north central Californian capless area. A distribution of this kind makes it obvious that it is a specific reason, and not mere failure of diffusion, that has kept the central Californians from use of the cap; and establishes some possibility that they once wore it and subsequently abandoned the custom.

The Great Basin type of cap is found among Cahuilla and Diegueño beside the coiled form. Both are shown in Plate 73, d.

The mortar hopper of the Cahuilla and other southerners is started on a hoop. Here is a truly interrupted distribution. The north twines its hopper, the south coils, the middle area dispenses with the article.

Uniformity of technique, material, pattern, and even fineness of finish of all coiled ware, irrespective of the nature of the basket, is almost absolute among the Cahuilla and their neighbors, and is one of the most marked traits of their art.

The commonest twined basket of southern California is a small or moderate sized openwork vessel of *Juncus* stems, used both as a receptacle and, after lining with leaves or similar material, for leaching. The weave is essentially simple twining, with considerable doubling and zigzagging of warp. The introduction of these variants seems random, the only apparent purpose being to keep the interstices approximately equal in area. No attention is paid to uniformity of mesh or to an even surface. The result is a basket that seems deliberately crude and unworkmanlike.

The seed beater has become a frame rather than a basket with the Cahuilla. It is nothing but a bundle of three, six, or a dozen sticks, wrapped together at one end to form a handle, and more or less spread fanwise at the other end over a hoop. A single crosspiece may bisect the circle and give stiffness, but is not always introduced. Modern pieces have the fan and hoop very roughly lashed together with cord, rag strips, or wire. As no old specimens have been preserved, this imperfect workmanship may possibly be ascribable to modern degeneracy. But the analogous crudeness of the openwork basket, as contrasted with the full maintenance of careful finish in all coiled ware to the present time, suggests that the Cahuilla beater was always made hastily and imperfectly. This is the more likely because on the one hand it is scarcely a true basket and on the other reaches its southernmost known range in southern California. The concept has become feeble, its execution half-hearted. (Fig. 57.)

The only other twined vessel known to have been made in the region of "mission" basketry is the pitched or asphalted water jug with constricted neck, and the occurrence of this is doubtful for the Cahuilla. The Chemehuevi and Kawaiisu manufacture a coated jug in diagonal twining and with pointed or round bottom, a type belonging to the Shoshonean Plateau and the western part of the Southwest. The Chumash made a bellied bottle that would stand up, and used simple twining. The Gabrielino, who also had no pottery, may have had the same type; the preserved description of their water vessel unfortunately is not clear. The Chumash and Chemehuevi forms probably met in the Serrano region, although here also exact knowledge fails. For Cahuilla, Luiseño, and Diegueño there is only a single and vague reference; and as these peoples made pottery, the occurrence of the basketry water bottle among them must be considered somewhat doubtful, and was probably at most occasional.

The southern California basket art thus reveals these traits. Twining is remarkably undeveloped. Types that are twined elsewhere in the State are either lacking in the south, replaced by coiled substitutes, or amazingly crude. The center of the art rests in coiling to a much higher degree than elsewhere. The coiled ware is connected with that of central California, especially of the San Joaquin Valley, but is reduced to a single well-maintained manner universally ap-

plied. The occurrence of pottery among the Cahuilla, Luiseño, and
Diegueño has unquestionably contributed to this condition of their
basketry. As soon as neighboring regions without pottery are entered, such as the Santa Barbara Channel or Tehachapi Mountain
district, the rigid restriction to a single style ceases, and twining
flourishes beside coiling.

POTTERY.

The pottery made by the Cahuilla, Luiseño, and Diegueño, which
did not extend to the Gabrielino but probably to the Serrano,
apparently had its immediate origin in the lower Colorado Valley,
from which it continues also in the opposite direction to the Seri.
It is a coiled and smoothed unslipped ware, made of clay that burns
red, with tempering of crushed rock; very thin walled, light, but
fragile and porous. Patterns are linear, solid areas being confined chiefly to fillings in of the favorite acute angle; and are
painted on in yellow ocher, which fires to a somewhat deeper red
than the clay. The Cahuilla and Luiseño more frequently omit designs, but when they add them, do so in typical Mohave style, which
is suggestive of tattoo and face-paint patterns; but they employ a
red substance in place of yellow ocher. Black designs occur (Pl. 62),
and though rare are of interest because unknown to the Mohave.
They are said to have been produced with black mineral; the surface is more highly polished and the lines finer. The forms of vessels seem to have been less numerous than with the Mohave; at least,
spoons, plates, and oval platters have not been found. The moderns
occasionally make specialties, like jars with three or four mouths,
which do not occur among the Mohave, where the art remained
vigorous in purely native condition until recently; but these may be
fanciful inventions under American stimulus. Something similar
has occurred among the Yuma, whose old pottery seems to have
nearly disappeared before crude and bastard forms made as
curiosities.

The introduction of this art from the Colorado River to the desert
and the coast is not altogether recent, as the presence of sherds in
the upper layers of an ancient site at La Jolla proves. The apparent
absence of pottery from the lower deposits can not yet be stressed,
because examination has been too far from exhaustive to make negative conclusions dependable. On the other hand, it can not be
doubted that the art came to the coast from the east at no very
remote period.

That the ultimate source of the pottery industry of the entire region
is from the Southwest proper is also certain. But again, hasty conclusions must be avoided. Nothing like the Mohave-Luiseño ware

has been found in any ancient or recent Pueblo culture; an area wholly or nearly without pottery separates the Colorado River from the westerly edge of the district of Pueblo architecture; and from the river to the coast there are no traces of any other form of the art.

The ware most nearly resembling that of southern California seems to be a red pottery with one-colored pattern found up the Gila and at least as far into Sonora as the Papago country. This similarity, together with the modern Seri one, points to Sonora rather than the Pueblos as the specific source of the southern California art.

HOUSES.

The Cahuilla house is thatched. Its original form has not been satisfactorily determined. At present it is rectangular and set on forked posts. There is a distinct ridge and considerable slope to the roof. The walls may be plastered with mud or adobe. This type of dwelling has unquestionably been influenced by the Mexican *jacal* or the American house; but to what degree is uncertain. On the desert larger and more nearly square houses with nearly flat roof and without sharp corners may be seen which somewhat suggest the Mohave house minus its covering of sand. These are probably more nearly aboriginal. The mud coating of the walls of the pitched-roof houses is certainly not native. The Mohave follow the same practice, but it is positively known to be recent with them.

In the mountains a type survived until recently which lacks walls. Two, four, or six posts are set up rather close together and connected across their crotched tops by short logs. From these, poles are then radiated to the ground, and some sort of thatch bound on. Such a dwelling suggests a reduction of the Miwok semisubterranean house or assembly chamber, but is probably more immediately connected with the Luiseño and Mohave houses; a covering of earth could be easily added or omitted. Stumps in abandoned settlements at the edge of the desert conform to this structural plan. But the question remains whether this type of house was built by all the Cahuilla or restricted to those in a certain topography; and further, whether it represents the standard house, or a form used in summer or for temporary purposes.

Uncertainty also surrounds the sweat house. The Serrano and Pass Cahuilla made this chamber. For the Mountain Cahuilla the sweat house has not been mentioned; but they may have had it. For the Desert Cahuilla the case is more doubtful. The next tribes to the east, those of the Colorado River, do not know the sweat house.[2]

---

[2] A recent study of the Cahuilla by L. Hooper (see bibliography) leaves the use of sweat houses and earth-covered houses somewhat obscure, but establishes the existence of sweat houses.

The sweat house of the Pass region is oval and small, about 12 by 8 feet, and of a man's height in the middle (Pl. 60). The only opening is the door on ground level. Inside from this is the fireplace, and beyond, two center posts, connected by a transverse beam. From this poles run down to the edge of the rather shallow excavation. The whole is then laid with brush and earth. The structure is too small for dancing or assemblies: all through southern California the sweat house is used only for sweating.

This sweat house agrees closely in plan with the old type of Cahuilla dwelling that has been discussed.

The ramada or shade is of the usual type: a roof of foliage on posts. In the desert it forms a sort of porch in front of the door, and is frequently surrounded in whole or part by a windbreak—both devices known also to the Mohave.

The brush inclosure for ceremonial purposes has not been reported from the Cahuilla, but may have been made by them.

WEAPONS.

The Cahuilla bow is that of all southern California—long, narrow, thick, and unbacked. It is made of mesquite, inferior specimens of willow, or palm-leaf stem; in the mountains probably of other materials. The arrow is of two kinds: cane with a wooden foreshaft, as among the Chemehuevi and Yokuts, or a single sharpened stem of *Artemisia*, without head, the Mohave type. The grooved straightener and polisher of steatite, which was heated, occurs throughout the south, and has already been mentioned as the regular accompaniment of the cane or reed arrow.

The thrusting war club with thick cylindrical head was used by the Cahuilla. This is a form found from the Pueblos to the Gabrielino.

The curved flat rabbit-killing stick of southwestern type was known to all the southern Californians (Fig. 55).

VARIOUS UTENSILS.

The Cahuilla cradle was a ladderlike frame like that of the Mohave and Diegueño. The relation of this generic southern California type to the other forms found in California has been discussed in the section dealing with the Yokuts. Whether the Cahuilla used a hooplike wickerwork hood of splints such as the Mohave attach to their frames is not recorded, but seems likely. (Pl. 39, *b*.)

The hammock-shaped carrying net (Fig. 59) is often suspended in the house to hold a sleeping baby. This may be an aboriginal custom, but there is no certainty on the point.

The desert habitat of most of the Cahuilla is probably responsible for their nonuse of the two commonest Californian string materials, *Apocynum* and *Asclepias*. Instead they employ the leaf fibers of the mescal, *Agave deserti*, and the bark of the reed, *Phragmites communis*. The latter plant is called *wish*, but this word in Luiseño denotes *Apocynum cannabinum*.

The mealing brush of soaproot fibers, *Chlorogalum pomeridianum*, is also replaced by one of agave among the Cahuilla.

The straight flute has four holes usually set roughly in two pairs by rule of thumb or eye, and therefore productive of arbitrary intervals rendering the instrument unsuited for accompaniment to the voice.

For strung shell money the Cahuilla are known to have used the *Olivella* type of thin, curving disks, but the more massive currency of clam must also have reached them.

SOCIETY.

The social organization of the Cahuilla has been less broken and altered in the past century than that of the Luiseño, and may therefore afford a truer picture of the society of the latter people than their own present institutions. At the same time the information about the Cahuilla is not wholly clear. As among the Serrano, the moieties stand out definitely, the "clans" are less certain.

The Cahuilla moieties are patrilinear, totemic, and exogamous. They are called *Istam*, after *isil*, the coyote, and *Tuktum*, after the wild cat, *tukut; -am, -um*, is the plural ending. Endogamy occurs now and then, as among the Miwok; it may or may not have been tolerated in native days.

The " clans " are very numerous, small, and associated with localities or named after places. All clan members insist on their direct kinship and descent in the male line from a comparatively recent ancestor. No recorded clan names and village names agree. Two or more clans might inhabit one village. The members of a single clan sometimes live in different villages, and the Cahuilla do not seem to regard this condition as a modern innovation. All this leaves it doubtful whether the clans are bodies of the kind usually implied by this term, or only families of actual blood kindred named after a spot with which they are or once were associated. Their moiety affiliations prove nothing in this matter, since under patrilinear moieties either patrilinear clans or patrilinear families must automatically form part of the moieties.

The recorded Cahuilla clans are nearly all from the desert division:

Coyote moiety.

Sawala-kiktum. Formerly with the Wild Cat *Nanha-yum* and *Ayelmukut* and Coyote *Ikoni-kiktum* in the village of Ekwawinet at La Mesa, 2 miles south of Coachella. Now at Torros Reservation.

Ikoni-kiktum. See last.

Taukat-im. Southwest of Coachella.

Wora'i-kiktum. At Indio.

Sewakil. South of Indio.

Masuvich-um. On Martinez Reservation. The name is said to refer to a sandy place.

Wiit-am, " grasshoppers." On Martinez Reservation.

Mumlait-im. On Martinez Reservation.

Wansau-wum. On Martinez Reservation. Named from *wanyish*, stream, because once flooded out.

Iviat-um. At Agua Dulce.

Sasalma-yum. At Agua Dulce.

Kaunakal-kiktum. At Agua Dulce. This group is said once to have lived at a place where *kaunakal* shrubs grew.

Kauwistamila-kiktum. At Agua Dulce.

A'atsat-um, " good ones." Formerly at Indian Wells.

Wanisiwau-yam. At Mecca.

Tevi-nga-kiktum. At Alamo.

Wiyist-am. At San Ysidro.

Havinawich-um. At Palm Springs.

Amna'avich-um, " large ones." Northwest of Palm Springs.

Hunavati-kiktum. Southeast of Banning. Perhaps Serrano.

Wild Cat moiety.

Palkausinakela, " seepage from a spring." Figtree John, west of Salton Sea.

Panatka-kiktum. Now at Thermal; came from west of there.

Tui-kiktum. Southeast of Thermal.

Isil-sivayauwich-um. South of Coachella.

Wanki-nga-kiktum. South of Coachella.

Nanha-yum, Tel-kiktum, and *Ayelmukut.* At La Mesa, south of Coachella.

Panasa-kiktum. Southeast of Coachella.

Wansinga-tamyangahuch-um. Northeast of Coachella.

Walpunidi-kiktum. At Alamo.

Palpunivikt-um. At Alamo.

Tamula-kiktum. Near Alamo.

Tamolanich-im. At Agua Dulce.

Awal-im, " dogs," a nickname. At Martinez.

Autaat-em. West or southwest of Coachella ; now at Martinez.

Waricht-em—warish, mesquite. At Indian Wells; now at Thermal and Mecca.

Kauwis-pawniyawich-em, "living in the rocks at Kauwis," *i. e.* at Palm Springs. Now at Mecca.

Kauwis-i-kiktum, " living at Kauwis." Perhaps one group with the last. Now at Palm Springs and Coachella.

Kilyi-nga-kiktum. On Mission Creek. Perhaps Serrano.

Iswet-um, "wolves," a nickname; in Spanish, Lobos, used in the form Lugo, as a modern family name. On Cahuilla Reservation. This is the only mountain Cahuilla clan recorded, and is so prominent on its reservation as to give the impression that *Iswetum* may have been a synonym for all the people of the district. The wolf is not an inhabitant of southern California.

Wakwai-kiktum. Formerly near Warner's ranch, that is, neighbors of the Cupeño. Now at Wakwi or Maulim on Torros Reservation.

The ending *-kiktum* on many of these names is from the stem *ki*, "live" or "house."

The Cahuilla word for "clan" is *tahelo*, which is probably from the stem *tah*, *atah*, "person," occurring in several Shoshonean languages of southern California.

The chief, *net*, and his assistant or ceremonial director, *paha*, held office in the clan, it is said.

The totemism of the moieties extends to ritual and myth. Images for the *nukil* or mourning anniversary are made by each moiety for the other. Temayowit and Mukat, the first gods, born in the Milky Way, are thought to have been companions of Coyote and Wild Cat, respectively. The moon is a woman of Coyote moiety, made by Temayowit, the sun a Wild Cat man who went to the sky.

Their possession of names and affiliation with the moieties render it probable that the enumerated groups of the Cahuilla approached the nature of clans. But the relation of the clans to the local or political units, to the moieties, to blood families, and to chieftainship and religious groups is far from clear for any of the southern California Shoshoneans.

RELIGION.

Considering the importance of the Cahuilla, their strength in survivors, and the interest attaching both on account of their varied environment and their position midway between the Gabrielino and the Mohave ceremonial foci, regrettably little is known of their religion.

Their creation myth seems to have been of Serrano type, but with the deities named as among the Cupeño.

The mourning anniversary was called *Nukil* or *Hemnukuwin.* Images were used.

The same may be said of the adolescence rite, *Aulolil* or *Pemiwoluniwom*, in which the girl was "roasted."

Whether the Chungichnish religion reached the Cahuilla of the pass is not certain. It probably obtained some foothold among those of the mountains. It did not exist in the desert. The Cahuilla there do not know Chungischnish, drink no toloache publicly, make no sand paintings, and hold no eagle ceremony. According to the Mohave, they sing several cycles analogous to their own song series.

There may be some forced native equating in this statement, but there is probably at least some basis of fact. The desert Cahuilla knew the toloache plant and admit that they drank it, but apparently only as occasional individuals intent on wealth or some other special aspect of fortune. This is very nearly the Mohave attitude toward the drug.[3]

On the whole, therefore, it would seem that the Cahuilla possessed the basic and generalized elements of southern California religion; lacked—at least in their most characteristic habitat—its developed Chungichnish form; and had come instead under a certain degree of Mohave or Colorado River influence. This influence is likely to have been indirect, since there is practically no mention of outright communications between the Cahuilla and the Mohave.

---

[3] L. Hooper, The Cahuilla Indians (see bibliography), gives, among other new data, an account of a Jimson-weed initiation which appears to refer to the Pass division.

CHAPTER 49.

THE DIEGUEÑO AND KAMIA.

THE DIEGUEÑO.

YUMAN STOCK.

With the Diegueño, more fully San Diegueños, we return once more to the much scattered Hokan family and enter upon consideration of the last of the stocks represented in California—the Yuman.

The Yuman stock is internally classified on the basis of speech as follows, Californian tribes being starred:

Lower California division: Kiliwi; Cochimi; Akwa'ala.

Central division, centering on the lower Colorado River: * Mohave; * Halchidhoma; * Yuma; Kohuana; Halyikwamai; Cocopa; * Kamia; * Dieguño; Maricopa.

Arizona Plateau division: Havasupai; Walapai; Tulkepai ("Tonto"); Yavapai.

TERRITORY AND DIVISIONS.

Dieguño land was washed by the ocean on the west and bordered by the holdings of the Luiseño, Cupeño, and Cahuilla on the north. For the east and south no precise limits can be set. The Dieguño of the north, about Mesa Grande and San Felipe, declare that they did not live beyond the eastern foot of the mountains. But what group owned the desert tract to the east, from Salton Sea to the now fertile Imperial Valley and New River district, has never been fully established. On the map most of the district in question has been assigned tentatively to the Kamia; in the section on whom the problem is discussed further.

Southward, the Dieguño shade off into the closely allied Yuman bands of northernmost Baja California. At Ensenada, 60 miles south of San Diego, the speech is still close to that of the Dieguño. The Indians through this stretch have no group names for each other, except by directions. They distinguish between the Diegueños, those formerly connected with the mission of San Diego, and the

Bajeños, the inhabitants of Lower or Baja California. But this is merely a reflection of the political separateness of American and Mexican. The congeners across the line have not thriven, and ethnologically they are wholly unknown, except for statements of the most general character; but the scant indications point to no ethnic demarcation of moment at or even near the international border.

Within the part of California occupied by the Diegueño two not very different dialects are spoken besides some minor subdialects. The two principal dialects have usually been designated as the northern and the southern, although " northwestern " and " southeastern " would be more exact. A number of differences of custom are known, but much of the available information concerns the two groups jointly, so that it is difficult to treat them other than as a unit. Their careful distinction by future students is indispensable.

Both dialects extended across the international boundary, but their position is such as to make it appear that the northern belonged primarily to American and the southern to Mexican California. The southern dialect includes, in American California, only the modern districts of Campo, La Posta, Manzanita, Guyapipe, and La Laguna.

It is probable that the Diegueño, or at least the northern branch, called themselves merely Ipai, people. They do sometimes call themselves " southern people," Kawak-upai, or " western people," Awik-upai, with reference to their neighbors; but these are not true national designations. Thus the Diegueño of Mesa Grande are Kawak-upai with reference to the Luiseño, and those of San Felipe as regards the Cupeño; but at San Felipe the real Kawak-upai should be the Campo people. The southern Diegueño sometimes call themselves Kamiai or Kamiyahi; which once more intrudes the vexed question of who the Kamia were.

To the Luiseño and Cupeño all the Diegueño are simply " southerners ": Kichamkuchum or Kichamkochem. The Mohave know them as Kamia'-ahwe, that is, " foreign " or remote Kamia.

Diegueño names for their neighbors are: Kohwai, perhaps also Hakunyau, the Luiseño; Hekwach, the Cupeño, and no doubt originally the Cahuilla also, although the latter are now known by their usual name, which the Indians declare to be of Spanish origin; Techahet, probably a place, is also recorded for the Cupeño or Cahuilla; Yuma or Yum (probably a recent name), Inyak-upai (" eastern people "), or Yakiyak, the Yuma; although some distinguish between the Kwichan or Yuma proper, said to be on the Colorado or beyond it, and the Yakiyak to the west of the Kwichan; Kwikapa, the Cocopa; Chimuwowo, the Chemehuevi; Humkahap, the Mohave; Mitlchus in the northern dialect, or Haiku in the southern, the Americans; Pinyai, the Mexicans.

The name Kamia seems to be unknown to the northern Diegueño, except, in the form Kamiai, as a designation for the inhabitants of the district of San Pascual, near the Luiseño frontier. The occurrence of this name at San Pascual may possibly be due to the settlement there of a group of southern Diegueño during or after mission times. With the Cupeño there was intimate association and considerable intermarriage, at least from the vicinity of San Felipe. The Cocopa are said not to have voyaged into northern Diegueño territory, but the Chemehuevi were occasional visitors in search of food. The Mohave seem very little known in the district of Mesa Grande and San Felipe. They probably made their journeys to Manzanita and other southern points, where references to their songs and sacred mountain occur.

The western portion of Diegueño territory is shown in detail on Plate 57. Other place names are Emitl-kwatai, Campo; Amat-kwa'-ahwat, farther up on the same stream; Amai'-tu, La Posta; Ewiapaip, from which we have made Guyapipe; Inyahkai and Aha-hakaik, La Laguna; Hawi, Vallecitos; Ahta, "cane," or Hapawu, Carrizo. Most of these are little reservations now; but it seems as if many of the reservations constituted by the government in this region, as among the Luiseño and Cahuilla, had an ancient village community as their nucleus.

Settled places that can not be located with any definiteness are Awaskal, Kohwat, Maktati, Maramoido, Matamo, Meti, Pokol, Shana, and Tapanke, mentioned in Spanish sources, Hanwi, Hasumel, Kamachal, Kokwitl, and Suapai in American. South of the boundary, some of them perhaps in what may be considered Diegueño limits, were Ahwat, Mat-ahwat-is, Hasasei, Hata'am, Hawai, Inomasi, Kwalhwut, Netlmol, and Wemura. The Hakum were inland near the border: that is, a village of this name evidently stood in or near Jacumba Pass.

Other settlements are given below in the clan lists under "Society."

Beyond their own territories the northern Diegueño knew Salton as Esily, "Salt," or Esilyeyaka; the mud volcanoes as Hakwicholol; Mount San Jacinto as Emtetei-Chaup-ny-uwa, "Chaup's house peak."

HISTORY AND NUMBERS.

San Diego was the first mission founded in upper California; but the geographical limits of its influence were the narrowest of any, and its effect on the natives comparatively light. There seem two reasons for this: first, the stubbornly resisting temper of the natives; and second, a failure of the rigorous concentration policy enforced elsewhere. Whether this second cause was itself the result of the first, or was due to an inability of the almost arid region to support a large population by agriculture without irrigation, is not wholly clear.

The spirit of the Diegueño toward the missionaries was certainly quite different from the passiveness with which the other Californians received the new religion and life. They are described as proud, rancorous, boastful, covetous, given to jests and quarrels, passionately devoted to the customs of their fathers, and hard to handle. In short, they possessed their share of resoluteness. Not especially formidable as foes, they at least did not shrink from warlike attempts. Within a month of the founding of the mission an attack was made for plunder. In its seventh year, the mission, meanwhile removed to its present site, was definitely attacked, partly burned, and three Spaniards, including one of the priests, killed. This was the only Franciscan to meet martyrdom at Indian hands in the entire history of the

California missions. Three years later it was necessary to send an expedition against the hostiles of Pamo.

Christianity also took hold of the natives very slowly. The initial year of the mission did not bring a single baptism; in the first five, less than a hundred neophytes were enrolled. After this, progress was more rapid: but the very success of the priests appears to have been the stimulus that drove the unconverted into open hostility. There can be little doubt that this un-Californian attitude can be ascribed to a participation by the Diegueño in the spirit of independence characteristic of the other Yuman tribes.

The Diegueño population, with the Kamia of American California included, may have reached 3,000. To-day there are between 700 and 800. This is a higher percentage of survival than is enjoyed by any other missionized group of California. The cause must be ascribed to the slowness of the Diegueño to submit and their retention of a greater degree of freedom of movement and residence. It was not until 55 years after its foundation that San Diego attained its maximum of converts. Other missions fell into heavy numerical decline in a much shorter period, and were only partly able to check the decrease by drawing upon importations from more and more remote districts. San Diego never harbored any Indians but Diegueños.

The total baptisms in 65 years were a few over 6,000. Three generations to a century would make this figure indicate a standing population of 3,000. But the native rate of reproduction may have been faster, and if so the numbers at a given time would have been less. Ten years before the mission reached its populational acme the annual death rate was 35 per thousand. This suggests more rapid breeding than is common to modern civilized communities; but it is probably not a high figure for a primitive community, and was certainly far below the mortality obtaining at other missions during their periods of activity.

RELIGION.

Diegueño religion is so largely compounded of the same elements as that of the Luiseño that its detailed consideration would be repetition. This is evident from the accompanying tabulation, the native names in which may serve as points of identification in future studies.

This similarity is probably in part ancient, but has undoubtedly been accentuated by the southeastward sweep of the Chungichnish toloache cult about a century ago. The southern Diegueño, in fact, did not come definitely under the influence of the movement until about the period of American occupation. It is characteristic of the effect of speech diversity in California that ceremonial names were translated or replaced by the Diegueño, not taken over. Only in the songs, the words and melody of which tend to form a close unit in the Indian mind, did outright borrowing of speech occur; and in these it took place on an extensive scale. A large proportion of Diegueño songs are in a foreign tongue; and this is generally not Luiseño or Cahuilla, as the singers believe, but Gabrielino.

TABLE 7.—ELEMENTS OF RELIGION IN SOUTHERN CALIFORNIA.

Religious elements.	Diegueño.	Luiseño.	Other groups.
Ceremonial enclosure...........	himak ("they dance"?), akiuch.	wamkish; hotahish, the fence.	Juaneño, wankech; Gabrielino yoba.
Ceremonial manager or dance leader.	kwaipal...........	paha'.............	Serrano, Cupeño, Cahuilla, paha'.
Toloache initiates.............	(1)...............	pumal-um........	Juaneño, pupl–em.
Shaman......................	kwasiyal..........	pula..............	Juaneño, pul.
"Tatahuila" dance (Pl. 55)....	tapakwirp........	morahash; totawish, the performer.	Juaneño, tobet (=towet?) the costume; Cupeño, pukavihat, the dance.
Eagle feather skirt.............	yipehai...........	palat..............	Juaneño, palet.
Headdress of owl feathers on stick.	tsekwirp, winyeyi.	cheyat............	
Erect headdress on band.......	talo...............	apuma; hainit....	Juaneño, eneat.
Stick headed with crystal......	kotat.............	paviut	
Toloache mortar................	kalmo.............	tamyush..........	
Net figure for initiation.........	minyu............	wanawut.........	
Toloache......................	kusi, kus.........	naktomush, the plant; mani, the preparation; pa'nish mani, the drinking.	Juaneño, pivat ("tobacco"); Cupeño manit paninil, the rite.
Bull-roarer....................	air...............	momlahpish......	
Sand painting..................	(1)...............	tarohaish.........	Juaneño,[1] Gabrielino.[1]
Clothes-burning rite...........	watlma...........	chuchamish......	Cupeño, süshomnil.
Image-burning rite.............	keruk, wukeruk...	tauchanish........	Cupeño, nangawil; Cahuilla, nukil, hemnukuwin.
Mourning rite for initiates......	ocham............	yunish matakish..	Gabrielino.[1]
Eagle mourning rite...........	ehpa ima ("eagle dance").	ashwut maknash ("eagle killing ")	Juaneño, panes, the bird.
Girls' adolsecence rite..........	atanuk, akil.......	wekenish, (yunish?).	Cupeño, aulinil, ülunika; Cahuilla, aulolil.
Fire dance.....................	(1)...............	(1)..............	
Initiates' dance.................	hortloi, (huitlui)..	tanish............	
Ordeal of stinging ants.........	(2)	antish............	Juaneno.[1]
Race at dying or new moon.....	(1)..., ...	(1)...............	Juaneño.[1]
Songs of invective and contempt.	(1)...............	nyachish..........	Gabrielino,[1] Cupeño, piniwahat.
Pole in Notush mourning......	(2)	kutumit..........	Fernandeño, kotumut.
Cannibal spirit, meteor, fireball.	Chaup, Kuyahomar.	Takwish..........	Cahuilla, Takwish; Juaneño, Takwich ("Tacuieh").

[1] Occurs, but name unrecorded.   [2] Lacking.

The name Chungichnish did not enter the Diegueño idiom. While it is difficult to believe that they took over the ritual without the least knowledge of the associated deity, such knowledge can not have been profound, since there is no trace of it in the available myths. The Diegueño call the Chungichnish practices simply *awik*, " western."

Being recent among them, this cult has not invaded all rites to the same extent as among the Luiseño. The girls' adolescence ceremony, for instance, is totally free from Chungichnish coloring, and must be regarded as belonging to an older stratum of religion, although not necessarily an originally Diegueño one, since the Diegueño elements of this rite recur among the Luiseño plus Chungichnish additions. The adolescence ceremony, in fact, seems to have been worked out and to have spread over the entire coastward part of southern California so long ago that it became wholly naturalized among each group with a nearly uniform character.

Apart from the stronger hold of the Chungichnish cultus among the Luiseño, the two peoples differ definitely in religious outlook. This diversity has been noted by all careful observers, and is the more marked because of the close similarity of the concrete elements making up the two religions and the practical identity of the cultures on their material and economic side. The Luiseño are mystics, crude but earnest. The Diegueño are left untouched by the abstruse. The actual—picturesque or decorative but either visible or tangible—is what interests them. The sacred order of births of the essences of things does not occur in their narrow cosmogony. The dying god Wiyot, representative of humanity, is slighted in their traditions for the sea serpent that was beheaded, the wonder-working boy Chaup, the blind brother of the creator, or other individuals remarkable only for their peculiarities of magic. The relation of the two mythologies, with reference to those of all southern California, is discussed in detail in the chapter on the Yuma. No trace of the Luiseño esoteric system of double terms for all sacred objects or concepts has been found among even the most immediately contiguous Diegueño. The sand paintings of the two peoples have already been described as perceptibly different workings out of a single idea.

In some measure these differences may be due to the Diegueño having been subject to an eastern influence from their Yuman kinsmen of the lower Colorado River, from which the Luiseño were guarded by the intervening Cahuilla. This influence undoubtedly existed. Its spring was probably in large measure the Mohave nation; but wherever it originated, it was chiefly transmitted to the Diegueño proper by the Yuma and Kamia. As between the river tribes and the Diegueño, there is no doubt that the current flowed from the former to the latter.

The effects of this stimulation or borrowing are visible at several points. The Diegueño, in the mythic basis of part of their ritual, make much of the sacred mountain of the Mohave, Avikwame, which they called Wikami, although sometimes they relocate it at a lower peak near Yuma. They sing song cycles admitted by the Mohave as equivalent to their own, in part as identical. *Orup* and *Tutomunp* songs phonographed among the southern Diegueño have been promptly recognized and correctly named by the Mohave. Whether they would have similarly known Luiseño songs of *Temenganesh, Pïmukvul*, or *Nokwanish* is very doubtful. The Diegueño mourning rite with images is called *Keruk*—it is said after the name of the booth which is burned at the climax. The Yuma also consume a shade at their anniversary and call one of the two kinds of songs in the rite *Karu'uka*. That the Luiseño, whose speech is radically diverse, do not know this name, proves nothing; but it is significant that they are not mentioned as burning any structure. More intimate knowledge may bring to light hundreds of other points of contact.

It is extremely desirable, in this connection, that something intimate may yet be ascertained as to the religion of the Cahuilla. In origin, they are one with the Luiseño and Gabrielino. Their position is such that they may well have received ritual influence from the river tribes to the same degree as the Diegueño. The Mohave speak of the Cahuilla cults in terms of their own; but this may be because they themselves, situated at the center of an area of religious dispersion, know no other rites. The Diegueño refer to the Cahuilla as if in their beliefs and practices they were one with the Luiseño. Yet this may indicate nothing much more than that they recognized the Cahuilla and Luiseño as allied nations distinct from themselves. Moreover, the Mohave have in mind the Cahuilla of the desert, the Diegueño probably those of the mountains, immediate neighbors and associates of the Luiseño. We, on the other hand, are so little informed about the Cahuilla that we do not know positively how far the respective influences of Avikwame and Chungichnish prevailed among them.

A complete list of the known song series or cycles of the southern Diegueño is included in a comparative discussion in the chapter on the Yuma (Table 8).

As to the Diegueño, once more, a distinct eastern and Yuman importation can accordingly be recognized in their religion in addition to a more recent northwestern and Shoshonean one. When both are accounted for, we are face to face with a native Diegueño

basis. But how much of this is original Diegueño it is impossible
to say. Its outstanding elements—the girls' rite with its roasting,
the use of toloache in some way, the mourning anniversary with
images, the stringing of songs into cycles or classes, a type of cosmogony—are all common to an array of tribes, stretching in some
cases into central California and in others into Arizona. There is
nothing to suggest that the Diegueño were especially prominent or
creative among this group of nations. We may rather conclude
from their marginal position, with the unnavigable sea at their back
and the extremely poor and hard-pressed peoples of Baja California
on their right hand, that, other things equal, they received more
often than they gave; and, as one people among many, conditions
were far from equal. Most of the substratum even of their religion,
then, is likely to have had its ultimate devising in the hands of
other nations; and all that we can point to as specifically Diegueño
in source are the superficial details peculiar to them. Fuller knowledge will no doubt add to the number of these, but, on the other
hand, is also certain to reduce the number at other points as it un-
covers the presence of this or that trait, as yet recorded only for
the Diegueño, among their neighbors also.

The following are the principal of these peculiarities:

The Diegueño girls' ceremony being free of the Chungichnish atmosphere, and therefore containing more magic and less religion,
refers primarily to the girls' physiological well-being during life,
whereas the Luiseño, having more nearly equated the ceremony
with that for boys, make of it almost an initiation into a cult, with
sermons over the sand painting, an ordeal of retaining swallowed
tobacco, foot racing, and painting of rocks by the candidate. In
place of these features, the Diegueño use the *atulku*, a large crescentic stone, heated and placed between the girls' legs to soften the
abdominal tissues and render motherhood easy and safe. These
stones have been spoken of as sacred. No doubt they were. But
their use was a practical one, in native opinion, not symbolical or
esoteric.

Cremation among the Diegueño was followed by a gathering of the
ashes, which, placed in a jar of pottery, were buried or hidden among
remote rocks. The apparel of the dead person was saved for the
clothes-burning ceremony, but no mention is made of the preliminary
rite of washing called *Tuvish* by the Luiseño.

The image ceremony begins with a night of wailing. On the six
succeeding nights the images are marched around the fire and dancing and singing continue until morning. The figures are of mats
stuffed with grass, the features indicated in haliotis shell. The faces
of those representing men are painted black, of women, red. On

the last of the six nights, at daybreak, the images, together with a great quantity of property, are put into the *keruk*, a small semi-circular house of brush open to the east in which the images have previously been stored, and the whole is burned to a song "Goes *katomi* to your house." *Katomi* may denote essence, or spirit; the meaning is not certainly known. The purpose of the rite is said to be to keep the dead content, prevent their return, and assuage the grief of the survivors, who at once cease mourning.

The Diegueño danced and raced for the revival of the moon toward the end of its waning; the Juaneño when it was new; for the Luiseño, both periods are mentioned.

The Diegueño keep or don their ceremonial paraphernalia in a "house" or enclosure called *kwusich-ny-awa*. The meaning of this term is not known but *kwusich* recalls *kwasiyai*, shaman, and *awa* is house. It is not recorded whether the *kwusich-ny-awa* was a special religious structure or a living house temporarily set apart for sacred purposes. It may have been nothing but a small brush fence such as the Luiseño built near the main *wamkish*.

East is the primary ceremonial direction to the Diegueño, as north is to the Luiseño and usually to the Mohave. The ceremonial enclosures open in these directions, but both Diegueño and Luiseño occasionally state the entrance to have been on the side characteristic of the other tribe.

The Diegueño are the only tribe in California as yet known to possess a system of color-direction symbolism. This is: East, white; south, green-blue; west, black; north, red. It is interesting that there is little if any idea of a circuit of the directions or fixed sequence of the colors, as in the Southwest. The Diegueño thinks of two pairs of directions, each with its balance of colors, white-black or red-blue. If he falters, which is not infrequently, the confusion is within the pair.

From this directional symbolism it might be inferred that the ceremonial number of the Diegueño was four, as it is to a very marked degree among the Mohave and Yuma. This, however, is true chiefly of Diegueño mythology; and it may be remarked that the color symbolism has so far been found only in traditions. In ritual, things are done three times, or six times in a pair of threes, almost always; four is rare, five and seven do not occur. This conflict is rather remarkable and seems very un-Indian. It has an analogue in an indeterminateness of sacred number among the Luiseño, where three and four both occur, but the feeling for number seems curiously deficient. With the Juaneño, five rather looms up, but there is no certainty. With the Gabrielino, 4 and its multiple 8 secure primacy once more; but there is also a tendency toward 6 and 12, and perhaps 7, which in turn prevail among the Serrano and Yokuts.

SHAMANISM.

The shaman, *kwasiyai*, is said by the Diegueño to have been born
as such. He may have owned guardian spirits, but information to
this effect is very vague. There were bear doctors as well as shamans
who could turn themselves into eagles. The weather maker was
called *kwamyarp*.

Curing was effected by sucking blood or the disease object, either
with the mouth or through a pipe; by kneading and pressing; and
by blowing tobacco smoke. Suspected shamans were done away
with.

CALENDAR.

The Diegueño calendar had six named divisions and no more,
which have been independently recorded twice.

Season.	Weather.	First count.	Second count.
November	cold	ilya–kwetl	
December	snow	heha–nimsup	namasap (white).
January	cold	hatai	tai.
February	rain	heha–psu	pswi, kwurh.
March	rain	hatya–matinya	matanai.
April	growth	ihy–anidja	anaha.

Kwurh of the second count may possibly stand for *-kwetl* of the
first and have been misplaced.

The round of six was gone through twice each year. Although the
month names refer to wintry phenomena, they were repeated in
summer. That the divisions were lunar is shown by the fact that
the names in the second list were obtained with the prefix *hatlya*,
"moon."

The Diegueño reckoning is an exact duplicate of the Zuñi calendar,
except for appearing not to begin at the solstices. This default may
be an error, or due to an imperfect adjustment. The Luiseño and
Juaneño calendar was almost certainly based on the solstices, and
the annual repetition of the Diegueño count very strongly suggests
a primary recognition of two fixed points within the year; and these
can hardly have been any events other than the solstices. The Zuñi-
Diegueño reckoning flows more evenly for short periods than the
Juaneño-Luiseño system of combining four or five months with two
longer solstitial periods; but after each few years it must require
a violent wrench to readjust it. The Juaneño plan seems rather more
advanced in that it has departed farther from a mere seasonal year
divided by lunations toward a true solar year.

SOCIETY.

The Diegueño were divided into exogamous patrilineal clans. Their system, like that of the Luiseño, is, however, a vestigial or rudimentary one, evidently because they were situated at the edge of the Californian area of clans. The totemic moieties of more northerly nations are lacking. So are the totemic names of the cognate Yuman tribes to the east. The clans are definitely associated with localities in the native mind. Their names, so far as translatable, give the impression of being place names, perhaps of narrowly limited spots. Married women went to live with their husbands' people. The following are the known clans. There were undoubtedly others:

Northern Diegueño " clans."

Matuwir ("hard"), south of Mesa Grande.
Shrichak ("an owl"), at Pamo in winter, Mesa Grande in summer.
U'u ("an owl"), at Pamo and Mesa Grande.
Kwitlp, at Pamo and Mesa Grande.
Hesitl ("manzanita"), at Tauwi, San Jose, on Warner's ranch, adjoining the Cupeño.
Paipa, at Santa Ysabel.
Esun, at Santa Ysabel.
Kwaha ("estafiate"), at Santa Ysabel.
Hipuwach, at Santa Ysabel.
Tumau ("grasshopper"), now at Capitan Grande, formerly at Mesa Grande, Santa Ysabel, and elsewhere. Reckoned as distinct from the Tumau clan of the southern Diegueño.
Kukuro ("dark, shady"), now at Mesa Grande, formerly at Mission San Diego and Tiajuana, original location uncertain.
Lachapa (short?), location uncertain.

Southern Diegueño " clans."

Kwitak, at Campo.
Nahwach, at Miskwatnuk, north of Campo.
Yachap, at Hakisap, northeast of Campo.
Hitlmawa, at Snauyaka, Manzanita.
Kwamai ("wishing to be tall"), at Pilyakai, near La Posta.
Saikul, at Matajuai.
Kwatl ("hide"), at Hakwaskwak, in Jacumba Valley.
Hetmiel, at Hakwasik, east of Tecate Divide below Jacumba Valley on American soil; now near Campo.
Kanihich or *Kwinhich*, in southwestern Imperial Valley; now at Campo.
Hayipa, at Hakwino, Cameron Lake, in southwestern Imperial Valley.
Hakisput, at Hachupai in Imperial Valley.
Tumau ("grasshopper"), near Brawley in Imperial Valley; now among the Yuma.
Miskwis, location unknown.

These locations tend to connect the southern Diegueño with the nonfarming division of the elusive Kamia. ·That Imperial Valley was owned by a group called Kamia is clear; whether these were more nearly allied to the agricultural totemic Kamia on the Colorado or to the hunting, nontotemic Kamiai or "southern Diegueño" of the mountains of San Diego County is less certain.

The southern Diegueño having been less disturbed by civilization, their list probably represents the aboriginal status more closely. From this it would appear that each "clan" owned a tract and that each locality was inhabited by members of one clan, plus their introduced wives. The *kwaipai* or chief of the clan had direction of ceremonies, which were largely or wholly made by clans as such. This is a gentile system reduced to a skeleton; the only unquestionable clan attribute is the exogamy. Patrilinear descent proves nothing, since the wholly ungentile tribes of California reckon and inherit in the male line. It is not unlikely that the scheme had its origin in pure village communities or small political groups among whom a prevalent exogamy hardened into a prescription, while the name of one of a number of spots in their habitat became generally accepted as their appellation. Only a slight readjustment in these directions would be required to convert the Yurok villages, the Pomo communities, or the Yokuts tribes into "clans." In short, it is doubtful whether the term clan is applicable.[1]

The northern Diegueño data suggest a more definitely social system. Pamo had a chief (*kwaipai*) for the village or community as well as for each clan living there, besides *koreau* or assistant chiefs in the clans. But the northern Diegueño were shuffled into the mission and mission stations and out again after secularization, and it would be venturesome to draw inferences from statements that may refer to conditions either 50 or 150 years old.

The Diegueño word for clan is *simus*, which may be from a Yuman stem meaning "name."

CUSTOMS.

The semicouvade was practiced by Diegueño and Luiseño alike. For a month after a birth father and mother alike did no avoidable

---

[1] Spier (see bibliography) lists the following southern Diegueño clans: Kwaha, Waipuk ("kingsnake"), Huhlwa ("twined basket"), Oswai, Illich ("worthless"), Kalyarp ("butterfly"), Hotum ("drum"—an object learned from the Spaniards), Kwainyitl ("black"), Paipa, Nihkai; plus several previously recorded: Tuman, Lyacharp, Neeihhawach, Hitlmiarp, Kwatl, Kwitark, Kwamai, Miskwis, Kwinehich, Hitlmawa, Saikur. A map gives their situations, which seem to be their summer haunts, hunted and gathered over from spring to autumn. Winter was spent in mixed groups in the eastern foothills, at the desert's edge. Clans sometimes fought; they owned eyries and most food products of their tract, but not acorns. Local exogamy was normal but not studied; there was no preferential marriage between clans; residence after marriage was patrilocal. Clans seem to have been without totemic associations. Each had a chief, the office being generally hereditary, but with some selection among heirs by the people. The principal functions of the chief were to admonish and to hold the mourning ceremony; his necessary qualification, generosity. Other than their names, there is little in all this to mark the "clans" as being more than local bands or miniature "tribes" of the usual Californian type.

work, shunned exposure, and refrained from meat and salt—the usual food taboos of the region.

The umbilical cord, after severing, was coiled on the infant's abdomen. After it fell off, it was carefully buried. This is also a Luiseño custom.

Suicide by jealous women is said to have been not rare.

The entire scalp, including the ears, was cut from fallen foes and preserved. The event was celebrated in a night of dancing by men and women in the ceremonial inclosure. It is said that the dancers took turns at setting the scalp on their own heads.

The standard game of the Diegueño is guessing, *homarp*, Spanish peon, played as by the Luiseño. The hoop and poles have gone out of use. Women's dice are of Mohave type: four little boards, painted or burned. These are said to be in use only among the southern division, and to be a " Mohave " importation.

DRESS.

Men went naked. A braided girdle of agave fiber evidently served for carrying and not to support a breechclout. Women's wear was the usual two-piece petticoat. The hinder garment, *teparau*, was of willow bark; the front apron, of the same material or of close strings, perhaps partly braided or netted. The footgear, which was worn only on rough or thorny ground, was a sandal of agave fiber, cushioned to the thickness of a half inch or more.

Both sexes wore their hair long. The men bunched it on their crowns. The women allowed it to hang loose, but trimmed the front at the eyebrows, and often set on their heads a coiled basketry cap.

Tattooing, *ukwich*, was somewhat random and variable. Women bore more designs than men, as a rule, and two or three vertical lines on the chin were the commonest pattern, but forehead, cheeks, arms, and breast were not exempt. Women were tattooed in connection with the adolescence ceremony. A cactus thorn pricked charcoal into the skin.

HOUSES.

The house in the mountains, and apparently on the coast also, was earth covered. Three posts, planted in a row, were connected by a short ridge log, on which poles were then leaned from the sides. A layer of *hiwat* brush kept the superimposed soil from sifting or washing in. The door was not oriented. The elliptical outline, sharp roof, and absence of walls approximate this structure to the Luiseño and Cahuilla house; but the regular roofing with earth, exacted by neither the mild climate of the coast nor the heat of the desert edge, points to an influence of the cognate tribes on the Colorado River.

The sweat house, *tawip*, is described as smaller but higher than the dwelling. Its center rested on four posts set in a square. The roof was like that of the living house. The fire was between the posts and the door. Men sweated regularly in the evening; women did not enter at any time. This is the farthest known occurrence of the typical Californian sweat house; the Mohave and Yuma did not know any device of the kind.

Wells, *setlmehwatl*, were dug with sticks. Like the Cahuilla, the Diegueño declare this to have been a practice of the pre-Spanish days. Permanent springs are not numerous on the eastern slope of the mountains.

FOOD, ARTS, AND IMPLEMENTS.

About San Diego Bay fish and mollusks formed the basis of subsistence. Inland the range of food was similar to that of the mountain Luiseño and Cahuilla. Toward the desert baked " mescal," *amatl*, looms up as a staple. In spite of their affinity to the farming Kamia, the Diegueño never attempted the practice of agriculture.

The mortar was that of the Luiseño, but usually made in a smaller bowlder, and often sunk into the ground. The bed-rock mortar was also known.

The same pottery is made by the Diegueño as by their neighbors. A reddish clay is mixed with finely crushed rock, coiled, shaped with a stone and a wooden paddle called *hiatltut*, and fired. Nowadays it is usually unornamented. Formerly patterns were customary, it is said; but this seems doubtful. Cook pots and water jars are the common forms. Bowls and plates of clay seem to be largely replaced by baskets.

Basketry is of the type general in southern California; but in addition a variety of soft textiles in basket shape, close-twined sacks or wallets, were made of string materials, especially milkweed. These are unparalleled in California except for some ancient specimens found in the southern San Joaquin Valley (Pl. 63), and for somewhat similar wares made by the Mohave and Yuma, but executed to-day in civilized materials and coarsened technique.

The war club, *hitlchahwai*, was of heavy mesquite wood, and of typical southwestern form, that is, with a cylindrical enlargement at the head.

String was either red or white, apparently as it was made of milkweed, *hotl*, or yucca, *pyatl*. Heavier cordage, and the burden net, *katari*, were usually of yucca.

Carrying nets and sacks are made in the " bowline on a bight " stitch among the northern Diegueño, with the double loop or square knot among the southern Diegueño. This is but another of several indications that the two groups were further cleft in culture than their similarity of dialect and inclusion under a common Spanish name would indicate.

On San Diego Bay tule balsas were used; perhaps canoes also. The paddles were double bladed, as among the Chumash.

What appear to be olivella or other small univalve shells were dug out of the ground in the eastern desert and made into necklaces by the interior Diegueño. They were called *ahchitl*. These may have been living shells in the banks of New River, but are more likely to have been ancient remains from former lake beds or overflowed districts in the region below sea level.

Pipes, *mukwin*, were 6 or 8 inches long, tubular, and either of stone or of pottery. The former may be presumed to have been used in religion, the latter for every-day smoking. The Mohave also make pipes of clay, but they are much shorter. A pipe of cane is also mentioned by the Diegueño.

Like all the tribes of southern California, the Diegueño had no drum. The rattle was a gourd or turtle shell, both of which were called *ahnatl*. The gourd is probably recent. A deer-hoof rattle was used in the mourning anniversary.[2]

THE KAMIA.

The Kamia, Kamya, Comeya, or Quemaya are a Yuman tribe between San Diego and the lower Colorado whose identity is not altogether clear, while their territory is even more doubtful.

These are the facts about them.

In 1775 the Quemaya were said by Garcés to live in the mountains from about the latitude of the south end of Salton Sea to San Diego, to eat mescal like a hunting group, but to visit the lower Colorado River for agricultural food. Hardy in 1826 described the Axua (ahwe, "foreign") as on the Colorado,

---

[2] Spier (see bibliography) has recently added important notes on the southern Diegueño. There are no bear or weather shamans, though both are known from northern neighbors. The Jimson-weed initiation is made by a "clan," viz, the people of a locality, mostly of one clan; members of any clan are included among the initiates. The ceremony is simple: The ground painting contains no figures of animals; the net figure (Luiseño *wanawut*) is not used; the whirling dance (*tipkwirp*) is not made; the fire ceremony is made after the Jimson-weed drinking. There is no clothes-burning ceremony separate from the image ceremony. Wild plums are pounded, leached, and cooked like acorns. The metate is often unsquared, its hollow oval. Rabbits are netted; small rodents taken in a stone deadfall baited with an acorn; snares are not used. Houses are for winter use only, gabled with a ridgepole in two forked posts, and covered with earth. The flat-roofed shade is not built. The diagonally twined cap is said to be for women, the coiled cap for men. Good blankets contain an average of 20 jack-rabbit or 40 cottontail skins. They serve mainly as bedding, but are also worn as ponchos. Trees are felled by fire, wedges not used. Cord is of mescal, milkweed, or human hair, not of yucca, nettle, or reed. The old rattle was of deer hoofs or clay, gourds being a Mohave importation, and turtle shells not used. Sinew-backing of the bow is known as a Chemehuevi trait. Soapstone arrow straighteners are preferable to clay ones. Arrowheads of stone are for large game only. Clubs were curved or spiked, not cylinder headed. The "moons" of the year have six names only, repeated, and seem to denote seasons rather than lunations. Other recent papers on the Diegueño, by G. G. Heye and E. H. Davis, are also cited in the bibliography.

above the mouth of the Gila, fishing and farming. Whipple in 1849 distinguished
the Comaiyah from the Yuma or Kwichyana and put them on New River near
Salton Sea. The modern Yuma know the eastern or "southern" Diegueño,
as they have been called in the present work, as Kamya, and appear to include the western or "northern Diegueño" with the Shoshonean Cahuilla under
the designation Hakwichya. The Mohave distinguished between the Kamia,
and the Kamia ahwe or foreign, strange Kamia, whose dialects, habits, and
territory were distinct. The Kamia they describe as farmers, and as living
on the Colorado below the Yuma, but wholly on the west side; which may mean
that they ranged considerably back from the river. The Kamia ahwe they
identify with the Diegueño, state that they did not farm, but ate snakes and
other strange foods, and place them in the mountains that run south of San
Jacinto Peak. Alone of all the Yuman tribes, they did not travel or visit—
hence their name as "foreign" people; and captive women from them made
no attempts to escape.

This evidence points to a group that held the New River district,
the depressed desert valley—anciently an arm of the Gulf of California extending over most of Cahuilla territory also—that slopes
from the lowest course of the Colorado northwest to the sink, nearly
300 feet below sea level, called Salton Sea, which is at irregular times
dry and flooded. The people in this area, particularly in its southern
or Baja California part, would naturally have had an outlet toward the
great river; and may have had a foothold, perhaps even their main
seats, on its nearer bank. These people are here identified as probably the Kamia. Their chief residence must have been across the
line in Mexican California; on the map they have been given the
tract between Diegueño, Yuma, Cahuilla, and the international
boundary. (Pl. 1.)

The old ownership of this stretch, which forms part of the Colo
rado Desert and was formerly as utterly arid as portions of it are
fertile under irrigation at present, is, however, by no means estab
lished. Although likely to have been only seasonally inhabited, and
in any event harboring only the slenderest population, it must nevertheless have belonged to some group. Yet what this group was
remains open to some doubt. It was not the northern Diegueño,
who, by the common account of themselves, the Yuma, and the
Mohave, did not own beyond the eastern foot of the mountains. It
was not the Cahuilla, who profess to have reached south only to
Salton Sea or at most a little beyond its farther end. It may have
been the Yuma, who sometimes claimed eastward to the Diegueño,
and who may have visited the desert for one purpose or another,
though they certainly never lived in it. In favor of this supposition
is the fact that the northern Diegueño, little as they know of the
Yuma, place no other group between them and themselves. On the
other hand, there undoubtedly was a Kamia tribe with its distinctive dialect and a range on New River as well as on the nearer side
of the lowest Colorado.

It is also possible that the owners of what is given as Kamia territory on the map and the southern Diegueño of Campo, Manzanita, and Jacumba, are the same people. These "southern Diegueño" are really southeastern and might just as correctly have been called "eastern." They call themselves Kamiai or Kamiyahi. Their situation on the map of the American State is such that they give the impression of being but the spur of a group that lives mainly in Mexican territory. From what is known of their customs, they are in fairly close affiliation with the Colorado River tribes, and under their religious influence, to nearly the same degree as the northern Diegueño cults have been shaped by the Shoshoneans beyond. All this agrees splendidly with the Yuma terminology: Kamya for the eastern Diegueño, Hakwichya for the western Diegueño together with the Shoshonean Cahuilla, to whom alone it properly refers. The application of the name Diegueño to both the southern-eastern and the northern-western group proves nothing, since it is of Spanish origin and indicative of mission affiliation, with only a secondary ethnic significance. In any event it is balanced by the similar Mohave terms for the Kamia and the Diegueño.

It may be added that the modern Diegueño of the "southern" branch voice some claim to a former ownership of the Imperial Valley. There are individuals among them who were born, or whose parents were born, in this valley, and along the eastern foot of the mountains in a latitude where these mountains belong to the northern Diegueño.

All this looks as if the southern Diegueño Kamia and the Colorado River Kamia south of the Yuma might have been a single people that stretched across the greater part of the State at its southern end and in Mexican California. The difficulty, however, is to accept as a single nation a group which at one end farmed, was divided into totemic clans, and closely resembled the Yuma in all customs, and at the opposite end of its territory was nonagricultural, nontotemic, and so similar to the northern Diegueño that it has been usually considered a part of the latter.

Enough of speculation, however. Knowledge is so scant that a certain amount of conjecture is admissible. But what is really desirable is information, which can undoubtedly still be secured, especially in Baja California. And with that statement we must leave the Kamia.

CHAPTER 50.

THE MOHAVE: CONCRETE LIFE.

HABITAT AND OUTLOOK.

With the Mohave, the third Yuman tribe to be considered, we reach for the first time a people living on a large river. The Colorado is one of the great streams of the continent, voluminous, and far longer than any within the boundaries of California. From the Mohave to its mouth its shores were occupied by a line of Yuman tribes, similar in speech, in habits, in appearance, and in disposition. This enormous Nile, flowing through narrow bottom lands bordered sharply by sandy stretches, high mesa rims, and barren mountains rising on both sides from an utterly arid desert, provides a setting wholly unlike any heretofore encountered. And its civilization is equally distinct.

The country of the Mohave is the valley which bears their name, the uppermost of a number that stretch at intervals to the sea. Above is the great defile known as Eldorado Canyon, visited now and then by Chemehuevi and Walapai, who lived above it on west and east, but unfit for habitation; and beyond comes a bend and the vast gorge that culminates in the Grand Canyon. The river civilization thus comes to a sudden upstream stop with the Mohave.

Their valley lies in what is now three States: California, Nevada, and Arizona. As the channel has flowed in recent years, most of the bottom lands lie on the eastern side; and there the bulk of the settlements were. But the land is so shut in by the high desert and so dependent on the river that it is an inevitable unit. East and west, the left bank and the right, are incidental. The stream course is a furrow that separates Arizona from California, as culturally it divides the Southwest from California; and whoever lived in the trench belonged as much, and as little, to one area as to the other.

Cottonwood Island, above Fort Mohave, was but intermittently inhabited by the Mohave. The same is true, perhaps in even greater measure, of Chemehuevi Valley below them. After the Mohave drove the Halchidhoma out of the country about Parker and below, the Chemehuevi began to drift into the valley now named after them. The Mohave probably maintained some claim to the land, although they did not use it; for they tell that they came in numbers, and by persuasion or compulsion induced the Chemehuevi to remove to Cottonwood Island at their northern limit. Here Chemehuevi and Mohave lived more or less together until about 1867, when, war breaking out between them, these Mohave outposts felt it safest to rejoin their main body below, just as certain Chemehuevi who had reoccupied Chemehuevi Valley fled from it back to the desert from which they had come. The most frequent references of the Mohave to their habitations are to the vicinity of Fort Mohave; but they lived down to the lower end of Mohave Valley, where the river enters the narrow gorge above which rise the jagged peaks known as the Needles.

For every people hitherto mentioned in this book a list of towns or villages has had some significance. When such information has not been given, ignorance has been the sole cause. The settlement is the political and social basis of life in California. The tribe, at least as a larger unit, exists hardly or not at all. The reverse is the case with the Mohave. They think in terms of themselves as a national entity, the *Hamakhava*. They think also of their land as a country, and of its numberless places. They do not think of its settlements. Where a man is born or lives is like the circumstance of a street number among ourselves, not part of the fabric of his career. The man stands in relation to the group as a whole, and this group owns a certain tract rich in associations; but the village does not enter into the scheme. In fact, the Mohave were the opposite of clannish in their inclinations. Their settlements were small, scattering, and perhaps often occupied only for short times; the people all mixed freely with one another.

With such proclivities, it is small wonder that the petty Californian feuds of locality and inherited revenge have given way among the Mohave to a military spirit, under which the tribe acted as a unit in offensive and defensive enterprise. Tribes hundreds of miles away were attacked and raided. Visits carried parties of Mohave as far as the Chumash and Yokuts. Sheer curiosity was their main motive; for the Mohave were little interested in trade. They liked to see lands; timidity did not discourage them; and they were as eager to know the manners of other peoples as they were careful to hold aloof from adopting them.

These journeyings brought with them friendships and alliances as well as enmities. The Mohave were consistently leagued with the Yuma against the Halchidhoma and Maricopa and Kohuana and Cocopa; and these belligerencies led them into hostile or amicable relations with people with whom they had but few direct contacts.

Thus the Pima and Papago, the friends of the Maricopa, became normal foes, the Yavapai and western Apache nominal friends. Against tribes of the desert and mountains the Mohave carried on few wars. Perhaps the nomads were too elusive. On the other hand, reciprocal raids into a valley thickly settled by an aggressive people thirsting for adventure and glory did not appeal to the scattered mountaineers. Thus the Chemehuevi and Mohave got along well. The Mohave constantly traversed the Chemehuevi territory that began at the western border of their own valley; and the smaller and wilder people came to be profoundly influenced by the more dominant one, as has already been recounted.

APPEARANCE.

The Mohave men are tall, long footed and limbed, large boned, and spare. The common California tendency toward obesity is rare. Their carriage is loose, slouching at times and rapid at others. They lack the graceful dignity of the Pueblo and the sedate stateliness of the Plains warrior, but are imposing to look at. In walking, they are apt to stoop and drag, but break readily into an easy trot in which they travel interminably. The women have the usual Indian inclination toward stoutness after they have borne several children, and in comparison with the men seem dumpy, but carry themselves very erect and with a pleasingly free and even gait. The color of both sexes is distinctly yellowish—as often appears in the women when they wash—but ordinarily is turned a very dark brown by dirt and exposure to the sun. (Pls. 64, 65.)

Mohave men sit with their thighs on their calves and heels, or with legs bent to one side on the ground. These are women's fashions among the Indians of the western Plains. Women at rest stretch their legs straight out, and sometimes cross their feet. This is Pueblo style, but a most indecent position for a woman among the majority of American Indians. At work, a Mohave woman tucks one leg under her, with her other knee up. This is a common female attitude in California, and convenient for certain kinds of sedentary work. When she pleases, the Mohave woman also sits with her legs folded in oriental style—the normal attitude of Navaho and Plains men. Dress may have had much influence in determining the adoption of some of these styles. Thus the " Turk position " is easily taken in the loose fiber petticoat of California, but is awkward or likely to lead to exposure in the rather long gown of unyielding buckskin worn by the eastern women. But factors other than fashion of garment have certainly been operative, particularly for men. This is one of the most interesting matters in the whole range of customs. and further knowledge for California is a great desideratum.

A very frequent Mohave gesture, apparently of embarrassment, is the quick placing of the hand over the mouth. Men especially seem addicted to this movement.

In many individuals the fingers habitually hang straight, except for a sharp bend at the farthest joint, which gives the hand a curious effect as of the legs of a crab.

Men wore, and sometimes still wear, their hair long, rolled or rather pasted into 20 or 30 ropes of about the thickness of a lead pencil. The greater the mass of these strands hanging down the back to the hip, the prouder the owner. The women trim the hair square above the eyes and let the remainder flow free, spread out over the shoulders. In mourning they cut it a little below the ears; the men clip a trifle from the ends. The hair is sometimes tied up in clay mixed with mesquite gum, to stain it black and glossy; or plain clay is allowed to dry on it in a complete casing and left for a day or two, in order to suppress parasites. As the nits survive and hatch out, the treatment requires frequent repetition.

The Mohave tattoo somewhat irregularly, although their own saying is that an untattooed person goes into a rat's hole at death instead of the proper place for spirits—as the Yahi pierce their ears with a similar purpose. Another account is that the ghosts are asked to point to the pole star, *umasakahava*, which in their new country is south; if they point northward, the rat's hole is their fate. Both sexes most commonly mark lines or rows of dots down the chin, and may add a little circle, a stripe, or a few spots on the forehead. The men are the more sparsely ornamented. Women sometimes draw a few lines across the cheeks or on the forearms. The absence of any standardized style is notable. (Fig. 46.)

The Mohave paint the face far more frequently and effectively than other California Indians. Young women in particular hardly appear at a gathering or public occasion without striking red or yellow patterns across the cheeks. Forking lines are drawn downward from the eyes, or a band passes squarely across the cheeks, and the like. The style is obviously kindred to that followed by the Seri, though not quite so inclined to fineness of execution. (Figs. 60, 61, 62.)

DISPOSITION.

The Mohave are noticeably more responsive and energetic than the other Indians of California. They are an obstinate people—amiably so, but totally unable to see anything but their own view once this has set. They are rarely sullen; although they sometimes

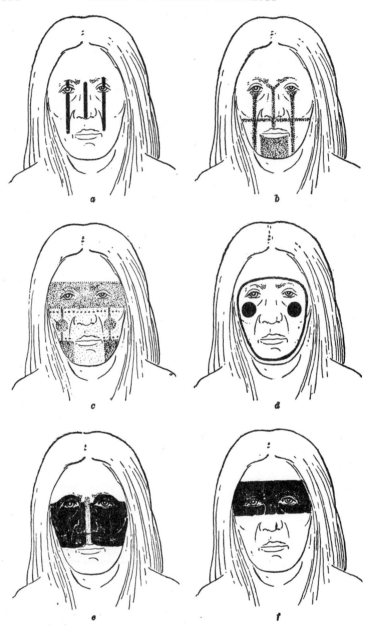

Fig. 60.—Face paints: Mohave men. *a*, Ha'avkek; *b*, "cut"; *c*, modern; *d*, for male twin; *e*, for elderly man; *f*, "lie at back of house," for old man. (Heavy and light stippling indicate red and yellow, respectively.)

sulk like children, they are more given to outbursts of temper. The women scold freely on occasion. The Californian trick of eating in a grievance is foreign to them. Ordinarily they are idle minded and therefore readily persuaded, until some prejudice is stirred. Then they become immovable, although usually without resentment. Normally they are frank, inquisitive, and inclined to be confiding. They are untidy, careless of property, and spend money freely, like eastern Indians. Only the old women evince some disposition to hoard for their funerals.

The slow, steady labor to which the Californian and the Pueblo are inclined is rarely seen among the Mohave. They either lounge in complete relaxation or plunge into sudden and strenuous activity. No physical exertion is too great for them. They make valuable laborers, except that they are rarely dependable for long periods. When they have enough, nothing can hold them to the job. In their own affairs, such as house building and farming, they often work with a veritable fury, and even when hired do not spare themselves. They eat voraciously, but endure hunger without trace of complaint. The demeanor of the men in repose has a certain reserve, as befits a people that fought for pleasure, but they unbend readily, talk volubly, and laugh freely. Jokes are greeted uproariously. All ages and sexes demonstrate their feelings openly. Young men may be seen walking with their arms around each other, fathers kiss their children irrespective of who is about, girls in love manifest their sentiment in every action. There is something very winning in the instantaneousness of the generous Mohave smile. The habitual and slow-dying distrust typical of most of the California Indians does not rest on the Mohave's mind; when he suspects, he complains or accuses. The children are remarkably free from the unconquerable shyness that most Indian youngsters, in California as elsewhere, can not shake off. They often answer even a strange white man readily. Altogether it is a nation half child, half warrior, likable in its simple spontaneity, and commanding respect with its inherent manliness—as far different from the usual California native as Frenchman and Englishman stand apart.

HOUSES.

The house has a frame of logs and poles, a thatch of the arrow weed that serves so many Mohave needs, and a covering of sand. The latter blends so gradually into the surrounding soil that it is practically impossible to give outside measurements, and the old description of the domicile as dug into a sand hill is a natural mistake. The structure has a rectangular interior, and is substantially square on a line of 20 to 25 feet. The door or front is always to the

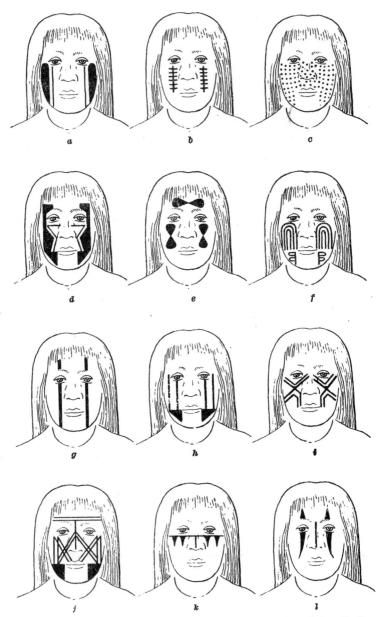

Fig. 61.—Face paints: Mohave women. a, "Rainbow"; b, "coyote teeth"; c, "yellow-hammer belly"; d, "butterfly"; e, "atalyka leaf"; f, "bent over"; g, h, hatsiratsirk; i, j, hotahpava; k, l, tatsirkatsirka. All in red or yellow.

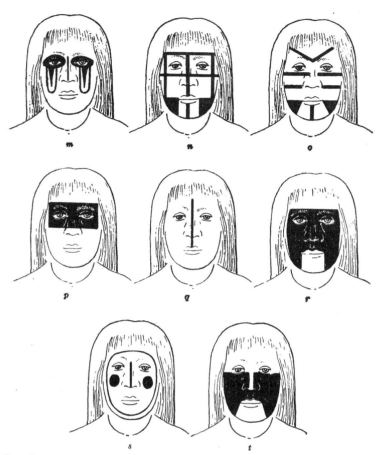

FIG. 62.—Face paints: Mohave women. *m*, "Tatsirkatsirka enclosed"; *n*, *o*, *r*, without names; *p*, "at edge of nose"; *q*, humturk; *s*, for female twin; *t*, mourning for a child. All in red or yellow except *t*, which is black.

south on account of the coldness which the frequent north wind seems to the desert dwellers to bear. (Pl. 56; Fig. 63.)

So few of the native houses of the Californians have been described accurately that the following details may not be amiss.

In the center are either four posts or two placed longitudinally, that is, in north and south line; or one; or two set transversely. The last arrangement is the commonest, but there is a name for each design. The tops of the posts are slightly hollowed, and the connecting logs laid on. The south or front wall has eight or ten posts of varying length; the back, two principal ones in the middle; the sides, about five that are still shorter. The tips of these are all connected. From the log above the center posts six or eight beams run to the back wall and an equal number forward. The latter spread into two sets of threes or fours to clear the door. From these 12 or 16 beams about 20 smaller rafters extend to each of the sides. Across these rafters sticks are laid longitudinally. The thatch in turn runs across the house. In the middle the 12 or 16 beams are directly overlaid with transverse sticks close together. In this part of the house, therefore, the sticks and the thatch run in the same direction.

The low side walls slope. About two dozen light poles are leaned against the logs that connect the five vertical posts on each side. On these leaning poles four or five long sticks are laid horizontally, and against these arrow-weed thatch is set upright, outside of which comes the banking of sand. The rear is similarly constructed. The front wall is higher, vertical, and unbanked. Sticks run across the inner as well as outer faces of its posts. In the space thus formed thatch is set and sand poured in. In the old days a mat of woven cottonwood bark closed the door at night. In front there is often a space enclosed with a windbreak of arrow weed, and almost invariably a flat shade on posts.

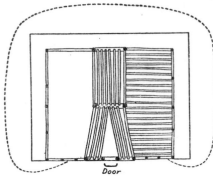

Fig. 63.—Plan of Mohave earth house.

Seen from the front, the roof is nearly level in the center, slopes about 10 degrees to the side posts, and then falls more steeply, but still at no great angle, to the ground. The profile is gently rounded, especially toward the rear, but of course terminates vertically in front. The floor is fine soft sand. (Pl. 56.)

The following are details of two houses:

Inside length to rear posts_____feet__	22	23
Inside length to base of rear wall_____do____	24	26
Inside width, side posts to side posts_____do____	22	24
Inside width, wall to wall base_____do____	24	30
Distance between 2 transversely set center posts_____do____		7
Width of door_____do____		2½
Height—center posts_____do____	6	6
middle of roof _____do____	7½	
front posts at door_____do____		5
at ends_____do____		3
back posts_____do____	4	4
side posts _____do____	3	3
door_____do____	6	6
Diameter—center posts_____inches__	10+	
door posts_____do____	10+	
2 middle rear posts_____do____	10+	
side posts_____do____	7–8	
log on center posts_____do____	12	
beams _____do____	5–9	
rafters_____do____	4–5	
Number of beams_____	12	16
Number of rafters _____	39	
Number of side posts, each side_____	5	5

The Mohave were without sweat houses. Prominent men put up large houses in which considerable groups of people slept. Such a house was the owner's dwelling; the others lived near by in smaller houses, but these were considered too cold for comfortable sleeping. The big houses can not be regarded as more than a sort of Mohave substitute for the sweat house, since women and children assembled there with the men—a quite un-Californian practice.

A prospective builder summoned his friends and kin to do the work, and fed them while they were busy on his behalf. His place, and that of his wife, was the corner west of the door. Other couples occupied the other corners. Girls slept along the walls, unmarried men in the center. Late in the afternoon a fire was built just inside the door. At night this was covered with sand. Smoke hung through the house, but above the heads of the reclining inmates. The myths frequently mention such houses as crowded with people.

AGRICULTURAL AND OTHER FOODS.

Mohave agriculture according to aboriginal methods began quickly to go into disuse after Americans settled among them, and it is already somewhat difficult to estimate the importance of the art to them. It may have furnished half their subsistence. The rainfall is too nominal to support any cultivated plant, and the Mohave seem to know nothing of irrigation. Annually, about May and June, the Colorado rises and floods large stretches of the bottom lands, sometimes to a distance of a mile or two. Sloughs from this overflow remain for months or through the year. The level tracts are left drenched and coated with soft mud. In this the Mohave plant; and under the fierce sun their produce shoots and ripens with marvelous rapidity. The relation of the tiller to his strip of fertile soil in the vast burning desert is therefore similar to that which obtained in primitive Egypt, and gives Mohave agriculture a character unique in native America.

Corn is planted irregularly, not in rows. The planter takes one long step more or less at random from his last hole and rams his stick into the ground for another hole. Half a dozen kernels are sunk from half a foot to a foot deep.

The wheat planter sits on the ground and makes holes at the limit of his reach a foot or two apart, and drops a number of seeds into each. This is, of course, a plant introduced by the Spaniards, but the Mohave regard it as indigenous.

Beans, pumpkins, watermelons, and cantaloupes were also planted by the Mohave. Their corn is usually white and long eared, but they distinguish blue, red, yellow, and spotted yellow and white varieties

also. Beans are called white, yellow, " deer droppings" (black), and
" Pleiades" (spotted). Bean-stalk fiber was a common material for
cordage.

The farming implements were two: A hard, heavy staff for planting, which is nothing but the California root-digging stick somewhat
enlarged and slightly flattened at the sharp end; and the cultivator,
a broader piece, whose square edge is pushed flat over the ground to
cut the weeds off as they sprout. The cultivator handle is usually
somewhat crooked in the plane of the working edge. (Pl. 67, *a*, *b*.)

Women perhaps did most of the farm work, but the men were not
averse to participating, and there may have been no formal division
of labor. Even in recent years an old Mohave and his wife can frequently be seen going to their patch together—he carrying an
American hoe, she preparing to pull weeds with her hands.

It is rather interesting that pottery and agriculture are definitely
associated in the Mohave mind, their myths telling how the god
Mastamho thought farmed food incomplete until vessels were provided to cook and eat it in. The Pueblo has little feeling of this sort.
Corn is to him something so basic that it was primal; the method of
causing it to flourish is his gravest concern; but he is little
interested in vessels. The Mohave thinks of both as something given
to him. Perhaps this sense is intensified by his situation among
nations that neither farm nor bake pots.

Besides the usual native American farm products, the Mohave
planted several wild herbs or grasses in their overflowed lands and
gathered the seeds. These they call *akatai*, *aksamta*, *ankithi*, and
akyesa. They are unidentified except for the last, which appears to
be a species of *Rumex*.

A larger variety of seeds were collected from plants that sprang
without cultivation after the recession of the river from certain tracts
of the bottom lands. These include *akwava*, *kupo*, *aksama*, *ham-
askwera*, *koskwaka*, and *ankika*.

The Mohave metate for corn, wheat, and beans is a rectangular
block of lava on which a cylindrical muller is rubbed back and forth.
It is therefore the Pueblo type of implement, except for not being
boxed or set into the ground. A myth describes the metate first used
by Turtle woman, in Mastamho's presence, as " rounded, not square
like the metate of to-day." The narrator may have been merely
thinking of a ruder implement, as would befit the time of beginnings;
or it is conceivable that the native Mohave metate was of the oval
Californian type, which went out of use after steel axes allowed the
readier shaping of stone. (Pl. 66.)

Mesquite beans are crushed with a stone pestle in a wooden mortar,
the hard seeds remaining whole. The meal is sometimes eaten raw,

the seeds being shaken out of it in the hand. More commonly, water is poured on the flour to extract the sugar, and then drunk off. The dough that is left is carried to the mouth in handfuls, sucked out, and replaced, to be steeped a second time before being thrown away. Sometimes the fresh dough is patted into a huge jar-shaped cake, covered with wet sand, and baked. It comes out so hard that it has to be cracked with a stone. The seeds are spat out or swallowed whole. Mesquite screw meal is baked in the same fashion.

Fresh mesquite screw bean is " cooked " by being stored in an immense pit, perhaps 15 feet across and 4 or 5 deep, lined and covered with arrow weed. From time to time water is sprinkled on the mass. After about a month the screws turn brown and very sweet.

Mesquite of both varieties formed an important part of Mohave food. Trees are said to have been owned. In other cases a bunch of arrow weeds was hung on a tree to indicate that its yield was claimed.

Long wooden pestles were also used (Pl. 67, c)—an unknown implement in the remainder of California.

Fish were taken with seines, or driven up shallow sloughs into scoops, *kwithata* (Pl. 59), as large as a canoe, that were quickly lifted up. The fish of the muddy Colorado are rather soft and unpalatable to the white man, but the Mohave caught quantities and relished them. Game is very scarce in the valley, and the Mohave rarely left their country to hunt. They can have eaten meat only occasionally. They refused to touch the turtles and lizards of which the Chemehuevi and other tribes made use.

Fish are sometimes broiled on charcoal, but more often cooked into a disintegrated stew with or without corn. The tails, heads, scales, and guts are left in, only the " gall " being taken out. Such a mess is stirred and tasted with three little rods tied together in the middle, and is scooped to the mouth with the fingers. Sometimes the viscera are removed to be cooked separately.

POTTERY AND BASKETRY.

Clay is tempered with sandstone crushed on the metate, and built up by coiling. The start of a vessel may be spiral, but its body consists of concentric rings. The paste is rolled out into a slim sausage, the length of which is roughly estimated on the vessel. It is then laid on the last coil, and any excess pinched off. It is beaten, with a light and rapid patting with a wooden paddle, against a smooth cobble held inside, and its edge finished flat by scraping between the thumb-nail and index finger. Then the next coil is added. The maker sits with the growing vessel on the thighs of her stretched legs, or with one leg flat in front of her and the other doubled under.

The paint is yellow ocher, which is put on with a little stick and burns dull red. The firing is by an open wood fire. The patterns are carelessly done and often shaky. (Pl. 68; Figs. 64, 65.)

The following are enumerated as pottery vessels:

hapurui, the water jar.

taskyena, the cook pot.

chuvava, a large cook pot, rested on three conical supports of pottery.

kam'otta, a spoon or ladle, with the handle often in the rude shape of a quail's head and hollowed to rattle. (Fig. 64.)

kayetha, a flat bowl or lipless plate. (Fig. 65.)

kakapa, an oval platter.

katela, a parcher for corn and wheat, pointed at two ends.

kayuka, an open bowl. (Fig. 64.)

The water jar is sometimes made asymmetrically and is then known as *hanemo*, "duck," from its resemblance to a swimming water bird.

kwathki seems to be the generic name for pottery.

FIG. 64.—Mohave bowl and ladle with "rain" and "fish backbone" designs.   (Cf. Pl. 68.)

Designs on vessels are named spider, rain, rainbow, fish backbone, melon markings, turtle, cottonwood leaf, coyote tooth, yellow-hammer belly, tattoo, and *hotahpam*, a style of face paint that crosses under the eye.

Mohave basketry was easily the poorest of any in California. Coiled baskets are still used in every house and their employment as drums to certain kinds of singing proves the habit to be old; but they are Chemehuevi or Maricopa trays. The Mohave made only a few flat receptacles in an irregular plain twining or open-stitch coiling (Pl. 55, *b*); fish traps or scoops in twining (Pl. 59); wicker hoods of splints for their cradles (Pl. 39, *b*); and the *kupo* carrying frame of two U-shaped sticks surrounded with thin string—a far derivation from the burden basket of California. One textile art they followed with more skill: the weaving of bags or wallets from string of bean and *akyasa* fiber, much as the Diegueño wove, it appears. At present such receptacles are made only in American yarns. Braided or woven belts with which the baby was lashed into the cradle have deteriorated similarly.

VARIOUS UTENSILS.

Now and then a stone ax made its way into the Mohave country from the Southwest, but rarely; and the implement is associated by the tribe with eastern nations. There was also no adze, and the general Californian horn wedge seems to have been unknown. Trees were not felled. If land was to be made arable, split stones were tied to handles, and with this rude tool the smaller limbs and foliage were hacked from willows. The brush was then burned about the butt to kill the tree, the stump being left standing. (Fig. 66.)

FIG. 65.—Mohave pottery bowl. Design: " Cottonwood leaf " and " rain."

The rush raft of the Mohave was a crude affair of two bundles, with about three sticks skewered through, and some lashings of willows. The material was the flat tule, *atpilya* (probably *Typha* rush), not the round stemmed *kwaľinyo* (*Scirpus lacustris*). Loose tules might be laid on top. Four to six persons could be carried, those in the middle remaining dry. The balsa was pushed with a long pole. It was made for crossing the river. If the current carried it far downstream it was easier to put a new one together than to drag the old one up against the current. The men were all good swimmers. Children were some-

FIG. 66.—Mohave fire drill.

times pushed across the river in pots a yard in diameter. These vessels were made for the purpose, being too large, the Mohave say, to utilize for cooking.

Shell currency seems to have been held only in small quantity. A horse was given for half a fathom of typical Californian disk beads—a very high valuation. Most old women wore at the throat a clam shell cut into frog shape and called simply *hanye*, frog. These also were valuable. On the whole, the Mohave appear to have used shells as jewelry rather than money; in which they resembled the southwesterners. They took to imported glass beads more eagerly than most Californians. Men as well as women coiled strands of blue and white Venetian beads in thick masses around their necks; women wound them around their wrists; and donned showy shoulder capes of a network of beads. A definite style seems to have been evolved early, which made use almost wholly of the two colors mentioned; and these, it must be admitted, match pleasingly with ˙the brown of the Mohave skin. The women's lacelike bead capes that fit snugly around the shoulders are shown in Plates 54 and 69.

GAMES.

The favored game of the Mohave was between two players, each of whom cast a long pole at a rolling hoop. The ring was thrown by the winner of the last point, and either runner was at liberty to dart his pole when he pleased. If the hoop was pierced, nothing was counted. If the ring rested on the pole with sufficient overlap that a space was visible, one point was made. Should the ring lie on the end of the pole, the score was double. If both players cast successfully, both scored. Four points won the stakes. A favorite device was to hurl one's pole between the opponent's and the hoop.

Thus the Mohave describe the game. The following record presents some discrepancies:

Two elderly men bet three dollars, as the Indians say, that is, a dollar and a half each, on a game of five points. When the score stood 2 to 1, the leader threw the tip of his pole under the ring. His opponent insisted that this was worth only 2 points, but 3 were allowed, running out the game. The players immediately bet two dollars and a half each and resumed. When the winner had scored 2 points to 3, he apparently feared to lose and quit; whereupon the new stakes of five dollars were divided in the proportion of 2 to 3.

A football race was run by two men, each with a ball of willow root.

Shinny was played with a slender curved stick and small wooden ball by "old," that is, middle aged, men, seven or eight to a side, between goal lines a third of a mile apart. Betting was public, but by individuals, the stakes being matched and deposited in pairs. The ball was put into a hole in the middle of the field, covered with soil, and trod down. Half a dozen players struck at the pit until the billet flew out. The play was fast, wild, and random, without stations or order, each contestant and many younger spectators following the ball as closely as they could. Other people stood where they pleased and stepped aside when the ball.traveled toward them. Boys pointed it out in the confusion and clouds of desert dust. The striking was clean, hard, and generally successful, the aim not so good, nursing of the ball scarcely attempted. If it entered a mesquite thicket from which it could not be struck, it was picked out and play resumed from a pit as at the start.

The guessing game was played by four men on a side, each with one piece of cane which he hid in his hand under a mat or blanket. Pointing was at one or two of the players. An umpire stood in the middle, parceled out the twelve stick counters as they were lost, held the stakes, and threatened to burn them if the contestants quarreled too violently.

Another variety, less formal, was played between two persons, one of whom hid a bit of stick in one of four little heaps of sand. Each wrong guess lost one of the five counters from which the game was played; if the stick was found, the play was transferred.

Women played dice with four willow staves, painted in three different patterns on one side. The score has not been recorded. In the myths, boys sometimes play this game.

Women also swung the ring-and-pin. The rings were the butts of pumpkin rinds. Each ring caught counted one point, except the last one, which went for ten. When none was caught, play passed to one of the pair of opponents. A long spiral was drawn on the sand, and a mark made across this for each point, the two sides beginning at opposite ends of the line. When the tallies met, they were counted, and the victors were considered to have won the anuses of their opponents.

TOTEMIC CLANS.

The Mohave share with the other Yuman tribes of the Colorado a peculiar clan system. This comprises patrilinear, exogamous, nameless groups of totemic reference. All the women born in a clan bear an identical name, although they may in addition be known by nicknames or other epithets. These clan names are of totemic import, though they are not the word which is in common use to denote the totemic object. Thus *anya* is "sun," but the woman's clan name that "means" sun, as the Mohave say, is *Nyo'ilcha*. In a few instances there is a resemblance, as in Yuma *ave*, rattlesnake, and *Mave*, rattlesnake clan name. But in general the names appear to be archaic stems, disguised descriptions or allusions, or equivalents from other dialects. Many of the younger men and women seem to be ignorant of the totemic import of the names, and totem taboos are either lacking or slight, although the Cocopa do not kill their totem. The clans do not enter into religious activities, so far as known. In fact, the ceremonial scheme of these tribes is such that it is difficult to see how the natives could have found serious points of contact between their clan organization and cult practices if they had been so inclined. The impress which this gentile scheme makes is that it rests lightly on society and not at all on cults.

The clans are mentioned in mythology, but in a bald and formal way. At a certain point in some long myth dealing with other things a man called so and so announces or is instructed that he will take such and such a name for his daughters and his sons' female descendants. Sometimes it is added that he will settle or "take land" at a specified place. Such references can scarcely be interpreted as any strong indication of an original local basis for the clans. They seem rather to reflect the custom of the river Yumans of living in little groups of kinsmen, and therefore incidentally of clan mates, at more or less shifting sites determined by the farming fields, and scattered rather randomly through the cultivable portions of the tribal territory. At the same time it is well to remember that the "clans" of the Diegueño and southern California Shoshoneans were essentially local in native consciousness and perhaps in fact.

The known clans of the Mohave and Yuma are here listed according to their women's names and totemic implications, with the corresponding data added for several cognate tribes of Arizona and Baja California. Of these, the Kamia are the group of that name actually on the Colorado, while a series of names reported as "Maricopa from the Cocopa" have been interpreted as belonging to one of the refugee tribes formerly on the Colorado, probably the ancient "Cajuenche" or Kohuana neighbors of the Cocopa.

Nyo'itcha, Mohave: sun, fire, deer, eagle, or beetle.

Hoalya, Mohave: moon (*haly'a*).

Mat-hachva, Mohave: wind (*mat-ha*).

Owich, Mohave: cloud.

Hipa, Mohave, Yuma, Maricopa: coyote; Maricopa also: cholla cactus.

Moha, Mohave: mountain sheep.

Siulya, Mohave: beaver.

Malyikha, Mohave: wood rat.

Kutkilya, Mohave: owl; Kohuana: yellow animal.

Mothcha, Mohave: screech owl.

Masipa, Mohave: quail, possibly also coyote.

Maha, Mohave: a small bird; *Sikuma*, Yuma, Kamia: dove; Kohuana: "pigeon"; *Sakuma*, Cocopa: dove, buzzard.

Halypota, Mohave: frog; Yuma: already done; Kohuana: a shrub.

Nyikha, Mohave: a caterpillar or worm.

Kata, Mohave: tobacco, perhaps also mescal, that is agave.

Vahadha, Mohave: tobacco.

Tilya, Mohave: mescal.

Vimaka, Mohave: bean mesquite.

Musa, Mohave: screw mesquite; *Kalsmus*, Kamia: screw mesquite; *Alymos*, Yuma: bean (?) mesquite, deer: *Kasmus*, Cocopa: beaver.

Kumadhiya, Mohave: ocatilla cactus; *Kimithi*, Maricopa: ocatilla, roadrunner.

Kwinitha, Mohave: prickly pear cactus.

Chacha, Mohave: corn or food; *Harchach*, Maricopa: white corn; Yuma: agricultural food, frog.

Waksi, Haksi, Yuma: hard earth; Kamia, undetermined; *Ksila,* Maricopa, sand.

Sinykwatl, Yuma: deer or skin; also eagle; *Sinikwus,* Kohuana: red ant; Kamia: undetermined; *Sikupas,* Yuma: red ant.

Kwaku, Maricopa: deer (Mohave: *akwaka*).

Wahas, Yuma: beaver.

Liach, Liots, Yuma: buzzard, cloud, also called "Pima" clan; Maricopa, buzzard, sun, fire; Kamia, buzzard.

Met'a, Yuma: road-runner.

Chia, Yuma: night-hawk.

Mave, Smawi', Yuma, Kohuana, Cocopa: rattlesnake (*ave*).

Estamadhun, Yuma: an insect.

Kwisku, Yuma: grasshopper, willow bark for skirt.

Sikus, Yuma, undetermined; Cocopa: salt, coyote, and two undetermined meanings.

Niu, Cocopa: deer; *Kwinis,* Kohuana: deer.

Nimi, Cocopa: wild cat.

Uru, Cocopa: night hawk (Mohave: *orro*).

Kapsas, Cocopa: frog.

Kwas, Cocopa: "Colorado river".

Kuchal, Cocopa: bark.

Wachuwal, Cocopa: undetermined.

Hutpas, Kohuana: sedge.

Salal, Kohuanà: bean mesquite.

Namituch, Maricopa: bean mesquite.

Pakit, Maricopa: "buzzard."

Kunyih, Kamia: coyote, fox.

Witah, Kamia: undetermined.

Itlkamyap, Kamia: undetermined.

It is rather remarkable how divergent the lists for the several tribes are. More than two-thirds of the names are confined to a single nation. Only a sixth are found among three of the six. Not one is established among all of the tribes. The only names of any notable distribution are:

Hipa, coyote.
Sikuma, dove.
Liach, buzzard.
Mave, rattlesnake.
Sinikwus-Sikupas, red ant.
Havchacha, corn.
Kalymusa, screw mesquite.
Halypota, of variable significance.

Frequently a single name has two, three, or even five totemic implications: compare *Nyo'ilcha* at the head of the preceding list.

Analogously, the same "totem" often has entirely diverse names attached to it, sometimes perhaps within a single tribe, certainly among different tribes. For instance:

Deer: Mohave, *Nyo'ilcha;* Yuma, *Alymos;* Cocopa, *Niu;* Kohuana, *Kwinis;* Maricopa, *Kwaku.*

Coyote: Mohave, Yuma, Maricopa, *Hipa;* Cocopa, *Sikus;* Kamia, *Kunyih.*

Bean mesquite: Mohave, *Vimaka;* Yuma, *Alymos;* Kohuana, *Salal;* Maricopa, *Namituch.*

It is clear that all the agricultural Yuman tribes adhered with rather rigid uniformity to the scheme of the system, but varied its precise content freely. This is a situation of some interest, because the tendency of scholars has been to observe frequent transmission of individual elements from culture to culture, at least among primitive peoples, whereas the combinations made of these elements by individual nations have seemed much more fluctuating. In the present case the probability of diverging growths from a single source is very high.

It may be added that the indirectness of the totemic reference in this clan system finds an analogue among the Pima and Papago, whose totemic clans and moieties are also nameless, but are distinguished by their appellations for " father; " and among the Miwok, whose individual personal names connote totemic objects without expressing them.

Among the Yuma and Cocopa gray-haird women are called by their clan name with *akoi* or *wakui,* " old woman," prefixed: thus, *Akoi-hipa, Wakui-niu.* In other instances the ordinary word denoting the totem replaces the clan name: *Akoi-akwak* (deer) for *Alymos, Akoi-uru* (night-hawk) for *Chia, Wakui-panapala* (buzzard) for *Sakuma, Wakui-sih* (salt) for *Sikus.* In still other cases a third stem appears, as *Wakui-chayil* for *Kapsas* (*hanye,* frog), and *Wakui-mas* for *Kwiye* (*ihwi,* cloud). This plan is not known to be followed by the Mohave; but this people changes *Nyo'ilcha* to *Nyocha* and *Siulya* to *Kusuvilya* for a woman who has lost a child.

LAND OWNERSHIP.

Farm land was owned and could be sold for beads or other property. A brave man, the Mohave say, brought captives and spoils back from war and gave them to other men in return for tracts of land.

Quarrels of various sorts were settled by a sort of combat calculated to prevent fatalities. For instance, when the river flooded the valley, it sometimes changed the configuration of the land or washed away landmarks. A group of people might then assert the boundary of their holdings to have been at a point which their neighbors regarded as well within their own limits. A sort of pushing match, *thupirvek,* was then arranged. One man was surrounded by his friends, who tried to shove or drag him across the disputed territory, whereas their opponents struggled to carry a champion of theirs to the farthest end of the land of the aggressors. In this scuffle legs were sometimes broken and the human footballs nearly crushed and pulled to death. The stake of the contest may sometimes have been not only the stretch first in dispute but the entire arable holdings of both contestants.

If the losers were dissatisfied, they reappeared next morning at their asserted boundary, armed with willow poles a couple of inches thick and 5 or 6 feet long. Each man held a shorter stick in his left hand. The victors met them, and a stick fight, *chetmana'ak*, ensued, which might last hours. The contestants beat each other over the heads till they were weary. As they parried with their staves, no one was killed, say the Mohave, but men sometimes died afterwards, especially when they fought long on a summer's day and maggots bred in the wounds. The object of each party was to drive the other back across the disputed tract, whereupon title to it was definitely established. The dispossessed losers went to friends elsewhere and might have fields lent to them.

Such a system would have been impossible among other Californians. If these raised their hands against an opponent at all it was to kill, and the losers would scarcely have ceased to plan injury for their wrongs unless formal settlement were made.

CHIEFTAINSHIP.

The Mohave had hereditary chiefs, in the male line, whom they call *hanidhala* (from Spanish *general*); but their functions are obscure. They are much less often mentioned than the brave man or war leader, who ranked in estimation much like his counterpart among the eastern tribes of the continent, and for whom alone an anniversary mourning rite was performed; less, too, than the *kohota* or manager of entertainments, somewhat recalling the Luiseño *paha';* and the *kwathidhe*, the "doctor" or shaman. All three of these characters acquired their prominence individually—through their dreaming, the Mohave say. Only the chief inherited—but counted for little, it would seem.

The Mohave say that when a man, instead of joining in a feast, orated while the others ate, or if he allowed his dishes, property, or house to be destroyed—presumably by those whom he had offended— he gained prestige and authority. Early travelers tell how the "chiefs" to whom they made presents promptly distributed these, keeping nothing for themselves. It is doubtful whether these accounts refer to the official hereditary chiefs or to men of influence. But it is clear that liberality and abnegation were qualities required of him who aspired to leadership.

The following narrative, which appears to relate to about 1855, illustrates the position of the *kohota* or festival chief, the nature of Mohave dances, and the attitude toward captives:

When I was a boy I saw a war party set out to help the Yuma, who had issued an invitation for a raid on the Cocopa. They killed two of the enemy and took two women captives. They returned to a place some miles south of Fort Mohave, where the entire tribe assembled. This place was among the *Mat-halya-dhoma* or northern Mohave, who already had several captives, whereas the *Kavilya-dhoma* or southern Mohave were without. The two women were brought to the *kohota* at this place, because he had asked some of his kinsmen to join the party and if captives were made to carry food and water for them and guard them so that they· could be taken home to himself.

The *kohota* is a man who constantly works, builds a large house, makes dances, and provides food for all who come. When he undertakes anything, people say: " Let us help him because he works for us all." When he has nothing left, everyone contributes blankets or other property. Captives are given to him to keep. Every year he says: " Let us sing," and then the people gather and are happy.

This *kohota* sang " Pleiades." In the morning the men and the women would dance to this, facing each other. About noon they all ate. Then in the afternoon the *kohota* would call on someone who sang *Chutaha*. When the jar began to resound, the people would leave off their play or gambling and come together, the young men with feathers in their hair. Then they would dance to this, three rows of young men, one of old, and two women, until the sun had nearly set.

Then the *kohota* might say: " Let who wishes to, sing; I name no one. Let any woman sing." He would bring out his rattles. Then if women wanted to dance *Tumanpa*, they brought a rattle to a man who sang *Tumanpa*, and so for " Raven " and *Vinimulya* and *Vinimulya-hapacha*. But *Nyohaiva* is sung without rattle. The singer holds a long stick. Sometimes one other man sings with him. Many women stand about him, shoulder to shoulder, moving one foot at a time sidewise to the left, their hands hanging, the circle revolving. When the singer swings his stick, they step with their knees bent. All five of these dances may be going on at the same time. As soon as one song is finished, another is begun; they dance fast because the sun is nearly gone, and the women sweat.

So they did this time when the captives were brought in. As it began to be dusk, they stopped, and all went to the river and washed off their paint in order that the two captives might not cause them to be sick. Having returned and dried themselves, they ate, and then began dancing again. They sang the same songs as before, and sometimes also *Chuhuecha*, or " Cane," though these are not danced to; or *Ohuera*.

And some men sang *Tudhulva*, and they gambled to that by a fire. They played that all night. I was a boy but I was there.

In the morning the *kohota* said: " Now all bathe. Then come back in two days and we will dance again."

So in two days they all assembled once more, and danced again the whole day and the whole night. In the morning they continued singing while the *kohota* took the two slaves, one in each hand, and started toward the river. Behind him came those who were singing *Tumanpa*, then the *Vinimulya-hapacha* singers. All the people followed him. When he came near the river, he ran and leaped in with the captives. Everyone plunged after him. This was to make the two Cocopa women Mohaves, so that they would not bring sickness on the people. They had waked me at daybreak to take part. Being a small boy, I did not want to jump into the water, but they compelled me.

Then the *kohota* sent the people home and took the two captives into his house. He said: " Perhaps these young women will bear children. These children will grow up half Mohave and half Cocopa, and because they belong to both tribes, there may be no more fighting."

The captives were sisters, both called *Orro*, which is a Cocopa name for women and means nighthawk in Mohave. After two or three years one of them was married and had a child. The other one did not marry. Then, after a time, the *kohota* said: "Everything is peaceable. Fighting has stopped. Let us not keep her since all tribes are friends. We will send her home." So a party of men took the unmarried girl to the Yuma, where the Cocopa met her and brought her home. Her sister remained with the Mohave and is living yet and her son is a man. She is still called Orro.

MARRIAGE AND SEX.

The Mohave are at least as loose as any California Indians, and far franker about sexual relations. Marriage is a living together at will, and divorce is separation when either is so inclined. No mention is made of any bride purchase or wedding ceremony. A woman that is notoriously unstable becomes conspicuous and is called *kama-luik*, but there seems to be no serious criticism of either men or women on the score of conduct dictated by sex feeling. The old do not exhort the young to be continent, but urge them to enjoy themselves while they may. This indiscriminateness has perhaps contributed to a higher social position, or at least greater freedom, of women among the Mohave than is usual. They sit, eat, laugh, work, and converse freely with the men, and the children display little less bashfulness. In the realm of religion, however, women are very subsidiary. They rarely join the men's singing, tell myths, or become shamans; and there is not a single song series for women.

A Mohave brought a second wife into his house, where she occupied a separate corner. The first wife was urged by her kin to be silent and put up with the unwelcome situation. After a time she left her husband for another. This one soon displayed an ugly disposition, and when angry would throw out her property or tear up her new front petticoat of bean strings. Finally she buried her food, packed up, and left, telling him to save persuasion as she would not return. They have now become old, but still do not speak. If he comes where she is, she looks away.

If two half-sisters had sons and the children of these sons married (that is, the second half-cousins) the father of the girl would say to the father of the boy: "It is not long ago that our mothers were related. You knew it. Why did you allow this?" Then he would take a horse or something from the boy's father, and the young people were permitted to remain married, not being considered relatives any longer.

Women gave birth seated. They leaned backward, but without support, and held neither rope nor stick. Another woman received the child. For a month the mother ate no salt or flesh; and, together with her husband, refrained from smoking.

Twins, *havak*, were thought to come from the sky. "We have only come to visit," they said. "Our relatives live above. Give us something and we shall stay with you for a time." They possessed clairvoyance and knowledge of supernatural things; but their "dreams" were of the sky, not of the mountain Avikwame. They must be treated alike. If one were given more of something than the other, at least in childhood, the latter became angry and went where he had come from. If one died, the other lay down and, without sickness, followed him.

The Mohave appear not to make a dance for adolescent girls: dancing is not a characteristic social form with them. The maiden is kept covered with hot sand for four nights. There is no actual pit, as among the Shoshoneans, but sand is taken from next the fire. It is likely that she is sung for, but this has not been reported. During the four days her acts are symbolical of her future. She goes about plucking leaves from arrow-weed brush—a perfectly useless labor—merely because she would forever be lazy if she remained sitting in the house. She is silent, so as not to turn gossip. If she moved her head to look about she would soon become immodest. So that she may have a clean head the remainder of her life, her mother louses her and assembles the catch in a small pot.

For 40 days the girl eats no salt, drinks only warmed liquids, and washes herself with hot water. On her next illness the period is the same; on successive occasions, 10, 8, 6, and 4 days.

The Mohave call transvestites *alyha* and hold a ceremony inducting youths into this condition. They say that a boy dreams that he is an *alyha* and then can not do otherwise. Four men who have dreamed about the ceremony are sent for, and spend the night in the house, twisting cords and gathering shredded bark for the skirt the prospective *alyha* will thereafter wear. The youth himself lies, with two women sitting by him. As they twist the cords, the men sing:

ihatnya vudhi	roll it this way.
ihatnya va'ama	roll it that way.

When the petticoat nears completion:

istum	I hold it.
icham	I place it.
hilyurik	it is done.
havirk	it is finished.
ka'avek	hear!
kidhauk	listen!

These songs the singers dreamed when they were with the god Mastamho, and during the night they tell and sing of how they saw him ordering the first performance of this ceremony.

In the morning the two women lift the youth and take him out-doors. One of the singers puts on the skirt and dances to the river in four stops, the youth following and imitating. Then all bathe. Thereupon the two women give the youth the front and back pieces of his new dress and paint his face white. After four days he is painted again and then is an *alyha.* Such persons speak, laugh, smile, sit, and act like women. They are lucky at gambling, say the Mohave, but die young. It is significant that a variety of venereal sickness which they treat is also called *alyha.*

Sometimes, but more rarely, a girl took on man's estate, among both Yuma and Mohave, and was then known as *hwami,* and might marry women. There was no ceremony to mark her new status.

NAMES.

The Mohave are vehement in their observance of the name taboo of the dead, and are bashful about their names before strangers, but readily accept and even take for themselves names of the most un-dignified sort. A phrase that strikes as apt or novel or alludes to a trivial incident is the basis of many names. There is not the least shrinking from obscenity, even in such personal connection as this. The other Californians are sufficiently shameless in their conversa-tion on occasion, but the Mohave delight in filthy speech habitually. Some men assume names of this character in the hope of attracting or impressing women. These are typical men's names: Earth-tongue, Proud-coyote, Yellow-thigh, Foreign-boy, Girl's-leg, Hawk's-track, Doctor's-sack, Shoots-mountain-sheep, Sells-eagle, Muskmelon, Rope, Gartersnake, Man-dies-bone-castrated-coyote.

Kweva-namaua-napaua, of which the second element means "father's mother" and the third "father's father," is a violent insult uttered by angry women, evidently because of its reference to an-cestors normally dead. In a contrary spirit of delicacy the Mohave referred to the father's settlement or kin as on the right, the mother's as on the left, or designated the places from which the father's kin sprang as *ny-amata-kothare,* and the mother's as *hanavasut.* The indirectness of the allusion allowed these phrases to be used on cer-tain occasions without sting.

DEATH.

The Mohave have the appalling habit of beginning their wailing and singing some hours before an expected death. If the patient possesses unexpected vitality, the singing may go on for two or three days. In certain crucial cases the effect must be adverse; but the probability is that the mourning usually commences only after the sick person has indicated his expectation of dying, and that he is comforted by the unrestrained solicitude and grief of the crowd of his kinsmen and friends. General mourning after death goes on only for a very few hours; unless a death has occurred suddenly, when time must be allowed to assemble the relatives. A trench is scooped out near the house, willow or cottonwood logs piled above it, the body laid on with its head to the south, burning arrow weeds applied, and when the fire has sunk into the pit, sand is pushed over it. There are no cemeteries. The house and shade are immediately set on fire with all their contents. While the pyre is blazing, the shouts and lamentations are at their height, property is thrown into the flames, and people even strip themselves of their garments. All relatives, however remote, attend the cremation and weep; afterwards, only the closest kin cry for a few days, then go about their affairs as if nothing had happened. The loud lamentations must be extremely exhausting. For an entire night a father may sing *Tumanpa*, or whatever he knows, at the top of his voice for a dying son, while the mother alternates wails with speaking aloud until her voice comes in a whisper. An uncle shouts in jerky sentences how Mastamho made the river, or some other myth that he has dreamed, while others seem to " preach " in competition with him, or lament more inchoately, and the sitting women cry *alalalai* or weep mutely. Of course grief is not spontaneous in all, but it is expressed most unrestrainedly; the cries that arise at the moment of death are piercing; and the quick fierce cremation with the circle of abandoned mourners makes a scene whose intensity is unforgettably impressive. (Pl. 69.)

For four days after a death the kin eat no salt, fish, flesh, or fat, incense themselves with the smoke of arrow weed, and wash with steepings of the peeled root of the same plant, in order not to fall ill.

The Mohave enact a special mourning for men with an illustrious war record and perhaps for chiefs. This seems to be held either immediately after cremation or some days or weeks later; but strangely enough is called "Annual" by them in English, as if it were an anniversary. The native name is *Nyimich*, "mourning," or *Hitpachk*, which seems to refer to the running in the rite, or *Nyimi-chivauk*, " cry-put." The mourners, distinguished men, and old people sit crowded close under a shade, crying and singing for a night, or a day and a night. Almost constantly there is some old man " preaching "—speaking on mythological subjects in loud, detached, jerky words or pressed-out phrases. This is called *nyimi-chekwarek*, " mourning-talk." For hours 12 men run back and forth over a cleared and dampened space south of the shade. One shouts and directs; one holds a war club and is the leader; two carry bows and arrows; four have sticks with loops of beads; and four others carry sticks from which feathers dangle in pairs. Sometimes a woman and a mounted man are stationed on each flank of the 12 runners, several of whom wear large bunches of feathers on their heads. The running back and forth is a conventionalized representation of warfare, and occasionally an imitative act may be recognized. In the morning the dead warrior's house, his property, the shade, and all the paraphernalia of the runners are burned, and the entire assemblage bathes.

The destroying of property with the dead is a subject of much concern to most Mohave, and frequently discussed. It is called *upily-m* or *ch-upily-k*. One man wants his flute laid on his breast when he is burned, another his rattle, a third his feathers. Old women with difficulty keep a horse alive on gathered mesquite in order that it may be killed and eaten at their funeral. When a man has sung for his dying or dead son. he throws away and gives him—*chupilyk*—his songs.

An old woman had saved some odds and ends of property for *chupilyk* for herself. When she sold them, she declared her intention of buying food, which would pass into her body and thus be destroyed with her. She was perhaps half humorous in her remarks, but at the same time evidently explaining to her conscience.

WAR.

War was carried on with four weapons, according to native reckoning: the unbacked bow of willow, *otisa*, a little less than a man in length; the arrow, *ipa*, of *Pluchea sericea*, the arrow-weed which serves so many uses, feathered but unforeshafted and untipped; the mallet headed club, *halyahwai*, of mesquite wood; and the *tokyeta* or straight stick club of screw mesquite wood. Shields and lances were known, but very little used. At long-range fighting, the headless arrow penetrated but a short distance, and many a warrior returned covered with wounds, the Mohave say. Their myths make some of their heroes bristle like a porcupine at the end of a battle, and speak of men dying subsequently from wounds more frequently than during a fight. The ambition of combatants was to come to close quarters, and here execution was often deadly. No man was accounted really brave who had not distinguished himself in this hand-to-hand fighting; and in surprise attacks on settlements it was the rule. A leader sometimes rushed into the opposing ranks, grasped an opponent, and threw him over his shoulders, thus at the same time shielding his own head from the foe and exposing his victim to the blows of his followers. Such struggles often ceased when one or two had been slain and their heads secured as trophies to be scalped at leisure; but at other times the mêlée became general and losses were heavy. The straight club was for breaking heads; the mallet was thrust upward endwise to crush in an opponent's face after his long hair had been seized with the free hand. This style of fighting was not confined to ambuscades and desperate resistances of those who had been trapped, but sometimes marked the termination of an open combat. The Mohave prized courage above all other virtues, and it can not be denied them.

Brave men dreamed especially of the morning star and of certain hawks.

When war parties went out, each man carried a gourd of water and a gourd of ground wheat which furnished his sole subsistence for 15 days. Travelers professed to journey four days without any food. Horses were rarely used in war or travel, in fact seem to have been kept chiefly for food and show. The Mohave move across the country in a trot that carries them over long distances rapidly. They seem not inferior to the southwestern and Sonora Indians in this ability. Bits of *ihore* willow were often chewed to keep the mouth moist. If hail or showers threatened, the bow was sometimes cased to protect the string. In battle and at other times a belt was worn; under the back of this, arrows were thrust.

Triumphal scalps consisted of the entire skin of the head except a triangle consisting of nose, mouth, chin, and throat; and with their long locks they must have made magnificent trophies. They were celebrated over in the *Yakatha'alya*. The scalp was put on a pole set up in an open field or playground, *mat'ara*. Near by was a shade, under which the old people sat, the women calling *pilelelelele*. Young men and women painted their hair white and danced for four days and nights. The songs were from any of the standard series, irrespective of their content. After each period of dancing, the youths and girls bathed and smoked themselves over a fire of human dung to escape sickness. The celebration was directed by the *kohota*, and was held near his house. He alone could touch the scalp, and might keep it for another dance a year later; but even he had to incense himself eight times each of the four days.

A constant object of Mohave war parties was the capture of girls or young women. Other prisoners were not taken. The Mohave speak of these captives as "slaves," but the word by which they were designated, *ahwe*, means only " strangers." They were not violated; in fact, a ceremony had to be made over them else they would bring sickness into the land; and even after this purification they seem more generally not to have been married. They were given work, but not often abused, except under suspicion of trying to escape. In fact, their usual treatment appears to have been rather kindly, and they were sometimes assigned seed and a patch of field for their personal subsistence. The economic life was far too simple to allow of such captives being seriously exploited, and they needed constant watching to keep; yet the Mohave were sufficiently intent to hold them to even purchase the captives of other tribes. Their curious attitude in the matter is distinctly southwestern.

The last great fight of the Mohave occurred in 1857 or 1858, a short time after their successful raid against the Cocopa, the celebration of which has been described. The same five leaders were at the head of this more disastrous expedition, which was directed against their hereditary foe, the Maricopa. The Mohave, in a party whose numbers are not exactly known but estimated by themselves at about 200, were joined at Avi-kwa-hasala by 82 Yuma and a considerable body of Yavapai and a contingent from a more remote tribe whom the Mohave call *Yavapaya-hwacha*, "traveling" or "nomadic Yavapai," and the description of whose appearance and manners exactly fits the Apache. The Maricopa summoned the Hatpa or Pima, "a large tribe of many villages," as the Mohave found to their cost. The battle took place at Avi-vava, in an open plain. The Apache fought fiercely for a time but fled when things turned against them, and escaped without a fatality. The Yavapai followed but lost seven. The majority of warriors of these tribes were probably mounted, whereas the river nations fought on foot. A part of the Mohave and all the Yuma were surrounded and exterminated after a most determined hand-to-hand fight. Sixty Mohave fell and 80 of the 82 Yuma—Humara-va'acha and Kwasanya being the only survivors of the latter. The Yuma refused to flee and stood in a dense mass. When the foe charged, they attempted to grasp and drag him into their body, where he was hacked to pieces with great knives.

It is this style of fighting, based on a readiness to clinch with the enemy in mortal issue, that was characteristic of the Yuman river tribes, as well as the Pima, and that allowed the latter people, quiet farmers as they were, to more than hold their own against the untiringly aggressive but unstable Apache. The same quality of fortitude has found notable expression among another agricultural tribe, the Yaqui of Sonora.

The Mohave reckon that a war party returning from an attack on the Maricopa sleeps one night on Maricopa soil, five in Yavapai territory, one among the Walapai, and on the eighth evening reaches the foot of Mohave Valley. The distance is 150 miles by air, considerably more over the ground, and most of the country totally desert.

CHAPTER 51.

THE MOHAVE: DREAM LIFE.

DREAMING.

The Mohave adhere to a belief in dreams as the basis of everything in life, with an insistence equaled only by the Yurok devotion to the pursuit of wealth. Not only all shamanistic power but most myths and songs, bravery and fortune in war, success with women or in gaming, every special ability, are dreamed. Knowledge is not a thing to be learned, the Mohave declare, but to be acquired by each man according to his dreams. For "luck" they say *sumach ahot*, "good dreaming," and "ill starred" is "bad dreams." Nor is this a dreaming by men so much as by unconscious infants in their mothers or even earlier, when their *matkwesa*, their shadows, stood at Avikwame or played at Aha'av'ulypo. "I was there, I saw him," a myth teller says of his hero, or of the death of the god Matavilya; and each shaman insists that he himself received his powers from Mastamho at the beginning of the world. So deep are these convictions, especially as old age comes on, that most Mohave can no longer distinguish between what they have received from other men and what is their own inward experience. They learn, indeed, as much as other people; but since learning seems an almost valueless nothing, they dream over, or believe they have first dreamed, the things which they in common with every Mohave know. It is a strange attitude, and one that can grow only out of a remarkable civilization.

There is, too, an amazing timelessness in these beliefs, which finds reflection in every myth. The precise time of day or night of each trivial supernatural event is specified, but the briefest moments suffice for the growth from boyhood to adult age, for the transformation from person to animal, for the making of a mountain or the ordering of an everlasting institution. Just so a Mohave can not

754

tell a story or a dream without naming the exact spot at which each character journeyed or slept or stood or looked about; but four steps bring the god to the center of the earth or the source of the river, and his arms reach to the edges of the sky.

Dreams, then, are the foundation of Mohave life; and dreams throughout are cast in mythological mold. There is no people whose activities are more shaped by this psychic state, or what they believe to be such, and none whose civilization is so completely, so deliberately, reflected in their myths.

SONG SERIES.

Public ceremonies or rituals as they occur among almost all native Americans can not be said to be practiced by the Mohave. Even dances are little developed among them, being little more than an occasional addition to certain cycles of familiar songs. These cycles or series number about 30, each designated by a name. The songs in each are comparatively uniform, in fact little more than variations on a single theme; and although no two of the 100 or 200 songs of one series are identical, the Mohave need hear only a few bars of any song to recognize its kind. All the cycles have their songs strung on a thread of myth, of which the singer is conscious, although practically nothing of the story appears in the brief, stylistically chosen, and distorted words of the songs. Sometimes a night is spent by a singer entertaining a houseful of people with alternate recital and singing; but such occasions seem not to have been common. Many singers declare that they have never told their whole tale through and sung their songs from beginning to end at one sitting. It is in accord with this statement that some men appear to know the whole of a song cycle but only parts of its myth; and that to the public at large all the songs are more or less familiar, but the stories much less known.

The singers generally state that they have dreamed the myth and cycle; sometimes admit that they have learned them from listening to older relatives; and occasionally declare that they first learned them in part and then dreamed the whole. One or more of an old man's sons or brothers or brothers' sons usually sing the same cycles; others have dreamed a different one. Some men, and they are not a few, profess to know, and sing and tell, three or four series. The same cycle is often sung quite differently by men not connected in blood or by personal association, and the story appears to vary to a nearly equal degree.

At funerals, and in case of an anticipated death for many hours before, mourning consists largely of singing from these cycles. A dying man's kin know his songs and sing them; for a man not given to singing, or a woman, or a child, the chief mourners sing from their own cycles. The Mohave appear to be aware, and tell readily, what songs will be sung at the funeral of any person with whom they are well acquainted. As the same songs are substantially the only ones which they use for pleasure, this definite association with death seems strange; but the content, or rather implication, of all of them is so mythological, and at the same time so vague and so conventionalized according to familiar patterns, that any song is intrinsically about equally suitable for any occasion. A singer evidently does not think of the reference or lack of reference of his song to the funeral or the celebration which is going on at the moment. Music is proper, and he sings what he knows. The mythology that is touched upon is one of the materials of which his fabric is made, and nothing more. When a man has sung for his dead son, he breaks the rattle and declares that he has thrown his song away; but after a time his association of grief vanishes, and when next he sings, it is from the same series. He certainly would recur to it at the next death.

About a third of the cycles are said by the Mohave to belong to shamans and to serve the curing of particular sicknesses. These seem to be regarded with some disfavor and to be little used on other occasions; but all that is known of them shows them to be nearly the same as the nonshamanistic cycles, and to be based on myths of the identical type. The remainder are variously classified, according to the proper instrument that accompanies the singing, whether or not they can be danced to, whether the tale contains episodes of war, and so on. *Hacha* and *Chutaha*, for instance, are sung chiefly as an occasion for dancing. But again, neither their songs nor story appear to present any marked peculiarities.

The myths are enormously long, and almost invariably relate the journey of either a single person, or of a pair of brothers with or without a following, beginning with their coming into existence and ending with their transformation into an animal or a landmark. This journey, which is sometimes described as occupying two or three days, but is really a timeless life history of the hero, is given with the greatest detail of itinerary; but incidents of true narrative interest are few, often irrelevant to the main thread of the story, and usually can be found in very similar form in entirely distinct cycles. But each locality reached, whether on the river, in the desert, or among distant mountains, is named, and its features are frequently described. All that happens, however, at most of these stops is that the hero thinks of something that he has left behind or that will happen, marvels at the appearance of a rock, sees a badger, catches a wood rat, has night come on and watches the stars, or suddenly, and in the same vein, plots the death of his brother and companion. As a story the whole is meaningless. In fact, the narrator is sometimes guilty of gross inconsistencies as he goes along, and when asked to resummarize his tale, usually outlines it altered. The plot is evidently a framework on which episodes of ornamental significance can be hung.

We are thus face to face with a style of literature which is as frankly decorative as a patterned textile. The pattern is far from random; but it is its color and intricacy, its fineness or splendor, that have meaning, not the action told by its figures; and as a simple but religious people don the same garment for festivity or worship, for dress or interment, provided only it is gorgeously pleasing enough, so the Mohave weave their many myths in one ornamental style and sing them on every occasion that calls for music. Something of this quality has already been found in the tales of the Gabrielino and chants of the Luiseño. But the Mohave are perhaps more single-minded, more extreme and less conscious, and therefore more expert, in their national manner.

The same with the songs. As a narrator comes to each spot in his story, he sings so many songs. If, after his conclusion, he is asked to repeat the songs that belong to a certain place, he may sing four instead of six, and insist that there were no more. He is truthful: comparison shows that he is now singing other variations of his fundamental theme; and the words are likely to be different. What he has in mind is clearly only the theme, certain manners of varying it, a certain stock of words to be fitted to the melody. This might be anticipated. It would be impossible for ordinary men to remember definitely the sequence and the precise minor shadings of the varying rhythms and melodic embellishments of 150 songs all cast in the same mold. The gifted individual might do this; but it does not attract him. In short, the skeleton of the plot, its geography, the basic tune and the kind and scope of its variations, are held somewhat plastically in mind; everything else is more or less improvised, with frequent recourse to remembrances of other singers and even diverse series.

Some examples of songs will illustrate:

Tumanpa-vanyume:

Words of song.	Mohave.	English.
tiyakayami	tayamk	move
kachaik	hacha	Pleiades
hayangamanui varam	(=kiyuk)	(see!)

Goose:

nahaiyamim	nyahaim–	At Nyahaim–
kuvayanghim	kuvara	kuvara
tinyamauch	tinyam	night
kwidhauvangai	kuvidhauk	have

Another:

himangauch	*iamk*	go
tawimangai	*matawemk*	travel to
inyamaut	*iny-amata*	my land
hangaii.		

Turtle:

kwinyavai	At Hakwinyava
kutinyam hakwinyk	dark imagine (make a dark place—a house—by thinking)
havasu	blue

The same:

hinyora	is marked
hiama (for *himata*)	her body (the turtle's)
akwatha	yellow

Nyohaiva:

amatuanga	at Amataya'ama
sumakwanga	dream
sumakahuwam	dream

Raven:

ahnalya	gourd-rattle
oalya	I show
viv'aum	standing

The following song is:

ahnalya	gourd-rattle
idhauk	I hold
amaim ichiak	upward raise it
viv'aum	standing

And the one after:

idhauk	I hold it
akanavek	I tell of it
viv'aum	standing
achidhumk	I look hither
achikavak	I look thither
viv'aum	standing

The next song, the first of the following group:

tinyam-kalchieska	the night bat
himan kuyamk	rising flies
akanavek	I tell it
sivarek	I sing it

Another Raven song:

ahpe	metate
hamuchye	muller
tawam	grinding
tadhi (*cha*) *tawam*	corn grinding

The first song of this cycle:

humik	Now both
pi'ipaik	being persons (*i. e.,* alive)
nakwidhauk	we sit here

And the last:

matahaik (for *mat-hak*)	the wind
ikwerevik	whirls

It is clear that very little of the plot gets into the song: insufficient to render it intelligible to those who have not learned or heard the story; although the words themselves may be readily recognizable.

THE SEVERAL SERIES: TUMANPA TYPE.

Tumanpa comes in three varieties: *Tumanpa akyulya*, long; *Tumanpa uta'uta, atatuana, taravika*, or *halyadhompa*, short, odd, or crooked; and *Tumanpa Vanyume*, of the Vanyume or Serrano of Mohave River. The first two differ in the length of their songs. The myth is the same and takes, with the songs, a night to go through. The story begins at Aha'av'ulypo at the death of Matavilya and then relates the rather eventless journey of an old man and woman, brother and sister, first north to Okalihu, then south along the river past Bill Williams Fork, then eastward, until at Chimusam-kuchoiva, near Aubrey in Arizona, the two marry and turn into rock. Another version takes them first into the Providence Mountains west of Aha'av'ulypo, omits the marriage, but ends at the same locality. There are practically no events except the journey itself. Instead, the things which the Tumanpa see, their thoughts about them and names for them, are entered into at length: a battle, scalping, the newly made river, driftwood, rats and other animals, the constellations, and so on indefinitely and no doubt differently in the mouth of each reciter.

Tumanpa Vanyume has an obscure history. Some Mohave say that it was learned by them from Tavaskan, a chief at Tejon. This would make him a Kitanemuk, but this dialect and Vanyume are both Serrano and not very different. Others declare that the songs were learned from certain Mohave-speaking relatives of Tavaskan and are therefore in Mohave, although the myth is told in the Vanyume language and is unintelligible; much as the Cocopa sing another variety of the same cycle, *Tumanpa ahwe*, "foreign Tumanpa," in words intelligible to the Mohave and believed by them to be in their own speech, whereas they can not understand the accompanying story. Cocopa is Yuman speech, and it may well be that the phrases which occur over and over in all Yuman songs are sufficiently similar to be recognizable; but Serrano is a Shoshonean language. In any event the *Tumanpa Vanyume* songs sung by the Mohave have Mohave words; and they agree that the inevitable journey narrated in the story begins at Aha'av'ulypo, progresses to Matavilya-vova near Barstow, and ends at Aviveskwikaveik, south of Boundary Cone at the rim of Mohave Valley. Barstow is Vanyume territory, and possibly that is all that this tribe has to do with the cycle.

Vinimulya and *Vinimulya-hapacha*—the first is also called *Vinimulya-tahanna*, "Vinimulya indeed "—are stories of fighting. They are often coupled with *Tumanpa*, " Raven," and *Nyohaiva* as a group of series that are sung at celebrations, even the women participating, and men and women dancing. These cycles tell of war, lend themselves to play, and are free from any suspicion of shamanistic powers in the Mohave mind.

Vinimulya-hapacha lasts from near sunset to the middle of the following afternoon. One version begins at "Gourd mountain" in Chemehuevi or other Shoshonean territory, 200 or 300 miles northwest of Avikwame; comes into Mohave Valley; and ends " at " Aviwatha (New York Mountains), Savetpilya (Charleston Peak), Harrakarraka, and Komota, four widely separated places belonging to the Chemehuevi.

Another account makes the hero Umas-kwichipacha, a Mohave, leave his home, Aha-kwa'a'i, in Mohave Valley and settle for a year with his people in the Providence Mountains, historic Chemehuevi territory. On his impending return, the people in Mohave Valley crediting him with warlike intent, he goes first past Hatalompa far downstream to Aha-kwatpava below Ehrenberg, then turns back and after a number of days' marches reaches Kwaparveta at the lower end of the valley. The residents there flee up the valley and Umas-kwichipacha with all his followers, men, women, and children, pursues, until he reaches his old home Aha-kwa'a'i. There he gathers booty and settles. His daughter Ilya-owich-maikohwera, angered at his suggestion that she take a husband, runs off to the Walapai for a year. On her return, Umas-kwichipacha starts up the valley, the residents fleeing before him under the leadership of his younger brother Savilyuvava to Sokwilya-hihu near Fort Mohave. There they make a stand, Savilyuvava is killed and scalped, his daughter made captive, and his people driven across the river. Next the hero attacks the Ipa'ahma, "quail people," who also flee across the river and join the defeated party of Savilyuvava at Avi-kutaparva, a few miles above. There they and Umas-kwichipacha defy and revile each other across the river, mentioning each other's kin. Then he returns to the Providence Mountains, where one of his people, Umas-elyithe, dies from wounds received in the battle.

This is clearly a "clan legend," though of the peculiar form favored by the Mohave. While the narrator does not regard it necessary to mention the fact in his story, he thinks of all Umas-kwichipacha's people—as well as his brother's—as having daughters named Owich.

Akaka, "Raven," tells of the birth from the ground, where Matavilya's house was burned after his death at Aha'av'ulypo, of the two raven brothers, Humar-kwidhe and Humar-hanga. They move toward the door and sing of their toys, buzzers of cane; then, that there will be war; then face and reach out in the four directions and thereby obtain gourd rattles. Then they sing of the bat of night, Orion and the Pleiades, hostile tribes in the south, the dust of an approaching war party, the battle at dawn, captive women, scalped foes, the return journey northward past Bill Williams Fork, announcement of victory, gathering of the people, and the dance of celebration. They continue singing, telling of the birds to be heard before dawn, of food in the grinding, of people gathering to play at

Miakwa'orva. Now they move nearer the door, are able to stand and walk, and tell of their bodies and what those who dream of them will sing. They go outside the door, wondering what their shape will be and where they shall go, and take new names. Feathers begin to grow on them and they commence to fly. It dawns, and the older brother announces that he will follow the darkness as it passes from east to west, and go southwestward to live, as the crow, with the Kamia. The younger takes the name Tinyam-hatmowaipha, "dusky night," will be the raven, and stay in the Mohave land. The wind puffs and they soar off with it.

This is a curious tale within a tale, if it can be called a story at all. The heroes do nothing but move 30 feet, sing all night, and disappear at daybreak. What they sing of is precisely what any Mohave would be likely to sing of if he sat up. The story is thus but a pallid reflection of the conventional subjects of Mohave singing. The version outlined comprises some 186 songs in about 32 groups.

Nyohaiva differs from those that precede in being sung without gourd rattle accompaniment. The singer stands leaning on a stick. The tale is one of war.

Nyohaiva, the insect called *yanathakwa'ataya*, was a woman who grew out of the ground at Miakwa'orva, near the northern end of Mohave Valley. She moved southward, went east from opposite Needles into the mountains, gave a bow and knife to Hamatholaviya that the Walapai might live by hunting, returned to the river, leaped far down, accepted a new name, Ath'inkumedhi, from Nyahunemkwayava, but rejected several men who claimed her as sister. At Akwaka-hava, somewhere in the old Halchidhoma country, she was offered food and plotted against by Kimkusuma, Ochouta, and their two brothers, who wished to eat her. She found her relatives' bones, beat the people of Akwaka-hava in a contest for them, and defied them to war. She went downstream to Avi-haly'a and Avenyava and prepared the people for war. They assembled, and she appointed three leaders besides herself. On the way up they met her brother, on whom horns were growing, and she sent him to the east to become a mountain sheep. As the party approached Akwaka-hava, Nyohaiva put the foe to sleep with a magic ball, entered the house with her three companions, carried off the sleeping Ochouta, and decapitated him with her thumb-nail. She took the head northward to Amata-ya'ama, near Parker, still in old Halchidhoma territory, where four *alyha* men-women lived, and made the scalp dance. Ochouta's skull she threw far south, where it became the rock Avi-melyakyeta at Picacho near Yuma. Then she herself turned into a black rock near Amata-ya'ama.

One narrator sang 33 groups of from 1 to 5 songs, 107 in all, in reference to the myth outlined.

"SALT" TYPE.

"Salt," "Deer," and "Turtle" are sometimes mentioned with "Tumanpa short" as sung indoors during the long winter nights, apparently in contrast to "Tumanpa long," the two *Vinimulya*,

" Raven," and *Nyohaiva*, which lent themselves to outdoor dancing when the people gathered for amusement. All the singings of the present group except "Turtle," which uses no rattle, were also danced to, but only on the limited scale which a crowded house allowed. Thus in "Deer," women accompanied the singer, and a few men danced. In "Salt," three men stood by the singer facing four women inside the door, and the two lines danced four steps forward and back. The singer might make a knot in a string of his own length as he finished each song.

"Salt," *Ath'i*, uses the rattle. One version begins at Aha'av'ulypo and ends at Yava'avi-ath'i, near Daggett, in Vanyume country. Another, whose 25 groups of 115 songs take a night and a day to traverse, tells of four mountain-sheep brothers who journeyed from Aha'av'ulypo, after Matavilya's death, eastward and then north through the Walapai country to Ati'siara, where the two oldest sank into the ground and blew back their brothers, who wished to follow them. The younger brothers went north, then west, crossed the course of the future river at Ukaliho, passed the Providence Mountains, and reached Hayakwiranya-mat'ara, east of Mojave station in Kawaiisu or Vanyume land. On the way they saw and talked or disputed about their tears, their powers and future, several insects, rats, birds, and tobacco plants, meteors and constellations, and a lake which they took to be the sea. Then they turned southeastward across the desert, and finally at Himekuvauva, a day's journey west of Parker, their tears turned into salt and they into stone. The Chemehuevi now gather salt there, the Mohave say, and sing what they have dreamed about Salt, beginning at the point where the Mohave leave off.

Akwaka, "Deer," is sung to the gourd rattle. It seems to be of no great length, so that it can be completed within a night. Most of the songs are those of the deer, but the last of the cycle are put in the mouths of the true heroes of the myth, Numeta the older brother and Hatakulya the younger. These seem to be the mountain lion and the jaguar; wild cat is *nume*. The Mohave say that Numeta's tail stands up, Hatakulya's hangs.

When Matavilya died, the two feline brothers sank into the ground at Aha'av'ulypo, emerged to the north at Hatakulya-nika, sank in again, and reappeared far west at Avi-kwinyehore, beyond San Bernardino. There they made two deer of clay, cleansed them by rain, and thought of the bow and hunting of the eastern mountain tribes. The deer stood and looked at the earth, sun, sky, and coming of night, and then journeyed eastward across the San Bernardino Range, through the Mohave Desert, past the New York Mountains and Avikwame, across the Colorado River at Idho-kuva'ira and Karaerva near Fort Mohave, by the foot of Boundary Cone, south, then up by Aha-kuvilya wash, and east to Amata-kwe-hoalya, "pine land," the Walapai Mountains. Their experiences are of the sort conventional in Mohave song myths; they find grass, see the morning star, swim with difficulty across the river, meet antelopes and wild cats.

From the Walapai Mountains a path led eastward which Numeta and Hatakulya had made for them. The female believed the tracks to be left from the beginning of the world, but the male knew that his makers were waiting for him and that disaster portended: he had "dreamed badly." Where the trail stopped, Numeta and Hatakulya were in wait: the older unskillfully made a noise with his bow, but the younger shot and wounded the male deer, which ran eastward and died at Amata'-ahwata-kuchinakwa. The brothers followed, so that the Walapai and Yavapai of that country might know how to hunt, found the dead body, but quarreled about its division. Numeta went back to the Walapai Mountains; Hatakulya, taking only the deer's heart, to Ahta-kwatmenva, east of Kingman, also in Walapai country. The female deer went on to Avi-melyahweke, mountains also in Arizona, but far south, opposite Parker. Such is the myth: the songs begin only at the New York Mountains, Aviwatha, and end at Amata'-ahwata-kuchinakwa. The last song is:

kwora'aka'o'cwich	old man (brother)
achwodhavek	divide
himata	its body
hikwiva	its horns
chathkwilva	skin
kosmava	sinews

Kapeta, " Turtle," is sung to the beating of a basket with a rod. This person was born last in the great house of Mastamho on Avikwame. She came into existence on the west side of the house, hence the Chemehuevi, who live in that direction, eat turtle. The singing seems to be thought to begin at Aha-kwi'-ihore, near the New York Mountains. The story progresses through the various mountains west of the river belonging to the Chemehuevi. Then it tells how Turtle went east to Hakwinyava, in Pima land, and built herself a house.

CHUHUECHA TYPE.

Chuhuecha, Ohwera, Ahta, and *Satukhota* are also classed by the Mohave as good singings because those who know them do not become shamans in old age.

The heroes of *Chuhuecha* are the two brothers called *Hayunye,* an insect, perhaps the cricket, that is said to sing *Chuhuecha* now as it chirps. A record obtained includes 169 songs in 83 groups. The singer begins in the evening to beat his basket with a bundle of stems and tells of Aha'av'ulypo and the sickness and funeral of Matavilya. By the middle of the night his story is at Analya-katha, northwest of the Providence Mountains, in Chemehuevi land; in the morning at Kwiya-selya'aya, where the river flows through Chemehuevi Valley. In the evening he begins again, but sings only a short time and ends his tale at the sea—the Gulf of California, in Papago land. At first the two brothers' experience are of the usual insignifi-

cant and descriptive kind. Later in the story, the elder wins the
younger at gambling and maltreats him. From their house at Avi-
melyahweke in Arizona the younger goes far down river and gets a
wife among the Alakwisa, then kills much game, wins his brother's
body at dice, kills him, and throws his corpse south to grow as cane.
Then he turns to stone. His wife goes far east to the Pima country,
and bears a miraculous boy, who grows up in four days, journeys to
the sea, and turns into low cane. His mother follows and becomes
the shore bird *minturisturisa* (the snipe?). Where the plot is nominal, the songs are numerous; as the story becomes humanly interesting, the songs are few and hurried. *Chuhuecha* is not danced to.

Ohwera has the eagle as its hero, and revolves at least in part
about the New York Mountains and the Chemehuevi country northwest of the Mohave. The singer strikes together two bundles of
stems. A sort of dance can accompany the singing. Six men and
two women kneel on one leg, then stamp the forward foot slightly
to each beat of the music.

Ahta, or "Cane," also called "tall cane," *Ahta'-amalya'e*, is a long
story, with more plot than most cycles. The singer strikes a double
beat on a Chemehuevi basket with a stick. There is no dancing.

Satukhota has much the same plot as the Diegueño story of *Kuya-
homar*, but the Mohave know nothing of this, and connect their
series with a Maricopa version called *Satukhota*. Its geographical
setting indicates that they are right. The story is said to begin
at Aha-kutot-namomampa near the Bill Williams Fork of the Colorado. Kwa'akuya-inyohava, "west old woman," surviving alone
after a flood, gives birth to two boys, Para'aka and Pa'ahana, who
grow up, take cane, make flutes, and attract the two far-away daughters of Masayava-kunauva, who lives at Koakamata, near Maricopa
Wells. They marry the girls, go off with them, and are killed by
their wives' kin in the Papago country, but are avenged by their
son Kwiya-humar. *Satukhota* and "Cane" appear to have much
plot in common. The *Satukhota* singer smites his palm against his
breast.

"PLEIADES" TYPE.

Hacha or "Pleiades," and *Chutaha*, which refers to the long-billed
wading bird *minsakulita*, stand apart from all others in being primarily dance singings, although the Mohave list them indiscriminately with the others. There is some justification for this attitude
because there are long myths for both, beginning at Aha'av'ulypo.
There are only two Pleiades songs and two *Chutaha*, these being
sung over and over for hours. There seems to be no instrument
of percussion used in the former. For *Chutaha*, a trench perhaps
4 feet long and a few inches wide is scooped out with the foot and

sprinkled to compact its walls. At one end a tray-shaped Chemehuevi basket is laid and beaten; at the other, a large pot is set as a
resonance chamber. The dances, which are made at least primarily
for the fun of them, are conducted as follows:

The Pleiades singer stands under a shade with his back to the
sun. Behind him young men stand abreast, and behind these, their
elders. They wear feather-hung rabbit skin ropes over their
shoulders. Facing the singer are a row of girls and one of older
women. All sing with him for a time. Then he ceases, but they
continue to dance. They bend and raise the body, make a long
stride forward with the right knee elevated, bend again, and step
back. As the men step backward, the women step forward, and
vice versa.

In *Chutaha*, when the basket is struck with the palm, the jar
gives out a deep booming, and the people assemble. Abreast with
the singer is a kneeling line of elderly men facing east; behind him,
two women selected for their loud voices, their bodies painted red,
their hair white; in front, looking toward the sun, sit three rows
of younger men. They wear tufts of white heron or crane feathers on
their heads, or strings of these feathers down their backs. A passage is left through their ranks. Down this path runs an old man,
one arm raised behind him, the other pointing forward and down.
He shouts: " Hu! once, once, once," the drummer smites his basket,
and all clap hands. Again the runner comes, but calls: " Twice,
twice, twice (*haviktem*)," and as all answer " Yes," and clap again,
the drummer and singer begin. Soon the singer raises his hand and
the row of old men arises. Each one holds a stick of his own length
and merely nods his head to the music. Again the singer signals,
and the three rows of young men, 40 or 50 in number, kneel, and the
first rank stands and sings. One of them raises his arms and the
second row rises and joins in the song; and then the third on signal
from the second. Finally the two women sing, their shrill voices
rising above the great chorus. The young men's dancing is a slight
flexing of the knees, the arms hanging slack. As the leader in the
middle of each row raises his hand, they drop farther, perhaps a foot
each time. The dance is continued until everyone is tired. It is very
clear that the Mohave are not dance specialists. Unison mass effect
makes up to them for variety and meaning of movement.

It is doubtful whether either Pleiades or *Chutaha* is sung at funerals. Their four songs are known to every one, but their public execution seems to be left to the dance or play director, the *kohota*.

VARIOUS SERIES.

Nyavadhoka, *Halykwesa*, *Ohulya*, and *Kamtoska* are little known.
The first has its myth begin at Aha'av'ulypo. The singer slaps his

thigh. In *Halykwesa* he kneels before a basket and beats it with a stick. There is no dancing. The singing is considered short, lasting only part of the night. The story begins at Av'athamulya; the hero traveled to the sea, presumably the Gulf of California, and became a univalve shell. In *Ohulya* the basket is beaten both with the stick and with the hand, which suggests a double or syncopated rhythm. The hero of the tale is the rat, who began his career at Avihalykwa'ampa. The *Kamtoska* singer also uses a basket. This singing tells of an unidentified brownish bird with the cry "*tos, tos.*"

Some of the Mohave count *Tudhulva*, the hand game, as a song series. There seems to be an associated story into which coyote enters. When besides dances, traditions, funeral rites, and shamanistic practices, even games are reckoned in one common group, it is clear that the standardized formula into which these varied activities have been fitted must have deeply impressed the civilization.

In addition to *Tumanpa Vanyume*, the Mohave follow several other foreign singings. *Chiyere*, "birds" (that is, in general), was learned by one or more individuals from the Yuma. They are said not to know the story. The rattle is used and the songs can be danced to. *Av'alyunu* is also from the Yuma. The myth begins at Aha'av'ulypo. *Alysa* is from the Kamia. The singer rattles, and men and women dance in a circle, an arrangement that is rare in native Mohave dances.

" GOOSE " SERIES.

The shamanistic song series that follow seem to comprise only a portion of the curative practices of the Mohave, and on the other hand to be only partly shamanistic, since some of them are in dispute as "doctor" singings, and the myths that accompany them are, in some cases, of the same tenor as the stories of the nonshamanistic series. Perhaps the present group, or some of its cycles, are shamanistic in association rather than practice. Thus the Mohave say that those who sing them become doctors when they grow old. At the same time these cycles are not danced to, do not use the rattle, and seem not to be sung at funerals, so that they must present a quite different aspect to the native mind from the preceding ones.

Yellaka or "Goose" is one of these "doctor's singings," but the cure which it serves is not known. It begins at the source of the river, and describes, with much detail but little incident, the journey to the sea of a company of birds with the goose and later the grebe as their leader. The musical theme is unusually simple in one of the renditions; a second is rather different in melody and rhythm. The stories of these two versions seem to be similar in scheme, but far apart in particulars. Since other cycles probably vary equally in the mouths of different individuals, a synopsis of the two Goose versions may be of interest. It may be added that the two singers who gave the information were relatives, although not close kin. The first was a young man, who also knew and sang *Nyohaiva*. His rendition, according to his own itemizing, comprised over 400 songs in 66 groups. The second was an old man, who professed to sing no other series. His Goose songs fell into 89 groups, and required two nights and a half to complete.

Version 1.

Song-group 1: at Nyahaim-kwidhik (" wet-lie ") or Nyahaim-kwiyuma (" wet-see "). Pahuchacha (Mastamho) makes the river and Goose (Yellaka) comes out followed by other birds, still unformed. (8 songs.)

2: they go to Nyahaim-kuvara, in the San Francisco Mountains in Arizona and return. (6 songs.)

3: they go to Kwathakapaya, Mount San Gorgonio near San Bernardino. (4.)

4: they return to Nyahaim-kwidhik. (10.)

5–8: south to Nyahaim-korema, Nyahaim-kumaika, Nyahaim-kuchapaiva, Nyahaim-kwattharva. (4, 4, 8, 10 songs.)

9–11: started on their long journey down the Colorado River, the birds think themselves equal to Goose; he teaches them to know right and left, and shows them foam. (8, 5, 10.)

12, 13: at Nyahaim-kwachava. They think he will die, and Raven, Road-runner, and Gold-eye ask him for names. (4, 2.)

14: at Hatakulya-nikuya. Raven is named and flies off. (5.)

15, 16: at Hatavilya-kuchahwerva. Roadrunner and Gold-eye are named. (4, 5.)

17: at Amata-hamak. Goose is sick but bars the way to the others by stretching his wings. (15.)

18: at Thaweva. He sinks and they think him dead. (6.)

19–21: at Aha'av'ulypo. Only his heart still lives. He dies, Halykupa (Grebe) takes his place, and orders the insect Han'ava to wail for him. (10, 10, 10.)

22, 23: at Ahakekachvodhauva Grebe gives half the birds to Minse'atalyke to lead, but the channel rejoins at Wathalya. (10, 14.)

24–27: going on, Grebe hears a supernatural noise from Avikwame, makes the birds swim in a straight row, and names the places Ahaikusoerva and Avikunu'ulya. (5, 5, 4, 5.)

28–31: approaching Avikwame, Grebe tells four names of Pahuchacha, warns the birds not to heed him as his power is antagonistic to theirs, and succeeds in passing the mountain. (8, 6, 10, 10.)

32: at Akwaka'iova, near Fort Mohave, they sleep. (13.)

33: Halykupa pretends to hear a noise of Goose far ahead. (18.)

34: at Hachiokwatveva. Four birds, led by Han'avachipa (Gnat catcher?), select land to become people. (10.)

35: at Avihalykwa'ampa. Grebe resolves to take the land. (10.)

36: at Hayakwira-hidho. A white beaver dams the river with its tail, but Grebe passes. (6.)

37: at Idholya-idhauva they land. (4.)

38: at Himekoata they sleep and Grebe makes a rock for them to breed on in future. (10.)

39–41: at Hachehumeva, Omaka, Aspalya-pu'umpa, their feathers sprout, they look back where they have come from, and think of that place. (5, 6, 4.)

42: at Selya'aya-kwame. Grebe tells them they are birds, but they do not understand. (6.)

43: at Hakuchyepa, Bill Williams fork, Woodpecker flies off. (4.)

44–47: at Avi-sokwilya-hatai, where they sleep, Quail, Oriole, Nighthawk, and Mockingbird take their characteristics and the last announces day break. (6, 6, 6, 10.)

48, 49: at Avi-vataya and Avi-vera Grebe has them try walking on land and tells them they are not yet fully formed. (6, 8.)

50, 51: at Aha-kutinyam he tells them how to lay eggs and Mud-hen does so. (8, 4.)

52–54: at Aha-takwatparva and Kuvukwilya they hear a noise far in the south and Grebe tells them it comes from their brothers who have come into existence from Goose's body which floated south to the sea. They try to walk on land, but faint, and Grebe makes wind and hail for them. (3, 3, 4.)

55, 56: at Aha-kumitha the wet from their feathers makes a spring and as they go on Grebe names a place To'oska. (4, 3.)

57–59: at Yellaka-hime ("goose-foot") they try to fly but their gooselike toes fail to leave the ground. At Aha-dhauvaruva they return to the water and hear a noise ahead near Yuma. (6, 4, 4.)

60: at Avi-kunyura they speculate over their ultimate appearance. (4.)

61–64: at Hukthilya they hear Pakyetpakyet, at Kwenyokuvilyo Ahanisata, at Amata-kutkyena Kwilolo, who have grown from Goose's body. They go on and see the ocean. (4, 2, 4, 5.)

65–66: at the sea, Minturisturisa (Snipe?) dives and arises with a necklace of shells. All go on the ocean except Grebe, Wood-duck, and Sakatathera. The latter wishes to return north and become a person. (6, 4.)

Here end the songs, but as in many Mohave singings, the story continues. The three birds rise halfway to the sky, where they can see the ocean on all sides of the earth, and try to alight on Avikwame, but come down on Avi-kw-ahwata, farther south. They proceed upstream, sleep at Savechivuta, go on to Hachiokwatveva near Fort Mohave where the four birds led by Han'avachipa have chosen tracts of land and become people. The three are unable to eat the edible food offered them. They announce that they have come to take the land. The first settlers resist successfully and Wood-duck and Han'-avachipa are wounded. The three wanderers think Mastamho may be able to do something for them, go on north, and meet him at Hokusava, where the god is turning various beings into finished birds. He gives mythic names to the three, who go off as birds. Mastamho returns in four steps to the head of the river, makes fish, sand, and rocks, deliberates, turns into the bird Sakwithei, and flies away.

Version 2.

Song-group 1: at Nyahaim-kwiyuma ("wet-see"), the mythical source of the river, where many eggs hatch.

Groups 3 to 5 and 11 to 12 are devoted to the names of Goose.

15: at Avi-kwatulya.

19: at Avak-tinyam. Tinyam-hwarehware and Han'ava, two insects, cry in their house when they see Goose, here called Masahai-tachuma, coming at the head of many birds.

24: at Selya'aya-ita.

28: at Avi-kutaparva.

29: at Kara'erva, near Fort Mohave.

32: at Avi-halykwa'ampa.

33: at Mat'ara ("playing field"), near Needles.

36: at Hokyampeva.

40: at Sankuvanya. Goose turns white and thinks himself like the gulls he sees.

43: at Hakuchyepa, the mouth of Bill Williams fork, Goose takes the main channel, other birds follow a blind slough and must return.

44: at Amata-kutudhunya. It becomes night and the birds quarrel whether it will be light again. Goose tells of the owl and night birds.

47: he tells of Orion and the Pleiades.

48: Goose awakes and tells of a dream in which they were at the sea.

51: the birds swim on downstream abreast, they being now where the river is widest.

55 to 56: at Hatusalya. Goose tells of sitting on the beach of the sea.

59: at Kuvukwilya. Mastamho is there, but Goose announces that they will pass on.

69: Goose dreams he sees the ocean, the others say that it is a mesa; they quarrel.

70: at Yiminalyek, in Yuma country.

77: at Avi-aspa or Amata-kutkyena, below Yuma territory.

81: they have gone to Amata-hakwachtharva, apparently another name for the place at which they began.

86: they grow feathers and begin to fly.

88: at Hokusava.

89: at Amata-minyoraiva, north of Mastamho's mountain Avikwame.

OTHER SEMI-SHAMANISTIC SERIES.

Halykupa, "Grebe," is the chief character of the latter part of the Goose story. There seems to be a distinct *Halypuka* or "Loon" singing, for which a basket is beaten. Those who dream this shout like the bird at the "annual" mournings and have the repute of not living long.

Ahakwa'ilya seems to be named from the dragon-fly larva. A basket is beaten. This is both specified and denied as a shamanistic cycle.

Sampulyka, "Mosquito," also uses a basket as instrument.

Wellaka cures diarrhea.

Hikupk has to do with venereal disease.

Apena, "Beaver," begins its story with Matavilya still alive at the source of the river. It is sung by shamans who cure neck swellings caused by the beaver, can smoke tobacco while diving, and prevent the river from washing away banks on which houses stand. *Ichul-yuye* may be another singing connected with the beaver, or perhaps is only the name of the sickness which the *Apena* dreamer cures.

Humahnana, a hard, black, malodorous beetle, and *Ipam-imicha*, "person cries," begin their tale at Aha'av'ulypo, use no accompaniment to their songs, and serve to cure the sickness *ichudhauva* caused by eating a bird wounded by hawks, as well as the *ichiekanyamasava*, diarrheal illness which befalls infants whose fathers eat game killed by themselves instead of giving it away. *Ipam-imicha* also has to do with the "foreign-sickness" caused by eating strange food, and is thus connected with *Yaroyara*, which serves the same purpose and also commences at Aha'av'ulypo. All four of these singings, if they are indeed distinct, are held by the Mohave to be truly shamanistic in their details of Matavilya's sickness and funeral.

Hayakwira is a cycle concerned with another kind of rattlesnake than the *Ave* songs and story described below under "Shamanism." *Chamadhulya* is allied to *Hayakwira*.

MYTHOLOGY.

Besides the tales that form the thread of their song cycles, the Mohave tell at least three other kinds of myths, which ordinarily are not sung to. There is, first, an origin myth, of a type generic in southern California. Second, there are long pseudohistorical narrations, which contain suggestions of migration legends and clan traditions, but are too thoroughly cast in the standard molds of Mohave mythology to evince these qualities very clearly. Lastly, there are coyote stories and miscellaneous tales, which, if they do nothing else, prove that the Mohave can on occasion be reasonably brief.

This is the cosmogony; for which the Mohave seem to have no name other than "dream tale" or "shaman's tale":

The first were Sky and Earth, male and female, who touched far in the west, across the sea. Then were born from them Matavilya, the oldest; Frog, his daughter, who was to cause his death; his younger brother or son Mastamho, his successor and greater than he; and all men and beings. In four strides Matavilya led them upward to Aha'-av'ulypo, "house-post water," in Eldorado Canyon on the Colorado, above Mohave land; the center of the earth, as he found by stretching his arms. There he made his "dark round," the first house. With an unwitting indecency he offended his daughter, and plotting against him, she swallowed his voidings, and he knew that he should die, and told the people. Coyote, always suspected, was sent away for fire, and then Fly, a woman, rubbed it on her thigh. Coyote raced back, leaped over Badger, the short man in the ring of people, snatched the god's heart from the pyre, and escaped with it. Mastamho directed the mourning, and Han'ava, the cicada, first taught how to wail. Korokorapa, also called Hiko or Haiko, "white man," alone had sat unmoved as Matavilya lay dying, now sank into the ground with noise, and returned westward to Pi'in, the place of universal origin.

Matavilya's ashes offended, and wind, hail, and rain failed to obliterate them. In four steps Mastamho strode far north, plunged his cane of breath and spittle into the earth, and the river flowed out. Entering a boat, Mastamho journeyed with mankind to the sea, twisting and tilting the boat or letting it run straight as he wished wide bottom lands or sharp canyons to frame the river. He returned with the people on his arms, surmounted the rising waters to the mountain Akokahumi, trod the water down, and took his followers upstream to the northern end of what was to be the Mohave country. Here he heaped up the great pointed peak Avikwame—more exactly Avi-kwa'ame—Newberry or Dead Mountain as the Americans call it, where he, too, built himself a house. It is of this house that shamans dream, for here their shadows were as little boys in the face of Mastamho, and received from him their ordained powers, confirmed by tests on the spot. Here, too, Mastamho made the people shout, and the fourth time day and sun and moon appeared.

Then he plotted the death of "sky-rattlesnake," Kammay-aveta, also called Umas-ereha, a great power far south in the sea. Message after message was sent him; he knew that the sickness which he was summoned to cure was pretended; but at last he came, amid rain and thunder, stretching his vast length from ocean to mountain. As his head entered the great house it was cut off. It rolled back to the sea in the hope of reconstituting its living body, but became only an ocean monster; while from his blood and sweat and juices came rattlesnakes and noxious insects whose powers some shamans combat. This was the first shaman killed in the world.

Now Mastamho's work was nearly done. To Walapai, Yavapai, Chemehuevi, Yuma, and Kamia he gave each their land and mountains, their foods, and their speech, and sent them off. The youngest, the Mohave, he taught to farm, to cook in pottery, to speak and count as was best fit for them, and to stay in the country. Then, meditating as to his own end, he stretched his arms, grew into *saksak* the fish eagle, and flew off, without power or recollection, ignorant and infested with vermin.

"GREAT TALES."

The migration or war myths are of the type of the *Vinimulya-hapacha* cycle stories. Their groups of people who travel and fight seem all to be regarded as Mohave, and each of them to stand in the narrator's mind for a body of kinsmen in the male line; but his interest is in their doings, not in their organization, and their clan affiliations are rarely mentioned, or sometimes contradictorily. The geography, as always among the Mohave, is gone into very minutely, and centers in Mohave Valley, but the marches and settlements are made to extend for long distances in all directions. These stories are called *ich-kanava*, "great tellings," and while of similar tenor, appear to vary greatly according to the narrator. They are, of course, dreamed, in native opinion, and are staggeringly prolix. One, which the narrator, a blind old man, had sometimes told from for a night, or until his hearers went to sleep, but never completely through, he recited on six days for a total of 24 hours, and then was still far from the end. He evidently was wholly unable to estimate its length.

Such stories simply can not be condensed. An outline becomes as dry a skeleton of names and places as certain passages of the priestly writer of the Pentateuch. The central events, the battles themselves, are trivial. The point, and to the native the interest of the whole, evidently lies in the episodes and a certain treatment of them; which

is so peculiar, so uninteresting even, to those habituated to other
literary manners, that it must be admitted as a very definite style,
in the inward sense of that word. A comparison with the Iliad
with the wrath of Achilles omitted, or the Mahabharata without the
careers of its five brother heroes, gives some rude suggestion of the
quality. If Mohave civilization had been advanced enough to allow
of their finding some clear central theme to hold together the welter
of detail and names, their "great tales" would no doubt seem impressive to us. A fragment of one may serve to give some hint of
the epic breadth of manner.

Part of a Hipahipa Legend.

Amainyavererkwa and Ichehwekilyeme, his son, were at Amata-tasilyka. They
were there four days. Then Ichehwekilyeme went fishing. He visited his
friends, some to the north and some to the south, through the whole Mohave
Valley, and gave them fish. The next day he went again. His people said:
"Take food with you," and wanted to give him mixed corn and pumpkin seeds,
but he said: "I will not carry a load. I shall travel light." So he took
only his fish net and went off on a run. On his way he followed a lake (or
slough), Aha'-inya (some miles south of Fort Mohave). When he had caught
fish, the people there crowded around him. He gave them his catch and they
cut up the fish and ate them. When they had thus pleased themselves, they
killed Ichehwekilyeme with a club and hid his body and ran off. The men
who did this were Hinyorilya-vahwilya, Hinyorilya-vanaka, Hinyorilya-vapaya,
and Hinyorilya-va'ava. When the people (at large) had scattered abroad, these
four had returned and settled at Avinya-kapuchora and Kwinalya-kutikiorva,
near Aha'-inya. They were Hipahipa (the mythic name of a clan, whose women
bore the name Kutkilya, which is still in use). Now that they had killed
Ichehwekilyeme, they ran off far to the east to Chivakaha, Aha-kupone, Aha-
kuvilya, and Avinyesko.

Amainyavererkwa became distressed about his son and searched for him.
As he had friends everywhere, he thought perhaps the young man might be at
Aha-talompa (near the southern end of the valley), or perhaps at Kuhuinye.
Or he thought he might be at Avi-kw-ahoato, or Avi-kutaparva, or Kwiya-kavasu,
or Kwiya-kulyike, or Hu'ulyechupaiva, or at Avi-tutara (apparently all in
Mohave Valley). As he had friends at all these places he thought of them,
and in the morning put on his sandals and went southward. As he traveled,
he looked over these places. By noon he had come down to the last one.
Then he returned and by night reached his house in the north (of the valley)
without having found his son. His people crowded thickly around him, but
he said that he had not heard news nor seen tracks. He felt very bad.

Then Ampotakerama was the only one there who thought: "Perhaps the
young man became as if crazy or blind. Perhaps he was drowned, or ran off."
Ampotakerama thought thus all that night.

Now Umase'aka lived at Amata-tasilyka also. But he said nothing. Ahalya'-
asma was chief there also, and so were Ahamakwinyuenyeye, Nyemelyekwesi'ika,
and Ha'ampa-kwa'akwenya. They too thought. But Amainyavererkwa said
nothing. He only lay and slept while the others were thinking.

When the sun was up, the others all told him: "Eat a little." But
Amainyavererkwa said: "I feel bad. I want to go north. When I come
back and have found my boy I shall eat." So he started.

When he returned, all crowded around him again. He said: "I have looked everywhere. I have no more friends among whom I can search. I think my son is lost." Then all cried and had tears in their eyes.

In the morning Amainyavererkwa went up river once more. This time he went farther and traveled until he came to Asesmava. There he slept. In the morning he went on. He visited all his friends and received to eat whatever kinds of food they ate different from his own. He thought that perhaps his son had gone up for the purpose of eating these strange foods. Late in the afternoon he came to Amata-akwata, Kukake, Ahtanye-ha, and Avinyidho. He inquired there among his friends. It was now sunset and his friends gave him to eat, but told him they had not seen his son. He ate a little and slept there that night.

In the morning he ate a little again. His friends gave him red paint and feathers which he packed and put on his shoulder and then he started (south) homeward.

At sunset he came to Akwereha. He had no one living there, but lay and slept there. He thought: "I will call this place Akwereha, and all will call it by this name when they tell stories. And I will leave my paint and feathers here, and will call it also Amata-sivilya-kwidhaua (feather-having-place)."

In the morning he went on, and while it was still early came to Kwakitupeva and Kwasekelyekete (Union Pass, north of Fort Mohave). There he drank a little. He was now feeling very bad on account of his son. Then he began to run until he came to Amata-kamota'ara. There he drank again and then ran on until he came to Ammo-heva (Hardyville). Having drunk once more, he went on until he came to Ismavakoya and Mach-ho. There he looked to see how far he still had to go. Then he began running again. He ran until he came to Akweretonyeva. Then he thought: "I am nearly at my house now." So he walked fast until he came to Selya'aya-kumicha, and then to the top of Amai-kwitasa. Then he looked toward his house at Amata-tasilyka. As he stood, he saw that it was dusty about his house as if there were wind there. The dust was from the many people.

When he returned home he again thought of the north. He wanted to go north once more to look for his son. Then in the morning he took his sandals and started. He came to Oachavampeva, Asmalya-kuvachaka, Amata-kumata'ara, and Avi-tunyora. At Avi-tunyora lived Himekuparakupchula. He was a shaman and knew everything that happened. It was he that Amainyavererkwa went to see. Himekuparakupchula had two sons, Thumeke'-ahwata, the older, and Ahwe-mestheva, the younger. He himself was too old to walk. When Amainyavererkwa came, his two sons set him up and leaned against him to support him. He was so old that he could hardly talk.

Amainyavererkwa sat down near him and said: "My son is lost." Himekuparakupchula said: "I am the man who knows everything. No one has told me of this matter, but I know it. Here are my two sons. The oldest is not very able. The younger knows something. Call him. He is playing about with a bow. Call him and ask him. He knows. He has dreamed like myself." So they called Ahwe-mestheva, and the boy came. He said: "I know. I am like the old man, my father." He was ready to go back with Amainyavererkwa. But he only sat and said that he knew and made no movement. Amainyavererkwa asked: "You will be sure to come?" Ahwe-mestheva said: "Yes; I shall surely come southward."

Then Amainyavererkwa started back to his house. When he had gone a short way he looked back but did not see the boy coming. He went on, looking back, but still Ahwe-mestheva did not come. Then he thought: "I do

not think he will come. He has not seen. He is only a little boy. He is not
man enough and does not know and so will not come." But when he reached
Ammo-heva he looked again and saw the boy coming. Then he thought: " He
is really coming." When he reached Amata-kwilyisei he stood and looked
and again saw him coming. Then all at once the boy was no longer apparent.
He was traveling under the ground. Therefore Amainyavererkwa did not see
him. He kept looking back in vain. Then at last he saw him traveling
underground. He went on and reached his house in the afternoon and said:
"Ahwe-mestheva is coming. He will be here soon."

When Ahwe-mestheva arrived carrying bow and arrows everything was prepared. They had made a little hut of *idho* willows, sticking them into the
ground and tying the tops together. As the boy came in front of the hut he
threw his bow and arrows forward on the ground. Then he stood, kicked the
ground, and jumped up on the roof of the hut so that it shook. Then he
jumped up, then down on the ground again, and stood outside the hut. He
said: " I said that I knew everything. Now I shall sing. I shall sing four
times." Then he sang as follows (the words are distorted to fit the rhythm):

"Akwetinyam ithapikali, at night I see clearly."

"(Matkwesa) ikakorenye ikanamave, (my shadow) speaks and tells me
(all)."

"Akwetinyam ithapiwaye, at night I see brightly."

" Ikanavek kwanumadhe, I shall tell it (all) here (in time)."

When he had sung these four songs he went into the little house.

When he was inside he said: " I know the man's name. It is Ichehwekilyeme.
He went fishing. Four men killed him. Their names are Hinyorilya-vahwilya,
Hinyorilya-vanaka, Hinyorilya-vapaya, and Hinyorilya-va'ava. The people here
wanted to give him corn and pumpkin seeds to take with him, but he would
not. Then he went. These people found him fishing. He said to them:
' You are traveling and are hungry. Build a fire and I shall give you to eat.'
Then these four men answered: ' It is good.' Then they killed him. In the
water was a stump. There they dragged him and fastened his body down with
a stick so that no one would see and know."

Thus the boy Ahwe-mestheva knew and told everything, and so the people
discovered what had become of Ichehwekilyeme.

Then his father, Amainyavererkwa, went to Aha'-inya and found the body
and took it out of the water. Then they burned Ichehwekilyeme with his best
clothes and property, and cried at the house. Then the boy Ahwe-mestheva
said: "That is all. I go now." He shot an arrow northward and started
home.

When he returned, he told the old man Himekuparakupchula, his father:
" I found him." His father said: "It is good. Perhaps they will do something about it (fight). I do not yet know it, but perhaps they will." Then he
said to his oldest son, Thumeke'-ahwata: " Go down to them and let me know
what they will do." So the older son started. He reached Amata-tasilyka
at sunset. Amainyavererkwa said: " We do not yet know. I have nothing to
say. There is one man here who speaks and we follow. He is Ampota-kerama,
and he is thinking now. I know that people sometimes " steal" (ambush
shamans who have caused deaths). I have seen them doing that. But I think
that bad and we shall not do it. Perhaps Ampota-kerama will know something
to do."

And Ampota-kerama said: " I am trying to know how we shall start a fight.
Perhaps we shall play *kachoakwek* with them (a game of kicking at one another with the heels). Perhaps in that way we shall be able to pick a quarrel

and seize and kill them. Or perhaps we shall play *hachohwesavek* (a game in which balls of mud are put on the ends of poles and slung at the opposing party). If they beat us, we can become angry and fight. Perhaps we shall play with hoop and poles. If the ring lies so that the pole shows inside, we shall say that we can not see it clear. Then he who threw the pole will say: ' I can see it.' We shall say: ' No; it is not a score.' Perhaps in that way there will be a quarrel and a fight will begin." So they were thinking of that.

Here the recorded tale breaks off. The above is evidently little more than a beginning.

SHAMANISM.

Shamanism is deeply stained by the beliefs that pervade all Mohave thought. The shaman's experiences begin in myth at the world origin and are myth in form. The god Mastamho gave their special powers to all shamans of to-day, who own no private spirit allies. Their songs have words of the same cast as the myths on which are based all songs of pleasure or funeral. One class is dreamed like the other. There is no theory of disease objects projected into human bodies. Hence the physician sucks little if at all. The patient's soul, his "shadow," is affected or taken away; the shaman brings it back because he has dreamed, while Mastamho was regulating the world, of the mythical person that became a certain thing or animal, and saw the nature of its power of operation for human good or ill; and he counteracts this power with his own, with song or breath or spittle, blowing or laying on of hands or other action, as his own shadow then saw and was instructed. There is no philosophy of disease and treatment more diverse than this from the beliefs of the north and central Californians.

A single example, even though in condensation, may make this attitude plain.

A shaman's story.

At Aha'av'ulypo, the account begins, all the people were in the dark house that Matavilya made. "I shall die," he said when the Frog, the shaman, his daughter, had made him sick. Six persons were there and listened to him and grieved and went off when he had died: Tumanpa long, Tumanpa short, Chuhuecha, Salt, Nyavadhoka, and Av'alyunu (these song cycles are here personified).

Then follows the story of Matavilya's funeral, of the making of the river by Mastamho, and the killing of the gigantic Sky-Rattlesnake. From the glue in his joints, *himata-halai*, eggs, were formed, out of which came Achyeka, Yellow ant, the oldest, who took the name Humara-kadhucha. From *himata-haka-malya*, his "body form," grew Halytota, Spider, who called himself Ampota-nyunye, "road dust." Menisa, Scorpion, was born from Sky-Rattlesnake's sweat, and from his blood Ave, Rattlesnake, the youngest. These took the names Ampota-kuhudhurre and Ampota-himaika.

While these four took shape, Mastamho taught some of the people to know three sicknesses and their cure: *hayakwira* (a kind of rattlesnake distinct from *ave*), *isuma* (dream), and *ichhulyuye* (beaver). Of these sicknesses I know, says the narrator, but I do not treat them because they were not given to me. But Ave-rattlesnake, Scorpion, Halytota-spider, and Achyeka-ant are mine. Four rows of people stood at Avikwame before Mastamho, and these four sat there also, and my shadow was there. "Now he comes," Mastamho said of me. "Listen to him. What he says is true. I gave it to him." Then the four were ashamed and feared and hung their heads and did not want to hear, because I knew them and was above them.

Then Mastamho took all the people downstream to Avi-kutaparva, to the New York Mountains, and far west to Avi-hamoka, "three mountains," which is toward Tehachapi from Mojave station. The four went there too, but on the north, by their own road. There Rattlesnake marked himself with white dust, with dark dust, with white cloud, with dark cloud, and went with Mastamho and others eastward to Koskilya near Parker. There Mastamho ordained a line between the Mohave to the north and the Pima, the Halchidhoma, and the Kohuana to the south. There they prepared for war against the southerners, traveled against them at Ahpe-hwelyeve near Ehrenberg, attacked and fought, and took a Halchidhoma and a Kohuana scalp under Rattlesnake's lead. Then they returned to "Three Mountains" and made a dance over the scalps.

Rattlesnake lives there at Three Mountains. He has a road to every tribe. Often he thinks of war and wants to bite a person. "I like him," he says of a man, "I want him as a friend to be here." Then he asks the mountain. If the mountain says yes, the man will die; but if the mountain is silent, the man will be bitten and live. One road goes straight from Three Mountains to my heart, says the narrator, and I hear the singing and talking there. Then I know whether a person will live or die. When Rattlesnake or Spider has bitten him, he takes his shadow. If he brings it all the way to Three Mountains, the man dies. But if I can stop the shadow near Three Mountains, then I sing again at each place on the road and each time we are farther, until when I arrive with it here the man is well. At every place on the way I stand and sing and prevent the shadow's going on.

Spider also thinks of biting persons. He thinks (sings):

Oyach-kwa'-anyayi	my breath is bright.
iha-kwa'-anyayi	my spittle is bright.
iha-kwa'-akwithva	my spittle is tough.
oyach-kwa'-akwithva	my breath is tough.

"In the north, in the south, my breath is not hot. In the east my breath is hot. When the sun rises, I put up my hands. When they are warm, I lay them on my face, and my breath becomes hot. Hiha-nyunye, 'saliva-road,' is my name. My roads are four. They are not on earth, but high, in the sky. As Rattlesnake has done, so I will do. I am thinking of my friend whom I wish. I want his shadow on my road. My north road is cold, my south road is cold, but when I bite in the east it is hot. I do not want my friend at night, I want him when the sun rises in the east and my breath becomes hot in him," says Spider.

Then I see Spider start out on his sky road when he wishes to bite. North of Avikwame, at Lyehuta, lives the chief of Rattlesnakes, Ampota-nyamatham-tamakwa. Him I hear Spider asking; and if he will not allow, Spider can do nothing. When he permits, Spider bites with his four teeth, and bright-spittle and hot-spittle go into the person's body and make it clear. Then I can look through the man, and he rolls about in sweat. Spider ties his heart around with spittle. I see it like that. If I am summoned from far away, the heart may be wrapped twice when I arrive. Then I walk four times around the man on the left side (sunwise) and break the roads that Spider has made to his heart, and he sits up and spits out what Spider has put into him, and is well. But if Spider has tied his heart four times around when I arrive and it is tight, the man is killed. I can do nothing then.

If Spider has bitten a person without the assent of the mountain or of the great Rattlesnake, and the man is cured, Spider is full of breath, and goes off and dies somewhere. His shadow goes up, without legs, a round thing, *ampota-yara*, that rolls in the clouds, invisible, and makes rain.

There is another one, Halytota-kunemi, "brave spider," that brings on diarrhœa, and that warriors dream of. I know that one's name, but I did not dream about him. And so with Ave-hakthara, the short rattlesnake, that is brave and always wants to war: he too went off to one side from where I was, and knowledge about him was not given me.

But Scorpion at Three Mountains took the name Matkwesam-havika, "Shadow-companion," and meditated what his form would be. He too made four roads, but they are underground. At the end of the road to the east, he made Tarantula by his word; at the north, Rock Spider; west, Firefly; south, Kwithohwa, a longish yellow spider. These four own the winds and clouds, which are their breath. But the rain from these clouds is bitter. I can make it fall, and sometimes when the crops are dry, people ask me to make it, but I refuse because it is not good. Scorpion asked these four at the ends for the power to kill. But they did not answer him, hence he only wounds, and a man who is strong needs no treatment. Sweat is harmless, and that is what Scorpion was born from. He also went down the river to ask four great rattlesnakes for power, but one after the other would not give it to him.

Achyeka-ant was the oldest of the four. He, too, made four roads of spittle and breath. Then he called himself "night body," Kutinyam-himata, and sank down to the heart of the earth, *amata-hiwa*. There he was no longer a person, but a yellow ant; and there he made four more roads in the darkness. He emerged, and now called himself "bright body," Himata'-anyayi, who would live in the roots of a tree, the heart of a tree, and make his house there. His body is here on earth, his shadow below. It is his night body, the underground shadow, that bites men. It goes through the veins, of which one leads to the heart. He eats the heart and the man begins to die. He is a long time dying; but at last Achyeka takes the man's shadow with him to his house. But he failed to make stone and earth alive as he tried. So I take a very fine earth, rub it between my hands, and put it on the sick person's body. So I stop the roads to the middle place of Achyeka, and bring the person's shadow back to him, and he becomes well.

The complete interweaving of shamanistic beliefs and curative practices with the national mythology, and the complete dependence, in native opinion, of both on individual dreaming, are fully exemplified by the foregoing personal narrative.

The following is a purely objective description of the treatment extended for snake bite by another shaman.

When the shaman is notified, he immediately begins to sing where he is, in order to produce a cooling wind and sprinkle of rain for the wounded man. When he arrives where the patient is lying with his head to the south in front of his house, he sings standing at a little distance from him, first on his north, then on his west, south, and east. Should he sing a fifth song, the sick man would die. Only the man's wife may sit by him; all others are at a distance.

The shaman forbids everyone to drink until the sun has set, and takes no water himself, because the rattlesnake does not drink. He sits awake, and at midnight and in the morning sings his four songs over again. Then he goes home and the patient is cured.

If a man eats fish caught in his own net while this is new, the ghosts, *nyavedhi*, of the fish take away his shadow, *matkwesa*. Then he becomes drowsy and feeble, and a shaman must sing the soul back. But the shaman must not stay too long in the village of the dead, or the departed among his own kin are likely to seize and try to hold him with them in affection.

STATUS OF THE SHAMAN.

The Mohave are astoundingly frank in telling of how they kill their doctors or shamans, and some of the latter reciprocate with unforced declarations of the harm they have done. This is a native summary:

Doctors are despatched for blighting the crops; for repeatedly attending a patient but killing instead of curing him; for having said about a sick person: "I wish you would die;" and for admitting responsibility for deaths. There is a doctor now who stands at funerals and says aloud: "I killed him." Doctors and brave men are alike. The latter say: "I do not wish to live long." A doctor says: "I shall not live a long time. I wish to die. That is why I kill people. Why do you not kill me?" Or he may hand a stick to a man and say: "I killed your father." Or he may come and tell a sick person: "Don't you know that it is I that am killing you? Must I grasp you and despatch you with my hands before you will try to kill me?"

The Mohave tell of such utterances as if they were frequent, and there is little doubt that certain shamans, particularly those under suspicion, now and then launched into a very delirium of provocation and hate—an intensity of emotion rare among other Californians. In general, they unquestionably believe their spirit experiences and power to be actual.

The following autobiographical anecdote well illustrates the native attitude:

When I was young, I was once with a friend at a shaman's house. My friend proposed that we kill him. I took my bow and four arrows and said to the shaman: "I am going to shoot doves." He assented. When I returned, the shaman seemed to be asleep under the shade before his house. My friend was indoors, and said: "He is sleeping." I took a (steel) ax and swung at the shaman's head. I struck him in the cheek. As he sat up, no blood came from the wound. Then suddenly a torrent gushed out. My companion became frightened, ran off, returned, struck at the shaman's head, but hit only his legs, and ran off, hardly able to drag his own. Two women had been sitting near, lousing each other, and at first had not seen what we did. Then they began to cry and wail. I crossed the river, and found some men gambling, and sat with them. In the afternoon I said: "I have killed so and so." They thought I was boasting. "Yes, do it," they said. "That

will be good. Too many people are dying." "I have done it already," I
answered. Soon the dead man's relatives came, and it seemed that we should
fight with sticks. But on the next day the shaman's son announced that he
would not fight, and nothing further happened.

TOLOACHE.

The Mohave know the Jimson weed and its qualities, but give no
evidence of having been at all influenced by the toloache cult of the
Shoshonean tribes. They make no ceremony connected with the
plant. Individuals drink a decoction of the leaves taken from the
west side of the bush—those on the east are considered ·poison—become unconscious for four days, dream, and thus acquire luck in
gambling. This appears to be similar to the desert Cahuilla practice and indicates a semishamanistic use of the drug analogous to its
status among the Pueblos.

THE GHOST DANCE.

The Mohave took up the later or eastern ghost dance, whereas most
California tribes either were influenced by the less known first wave
or escaped both. The movement was introduced by a Southern
Paiute, and appears to have left no impress at all on the Mohave consciousness. They had their own peculiar and satisfying scheme of
dreaming, and by 1890 were .still so wholly absorbed in their native
way of doing things that they hardly realized that they were living
in a new and destructive atmosphere.

RELIGION AND KNOWLEDGE.

It is interesting that the Mohave are frequently in argument about
each other's religious knowledge. Some one announces that he has
dreamed one of the less common cycles: others deny that there is
such a myth or cycle, or refuse to admit more than that the assertor
says so. A man begins a story. Suddenly another interrupts with
the reproof that what is being told is nothing, a mere mixture of
things as diverse as *Chutaha* and coyote tales. The narrator insists
that he has dreamed it so and it is correct. He is told that his
dreams are bad; and usually he subsides. Whether a certain man
is or is not a shaman, or is a legitimate one, or will become a shaman,
and what his power really is for, are all matters on which whoever
is minded expresses his opinion freely.

The Mohave display far more sense of the value of numbers than
the average Californian Indian. They are constantly using such
figures as "5 or 6"—"5, 6" they say—and "40 or 50," apparently
with a reasonably correct idea of the numbers denoted, especially

if persons are referred to. They are not much given to tallies, and one rarely sees them operating with counters or marks in the sand. Simple addition or subtraction of numbers below 100 they carry on readily in their heads.

The number 4 is brought into myth and religious act at every opportunity.

There is a word for year, *kwathe*, but its etymology is unknown.

The Mohave are utterly unlike the true southwestern Indians, and essentially in the status of the central and northern California tribes, in lacking fetishes or any artistic or concretely expressed symbolism. The Shoshoneans of southern California express the Pueblo spirit much more nearly in their sand paintings and ritualistic implements. In fact the gap between the southwesterners proper and the Yumans of the Colorado is profound as regards religion. There is no trace among the latter of kiva, altar, mask, offering, priest, initiation, fraternity, or color symbolism, all so characteristic of the town-dwelling tribes. Most of these elements recur, though in abbreviation or pallid substitute, among the Luiseño and Gabrielino; but among the Mohave they are replaced by the wholly predominant factor of dreaming.

CHAPTER 52.

THE YUMA.

RELATION OF THE YUMA AND MOHAVE.

The Yuma have provided a name not only for an Arizona city and county and a fort and reservation in California—all adjoining the great stream of the Colorado—but for the entire family of tribes to which they, the Mohave, the Diegueño, and many others belong. This does not mean that they were the central or prominent tribe of the group; for such nomenclatures become established by accident or by unconscious fancies of the civilized ear for designations of picturesque or facile sound. As a matter of fact, the Mohave seem to have been at least as numerous as the Yuma ever since they were known, equally solidary, rather more venturesome and addicted to travel to far parts, and probably more active in their inward life; since not only their religious concepts but their songs, the very words thereof, and their sacred places are known farther than Yuma influence penetrated. That the general lower Colorado culture to which both tribes adhered was in its origin and elementals more largely the creation of one tribe than of the other or of some still different group of the region, it is impossible to say. The original focus of the culture is almost certain to have been where there was the greatest agglomeration of tribes, about the mouth of the Gila, rather than at the upstream limit of the valley lands where the Mohave were situate. The lower river was also nearer to influences from the south and down the Gila from the east, the direction in which higher cultures lay. Yet one receives the impression that the most concentrated, energetic, and characteristic form of the river civilization in the past century or two has been that which it took among the Mohave.

It also happens that the Mohave are better known than the Yuma, so that even if a less extended description of the latter people were

not justified by circumstances, it would be inevitable. The following account is therefore limited to comparisons of the two tribes on
matters in which they are known to differ. In their agriculture,
manufacture, clothing, hairdress, houses, warfare, and tribal sense,
the Yuma and Mohave seem to be virtually identical.

TRIBAL AND HISTORICAL FACTS.

The Yuma call themselves Kwichyana or Kuchiana, and are
known to all the other Yumans by dialectic variants of this name,
whose meaning is not known to them. The Chemehuevi call them
Hukwats, the Apache denominate them together with other tribes
of the family: Hatilshe. A Spanish designation is Garroteros,
clubbers, perhaps with reference to their mallet or pestle-shaped
war clubs. The name Yuma first appears in Kino in 1702. Its
origin is not positively known. It has been thought a misapplica-
tion of *yamayo*, the word denoting a chief's son; but this interpretation seems only a conjecture. The existence of such titles for the
hereditary successors of chieftainship is, however, of interest as
parallel to Gabrielino and Juaneño custom.

The tribe may be estimated at 2,500 or more souls before contact
with the whites. Garcés in 1776 thought there were 3,000. The
number in 1905 was put at 900, in 1910 at 834.

The territory of the Yuma was the Colorado bottom about the
mouth of the Gila. They are said to have occupied the main stream
for 15 miles above and 60 miles below the confluence; but the latter
figure is almost certainly too high. It would bring the Yuma almost
to the Gulf of California, between which and themselves a number
of other tribes of allied lineage intervened. In distinction from the
Mohave, they seem to have inhabited chiefly the western bank of
the river; but such choices are probably dictated by considerations
of local topography.

The Yuma may have been among the first tribes discovered by
Caucasians in California. In 1540, two years before Cabrillo
sighted the channel islands, Alarcon, operating in conjunction with
the Coronado expedition to Zuñi, sailed up the great Rio de los
Tizones, the "Firebrand River" or Colorado, and established contact with the natives. He hardly penetrated as far as Mohave
territory—his 85 leagues would carry him there only if the river
flowed straight. But he certainly passed what were later the seats
of the Yuma, and may have seen their ancestors; although Oñate
in 1605 tells us nothing of any people in whom we can recognize

the Yuma, and the first positively identifiable mention of them is that of Kino, a century later. Alarcon's brief notices of the Indians accord well with the disposition and customs of the historic Yuman peoples of the river. It is also in agreement with what is known as to freedom of intertribal relations in the region, that Alarcon found the natives informed as to details of the equipment and appearance of the Spaniards who had reached New Mexico but a few months before.

While it has been asserted that Oñate reached the Yuma, his Cohuanas are the Kohuana, a separate tribe nearer the gulf; and the Ozaras whom he found at the mouth of the Gila are so described as to give the impression that they were a Piman rather than Yuman people. Kino and Garcés, like most lone travelers of resoluteness and tact, encountered few difficulties from the Yuma; but when two missions were soon after established among them they were wiped out within a year, in 1781. After the acquisition of California by the United States and the setting in of the overland tide of travel there were the usual troubles, and Fort Yuma was established to hold the tribe in check; but there was no notable resistance to the Americans.

In international friendships and enmities the Yuma belonged on the side of the Mohave and were hostile to the Maricopa in the great division that extended through the tribes of southern California and western Arizona, as already outlined with reference to the Chemehuevi. They seem, however, to have been more friendly to the Kamia, and through them with the Diegueño proper, than were the Mohave. It was probably their ancient feud with the Maricopa that embroiled them with the Pima, a peaceable but sturdy nation of farmers, against whom the volatile military ambition of the river tribes repeatedly dashed itself. The last great undertaking of the Yuma was against these people, and ended disastrously in 1858.

DREAMING.

The direct basis of all religion—tradition, ritual song, and shamanistic power—is individual dreaming, in the opinion of the Yuma. They hold to this belief as thoroughly and consistently as the Mohave. An autobiographic statement by one of their medicine men and myth narrators reveals this attitude more convincingly than it can be summarized in general statements:

Before I was born I would sometimes steal out of my mother's womb while she was sleeping, but it was dark and I did not go far. Every good doctor (*kwasidhe*, almost synonymous with *sumach*, "dreamer") begins to under-

3625°—25——51

stand before he is born. When a little boy I took a trip to Avikwame Mountain and slept at its base. I felt of my body with my two hands, but found it was not there (*sic*). It took me four days and nights to go there. Later I became able to approach even the top of the mountain. At last I reached the willow-roof (shade) in front of the dark-house there. Kumastamho was within. It was so dark that I could hardly see him. He was naked and very large. Only a few great doctors were in there with him, but a crowd of men stood under the shade before the house. I now have power to go to Kumastamho any time. I lie down and try, and soon I am up there again with the crowd. He teaches me to cure by spitting (blowing frothy saliva) and sucking. One night Kumastamho spat up blood. He told me: "Come here, little boy (this is a characteristic concept), and suck my chest." I placed my hands on his ribs and sucked his sickness out. Then he said: "You are a consumption dreamer. When anybody has consumption lay your hands on him and suck the pain out continually, and in four months he will be well." It takes four days to tell about Kwikumat and Kumastamho (the origin myth). I was present (*i. e.*, at the happenings told in this myth) from the very beginning (*sic*), and saw and heard all. I dreamed a little of it at a time. I would then tell it to my friends. The old men would say: "That is right! I was there and heard it myself." Or they would say: "You have dreamed badly. That is not right." And they would tell me right. So at last I learned the whole of it right.

Just so, the Mohave in general admit frankly that they have learned much of their knowledge of songs and stories from their older relatives, and yet insist that they possess all this knowledge through dreams; and like the Yuma, every narrator is convinced that he was present at the ancient events he tells of. If these tribes could express themselves in our abstract terminology, they would probably say that the phenomena of dreams have an absolute reality but that they exist in a dimension in which there is no time and in which there is no distinction between spiritual and material.

SONG-MYTH-RITES IN THE LOWER COLORADO REGION.

The narrative song cycles which largely take the place of dances among the Mohave, and have been mentioned for the Chemehuevi and Luiseño, are very much less known among the Yuma, the fragmentary information available being mostly from Mohave sources. The accessible data for all the Yuman tribes and some of their Shoshonean neighbors are gathered in the appended table. From this collocation it is clear that some song series have traveled widely and are so definitely international at present that their tribal origin can perhaps never be ascertained. It appears further that the Mohave have been most active in this religio-aesthetic manifestation. On the one hand they have borrowed freely, on the other they have probably been drawn upon by their neighbors to an at least equal extent.

At any rate, they possess much the largest number of cycles: 20 which they claim as their own, besides at least 10 more sung by doctors. Seven of the 20 are shared by one or more other tribes, and are likely to be of foreign devising. But the remainder are, so far as known, purely Mohave; and this is a greater number of series than has been recorded for any other people in the region. And it is not likely that the disproportion is altogether due to incompleteness of information. The Chemehuevi, for instance, themselves assert that they possess no more than four kinds of singings.

TABLE 8.—YUMAN SONG CYCLES.[1]

Mohave	Yuma	Maricopa	Cocopa	Kamia	Diegueño	Yavapai[2]	Chemehuevi	Serrano[3]	Cahuilla
Birds[4]	Birds								Birds
Av'alyumu[4]	Av'alyunu								
Alysa[4]			Alysa	Alysa					
Tumanpa			Tumanpa		Tu-tomump[5]			Tumanpa[6]	Tumanpa[7]
Raven				Raven					
Salt		Salt			Salt		Salt		
Turtle									Turtle
Deer		Deer					Deer		
Eagle[8]		Eagle							
Kwiya-humara[10]					(9)				
Shamar's[11]					Kuya-homar		Shamar's		
Frog									
Mat-hamuchicha		Taris[13]							
Chichohotchva		Buzzard			Orup[12]				
Harraupa		Mockingbird		P'ipa[14]					
						Rabbit	Mountain sheep		
					Keruk[16]				
Ohoma[16]					Kachahwar[17]				
Karu'uka[15]					Awi-kunchi[18]				
				Hakile	Akil[19]				
					Hortloi[20]				
					Tuharl				
					Tipai				
					Isa[22]				

(71)

[1] Data on Maricopa, Diegueño, and Chemehuevi from themselves; for all other tribes from Mohave informants. The tribes heading the last three columns are Shoshonean groups adjacent to Yumans. The Diegueño series except the Keruk are known only from the Southern division of the group. The Mohave add that the Maricopa sing the equivalent of their own *Satukhota* or *Kwiya-humara; Kampanyka,* bat; *Sakachara,* a bird called *sakachieka* in Mohave; and *Atadha,* an underground insect or chrysalis.

[2] And Walapai.

[3] The "Vanyume" of the Mohave. Possibly the Kawaiisu are meant.

[4] Borrowed by the Mohave from the Yuma.

[5] Said to be sung with Mohave words, and a phonographed song was promptly identified by the Mohave as their "Long Tumanpa." Also mentioned as *Tomanp.*

[6] The Mohave sing this "Vanyume Tumanpa," in addition to two kinds of their own.

[7] Said to be called *Tangiteve* by themselves, equated by the Mohave with Tumanpa.

[8] About the eagle; called *Ohuera.*

[9] The Diegueño practice a mourning rite in which an eagle is killed. This ceremony is practiced also by the Juaneño and Luiseño, and some of the Diegueño believe that it reached them from the latter people. Its songs, however, are in Diegueño, and appear to outline a story.

[10] Name of the hero; the story and songs are called *Satukhota.*

[11] The Mohave name ten or more kinds of doctor's singings.

[12] Or *Urop.* A phonographed song was recognized by the Mohave as from the Yuma *Harraupa.*

[13] Compare *min-turis-turisa,* the Mohave name of a waterbird.

[14] This word means "person" in Mohave.

[15] Two kinds of songs sung at the mourning commemoration.

[16] The commemorative mourning ceremony: *Wu-keruk* in the Southern dialect. The words seem to be Diegueño. The *Keruk* is said to contain *Cheyotai* or *Chayautai* songs, which perhaps should be reckoned separately.

[17] Or *Achauhai.* A basket is rubbed: *chahuar* is said to mean "rub." The words are Southern Diegueño from Jacumba. The story tells of two brothers. The younger loses a contest and is killed by the older who goes to Maricopa land.

[18] Sung to make fair weather. Diegueño words. The hero of the story is *Kwilyu.*

[19] *Atanuk* or *Akil* is the girls' adolescence ceremony. Perhaps *Atanuk* refers to the rite, *Akil* to the songs. The words are Diegueño: the songs are not recognized by the Mohave, who seem to perform no public ritual for their girls.

[20] *Hortloi, Hutltuyp,* or *Hurtburii* is the Diegueño name of the dance of the introduced toloache cult. While this does not seem to have been mythologized by them, they evidently fit it into the scheme familiar to themselves.

[21] Mohave cycles peculiar to themselves are omitted from this table. They are described in the preceding chapter.

[22] Spier (see bibliography) gives the following southern Diegueño song cycles: Hasa' (=Isa? birds); Tomanp (=Tu-tomanp); Ispa (eagle); Hahwar (scraping basket; =Kachahwar); Horhloi (=Hortloi); Tohar (rattle; =Tuharl); Tipai (people; =Tipai); Djokwar (speech); Tasitl (rattle); Hehltamataie (hair); Nyimi (wild-cat) and Parhau (fox), associated; Nyilkwar (crane?); also, of doubtful independence: Orup (sad, mourning) and Chaihotai (big song); and Nyiman-kumar (=Kuya-homar), equated with Tomanp. Tipai and Horhloi are recognized as of Shoshonean origin.

Mohave stimulation is further shown in the fact that their sacred peak Avikwame or Dead Mountain is sung about by the Yuma and Diegueño, and, according to the Mohave themselves, by the Walapai and Maricopa; although the corresponding mythic center of the Chemehuevi, Charleston Peak, is in their own territory. Aha'av'-ulypo or Eldorado Canyon to the north of Avikwame, which is al-most equally important in Mohave tradition, is also known to the Yuma. Some of the Mohave song narratives begin or end far afield, toward Tehachapi or in the Yavapai country or in Sonora; but the two places mentioned certainly dominate their mythic geography, and this point of view is reflected in Yuma story, and to a less degree among the Diegueño. It should be mentioned that some Diegueño accounts place their "Wikami" at Picacho Peak near Yuma.

A comparison of the songs—both words and tune—which appear to be the concrete elements most frequently and completely trans-mitted, should readily solve most of the interrelations of source and of borrowing by the several tribes. The narrative material has pre-sumably been much more thoroughly broken up and recombined in its wanderings from nation to nation; and the social use and ritual setting of the cycles are also likely to vary considerably according to tribe.

ORIGIN TRADITIONS OF SOUTHERN CALIFORNIA.

The account of origins of the Yuma, Mohave, Diegueño, and Maricopa is more or less completely known, for some of these tribes in several versions. All the stories agree sufficiently closely to allow of the recognition of a typical creation myth characteristic of the central Yuman tribes. It may be expected that the more remote northeastern and southwestern members of the family participated in this conglomerate of beliefs to a considerable extent. Much of the myth is shared with the neighboring Shoshoneans of southern California. The give and take between the two groups can not yet be determined fully. But certain distinctive Yuman and Sho-shonean ideas emerge clearly.

The Shoshonean creation has been designated as a myth of emer-gence, in the sense that mankind and all things in the world are born from mother Earth, with Sky or Night as father. The divinity Wiyot, or whatever he may be called, is not the maker but the first born, the leader and instructor, of men. As a matter of fact, such was the belief only of the Luiseño, Juaneño, and perhaps Gabrielino. The hinterland tribes—Cupeño, Cahuilla, and Serrano—evince only traces of cosmic interest. With them, the world begins with two quarreling brothers, of whom one causes and the other opposes death, and one retires to the sky, the other into the earth—is named Earth, even, in some accounts. One of the pair manufactures mankind.

This is also in general the Yuman idea; but these people add the fact that the two brothers, the creator and his death-instituting opponent, are born at the bottom of the sea, and that the younger emerges blinded by the salt water. In most Yuman accounts this concept of water origin is somewhat hesitatingly blended with earth-sky parentage. The Mohave alone have substituted for the ocean origin a direct birth from the great mother and father, have reduced the part of the antagonistic younger brother to a minimum, forgotten his blindness, and hold men to have been born with the gods, not made by them. Their cosmogony therefore assumes the same philosophy as that of the Luiseño-Gabrielino—a philosophy of distinctly Pueblo type; whereas the other tribes of the region, Yuman as well as Shoshonean, adhere to a more personalized and concrete conception. As the Mohave and Luiseño-Gabrielino are not in contact, in fact are separated by tribes like the Cahuilla, their cosmogonies can not be traced to a directly common source. They may be specializations, erected more or less independently, through a reweighting of particular ideas which in halting and ineffective form were once or are still the common property of all the Indians of southern California. Two mythological strata can therefore be recognized as regards cosmogony. The underlying one is represented by the Serrano, Cahuilla, Diegueño, and in the main by the Yuma and Maricopa. The upper crops out among the Gabrielino-Luiseño and, some distance away, among the Mohave, with some indications among the Yuma.

In the underlying stratum the Yuman names of the creator and his brother are Tuchaipa and Kokomat or Yokomatis. These designations are common to such distant tribes as the Diegueño and Maricopa, and must therefore be regarded as part of an old Yuman inheritance. But a curious inconsistence prevails. The Diegueño sometimes combine the names into Chaipa-Komat or Chakumat and apply this term to the creator, or call him Mayoha, which perhaps refers to the sky. At other times Chaipa-Kòmat is the earth from which the first man is made by the creator. The Yuma call the creator Kwikumat, whereas his companion, who is no longer his brother, is merely Blind Old Man. The Mohave introduce an entirely new name, Matavilya, for the leading divinity, and retain only faint traces of the concept of his companion who disappears under ground.

The creator makes men from clay: the younger brother attempts the same, but misshapes his creatures, who turn into web-footed birds—which, it may be added, play a considerable part in the song cycles of some Mohave shamans.

The great divinity, whether creator or leader, offends his daughter Frog, and is killed by her swallowing his voidings. This concept of the dying god, and of the mourning for him, is universal among Yumans and Shoshoneans, and is probably the dominant and most poignantly felt motive of every mythology in southern California. Its analogue in the Aztec Quetzalcoatl story has already been commented upon; but it is important that no parallel is known among the Pueblos or any true southwestern people. There may have been connections with the central and south Mexican story through Sonora. But except for dim suggestions, the development of the idea is probably local. All the Californians make much of the origin of death; and the Yuman and southern Shoshonean tale appears to think less of the impending end of the great god himself than of the fate of humanity as typified by him.

Everywhere there follows a concrete and circumstantial narration of the preparations for the divinity's cremation, of Coyote's plans to possess himself of his heart, of the measures taken to prevent this design, and of Coyote's success and consequent execration. The Juaneño are the only people known to have accompanied this story with a ritualistic practice; but the custom may have been more widely spread. This funerary cannibalism clearly rests upon generic Californian ideas of death and acts due the dead; and it is characteristic that its known occurrence is among those of the southern Californians nearest to the central part of the State, in which a similar custom is reported from the Pomo, although, of course, without a trace of the associated mythology. The custom further emphasizes what the flavor of the myth itself indicates: that the dying god motive is largely a native rather than an imported product.

Some Diegueño versions omit the death of Tuchaipa and consequently Coyote's theft also. This may be mere incompleteness of record; but as the myths in question are all from southerly Diegueño territory, it is not impossible that there existed a south Yuman area, centering in Baja California, in which these episodes were dispensed with. This would indicate that the dying god concept developed in southern California proper, where its ritualistic counterpart also has its seat, and inclines the balance toward a Shoshonean rather than a Yuman origin for the idea and its principal associations.

The Mohave rather slight Matavilya-Tuchaipa: his chief function is to die. His son, or, according to some accounts, younger brother, Mastamho, enters at far greater length into the narration, as the shaper and ordainer of things on the earth, and the instructor of men in all cultural relations. With the Yuma, the disproportion is not so marked; but Ku-mastamho is still of great importance.

Maricopa tradition, so far as it is fragmentarily known, does not mention this second great divinity; and the Diegueño do not know him. There is also no specific Shoshonean parallel: Chungichnish, who appears after Wiyot's death, is far too vague and shadowy a figure to compare with the practically active and more human Mastamho. This divinity seems therefore to be a creation of the Mohave; and this conclusion is confirmed by his definite association with the mountain Avikwame.

One other episode the Yuma and Mohave share with the Diegueño. Sky-Rattlesnake—Kammayaveta, Maihaiowit, Maiaveta, or Umas-ereha—is sent from his ocean abode to Avikwame, where, on entering the house, his head is chopped off or he is burned. . The motive is punishment of the doctor of evil design or the desire to acquire his ritualistic knowledge. This is an incident not recorded among any Shoshonean tribe; but the monster recurs in the Zuñi Kolowisi and is an ancient southwestern concept with water associations.

The specific common Yuman elements in this cosmogony are the rising out of the deep of the creator Tuchaipa, the blindness, opposition, and miscreations of his brother Kokomat, and the killing of Maiaveta. The complex of ideas associated with the dying god and Coyote's theft of his heart is a general Yuman possession, more likely to have originated among the Shoshoneans. Besides the fluctuating and often vague belief in Sky and Earth as the initial parents of all else, this set of Wiyot-Matavilya concepts is the principal theme of wide scope common to the two families of tribes. The Mohave have most largely developed the non-Yuman elements of the tradition, as well as the Mastamho cycle, which appears to be a special growth that has assimilated a variety of minor elements of Yuman origin. The Yuma stand next to the Mohave in both points. It does not seem that the contacts of these tribes with Shoshoneans were as numerous as the contacts of the Diegueño, but they evidently assimilated more because they were more inclined to mythologize. The difference is one between the comparatively active and specialized culture of the river tribes and a more generic, simple, and apathetic civilization among the Diegueño.

It is rather remarkable how closely the Maricopa adhere to the common Yuman tradition, if the record is to be trusted, whereas their national fortunes in the historic period have been intimately linked with those of the Pima, and the nearest of their kinsmen—the Yuma, Yavapai, and Mohave—have been their hereditary foes. The inference is that the Maricopa, like the Halchidhoma whom they subsequently received, were resident on the Colorado at no very ancient period. This is indicated also by their speech, which is said to be almost identical with Yuma, but perceptibly different from the dialects of the Yuman nomadic mountain tribes of western Arizona.

It has indeed often been asserted that the Maricopa were an offshoot from the Colorado River tribes; but all such statements appear to be assumptions based only on the knowledge that the tribe of Piman associations spoke a Yuman language, and to have been devoid, hitherto, of substantiation by definite historical evidence. How far the general civilization of the Maricopa retains its original cast, or, on the other hand, has yielded to the influences of their alien but allied neighbors, it is impossible to say, in the almost total absence of exact information about them; but, like the Havasupai, they bid fair to present valuable material for a study in the interesting problem of native American acculturation.

MOURNING AND ADOLESCENCE CEREMONIES.

The Yuma mourning ceremony, which is called *Nyimits*, "crying," and, like that of the Mohave, is generally known in English as an "Annual," appears to be made especially for distinguished warriors, and not for hereditary chiefs, rich men, or the dead of the community at large. This flavoring is distinctly eastern, although the commemoration concept itself is preeminently characteristic of California. The eastern cast appears in several features, such as mimic warfare and the use of a shield.

The rites are held under an open shade, where two lines of men sing *Karu'uka* and *Ohoma* songs during the night. The former are at the west end, the latter at the east, but both face toward the dawn. As this approaches, they dance in turn, and then, after it is day, dance again to the east of the shade. During the last Karu'uka singing, a handled skin drawn over a willow hoop and feathered at the edge, in other words a shield, is displayed; and as a climax, the shade is set on fire and an arrow shot against the shield, whereupon it and the bow and arrow are cast upon the blazing pile. There are other features of a dramatic character whose place in the rite is not clear. Two armed men run, another pair pursues shoulder to shoulder, the first turn and discharge an arrow which the hinder twain, separating, allow to pass between them. There is also said to be a pair of riders who avoid arrows; and apparently some symbolic taunting with death in war. The dualism that obviously pervades the performance, in spite of formal adherence to the fourfolding ceremonial pattern of the tribe, seems also connected with the idea of antithesis in combat.

The *Ohoma* singers carry a sort of arrow feathered at both ends; the *Karu'uka* party is led with a deer-hoof rattle. *Karu'uka* has already been mentioned as being the same word as the Diegueño *Keruk;* but the latter rite is a much more typical Californian mourning ceremony.

This, except for an allusion to its use by the Diegueño, is the most westerly known occurrence of the shield, whose distribution stretches through the Pima and Apache to the Pueblo and Plains tribes. Neither the Yuma nor the Mohave, however, appear to have used the implement very extensively in actual warfare, and there is no mention of any heraldry in connection with it. The true Californians fought naked, or, in the north, in body armor.

The Yuma hold an adolescence ceremony for girls, but its specific traits are too obscure to allow comparisons. As among the Mohave, there is no record of a tribal or societal initiation of boys. Since the coast tribes as well as the Pueblos on the other side practice initiations, even agreeing in such details as the employment of sand paintings, the absence of this set of customs among the Colorado River tribes is significant of their specialization in religion.

TOLOACHE.

The Yuma dreamers know and use Jimson weed, *smalykapita*,[1] Mohave *malykatu*, much as the Mohave do, to stimulate their dreams; in other words, as individual shamans. This differentiates the employment of the plant from its utilization by the Gabrielino and adjacent tribes, to whom it is the center of the initiation complex. The Yuma-Mohave attitude seems to be that of the Pueblos, to judge by the Zuñi, who use the drug in medical practice and to attain second sight. The Walapai and White Mountain Apache employ the plant. The association of Jimson weed with religion is probably continuous from the San Joaquin Valley to southern Mexico. Toloache is an Aztec word and the plant was worshipped. While little is known of its employment, it may be presumed to have been sacred to the tribes of northern Mexico, except where unobtainable or relegated to obscurity by the peyote cult. At bottom, therefore, the southern California toloache religion may confidently be ascribed to ideas that, like so much else in North America, originated in Mexico or Central America. On the other hand, as a specific growth this religion is unquestionably local, the Colorado Valley and Pueblo use of toloache being of much more elementary character in a more highly organized religious setting. In short, we are dealing here with an instance of connection between California and the Southwest in which historical priority must as usual be given to the more advanced region; and yet to regard the Californian manifestations as merely an imperfect loan from the Southwest would be erroneous. It is only the source that the Pueblos contributed, and a borrowed source at that. The growths upon it were independent: in fact, that of the humbler people the more luxuriant.

THE SWEAT HOUSE.

A parallel condition is presented by the sweat house, except that the discontinuity in recent times is emphasized by the lack of the institution among the spatially intermediate Yumans of the great

---

[1] Probably *Datura discolor* instead of the *D. meteloides* used in most of the remainder of California. See footnote, page 502.

river. Neither the Yuma, the Mohave, nor, it seems, the Pima and Papago of Arizona know the universal Californian sweat house. On the other hand, the sweat house correlates with the Pueblo kiva or estufa, which in spite of a possible augmentation of its sacred character under pressure from the Spaniard, retains some of its former functions of man's club and sleeping place; while even its religious associations are never wholly wanting in California. A failure to connect the kiva and the sweat house would be more than short-sighted. But an immediate derivation of the latter from the former would not only be hasty on general grounds, but directly contradicted by the Yuman gap. Here, too, then, we find entirely new associations clustering about the institution in its Pacific coast range; even possibly an enlargement of the sweat house into the dance house or assembly chamber of the Sacramento Valley tribes, and its definite affiliation with the masked society cult, every particular trait of which has obviously been devised on the spot. Again, also, we have the indication of an ultimate source in Mexico, the home of the temescal; and, to illustrate the principle one step farther, there is the Plains sweat lodge, the idea of which must be carried back to the same root, but whose concrete form, as well as its place in religion and daily custom, are markedly different from those of temescal, kiva, or California sweat house.

Incidentally, the cultural importance of the sweat house is one of the bonds that links the Yurok and Hupa to the Californian peoples, in spite of the numerous features which their civilization shares with that of the North Pacific coast in its narrower sense. The latter tract scarcely knows the sweat house.

The house is ritually significant to the Yuma and Mohave in myth, song, and symbolism, but is not itself ritually employed to any extent. It is referred to as " dark house " and " dark round." The open sided roof shade has similar though weaker associations as a concept; while actually used in cult, the structure is scarcely sacred. The ceremonial enclosure constructed by the group of peoples influenced by the Gabrielino is as foreign to the river tribes as the sweat house, but reappears among the Navaho, and may have a true homologue in the court or plaza in which most Pueblo dances are performed.

THE MOHAVE-YUMA CULTURE.

A balance may now be struck between the cultural affiliations of the lower Colorado tribes with the Indians respectively of the Southwest and of California, especially of southern California. Civilizational traits such as pottery and emergence myths, which are common to all three areas, may be left out of this consideration.

The Yuma and Mohave share with the southwestern peoples agriculture; totemic clan exogamy; a tribal sense; a considerable military spirit and desire for warlike renown; and the shield; all of which are un-Californian. They also agree with the southwesterners in lacking several generic or widespread Californian traits: a regard for wealth; basketry as a well-cultivated art; and the use of toloache in an organized cult.

On the other hand, they resemble the Californians and differ from the southwesterners in reckoning descent paternally; in holding public religious mourning commemorations; in hereditary chieftainship; and in the lack of architecture in stone, a priestly hierarchy, masks, depictive art, the loom, and body dress on a notable scale.

It is clear that there is substantially no less and no more reason for reckoning the river tribes in the Southwest than in the California culture area.

That they are more than merely transitional is revealed by a number of peculiarities. These, strangely enough for a people of intermediate location, are mostly negative: they lack the sweat house, the ceremonial enclosure, the initiating society, and the sand painting which the Gabrielino and Luiseño on their west share with the Pueblos and Navahos to the east.

The positive particularities of moment are all clearly and closely interrelated, and may be designated as the peculiar system of song-myth-rites with its reduction of dancing to a minimum and its basis of belief in an unusual form of dreams which also lend a characteristic color to shamanism. In this one association of religious traits, accordingly, rests the active distinctiveness of Yuma-Mohave culture; and to this growth must be attributed the local suppression of elements like the sweat house and the secret society.

It seems likely that when the culture of the Sonoran tribes shall be better known, it may link at least as closely as that of the Pueblos with that of the lower Colorado tribes and explain much of the genesis of the latter.

CHAPTER 53.

OTHER YUMAN TRIBES.

THE NATIONS ON THE COLORADO.

Besides the Mohave and Yuma, at least five other tribes of the same lineage once occupied the shores of the Colorado. Of these, only the Cocopa and Kamia retain their identity, and the latter are few. The others are extinct or merged. In order upstream these tribes were the Cocopa, Halyikwamai, Alakwisa, Kohuana, Kamia, Yuma, Halchidhoma, and Mohave.

THE COCOPA.

The Cocopa, called Kwikapa by the Mohave, held the lowest courses of the river, chiefly, it would seem, on the west bank. They have survived in some numbers, but have, and always had, their seats in Baja California. They are mentioned by name as early as 1605.

THE HALYIKWAMAI OR KIKIMA.

The Halyikwamai, as the Mohave call them, are the Quicama or Quicoma of Alacon in 1540, the Halliquamallas of Oñate in 1605, the Quiquima or Jalliquamay of Garcés in 1776, and therefore the first California group to have a national designation recorded and preserved. Oñate puts them next to the Cocopa, on the east bank of the Colorado, Garcés on the west bank between the Cocopa and the Kohuana. Garcés estimated them to number 2,000, but his population figures for this region are high, especially for the smaller groups. It seems impossible that three or four separate tribes should each have shrunk from 2,000 or 3,000 to a mere handful in less than a century during which they lived free and without close contact with the whites.

The discrepancies between the habitat assigned by one authority on the left bank and the other on the right, for this and other tribes, are of little moment. It is likely that every nation on the river owned both sides, and shifted from one to the other, or divided, according to the exigencies of warfare, fancy, or as the channel and farm lands changed. The variations in linear position along the river, on the contrary, were due to tribal migrations dependent on hostilities or alliances.

HALYIKWAMAI AND AKWA'ALA.

The Mohave, who do not seem to know the name Quigyuma or Quiquima, say that the Halyikwamai survive, but know them only as mountaineers west of the river. West of the Cocopa, that is, in the interior of northernmost Baja California, they say is Avi-aspa, " Eagle Mountain," visible from the vicinity of Yuma; and north of it another large peak called Avi-savet-kyela. Between the two mountains is a low hilly country. This and the region west of Avi-aspa is the home of the Akwa'ala or Ekwa'ahle, a Yuman tribe whose speech seems to the Mohave to be close to the Walapai dialect and different from Diegueño. They were still there in some numbers about 30 years ago, the Mohave say, and rode horses. They did not farm. They were neighbors of the Kamia-ahwe or Diegueño, and occasionally met the Mohave at Yuma or among the Cocopa.

The Halyikwamai, the Mohave say, adjoined the Akwa'ala on the north, near the Yuma, and, like the Akwa'ala, were hill dwellers. They also did not farm, but migrated seasonally into the higher mountains to collect mescal root, *vadhilya*. They did not, in recent times, come to the river even on visits, evidently on account of the old feuds between themselves and the Yuma and Kamia. In the last war expedition which the Yuma and Mohave made against the Cocopa, about 1855, the Akwa'ala and Halyikwamai were allied with the Cocopa.

It would seem, therefore, that the Halyikwamai or Quigyuma or Quiquima are an old river tribe that was dispossessed by its more powerful neighbors, took up an inland residence, and of necessity abandoned agriculture.

THE ALAKWISA.

The country of the Alakwisa is occasionally mentioned by the Mohave in traditions, but the tribe seems to have been extinct for some time, and fancy has gathered a nebulous halo about its end. Here is the story of an old Mohave.

When I was young an old Mohave told me how he had once come homeward from the Cocopa, and after running up along the river for half a day, saw house posts, charcoal, broken pottery, and stone mortars. He thought the tract must still be inhabited, but there was no one in sight. He ran on, and in the evening reached the Kamia, who told him that he had passed through the old Alakwisa settlements. His Kamia friends said that they had never seen the Alakwisa, the tribe having become extinct before their day, but that they had heard the story of their end. It is as follows:

There was a small pond from which the Alakwisa used to draw their drinking water, and which had never contained fish. Suddenly it swarmed with fish. Some dug wells to drink from, but these, too, were full of fish. They took them, and, although a few predicted disaster, ate the catch. Women began to fall over dead at the metate or while stirring fish mush, and men at their occupations. They were playing at hoop and darts, when eagles fought in the air, killed each other, and fell down. The Alakwisa clapped their hands, ran up, and gleefully divided the feathers, not knowing that deaths had already occurred in their homes. As they wrapped the eagle feathers, some of them fell over dead; others lived only long enough to put the feathers on.

Another settlement discovered a jar under a mesquite tree, opened it, and found four or five scalps. They carried the trophies home, mounted them on poles, but before they reached the singer, some of them dropped lifeless, and others fell dead in the dance. So one strange happening crowded on another, and each time the Alakwisa died swiftly and without warning. Whole villages perished, no one being left to burn the dead or the houses, until the posts remained standing or lay rotting on the ground, as if recently abandoned. So the Kamia told my old Mohave friend about the end of the Alakwisa.

Fabulous as is this tale, it is likely to refer to an actual tribe, although the name Alakwisa may be only a synonym of story for Halyikwamai or some other familiar term of history.

THE KOHUANA.

The Kohuana, Kuhuana, or Kahuene of the Mohave, are the Coana of Alarcón and the Cohuana of Oñate, who in 1605 found them in nine villages above the Halyikwamai. Garcés in 1776 called them Cajuenche, put them on the east side of the Colorado, also above the Halyikwamai and below the Kamia, and estimated there were 3,000 of them. Their fortunes ran parallel with those of the Halchidhoma, and the career of the two tribes is best considered together.

THE KAMIA AND YUMA.

Next above were the Kamia, also recorded as the Comeya, Quemaya, Comoyatz, or Camilya, who have already been discussed. There is much confusion concerning them, owing to the fact that besides the farming tribe on the river, who alone are the true Kamia of the Mohave, the Southern Diegueño call themselves Kamiai, and the Mohave call all the Diegueño " foreign Kamia." It is, however, well established that a group of this name was settled on the Colorado adjacent to the Yuma.

The Yuma have also been reviewed separately.

THE HALCHIDHOMA.

The Halchidhoma or Halchadhoma, as the Mohave know them, were unquestionably at one time an important nation, suffered reverses, and at last completely lost their identity among the Maricopa, although there are almost certain to be survivors to-day with that tribe. Oñate found them the first tribe on the river below the Gila. Kino, a century later, brings them above the Gila. They had no doubt taken refuge here from the Yuma or other adjacent enemies, but can have profited little by the change, since it brought them nearer the Mohave, who rejoiced in harrying them. Garcés makes them extend 15 leagues northward along the river to a point an equal distance south of Bill Williams Fork. He was among them in person and succeeded in patching up a temporary peace between them and the Mohave. He calls them Alchedum and Jalchedunes, but they can scarcely still have numbered 2,500 in 1776, as he reports.

The Mohave report that the Kohuana and Halchidhoma once lived along the river at Parker, about halfway between the Mohave and Yuma territories. This period must have been subsequent to 1776, since the location corresponds with that in which Garcés found the Halchidhoma, whereas in his day the Kohuana were still below the Yuma. Evidently they, too, found living too uncomfortable in the turmoil of tribes below the confluence of the Gila—the Mohave say that they lived at Aramsi on the east side of the stream below the Yuma and were troubled by the latter—and followed the Halchidhoma to the fertile but unoccupied bottom lands farther up. If they had been free of a quarrel with the Mohave, their union with the Halchidhoma brought them all the effects of one.

It must have been about this period of joint residence that the Halchidhoma, attempting reprisals, circuited eastward and came down on the Mohave from the Walapai Mountains. In this raid they captured a Mohave girl at Aha-kwa'-a'i, with whom they returned to their home at Parker, and then sold to the Maricopa. Subsequently, in an attack on the latter tribe, the Mohave found a woman who, instead of fleeing, stood still with her baby, and when they approached, called to them that she was the captive. They took her back, she married again, and had another son, Cherahota, who was still living in 1904. Her half-Maricopa son grew up among the Mohave, and becoming a shaman, was killed near Fort Mohave. This indicates that he reached a tolerable age.

But the preponderance of numbers and aggressions must have been on the side of the Mohave, because they finally drove both Halchidhoma and Kohuana south from Parker, back toward the

Yuma. The Halchidhoma settled at Aha-kw-atho'ilya, a long salty "lake" or slough, that stretched for a day's walk west of the river at the foot of the mountains. The Kohuana removed less far, to Avi-nya-kutapaiva and Hapuvesa, but remained only a year, and then settled farther south, although still north of the Halchidhoma.

After a time the Mohave appeared in a large party, with their women and children. They would scarcely have done this if their foes had retained any considerable strength. It was a five days' journey from Mohave Valley to the Kohuana. The northerners claimed the Kohuana as kinsmen but kept them under guard while the majority of their warriors went on by night. They reached the settlements of the Halchidhoma in the morning, the latter came out, and an open fight ensued, in which a few Halchidhoma were killed, while of the Mohave a number were wounded but none fell. In the afternoon, the Mohave returned—pitched battles rarely ended decisively among any of these tribes—and announced to the Kohuana that they had come to live with them. They also invited the Halchidhoma to drive them out; which the latter were probably too few to attempt. For four days the Mohave remained quietly at the Kohuana settlements doctoring their wounded. They had probably failed to take any Halchidhoma scalps, since they made no dance. The four days over, they marched downstream again, arrived in the morning, and fought until noon, when they paused to retire to the river to drink. The Halchidhoma used this breathing space to flee. They ran downstream, swam the river to the eastern bank, and went on to Ava-chuhaya. The Mohave took six captives and spoiled the abandoned houses.

After about two days, the Mohave account proceeds, they went against the foe once more, but when they reached Ava-chuhaya found no one. The Halchidhoma had cut east across the desert to take refuge with the Hatpa-'inya, the "East Pima," or Maricopa. Here ends their career; and it is because of this merging of their remnant with the Maricopa that when the Mohave are asked about the latter tribe they usually declare them to have lived formerly on the river between themselves and the Yuma: the Halchidhoma are meant. There can be little doubt that the Maricopa, too, were once driven from the river to seek an asylum near the alien and powerful Pima; but the Spanish historical notices place them with the latter people on the Gila for so long a time back—to at least the beginning of the eighteenth century—that their migration must far antedate the period which native tradition traverses.

The Mohave decided to stay on in the land above Aha-kw-atho'ilya, which the Halchidhoma had possessed, expecting that the latter would return. They remained all winter. There is said to have been no one left in the Mohave country. In spring, when the mesquite was nearly ripe and the river was soon to rise and open the planting season, they returned, traveling three days. The Kohuana went with them under compulsion, but without the Mohave having to use force.

For five years the Kohuana lived in Mohave Valley. Then they alleged an equally close kinship with the Yuma and a wish to live among them. The Mohave allowed them to go. Ten days' journey brought them to their ancient foes. After four years of residence here, one of their number was killed by the Yuma and his body hidden. His kinsmen found it and resolved to leave as soon as their going would not be construed as due to a desire for revenge—an interpretation that might bring an immediate Yuma attack upon them. They waited a year; and then their chief, Tinyam-kwacha-kwacha, "Night traveler," a man of powerful frame, so tall that a blanket reached only to his hips, led them eastward between the mountains Kara'epe and Avi-hachora up the Gila. They found the Maricopa at Maricopa Wells, recounted the many places at which they had lived, and asked for residence among their hosts. Aha-kurrauva, the Maricopa chief, told them to remain forever.

So the Mohave story, the date of which may refer to the period about 1820 to 1840. In 1851 Bartlett reported 10 "Cawina" surviving among the Maricopa. But this was an underestimation, as a further Mohave account reveals.

About 1883 the same Mohave who is authority for the foregoing, having been told by certain Kohuana who had remained among the Mohave, or by their half-Mohave descendants, that there were kinsmen of theirs with the Maricopa, went to Tempe and there found not only Kohuana but Halchidhoma, although the Americans regarded them both as Maricopa. The Kohuana chief was Hatpa'-ammay-ime, "Papago-foot," an old man, whom Ahwanchevari, the Maricopa chief, had appointed to be head over his own people. Hatpa'-ammay-ime had been born in the Maricopa country, but his father, and his father's sister, who was still living, were born while the Kohuana spent their five years among the Mohave. He enumerated 6 old Kohuana men as still living and 10 young men—36 souls in all, besides a few children in school.

These statements, if accurate, would place the Kohuana abandonment of the river at least as early as 1820; and the date agrees with the remark of an old Mohave, about 1904, that the final migration of the tribe occurred in his grandfather's time. It does not reconcile with the fact that a son of the Mohave woman taken captive by the Halchidhoma—who are said to have fled to the Maricopa 10 years earlier than the Kohuana—was yet living in 1904. In any event, in

1776 both tribes were still on the Colorado and sufficiently numerous to be reckoned substantially on a par with the Yuma and Mohave; in 1850, when the American came, they were merged among the Maricopa, and of the seven or eight related but warring Yuman nations that once lived on the banks of the stream, there remained only three, the Cocopa, Yuma, and Mohave, and a fragment of a fourth, the Kamia.   The drift has quite clearly been toward the suppression of the smaller units and the increase of the larger, a tendency probably influential on the civilization of the region, and perhaps stimulative in its effects.

TRIBES ENCOUNTERED BY OÑATE IN 1605.

The native information now accumulated allows the valuable findings of the Oñate expedition of 1605, as related by Zárate-Salmeron, to be profitably summarized, reinterpreted, and compared with those of later date.

In Mohave Valley, a 10 days' journey from the mouth of the river, as the natives then reckoned and still count, Oñate found the Amacavas or Amacabos.   This tribe has therefore occupied substantially the same tract for at least three centuries.   Their " Curraca," or " Lord," is only *kwora'aka*, " old man."

Five leagues downstream through a rocky defile brought Oñate to Chemehuevi Valley, where more Mohave lived.

Below the Mohave, evidently in the region about Parker or beyond, Oñate encountered an allied nation of the same speech, the Bahacechas.   This name seems unidentifiable.   Their head, Cohota, was so named for his office: he is the *kohota* or entertainment chief of the Mohave.

On the river of the Name of Jesus, the Gila, Oñate found a less affable people of different appearance and manners and of difficult speech, who claimed 20 villages all the way up that stream.   These he calls Ozaras, a name that can also not be identified.   The Relation gives the impression that this tribe stood apart from all those on the Colorado.   They do not seem to be the Maricopa, whose speech even to-day is close to that of the river tribes.   The most convincing explanation is that they were the Pima or Papago or at least some Piman division, who then lived farther down the Gila than subsequently.   This agrees with the statement that they extended to the shores of the sea.

Along the Colorado from the Gila to the ocean all the Colorado nations were like the Bahacechas in dress and speech—that is, Yumans.

The first were the Halchidoma, in 8 pueblos, the northernmost alone said to contain 160 houses and 2,000 people.

Next came the Cohuana in 9 villages, of 5,000 inhabitants, of whom 600 accompanied the expedition.

Below were the Agolle, Haglli, or Haelli, in 5 (or 100!) settlements, and next the Halliquamalla or Agalecquamaya, 4,000 or 5,000 strong, of whom more than 2,000 assembled from 6 villages.

Finally, in 9 pueblos, reaching down to where the river became brackish 5 leagues above its mouth, were the Cocopa.

The mythical island Ziñogaba in the sea sounds as if it might be named from "woman," *thenya'aka* in Mohave, and *ava*, "house." Its chieftainess, Ciñaca cohota, is certainly "woman-*kohota*." "Acilla," the ocean, is Mohave *hatho'ilya*. Other modern dialects have " s " where Mohave speaks " th." It is clear that the languages of the Colorado have changed as little in three centuries as the speech of the Chumash that Cabrillo recorded.

CHANGES IN THREE CENTURIES.

Apart from the Ozara, on the Gila, Oñate thus encountered seven Yuman nations on the left bank of the Colorado. Five of these are familiar, two appear under unknown designations, and the Yuma and Kamia are not mentioned. Possibly they remained on the California side of the river and thus failed of enumeration. But if the foreign Ozara held the Gila to its mouth there would have been no place for the Yuma in their historic seats.

Alarcón's data, the earliest of all for the region or for any part of California, specify the Quicama (Halyikwamai), Coana (Kohuana), and Cumana (Kamia?), and allude to many elements of the culture of later centuries: maize, beans, squashes or gourds, pottery, clubs, dress, coiffure, transvestites, cremation, intertribal warfare, attitude toward strangers, relations with the mountain tribes; as well as characteristic temperamental traits—enthusiasm, resistance to fatigue, stubbornness under provocation, an ebullient emotionality.

Alarcón and Melchior Diaz in 1540, Oñate in 1605, Kino in 1702, and Garcés in 1776, accordingly found conditions on the river much as they were when the American came. The tribes battled, shifted, and now and then disappeared. The uppermost and lowest were the same for 300 years: the Mohave and Cocopa. Among the conflicts, customs remained stable. If civilization developed, it was inwardly; the basis and manner of life were conservative.

CHAPTER 54.

ARTS OF LIFE.

This and the following two chapters on society and religion abandon the nationally descriptive presentation which has so far been followed for a comparative one. They are included for the convenience of those whose interest is generally ethnographic rather than intensive or local; but they make no attempts at completeness. On topics for which information is abundant or fruitfully summarizable it is collected here and reviewed. Subjects on which knowledge is irregular, or profuse but miscellaneous, or complicated by intricate considerations, have been omitted. For all such matter, the reader is referred to the appropriate passages in the tribal accounts which make the body of this book, and which can be assembled through the subject index.

DRESS.

The standard clothing of California, irrespective of cultural provinces, was a short skirt or petticoat for women, and either nothing at all for men or a skin folded about the hips. The breechclout is frequently mentioned, but does not seem to have been aboriginal. The sense of modesty as regards men was very slightly developed. In many parts all men went wholly naked except when the weather demanded protection, and among all groups old men appear to have gone bare of clothing without feeling of impropriety. The women's skirt was everywhere in two pieces. A smaller apron was worn in front. A larger back piece extended at least to the hips and frequently reached to meet the front apron. Its variable materials are of two classes, buckskin and plant fibers. Local supply was the chief factor in determining choice. If the garment was of skin, its lower half was slit into fringes. This allowed much greater freedom of movement, but the decorative effect was also felt and made use of. Of vegetable fibers the most frequently used was the inner bark of trees shredded and gathered on a cord. Grass, tule, ordinary cordage, and wrapped thongs are also reported.

As protection against rain and wind, both sexes donned a skin blanket. This was either thrown over the shoulders like a cape, or wrapped around the body, or passed over one arm and under the other and tied or secured in front. Sea-otter furs made the most prized cloak of this type where they could be obtained. Land otter, wildcat, deer, and almost every other kind of fur was not disdained. The woven blanket of strips of rabbit fur or bird skin sometimes rendered service in this connection, although primarily an article of bedding.

There was not much sewing. It was performed with bone awls, apparently of the same types as used in basket coiling (Fig. 67, *a–h*). In the northwest, where no coiled baskets were made, awls were used to slit lamprey eels.

The typical California moccasin, which prevailed over central and northwestern California, was an unsoled, single-piece, soft shoe, with one seam up the front and another up the heel. This is the Yurok, Hupa, and Miwok type. The front seam is puckered, but sometimes with neat effect. The heel seam is sometimes made by a thong drawn through. The Lassik knew a variant form, in which a single seam from the little toe to the outer ankle sufficed. The draw string varied: the Miwok did without, the Lassik placed it in front of the ankle, the Yurok followed the curious device of having the thong, self-knotted inside, come out through the sole near its edge, and then lashing it over instep and heel back on itself. This is an arrangement that would have been distinctly unpractical on the side of wear had the moccasins been put on daily or for long journeys. Separate soles of rawhide are sometimes added, but old specimens are usually without, and the idea does not seem to be native. The moccasin comes rather higher than that of the Plains tribes, and appears not to have been worn with its ankle portion turned down. Journeys, war, wood gathering are the occasions mentioned for the donning of moccasins; as well as cold weather, when they were sometimes lined with grass. They were not worn about the village or on ordinary excursions.

The Modoc and Klamath moccasin stands apart through eastern modification. It appears to have been without stiff sole, but contained three pieces: the sole and moccasin proper, reaching barely to the ankle; a **U**-shaped inset above the toes, prolonged into a loose tongue above; and a strip around the ankles, sewed to the edge of the main piece, and coming forward as far as the tongue. The main piece has the two seams customary in California. The ankle piece can be worn turned down or up; the draw string passes across the front of the tongue. The Atsugewi moccasin is also three-piece and therefore probably similar in plan.

Southern California is a region of sandals; but the desert Cahuilla wore a high moccasin for travel in the mountains. The

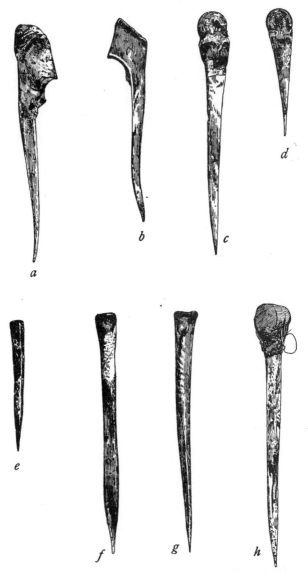

FIG. 67.—Bone awls. *a*, Pomo; *b*, Maidu; *c*, *d*, *e*, Yokuts; *f*, Yuki;
g, *h*, Miwok.

hard sole curls over the thick but soft upper, and is sewed to it from the inside by an invisible stitch. The upper has its single seam at the back. The front is slit down to the top of the instep, and held together by a thong passed through the edges once or twice. The appearance of this moccasin is southwestern, and its structure nearly on the plan of a civilized shoe. It reaches well up on the calf.

Moccasins and leggings in an openwork twining of tule fibers were used in northeastern California and among the Clear Lake Pomo as a device for holding a layer of soft grass against the foot for warmth.

The skin legging is rarer than the moccasin. It was made for special use, such as travel through the snow.

The only snowshoe used in California is a rather small oval hoop, across which from one to three thongs or grapevines are tied longitudinally and transversely (Fig. 68, a–d). The nearest parallels are in prehistoric pieces from the cliff-dweller area (Fig. 68, e).

In southern California the sandal of the Southwest begins to appear. In its characteristic local form it consists of mescal fiber, untwisted bundles of which are woven back and forth across a looped cord, forming a pad nearly an inch thick. (Pl. 62.) The Colorado River tribes have abandoned the use of this form of sandal, if ever they possessed it. In

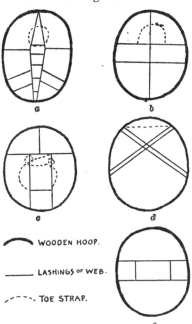

FIG. 68.—The Californian snowshoe. a, Klamath-Modoc, two-ply rawhide thong; b, Maidu, wrapped thong; c, Yurok, two-ply or four-ply grapevine; d, Nongatl, double thong, untwisted; e, prehistoric, Mesa Verde, Colo.

recent years they have worn simple rawhide sandals; but their very slender opportunities to hunt render it doubtful whether this is a type that antedates the introduction of horses and cattle among them. The Chemehuevi are said to have worn true moccasins. There is no clear report of any sandal north of Tehachapi.

The woman's basketry cap, a brimless cone or dome, is generally considered a device intended to protect against the chafe of the pack strap. That this interpretation is correct is shown by the fact that in the south the cap is worn chiefly when a load is to be carried; whereas in the north, where custom demands the wearing of the cap at all ordinary times, it is occasionally donned also by men when it becomes of service to them in the handling of a dip net which is steadied with the head. The woman's cap is not, however, a generic California institution. In the greater part of the central area it is unknown. Its northern and southern forms are quite distinct. Rather surprisingly, their distribution shows them to be direct adjuncts or dependents of certain basketry techniques. The northern cap coincides with the *Xerophyllum* technique and is therefore always made in overlaid twining. (Pls. 14, 70, 71, 73, *f*.) The range of the southern cap appears to be identical with that of baskets made on a foundation of *Epicampes* grass, and is accordingly a coiled product. (Pls. 53, 73, *d*.) There can be no question that tribes following other basketry techniques possessed the ability to make caps; but they did not do so. It is curious that an object of evident utilitarian origin, more or less influenced by fashion, should have its distribution limited according to the prevalence of basketry techniques and materials.

Two minor varieties of the cap occur. Among the Chemehuevi the somewhat peaked, diagonally twined cap of the Great Basin Shoshoneans was in use. It also occurs among the typical southern California tribes as far as the southern Diegueño by the side of the coiled cap. (Pl. 73, *d*.) This is likely to have been a comparatively recent invasion from the Great Basin, since coexistence of two types side by side among the same people is a condition contrary to prevailing ethnic precedent.

The Modoc employ but little overlay twining, and most of their caps are wholly in their regular technique of simple twining with tule materials. The Modoc cap averages considerably larger and is more distinctly flat topped than that of the other northern Californians.

The hair net worn by men (pls. 55, *a*, 72) centers in the region of the Kuksu religion, but its distribution seems most accurately described as exclusive of that of the woman's cap. Thus the Kato probably used the net and not the cap; the adjacent Wailaki reversed the situation. There are a few overlappings, as among the Yokuts, who employed both objects. The head net is also reported for the Shasta of Shasta Valley, but may have penetrated to them with the Kuksu elements carried into this region in recent years by the ghost dance.

Some tattooing (Figs. 45, 46) was practiced by most groups; facially more often than on the body, and more by women than by men. The most abundant patterns, taking in the whole cheeks, are found in the region of the Yuki and Wailaki; elsewhere the jaw is chiefly favored.

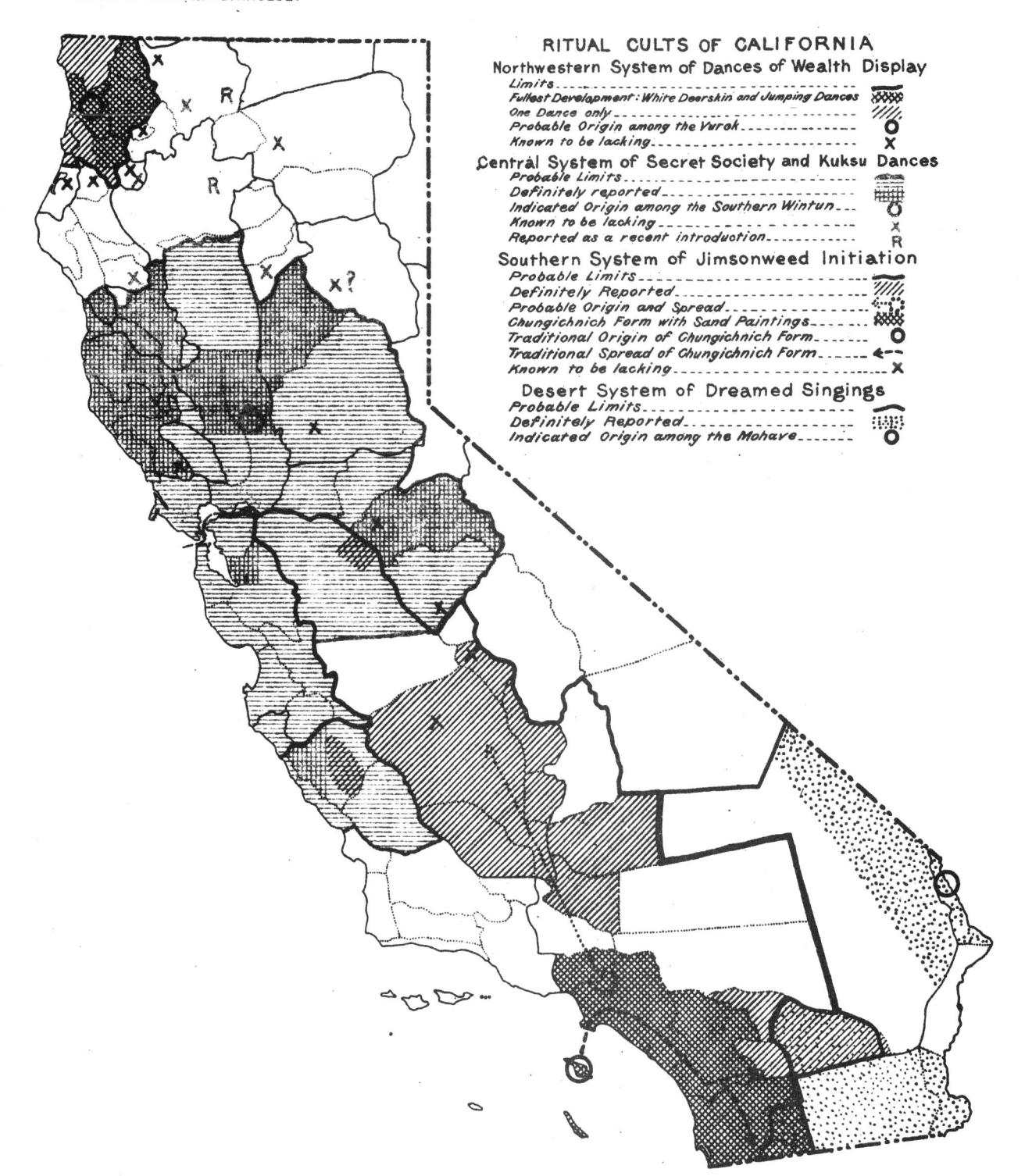

RITUAL CULTS OF CALIFORNIA

Northwestern System of Dances of Wealth Display
Limits..
Fullest Development: White Deerskin and Jumping Dances
One Dance only...
Probable Origin among the Yurok......................
Known to be lacking......................................

Central System of Secret Society and Kuksu Dances
Probable Limits...
Definitely reported......................................
Indicated Origin among the Southern Wintun...
Known to be lacking......................................
Reported as a recent introduction...................

Southern System of Jimsonweed Initiation
Probable Limits...
Definitely Reported......................................
Probable Origin and Spread............................
Chungichnich Form with Sand Paintings...........
Traditional Origin of Chungichnich Form..........
Traditional Spread of Chungichnich Form.........
Known to be lacking......................................

Desert System of Dreamed Singings
Probable Limits...
Definitely Reported......................................
Indicated Origin among the Mohave...............

HOUSES.

The houses of native California are difficult to classify except in summary fashion. The extreme forms are well differentiated, but are all connected by transitions. The frame house of the Yurok and Hupa is a definite type whose affinity with the larger plank house of the North Pacific coast is sufficiently evident. Southward and eastward from the Yurok it becomes smaller and more rudely made. Bark begins to replace the split or hewn planks, and before long a conical form made wholly of bark slabs is attained. This in turn, if provided with a center post, need only be covered with soil to serve as the simple prototype of the large semisubterranean house of the Sacramento Valley. Again, the bark is often partly replaced by poles and sticks. If these are covered with thatch we have a simple form of the conical brush house. This in turn also attains the gabled, rectangular form of the plank house, as with the Cahuilla, or again is made oval, or round and domed, as among the Pomo and Chumash. In the latter case it differs from the semisubterranean house only in the lack of earth covering and its consequent lighter construction. A further transition is afforded by the fact that the earth house almost invariably has foliage of some kind as its topmost covering immediately below the dirt surfacing of the roof. The brush house is often dug out a short distance. The Chumash threw the earth from the excavation up against the walls for a few feet. The earth-covered house proper is only a little deeper and has the covering extending all the way over.

Neither shape, skeleton structure, nor materials, therefore, offer a satisfactory basis for the distinction of sharp types. A classification that would be of value would have to rest on minute analysis, preceded in many cases by more accurate information than is now available. Among numerous tribes the old types of houses have long since gone out of use. Among most of the remainder they have been at least partly modified, and the majority of early descriptions are too summary to be of great service.

Nor does a consideration of distributions hold much present promise of fuller understanding. The earth-covered house was made from the Modoc, Achomawi, and Yuki south to the Miwok; then again in the extreme part of southern California. The bark house is found chiefly among mountain tribes, but no very close correlation with topography appears. The well-fashioned plank house is definitely to be associated with the northwestern culture. The earth lodge of the Sacramento Valley region is evidently connected with the Kuksu religion on one side, since the southward distribution of the two appears to coincide. Northward, however, this form of house extends considerably beyond the cult. The southern earth lodge probably has the center of its distribution among the Colorado River tribes. It appears to have penetrated somewhat farther west than the religious influences emanating from this district. From the Chumash to the southern valley Yokuts communal houses were in use. But the larger specimens of the earth lodges of the Sacramento Valley district must also have sheltered more people than we reckon to a family, and the same is definitely stated for the thatched houses of some of the Pomo.

As regards outward affiliations, there is the same uncertainty. Are we to reckon the semisubterranean house of interior British Columbia as one in type with the Navaho hogan simply because the two are roofed with earth; or is the hogan essentially of the type of the Plains tepee by reason of its conical shape and tripod foundation? Until such broader problems are answered, it would probably be premature to interpret the history of dwellings in aboriginal California.[1]

Views and plans of dwellings and dance houses will be found in Plates 9, 11, 12, 13, 46, 56, and Figures 4, 19, 23, 24, 25, 35, 39, 63.

The separate hut for the woman in her periodical illness seems to be a northern Californian institution. Information is irregular, but the groups who affirm that they formerly erected such structures are the Yurok, Karok, Hupa; probably the other northwestern tribes; the Shasta and Modoc; the northern Maidu; and apparently the Pomo. The Yuki and Sinkyone deny the practice, but their position renders unconfirmed negative statements somewhat doubtful. South of the Golden Gate there is no clear reference to separate huts for women except among the Luiseño, and the Yokuts specifically state that they did not build them.

SWEAT HOUSES.

The sweat house is a typical California institution, if there is any; yet, characteristically, it was not in universal use. The Colorado River tribes lacked it or any substitute; and a want of reference to the structure among a series of Shoshonean desert tribes—the easternmost Cahuilla, the Chemehuevi, the eastern Mono—indicates that these must perhaps be joined to the agricultural Yumans. The nonuse of the sweat house among the Yuma and Mohave appears to be of considerable significance, since on their other side the edifice was made by some of the nomadic tribes of the Southwest, and—as the kiva or estufa—a related type is important among the Pueblos.

The Californian sweat house is an institution of daily, not occasional, service. It is a habit, not a medicinal treatment; it enters into

---

[1] A searching analysis of house types in California has recently been made by F. Krause (see bibliography).

ceremony indirectly rather than specifically as a means of purification. It is the assembly of the men and often their sleeping quarters. It thus comes to fulfill many of the functions of a club; but is not to be construed as such, since ownership or kinship or friendship, not membership, determines admission; and there is no act of initiation.

In line with these characteristics, the California sweat house is a structure, not a few boughs over which a blanket is thrown before entry is made. It is earth covered, except in the northwest, where an abundance of planks roof a deep pit. Consequently, a substantial construction is requisite. A center post is often, or always, set up; logs, at any rate, have to be employed.

Warmth was produced directly by fire, never by steam generated on heated stones. While the smoke was densest the inmates lay close to the floor. Women were never admitted except here and there on special ceremonial occasions, when sweating was a subsidiary feature or wholly omitted.

In general, the sweat house was somewhat smaller than the living house. This holds of the northwestern tribes, the Yokuts, and those of southern California. In the region of the Kuksu religion the dance house or ceremonial assembly chamber, built much like the sweat house elsewhere but on a much ampler scale, has come to be known as "sweat house" to both Indians and whites. It is not certain how far this large structure really replaced the true sweat house in and about the Sacramento Valley. The two seem generally to have existed side by side, as is known to have been the case among the Pomo and Patwin, but the smaller edifice has lost its proper identity in description under the unfortunate looseness of nomenclature; much as among tribes like the Yana and Achomawi the Indians now speak of "sweat houses" inhabited by families. In these latter cases, however, there is some indication that the earth-covered dwellings were on occasion used for sweating. Some careful, because belated, inquiries remain to be made.

In extreme northeastern California the Plains form of sweat house has obtained a foothold: a small dome of willows covered with mats, large enough for a few men to sit up in, heated by steam. This is established for the Modoc, while less complete descriptions suggest the same for the Shasta, Achomawi, and Washo; but among at least some of these groups the steam sweat house is of modern introduction.

It is rather notable that there is no indication of any fusion or hybridization of the Californian and the eastern types of sweat house, even in the region where they border. This condition is typical of cultural phenomena in native America, and probably throughout the world, as soon as they are viewed distributionally rather than in their developmental sequence. Civilizations shade by endless transitions. Their elements wander randomly, as it seems, with little reference to the circumstances of their origin. But analogous or logically equivalent elements rigidly exclude each other more often than they intergrade.

Sweat houses are illustrated in Plates 10, 13, 14, 56, 60, and Figures 5, 6.

BOATS.

Native California used two types of boat—the wooden canoe and the tule balsa or shaped raft of rushes. Their use tends to be exclusive without becoming fully so. Their distribution is determined by cultural far more than by physiographic factors.

The northwestern canoe was employed on Humboldt Bay and along the open, rocky coast, but its shape as well as range indicate it to have been devised for river use. It was dug out of half a redwood log, was square ended, round bottomed, of heavy proportions, but nicely finished with recurved gunwales and carved-out seat. A similar if not identical boat was used on the southern Oregon coast beyond the range of the redwood tree. The southern limit is marked by Cape Mendocino and the navigable waters of Eel River. Inland, the Karok and Hupa regularly used canoes of Yurok manufacture, and occasional examples were sold as far upstream as the Shasta. This boat is a river type, only secondarily used on the ocean, and evidently a local specialization of an old North Pacific coast form. (Pls. 3, 5, 13, 15.)

The southern California canoe was a seagoing vessel, indispensable to the Shoshonean and Chumash islanders of the Santa Barbara group, and considerably employed also by the mainlanders of the shore from Point Concepcion and probably San Luis Obispo as far south as San Diego. It was usually of lashed planks, either because solid timber for dugouts was scarce, or because dexterity in woodworking rendered such a construction less laborious. The dugout form seems also to have been known, and perhaps prevailed among the manually clumsier tribes toward San Diego. A double-bladed paddle was used. The southern California canoe was maritime. There were no navigable rivers, and on the few sheltered bays and lagoons the balsa was sufficient and generally employed. The ends of this canoe seem to have been sharp and raised and the beam narrow. It is not certain whether the Chumash canoe was built entirely of planks or was a dugout with planks added.

A third type of canoe had a limited distribution in favorable localities in northern California, ranging about as far as overlay twining, and evidently formed part of the technological culture characteristic of this region. A historical community of origin with the northwestern redwood canoe is indubitable, but it is less clear whether the northeastern canoe represents the original type from which the northwestern developed as a specialization, or whether the latter, originating under northern influences, gave rise to the northeastern form as a marginal deterioration. This northeastern canoe was of pine or fir, burned and chopped out, narrow of beam, without definite shape. It was made by the Shasta, Modoc. Atsugewi, Achomawi, and northernmost Maidu.

The balsa has a nearly universal distribution, so far as drainage conditions permit, the only groups that wholly rejected it in favor of the canoe being the group of typical northwestern tribes. It is reported from the Modoc, Achomawi, Northern Paiute, Wintun, Maidu, Pomo, Costanoans, Yokuts, Tübatulabal, Luiseño, Diegueño, and Colorado River tribes. For river crossing, a bundle or group of bundles of tules sufficed. On large lakes and bays well-shaped vessels, with pointed and elevated prow and raised sides, were often navigated with paddles. The balsa does not appear to have been in use north of California, but it was known in Mexico, and probably has a continuous distribution, except for gaps due to negative environment, into South America.

Except for Drake's reference to boats among the Coast Miwok—perhaps to be understood as balsas—there is no evidence that any form of boat was in use on the ocean from below Monterey Bay to Cape Mendocino. A few logs were occasionally lashed into a rude raft when seal or mussel rocks were to be visited.

A number of interior groups ferried goods, children, and perhaps even women across swollen streams in large baskets or—in the south—pots. Swimming men propelled and guarded the little vessels. This custom is established for the Yuki, Yokuts, and Mohave, and was no doubt participated in by other tribes.

The rush raft was most often poled; but in the deep waters of San Francisco Bay the Costanoans propelled it with the same double-bladed paddle that was used with the canoe of the coast and archipelago of southern California, whence the less skillful northerners may be assumed to have derived the implement. The double paddle is extremely rare in America; like the "Mediterranean" type of arrow release, it appears to have been recorded only from the Eskimo. The Pomo of Clear Lake used a single paddle with short, broad blade. The northwestern paddle is long, narrow, and heavy, having to serve both as "pole" and as "oar"; that of the Klamath and Modoc, whose waters were currentless, is of more normal shape. (Pl. 67, *f–h*.) Whether the southerners employed the one-bladed paddle in addition to the double-ended one does not seem to be known.

FOOD.

Plants appear to have furnished a larger part of the diet than animals in almost all parts of California. Fish and mollusks were probably consumed in larger quantities than flesh in regions stocked with them, especially the salmon-carrying rivers of northern California, the Santa Barbara Archipelago, Clear and Klamath Lakes, the larger bays like that of San Francisco, and in a measure the immediate coast everywhere. Of game, the rodents, from jack rabbits to gophers, together with birds, evidently furnished more food the seasons through than deer and other ruminants. Foods rejected varied locally, of course, but in general northern California looked upon dog and reptile flesh as poisonous, but did not scruple to eat earthworms, grasshoppers, hymenopterous larvæ, certain species of caterpillars, and similar invertebrates when they could be gathered in sufficient masses to make their consumption worth while. In south central California the taboos against dogs and reptiles were less universal, and south of Tehachapi and east of the Sierra snakes and lizards were eaten by a good many groups. In much the greater part of the State acorns constituted a larger part of the diet than any other food, and a lengthy though simple technique of gathering, hulling, drying, grinding, sifting, leaching, and cooking had been devised. Many other seeds and fruits were treated similarly; buckeyes (*Aesculus*), for instance, and the seeds of various grasses, sages, compositæ, and the like. These were whipped into receptacles with seed beaters, which varied only in detail from one end of the State to the other (Pls. 24, *b*, 29, 50; Fig. 57); collected in close-woven or glue-smeared conical baskets (Pl. 73, *a;* contrast the open-work basket for acorns and loads, Pls. 9, 14, 23, *b*); parched with coals in trays; winnowed by tossing in trays; ground; and then eaten either dry, or, like acorn meal, as lumps of unleavened bread baked by the open fire or as boiled gruel. Leaching was on sand which drained off the hot water. In the north, the meal was spread directly on the sand (Pl. 14); in central California fir leaves were often interposed; in the south, also an openwork basket. Pulverization was either by pounding in a mortar or rubbing on the undressed metate or oval grinding slab (Pls. 16, 44, 45, 60, 66; Figs. 27, 58). The history and interrelations of the various types of these implements is somewhat intricate and has been discussed in the chapters on the Maidu, Chumash, Luiseño, and Cahuilla. The grinding process had become a well-established cultural pattern. Besides seeds, dried salmon, vertebræ, whole small rodents, berries, and fruits were often pulverized, especially for storage. In analogous manner, other processes of the acorn and seed preparation complex were extended to various foods: leaching to wild plums, parching to grasshoppers and caterpillars (Pl. 61). This complex clearly dominates the food habits of California.

Where the acorn fails, other foods are treated similarly, though sometimes with considerable specialization of process; the mesquite bean in the southern desert, the piñon nut east of the Sierra, the water lily in the Klamath-Modoc Lakes.

Agriculture had only touched one periphery of the State, the Colorado River bottom, although the seed-using and fairly sedentary habits of virtually all the other tribes would have made possible the taking over of the art with relatively little change of mode of life. Evidently planting is a more fundamental innovation to people used to depending on nature than it seems to those who have once acquired the practice. Moreover, in most of California the food supply, largely through its variety, was reasonably adequate, in spite of a rather heavy population—probably not far from one person to the square mile on the average. In most parts of the State there is little mention of famines.

. More detailed reflections on the food quest of the California Indian have been expressed in the last of the chapters on the Yokuts.

FISHING.

In fresh-water and still bays fish are more successfully taken by rude people with nets or weirs or poison than by line. Fishhooks are therefore employed only occasionally. This is the case in California. There was probably no group that was ignorant of the fishhook, but one hears little of its use. The one exception was on the southern coast, where deep water appears to have restricted the use of nets. The prevalent hook in this region was an unbarbed or sometimes barbed piece of haliotis cut almost into a circle. Elsewhere the hook was in use chiefly for fishing in the larger lakes, and in the higher mountains where trout were taken. It consisted most commonly of a wooden shank with a pointed bone lashed backward on it at an angle of 45° or less. Sometimes two such bones projected on opposite sides (Fig. 28). The gorget, a straight bone sharpened on both ends and suspended from a string in its middle, is reported from the Modoc, but is likely to have had a wider distribution.

The harpoon was probably known to every group in California whose territory contained sufficient bodies of water. The Colorado River tribes provide the only known exception. The type of harpoon is everywhere substantially identical. The shaft, being intended for thrusting and not throwing, is long and slender. The foreshaft is usually double, one prong being slightly longer than the other, presumably because the stroke was most commonly delivered at an angle to the bottom. The toggle heads are small, of bone and wood tightly wrapped with string and pitched. The socket is most frequently in or near the end. The string leaving the head at or near the middle, the socket end serves as a barb. This rather rude device is sufficient because the harpoon is rarely employed for game larger than a salmon. The lines are short and fastened to the shaft.

A heavier harpoon which was perhaps hurled was used by the northwestern coast tribes for taking sea lions. Only the heads have been preserved. These are of bone or antler and possess a true barb as well as socket. A preserved Chumash harpoon has a detachable wooden foreshaft tipped with a flint blade and lashed-on bone barb. The foreshaft itself serves as toggle.

There is one record of the spear thrower; also a specimen from the Chumash. This is of wood and is remarkable for its excessively short, broad, and unwieldy shape. It is probably authentic, but its entire uniqueness renders caution necessary in drawing inferences from this solitary example.

The seine for surrounding fish, the stretched gill net, and the dip net were known to all the Californians, although many groups had occasion to use only certain varieties. The form and size of the dip net, of course, differed according as it was used in large or small streams, in the surf, or in standing waters. The two commonest forms of frame were a semicircular hoop bisected by the handle, and two long diverging poles crossed and braced in the angle (Pls. 4, 7). A kite-shaped frame was sometimes employed for scooping (Pl. 6). Nets without poles had floats of wood or tule stems. The sinkers were grooved or nicked stones, the commonest type of all being a flat beach pebble notched on opposite edges to prevent the string slipping. Perforated stones are known to have been used as net sinkers only in northwestern California, and even there they occur by the side of the grooved variety. They are usually distinguishable without difficulty from the perforated stone of southern and central California which served as a digging stick weight, by the fact that their perforation is normally not in the middle (Fig. 7). The northwesterners also availed themselves of naturally perforated stones.

Fish weirs were used chiefly in northern California, where the streams carry salmon. In the northwest such "dams" sometimes became the occasion of important rituals. Fish traps are shown in Plates 33 and 59.

Fish poison was fed into small streams and pools by a number of tribes: the Pomo, Yana, Yokuts, and Luiseño are mentioned, and indicate that the practice was widely spread. Buckeyes, the squirting cucumber, and soaproot (*Chlorogalum*) as well as probably other plants were employed.

HUNTING.

Among hunting devices, the bow was the most important. Deer were frequently approached by the hunter covering himself with a deer hide and putting on his own head a stuffed deer head (Pl. 8; Fig. 31). This method seems not to have been reported from the south. This area also used snares little, if at all; whereas in the northwest deer were perhaps snared more often than shot. Dogs seem to have been used in hunting chiefly in northern California. Driving large game into a brush fence or over a cliff was a rather unusual practice, though specifically reported from the Mountain Maidu. The surrounding of game—rabbits, antelope, occasionally deer or elk—was most practicable in relatively open country and is therefore reported chiefly from the southern two-thirds of the State. Rabbits were frequently driven into long, low, loose nets. Through southern California a curved throwing stick of southwestern type, of boomerang shape but unwarped (Fig. 55), was used to kill rabbits, other small game, and perhaps birds. Traps, other than snares for deer, quail, and pigeons, were little developed. Deadfalls are occasionally reported for rodents. The Achomawi caught large game in concealed pits.

BOWS.

The bow was self, long, and narrow in the south, sinew-backed, somewhat shorter, thin, and flat in northern and central California. Of course, light unbacked bows were used for small game and by boys everywhere. The material varied locally. In the northwest the bow is of yew and becomes shorter and broader than anywhere else; the wood is pared down to little greater thickness than the sinew, the edge is sharp, and the grip much pinched. Good bows, of course, quickly went out of use before firearms, so that few examples have been preserved except low-grade modern pieces intended for birds and rabbits. But sinew backing is reported southward to the Yokuts and Koso. The Yokuts name of the Kitanemuk meant "large bows." This group, therefore, is likely to have used the southern self bow. On the other hand, the short Chemehuevi bow was sinew backed, and a backed Chumash specimen has been preserved.

The following are measurements of the California bows in one museum:

	Length in inches.	Width in sixteenths of inches.	Thickness in sixteenths of inches.
Sinew-backed:			
Yurok (6)	32–52	[1] 22–40	5–9
Tolowa (2)	39	[1] 24–30	9–10
Yahi (2)	44–54	[1] 28–30	10–12
Northern Wintun? (2)	44–45	22–24	11–12
Miwok? (1)	44	22	14
Self:			
Klamath–Modoc (3)	40–43	[1] 25–35	9–14
Pomo (1)	56	[1] 20	13
Yokuts (8)	40–56	19–24	8–14
Luiseño (1)	64	19	16
Cahuilla (6)	52–56	17–20	10–15
Mohave (7)	53–70	18–22	12–17

[1] Grip pinched in from this maximum.

The arrow was normally two-pieced, its head most frequently of obsidian, which works finer and smaller as well as sharper than flint. The butt end of the point was frequently notched for a sinew lashing. The foreshaft was generally set into the main shaft. For small game shot at close range one-piece arrows frequently sufficed; the stone head was also omitted or replaced by a blunted wooden point. Cane was used as main shaft wherever it was available, but nowhere exclusively. From the Yokuts south to the Yuma the typical fighting arrow was a simple shaft without head, quantity rather than effectiveness of ammunition appearing the desideratum. The same tribes, however, often tipped their deer arrows with stone.

The arrow release has been described for but three groups. None of these holds agree, and two are virtually new for America. The Maidu release is the primary one, the Yahi a modification of the Mongolian, the Luiseño the pure Mediterranean, hitherto attributed in the New World only to the Eskimo. This remarkable variety in detail is not wholly uncharacteristic of California.

The arrow, in the north, was bent straight in a hole cut through a slab of wood (Pl. 16). and polished with *Equisetum* or in two grooved pieces of sandstone. The southern straightener and polisher is determined by the cane arrow: a transversely grooved rectangle of steatite set by the fire. Among pottery-making tribes clay might replace steatite. This southwestern form extends north

to the Yokuts and Mono (Pl. 49); the Maidu possessed it in somewhat aberrant form.

TEXTILES.

Basketry is unquestionably the most developed art in California.
It is of interest that the principle which chiefly emerges in connection with the art is that its growth has been in the form of what
ethnologists are wont to name "complexes." That is to say, materials, processes, forms, and uses which abstractly considered bear
no intrinsic relation to one another, or only a slight relation, are in
fact bound up in a unit. A series of tribes employs the same forms,
substances, and techniques; when a group is reached which abandons
one of these factors, it abandons most or all of them, and follows a
characteristically different art.

This is particularly clear of the basketry of northernmost California. At first sight this art seems to be distinguished chiefly by
the outstanding fact that it knows no coiling processes. Its southern
line of demarcation runs between the Sinkyone and Kato, the Wailaki
and Yuki, through Wintun and Yana territory at points that have
not been determined with certainty, and between the Achomawi (or
more strictly the Atsugewi) and the Maidu. Northward the art extends far into Oregon west of the Cascades. The Klamath and
Modoc do not fully adhere to it, although their industry is a related one.

Further examination reveals a considerable number of other traits
that are universally followed by the tribes in the region in question.
Wicker and checker work, which have no connection with coiling,
are also not made. Of the numerous varieties of twining, the plain
weave is substantially the only one employed, with some use of subsidiary strengthening in narrow belts of three-strand twining. The
diagonal twine is known, but practiced only sporadically. Decoration is wholly in overlay twining, each weft strand being faced with
a colored one. The materials of this basketry are hazel shoots for
warp, conifer roots for weft, and *Xerophyllum*, *Adiantum*, and alder-
dyed *Woodwardia* for white, black, and red patterns, respectively.
All of these plants appear to grow some distance south of the range
of this basketry. At least in places they are undoubtedly sufficiently
abundant to serve as materials. The limit of distribution of the art
can therefore not be ascribed to botanical causes. Similarly, there
is no reason why people should stop wearing basketry caps and
pounding acorns in a basketry hopper (Pl. 24, *a*) because their
materials or techniques are different. That they do evidences the
strength of this particular complex. (Compare Pls. 23, 24, 73, *e*, *f*.)

In southern California a definite type of basket ware is adhered to
with nearly equal rigidity. The typical technique here is coiling,

normally on a foundation of straws of *Epicampes* grass. The sewing material is sumac or *Juncus*. Twined ware is subsidiary, is roughly done (Pl. 73, *b*), and is made wholly in *Juncus*, a material that, used alone, forbids any considerable degree of finish. Here again the basketry cap (Pl. 73, *d*) and the mortar hopper (Pl. 44, *a*) appear, but are limited toward the north by the range of the technique. (Compare Pls. 55, *c, e;* 73, *c*.)

From southern California proper this basketry has penetrated to the southerly Yokuts and the adjacent Shoshonean tribes. Chumash ware also belongs to the same type, although it generally substitutes *Juncus* for the *Epicampes* grass. Both the Chumash and the Yokuts and Shoshoneans in and north of the Tehachapi Mountains have developed one characteristic form not found in southern California proper—the shouldered basket with constricted neck. This is represented in the south by a simpler form—a small globular basket. The extreme development of the "bottle neck" type is found among the Yokuts, Kawaiisu, and Tübatulabal. The Chumash on the one side, and the willow-using Chemehuevi on the other, round the shoulders of these vessels so as to show a partial transition to the southern California prototype. (Compare Yokuts, Pl. 50; Mono and Kawaiisu, Pl. 55, *d, e;* Chumash, Pls. 50, 52, 53, 54; Chemehuevi, Pls. 59, 73, *a*.)

The Colorado River tribes slight basketry to a very unusual degree. (Pl. 55, *b*.) They make a few very rude trays and fish traps. The majority of their baskets they seem always to have acquired in trade from their neighbors. Their neglect of the art recalls its similar low condition among the Pueblos, but is even more pronounced. Pottery making and agriculture are perhaps the influences most specifically responsible; although it is observable that the river tribes show little skill or interest in anything mechanical or economic.

Central California from the Yuki and Maidu to the Yokuts is an area in which coiling and twining occur side by side. There were probably more twined baskets made but they were manufactured for rougher usage and were generally undecorated. Show pieces were almost invariably coiled. The characteristic technique is therefore perhaps coiling, but the two processes were nearly in balance. The materials are not as uniform as in the north or south. The most characteristic plant is perhaps the redbud, *Cercis occidentalis*, which furnished the red and often the white surface in coiling and twining. Willows are also widely used; and *Carex* root fibers provide the Pomo and Yokuts with a splendid material for weft and especially wrapping. Dogwood, maple, hazel, pine, tule, and grape are also employed, some rather consistently by a single group or two, others only occasionally, but over a wide area. The most common techniques are coiling with triple foundation and plain twining. Diagonal twining is, however, more or less followed, and lattice twining, single-rod coiling, and wickerwork all have a local distribution, including in each case the Pomo. Twining with overlay is never practiced. Forms are variable, but not to any notable extent. Oval baskets were made in the Pomo region, but there was no shape of as pronounced a character as the southern Yokuts bottle neck.

It is rather clear that a number of local basketry arts developed in central California on this generic foundation. The most complex of these is without any question that of the Pomo and their immediate neighbors. The many specialties and peculiarities of this art have been set forth in detail in the account of this group. It may only be added that the Pomo appear to be the only central Californian group that habitually makes twined baskets with patterns.

Another definite center of development includes the Washo and in some measure the Miwok. Both of these groups practiced single-rod coiling and have evolved a distinctive style of ornamentation characterized by a certain lightness of decorative touch. (Pls. 76, 55, f.) This ware, however, shades off to the south into Yokuts basketry with its southern California affiliations, and to the north into Maidu ware.

The latter in its pure form is readily distinguished from Miwok as well as Pomo basketry, but presents few positive peculiarities. Costanoan and Salinan baskets have perished so completely that no very definite idea of them can be formed. It is doubtful whether a marked local type prevailed in this region. The Yuki, wedged in between the Pomo and tribes that followed the northern California twining, make a ware which in spite of its simplicity can not be confounded with that of any other group in California (Pl. 75); this in spite of the general lack of advancement which pervades their culture.

It thus appears that we may infer that a single style and type underlies the basketry of the whole of central California; that this has undergone numerous local diversifications due only in part to the materials available, and extending on the other hand into its purely decorative aspects; and that the most active and proficient of these local superstructures was that for which the Pomo were responsible, their creation, however, differing only in degree from those which resulted from analogous but less active impulses elsewhere. In central California, therefore, a basic basketry complex is less rigidly developed, or preserved, than in either the north or the south. The flora being substantially uniform through central California, differences in the use of materials are generally in themselves significant of incipient national diversifications.

The Modoc constitute a subtype within the area of twining. They overlay chiefly when they use *Xerophyllum* or quills, it would seem; and the majority of their baskets, which are composed of tule fibers of several shades, are in plain twining. But the shapes and patterns of their ware have clearly been developed under the influences that guide the art of the surrounding tribes, and the cap and hopper occur among them.

It is difficult to decide whether the Modoc art is to be interpreted as a form of the primitive style on which the modern overlaying complex is based, or as an adaptation of the latter to a new and widely useful material. The question can scarcely be answered without full consideration of the basketry of all Oregon.

The awl with which coiled basketry was made, and with which such little sewing as existed was performed, was usually of bone, in the desert south also of spines. Figure 67 shows a series of central Californian forms. Among the northwestern tribes, who did not coil, a blunter awl survives in use for dressing lamprey eels; and buckskin was presumably sewn with sharp specimens.

Cloth is unknown in aboriginal California. Rush mats are twined like baskets or sewn. The nearest approach to a loom is a pair of sticks on which a long cord of rabbit fur is wound back and forth to be made into a blanket by the intertwining of a weft of the same material, or of two cords. The Maidu, perhaps the Chumash, and therefore probably other tribes also, made similar blankets of strips of goose or duck skin, and in other cases of feather-wrapped cords. The rabbit-skin blanket has, of course, a wide distribution outside of California; that of bird skins may have been devised locally.

POTTERY.

The distribution of pottery in California reveals this art as due to southwestern influences. It is practiced by the Yuma, Mohave, and other Colorado River tribes; sporadically by the Chemehuevi; more regularly by the Diegueño, Luiseño, Cupeño, Serrano, and Cahuilla; probably not by the Gabrielino; with the Juaneño status unknown.

A second area, in which cruder pottery is made (Pl. 51), lies to the north, apparently disconnected from the southern California one. In this district live the southern and perhaps central Yokuts, the Tübatulabal, and the western Mono. This ware seems to be pieced with the fingers; it is irregular, undecorated, and the skill to construct vessels of any size was wanting.

The southern Californians tempered with crushed rock, employed a clay that baked dull reddish, laid it on in thin spiral coils, and smoothed it between a wooden paddle and a pebble. They never corrugated, and no slipped ware has been found in the region; but there is some variety of forms—bowls, jars, pots, oval plates, short-handled spoons, asymmetrical and multiple-mouthed jars, pipes—executed in a considerable range of sizes. Designs were solely in yellow ocher, and frequently omitted. They consisted chiefly of patterns of angular lines, with or without the corners filled in. Curves, solidly painted areas, and semirealistic figures were not attempted. (Pls. 49, 62, 68; Figs. 64, 65.) The ware is light, brittle, and porous. The art during the last generation has been best preserved among the Mohave, and seems at all times to have attained greatest development on the Colorado River. But the coast tribes may have been substantial equals before they came under Caucasian influence; except that they decorated less. An affinity with Pima and Seri ware is unmistakable; but it is far from attaining identity. There is no direct or specific resemblance to any present or ancient Pueblo pottery; but rather close parallels in prehistoric ware from the Papago and Gila country. This argues either a local origination of Colorado River pottery under generic southwestern influence or a more direct stimulus or importation from Sonora. Potsherds indistinguishable from the modern ware occur on the surface of ancient sites on the Diegueño coast. Whether they extend to the earlier deposits remains to be ascertained; but they testify that the art is not an entirely recent one. Pottery was not established in California as a direct adjunct of agriculture, its distribution being considerably greater.

MUSICAL INSTRUMENTS.

The rattle is of three kinds in the greater part of California: the split clap stick for dancing (Pls. 67, c, 77), the gravel-filled cocoon bunch for shamanistic practices and ritualistic singing (Fig. 37; Pl. 67, d), and the bundle of deer hoofs for the adolescent girl. South of Tehachapi these are mostly replaced by a single form, whose material varies between turtle shell and gourd according to region. The northwest does not use rattles except in the adolescence ceremony; in which some tribes, such as the Hupa and Sinkyone, employ a modification of the clap stick, the Karok, Tolowa, and others the more general deer hoofs. The latter are known as far south as the Diegueño, but seem to be associated with hunting or mourning ceremonies at this end of the State. The clap stick penetrated south to the Gabrielino.

The notched scraper or musical rasp has been reported only from the Salinans.

. California is a drumless region, except in the area of the Kuksu cult. There a foot drum, a segment of a large cylinder of wood, is set at the back of the dance house, and held very sacred. Various substitutes exist elsewhere: the Yurok beat a board with a paddle, the Maidu and Diegueño strike or rub baskets, the Mohave do the same before a resounding jar. But these accompaniments belong to gambling or shamans' or narrative songs; none of the substitutes replace dance drums.

Whistles of bone or cane are employed far more frequently in dances than the drum by practically all tribes, in fact, although of course in quite different connections.

The bull-roarer has been reported from several scattered tribes. (Pl. 44, *d–f*.) As might be expected, its function is religious, but is not well known and seems to have varied. To the Luiseño it was a summons. It was not used by the northwestern nations.

The only true musical instrument in our sense is the flute, an open reedless tube, blown across the edge of one end. Almost always it has four holes, often more or less grouped in two pairs, and is innocent of any definite scale. It is played for self-recreation and courtship. (Pl. 43.) The Mohave alone know a reeded flageolet.

The musical or resonant bow, a sort of jew's-harp, the only stringed instrument of California, has been recorded among the Pomo, Maidu, Yokuts, and Diegueño, and no doubt had a wider distribution. It was tapped as a restful amusement, and sometimes in converse with spirits.

It is remarkable, although abundantly paralleled among other Indians, that the only two instruments capable of producing a melody were not used ceremonially. The cause must be their imperfection. The dance was based on song, which an instrument of rhythm could enrich, but with which a mechanically produced melody would have clashed.

It is also a curious fact that the comparatively superior civilization of the northwestern tribes was the one that wholly lacked drum, bull-roarer, and musical bow, and made minimal employ of rattles.

MONEY.

Two forms of money prevailed in California: the dentalium shell, imported from the far north; and the clamshell disk bead. Among the strictly northwestern tribes dentalia were alone standard. In a belt stretching across the remainder of the northern end of the State, and limited very nearly, to the south, by the line that marks the end of the range of overlay twined basketry, dentalia and disks were used side by side. Beyond, to the end of the State, dentalia were so sporadic as to be no longer reckoned as money, and clam currency was the medium of valuation. It had two sources of supply. On Bodega Bay the resident Coast Miwok and neighboring Pomo gathered the shells of *Saxidomus aratus* or *gracilis*. From Morro Bay near San Luis Obispo to San Diego there occurs another large clam, *Tivela* or *Pachydesma crassatelloides*. Both of these were broken, the pieces roughly shaped, bored, strung, and then rounded and polished on a sandstone slab. The disks were from a third of an inch to an inch in diameter, and from a quarter to a third of an inch thick, and varied in value according to size, thickness, polish, and age. The Pomo supplied the north; southern and central California used *Pachydesma* beads. The southern Maidu are said to have had the latter, which fact, on account of their remoteness from supply, may account for the higher value of the currency among them than with the Yokuts. But the Pomo *Saxidomus* bead also reached them.

From the Yokuts and Salinans southward, money was measured on the circumference of the hand. The exact distance traversed by the string varied somewhat according to tribe; the value in our terms appears to have fluctuated locally to a greater degree. The available data on this system have been brought together in Table 6 in the chapter on the Chumash. The Pomo, Wintun, and Maidu seem not to have known the hand scale. They measured their strings in the rough by stretching them out, and appear to have counted the beads when they wished accuracy.

Associated with the two clam moneys were two kinds of valuables, both in cylindrical form. The northern was of magnesite, obtained in southeastern Pomo territory. This was polished and on baking took on a tawny or reddish hue, often variegated. These stone cylinders traveled as far as the Yuki and the Miwok. From the south came similar but longer and slenderer pieces of shell, white to violet in color, made sometimes of the columella of univalves, sometimes out of the hinge of a large rock oyster or rock clam, probably *Hinnites giganteus*. The bivalve cylinders took a finer grain and seem to have been preferred. Among the Chumash such pieces must have been fairly common, to judge from grave finds. To the inland Yokuts and Miwok they were excessively valuable. Both the magnesite and the shell cylinders were perforated longitudinally, and often constituted the center piece of a fine string of beads; but, however displayed, they were too precious to be properly classifiable as ornaments. At the same time their individual variability in size and quality, and consequently in value, was too great to allow them to be reckoned as ordinary money. They rank rather with the obsidian blades of northwestern California, as an equivalent of precious stones among ourselves.

The small univalve *Olivella biplicata* and probably other species of the same genus were used nearly everywhere in the State. In the north they were strung whole; in central and southern California, frequently broken up and rolled into thin, slightly concave disks, as by the southwestern Indians of to-day. Neither form had much value. The olivella disks are far more common in graves than clam disks, as if a change of custom had taken place from the prehistoric to the historic period. But a more likely explanation is that the olivellas accompanied the corpse precisely because they were less valuable, the clam currency either being saved for inheritance, or, if offered, destroyed by fire in the great mourning ceremony.

Haliotis was much used in necklaces, ear ornaments, and the like, and among tribes remote from the sea commanded a considerable price; but it was nowhere standardized into currency.

TOBACCO.

Tobacco, of two or more species of *Nicotiana*, was smoked everywhere, but by the Yokuts, Tübatulabal, Kitanemuk, and Costanoans it was also mixed with shell lime and eaten.

The plant was grown by some of the northern groups: the Yurok, Hupa, and probably Wintun and Maidu. This limited agriculture restricted to the people of a small area remote from tribes with farming customs is remarkable. The Hupa and Yurok are afraid of wild tobacco as likely to have sprung from a grave; but it is as likely that the cultivation produced this unreasonable fear by rendering the use of the natural product unnecessary, as that the superstition was the impetus to the cultivation.

Tobacco was offered religiously by the Yurok, the Yahi, the Yokuts, and presumably by most or all other tribes; but exact data are lacking, offering being a rather limited practice of the Californians.

The pipe is found everywhere, and with insignificant exceptions is tubular. In the northwest it averages about 6 inches long and is of hard wood scraped somewhat concave in profile, the bowl lined with inset soapstone. For some distance about the Pomo area the pipe is longer, the bowl end abruptly thickened to 2 inches, the stem slender. In the Sierra Nevada the pipe runs to only 3 or 4 inches and tapers somewhat to the mouth end. The Chumash pipe has been preserved only in its stone exemplars. These usually resemble the Sierra type, but are often longer, normally thicker, and more frequently contain a brief mouthpiece of bone. Ceremonial specimens are sometimes of obtuse angular shape. The pottery-making tribes of the south used clay pipes most commonly. These were short, with shouldered bowl end. In all the region from the

Yokuts south, in other words wherever the plant was available, a simple length of cane frequently replaced the worked pipe; and among all tribes shamans had all-stone pieces at times. The Modoc pipe was essentially eastern: a stone head set on a wooden stem. The head is variable, as if it were a new and not yet established form: a tube, an L, intermediate forms, or a disk. (Compare Fig. 29 with Pl. 30.)

The Californians were light smokers, rarely passionate. They consumed smaller quantities of tobacco than most eastern tribes and did not dilute it with bark. Smoking was of little formal social consequence, and indulged in chiefly at bedtime in the sweat house. The available species of *Nicotiana* were pungent and powerful in physiological effect, and quickly produced dizziness and sleep.

VARIOUS.

The ax and the stone celt are foreign to aboriginal California. The substitute is the wedge or chisel of antler—among the Chumash of whale's bone—driven by a stone. This maul is shaped only in northwestern California. (Pl. 19.) The extreme south and southeast of the State seem to have lacked even the wedge. An adz of shell lashed to a curved stone handle is restricted to the northwestern area. (Pl. 19.)

The commonest string materials are the bark or outer fibers of dogbane or Indian hemp, *Apocynum cannabinum*, and milkweed, *Asclepias*. From these fine cords and heavy ropes are spun by hand. Nettle string is reported from two groups as distant as the Modoc and the Luiseño. Other tribes are likely to have used it also as a subsidiary material. In the northwest, from the Tolowa to the Coast Yuki, and inland at least to the Shasta, Indian hemp and milkweed are superseded by a small species of iris, *I. macrosiphon*, from each leaf of which thin, tough, silky fibers are scraped out. The manufacture is very tedious, but results in an unusually fine, hard, and even string. In the southern desert *Agave* fibers yield a coarse, stiff cordage, and the reed, *Phragmites*, is also said to be used. Barks of various kinds, mostly from unidentified species, are used for wrappings and lashings by many tribes, and grapevine is a convenient tying material for large objects. Practically all Californian cordage, of whatever weight, was two-ply before Caucasian contact became influential; although three-ply bow strings have been reported.

The carrying net is essentially southern so far as California is concerned, but connects geographically as well as in type with a net used by the Shoshonean women of the Great Basin. It was in use among all the southern Californians except those of the Colorado River and possibly the Chemehuevi, and extended north to the

Yokuts and Koso. (Figs. 53, 59.) The shape of the utensil is that of a small hammock of large mesh, gathered at the ends on loops which can be brought together by a heavy cord. A varying type occurs in an isolated region to the north among the Pomo and Yuki. Here the ends of the net are carried into a continuous headband. This arrangement does not permit of a contraction or expansion to accommodate the load as in the south. The net has also been mentioned for the Costanoans, but its type there remains unknown. It is possible that these people served as transmitters of the idea from the south to the Pomo. A curious device is reported from the Maidu. The pack strap, when not of skin, is braided or more probably woven. Through its larger central portion the warp threads run free without weft. This arrangement allows them to be spread out and to enfold a small or light load somewhat in the fashion of a net.

The carrying frame of the Southwest has no analogy in California except on the Colorado River. Here two looped sticks are crossed and their four lengths connected with light cordage. Except for the disparity in weight between the frame and the shell of the covering, this type would pass as a basketry form, and at bottom it appears to be such. The ordinary openwork conical carrying basket of central and northern California is occasionally strengthened by the lashing in of four heavier rods. In the northeastern corner of the State, where exterior influences from other cultures are recognizable, the carrier is sometimes of hide fastened to a frame of four sticks.

The storage of acorns or corresponding food supplies is provided for in three ways in California. All the southern tribes construct a large receptacle of twigs irregularly interlaced like a bird's nest. This is sometimes made with a bottom, sometimes set on a bed of twigs and covered in the same way. The more arid the climate, the less does construction matter. Mountain tribes make the receptacle with bottom and lid and small mouth. In the open desert the chief function of the granary is to hold the food together, and it becomes little else than a short section of hollow cylinder. Nowhere is there a worked-out technique. The diameter is from 2 to 6 feet. The setting is always outdoors, sometimes on a platform, often on bare rocks, and occasionally on the ground. (Pl. 60.) The Chumash seem not to have used this type of receptacle.

In central California a cache or granary is used which can also not be described as a true basket. It differs from the southern form in usually being smaller in diameter but higher, in being constructed of finer and softer materials, and in depending more or less directly in its structure on a series of posts which at the same time elevate it from the ground. This is the granary of the tribes in the Sierra

Nevada, used by the Wintun, Maidu, Miwok (Pl. 38), and Yokuts, and in somewhat modified form—a mat of sticks covered with thatch—by the western or mountain Mono. It has penetrated also to those of the Pomo of Lake County who are in direct communication with the Wintun.

In the remainder of California large baskets—their type, of course, determined by the prevailing style of basketry (Pls. 9, 54)—are set indoors or perhaps occasionally in caves or rock recesses. In the desert south there was some storage in jars hidden in cliff crevices.

The flat spoon or paddle for stirring gruel is widely spread in California, but far from universal. It has been found among all the northwestern tribes, the Achomawi, Atsugewi, Shasta, Pomo, Wappo, southern Maidu, northern Miwok, Washo, and Diegueño. The Yokuts and southern Miwok, at times also the Washo, use instead a looped stick, which is also convenient for handling hot cooking stones. The Colorado River tribes, who stew more civilized messes of corn, beans, or fish in pots, tie three rods together for a stirrer. Plates 17, 44, and Figure 38 illustrate types of stirrers.

Cradles or baby carriers (Pls. 35, 39, 40) have been discussed in one of the chapters on the Yokuts.

Fire was made only by the drill, except that the Pomo are said sometimes to have scraped together two rough pieces of quartz. The materials of the fire drill (Pls. 77, 78; Fig. 66) varied considerably according to locality; borer and hearth were sometimes of the same wood. The drill, whether for fire or for perforation, was always twirled by hand rubbing. The Pomo pump-drill is taken over from the Spaniards.

CHAPTER 55.

SOCIETY.

POLITICAL ORGANIZATION.

Tribes did not exist in California in the sense in which the word is properly applicable to the greater part of the North American Continent. When the term is used in the present work, it must therefore be understood as synonymous with "ethnic group" rather than as denoting political unity.

The marginal Mohave and the Yuma are the only Californian groups comparable to what are generally understood as "tribes" in the central and eastern United States: namely a fairly coherent body of from 500 to 5,000 souls, usually averaging not far from 2,000; speaking in almost all cases a distinctive dialect or at least subdialect; with a political organization of the loosest, perhaps; but nevertheless possessed of a considerable sentiment of solidarity as against all other bodies, sufficient ordinarily to lead them to act as a unit. The uniquely enterprising military spirit displayed by the Yuma and Mohave is undoubtedly connected with this sense of cohesion.

The extreme of political anarchy is found in the northwest, where there is scarcely a tendency to group towns into higher units, and where even a town is not conceived as an essential unit. In practice a northwestern settlement was likely to act as a body, but it did so either because its inhabitants were kinsmen or because it contained a man of sufficient wealth to have established personal relations of obligation between himself and individual fellow townsmen not related to him in blood. The Yurok, Karok, and Hupa, and probably several of the adjacent groups, simply did not recognize any organization which transcended individuals and kin groups.

In north central California the rudiments of a tribal organization are discernible among the Pomo, Yuki, and Maidu, and may be assumed to have prevailed among most other groups. A tribe in this region was a small body, evidently including on the average not much more than 100 souls. It did not possess distinctive speech, a number of such tribes being normally included in the range of a single dialect. Each was obviously in substance a "village community," although the term "village" in this connection must be understood as implying a tract of land rather than a settlement as such. In most cases the population of the little tribe was divided between several settlements, each presumably consisting of a few households more or less connected by blood or marriage; but there was also a site which was regarded as the principal one inhabited. Subsidiary settlements were frequently abandoned, reoccupied, or newly founded. The principal village was maintained more permanently. The limits of the territory of the group were well defined, comprising in most cases a natural drainage area. A chief was recognized for the tribe. There is some indication that his elevation was normally subject to popular approval, although hereditary privileges are likely to have limited selection to particular lineages. The minor settlements or groups of kinsmen had each their lesser chief or headman. There was usually no name for the tribe as such. It was designated either by the name of its principal settlement or by that of its chief. Among foreigners these little groups sometimes bore names which were used much like true tribal names; but on an analysis these generally prove to mean only "people of such and such a place or district." This type of organization has been definitely established for the Wailaki, Yuki, Pomo, and Patwin, and is likely to have prevailed as far south as the Miwok in the interior and the Costanoans or Salinans on the coast and inland to the Maidu and Yana. In the northeast, among Shasta, Atsugewi, and Achomawi, there are reports of chiefs recognized over wider districts, which would suggest somewhat larger political units.

The Yokuts, and apparently they alone, attained a nearer approach to a full tribal system. Their tribes were larger, ranging from 150 to 400 or 500 members, possessed names which do not refer to localities, and spoke distinctive dialects, although these were often only slightly divergent from the neighboring tongues. The territory of each tribe was larger than in the region to the north, and a principal permanent village rarely looms up with prominence.

The Shoshoneans of Nevada, and with them those of the eastern desert fringe of California, possessed an organization which appears to be somewhat akin to that of the Yokuts. They were divided into groups of about the same size as the Yokuts, each without a definite metropolis, rather shifting within its range, and headed by a chief possessing considerable influence. The groups were almost throughout named after a characteristic diet: thus, "fish eaters" or "mountain-sheep eaters." It is not known how far each of these tribes possessed a unique dialect: if they did, their speech distinctness was in most cases minimal. Owing to the open and poorly productive nature of the country, the territory of each of these Shoshonean groups of the Great Basin was considerably more extensive than in the Yokuts habitat.

Political conditions in southern California are obscure, but are likely to have been generally similar to those of north central California. Among the Chumash, towns of some size were inhabited century after century, and these undoubtedly were the centers if not the bases of political groups. Among the Serrano and Diegueño, groups that have been designated as "clans" appear to have been pretty close equivalents of the Pomo tribelets or "village communities" in owning a drainage territory, in the size of this area, and in their numbers. Cahuilla, Cupeño, and Luiseño may also prove to conform. The larger towns of the Gabrielino and Chumash may represent concentrations like those of the Patwin and Clear Lake Pomo. In at least part of southern California, however, the local groups were assigned to totemic moieties and practiced habitual if not rigorous exogamy. They may therefore be the typical tribelets of other parts of the State somewhat remodeled under the influence of a social pattern.

The Mohave and other Yuman tribes of the Colorado Valley waged war as tribal units. Their settlements were small, shifting, apparently determined in the main by the location of their fields, and enter little into their own descriptions of their life. It is clear that a Mohave's sense of attachment was primarily to his people as a body, and secondarily to his country. The California Indian, with the partial exception of the Yokuts, always gives the impression of being attached first of all to a spot, or at most a few miles of stream or valley, and to his blood kindred or a small group of lifelong associates and intimates.

It should be added that the subject of political organization and government is perhaps in as urgent need of precise investigation as any other topic in the field of California ethnology.

THE CHIEF.

Chieftainship is wrapped in the obscurity of the political organization to which it is related. There were hereditary chiefs in most parts of California. But it is difficult to determine how far inheritance was the formally instituted avenue to office, or was only actually operative in the majority of instances. In general, it seems that chieftainship was more definitely hereditary in the southern half or two-thirds of the State than in the north. Wealth was a factor of some consequence in relation to chieftainship everywhere, but its influence seems also to have varied according to locality. In the south, liberality perhaps counted for more than possession of wealth. The northwestern tribes had rich men of great influence, but no chiefs. Being without political organizations, they could not well have had the latter.

The degree of authority of the chief is difficult to estimate. This is a matter which can not be judged accurately from the relations between native groups and intruders belonging to a more highly civilized alien race. To understand the situation as between the chief and his followers in the routine of daily life, it is necessary to have at command a more intimate knowledge of this life before its disturbance by Caucasian culture than is available for most Californian groups. It seems that the authority of the chief was considerable everywhere as far north as the Miwok, and by no means negligible beyond; while in the northwest the social effect of wealth was so great as to obtain for the rich a distinctly commanding position. Among certain of the Shoshoneans of southern California the chief, the assistant or religious chief, and their wives or children, were all known by titles; which fact argues that a fairly great deference was accorded them. Their authority probably did not lag much behind. Both the Juaneño and the Chumash are said to have gone to war to avenge slights put upon their chiefs. The director of rituals as an assistant to the head chief is a southern California institution. Somewhat similar is the central Yokuts' practice of having two chiefs for each tribe, one to represent each exogamous moiety. The chief had speakers, messengers, or similar henchmen with named offices, among the Coast Miwok, the interior Miwok, the Yokuts, the Juaneño, and no doubt among other groups.

The headman of a settlement seems to have been head of a group of kinsmen and must be distinguished from the heads of political groups, although this is usually difficult in the absence of detailed information because the same word often denotes both offices.

The chief was everywhere distinctly a civil official. If he commanded also in battle, it seems to have been only through the accident of being a distinguished warrior as well. The usual war leader was merely that individual in the group who was able to inspire confidence through having displayed courage, skill, and enterprise in combat. It is only natural that his voice should have carried weight even in time of peace, but he seems not to have been regarded as holding an office. This distinction between the chief and the military leader appears to apply even to the warlike Yuma and Mohave.

There were no hereditary priests in California. A religious office often passed from father to son or brother's son, but the successor took his place because his kinship had caused him to acquire the necessary knowledge, rather than in virtue of his descent as such.

The shaman, of course, was never an official in the true sense of the word, inasmuch as his power was necessarily of individual acquisition and varied directly according to his supernatural potency, or, as we should call it, his gifts of personality.

SOCIAL STRATIFICATION.

Social classes of different level are hardly likely to develop in so primitive a society as that of California. It is therefore highly distinctive of the northwestern area that the social stratification which forms so important an element in the culture of the North Pacific coast appears among these people with undiminished vigor. The heraldic and symbolic devices of the more advanced tribes a thousand miles to the north are lacking among the Yurok: the consciousness of the different value of a rich and a poor man is as keen among them as with the Kwakiutl or the Haida.

The northwest perhaps is also the only part of California that knew slavery. This institution rested wholly upon an economic basis here. The Chumash may have held slaves; but precise information is lacking. The Colorado River tribes kept women captives from motives of sentiment, but did not exploit their labor.

Wealth was by no means a negligible factor in the remainder of California, but it clearly did not possess the same influence as in the northwest. There seems to have been an effort to regulate matters so that the chief, through the possession of several wives, or through contributions, was in a position to conduct himself with liberality, especially toward strangers and in time of need. On the whole, however, he was wealthy because he was chief rather than the reverse. Among the Colorado River tribes a thoroughly democratic spirit prevailed as regards property, and there is a good deal of the Plains sentiment that it behooves a true man to be contemptuous of material possessions.

EXOGAMY AND TOTEMISM.

California was long regarded as a region lacking clans, group totems, or other exogamous social units. The Colorado River tribes were indeed known to be divided into clans, and the Miwok into moieties, both carrying certain rather indirect totemic associations. But these seemed to be isolated exceptions. More recent information, however, shows that some form of gentile organization was prevalent among nearly all groups from the Miwok south to the

Yuma; and the principal types which this organization assumes have become clear in outline.

In brief, the situation, which is reviewed in Figure 69, is this: Almost everywhere within the area in question the units are exogamous. Nearly always they are totemic. Descent is invariably patrilinear. In the extreme south or southeast the division of society is on

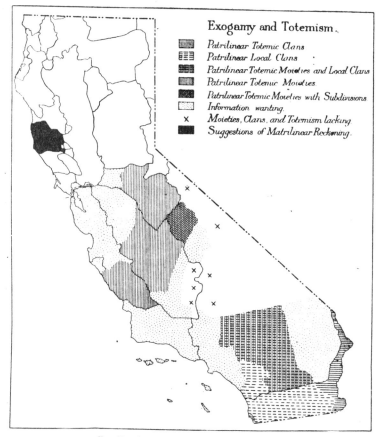

Exogamy and Totemism.

▤   *Patrilinear Totemic Clans*
▦   *Patrilinear Local Clans*
▨   *Patrilinear Totemic Moieties and Local Clans*
▥   *Patrilinear Totemic Moieties*
▩   *Patrilinear Totemic Moieties with Subdivisions*
▫   *Information wanting.*
×   *Moieties, Clans, and Totemism lacking.*
■   *Suggestions of Matrilinear Reckoning.*

FIG. 69.—Exogamy and totemism in California.

the basis of multiple clans, in the San Joaquin Valley of moieties, in the middle—that is, roughly in the region of the northern part of southern California—there are clans and moieties. Toward the head of the San Joaquin Valley there is a tract over which clans, moieties, and totems are all lacking. This tongue of clanless area seems to represent an intrusive influence from the desert Shoshoneans on the east. It perhaps did not disrupt the continuity of totemic social organization between central and southern California, since there is no definite information available on the most south-westerly group of the Yokuts, the Chumash, the Kitanemuk, or the Gabrielino. The map suggests the possibility that at least some of these groups possessed moieties or totems and thus served to link central and southern California into one continuous chain.

It is hardly possible to doubt that this totemic clan or moiety system of California stands in a positive historic relation to that of the Southwest. The fact of its being a patrilinear system, whereas the southwestern Indians reckon descent in the female line, indicates only that the connection is ancient and indirect. Both the other North American regions in which totemic clans or moieties prevail, the North Pacific coast and the eastern side of the continent, are divided into patrilinear and matrilinear subareas. The continental distribution is such that it would be more than hazardous to assume the patrilinear institutions of the North Pacific, the East, and the Southwest-California area to have been derived from one common source, and the matrilinear institutions of the same three regions from a second origin. It is as clear as such matters can be that a system of gentile organization developed around three centers— of which at least that of the north Pacific coast is likely to have been independent of the others—and that within each area, with the growth and diversification of the institution, paternal and then maternal reckoning grew up. Such seeming to be the course of development, we need be under no hesitation in linking the totemic exogamy of California with that of the Southwest, in spite of its decisive patrilinear character; and this conclusion holds even if the exogamy should prove to be but slightly or brokenly connected on the map with that of the Southwest.

As to the age of exogamy in the two regions, there can be little doubt that as in most matters probable precedence should be given to the Southwest on the ground of the generally greater richness of its culture. It is only necessary to guard against the hasty inference that, because the connection is almost certain, and the radiation from New Mexico and Arizona into California probable, this movement has been a recent one whose course can still be traced by the present location of this or that particular tribe. As between the patrilineate of the Californians, on the other hand, and the matrilineate of the Pueblos, the former, representing a presumably older type, may well prove to be at least equally ancient in absolute time.

The clans of the Colorado River tribes are fairly numerous, a dozen or more for each group. They have no names as such, but are each characterized by the use of a single name borne by all the women of a clan. These women's names can often not be analyzed, but are understood by the Indians as denotive of an animal or object which is clearly the totem of the clan. This system is common without material modification to all the Yumans of the river, but the totemic references vary considerably, and the women's names even more. The latter must have fluctuated with considerable readiness, since only a small proportion of the total number known are common even to two tribes. The clans enter into myth, but are without ritual function. Details will be found in the first of the chapters on the Mohave.

With the Diegueño and Luiseño the system loses many of its characteristics. Totemism, direct or indirect, is wholly lacking. The groups are numerous and small. Their names when translatable are mostly those of localities, or have reference to a locality. The native theory is clearly that each clan is a local kin group. How far this was actually the case is difficult to determine positively.

With the Cupeño, Cahuilla, and Serrano, the institution is reinvigorated. The local groups persist as among the Luiseño and Diegueño and bear similar names. They are classed, however, in two great totemic moieties, named after the coyote and wild cat. With the Serrano, at least, the moieties do not determine marriage, groups of the same moiety sometimes intermarrying more or less regularly.

From here on northward follows the gap in our knowledge. It is, however, certain that the Shoshonean Kawaiisu and Tübatulabal, and the southern Yokuts such as the Yaudanchi and Yauelmani, were at least substantially free from the influence of any exogamous system.

When this negative or doubtful zone has been passed through, we find ourselves well in the San Joaquin Valley. Here, among the central Yokuts, according to some slender indications among the Salinans, probably among the northern Yokuts, and among all the Sierra Miwok, clans have wholly disappeared. The exogamous moiety, however, remains, and its totemic aspects are rather more developed than in the south. The Miwok carry the totemic scheme farthest, dividing the universe as it were into totemic halves, so that all its natural contents are potential totems of one or the other moiety. Among the other groups of this region the totemism is generally restricted to a limited number of birds or animals. Moieties are variously designated as land and water, downstream and upstream, blue jay and coyote, bullfrog and coyote, or bear and deer. The totem is spoken of as the "dog," that is, domestic animal or pet, of each individual. Among the Miwok the personal name refers to an animal or object of the individual's moiety, but the totem itself is hardly ever expressed in the name, the reference being by some implication which can hardly be intelligible to those who do not know the individual and his moiety.

The western Mono, at least in the northern part of their range, have come under the influence of the Miwok-Yokuts system, but this has assumed a somewhat aberrant shape among them. They subdivide each moiety into two groups which might be called clans except for the fact that they are not exogamous. The names of these groups have not yielded to certain translation. The Mono themselves seem to identify them with localities, which may be a correct representation of the facts, but is scarcely yet established.

Matrilinear descent has once been reported for a single Yokuts tribe, the Gashowu, but is so directly at variance with all that is known of the institutions of the region as to be almost certainly an error of observation. On the other hand, there are more positive indications of a reckoning in the female line among some of the Pomo and Wappo; and these are the more credible because the Pomo lie outside of the exogamic and totemic area of California. The facts pointing to Pomo matrilineate are, however, slight; and it is clear that the institution was at most a sort of suggestion, an undeveloped beginning or last vestige, and not a practice of much consequence.

Totemic taboos were little developed in California. Among most groups the totem seems to have been killed and eaten without further thought. Belief in descent from the totem is also weak or absent, except for some introduction of the moiety totems into the cosmogony of the Shoshoneans of the south.

The exogamic groups of California have rather fewer religious functions than is customary in North America. The Colorado River clans seem to have no connection with ritual. The clans of the Shoshoneans were perhaps, in some tribes, the bodies that conducted ceremonies, the instruments for ritual execution; although the rites were in no sense peculiar, but substantially identical for each clan. It appears also that these ritually functioning groups or "parties" sometimes included several "clans" and admitted individuals who had broken away from their hereditary bodies. It is thus likely that these religious bodies really crystallized around chiefs rather than on a clan basis. Indeed, the word for such a religiously functioning group is merely the word for chief. In the San Joaquin Valley the moieties assume ceremonial obligations, usually reciprocal, and evidently in the main in connection with the mourning anniversary; but these arrangements begin to fade out toward the north, among the Miwok.

MARRIAGE.

Marriage is by purchase almost everywhere in California, the groups east of the Sierra and those on the Colorado River providing the only exceptions. Among the latter there is scarcely a formality observed. A man and woman go to live together and the marriage is recognized as long as the union endures. While some form of bride purchase is in vogue over the remainder of the State, its import is very different according to locality. The northwestern tribes make it a definite, commercial, negotiated transaction, the absence of which prior to living together constitutes a serious injury to the family of the girl, whereas a liberal payment enhances the status of both bride and groom. In the southern half of the State, and among the mountaineers of the north, payment has little more significance than an observance. It might be described as an affair of manners rather than morals. Formal negotiations are often omitted, and in some instances the young man shows his intentions and is accepted merely on the strength of some presents of game or the rendering of an ill-defined period of service before or after the union. Even within comparatively restricted regions there is considerable difference in this respect between wealthy valley dwellers and poor highlanders: the northern Maidu furnish an interesting case in point.

So far as known the levirate or marriage of the widow by her dead husband's brother was the custom of all California tribes except those of the Colorado River. The same may be said of the widower's marriage to his dead wife's sister, or in cases of polygamy to two sisters or to a mother and daughter. These customs must therefore be looked upon as basic and ancient institutions. The uniformity of their prevalence is in contrast to the many intergrading forms assumed by the marriage act, and in contrast also to the differences as regards exogamy, render it probable that if an attempt be made to bring the levirate and marriage with the wife's sister into relation with these other institutions, the former must be regarded as antecedent—as established practices to which marriage, exogamy, and descent conformed.

VARIOUS SOCIAL HABITS.

A rigid custom prescribes that the widow crop or singe off her hair and cover the stubble as well as her face with pitch, throughout a great part of central California. This defacement is left on until the next mourning anniversary or for a year or sometimes longer. The groups that are known to follow this practice are the Achomawi, Shasta, Maidu, Wintun, Kato, Pomo, and Miwok: also the Chukchansi, that is, the northern hill Yokuts. Among the southern

Yokuts the widow merely does not wash her face during the period in which she abstains from eating meat. Beyond the Yokuts, there is no reference to the custom; nor is it known from any northwestern people.

A mourning necklace is northern. The northwestern tribes braid a necklace which is worn for a year or longer time after the death of a near relative or spouse. The Achomawi and northwestern Maidu, perhaps other groups also, have their widows put on a necklace of lumps of pitch.

A belt made of the hair cut from her head was worn by the widow among the Shastan tribes, that is the Shasta, Achomawi, and Atsugewi. With the Yokuts and in southern California belts and hair ties and other ornaments of human hair reappear, but do not have so definite a reference to mourning.

The couvade was observed by nearly all Californians, but not in its "classic" form of the father alone observing restrictions and pretending to lie in. The usual custom was for both parents to be affected equally and for the same period. They observed food restraints and worked and traveled as little as possible in order to benefit their child; they did not ward illness from the infant by shamming it themselves. The custom might well be described as a semicouvade. It has been reported among the Achomawi, Maidu, Yuki, Pomo, Yokuts, Juaneño, and Diegueño. Among the Yurok, Hupa, Shasta, and with them presumably the Karok and other northwestern tribes, there are restrictions for both parents, but those for the father are much shorter.

Fear toward twins is known to be felt by the Yurok, Achomawi, and northwestern Maidu of the hills. It is likely to have prevailed more widely, but these instances suggest a most acute development of the sentiment in northern California.

The child's umbilical cord was saved, carefully disposed of, or specially treated. The Diegueño, Luiseño, Juaneño, and Chukchansi Yokuts buried it. The Tachi Yokuts tied it on the child's abdomen. The Hupa and Yurok kept it for a year or two, then deposited it in a split tree.

KINSHIP TABOOS.

The taboo which forbids parents-in-law and children-in-law to look each other in the face or speak or communicate was a central Californian custom. It is recorded for the Kato, Pomo, Maidu, Miwok, Yokuts, and western Mono; with whom at least the southerly Wintun must probably be included. The Yuki, the eastern Mono, the Tübatulabal, and the Kawaiisu seem not to have adhered to the practice, whose distribution is therefore recognizable as holding over a continuous and rather regular area. There is no mention of the habit in regard to any northwestern or southern tribe. Actually, the mother-in-law is alone specified in some instances, but these may be cases of loose or incomplete statements. Accuracy also necessitates the statement that among the Kato and Pomo the custom had rather a feeble hold, and that these people did not hesitate to address a parent-in-law as long as they spoke in the plural or third person— a device which the Miwok and western Mono also made use of as an allowable circumvention of the taboo when there was the requisite occasion.

It may be added that among the Yana and the western Mono, two far-separated and unrelated peoples, brother and sister also used plural address. For the Yana it is stated that a certain degree of avoidance was also observed; but this was not very acute. This custom can be looked for with some likelihood among the intervening nations, but to predict it would be rash. There are many purely local developments in Californian culture: witness the sex diversity of speech among the Yana.

As in other parts of America, no reason for the custom can be obtained from the natives. It is a way they have, they answer; or they would be ashamed to do otherwise. That they feel positive humiliation and repugnance at speaking to a mother-in-law is certain; but this sentiment can no more be the cause of the origin of the custom than a sense of shame can itself have produced the manifold varieties of dress current among mankind. It can hardly be doubted that a sense of delicacy with reference to sexual relations lies at the root of the habit. But to imagine that a native or unhistorically minded civilized person might really be able to explain the source of any of his institutions or manners is to be unreasonable.

DISPOSAL OF THE DEAD.

The manner of disposing of the dead fluctuated greatly according to region in California. The areas in which cremation was practiced seem to aggregate somewhat larger than those in which burial was the custom, but the balance is nearly even, and the distribution quite irregular. Roughly, five areas can be distinguished. (Fig. 70.)

Southern California burned.[1]

Interment was the rule over a tract which seems to extend from the Great Basin across the southern Sierras to the Chumash and Santa Barbara Islands. This takes in the Chemehuevi, the eastern Mono, the Tübatulabal, the southern Yokuts, the Chumash, and perhaps a few of the adjacent minor Shoshonean groups.

A second region of cremation follows. This consists of the entire central Sierra Nevada, the San Joaquin Valley except at its

---

[1] The Vanyume should be added to the southern cremation area delineated in Figure 70.

head, the lower Sacramento Valley, and the coast region for about
the same distance. Roughly, the range is from the Salinans and
central Yokuts to the Pomo and southern Maidu.

The second area of burial takes in all of the tribes under the influence of the northwestern culture, and in addition to them the

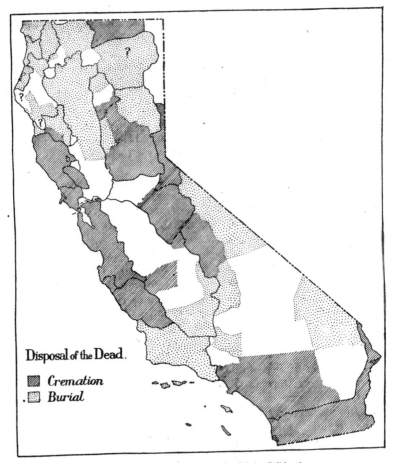

FIG. 70.—Cremation and earth burial in California.

Yuki, at least the majority of the Wintun, and most of the northern
Maidu.

The Modoc in the northeastern corner of the State again cremate.
For the adjoining Achomawi the evidence conflicts. It is possible
that this northern region was connected with the central area of
cremation through the Yahi and northwestern Maidu of the foothills.

It seems impossible to establish any correlation between custom and environment in this matter. Treeless and timbered regions both cremated and in other cases interred.

It does appear that the southern and central culture areas can be described as regions of prevailing cremation, the northwestern culture as one of burial. The practice of each of the two interring regions has to some extent penetrated the adjacent parts of the central area. Interment, however, extends farther beyond the outer limits of the northwestern culture than almost all other institutions or elements which are definitely characteristic of the northwest—basketry and dentalia for instance. Furthermore, there is the curious tongue of burying peoples from the Santa Barbara Islands to the eastern Mono. This group can scarcely correspond to any primary cultural stratum.

WAR.

Warfare throughout California was carried on only for revenge, never for plunder or from a desire for distinction. The Mohave and Yuma must, indeed, be excepted from this statement, but their attitude is entirely unique. Perhaps the cause that most commonly originated feuds was the belief that a death had been caused by witchcraft. No doubt theft and disputes of various sorts also contributed. Once ill feeling was established, it was likely to continue for long periods.

Torture has been reported as having been practiced by several tribes, such as the Maidu and the Gabrielino. It appears to have been considered merely a preliminary to the execution of captives, which was the victors' main purpose. As a rule, men who could be seized in warfare were killed and decapitated on the spot. Women and children were also slaughtered more frequently than enslaved. The Colorado River tribes made a point of capturing young women, but did not abuse them. There is no record of any attempt to hold men as prisoners.

Scalps were taken in the greater part of California, brought home in triumph, and celebrated over, usually by a dance around a pole. Women as well as men generally participated. Some tribes made the dance indoors, others outside. There was no great formality about this scalp dance of victory. It may often have been celebrated with great abandon, but its ritual was loose and simple. The Mohave and Yuma alone show some organization of the ceremony, coupled with a considerable manifestation of dread of the scalps themselves —a southwestern trait.

It is rather difficult to decide how far the scalp taken was literally such and how far it was the entire head. A fallen foe that could be operated upon in safety and leisure was almost always decapitated, and his head brought home. Sometimes it is said that this head was danced with. In other localities it was skinned at the first opportunity and the scalp alone used in the dance. The scalp, however, was always a larger object than we are accustomed to think of with the habits of eastern tribes in mind. The skin taken usually extended to the eyes and nose, and included the ears. There is no evidence of an endeavor to preserve scalps as permanent trophies to the credit of individuals; nor of a feeling that anything was lost by a failure to secure scalps, other than that an occasion for a pleasant celebration might be missed thereby.

It is significant that it remains doubtful whether the Yokuts, the Valley Maidu, and the Pomo took scalps or performed a scalp dance. If they did so, it was clearly with less zest than most of their neighbors. All of the tribes in question are peoples of lowland habitat, considerable wealth, and comparative specialization of culture.

In the northwestern area no scalps were taken, and the victory dance was replaced by one of incitement before battle. In this dance the fully armed warriors stood abreast, with one or more of their number moving before them. With the Yurok and Hupa, and perhaps some of their immediate neighbors also, this dance was also or particularly made when two hostile parties gathered for settlement of a feud; and, as might be expected, as often as not resulted in a new fight instead of the desired peace. The northwestern habit of not scalping extended at least as far south as the Sinkyone and as far east as the Shasta. The Wintun on the Trinity River are also said to have taken no scalps and may therefore be supposed to have practiced the associated form of incitement dance. Finally, there is an echo of the Yurok custom from as far away as the Maidu of the northern Sacramento Valley, who it is said had a war dance performed by armed negotiators.

The battle weapon of California was the bow. Spears have been mentioned as in use by a number of tribes, but all indications are that they were employed only sporadically in hand-to-hand fighting and not for hurling from the ranks. It is probable that they were serviceable in an ambush or early morning rush upon the unsuspecting sleepers in a settlement. In a set fight the spear could not be used against a row of bowmen by unarmored and unorganized warriors.

Southern California used the Pueblo type of war club, a rather short, stout stick expanded into a longitudinal mallet head. This seems to have been meant for thrusting into an opponent's face rather than for downright clubbing. The Mohave, at any rate, knew a second form of club, a somewhat longer, straight, and heavy stick, which served the specific purpose of breaking skulls. In central California mentions of clubs are exceedingly scarce. If they were used they were probably nothing but suitable sticks. When it came to hand-to-hand fighting the central Californian was likely to have recourse to the nearest stone. Rocks were also favored by the northwestern tribes, but in addition there are some examples of a shaped war club of stone in this region. This club was a little over a foot long and rudely edged, somewhat in the shape of a narrow and thick paddle blade. This type has affiliations with the more elaborate stone and bone clubs used farther north on the Pacific coast.

Slings seem to have been known to practically all the California tribes as toys, and in some parts were used effectively for hunting water fowl. The only definite reports of the use of slings in warfare are from the Wintun of Trinity River and the western Mono, both mountaineers.

The shield, which is so important to the Plains Indian and to the southwestern warrior, was known in California only to the Mohave, Yuma, and perhaps Diegueño—that is to say, the local representatives of the Yuman family. It was a round piece of unornamented hide. There is no reference to symbolism, and it appears to have been carried only occasionally. Not a single original specimen has been preserved. Much as tribes like the Mohave speak of war, they rarely mention the shield, and its occurrence among them and their kinsmen is of interest chiefly as an evidence that the distribution of this object reached the Pacific coast at one point at least.

Armor enters the State at the other end as an extension from another extra-Californian culture. It is either of elk hide or of rods twined with string in waistcoat shape. (Pl. 18.) The rod type is reported from the northwestern tribes, the Achomawi, and the northern mountain Maidu. Elkskin armor has been found among the same groups, as well as among the Modoc, Shasta, northern valley Maidu, and Wailaki. These closely coincident distributions indicate that the two armor types are associated, not alternative; and that, confined to the northernmost portion of the State, they are to be understood as the marginal outpost of a custom that centers in the culture of the North Pacific coast.

The greater part of central California appears to have been armorless and shieldless.

GAMING.

The endless games of the North American Indians have been reduced by Mr. Stewart Culin to a few fundamental types:

> Games of dexterity:
>> With a dart—
>>> Outdoor—Hoop and pole.
>>> Hand—Ring and pin.
>> With a ball—Shinny, lacrosse, etc.
> Games of chance:
>> Pure chance—Dice.
>> Guessing—Hand or stick.

Among amateurs, the guessing games come out entirely according
to luck; among skillful players they depend on concealment and
reading of facial and bodily expression, and are therefore in reality
games of mental ability, or rather of will and character.

As a rule, all of these games were known to all the California
Indians, and, with some exceptions, no game existed in more than
one form among the same group.

The hoop-and-pole game was perhaps the chief one which was entirely unknown in some districts. The Yurok and Hupa did not possess it, and it seems to have been lacking also through the remainder of
the northwestern part of the State. It is an interesting circumstance,
illustrating in one of several concrete ways the fact that at the northwestern corner of California is ethnographically the last southern
frontier of the North Pacific coast "culture area," that this hoop-
and-pole game, favorite over a large part of the continent, also holds
but a small part in the amusements of most of the coast tribes from
Oregon to Alaska.

The dignity of this game is upheld at the opposite end of the State,
where the Mohave deem it the means of gambling best befitting a
man. They play it with a small string-wound hoop, and long poles
that are slid so as to fall, if possible, on or under the rolling hoop
when this finally comes to rest. The Luiseño and Diegueño, the
other tribes of the south, the Salinan and Costanoan groups, the
Maidu, the Pomo, the Shasta, and the Modoc, played substantially
the same game. Among the Yokuts, Mono, and Miwok of the Sierra
Nevada, youths and boys played a simpler and typically Californian
variety. A small block was thrown or slid, and then poles darted
after it. This must be a slovenly degeneration of an original hoop
game.

The ring-and-pin or hand variety of the same game, in which
several rings or loops are strung to the butt end of a pin on which
they are to be caught, is widespread in California, but varies characteristically according to habits of life and, ultimately, environment.

The fishing tribes of the northwest, as far south as the middle course of Eel River, including the Tolowa, Yurok, Hupa, Chimariko, Shasta, and Sinkyone (Fig. 14), employed salmon vertebræ as "rings." On the headwaters of Eel River, where the streams run smaller and hunting must largely replace fishing, the Wailaki used deer bones. In the South, the Luiseño favored acorn cups; while the agricultural Mohave made their rings of pumpkin rind. The Klamath and Modoc employed a single-looped ball, made of the same tule rush that is the material of most of their industries. Maidu and Yokuts did without this game, so far as known.

Of the many possible varieties of ball games, each group usually specialized on one. The Pomo played a kind of lacrosse, with a rude small net. Still simpler rackets are found among the southern Maidu. With the Miwok and Yokuts the net has degenerated into a mere loop at the end of a stick, serving to pick up or pocket the ball rather than bat it. Among both these groups this rudimentary form of the racket is perhaps due to the shinny stick being the standard form of ball-propelling implement. The Miwok women, but not the men, also batted a soft hair-stuffed ball with baskets resembling the common utilitarian seed beater.

The Mohave knew nothing of lacrosse, but clung to simple shinny, played with a small block or ball and plain curved sticks. With these they played as our boys play shinny or hockey on the ice.

It would have been difficult to find many suitable fields for such an active free-running game in the rocky canyons of the northwestern tribes; even the bars and river benches are narrow, rough, and uneven. Here, accordingly, the game was played with a double ball of two string-tied blocks of wood, impossible to propel far by striking, and requiring to be picked up with the end of the stick and thrown. Maneuvering thus took the place of speed; the players grappled like wrestlers, and a number of men could participate within a small area. (Pl. 79.)

Elsewhere than in the northwest the double-ball game is essentially or wholly one for women, as over most of the continent. This is the case among the Shasta, Modoc, Achomawi, Washo, Maidu, and Miwok. Among the last three groups the "ball" has degenerated into merely the connecting string, though this is heavy and sometimes knotted at the ends.

Through most of the south, and along the coast as far north at least as Monterey, sticks or bats were often dispenesd with, and the game became essentially a football race. The contestants covered a long distance, each hurling, with his feet only, his little wooden ball. Speed and endurance were counted as even more valuable factors toward victory than skill in manipulation. Diegueño, Luiseño, Costanoan, and presumably the intervening groups competed in this way, which was familiar also to the Indians of Arizona. The Chumash, however, knew shinny; and in the interior the ball race had penetrated to the Maidu and Miwok. This latter people followed all the varieties of ball play: rackets for men and for women, shinny, double ball for women, and football race.

Dice· were everywhere preeminently if not entirely a woman's game. A set numbered four, six, or eight, each only two-sided; the count of the various combinations of pieces falling face up or face down varied locally.

The Yurok, Tolowa, Wiyot, and Hupa used four mussel-shell disks; the Pomo, Wailaki, and northern Yokuts, six split sticks; the Mohave, Diegueño, and Luiseño, four painted boards; the southern Yokuts, Chumash, and Chemehuevi, filled walnut shells. (Fig. 54.) Among the Miwok split acorns were employed; and among the Mono, acorn cups. The Modoc used either the Californian sticks or a northern type consisting of four beaver teeth. Some tribes played on a flat basket, others on a stone.

The ball game, whatever its character, was well fitted for competition between towns or districts, and was often heavily backed with stakes; but, except with the Mohave and perhaps the Yokuts, who favored respectively the rolling hoop and the shinny stick, the gambling game above all others, and therefore the man's game par excellence, among the California tribes, was the "hand" or "grass" game, a contest of guessing. Tremendous energy and concentration were thrown into this play, which was passionately followed. Songs and sometimes drumming were regular features, without which the stimulus to play hard would be weakened, and the contestants' luck magically diminished. Actually, the singing and rhythmic swaying aided the hiding player to conceal his knowledge of the location of the "ace" by enabling him better to control his expression.

A public ritual, a dance, even a mourning ceremony, could hardly take place without the accompaniment, at least at the conclusion, of the guessing game. It is hard for us to realize to the full the large degree to which this amusement or occupation entered into the life not so much of a professional class of gamblers as of all the California Indians. Their avarice, and the importance to them of their wealth, hardly allowed them to bet as recklessly, and to strip themselves as completely of all belongings on a run of ill luck, as some of the eastern tribes, with whom liberality rather than possession carried prestige; but they made up in the frequency, the duration, and the tenacity of their play.

Two types of the game occur, and these do not differ fundamentally. In the northwest a bundle of 25 or 50 slender rods is used, one being painted in the center. These sticks are shuffled, in sight of the opponent, with a peculiar rolling twist, divided behind the back, and then shown, the middle portions concealed in the hands. After some deliberation, and frequent false or pretended starts, the opponent guesses for the hand containing the one marked stick, indicating his decision by pointing past the other hand. If he is right, he wins nothing but the privilege of playing; if wrong, one counter goes to the player, who shuffles again. An expert player always knows the place of the marked rod among its many plain fellows, even behind his back, and frequently displays it alone against the pack in his other hand, to tempt his opponent to incline to the latter; or, divining the tendency of his mind, misleads him with a single unmarked rod.

Shasta women, the northern Wintun, and the Modoc play like the northwestern tribes; but through the remainder of the State, from the Shasta men and Achomawi to the Diegueño, the implements are two small bones, or short sticks, one of them marked with a band. These are concealed in the two hands behind the back, under a mat, or often wound in two wisps of grass in view of the opponent, whence the popular American name of the game. Some tribes use only one small bone, guessing for the full hand; mostly they employ four, handled by two men on a side; the southern Indians usually attach string loops to pass over the fingers; but such differences do not seriously alter the course of the play.

The counters are everywhere sticks. Contrary to our custom, the Indians rarely begin with an equal number of markers on the two sides, but with a neutral pile from which winnings are allotted to this or that contestant. Only after this stock is exhausted do they begin to win from each other; and the game continues until one side is without sticks. This may be an affair of minutes. But if fortunes are fluctuating and ability even, one contest may be prolonged for hours. If the losers, without a word, continue to play, they are understood to bet in the ensuing game an amount the equal of that which was staked by both parties in the first game. At least such is the Hupa custom.

Among the Mohave several varieties of the guessing games are played. One of these, shared by them with some of the tribes of the Southwest, is a smaller informal affair pertaining to idle moments. A bit of stick is hidden in one of four little hillocks of sand. Dexterity of manipulation and perception seems the deciding factor instead of control of the features.

The Coast Miwok, some of the Maidu, and the Washo, played the regular "hand" game, but also guessed whether the number of a handful of manipulated sticks was odd or even. Among the Pomo the sticks were counted off by fours after the remainder had been guessed at. This procedure is suggestive of a Chinese form of gambling, but the geographical compactness of the area over which this subtype of guessing game is found indicates its distribution from a native origin.

The "four-stick game" of Mr. Culin is another local variety, which has been found only among the Lutuami, Achomawi, northern Paiute, and Washo—all at least partly Californian—and possibly the Chinook of Oregon. Among most or all of these tribes it does not replace but occurs by the side of the usual guessing game. Two of the sticks are heavy, two short and thin. The guessing is for the order in which they are grouped under a basket or mat.

When one reflects that in reality chance is no greater factor in the standard forms of the guessing game than in the American national card game, the decisive element being the match of character against character, the fascination which the game exercises on the Indian's mind is easy to understand.

The economic basis of life and the estimation of the purpose of wealth among the Indians are so different from our own, that gambling, instead of incurring odium, was not only sanctioned but approved. Nevertheless the underlying human similarity of the emotional processes connected with the practice is revealed in a most interesting way by the common belief in a connection between success at play and in relations with the opposite sex: "Luck in love," the reverse at cards, and vice versa, is our proverbial superstition. But the Indian, regarding, like the ancient Hebrew and ourselves, sexual affairs as normally destructive of supernatural or magical potency, draws in a particular case an opposite inference. Two Yokuts myths relate how the favorite hero of these tales, Limik, the prairie falcon, was uniformly successful in winning all stakes, in the one case at shinny, in the other with the hoop and poles, until the coyote was induced to disguise himself as the victor and thus take advantage of the latter's wife. As soon as this misfortune, although unknown, befell the falcon, his luck turned, until he had lost everything. The modern gambler would perhaps expect the opposite event.

CHAPTER 56.

RELIGION AND KNOWLEDGE.

SHAMANISM.

The shamanistic practices of most California groups are fairly uniform, and similar to those obtaining among the North American Indians generically. The primary function of the California shaman is the curing of disease. The latter is almost always considered due to the presence in the body of some foreign or hostile object, rarely to an abstraction or injury of the soul. The Mohave are the only tribe for whom there is definite record that shamans recovered souls, though the attitude of other southern Californians is such that the belief may well have prevailed among them also. Over most of California the shaman's business is the removal of the disease object, and this in the great majority of cases is carried out by sucking. Singing, dancing, and smoking tobacco, with or without the accompaniment of genuine trance conditions, are the usual diagnostic means. Manipulation of the body, brushing it, and blowing of breath, saliva, or tobacco smoke are sometimes resorted to in the extraction of the disease object.

As contrasted with the general similarity of the practices of the established shaman, there is a considerable diversity of methods employed by the prospective shaman in the acquisition of his supernatural powers. This diversity is connected with a variety of beliefs concerning guardian spirits.

In central California, from the Wailaki and Maidu to the Yokuts, the guardian spirit is of much the same character as with the Indians of the central and eastern United States, and is obtained in much the same way. A supernatural being in animal or other form is seen and conversed with during a trance or dream. Sometimes the spirits come to a man unsought, sometimes there is a conscious attempt to acquire them.

For southern California information on these matters is tantalizingly scant and vague. The few statements recorded from Indians seem mostly made under the pressure of questioning. It remains to

be established that a definite belief in personal guardian spirits
obtained in southern California. This doubt is strengthened by the
fact that the concept of the guardian spirit, and, consequently, the
institution of shamanism in its most commonly accepted form, seem
to have been very weak among the tribes of the southwestern United
States, especially the Pueblos.

Among the Colorado River tribes it is certain that there was no
belief in a guardian spirit of the usual kind. Shamans derived
their power by dreaming of the Creator or some ancient divinity, or,
as they themselves sometimes describe it, from having associated before their birth—in other words, during a previous spiritual existence—with the gods or divine animals that were on earth at the beginning. The culture of the Colorado River tribes is so specialized
that a positive inference from them to the remaining southern Californians would be unsound; but it must be admitted that their status
increases the probability that the latter tribes did not share the central Californian and eastern ideas as to the source of shamanistic
power.

In northern California, and centering as usual among the northwestern tribes, beliefs as to the source of shamanistic power take a
peculiar turn. Among peoples like the Yurok the guardian in the
ordinary sense scarcely occurs. The power of the shaman rests not
on the aid or control of a spirit, but upon his maintenance in
his own body of disease objects which to nonshamans would be
fatal. These "pains" are animate and self-moving, but are always
conceived as minute, physically concrete, and totally lacking human
shape or resemblance. Their acquisition by the shaman is due to a
dream in which a spirit gives them to him or puts them in his body.
This spirit seems most frequently to be an ancestor who has had
shamanistic power. The dream, however, does not constitute the
shaman as such, since the introduced "pain" causes illness in him as
in other persons. His condition is diagnosed by accepted shamans,
and a long and rigorous course of training follows, whose object is
the inuring of the novice to the presence of the "pains" in his body
and the acquisition of control over them. Fasting and analogous
means are employed for this purpose, but the instruction of older
shamans seems to be regarded as an essential feature, culminating in
what is usually known as the "doctors' dance." This dance is therefore substantially a professional initiation ceremony. There is no
doubt that it provided the opportunity for the establishment of shamans' societies as organized bodies, but this step seems never to have
been taken in California.

From the Yurok and Hupa this peculiar type of shamanism
spreads out gradually, losing more and more of its elements, to at

least as far as the Maidu. Already among the Shasta the shaman
controls spirits as well as "pains," but the name for the two is
identical. With the Achomawi and Maidu the "pain" and the spirit
are differently designated. Here the doctor's concern in practice
still is more largely with the "pains," but his control of them rests
definitely upon his relation to his spirits and their continued assist-
ance. The doctor dance persists among all these tribes. It is practiced
also by the northerly Wintun and Yuki. The Yuki shamans possess
and acquire spirits very much like the central Californians, and the
spirits are sometimes animals. The "pain" is still of some importance among them, however, and they and the Wintun agree in
calling it "arrowhead." A line running across the State south of
the Yuki, and probably through Wintun and Maidu territory about
its middle, marks the farthest extension of remnants of the northwestern type of shaman.

Among the Pomo there is no mention of the doctor dance, while
indications of a considerable use of amulets or fetishes suggest that
entirely different sets of concepts obtain.[1] The Miwok and Yokuts
also knew of nothing like a " doctor dance," and with them it would
seem that the Maidu of the south may have to be included.

It may be added that central and southern California are a unit in
regarding shamanistic power as indifferently beneficent or malevolent. Whether a given shaman causes death or prevents it is merely
a matter of his inclination. His power is equal in both directions.
Much disease, if not the greater part, is caused by hostile or spiteful
shamans. Witchcraft and the power of the doctor are therefore in-
dissolubly bound up together. The unsuccessful shaman, particularly if repeatedly so, was thought to be giving prima facie evidence
of evil intent, and earnest attempts to kill him almost invariably
followed.

In the northwest this intertwining of the two aspects of supernatural power was slighter. Shamans were much less frequently
killed, and then rather for refusal to give treatment or unwilling-
ness to return pay tendered for treatment, than for outright witchcraft. A person who wished to destroy another had recourse to
magical practice. This northwestern limitation of shamanism is
perhaps connected with the fact that among the tribes where it was
most marked the shaman was almost invariably a woman. In these
matters, too, tribes as far as the Maidu shared in some measure in
the beliefs which attained their most clear-cut form among the Yurok
and Hupa.

---

[1] See footnote, p. 259.

The use of supernatural spirit power was on the whole perhaps more largely restricted to the treatment or production of disease in California than in most other parts of aboriginal North America. There is comparatively little reference to men seeking association with spirits for success in warfare, hunting, or love, although it is natural that ideas of this kind crop out now and then. There are, however, three specialties which in the greater part of the State lead to the recognition of as many particular kinds of shamans or "doctors," as they are usually known in local usage. These are rain or weather doctors, rattlesnake doctors, and bear doctors.

The rain doctor seems generally to have exercised his control over the weather in addition to possessing the abilities of an ordinary shaman. Very largely he used his particular faculty like the prophet Samuel, to make impression by demonstrations. All through the southern half of the State there were men who were famous as rain doctors, and the greatest development of the idea appears to have been in the region where central and southern California meet. Control of the weather by shamans was, however, believed in to the northern limit of the State, although it was considerably less made of there. The groups within the intensive northwestern culture are again in negative exception.

The rattlesnake doctor is also not northwestern, although tribes as close to the focus of this culture as the Shasta knew the institution. His business, of course, was to cure snake bites; in some cases also to prevent them. Among the Yokuts a fairly elaborate ceremony in which rattlesnakes were juggled with was an outgrowth of these beliefs. Less important or conspicuous demonstrations of the same sort seem also to have been made among a number of other tribes, since we know that the northern Maidu of the valley had some kind of a public rattlesnake ceremony conducted by their shamans. There appears to have been some inclination to regard the sun as the spirit to which rattlesnake doctors particularly looked.

The bear doctor was recognized over the entire State from the Shasta to the Diegueño. The Colorado River tribes, those of the extreme northwest, and possibly those of the farthest northeastern corner of the State, are the only ones among whom this impressive institution was lacking. The bear shaman had the power to turn himself into a grizzly bear. In this form he destroyed enemies.

The most general belief, particularly in the San Joaquin Valley and southern California, was that he became actually transmuted. In the region of the Wintun, Pomo, and Yuki, however, it seems to have been believed that the bear doctor, although he possessed undoubted supernatural power, operated by means of a bear skin and other paraphernalia in which he encased himself.[2] Generally bear shamans were thought invulnerable, or at least to possess the power of returning to life. They inspired an extraordinary fear and yet seem rather to have been encouraged. It is not unlikely that they were often looked upon as benefactors to the group to which they belonged and as exercising their destructive faculties chiefly against its foes. In some tribes they gave exhibitions of their power; in others, as among the Pomo, the use of their faculties was carefully guarded from all observation. Naturally enough, their power was generally considered to be derived from bears, particularly the grizzly. It is the ferocity and tenacity of life of this species that clearly impressed the imagination of the Indians, and a more accurately descriptive name of this caste would be " grizzly bear shamans."

Throughout northern California a distinction is made between the shaman who sings, dances, and smokes in order to diagnose, in other words, is a clairvoyant, and a second class endowed with the executive power of sucking out disease objects, that is, curing sickness. This grouping of shamans has been reported from the Hupa, Wiyot, Nongatl, Yuki, Pomo, and Maidu. It has not been mentioned among more southerly peoples. It thus coincides in its distribution with the concept of the " pain " as a more or less animate and self-impelled thing, and the two ideas can scarcely be interpreted as other than connected. The sucking shaman seems to be rated higher than the one that only sings; as is only natural, since his power in some measure presupposes and includes that of his rival. It is not unlikely, however, that certain singing shamans were believed to possess an unusual diagnostic power against illness, and no doubt all such matters as finding lost objects and foretelling the future were their particular province.

CULT RELIGIONS.

The cults or definitely elaborated religions of California have been described in detail in the accounts given of the peoples among whom they are perhaps most intensively practiced, and who may be assumed to have had somewhat the largest share in their development: the Yurok, Wintun (compare especially Tables 1–4), Gabrielino and Luiseño (see also Table 7), and Mohave (Table 8). The respective ranges of the four systems are plotted on Plate 74. Certain comparative aspects of these cult types will be considered here.

It appears from Plate 74 that the specific northwestern cultus is separated from that of north central California by a belt of tribes that participate in neither.

---

[2] There may be confusion as regards this area, either in the customs themselves or in the information about them, between true bear shamans and bear impersonators in Kuksu rituals.

The religions of north central and southern California, or Kuksu and "toloache," on the other hand, seem to have overlapped in the region of the northern Yokuts and Salinans. It is unlikely that the two cults existed side by side with undiminished vigor among the same people; one was probably much abbreviated and reduced to subsidiary rank, while the other maintained itself in flourishing or substantially full status. Unfortunately the tribes that seem to have shared the two religions are the very ones whose institutions have long since melted away, so that data are exceedingly elusive. It is not improbable that fuller knowledge would show that the two religions reacted toward each other like the basketry complexes that have been discussed: namely, that they were preserved integrally, and normally to the exclusion of each other.

This seems on the whole to be what has happened in southern California, where the Jimson-weed religion emanating from the Gabrielino and the system of song-myth cycles issuing from the Colorado River tribes existed side by side to only a limited extent among the Diegueño and perhaps some of the Cahuilla and Serrano. Even in these cases of partial mixture it is possible that the condition is not ancient. A recent wave of propaganda for the Jimson-weed cult radiated southward and perhaps eastward from the Gabrielino during mission times—may in fact have succeeded in then gaining for the first time a foothold—particularly because civilization had sapped the strength of the older cults in regions where these had previously been of sufficient vitality to keep out this "toloache" religion.

In any event there are certain ceremonies of wide distribution in California which must be considered as belonging to a more generalized and presumably older stratum of native civilization than any of the four great cults referred to. Most prominent among these simpler rituals is the adolescence ceremony for girls. The dance of war or victory occupies second place. To these must be added in northwestern and north central California the shamans' dance for instruction of the novice, and in north and south central California various exhibitions by classes or bodies of shamans. Generally speaking, all these rites are dwarfed among each people in proportion as the nation adheres to one of the four organized cults; but they rarely disappear wholly. They are usually somewhat colored by ritualistic ideas developed in the greater cults. Thus the adolescence rites of the Hupa, the Maidu, and the Luiseño are by no means uniform. And yet, with the partial exception of the latter, they have not been profoundly shaped by the cults with which they are in contact, and can certainly not be described as having been incorporated in these cults. In short, these old or presumably ancient rites, which are all animated by essentially individual motives as opposed to communal or world purposes, evince a surprising vitality which has enabled them to retain certain salient traits with but little modification during periods when it may be supposed that the more highly florescent religions grew or were replaced by others.

The mourning anniversary belongs to neither class and is best considered separately.

The Kuksu and toloache systems shared the idea of initiation into a society. This organization was always communal. The organization of the society was also of very simple character, particularly in the south. In the Kuksu society two grades of initiates were recognized, besides the old men of special knowledge who acted as directors.[3]

The Kuksu cult impersonates spirits and has developed a fair wealth of distinctive paraphernalia and disguises for the several mythic characters. This is a feature which probably developed on the spot. It can not well have reached central California from either the Southwestern or the North Pacific coast areas, since the intervening nations for long distances do not organize themselves into societies; not to mention that the quite diverse northwestern and toloache religions are present as evidences of growths that would have served to block the transmission of such influences.

The dances and costumes of the toloache cult are extremely simple. Ritual actions refer unceasingly to mythology, and the ground painting is only one of several manifestations of an actively symbolizing impulse, but there are no disguises or impersonations. The vision-producing drug gives the cult an inward-looking and mystic character and discourages meaningless formalism.

The cults of the Colorado River tribes are bare of any inclination toward the formation of associations or bodies of members. They rest on dreams, or on imitations of other practitioners which are fused with inward experiences and construed as dreams. These dreams invariably have a mythological cast. Ritually the cults consist essentially of long series of songs, but most singers know a corresponding narrative. Dancing is minimal, and essentially an adjunct for pleasure. Concretely expressed symbolism is scarcely known; disguises, ground paintings, altars, religious edifices, drums, and costumes are all dispensed with.

The northwestern cults adhere minutely to certain traditional forms, but these forms per se have no meaning. There is no trace of any cult organizations. The esoteric basis of every ceremony is the recitation of a formula, which is a myth in dialogue. The formulas are jealously guarded as private property. Major rites

---

[3] It is doubtful whether the Miwok, Yokuts, Costanoans, and Salinans—in other words, the southern Kuksu dancing tribes—possessed a society.

always serve a generic communal or even world-renewing purpose and may well be described as new year rites. Dance costumes and equipments are splendid but wholly unsymbolic. All performances are very rigorously attached to precise localities and spots.

It is clear that as these four cults are followed from northwestern California southeastward to the lower Colorado, there is a successive weakening of the dance and all other external forms, of physical apparatus, of association with particular place or structure; and an increase of personal psychic participation, of symbolism and mysticism, of speculation or at least emotion about human life and death, and of intrinsic interweaving of ritualistic expression with myth. The development of these respective qualities has nothing to do with the development of principles of organization, initiation, and impersonation or enactment, since the latter principles are adhered to in the middle of our area and unknown at the extremities.

As organizations, the Kuksu and toloache cult associations are decidedly weak. They aim usually to include all adult males, and even where some attempt at discrimination is made, as perhaps among the Wintun, the proportion of those left out of membership seems to be small. There is no internal hierarchy; recognized priests can scarcely be spoken of with propriety; and there never is an elaboration of structure through the coexistence of parallel and equivalent societies within the community. On all these sides, the Californian religious bodies are much less developed than those of the Southwest and the Plains.

To compensate for the simplicity of organization in the Kuksu and toloache religions, initiation looms up largely, according to some reports almost as if it were the chief function of the bodies. Novices were often given a formal and prolonged education. Witness the *woknam*, the "lie-dance" or "school" of the Yuki, the orations of the Maidu and Patwin, the long moral lectures to Luiseño boys and girls. That these pedagogical inclinations are an inherent part of the idea of the religious society is shown by the fact that the Yurok and Mohave, who lack societies, do not manifest these inclinations, at least not in any formal way. In the Southwest, education seems less important than in California, relatively to the scheme of the whole religious institution; and for the Plains the difference is still greater. It appears, therefore, that these two aspects, initiation and organization, stand in inverse ratio of importance in North American cult societies.

Police and military functions of religious societies are very strongly marked among the Plains tribes; are definitely exercised by the bow or warrior societies of the Southwest, and perhaps stand out larger in native consciousness than in our own, since ethnologists have usually approached the religious bodies of this area from the side of cult rather than social influence; but such functions are exceedingly vague and feeble in California. There may have been some regulation of profane affairs by the body of initiates; but the chiefs and other civil functionaries are the ones almost always mentioned in such matters in California. There certainly was no connection of the cult societies with warfare. The first traces of an association of cult and war appear on the Colorado River, where societies do not exist. The negativeness of the California religious bodies in this regard is to be construed as an expression of their lack of development of the organization factor.

In spite of their performance of communal and often public rituals, American religious societies are never wholly divorced from shamanism, that is, the exercise of individual religious power; and one of their permanent foundations or roots must be sought in shamanism. On the Plains there is a complete transition from societies based on voluntary affiliation. purchase, age, war record, or other nonreligious factors, to such as are clearly nothing but more or less fluctuating groups of individuals endowed with similar shamanistic powers. Farther east the Midewiwin is little more than an attempt at formal organization of shamanism. In the Southwest, among the Pueblos, the fraternal as opposed to the communal religious bodies can be looked upon, not indeed as shamans' associations, but as societies one of whose avowed purposes—perhaps the primary one—is curative, and which have largely replaced the shaman acting as an individual. Among the Navaho the greatest ceremonies seem to be curative. In California we have the similarity of name between the Luiseño shaman and initiates, *pul–a* and *pu–pl–em*, already commented on; and the *lit* or doctoring of the Yuki societies as practically their only function besides that of perpetuating themselves by initiation. In spite of their loose structure and comparative poverty of ritual, it can not, however, be maintained that the societies of California are more inclined to be shamanistic than those of the other two regions.

Perhaps the most distinctive character of the two Californian cult societies is their freedom from any tendency to break up into, or to be accompanied by, smaller and equivalent but diverse societies as in the Plains. Southwest, and North Pacific coast regions.

Dance costumes and ornaments are illustrated in Plates 3, 42, 58, 59. 61. 77. 80. and Figures 20, 21, 44.

THE MOURNING ANNIVERSARY.

The anniversary or annual ceremony in memory of the dead bulks so large in the life of many California tribes as to produce a first impression of being one of the most typical phases of Californian culture. As a matter of fact, the institution was in force over only about half of the State: southern California and the Sierra Nevada region. There can be little doubt that its origin is southern. The distribution itself so suggests. The greatest development of mourning practices is found among the Gabrielino and Luiseño. It is not that their anniversary is much more elaborate than that of other groups—the use of images representing the dead is common to the great majority of tribes—but it is that these southerners have a greater number of mourning rites. Thus the Luiseño first wash the clothes of the dead, then burn them, and finally make the image ceremony. Of this they know two distinct forms, and in addition there are special mourning rites for religious initiates, and the eagle dance, which is also a funerary ceremony. Another circumstance that points to southern origin is the fact that the anniversary is held by nearly all tribes in the circular brush enclosure, which is not used by the Miwok and Maidu for other purposes, whereas in southern California it is the only and universal religious structure. Finally, there are no known connections between the anniversary and the Kuksu cult of the Miwok and Maidu, whereas the Jimson-weed religion of southern California presents a number of contacts with the mourning ceremony.

It is a fair inference that the anniversary received its principal development among the same people that chiefly shaped the Jimson-weed cult, namely, the Gabrielino or some of their immediate neighbors. It is even possible that the two sets of rites flowed northward in conjunction, and that the anniversary outreached its mate because the absence of the Jimson-weed plant north of the Yokuts checked the invasion of the rites based upon it.

The Mohave and Yuma follow an aberrant form of mourning which is characteristic of their general cultural position with reference to the remainder of southern California. Their ceremony is held in honor of distinguished individual warriors, not for the memory of all the dead of the year. The mourners and singers sit under a shade, in front of which young men engage in mimic battle and war exploits. There are no images and no brush enclosures. The shade is burned at the conclusion, but there is no considerable destruction of property such as is so important an element of the rite elsewhere in California.

An undoubted influence of the anniversary is to be recognized in a practice shared by a number of tribes just outside its sphere of distribution: the southern Wintun, Pomo, Yuki, Lassik, and perhaps others. These groups burn a large amount of property for the dead at the time of the funeral.   Somewhat similar are the eastern Mono practices.

Some faint traces, not of the mourning anniversary itself, indeed, but rather of the point of view which it expresses, are found even among the typical northwestern tribes. Among the Yurok and Hupa custom has established a certain time and place in every major dance as the occasion for an outburst of weeping. The old people in particular remember the presence of their departed kinsmen at former presentations of this part of the ceremony, and seem to express their grief spontaneously.

On the question of the time of the commemoration, more information is needed. It appears rather more often not to fall on the actual anniversary. Among some of the southern tribes it may be deferred several years; with the Mohave it seems to be held within a few weeks or months after death; the Sierra tribes mostly limit it to a fixed season—early autumn.

GIRLS' ADOLESCENCE CEREMONY.

Probably every people in California observed some rite for girls at the verge of womanhood: the vast majority celebrated it with a dance. The endless fluctuations in the conduct of the ceremony are indicated in Table 9. It appears that in spite of a general basic similarity of the rite, and the comparatively narrow scope imposed on its main outlines by the physiological event to which it has reference, there are very few features that are universal. These few, among which the use of a head scratcher and the abstention from flesh are prominent, are of a specifically magical nature. The wealth of particular features restricted to single nations, and therefore evidently developed by them, is rather remarkable, and argues that the Californians were not so much deficient in imagination and originality as in the ability to develop these qualities with emotional intensity to a point of impressiveness. There is every reason to believe that this inference applies with equal force to many phases of Californian civilization. It merely happens that an unusually full series of details is available for comparison on the rite for girls.

It has been noted several times that poor and rude tribes make much more of the adolescence ceremony in California than those possessed of considerable substance and specialized institutions. In this connection it is only necessary to cite the Yurok as contrasted with the Sinkyone, the Pomo as against the Yuki, valley Maidu against those of the mountains, Yokuts against Washo, Mohave against Diegueño. Precedence in general elaboration of culture must in every instance be given to the former people of each pair; and yet it is the second that makes, and the first that does not make, an adolescence ceremony. This condition warrants the inference that the puberty rite belongs to the generic or basic stratum of native culture, and that it has decayed among those nations that succeeded in definitely evolving or establishing ceremonials whose associations are less intimately personal and of a more broadly dignified import.

In the northern half of the State the idea is deep rooted that the potential influence for evil of a girl at the acme of her adolescence is very great. Even her sight blasts, and she is therefore covered or concealed as much as possible. Everything malignant in what is specifically female in physiology is thought to be thoroughly intensified at its first appearance. So far as known, all the languages of this portion of California possess one word for a woman in the periodic illness of her sex, and an entirely distinct term for a girl who is at the precise incipiency of womanhood.

A second concept is also magical: that the girl's behavior at this period of intensification is extremely critical for her nature and conduct forever after. Hence the innumerable prescriptions for gathering firewood, industry, modest deportment, and the like.

This concept pervades also the reasoning of the tribes in the southern end of the State, but is rather overshadowed by the more special conviction that direct physiological treatment is necessary to insure future health. Warmth appears to be considered the first requisite in the south. Cold water must not be drunk under any circumstances, bathing must be in heated water; and in the sphere of Gabrielino-Luiseño influence, the girl is cooked or roasted, as it were, in a pit, which seems modeled on the earth oven. The idea of her essential malignancy is comparatively weak in the south.

The southern concepts have penetrated in diluted form into the San Joaquin Valley region, along with so many other elements of culture. On the other hand, the Mohave, and with them presumably the Yuma, practice a type of ceremony that at most points differs from that of the other southern Californians, and provides an excellent exemplification of the profound aloofness of the civilization of these agricultural tribes of the Colorado River.

The deer-hoof rattle is consciously associated with the girls' ceremony over all northern California. Since there is a deep-seated antithesis of taboo between everything sexual on the one hand, and everything referring to the hunt, the deer as the distinctive game animal, and flesh on the other, the use of this particular rattle can hardly be a meaningless accident. But the basis of the inverting association has not become clear, and no native explanations seem to have been recorded.

A few Athabascan tribes replace the deer-hoof rattle by a modification of the clap-stick which provides the general dance accompaniment throughout central California, but which is not otherwise used in the northwest. In southern California the deer-hoof rattle is known, but is employed by hunters among the Luiseño, by mourners among the Yumans.

The scarcity of the ritualistic number 4 in Table 9 may be an accident of tribal representation in the available data, but gives the impression of having some foundation in actuality and a significance.

3625°—25——56

TABLE 9. THE ADOLESCENCE CEREMONY FOR GIRLS.

[Present, x; absent, o.]

	Singing	Dancing	Women dance	Men dance	Girl dances	Dance in circle	Dance abreast	Dance outdoors	Dance indoors	Deerhoof rattle	Eyeshade	Girl covered	"Roasting" in pit	Girl runs	Girl carries wood	Girl works	Girl bathes	Head scratcher	Fasts from meat	Fasts from salt	Drinks no water	Ears pierced	Tattooed	General license	Duration: nights	Repetitions of ceremony	Special features
Yurok		o		x	x	x	x	x	o	x	x		o	o	x		x	x	x		x				10		
Karok	x	x	x	x	o	o		o	x	o		x		x	x		o		x		x				10	3	Leaps toward morning star.
Hupa	x	x		x				x	x	x					x		x	x	x		x				10		Pared stick rattle; painted boards; girl peers into haliotis shells.
Tolowa	x	x	x	x					x	x		x							x								
Wiyot	x	x	x				x	x	x	o		x							x					x	10		
Sinkyone	x	x	x	x	x		x		x										x	x					5	2	10 or 5 nights; concluding dance by women in water.
Yuki	x	x	x	x	x	x	x			x		x						x	x	x				x			Pared stick rattle; girl keeps awake; hair over her eyes.
Pomo		o								o																	
Modoc	x	x	x	x	x	x	x			x					x		x	x	x		x	x		x	5	3	
Shasta	x	x	x	x	x	x	x	x	o	x	x				x	x	x	x	x			x			10	3	Girl keeps awake; does not look about; east is symbolic direction.
Achomawi	x	x	x	x	x	x	x	x		x		x		x	x	x		x	x			x		x		2	Girl must not look at world.
Mountain Maidu	x	x	x	x	x	x	o	x	o	x		x		x	x	x	x	x	x			x			5		Girl in ring of fire.
Hill Maidu	x	x	x	o								x						x	x						10		
Valley Maidu	x	o		x					o			x															Girl in trench in house.
Central Miwok	x	x							x										x						5		
Washo	x	x			x	x	o			o									x						4		
Yokuts		x		x						x			x														Girl uses no cold water.
Tibatulabal										o			x						x								Girl in pit; roasting not sure.

Girl forbidden all work; tobacco drunk.

Sand painting; tobacco eating ordeal, rocks painted; girl forbidden all work.

Crescentic stone applied; girl forbidden all work; tobacco drunk; period in pit indefinite.

Girl washes 40 days with warm water; drinks no cold water; loused by mother; lies in hot sand.

Cahuilla	x	x		x	x	x				x	x		x	x	o	x	x	x	2
Luiseño	x	x		x	x	x	o	o	o	x	x	o	x		o	x	x	x	3
Diegueño	x		x	x	x	x	o	o	o	x		o		x		x	x	x	3?
Mohave				x			x	x		[x]		o	o	o	o	o	o	o	6

BOYS' INITIATIONS.

The description which has sometimes been made of Californian religion as characterized by initiation and mourning rites does not appear to be accurate. Mourning customs, so far as they are crystallized into formal and important ceremonies, are confined to a single wave of southern origin and definitely limited distribution—the mourning anniversary. The girls' adolescence rite, on the other hand, is universal, and clearly one of the ancient constituents of the religion of all California as well as considerable tracts outside.

Boys were initiated into the two great organized religions of the State, the Kuksu and the toloache cult. Important as the initiation ceremonies were in these cults, it would, however, be misleading to regard them as primary: logically, at any rate, the cult comes first; the initiation is a part of it. When, therefore, we subtract these two religions, there is left almost nothing in the nature of initiations for boys parallel to the girls' adolescence ceremony.

The only clear instance is in the northeastern corner of the State among the Achomawi and Shasta, primarily the former. These people practice an adolescence rite for boys comparable to the more widespread one for girls. Among each of them a characteristic feature is the whipping of the boy with a bow string. The Achomawi also pierce the boy's ears and make him fast, besides which he performs practices very similar to the deliberate seeking after supernatural power indulged in by the tribes of the Plains. The entire affair is very clearly an adolescence rather than an initiation rite, an induction into a status of life, and not into an organized group. It may be looked upon as a local extension to boys of concepts that are universal in regard to girls.

In southern California there is sometimes a partial assimilation of the boys' toloache initiation and of the girls' adolescence ceremony. Thus the Luiseño construct ground paintings for both, deliver analogous orations of advice to both, and put both sexes under similar restrictions. The Kawaiisu are said to give toloache to both boys and girls.

But these local and incomplete developments are very far from equating the initiations for the two sexes; and neither balances with mourning ceremonies. The girls' adolescence, the boys' initiation into a society, and the mourning anniversary clearly have distinct origins so far as California is concerned, and represent separate cultural planes.

NEW YEAR OBSERVANCES.

A first-salmon ceremony was shared by an array of tribes in northern California. The central feature was usually the catching and eating of the first salmon of the season; after which fishing was open to all. These features constitute the ceremony one of public magic. The tribes from which some observance of this kind has been reported are the Tolowa, Yurok, Hupa, Karok, Shasta, Achomawi, and northern mountain Maidu. The list is probably not complete; but it may be significant that all the groups included in it are situated in the extreme north of the State, whereas salmon run in abundance, wherever there are streams of sufficient size to receive them, as far south as San Francisco Bay. It thus seems probable that the distribution of the rite was limited not only by the occurrence of the fish but also by purely cultural associations. Its range, for example, is substantially identical with that of the northern type of overlaid basketry.

The first-salmon ceremony is clearly of the type of new year's rituals, but is the only well-marked instance of this type yet found in California outside of the hearth of the northwestern culture. The idea of ceremonial reference to the opening of the year or season seems not to have been wholly wanting in north central California, especially where the Kuksu religion prevailed, but there is no record of its having been worked out into a definite ritual concept. In the northwest there were first-acorn and world-renewing ceremonies as well as the first-salmon rite. With the Karok these contained the superadded feature of new-fire making. All this, however, was an essentially local development among the small group of tribes who had advanced the northwestern culture to its most intense status.

In other words, an annual salmon producing or propitiating act of magical nature and of public rather than individual reference is usual in the northern part of the State, as well as in Oregon, and is therefore presumably an ancient institution. Among the specifically northwestern tribes this act later became associated with a ritualistic spectacle, either the Deerskin or the Jumping dance, which probably had no original connection with the magical performance; after which the combination of magic act and dance was applied to other occasions of a first fruits or New Year's character.

OFFERINGS.

Offerings of feathered wands are reported from the Chumash, the Costanoans, and the Maidu, and may therefore be assumed to have had a considerably wider distribution in the central parts of California, although neither Yuki nor Pomo seem to know the device. The idea is that of the prayer stick or prayer plume of the Southwest, and there is probably a connection between the practices of the two regions; although this may be psychological, that is, indirectly cultural, rather than due to outright transmission. This inference is supported by the fact that there is no reference to anything like the offering of feather wands in southern California where southwestern influences are, of course, most immediate. In fact, the practice of setting out offerings of any kind is so sparsely mentioned for southern California that it must be concluded to have been but slightly developed. The Californian feather wand was of somewhat different shape from the southwestern prayer plume. It appears usually to have been a stick of some length from which single feathers were loosely hung at one or two places. The northwestern tribes are free from the practice.

Another ultimate connection with the Southwest is found in offerings or sprinklings of meal. These have been recorded for the Pomo, the Maidu, the Costanoans, and the Serrano. In some instances it is not clear whether whole seeds or flour ground from them was used, and it is even possible that the meal was sometimes replaced by entire acorns. The southern California tribes should perhaps be included, since the use of meal or seeds in the ground painting might be construed as an offering. The custom seems, however, to have been more or less hesitating wherever it has been reported. It certainly lacks the full symbolic implications and the ritualistic rigor which mark it in the Southwest. Among the Yokuts and probably their mountain neighbors offerings of eagle down appear to have been more characteristic than of seeds or meal. The northwestern tribes can again be set down with positiveness as not participating in the custom.

THE GHOST DANCE.

The ghost dance, which swept northern California with some vehemence from about 1871 to 1873 or 1874, is of interest because of its undoubted connection with the much more extensive and better known wave of religious excitement that penetrated to the Indians of half of the United States about 1889 and 1890, and which left most of the Californians totally untouched. Both movements had their origin among the Northern Paiute of Nevada, and from individuals in the same family. The author of the early phophesies may have been the father and was, at any rate, an older kinsman of Wovoka or Jack Wilson, the later prophet or Messiah. The ideas of the two movements and their ritual were substantially identical. There is thus little doubt that even their songs were similar, although, unfortunately, these were not recorded for the earlier movement until after its fusion with other cults.

The question arises why the religious infection which originated twice in the same spot in an interval of 15 or 20 years should at the first occasion have obtained a powerful, although fleeting, foothold in northern California alone, and on its recrudescence should have spread to the Canadian boundary and the Mississippi River. That the Californians remained impassive toward the second wave is intelligible on the ground of immunity acquired by having passed through the first. But that a religion which showed its inherent potentiality by spreading to wholly foreign tribes should in 1870 have been unable to make any eastward progress and in 1890 sweep like wildfire more than a thousand miles to the east is remarkable. The only explanation seems to be that the bulk of the Indian tribes in the United States in 1870 had not been reduced to the necessary condition of cultural decay for a revivalistic influence to impress them. In other words, the native civilization of northern California appears to have suffered as great a disintegration by 1870, 20 or 25 years after its first serious contact with the whites, as the average tribe of the central United States had undergone by 1890, or from 50 to 100 years after similar contact began. As regards the Plains tribes, among whom the second ghost dance reached its culmination, there may be ascribed to the destruction of the buffalo the same influence on the breaking up of their old life as the sudden overwhelming swamping of the natives by the California gold seekers. In each case an interval of from 10 to 20 years elapsed from the dealing of the substantial death blow to the native civilization until the realization of the change was sufficiently profound to provide a fruitful soil for a doctrine of restoration.

Individual tribes had, of course, been subject to quite various fortunes at the hands of the whites when either ghost dance reached them. But it is also known that they accorded the movement many locally diverse receptions. Some threw themselves into it with an almost unlimited enthusiasm of hope; others were only slightly touched or remained aloof. This is very clear from Mooney's classical account of the greater ghost dance, and it can be conjectured that an intensive study would reveal the skeptical negative tribes to have been so situated that their old life did not yet appear to themselves as irrevocably gone, or as so thoroughly subject to the influences of Caucasian civilization that they had accepted the change as final. Then, too, it must be remembered that the wave, as it spread, developed a certain psychological momentum of its own, so that tribes which, if left to themselves or restricted to direct intercourse with the originators of the movement, might have remained passive, were infected by the frenzy of differently circumstanced tribes with whom they were in affiliation.

The same phenomena can be traced in the history of the California ghost dance, imperfect as our information concerning it is. The Karok and Tolowa seem to have projected themselves into the cult with greater abandonment than the Yurok. The Hupa, at least to all intents, refused to participate. This is perhaps to be ascribed to the fact that they were the only tribe in the region leading a stable and regulated reservation life. But it is not clear whether this circumstance had already led them to a conscious though reluctant acceptance of the new order of things, or whether some other specific cause must be sought.

On many of the northernmost tribes the effect of the ghost dance was quite transient, and it left no traces whatever. It was perhaps already decadent when the Modoc war broke out. At any rate it is no longer heard of after the termination of that conflict. How far the Modoc war may have been indirectly fanned by the doctrine remains to be ascertained. Its immediate occasion seems not to have been religious.

Somewhat farther south the ghost dance took firmer root among tribes like the Pomo and southern Wintun, which were beyond the most northerly missions but which had been more or less under mission influence and whose lands had been partly settled by Mexicans in the period between secularization and the Americanization of California. The old Kuksu ceremonies were now not only revived but made over. A new type of songs, paraphernalia, and ritual actions came into existence; and these have maintained themselves in some measure until to-day they are strongly interwoven with the aboriginal form of religion. The Wintun at least, and presumably the Pomo also, are still conscious, however, of the two elements in their present cults, and distinguish them by name. *Saltu* are the spirits that instituted the ancient rites, *boli* those with whom the modern dances are associated.

This amalgamation, strangely enough, resulted in the carrying of the Kuksu religion, at a time when it was essentially moribund, to tribes which in the days of its vitality had come under its influence only marginally or not at all. Evidently the ghost dance element acted as a penetrating solvent and carrier. The central Wintun took the mixed cult over from the southern Wintun, and the use since 1872 of typical Kuksu paraphernalia as far north as the Shasta of Shasta Valley evidences the extent of this movement.

None of the tribes within the mission area seems to have been in the least affected by the ghost dance. This is probably not due to their being Catholics or nominal Catholics, but rather to the fact that their life had long since been definitively made over. Groups like the Yokuts, of which only portions had been missionized and these rather superficially, also did not take up the ghost dance. The cause in this case presumably lies between their geographical remoteness and the fact that most of their intercourse was with missionized tribes.

The Modoc were perhaps the first Californian people to receive the early ghost dance from the Northern Paiute. It is hard to conceive that the Achomawi should have been exempt, but unfortunately there appear to be no records concerning them on this point. The

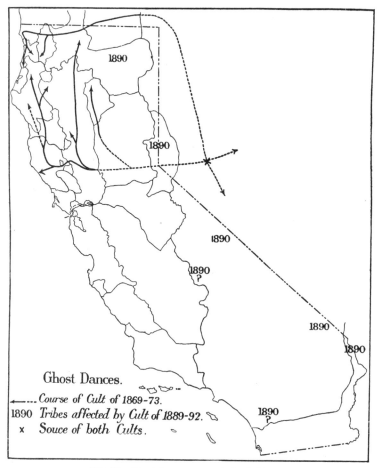

Fig. 71.—Ghost dance movements in California.

same may be said of the mountain Maidu. From the Modoc, at any rate, the cult was carried to the Shasta. These transmitted it still farther down the Klamath to the Karok. From there it leaped the Siskiyou Mountains to the Tolowa, from whom the lower Yurok of the river and of the coast took their beliefs. The upper Yurok were less affected and the Hupa scarcely at all. Here we lose track of the spread of the dance. Probably all the Athabascan tribes between the Whilkut and the Wailaki, at least those that survived in sufficient numbers, came under ghost dance influence, but the direction in which this influence progressed seems to have been from the south northward. Their dance appears to have been associated with the erection of large round dance houses of central Californian type. The traced course of the movement is: southern Wintun of the Sacramento Valley; Long Valley Wintun; southeastern Pomo; eastern Pomo; southern, central, and northern Pomo; Huchnom; Yuki, Kato, and Wailaki; and north to the Hayfork Wintun, Whilkut, and perhaps Chilula. (Fig. 71.)

It has already been mentioned how in the Sacramento Valley the ghost dance spread from south to north. To this it may be added that the Yana received the cult from the valley Maidu to the south of them. The question then arises how the dance reached the southern Wintun. There is no known information on this point. The movement may conceivably have traveled directly westward from the Northern Paiute through Washo and southern Maidu. Yet, on the whole, it is likely that the entry into California was at a single point; that is, through the Modoc and Klamath tribes, from whom the cult spread southward until, reaching its extreme limit among the southern Wintun, it recrystallized and then flowed back northward. Inquiry among the southern Maidu and northern Miwok would probably determine this issue.

It is not known whether any of the Miwok took up the ghost dance. In a number of localities they have during the last generation or so erected circular or octagonal dance houses of wood without earth covering. These look very much like a ghost dance modification of the old semisubterranean dance house of the Kuksu cults. Forty or fifty years ago—that is, about the time of the ghost dance—the hill Miwok received a number of new dances, including some of the Kuksu series. These came from Costanoan territory to the west, but quite possibly represent a cult revival of the imperfectly missionized northernmost valley Yokuts or Plains Miwok, original neighbors of the hill Miwok, but later domiciled at the Costanoan missions.[1]

The 1890 ghost dance is reported by Mooney, specifically or by implication, for the Achomawi, Washo, Mono, Koso, Yokuts of Tule River, Luiseño or other "mission" groups. Chemehuevi, and Mohave. The Washo, eastern Mono, Chemehuevi, and perhaps Koso could hardly have escaped participation. The Achomawi may have been rendered susceptible by a failure to take part in 1872. The Mohave were never seriously affected. The Yokuts and Luiseño were no doubt interested, but seem never to have practiced the cult.

---

[1] The northern Miwok of 1923 know nothing of the ghost dance.

No tribe in California retained for more than a very short time any phase of this second ghost dance religion.

The California Indian did not record the passage of long intervals of time. No one knew his own age nor how remote an event was that had happened more than two or three years ago. Tallies seem not to have been kept for any purpose, and no sticks notched annually have been found or reported in the State. Most groups had not even a word for " year," but employed " world," " summer," or " winter " instead. Where there appear to be words meaning " year," they seem as often as not to denote " season," that is, a half year.

Probably every tribe, however, had a system of measuring time within the year. This was by the universally known method of naming and reckoning lunations in the round of the seasons. The point of interest in this method to the historian of culture rests in the means taken to adjust the eternally varying and essentially irreconcilable lunar and solar phenomena. Half a dozen such calendars are known from California. These clearly belong to three types, evidently representative of the three cultures of which so much mention has been made in this book.

The Maidu knew 12 moons, named after seasonal occurrences. The series began in spring, and appears not to have been controlled by any solar phenomenon. There can accordingly scarcely have been a consistent method, however rude, of adjusting the moon count to the year. When the discrepancy became too insistent, something was presumably stretched or the reckoning simply suspended until matters seemed to tally again. The whole scheme is essentially descriptive of terrestrial events, and has as little reference to astronomical events as a system can have and still be called a calendar. In line with this attitude of the Maidu is the fact that they made definite recognition of the seasons, as shown by a neat nomenclature. It should also be added that the upland Maidu counted only the winter moons, those of the summer being left unnamed.

The Yurok calendar has a more astronomical basis, although simple enough; and the descriptive element is almost lacking. The moons are numbered, not named, at least up to the tenth; the remaining ones have descriptive appellations. The year begins definitely at the winter solstice. The summer solstice may have been noted also, but does not enter into the system. There was a clear recognition of the essential problem of a year calendar, some individuals counting twelve moons and others thirteen. The solution must have been less clearly formulated, since it is stated that disputes often took place as to the proper designation of the current moon. Yet recognition of the solstice as a primary point, however inaccurately it may have been determined by offhand appearances without mechanically aided observations, would prevent any excessively gross errors or long-continued conflict of opinion.

The Yurok system is undoubtedly connected with that of the North Pacific coast, where the moons are also frequently numbered and fitted into the frame afforded by the solstices.

The Modoc calendar seems to be a weakening of the Yurok one. Basically, the moons are numbered, although their actual names are those of the fingers of the hand. But the beginning of the round is in summer and is determined by a seasonal harvest; there is no mention of the solstices; and none of an intercalary thirteenth month.

The Huchnom and Pomo mostly used descriptive moon names, but some "finger months" are included.[4]

In southern California the moon names are probably descriptive, but the fixed points of the calendar, and the means of its more or less automatic correction, are the two solstices. The Diegueño have only six month names; which means that the second half-year repeats and balances the first, and presumably that the two solstices are pivotal. The Juaneño and Luiseño do not repeat month designations within the year, but the former name only five and the latter but four periods in each half year. This scheme makes the nonlunar periods which include the solstices long and somewhat variable, but also accentuates them as primary.[5] All three varieties of this calendar must at times have been productive of difficulty within the haf-year, but as a perpetual system the scheme is obviously self-correcting. Whether any of the southern California tribes took actual observations of the solstices is not known.

This southern calendar is clearly allied to that of the tribes of the Southwestern States, who also deal in solstices but describe their moons. The Diegueño six-name plan is that of the Zuñi. The Pueblos definitely determined the solstices with fair accuracy by observations made on the horizon from established spots. It is possible that they were led to this procedure by their permanent residences. These would at least afford an advantage and perhaps a stimulus in this direction.

Astronomical knowledge not directly used in time reckoning was slight in northern and central California. The planets were too

---

[4] It appears (see footnote, p. 209) that both finger-count and descriptive calendars might coexist among one group in this region, and that the year sometimes began with the winter solstice. This suggests that central Californian and North Pacific coast customs have met in the Pomo area.

[5] It has been doubted whether the southern California periods tally with lunations in native consciousness, even though they are called "moons." See footnote, p. 723.

difficult to trouble with, except for Venus when it was the morning star. The Pleiades are the constellation most frequently mentioned, and seem to have had a designation among every tribe. Myths usually make them dancing girls, as in so many parts of the world. This may prove to be one of the concepts of independent or directly psychological origin which have so often been sought but are so difficult to establish positively. Orion's belt is probably recognized with the next greatest frequency, and then possibly Ursa Major. There are some references to Polaris as the immovable star. The Milky Way is known everywhere, and quite generally called the ghosts' road. In southern California stellar symbolism begins to be of some consequence, and half a dozen constellations and several isolated first magnitude stars are named in addition to those recognized farther north.

NUMERATION.

The round numbers familar to the Californians in ritual and myth are low, as among all American Indians. In the north, from the Tolowa and Sinkyone to the Achomawi and mountain Maidu, 5 or its multiple 10 is in universal use in such connections (Table 10). In the region of the well-defined Kuksu cult 4 takes its place, although the Pomo evince some inclination to supplement it by 6. To the south there is enough uncertainty to suggest that no one number stood strongly in the foreground. The Yokuts favor 6, but without much emphasis. The Gabrielino employed 5, 6, and 7 in addition to 4; among the Juaneño, 5 is most commonly mentioned; for the Luiseño, probably 3; among the Diegueño, 3 is clearly prevalent in ritual, 4 in myth. For a group of American nations with a definite ceremonial cult, and that comprising sacred paintings of the world, this is an unusually vague condition. Only the Colorado River tribes are positive: 4 is as inevitably significant to them as to all the Indians of the Southwest.

Directional reference of the ritualistic number is manifest in the Kuksu tribes, but everywhere else is wanting or at least insignificant, except with the Yuman groups. Here there is some tendency to balance opposite directions; single pairs are even mentioned alone. North or east has the precedence. In the Kuksu region there is a definite sequence of directions in sinistral circuit; but the starting point varies from tribe to tribe. Association of colors with the directions has been reported only from the Diegueño. Its general absence is an instance of the comparatively low development of ritualistic symbolism in California.

TABLE 10.—RITUAL NUMBERS AND METHODS OF NUMERATION.

Group.	Ritual number.				Units of count.		
					1–10	11–19	20+
Yurok		5, 10			10	10	10
Wiyot		5, 10			10	10	10
Karok		5, 10			5	10	10
Chimariko					5	10	10
Tolowa					10	10	10
Hupa, Chilula		5, 10			10	10	10
Sinkyone		5			5	.....	10
Wailaki					5	.....	10
Kato					5	5	10
Coast Yuki					5	5	10
Yuki	* 4		(6)		8	8	64
Wappo	*				5	10	10
Pomo	* 4		(* 6)		¹ 5	² 5	10, 20
Coast Miwok					10	10	10
Shasta		5, 10			5	10	10
Modoc		5			5	10	10
Achomawi		(5)			5	10	10
Yana		(5)			5	10	20
Wintun—							
Northern					5	10	.....
Central					5	5	.....
Southern	* 4				5	5, 10	20, 10
Maidu—							
Mountain		* 5			5	10	10
Hill	4	5			5	5, 10	20, 10
Valley	* 4	(5)			5	5	20
Southern					5	5	10
Miwok—							
Northern					10	5	20
Central	4				10	5	20
Southern					10	10	10
Yokuts—							
Central				6	10	10	10
Southerly	3		6, 12		10	10	10
Costanoan		(5)			³ 10	10	10
Esselen					5	.....	.....
Salinan					4	16	16
Chumash					4	16	16

* Referred to cardinal directions.   ² 10 among northeastern and southern Pomo.
¹ 10 among northeastern Pomo.   ³ 5 among southern Costanoans.

TABLE 10.—RITUAL NUMBERS AND METHODS OF NUMERATION—Continued.

Group.	Ritual number.					Units of count.		
						1–10	11–19	20+
Washo						5	10	10
Eastern Mono		4				10		
Tübatulabal						10		
Chemehuevi						10		
Serrano						5	10	10
Gabrielino		4. 8	(10)	6	(7)	5	5	5
Cahuilla						5	10	10
Luiseño	(3)	(*4)				5	5	5
Diegueño	4 3	* 4				5		10
Yuma						5	10	10
Mohave		* 4				5	10	10

* Referred to cardinal directions.   4 4 predominates in myth, 3 in ritual action

The same Table 10 shows also the distribution in California of methods of counting—the basis of all mathematical science. Mankind as a whole, and even the most advanced nations, count as the fingers determine. But it is obvious that the unit or basis of numeration can be one hand, or two, or the fingers plus the toes, that is, "one man." This gives a choice between quinary, decimal, and vigesimal systems. Whether from an inherent cause or because of a historical accident, practically all highly civilized nations count by tens, with hundred as the next higher unit. Peoples less advanced in culture, however, are fairly equally divided between a decimal numeration and one which operates somewhat more concretely or personally with fives and twenties. So, too, with the Californians. But to judge correctly their inclinations as between these two possibilities, it is necessary to distinguish between their use of low and high numbers.

For the first 10 numerals the majority of the Californians have stems only for 1 to 5. The words for 6 to 9 are formed from those for 1 to 4. This system is replaced chiefly in three regions by a truly decimal one, in which the word for 7, for instance, bears no relation to that for 2. The first of these three tracts holds the two Algonkin divisions of California, the Wiyot and Yurok; and a few immediately adjacent Athabascan groups, notably the Hupa and Tolowa. The second area comprises the Yokuts, Miwok, and most of the Costanoans—in short, the southern half of the Penutian family. In the third area are the Plateau Shoshoneans east of the Sierra Nevada.

These distributions reflect geographical position rather than linguistic affinities. The northern Penutians, southern Athabascans, and southern California Shoshoneans count by fives instead of tens. The map makes it look as if decimal numeration had been taken over by the Hupa and Tolowa in imitation of the method of their Algonkin neighbors; but the difficulty in this connection is that the great mass of eastern Algonkins count by fives instead of straight to ten.

For the higher numbers, the corresponding choice is between a system based on 20 and 400, or on 10 and 100. In this domain the decimal system prevails, showing that the quinary and vigesimal methods, even if inherently associated, are not inseparable. The situation may be summed up by saying that from 20 up, all California counts decimally except the people of two areas. The first comprises half or more of the Pomo, most of the southern Wintun, in general the western Maidu, and the northerly divisions of the interior Miwok. This is precisely the region of intensive development of the Kuksu cults. Here the count is by twenties. The second area is that of the Gabrielino and Luiseño, with whom the Fernandeño, Juaneño, and perhaps Cupeño must be included, but no others. (These peoples strictly do not count by twenties, but by multiplying fives.) Now, this, strangely enough, is precisely the tract over which the Chungichnish religion had penetrated in its full form. The connection between a system of religious institutions and a method of numeration in daily life is very difficult to understand, and the bonds must be indirect and subtle. That they exist, however, and that it is more than an empty coincidence that we are envisaging, is made almost indisputable by the fact that the northern tract of decimal counting for low numbers coincides very nearly with the area of the northwestern culture in its purest form as exemplified by New Year's rites and the Deerskin dance.

That the basing of the vigesimal on the quinary count, although usual, is by no means necessary, is shown by the northern and central Miwok, who count the first 10 numbers decimally, but proceed from 10 to 20 by adding units of 5, and beyond with units of 20. That a people should count first 5 and then another 5 and then proceed to operate systematically with the higher unit of 10, is not so very foreign to our way of thinking. But that our own psychic processes are by no means necessarily binding is proved by this curious Miwok practice of beginning with ten straight numeral words, then counting twice by fives, and finally settling into a system of twenties.

Two other totally divergent methods of counting are found in California. The Chumash and Salinans count by fours, with 16 as higher unit, the Yuki by eights and sixty-fours. The latter operate by laying pairs of twigs into the spaces between the fingers. Thus the anomaly is presented of an octonary system based on the hand. The Yuki operate very skillfully by this method: when they are asked to count on the fingers like their neighbors, they work slowly and with frequent errors. Both these systems run contrary to speech affinity: the Chumash and Salinans are the only Hokans that count by fours; and the Coast Yuki, Huchnom, and Wappo related to the Yuki know nothing of their system of eights.

Every count that can progress beyond one hand involves arithmetical operations of some sort, usually addition. But other processes crop out with fair frequency in California. Nine, fourteen, and nineteen are sometimes formed from the unit next above. The word for 4 is often a reduplicated or expanded 2; or 8 a similar formation from 4. Two-three for 6, three-four for 12, and three-five for 15 all occur here and there; and the Luiseño count by an indefinitely repeated system of multiplication, as "4 times 5 times 5."

The degree to which mathematical operations were conducted other than in the counts themselves has been very little examined into. The Pomo speak of beads by ten and forty thousands. Every group in the State, apparently, knew how to count into the hundreds; how often its members actually used these higher numbers, and on what occasions, is less clear. Rapid and extended enumeration argues some sense of the value of numbers, and it is likely that people like the Pomo and Patwin developed such a faculty by their counting of beads. Of direct mathematical operations there is less evidence. An untutored Yuki can express offhand in his octonary nomenclature how many fingers he has; he evidently can not multiply 10 by 2: for he finds it necessary to count his hands twice over to enable him to answer. An old Mohave knows at once that 4 times 4 is 16; but 4 times 8 presents a problem to be solved only by a sorting and adding up of counters. No Californian language is known to have any expression for fractions. There is always a word for half, but it seems to mean "part" or "division" rather than the exact mathematical ratio.

CHAPTER 57.

POPULATION.

PREVIOUS ESTIMATES AND COMPUTATIONS.

The strength of the aboriginal population is as difficult to estimate in California as in most parts of America. Early figures of general range, like Powers's 700,000, are almost invariably far too high, and those of more restricted application are either obvious impressionistic exaggerations or fail to specify accurately the areas really involved.

There has been only one attempt to approach the subject in a critical spirit, and to arrive at conclusions by computation in place of guess. This is a valuable essay by Dr. C. Hart Merriam, which takes the Franciscan mission statistics as a basis. The argument runs as follows:

In 1834 there were upward of 30,000 converted Indians. A ratio of one gentile to every three neophytes may be assumed for this period for the territory tapped by the missions. This gives 40,000. The population at the missions had, however, long suffered a heavy decrease. At least 10,000 must therefore be added to reach the true numbers before contact with the Spaniards: total, 50,000. The area in question comprises only one-fifth of the nondesert part of the State. Hence, natural conditions in the mission strip being on the average in no way superior to those elsewhere, there were 250,000 Indians in the fertile and semifertile portions of California. Add 10,000 for the deserts, and a grand total of 260,000 is reached.

Some of the factors in this computation are taken very conservatively; others must be gravely questioned. The assumption of the representativeness of the mission territory in productiveness seems fair. The proportion of four natives in 1834 where there had been five in 1769 is, if anything, too low, in view of the enormous mor-

tality at some of the missions. The proportion of converts to gentiles may be accepted as reasonable, statistics being totally lacking.
On the other hand, the vague report of over 30,000 in 1834, the year
of secularization, is less entitled to credence than the exact figure
of 24,634 for 1830.

That the tracts drawn upon for the missions covered only a fifth
of the nondesert parts of the State is, however, an undervaluation,
as can be seen by a glance at Figure 72. The outer, broken line on that
map, indicating the limits of partial missionization, is the one that
must be considered in this connection, since we are allowing for territory that still contained wild Indians as well as neophytes. It is
evident that this line includes very nearly a third of the whole State,
and certainly more than a third of the nondesert areas.

A recomputation then might start with 25,000; add a third for
gentiles, making 33,000; and possibly half to that as an allowance
for decrease from 1769 to 1830; total for the mission area about
1770, 50,000. Multiplying by 3 yields 150,000. An addition of
10,000 for desert areas might be insisted on; but if so, at least an
equal deduction would have to be made for the fertile portions of
the State being less than three times the mission area; so that the
result of 150,000 would stand. This cuts Dr. Merriam's total nearly
in half.

It must be pointed out that the mission data are of such a character that they can not be used with any accuracy except after a far
more painstaking analysis than they have yet been subjected to.
We hear constantly of a jumble of tribes at most of the establishments, and sometimes they are designated so as to be recognizable,
but their relative proportions remain obscure. A study of the bap-
tismal registers, where these give birthplaces, may provide some
notion of the strength of the various groups for certain periods at a
few of the missions; and from such conclusions an estimate of the
size of the tribes represented at all the establishments between 1769
and 1834 might be derivable. Before this can be done, however, the
location of the rancherias mentioned must be worked out with at
least approximate precision. Another difficulty is that the ratios
changed enormously. In 60, or even in 30 years, the unremitting
mortality undoubtedly shrank the numbers of the first converts from
the immediate vicinity very heavily; while neophytes from a distance
began to come in only gradually, but then, until a certain point was
reached, ever more rapidly. Thus, there were Yokuts at missions
founded on Costanoan, Salinan, Chumash, and perhaps Shoshonean
soil; but whether in 1810 and again in 1830 they constituted, at any
one point, 5 or 20 or 60 per cent of the converted population, there
is at present no means of deciding.

A RECONSIDERATION OF THE DATA.

For many years the present writer had set the native population of the State at 150,000. This was avowedly a guess, based on numerous scattered impressions, which, however, seemed at least as reliable as any computation can be at present. Later, he was inclined to shift the figure toward 100,000 rather than at 150,000. In the preparation of the present work the matter was once more gone into, and as exhaustively as possible. The method followed was to take up each group separately, giving consideration to all possible elements of knowledge, and checking these against each other. The variety of sources of information, unsatisfactory as most of these are separately, is considerable. There are, for instance, early estimates of travelers and settlers; the conclusions of ethnologists familiar with the people at a later time; the number of known villages or village sites; the tribal count in the Federal census of 1910, which was undertaken conscientiously and carried out very reasonably; the apparent rapidity of decrease in various areas; the availability of food supply in each habitat; and indications of the ratio of density of population in adjacent areas of differing surface and environment. The figures thus obtained more or less independently for each tribe, dialect group, or stock, were then brought together, rounded to the nearest half thousand, in Table 11, and yielded a total of 133,000.

TABLE 11.—INDIAN POPULATION OF CALIFORNIA, 1770 AND 1910.

Groups.	1770	1910	Groups.	1770	1910
Yurok.................	2,500	700	Northern Paiute in Cali-		
Karok................	1,500	800	fornia...............	500	300
Wiyot.................	1,000	100	Eastern and western		
Tolowa...............	1,000	150	Mono................	4,000	1,500
Hupa.................	1,000	500	Tübatulabal...........	1,000	150
Chilula, Whilkut........	1,000	(*)	Koso, Chemehuevi, Ka-		
Mattole...............	500	(*)	waiisu...............	1,500	500
Nongatl, Sinkyone,			Serrano, Vanyume,		
Lassik................	2,000	100	Kitanemuk, Alliklik.	3,500	150
Wailaki...............	1,000	200	Gabrielino, Fernan-		
Kato..................	500	(*)	deño, San Nicoleño..	5,000	(*)
Yuki..................	2,000	100	Luiseño...............	4,000	500
Huchnom..............	500	(*)	Juaneño...............	1,000	(*)
Coast Yuki............	500	(*)	Cupeño................	500	150
Wappo........	1,000	(*)	Cahuilla..............	2,500	800
Pomo.................	8,000	1,200	Diegueño, Kamia......	3,000	800
Lake Miwok...........	500	(*)	Mohave (total)........	3,000	1,050
Coast Miwok...........	1,500	(*)	Halchidhoma (emi-		
Shasta................	2,000	100	grated since 1800)....	1,000	......
Chimariko, New River,			Yuma (total)..........	2,500	750
Konomihu, Okwanu-					
chu..................	1,000	(*)		136,000	15,400
Achomawi, Atsugewi...	3,000	1,100	Total of groups marked *	....	450
Modoc in California....	500	(*)			
Yana..................	1,500	(*)			15,850
Wintun...............	12,000	1,000	Less river Yumans in		
Maidu.................	9,000	1,100	Arizona..............	3,000	850
Miwok (Plains and					
Sierra)...............	9,000	700			15,000
Yokuts................	18,000	600	Non-Californian Indians		
Costanoan.............	7,000	(*)	now in California.....	....	350
Esselen...............	500	(*)	Affiliation doubtful or		
Salinan.........	3,000	(*)	not reported..........	....	1,000
Chumash..............	10,000	(*)	Total...........	133,000	16,350
Washo in California.....	500	300			

It must be admitted that as each individual figure is generally nothing but an estimate, or an average of possible conjectures, the total can make no claim to precision. It represents only an opinion; but at least this opinion is the formulation of years of attention to all possible aspects of the question. A different impression may be truer, and perhaps can some day be verified.

Many of the figures for individual tribes in Table 11 may excite protest on the part of those specially familiar with a group. But it is believed that if some have been put too low, others are excessively liberal. Thus, 9,000 for the Maidu may seem a small total, but the student who has most carefully investigated these people judges 4,000 to be a conservative estimate. The numbers for the Mohave and Yuma are smaller than the prepioneer Garcés reported. Perhaps he was correct; but if so, the shortage is likely to be more than made up, in the State total, by the allowance of 9,000 for the Plains and Sierra Miwok, not to mention the high figure of 18,000 for the Yokuts. At any rate, the list represents the best that the writer conscientiously believes himself capable of proffering. And he is confident, in his own conviction, that he has not erred by more than a fourth from reality.

Of course there is no intention of offering the figure of 133,000 with the least idea of its specific correctness. It is meant only to indicate with some exactness the point near which the true value probably falls. A better expression might be to say that the population was from 120,000 to 150,000. But for broader computations, into which California might enter only as a small element, some precise formulation is necessary, and the 133,000 arrived at is the figure of all those in its vicinity that seems to have a little the greatest verisimilitude.

The plan of multiplicative calculation has been attempted on the basis of one people, the Yokuts. The computation can be followed in detail in chapter 32. The conclusion does not seem to have the same strength as that just arrived at, but it yields the interesting and perhaps significant corroboration of 130,000 maximum.

COMPARISON WITH THE POPULATION OF THE CONTINENT.

There is one other test that can be applied: Comparison with the remainder of the continent. Mr. James Mooney, who has devoted assiduous years to the problem of native population, arrives at a judgment of 846,000 souls for the United States and 202,000 in Canada, Alaska, and Greenland, or about 1,050,000 for America north of Mexico, with an estimate of error of less than 10 per cent. California covers a twentieth of the area of the country, or about a fortieth of the larger tract. On the basis of the present estimate of 133,000, this would allot to California nearly 16 per cent of the aboriginal population of the United States, as compared with 5 per cent of the area, or a relative density more than three times as great. This surely is liberal, no matter how highly we may rate the fertility of the Golden State and overlook its very considerable areas of minimal productivity.

In fact, the ratio is really higher, since Mr. Mooney's estimate of 846,000 seems to contain the figure of 260,000 for California. If for 260,000 we substitute 133,000, the total for the United States sinks to 719,000, and the California proportion rises to between 18 and 19 per cent. The density, similarly, is almost one person per square mile for California, as against one to every 4 plus miles over the remainder of the country. If we remember Death Valley, the Colorado and Mohave Deserts, the northern lava flows, and the high Sierra, this disproportion seems sufficient, if not excessive.

Comparison with outside territories therefore produces nothing to compel an enlargement of the estimate arrived at, in fact rather indicates that the reckoning of 133,000 is already thoroughly liberal. On the same basis, the result of Dr. Merriam's computation is incredible: 260,000 Indians in California, only 586,000 in all the other States and not more than 788,000 in the whole continent north of the Rio Grande, is a proportion that shatters conceivability. It is true that Mr. Mooney has evidently been thoroughly conservative in his estimates for the eastern and central United States with whose Indians he is most familiar from personal experience. But if this has been the inclination, for the larger part of the continent, of the admitted authority on the subject, a similar restraint is not only permissible but almost requisite in approaching the present more limited inquiry.

THE MISSION AREA.

A calculation made from Table 11 and Figure 72, of the number of Indians in the region affected by the missions, yields the following probabilities:

Pomo	3,000	Esselen	500
Yukian	1,000	Salinan	3,000
Miwok	4,000	Chumash	10,000
Maidu	1,000	Shoshonean	15,000
Wintun	4,000	Yuman	2,500
Yokuts	13,000		
Costanoan	7,000	Total	64,000

On the basis of the area involved being a third or not quite a third of the State, this figure of 64,000 would yield a total of very nearly 200,000, which is as near to Dr. Merriam's final conclusion as to the number advanced in the present work. Justice compels this admission; but the result thus attained seems not so much to compel an upward revision of the results already arrived at, as to indicate the unreliability of the multiplicative method.

POPULATION BY SPEECH FAMILIES.

The following compilation from Table 11 of the relative strength of the several native families in California may be of interest:

Families.		1770	1910
Penutian:			
Pen group: Maidu, Wintun, Yokuts	39,000		
Uti group: Miwok, Costanoan	18,000		
Total		57,000	3,500
Hokan:			
Northern group: Shastan, Chimariko, Karok, Yana	9,000		
Pomo	8,000		
Washo in California	500		
Southwestern group: Esselen, Salinan, Chumash	13,500		
Yuman (9,500, less 3,000 in Arizona)	6,500		
Total		37,500	6,000
Shoshonean:			
Plateau branch	6,000		
Kern River branch	1,000		
Southern California branch	16,500		
Total		23,500	4,050
Athabascan		7,000	1,000
Yukian		4,000	200
Algonkin (Yurok, Wiyot)		3,500	800
Lutuami in California		500	300
Total		133,000	15,850

DECREASE OF POPULATION.

There is one Indian in California to-day for every eight that lived in the same area before the white man came. To attain even this fractional proportion of one-eighth, half and mixed bloods, totaling nearly 30 per cent according to the census of 1910, must be included. It is true that a certain number of scattered individuals of much diluted blood, and individuals mainly of Indian blood but wholly Mexicanized in their mode of life, all of whom no longer habitually speak a native tongue, have probably succeeded in identifying themselves so completely with the Caucasian population as to have escaped the Indian census takers. But the total of such persons is not likely to exceed a few hundreds; and it seems only reasonable to omit them from any count of Indians.

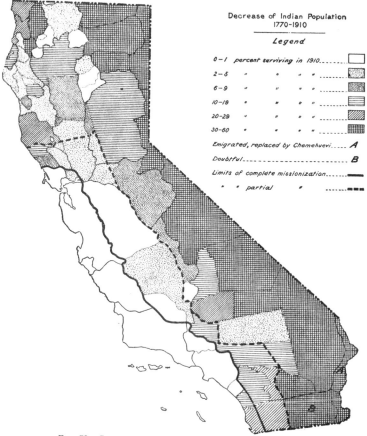

FIG. 72.—Decrease of native population from 1770 to 1910.

The causes of this decline of nearly 90 per cent within a period ranging, according to locality, from only 6 to 14 decades, are obscure. New diseases and alteration of diet, clothing, and dwellings have undoubtedly contributed largely. But civilized and semicivilized communities are often subject to similar influences, and thrive; whereas the native of low civilization, in many parts of the world, passes away. The ultimate explanation must therefore undoubtedly take into account, and perhaps in primary place, a set of cultural factors as well as the more obvious organic or physiological ones; and these cultural factors have never been determined, athough an untold quantity of conjecture and assertion has been formulated on the subject. But it may be of interest and service to set forth with some precision of detail those immediate conditions that appear in California to be associated with respectively greater tribal fatality or resistance.

CONDITIONS FAVORING SURVIVAL AND DECLINE.

The tribal figures have been already given in Table 11, and the ratio of decrease, or rather of survival, is graphically depicted in Figure 72.

From these compilations it is clear that, in general, decrease of the native race is directly in proportion to immediacy and fullness of contact with superior civilization. This fact would have been driven home even more emphatically by the map if it had been possible to present the tribal or dialectic areas in smaller subdivisions; but the data for the present time scarcely suffice for this, and those for the aboriginal period are unfortunately already too largely estimatory without being drawn fine and apportioned to minute districts.

First of all, it is established that the tribes that were completely devoted to mission life are gone. Many are wholly extinct; the most fortunate may amount to one-hundredth of their original numbers. In the extreme south, among the Luiseño and Diegueño, there seems to be an exception. It is not real; but due to the difficulty just mentioned: data are lacking to enable a separation of the wholly missionized from the partly missionized Luiseño and Diegueño. Both groups have therefore been treated as units. And yet all indications are that if we could discriminate in this region, there would be less than 5 per cent of survivors for the thoroughly missionized Luiseño and Diegueño districts, in place of the 20 to 30 or 40 per cent that the rough blocks of the map show.

The tracts from which part of the native population was drawn, or from which all of it was taken so short a time before secularization that a considerable proportion of the tribes was able to return to their old homes after 1834, tell the same story.

It must have caused many of the fathers a severe pang to realize, as they could not but do daily, that they were saving souls only at the inevitable cost of lives. And yet such was the overwhelming fact. The brute upshot of missionization, in spite of its kindly flavor and humanitarian root, was only one thing: death.

What the Franciscan commenced with his concentrations, the American finished by mere settlement, and extended to the hitherto unopened portions of the State. Where his cities sprang up, there was soon not an Indian within miles. In farming districts he lingered a little longer in scattered families. In the timbered hills, in the higher habitable Sierra, in the broken coast ranges, above all in the deserts and half deserts that skirt the eastern edge and make up a large part of the southern end of the State, the native maintained himself in some measure. The occasional homesteader, the cattle ranger, the lumberman, even the miner if he did not stay too long, were not present in force enough to blast him more than in partial measure. Outside of the mission district the preservation of the Indian population of California is in inverse ratio to the density of the white population. The tints of a map of one of these two factors need only to be reversed to serve as a substantially correct map of the other.

There are some exceptions: A number of hill tribes that have vanished completely in 60 years, or are on the very brink of extinction. Such are the Chimariko, New River Shasta, Konomihu, Okwanuchu, southern Yana, and Yahi in the north; and the Yokuts tribes of the Poso and Buena Vista foothill groups in the south; and, in only slightly less degree, all the Athabascan tribes between the Hupa and the Wailaki, the Shasta, the northern and central Yana, and the Vanyume. All these lived in remote places, where the white man never was abundant, and is still thinly sown; and yet they have perished. But they were small groups—all of them in numbers and many of them in territory as well. And they were all rude even in native culture; which is equivalent to saying that they were poor; in short, that the margin which they had established between themselves and the minimum limit of existence was narrower than that of other tribes. Thus, the maladjustment caused by even a light immigration of Americans was enough to push them over the precipice.

That this coincidence is no idle one is clear from the circumstance that neighboring tribes—in valleys or on larger streams, more populous, richer, and of more elaborated customs—have usually maintained themselves proportionally better in spite of heavier or at least equal contact with the whites. Compare the Yurok, Hupa, and Karok, the richest and most civilized tribes in the State, of whom from a quarter to a half survive, with the half dozen just-cited groups of Athabascan and Shastan mountaineers who inclose them on three sides, of none of whom even one person in twenty remains. Match, too, the wild Yana with the adjacent populous and comparatively refined Maidu and Wintun: at best a bare 5 per cent of maintenance in one case, 8 to 12 in the other. And so with the Yokuts Paleuyami, Chulamni, and Tuhohi, against their kinsmen the Yauelmani and Yaudanchi. Even as between the Yuki and the Pomo a similar relation prevails. The latter are more accessible lowlanders, they held rich farming lands, and were invaded by a much heavier stream of colonization; yet they have maintained themselves three or four times as successfully, relatively.

One further element is to be considered in this last class of cases. In the fifties and sixties the white settlers, however enterprising, were still sparse. Where a tribe numbered 2,000 or 3,000 closely concentrated people, it may sometimes have seemed venturesome to the whites to give way to passion and commence a warfare of extermination. Moreover, the natives furnished labor, services, perhaps even food, and soon acquired some means to make their trade worth while. Much, therefore, tended toward a preservation of amicable relations. A little group of hill men, however, was of small potential use; they were too scattered to be available for work, and too poor to buy much; they were likely to be so hungry as to kill cattle or horses on opportunity, and thereby to sow the seeds of a conflict; and however brave and desperate, they were not strong enough to be seriously feared.

RESERVATION INFLUENCE.

The first reservations established by Federal officers in California were little else than bull pens. They were founded on the principle, not of attempting to do something for the native, but of getting him out of the white man's way as cheaply and hurriedly as possible. The reason that the high death rate that must have prevailed among these makeshift assemblages was not reported on more emphatically is that the Indians kept running away even faster than they could die.

The few reservations that were made permanent have on the whole had a conserving influence on the population after they once settled into a semblance of reasonable order. They did little enough for the Indian directly; but they gave him a place which he could call his own, and where he could exist in security and in contact with his own kind. In this way the many scattered tracts in southern California that came under the jurisdiction of the Mission-Tule Agency have helped to preserve the numbers of Luiseño, Diegueño, and Cahuilla. The Hoopa reserve has done the same for the Hupa. Round Valley Reservation did not check a heavy decrease of the native Yuki, nor Tule River of the Yaudanchi; but, on the other hand, the number of introduced Wailaki, Wintun, and Maidu surviving on the former, and of Yauelmani on the latter, is almost certainly greater than if these people had been allowed to shift for themselves.

PROGRESSION OF THE DECLINE.

Doctor Merriam's estimate of the population at different dates in the nineteenth century tells a graphic story, even though the initial figures seem, for reasons already discussed, too high.

1800	260, 000	1860	35, 000
1834	210, 000	1870	30, 000
1849	100, 000	1880	20, 500
1852	85, 000	1890	18, 000
1856	50, 000	1900	15, 500

The decrease is saddening, however cautiously we may assume the absolute numbers. But excessive exaggerations need also be guarded against, such as the statement sometimes cited that 70,000 California Indians died of epidemic diseases in a few years following 1830.

INHABITED AND UNINHABITED AREAS.

The parts of native California which actually contained permanent settlements at one time or another formed a small fraction of the total area of the State. It is true that there were probably no regions which remained wholly unvisited, that most tracts were likely to be frequented seasonally for some food that they yielded, and that large areas came in this way to be wandered over and camped on. But there were no true nomadic tribes in California. Every group had some spot that it considered its home; here stood its most durable houses, and here the winters, or a considerable part of each year, were normally lived. It is these spots that were not distributed randomly over the whole extent of California, but clung to main water courses, valleys or their edges, and the more open canyons. The higher mountains, dense timber, rolling hills, the plains in the intervals between streams, and, of course, the vast preponderance of the deserts never held permanent settlements. In short, the Indian did not think of territory in terms of plane area as we do. Every representation of group lands as filling areas on the map is therefore misleading and must be considered a makeshift tolerable only as long as our precise knowledge of the facts remains inadequate for most regions.

CHAPTER 58.

PLACE NAMES.

TYPES OF PLACE NAMES.

It is well known to all who are sufficiently interested in the American Indian's point of view to make any inquiry into such matters, that the names which he gives to his settlements and to localities are normally descriptive, or at most based on some trivial but unusual happening. Romantic Indian names have been coined by romantic Americans through a species of prevalent self-deception. Just as we actually have Smithville or Warner or Leadville or Salmon Creek or Bald Mountain and leave Bridal Veil and Lover's Leap for occasional show places frequented by the idle and emotionally poor but hungry tourist, so the Indian will have his "clover valley" or "red rock" or "snow mountain" or "deer-watering place" or "bear fell down" and never dream of a "home of the mists" or "great Spirit's abode." His place names now and then are based on allusions to his mythology; but even in that case he is convinced that the event in question really happened, and that the formation of the ground or of a rock is evidence that it happened there.

All this applies to the California Indian as to the American Indian in general. There are, however, certain points in which native place names differ from our own. They are never based on the names of persons. They are also rarely if ever taken over from another language. The California Indian translates into his own tongue the place names of his neighbors or of the aliens whom his ancestors may long ago have gradually dispossessed; or he makes up a descriptive name of his own. Names of the type of our Washington, Philadelphia, Massachusetts, and Detroit are therefrore unrepresented among the Indians.

NORTH CENTRAL CALIFORNIA.

Some examples from tribes of the most diverse speech will illustrate.

The following are typical Yuki place names: Red rock, bent over, brush mouth, wide madroña, woodpecker sits on rock, for crossing water (a ford), salmon rock, snail rock, strong rock, peak, wormwood hole, water mouth, wide rock, dust flat, large dust, ground water, alder creek, flint hole, willow stream, deer eat pepperwood mouth, bear water, large water, sand, white rock ridge, white flower barrier, live-oak peak, good earth, tangled pines, wolf hole peak, pine-nut flat, wide water hole, skunk hole, hissing water drink (a hot spring), tan-oak hole, mountain-live-oak crotch, tree sifting-basket, rock, alder mouth, fir peak, large brush ridge, buckeye peak, large rocks together, sore canyon, large canyon, brush stands, cedars stand, windy rock.

Pomo names of settlements and camp sites run along similar lines: Wind tree (i. e., wind-bent tree), pine hole, hollow trail, tobacco hole, obsidian creek, shady, madroña flat, bear throws out, hand bog, grind pepperwood-nuts, hollow mussel, under the rock, east corner, milk-snake builds, dam mouth, willow valley, water-lily valley, string valley, rock mountain, scorched sweat-house, red-ant house, owl mountain, between the ground, clover corner, crow water, hand hangs, large, cold water valley, ground-squirrel water, valley end, between the rocks, north valley, old water place, rock house, large sand, mellow ashes, red mountain, river mouth, earth sweathouse, peeled tree, west point, south coyote gulch, bark fallen across, clover place, coyote house, west mountain, burned sweat house, pestle rock, west canyon, white-willow canyon, angelica mountain.

Some of these names evidently refer to episodes and to mythical incidents, and a few must be taken metaphorically, but the majority are directly descriptive of natural or conspicuous features or of the abundance of an animal or plant.

NORTHWESTERN CALIFORNIA.

A few Karok and Yurok town names: In the basket, upper dam, lower dam, make a dam, lake, ghosts, pepperwoods, great large, trail descends, clay, watch for ducks, they dance.

Athabascan place names frequently end in suffixes meaning " place " or " in "; but the body of the word is similar in character to those in other languages. Thus the towns shown on the Chilula map (Fig. 13), excepting the first, the eleventh, and the fifteenth, are named in order: Waterfall place, in the small glade, large timber point, near the large timber, down-hill ridge runs on, lying bones place, facing the water place, door upstream place, in the flat, flying dust place, among the willows place, projecting willows place, Yurok house place, in the slide, among the wild-syringa place.

SOUTH CENTRAL CALIFORNIA.

Yokuts place names seem unusually simple, because this language is averse to compounded words, but their meanings are nevertheless of the usual character. For instance, for villages: Cane, ground-squirrels' holes, salt grass, arrow, drink, markings, gate, deer's hole, clover, Jimson weed, bone, hole, sowing, wind, brush-shades. Most of these end in the locative -u in the original, but as this is only a case ending, it has not been translated. Yokuts place names are: Water's fall, dog's hole, rattlesnake's holes, eye, hot-spring, supernatural. Being tribally organized, the Yokuts also possess a few towns named in accord with their political divisions, though it is possible that these villages once bore specific local names. Thus: Tulamniu, Tahayu, Kochoyu, Dalinau, Suksanau, Kiawitnau: Tulamni place, Tuhohi place, Kechayi place, Dalinchi place, Chukchansi place, Koyeti place. It is not certain whether the spot was named after the tribe or the tribe after the village. The lack of exact agreement between the corresponding place and group names may be due to prevailing employment of the latter in the mouths of aliens of somewhat divergent dialect.

SOUTHERN CALIFORNIA.

Chumash names are also generally uncompounded: Bowstring, beach, moon, my eye, my ear, yucca, fish. These are all village names.

A few southern California Shoshonean place names can be added: Poison-oak, willow, doves drink, small woods, small roses, water, warm water, at the salt, river, pine water, alkali water, deer moon, cottonwood, pines, ears, road-runner's mortar.

With the Mohave elaborately compounded names are once more encountered. They are often of an unwieldly length. They are also more inclined to be colored by fancy than among the other Californians; that is, a fair proportion of the names are not directly descriptive of a visible feature, or of a practice customary there. For instance: Mortar mountain, three mountains, blue mountain, sharp mountain, lizard mountain, willow water, faecal sand, owls regarding each other, duck water, pine land rattlesnake tooth, hawk nose, see deer, yellow waterhole, fear slough, covered with sand, no water, water tears through, thick *akyasa* plants, lie in the middle, beaver house, tule water, football surmounts, dove's breast, whispering place, mosquito cannot, retches, cut earth, fat earth, gambling-ring place, four mortars, fight with club, yellow ocher washed open.

Diegueño names are sometimes simple, sometimes of Mohave type: hollow over, far above, my water, large valley, red earth, white earth, middle of the sky, lie on rock, flows in opposite, wrap around neck, hot water, rain above, large mountain, Chaup's house mountain, large, foam, pair of live oaks stands.

MEANINGLESS NAMES.

In all the native languages there are some place names that can not be translated by the Indians. The number of these, however, reduces rapidly in proportion to the degree to which the language has been studied and resolved into its elements. There is probably everywhere a residuum of unanalyzable names, which long usage has crystallized into a meaningless form. But there is also every indication that this residuum is smaller than among ourselves, and that in general the California Indian is more conscious, at least potentially, of the denotation of his place names than we are. Where we are content with an age-old term without inquiring into what it may signify, or when called upon for a new name, apply the name of a settler or repeat a geographical designation familiar from another part of the world, the Indian draws upon his imaginative faculties and makes a word. Only, this imagination is observant, practical and directly descriptive, and not intended to be exercised poetically

TABLE 12.—SOURCE OF SOME CALIFORNIA PLACE NAMES OF INDIAN ORIGIN.

Acalanes...... Costanoan (?) village (?).
Aguanga...... Luiseño place name.
Ahwahnee.... Miwok village in Yosemite valley.
Algootoon.... Perhaps Luiseño "raven."
Anacapa...... Chumash.
Anapamu.... Chumash.
Ausaymas.... Costanoan village.
Azusa......... Gabrielino place name; perhaps "skunk place."
Bally .... Wintun "peak."
Bohemotash.. Wintun "large —."
Bolbones..... Costanoan village.
Bully Choop.. Wintun "peak —."
Buriburi...... Costanoan village.
Cahto........ Pomo "lake" or "mush water."
Cahuenga.... Gabrielino place name.
Cahuilla...... Given as "master," but doubtful if Indian.
Calleguas..... Chumash "my head."
Calpella...... Pomo "mussel carrier."
Camulos...... Chumash "my mulus," a fruit.
Capay........ Wintun "stream."
Carquinez.... Wintun village.
Caslamayomi. Pomo or Coast Miwok "— place."
Castac........ Chumash "my eye."
Caymus...... Wappo village.
Chagoopa..... Probably Mono.
Chanchelulla. Probably Wintun.
Chemehuevi.. Probably the Mohave name of a Shoshonean tribe.
Choenimne... Yokuts tribe.
Cholame..... Salinan village.
Chowchilla... Yokuts tribe.
Cleone....... Pomo village.
Collayomi.... Coast Miwok "— place."
Coloma....... Maidu village.
Colusa....... Wintun village.
Concow....... Maidu "valley place."
Cosmit....... Diegueño place name.
Coso.......... Probably Shoshonean.
Cosumnes..... Miwok village.
Cotati........ Coast Miwok village.
Cucamonga... Gabrielino village.
Cuyama...... Chumash place name.
Cuyamaca.... Diegueño "rain above."

Guajome..... Luiseño place name.
Gualala....... Pomo "stream mouth."
Guatay....... Diegueño "large."
Guenoc....... Indian, but unidentified.
Guesisosi..... Probably Wintun.
Guilicos..... Coast Miwok name of a Wappo village.
Guyapipe..... Diegueño "rock lie on."
Hanaupah.... Shoshonean.
Hetch Hetchy Miwok name of a plant.
Hettenchow.. Wintun "camass valley."
Homoa...... Serrano place name.
Honcut...... Maidu village.
Hoopa....... Yurok name of Athabascan valley.
Horse Linto... Athabascan village.
Huasna...... Probably Chumash village.
Hueneme.... Chumash place name.
Huichica...... Coast Miwok village.
Hyampom... Wintun "— place."
Iaqua........ Athabascan, Yurok, Wiyot, etc., salutation.
Iñaja......... Diegueño "my water."
Inyo......... Possibly Shoshonean.
Ivanpah...... Probably Southern Paiute.
Jalama....... Chumash village.
Jamacha..... Diegueño name of a wild squash-like plant.
Jamul........ Diegueño "foam."
Jolon......... Probably Salinan.
Juristac...... Costanoan "— at."
Jurupa....... Serrano place name.
Kaweah..... Yokuts tribe.
Kaiaiauwa.... Possibly Miwok.
Kekawaka... Probably Indian, but unidentified.
Kenoktai..... Pomo "woman mountain."
Kenshaw.... Probably Wintun.
Kibesillah.... Pomo "rock flat."
Kimshew.... Maidu "— stream."
Klamath..... Probably either Lutuami "people" or Chinook name of the group.
Koip......... Probably Mono "mountain sheep."
Kuna........ Perhaps Mono "firewood."

TABLE 12.—SOURCE OF SOME CALIFORNIA PLACE NAMES OF INDIAN ORIGIN—Con.

Lasseck......	Name of an Athabascan chief.
Locoallomi...	Coast Miwok name of a Wappo village.
Loconoma....	Wappo "goose-town."
Lompoc......	Chumash village.
Lospe........	Possibly Chumash.
Malibu......	Chumash village.
Mallacomes...	Wappo village.
Marin........	Probably Spanish name of a Coast Miwok Indian headman.
Matajuai......	Diegueño "white earth."
Matilija......	Chumash place name.
Mattole......	Probably Wiyot or Athabascan.
Mettah......	Yurok village.
Modoc.......	Lutuami "south."
Mohave......	Mohave name of themselves.
Mokelumne...	Miwok "people of Mokel," a village.
Monache.....	Yokuts name of a Shoshonean division.
Mono........	Same as Monache.
Moorek......	Yurok village.
Moristul......	Wappo "north valley."
Morongo.....	Serrano local group.
Muah........	Probably Mono.
Mugu........	Chumash "beach."
Musalacon....	Pomo, perhaps a chief's name.
Muscupiabe...	Serrano place name.
Najalayegua..	Chumash village.
Napa.........	Probably Pomo "harpoon point."
Natoma......	Maidu "north place" or "upstream people."
Nimshew.....	Maidu "large stream."
Nipomo......	Chumash village.
Nojogui......	Probably a Chumash village.
Nomcult......	Wintun "west people."
Nopah.......	Perhaps Shoshonean.
Noyo.........	Pomo village.
Ojai..........	Chumash "moon."
Olanche......	Perhaps a form of Yaudanchi, a Yokuts tribe.
Olema.......	Coast Miwok "coyote valley."
Oleta........	Perhaps Miwok.
Olompali....	Coast Miwok "south —."
Omjumi......	Perhaps Maidu "rock —."
Omo..........	Miwok village.
Omochumnes.	Miwok "people of Umucha."
Ono.........	Possibly Wintun "head."
Orestimba ...	Perhaps Costanoan "bear —."
Orick........	Yurok village.
Osagon.......	Yurok place name.
Otay........	Diegueño "brushy."
Pacoima.....	Perhaps a Gabrielino place name.
Pala..........	Luiseño "water."
Pamo........	Probably a Diegueño place name.
Panamint.....	Name of a Shoshonean division.
Paskenta.....	Wintun "under the bank."
Pauba........	Perhaps a Luiseño place name.
Pauja........	Diegueño place name.
Pauma.......	Luiseño village.
Pecwan......	Yurok village.
Petaluma.....	Coast Miwok "flat back."
Piru..........	Shoshonean name of a Chumash village: a plant.
Pismo........	Perhaps a Chumash place name.
Piute, Pahute.	A Shoshonean division.
Pohono......	Probably Miwok.
Pomo........	Pomo "people."
Poonkiny....	Yuki "wormwood."
Poway.......	Diegueño or Luiseño.
Requa........	Probably a Yurok village.
Saboba.......	Luiseño place name.
Sanel.........	Pomo village: "dance house."
Saticoy.......	Chumash village.
Sequan.......	Diegueño name of a bush.
Sequit........	Chumash or Gabrielino.
Sespe........	Chumash village; perhaps "fish."
Shasta.......	Uncertain; most likely name of a Shasta headman.
Simi..........	Chumash place name.
Siskiyou.....	Uncertain; perhaps Oregon Indian.

TABLE 12.—SOURCE OF SOME CALIFORNIA PLACE NAMES OF INDIAN ORIGIN—Con.

Sisquoc	Probably a Chumash place name.	Tequepis	Chumash village.
Skukum	Chinook jargon "strong."	Tinaquaic	Perhaps a Chumash place name.
Somis	Chumash village.	Tinemaha	Perhaps Shoshonean.
Sonoma	Probably a Wappo suffix, meaning "village of."	Tishtangatang	Hupa village.
Soquel	Probably a Costanoan village.	Tissaack	Miwok place name of mythological origin.
Sotoyome	Pomo "place of Soto," a chief.	Tocaloma	Probably a Coast Miwok place name.
Suey	Perhaps a Chumash place name.	Tolenas	Wintun village.
		Tomales	Coast Miwok "bay."
Suisun	Wintun village or tribe.	Toowa	Probably a Mono word.
Surper	Yurok village.	Topanga	Gabrielino place name.
Suscol	Wintun village.	Topa Topa	Chumash place name.
Taboose	Perhaps a Mono Shoshonean word.	Truckee	Name of a Northern Paiute chief.
Tache	Yokuts tribe.	Tulucay	Wintun village, "red."
Tahoe	Washo "lake."	Tuolumne	Probably a Yokuts tribe.
Tahquitz	Luiseño divinity.	Ukiah	Pomo "south valley."
Taijiguas	Chumash village.	Ulatus	Wintun village or division.
Tajauta	Probably Gabrielino place name.	Ulistac	Costanoan "at ulis."
Tamalpais	Coast Miwok "bay mountain."	Un Bully	Wintun "— peak."
		Usal	Pomo "south —."
Tapu	Chumash "yucca."	Wahtoke	Yokuts "pine nut."
Tatu	Pomo name for the Huchnom.	Weeyot	Yurok name of the Wiyot.
Tecuya	Yokuts name of the Chumash.	Weitchpec	Yurok village: "at the forks."
Tehachapi	Yokuts, perhaps also Shoshonean, place name.	Winum Bully	Wintun "— peak."
		Yallo Bally	Wintun "snow peak."
Tehama	Wintun village.	Ydalpom	Wintun "north — place."
Tehipite	Perhaps a Mono Shoshonean word.	Yokohl	Yokuts tribe.
		Yolo	Wintun village.
Tejunga	Gabrielino place name.	Yosemite	Miwok: usually said to mean "grizzly bear;" perhaps "killers."
Temecula	Luiseño village; possibly "sun —."		
Tenaya	Miwok chief.	Yreka	Probably Shasta name for Mount Shasta.
Tepusquet	Perhaps a Chumash place name.	Yuba	Maidu village.
		Yucaipa	Serrano place name.
		Yuma	Probably Indian, but unidentified.

CHAPTER 59

CULTURE PROVINCES.

AREAS OF DISTINCTIVE CIVILIZATION IN CALIFORNIA.

Constant outright and implied reference has been made through this book to the three or four areas of culture, or ethnic provinces, distinguishable in native California. Roughly, the Tehachapi Range and the vicinity of Point Concepcion mark off the southern from the central type of civilization, while the northwestern extends south to a line running from Mount Shasta to Cape Mendocino or a little beyond. East of the crest of the Sierra Nevada the culture of central California changes into that of Nevada, or more properly of the Great Basin. In the south, the Colorado River, with some of the adjoining desert, must be set apart from the mountain and coast tracts.

Yet any map creates an erroneous impression of internal uniformity and coherence. Thus, all in all, the Yokuts are probably more similar to the Wintun in the totality of their life than to the Gabrielino. But innumerable cultural elements have reached the Yokuts from the south, and they themselves have very likely developed local peculiarities of which some have filtered across the mountains to the Gabrielino. Consequently any presentation which tended to create the impression that the Yokuts and Wintun belonged to a block of nations in which certain traits were standard and exclusive would mislead.

Just so in the northwest. The moment the Yurok and Hupa are left behind, central Californian traits begin to appear even among their most immediate neighbors. These increase in number and intensity among the peoples to the south and east. After a time

898

we find ourselves among tribes such as the Coast Yuki, who undoubtedly appertain to the central province. Yet these still make string or bury the dead or do various other things in the most distinctive northwestern manner.

CENTERS OF CIVILIZATION.

On the other hand, certain centers or hearths of the several types of culture become apparent rather readily and the increase of information, instead of distracting and confusing the impressions first formed, strengthens them: each focus becomes narrower and more distinct.

NORTHWESTERN.

Thus there seems no possible ground to doubt that the center of gravity and principal point of influence of the northwestern culture was the limited area occupied by the Yurok, Karok, and Hupa. Its precise point of gathering has been discussed in the first chapter of this book.

CENTRAL.

The heart of the central province is not quite so definite, but unquestionably lay between the Pomo, the more southerly Wintun or Patwin, and the Valley Maidu; with the Wintun, as the middle one of the three, the most likely leaders.

SOUTHERN.

In the south, one center is recognizable on or near the coast. The most developed peoples about this were the Chumash, Gabrielino, and Luiseño. As regards religion and institutions, we happen to know by far the most about the Luiseño; but there is direct evidence that a considerable part of Luiseño customs was imported from the Gabrielino, and precedence must therefore be given to this people. As to the choice between them and the Chumash, the Gabrielino must again be favored. Our knowledge of Chumash practices is scant, but there is so complete an absence of indications of their having seriously influenced the institutions of their neighbors that their civilization, at least on this side, can hardly have had the potency of that of the Gabrielino. A complication is indeed caused by material culture, which so far as it can be reconstructed from early descriptions, and particularly through the evidence of archaeology, was most developed among the Chumash and among a special branch of the Gabrielino who through their island habitat were in closest communication with the Chumash. Again, however, Chumash example did not reach far; and it is therefore likely that it is a localized development of technology which confronts us among the Chumash, as against a much more penetrating and influential growth of social and religious institutions among the Gabrielino.

COLORADO RIVER.

The hearth of the type of culture which radiated from the Colorado River must beyond doubt be sought either among the Mohave or the Yuma. As between the two, the Mohave are probably entitled to precedence, both because they were the more populous tribe, and because it appears to be solely their influence which has reached to northern groups like the Chemehuevi, whereas southern tribes like the Diegueño give unmistakable evidence of having been affected by the Mohave as well as by the nearer Yuma.

Geographical position, on the other hand, would point to the Yuma, who are not only more centrally situated than the Mohave with reference to tribes of the same lineage, but have their seats at the mouth of the chief affluent of the Colorado, the Gila, up and down which there must have gone on considerable communication with the Pima, the non-Yuman tribe of the Southwest which on the whole seems to be culturally most nearly related to the Yumans of the Colorado Valley. The Yuma had the Cocopa and other groups below them toward the mouth of the river; but above the Mohave as well as to their west there lived only Shoshoneans. Further, the Diegueño and the various Yuman groups of the northern half of Baja California are much more nearly in contact with the Yuma. General probability would therefore lead to an expectation of the focus of the Yuman culture of the Colorado being below the Mohave, among or near the Yuma. It seems not unlikely that if we could trace the history of this area sufficiently far back such would prove to have been the case, but that in recent centuries the Mohave, owing to an increase in numbers or for some other reason, have taken the lead in cultural productivity.

These four centers are indicated by crosses on the map in Figure 74.

AN IRREGULARITY.

Several peculiar traits, some of them positive and some of them negative, are found in a region which forms a sort of tongue separating the San Joaquin Valley from southern California. This region lacks pottery, which occurs on both sides of it; practices burial instead of cremation; is without exogamic institutions, which are also known both to the north and south; and is the area in which the so-called "bottle-neck" basket is dominant. The distribution of these several cultural elements is not identical, but in general they characterize the peoples from the southern Yokuts and Tübatulabal to the Chumash. A radiation from the latter people can scarcely be thought of because specifically Chumash features do not occur among the peoples inhabiting the more northerly part of the tongue. A possible Shoshonean influence from the Great Basin must be disallowed on parallel grounds. In fact, the traits in question are so few and diverse that it is doubtful whether they have any historical connection. If they are intrinsically associated it is perhaps chiefly through the fact that this middle and upland region failed to be reached in certain respects by both central and southern influences.

NATURE OF THE CENTERS.

It would, of course, be a grave mistake to assume that the whole of each type of culture had emanated from the group or small array of groups situated at its focus. Every tribe must be viewed as contributing to the civilization or civilizations of which it partakes. It is only that the most intensive development or greatest specialization of culture has occurred at the hearth. This renders it probable that more influences have flowed out from the center to the peripheries than in the opposite direction. But the movement must necessarily always have been reciprocal in considerable degree. What has probably happened in many cases is that the tribe which carried a certain set of practices and institutions farthest came thereby to attain a status in which it reacted more powerfully upon its neighbors in other respects, so that the civilizational streams which gathered into it were made over and caused to stream out again. In this sense the central or focal groups may have been influential in coloring to some degree the culture of their entire areas, while contributing in each case probably only a very small proportion of the substance thereof.

It will be seen that the cultural centers as here described are those indicated on the religious map (Pl. 74). In part this coincidence may be due to a rather heavy weighting of religious factors in the estimation of culture wholes—a procedure that seems necessary, since a definitely organized set of cults is like the flower to the plant—unquestionably one of the highest products of civilization. But the constitution of society, the use of wealth and attitude toward it, the material arts and industries, the type of mythology, music, and what may be called literature, correspond almost without exception, in the degrees of their complexity or specialization, to the elaborateness of religion. This cult map, then, although not an accurate geographical representation of the distribution of native civilizations in California, probably indicates their history about as well as would any averaged outline, and serves to balance or even correct the necessarily arbitrary delimitations which a culture province map like Figure 74 attempts.

It need hardly be added that a considerable concentration of population would be expectable at the focus of each province, together with a perceptible thinning out of numbers toward the margins. This, so far as can be judged, was the case. It is, however, of interest that diverse topographies are represented by the centers. In the northwest, the distinctive physiographic feature of the focal area is streams of sufficient size to be navigable and rich in salmon; in the central province it is the heart of a great valley; in the south a group of islands and a mainland shore washed by still ocean reaches; and at the southeast the vast Colorado with its annually overflowed bottom lands in the midst of a great desert. No single type of physical environment can therefore be said to have been permanently stimulative to concentration of numbers and the furtherance of civilization in California; except that there is a clear tendency for cultural focus to be situated on important drainage.

The annual run-off of the Klamath at Keno, before it has received notable affluents, is over $1\frac{1}{2}$ million acre-feet, which may be estimated to be perhaps doubled in its lower course. The Colorado at Yuma carries 16 millions; the Sacramento at Red Bluff over 10 millions, to which the Feather, Yuba, and American add nearly 13 millions. The total flow through Carquinez Straits, after considerable diversion for irrigation, is about 26 million acre-feet, derived probably more than three-fourths from the Sacramento and less than one-fourth from the San Joaquin half of the interior valley. It is evident that the Yurok, southern Wintun, and Yuma-Mohave centers of culture are closely correlated with the points of maximal flow of the three greatest drainage systems of California; although as between these three centers the degree of cultural advancement does not correlate with the relative amount of drainage. That is, on comparison of one area with another, inference that the one situated on the larger stream will be the more advanced in type of civilization does not hold for this part of the continent; but within one drainage or series of parallel and related drainages the advancement is greatest at the point of largest flow.

That the cultural importance of an ocean frontage must not be overestimated for California is clear from the relation of the Coast Yurok to the River Yurok, of the Wiyot to the Hupa, of the Pomo of the coast to those of Russian River and Clear Lake, of the Costanoans and Esselen to Yokuts, where, as discussed in previous chapters, the interior people seem in each case to have been the more prosperous.

NORTHWESTERN CALIFORNIA AND THE NORTH PACIFIC COAST CULTURE.

All of the cultures of California are without question at least partly related in origin to more widely spread civilizations outside the State.

The northwestern culture is obviously part of that generally known as the culture of the North Pacific coast. The center of this larger civilization is clearly in British Columbia, but this center is so remote that any specific comparison of the Yurok and Hupa with the Kwakiutl or Haida would be unprofitable. In Washington and Oregon, however, three subtypes of this culture are recognizable, after exclusion of three inland cultures: that of the Plateau east of the Cascades; the curiously simple' culture of the Kalapuya in the Willamette Valley; and of the Lutuamian Klamath and Modoc in the Klamath Lake basin. The three coastal provinces, which chiefly come into question in a comparison with north California, are, in order from the north, and as sketched in Figure 73:

(1) *Puget Sound*, with all or part of the Olympic Peninsula, and probably the southeastern portion of Vancouver Island and the opposite coast of British Columbia. The groups in this area are clearly

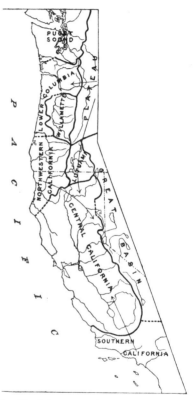

FIG. 73.—Subculture areas on the Pacific coast of the United States.

dependent for much of their culture on the Kwakiutl and other tribes to the north. Coast Salish groups are the principal ones in this province.

(2) *The Lower Columbia*, up to The Dalles, with the coast from about Shoalwater Bay on the north to lower Umpqua River on the south. The Chinook were nearly central and perhaps dominant. Other members were the Yakonan Alsea and Siuslaw, the most southerly of the coast Salish, and a few Athabascans.

(3) *Southwestern Oregon*, probably from the Umpqua and the Calapooya Mountains and inland to the Cascade Range. The principal stream is Rogue River, but the Coquille and upper Umpqua seem to have formed part. The abutment is on four ethnic subprovinces: the Lower Columbian just outlined, the Kalapuyan of the Willamette, the Lutuamian of the Klamath Lake drainage, and the northwest Californian of the Klamath River. The majority of the inhabitants were Athabascans; the other groups were the Kus and Takelma and a branch of the Shasta. The Takelma, except for being wholly off the coast, may be taken as typical.

Table 13 summarizes the principal comparable ethnic traits of these three regions and of northwestern California. It appears at once that northwestern California and southwestern Oregon are very closely related, so much so, in fact, as to constitute but a single area. They agree about three times out of four in the cases in which either of them differs from the Lower Columbia. The latter in turn seems rather more closely connected with Puget Sound than with southwestern Oregon, whether chiefly as a marginal dependent or, as seems more likely, as a separate center of some distinctness, can scarcely yet be decided, and need not be in the present connection. The important fact is that the general culture of the coast is decisively altered somewhere in the region of the Umpqua Mountains, and that thence south, as far as it prevails at all, that is, to Cape Mendocino, it is substantially uniform. In other words, we need not recognize three provinces of the coast culture in Oregon and Washington and a fourth in California: there were only three south of the forty-ninth parallel. The first lay in Washington with some extension into British Columbia; the second was mainly Oregonian with some overlap into Washington; the third centered in northern California but ran well into Oregon.

TABLE 13.—COAST CULTURES OF NORTHERN CALIFORNIA, OREGON, AND WASHINGTON.

	Northwestern California.	Southwestern Oregon.	Lower Columbia.	Puget Sound.
BODY AND DRESS.				
Head deformation	None.	None.	Universal; sign of free birth.	General.
Tattooing:				
Women	Chin almost solidly covered.	Three stripes on chin.	Little; none on face.	Little; none on face.
Men	Measuring lines on arm.	Measuring lines on arm.		
Women's hair	2 clubs in front.	2 clubs[1].	Parted, but flowing.	
Nose ornament	Dentalium[2].	Dentalium.	Dentalium.	Probably none.
Woman's hat	Brimless cap.	Brimless cap[3].	Brim, peak, and knob.	Same; or flattened cone.
Man's hat	None[4].	Fur cap.		None.
Man's deerskin shirt	None[4].	Worn.	None.	
Man's leggings	In snow only[4].	Reported.	Only inland.	
Man's robe	Of deer fur.	Of deer fur.	Twined fur strips or mountain goat wool.	Woven cedar bark or dog hair.
Woman's petticoat	Fringed deerskin; shaman's of fiber.	Fiber.	Fiber.	Fiber.
Woman's deerskin gown	None[4].	Mentioned as if customary[5].	Only inland.	
HOUSES.				
Material	Redwood where available.	Sugar pine, cedar; poor people: bark.	Cedar; inland: bark.	Cedar.
Position of planks	Vertical.	Vertical.	Vertical.	Horizontal.
Breadth (feet)	20.	12.	Up to 30 or 40.	Up to 60.

[1] Takelma: men shamans.
[2] Karok, Tolowa; Yurok and Hupa bore the nose of the dead.
[3] Takelma imported caps from California.
[4] The Shasta agree with the Oregonians.
[5] The Takelma speak of a gown with fringes of *Xerophyllum*: perhaps a hybrid of gown and Yurok petticoat, or a confused description of the latter.

TABLE 13.—COAST CULTURES OF NORTHERN CALIFORNIA, OREGON, AND WASHINGTON—Continued.

	Northwestern California.	Southwestern Oregon.	Lower Columbia.	Puget Sound.
HOUSES—continued.				
Length (feet)	23	15–20	Up to 100	Up to 500.
Subdivisions	None [6]	None	Present	Present.
Mat beds	On floor	On floor; girls on platform	On raised platform	On raised platform.
Excavation	Center of house only, 2–5 feet	Whole area, 1–5 feet	Whole area, 3–5 feet	Whole area, 3–5 feet.
Entrance	Round	Rectangular	Round or oval	Round or oval.
Door	Sliding	Sliding	Hung	
Ridges	Two	One	One	None; shed roof.
Carving or painting	None	None	Found	Found.
Summer house	No	Brush hut	Rush lodge	
Inmates	7–8	10+?	Several families	Several families.
SWEAT HOUSE.				
Permanent, sunk	Oblong, of planks, no earth covering	Rectangular, of planks, earth covered	Referred to in myths	Doubtful.
Movable [7]	None	For women only	None on coast; inland, doubtful	Doubtful.
Occupance	6–7 men sleep in	6 men sleep in		
Heat	Fire	Steam from hot stones	Doubtful	
CANOE.				
Material	Redwood		Cedar	Cedar.
Length (feet)	18		Up to 40 or 50	40–50.
Shape	Blunt prow	"Like butcher's tray"	Sharp prow; blunt inland	Sharp prow.

Painted or carved	No	Yes	Yes
Coasting voyages	No	Yes	Yes
BASKETRY.			
Twining:			
Warp	Hazel	Hazel or willow	
Weft	Split conifer roots	Split roots	Split roots
White patterns	Xerophyllum tenax	probably Xerophyllum	Xerophyllum tenax
Black patterns	Maidenhair fern	mud dyed	
Red patterns	Alder dyed	Alder dyed	
Decorating technique	Overlaid (faced) weft	Probably overlaid weft	Wrapped twining; false embroidery.
Checker and twill work	None	Not mentioned	Made.
Coiling	None	None	Inland; North of Columbia: imbricated.
Wallets and bags	None	Not mentioned	
Conical burden basket	Yes	Yes	
Mortar hopper	Yes	Yes	Not mentioned
Cradle	Twined	Twined	Wooden.
FOOD.			
Salmon	Staple	Important	Staple.
Acorns	Staple	Staple among Takelma	No.
Camass and bulbs	Some bulbs	Some bulbs	
Wasp larvæ	Eaten	Eaten	
Tobacco	Cultivated	Cultivated	Little used.

[6] Except a little anteroom for the storage of wood.

[7] The Plains type: low and small, of mats thrown over willows.

TABLE 13.—COAST CULTURES OF NORTHERN CALIFORNIA, OREGON, AND WASHINGTON—Continued.

	Northwestern California.	Southwestern Oregon.	Lower Columbia.	Puget Sound.
UTENSILS.				
Salmon harpoon	Two-pronged	Apparently two-pronged		
Seed beater	Of basketry	A stick		
Slab mortar	Used	Used		
Mush paddle	Used	Used		
Spoons	Elk antler; geometric carving.	Elk antler	Mountain sheep or goat; geometric carving.	Mountain sheep or goat; animal carving.
Wooden troughs or bowls	Rude, unornamented		Well made, ornamented	
Joined boxes	None		Probably only imported	Made.
Drum	None	None (among Takelma)		
SOCIETY.				
Cause of social rank	Possession of wealth	Possession of wealth	Possession of wealth	Birth plus wealth.
Foundation of slavery	Debt	Debt	War	War.
Slave sacrifice	No	No	Occasional	Occasional.
Village exogamy	No	No	No	
Clans	No trace	No trace	No trace	
Descent	Paternal	Paternal	Paternal	Paternal.
Potlatch	No	No record	Unimportant	Important.
Measurement of dentalia	By fives or number to arm length.	By tens	By number to fathom	
Burial	In ground, recumbent	In ground, sitting	In canoes; inland, in houses.	In canoes or boxes, often elevated.

WAR.				
Armor	Of rods or elk hide	"Elk hide over rods," hide helmets.	Of rods or elk hide	
Shield	None	Not reported	Few: probably inland only.	
War dance	Of incitement or settlement, not scalp dance.	Of incitement, apparently		
RELIGION.				
Masks or societies	None	None	None	Some.
Formulas	Long, narrative or dramatic.	Brief, type of prayers		
Girls' adolescence ceremony	Yes [8]	Yes [9]	Yes	Yes.
Ritual number	5, 10.	5	5	5.
Cause of disease	Pain object in body	Pain object in body	Pain object or theft of soul	
Source of shaman's power	Pain objects received from spirits.	Spirits	Spirits	Spirits.
Sex of shamans	Chiefly women	Men or women	Chiefly men	
Non-shamans own spirits	Rarely	Sometimes	Generally	

[8] Weakest among the Yurok.
[9] The Takelma ceremony is very similar to that of Karok and Shasta. The girl may not look about, wears a visor of bluejay feathers, sleeps with her head in a mortar hopper. For five days men and women dance in a circle.

NORTHWESTERN CALIFORNIA AND OREGON.

The cultural predominance of the California over the Oregon tract within this last area can scarcely be proved outright, because the life of the tribes of southwestern Oregon broke and decayed very quickly on contact with the Americans and has been but sadly portrayed. Yet this very yielding perhaps indicates a looseness of civilizational fiber. There may have been highly developed rituals held in southwestern Oregon comparable to the Yurok Deerskin dance, which have not only perished but been forgotten; but it is far more likely that the reason the ceremonies of this region vanished without a trace is that they never amounted to much nor had a deep hold on native life. The Gabrielino have been longer subject to Caucasian demoralization and are as substantially extinct as any Oregon group; but there is no doubt as to their religious and general cultural preeminence over their neighbors. The southern Wintun have been cuffed about for a century and are nearly gone, but it is reasonably clear that the Kuksu cult and culture centered among them. If the Rogue River tribes had cultivated a religion surpassing or even rivaling that of the groups on the Klamath, it is scarcely conceivable that its very memory should have dissolved in two generations.

Where direct evidence is available, it uniformly points the same way. The Yurok house is larger as well as more elaborate than that of the Takelma; the sweat house more specialized; the shamanism appreciably more peculiar; the formulas and myths show a much more distinct characterization. The Takelma give the impression of being not only on a level similar to that of the Shasta, but specifically like them in many features; and the Shasta have been seen to be culturally subsidiary to the Yurok and Karok. What holds for the Takelma there is no reason to doubt held for the Athabascans who nearly surrounded them. The lower Klamath thus is the civilizational focus of the drainage of the Rogue and probably of most of the Umpqua.

CAUSE OF THE PREDOMINANCE OF NORTHWESTERN CALIFORNIA.

This predominance could be laid theoretically to two causes: Exposure to external ethnic influences, or physiographic environment. Extraneous cultural influence can be dismissed in this case. The center of the coast civilization as a whole lay north; the Oregonians were the nearer to it. Central California has given too little to the Klamath region to be of moment—or at least gave only underlying elements, not those specializations that mark the cultural preeminence which is being considered. The latter quality it did not possess, as against northwestern California. Natural environment, therefore, must be the cause; and sufficient explanation is found in the fact that the Klamath is the largest stream entering the Pacific between the Sacramento-San Joaquin on the south and the Columbia on the north—the third largest, in fact, that debouches from this face of the United States. The large stream held the largest number of inhabitants; and, particularly on its lower reaches, allowed them to accumulate densely. This concentration provided the opportunity, or was the cause, however we may wish to put it, of a more active prosecution of social life.

CAUSE OF SOUTHWARD ABRIDGMENT.

It may seem strange that the peak or focus of this culture should be eccentric, that Yurok influence, to call it such, should have extended several times as far to the north as to the south, particularly that it should penetrate to remote parallel streams and not to the headwaters of its own drainage system. Such an objection may seem theoretically valid, but there is precedent to the contrary. The culmination of the North Pacific coast culture as a whole is probably found among the Haida, near the northern end of its long belt. In the Southwest the Pueblos of the Rio Grande have for centuries been culturally predominant, and yet they lie on the eastern edge of the province.

There is accordingly no reason for hesitating to accept as a fact the much more rapid southward than northward fading out of the northwestern culture.

There does not seem to be a satisfactory physiographic explanation for this unequal distribution. That the Trinity and the Eel soon become small streams in a rugged country as their course is followed should not have been sufficient to prevent unchecked spread up them of northwestern influences, since the northwestern culture is well established in a similar environment on the upper Rogue and Umpqua. It would seem, accordingly, that the cause has been a social one. Such a cause can only be sought in the presence of another civilization, in this case that of central California, as represented by the Kuksu dancing nations, and particularly the Pomo. The Pomo subtype of the central culture may therefore be considered as having been established about as long as that of the Yurok. This inference is corroborated by the fact that about the head of the Sacramento Valley, to which the Kuksu cult and basketry of Pomo type have not made their way and where most specific central Californian influences are weak, numerous elements of northwestern civilization have penetrated almost across the breadth of the State.

Physiography can, however, be called in to explain why the culture of the Yurok did not flow more freely east and northeast up its main stream, the Klamath, to the Lutuami. The elevated lake habitat of these people is very different from the region of coastal streams. Moreover, it is nearly shut off from them by the southern end of the great Cascade Range, but is rather open toward the Great Basin and the more northerly Plateau.

THE LUTUAMI SUBCULTURE.

The Lutuamian or Klamath Lakes culture or subculture, as represented in this work by the Modoc, corresponds well with this setting. It reveals some specializations, such as its *wokas* and tule industries, that are obviously founded on peculiar environment. There are some northwestern influences, but rather vague ones. The basis of the culture is perhaps central California, with some Great Basin or Plateau admixture. Since the introduction of the horse, the Lutuami mode of life has evidently been modified analogously to that of the Plateau peoples of the Columbia, although less profoundly; and with the horse came a number of cultural elements from the Plateau, if not from the Plains; of which some went on to the Shasta and Achomawi. This recent modification appears to have given Lutuami culture a more un-Californian aspect than it originally possessed. Neither the Kalapuya nor the Klamath-Modoc were a numerous enough people nor a sufficiently advanced one to have possessed a truly distinctive civilization. The Kalapuya are gone, but nearly a thousand Lutuami remain, and as soon as their society and religion are seriously inquired into, their cultural affiliations will no doubt become clearer.

DRAINAGE, CULTURE, AND SPEECH.

As regards the part of environment in general, it is clear that the culture provinces of the Pacific frontage of the United States are essentially based on natural areas, particularly of drainage. Thus the central Californian province consists of the great interior valley of that State with the adjacent coast. The Plateau is the drainage of the Columbia above the Cascade Range; the Great Basin, the area which finds no outlet to the sea. The one exception is northwestern California, whose ethnic boundary on the north cuts across the Umpqua, and on the south across the Klamath, the Trinity, and the Eel. The streams in this district have a northward trend, and it appears that both the Lower Columbia and the northwestern culture retained enough of the seaboard character of the British Columbia civilization to enable them better to cling along the coast than to push up the long narrow valleys that nearly parallel it.

At the same time there is not a single distinctly maritime culture in the entire stretch from Cape Flattery to Baja California, except in a measure that of Puget Sound. Lower Columbia and northwestern California clearly are river civilizations; that of central California evinces an almost complete negation of understanding or use of the sea. In southern California the acme of culture is indeed attained in and opposite the little Santa Barbara Archipelago; but the great bulk of the province is a canoeless, arid tract.

In nearly every case, too, the province is either composed mainly of people of one stock or family, or one such group dominates civilizationally.

Puget Sound: Salish preponderant, Wakash perhaps most characteristic.

Lower Columbia: Chinook most numerous and distinctive.

Willamette (distinctness doubtful) : wholly Kalapuyan.

Klamath Lakes (distinctness doubtful) : wholly Lutuami.

Northwestern California: Athabascans in the majority, Algonkins culturally dominant.

Central California: distinctly a Penutian province with Hokan fringes.

Southern California: Shoshonean, although the Chumash are not without consequence.

Lower Colorado: Yuman, with perhaps some Shoshonean margin.

Great Basin: Almost solidly Shoshonean.

Plateau: about balanced between Sahaptin and Salish.

It is also notable that in spite of this massing no province is populated wholly by people of one origin. The two apparent exceptions are areas so weak culturally that their proper independence is doubtful.

SOUTHERN CALIFORNIA AND THE SOUTHWESTERN PROVINCE.

Both the Southern California and Lower Colorado cultures present numerous relations to the great Southwestern province, and it is not open to doubt that many of their constituent elements can be traced back to an origin among the Pueblos or the ancestors or cultural kinsmen of the Pueblos. At the same time it would be a very summary and misleading procedure to consider these provinces an outright part of the Southwest. New foci have formed on the spot. If these are to be canceled out merely because they are secondary to an older, more active hearth of influences among the Pueblos, it would be equally justifiable to dismiss the culture of the latter as superficial and unimportant on the ground that its basic constituents have largely radiated out of Mexico. Understanding of the ultimate sources is, of course, indispensable to interpretation, but ramifications and new starts are of no less consequence to an understanding of the history of cultural growths. A direct merging of all the collateral branches into a single type merely on the ground of their relationship would lead to a prevention of the recognition of cultural individuality, as it might be termed, and thereby defeat the very end of truly historical inquiry. In the preceding pages it has been the constant endeavor to point out those elements in the native life of the southern end of California that can be considered as derived from the culture of the Southwest, and at the same time to determine how far the groupings of these elements and the social attitudes thereby established have remained specifically Southwestern or have become regionally peculiar.

The considerable distinctiveness that obtains in the south is perhaps most pregnantly illustrated by the fact that of the two subtypes there, the one geographically nearer to the Southwest proper, that of the Lower Colorado River, is on the whole not appreciably more similar to that of the Pueblos than is the one which has its center on the coast among the Gabrielino and their neighbors. Many things link the Mohave with the Pueblos and with the so-called nomadic tribes of Arizona. Other elements, such as the sand painting, have, however, been pointed out which are common to the Gabrielino and the Southwesterners proper and in which the Mohave and the Yuma do not participate. These elements may be somewhat the less numerous; but so far as can be judged in the present state of knowledge, as reviewed in the chapter on the Yuma, the balance between the two classes is nearly even. From this condition the only conclusion possible is that southwesern influences have infiltrated southern California slowly, irregularly, and disjointedly, with the result that these influences have been worked over into new combinations and even into new products faster than they arrived.

A searching examination of the relation of the southern California and Lower Colorado subcultures to the Southwest will prove of great interest because it will presumably unravel much of the history of civilization in all of these regions. Such an examination can not yet be conducted with satisfaction because the mother culture of Arizona and New Mexico, probably at once the greatest and the most compact native civilization of the continent north of Mexico, and the one which documents and archeology combine to illuminate most fully, has not yet been adequately conceptualized. Agriculture, pottery, stone architecture, clans, masked fraternities, dramatizing rituals are the ethnic activities that rise before the mind; but not one is universal in the Southwest. If the Apache and Havasupai are not southwestern, they are nothing at all; and yet one or both of them fail on every one of these supposed touchstones.

In fact, while ethnologists speak constantly of the Southwest as if it were a well-defined ethnic unit, what they generally have in mind is the Pueblos with perhaps the addition of their town-dwelling ancestors or of the interspersed and Pueblo-influenced Navaho. No satisfying picture that gives proper weight to the un-settled as well as the agricultural tribes has yet been drawn; at least not so as to serve for detailed comparative analysis. The Pima are closely linked with the Pueblos, and in other respects with the Lower Colorado tribes, but to unite them nonchalantly with either would be inadmissible. But so far as they are southwestern, the Papago are; and if the Papago, then, in some measure at least, the Yaqui and Seri also.

The truth is that the Southwest is too insistently complex to be condensed into a formula or surrounded with a line on the map. Essentially this is true of every culture. The Haida no more repre-sent the Chinook and the Yurok than the Hopi can be made to stand for the Pima, nor will an average struck in either case do justice to the essence of the Haida and Hopi ethnos. Such condensing efforts can be condoned only as preliminary steps to historical inquiry, as narrowly ethnological classifications which clear the way to an under-standing of civilizational events. Elsewhere in America cultures are often relatively simple and the time element not present to disturb a purely geographical view; hence the inadequacy of such reductions is less impressed on the student. But in the Southwest the factor of temporal order obtrudes instead of eluding us blankly. Two diverse strains, the life of the town dwellers and of the country dwellers, remain distinct yet are interminably interwoven. Regional differ-ences are striking in short distances and without notable environ-mental basis. And it is clear that the foundation of everything southwestern is Mexican, and yet that everything in the Southwest has taken its peculiar shape and color on the spot. In short, a history of southwestern civilization lies within measurable sight, but the antecedent analysis, which must include southern California, has not yet been made.

CENTRAL CALIFORNIA AND THE GREAT BASIN.

While the north and south of aboriginal California are to be con-strued as marginal regions of greater extraneous cultures, central California remains isolated. It can not be viewed as a subsidiary because the potent civilization on which it might depend does not exist. Its north and the south being accounted for, and the ocean lying on the west, the only direction remaining open for any set of influences is the east, and this is the area of the barren Great Basin, populated by tribes of no greater advancement than the central Cali-

fornians—perhaps even less developed. These tribes could not, therefore, well serve as carriers of culture into central California, if we
may judge by analogy with the spread of civilization in other parts
of the world. As a matter of fact, they did not. Specific culture
elements characteristic of the Plains have not penetrated into California. A few such traits that are discernible in northeastern Cali-

Fɪɢ. 74.—Major culture areas and centers of development within California.

fornia have evidently come in not across the Great Basin but down
the Columbia River and through the interior peoples of Oregon.
Moreover, it is questionable whether these elements have chiefly
entered California anciently or rather as an adjunct of the white
man and the horse. Nor have Southwestern influences penetrated
central California to any appreciable extent by way of the Great
Basin. Where Southwestern elements are traceable in central California, as in the San Joaquin Valley, it is usually probable that
they represent an immediate outflow from southern California.

Yet it is certain that central California and the Great Basin are regions of close cultural kinship. It is true that the food supply and material resources of the interior semidesert have enforced a mode of life which makes a quite different impression. Analogies have therefore been little dwelt upon. Absence of definite records concerning the Shoshoneans of the Great Basin render exact comparisons somewhat difficult even now. Both regions, however, lack in common most of the characteristic traits of the culture adjacent to them; and it is only necessary to set side by side their basketry, their houses, their technical processes or the schemes of their societies, to be convinced that the bonds between the two areas are numerous and significant. This kinship may be expected to be revealed convincingly as soon as a single intensive study of any Great Basin tribe is made from other than a Plains point of view.[1]

It has been the custom among ethnologists to recognize a " Plateau area " as possessing a common although largely negative culture. Our exact information to date regarding the peoples of this " Plateau " is almost wholly from the northern part of the area inhabited by the Salish. It is manifestly hasty to assume for the Shoshoneans of the Great Basin, which constitutes the southern half of this greater " Plateau," substantial cultural identity with the Sahaptin and interior Salish of the north. The latter have been subjected to powerful although incomplete influences from the North Pacific coast proper as well as from the Plains. Plains influences have penetrated also to the Shoshoneans, but the North Pacific coast could hardly have had much effect, and certainly not a direct one, in the Great Basin. The coastward tract here is central California; and we could therefore anticipate, on theoretical grounds, that it had affected the Great Basin Shoshoneans much as the North Pacific coast has influenced the Salish of the Plateau proper, that is, of the upper Columbia and Fraser.

This is exactly the condition to which the available facts point. The civilization of central California is less sharply characterized and less vigorous than that of the coast of British Columbia. Its influences could therefore hardly have been as penetrating. There must have been more give and take between Nevada and central California than between the interior and the coastal districts of British Columbia. But the kinship is clearly of the same kind, and the preponderance of cultural energy is as positively (though less strikingly) on the coast in one tract as in the other. The Kuksu cult and the institutions associated with it have not flowed directly into Utah and Idaho, nor even in any measure into Nevada, but they indicate a dominance of cultural effectiveness. which, merely in a somewhat lower degree. relates central California to the Great Basin substantially as the North Pacific coast is related to the northern Plateau.

---

[1] See Lowie in bibliography.

THE IDEA OF A CALIFORNIAN CULTURE AREA.

The "California culture area" of the older American ethnology therefore fades away. The north of the State, on broader view, is part of a great non-Californian culture; the south likewise. The middle region, on the other hand, is dominant, not dominated, within the larger area of which it forms part; but its distinctiveness is only a superstructure on a basic type of civilization that extends inland far beyond the limits of the California of to-day. Analogously, local cultural patterns have been woven on the fabric, respectively, of the far-stretched civilization of the north; and, twice, on that of the south. Thus, in a close aspect, not one but four centers of diffusion, or, in the customary phraseology, four types and provinces of culture, must be recognized in California. Figure 74 summarizes these conclusions.

PREHISTORY.

DATA.

California is a fairly rich field for prehistoric antiquities. There have probably been discovered since the American occupation at least a million specimens, about one in a hundred of which has found a resting place in a public museum or become available as a permanent record for science to draw on. But the ancient objects are widely scattered in the ground, and the absence of ruins and earthworks has made the discovery of inhabited sites largely a matter of accident. Systematic exploration is therefore comparatively. unremunerative, unless undertaken on an intensive scale. Only in two regions are artifacts and burials found in some concentration.

The more profitable and best exploited of these areas consists of the Santa Barbara Islands and the coast of the Santa Barbara Channel. The other takes in the winding shores of San Francisco Bay. In both instances the former inhabited sites are readily revealed by the presence of shell and sometimes of ashes. The channel district was the more heavily populated and the art of the natives distinctly more advanced. This region has therefore been extensively dug over by enthusiasts, and a number of really valuable collections have been amassed and deposited in public institutions. The San Francisco Bay shell mounds yield a smaller quantity of less interesting material. Now and then a nest of burials proves a fairly rich pocket, but in general not more than two or three implements can be secured for each cubic yard of soil turned over,[1] and the majority of these are simple bone awls, broken pestle ends. arrow points, and the like. On the other hand, some of the diggings in these northern mounds have been conducted in a scientific manner; with

---

[1] Artifacts secured per cubic yard of excavation: Emeryville shell mound, 2; Ellis Landing, 0.5; Castro, 0.2; Gunther Island (Humboldt Bay), 3.

the result that some attempt can be made to interpret the period, manner of life, and development of culture of the ancient inhabitants. It is likely that the southern area will allow of much more ample conclusions once it is investigated with definite problems in view.

ANCIENT SITES.

The number of prehistoric sites is known to have been very considerable wherever topography and climate and food supply encouraged settlement. Figures 75 to 77 suggest the density and continuity of occupation on San Diego Bay, as well as on two of the islands of the Santa Barbara group. For San Francisco and Humboldt Bays in the north, larger maps have been published. These districts comprise the principal shore lines in California that face on sheltered waters. The surf-beaten cliffs which constitute the remainder of the coast undoubtedly held a smaller population. Their numerous short transverse streams, most of them with half-filled mouths, offered the natives many sheltered sites, but the remains indicate that these were frequently occupied only as temporary or intermittent camps.

Away from the coast, the ancient sites are much more difficult to detect, and data are so scattering that any present endeavor to map the sites, even for restricted districts, is out of the question,

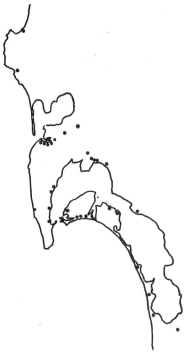

FIG. 75.—Prehistoric sites about San Diego Bay. (Data by Nelson and Welty.)

although painstaking investigation usually reveals abundant evidences of occupation.

On San Francisco Bay something over half of the bulk of the deposits left by the prehistoric occupants is shell. This, with the soil and rock and ash that have become mixed in, has usually accumulated to some height, forming a distinct and sometimes a conspicuous rounded elevation. The sites in this region are therefore well described by their common designation of "shell mounds."

Elsewhere, even on the coast, shell usually forms a smaller proportion of the soil or refuse left by ancient villages, except perhaps for certain localities in the Santa Barbara district. In consequence the mound formation is generally also less visible. Table 14 combines the available data on this point.

ANTIQUITY.

The shores of San Francisco Bay have been subsiding in recent periods, as the geologist reckons time. These shores are mostly low and frequently bordered by an extensive tidal marsh. Some of the mounds appear to have been established at the water's edge and have been affected by this subsidence. They grew up faster than the land sank, and thus remained convenient for occupation, but their bases have become submerged or covered with inorganic deposits. The exact depth to which this subsidence has taken place

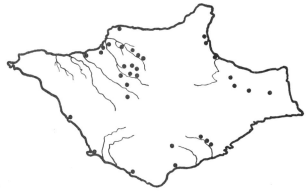

Fig. 76.—Prehistoric sites on Santa Rosa Island. (Data of P. M. Jones.)

is somewhat laborious to ascertain, and has been determined for only a few of the ten or more mounds known to be partly drowned. The bases of these range from 3 to 18 feet below the ocean level of to-day. This fact makes a respectable antiquity for the beginning of their occupation certain.

Some of the mounds on San Francisco Bay remained inhabited until the historic period. Early Spanish travelers, it is true, do not refer definitely to shell mounds, but it is only natural that as between a site and a group of houses filled with people, the latter would be the first to attract attention. A number of objects of European source have been found in the upper layers of these mounds, sometimes in association with burials: adobe bricks, a crucifix, medals, three-legged metates of Mexican type, and the like.

The Emeryville and Ellis Landing mounds, two of the largest and best explored on San Francisco Bay, have been estimated by their excavators to possess an age, respectively, of from one to several thousand and from three to four thousand years. The latter figure is arrived at by an ingenious computation. The Ellis Landing mound contains a million and a quarter cubic feet of material. About 15 house pits were recently still visible on it. If contemporaneously occupied, these would indicate a population of about a hundred. The Indians ate fish, game, acorns, seeds, and roots. A per capita allowance of fifty mussels a day, or an equivalent in other molluskan species, for adults and children, therefore seems liberal. Five thousand mussel shells crush down, per experiment, to a quarter as many cubic inches. Ash, rock, and other débris would bring the daily accumulation to about a cubic foot for the entire settlement. At a rate of deposition amounting to 300 to 400 cubic feet annually, 3,500 years would be required to build up 1,260,000 feet. There are too many indeterminate factors in such a calculation to allow its results

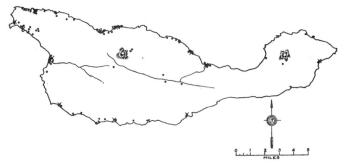

Fig. 77.—Prehistoric sites on Santa Cruz Island. The largest middens are crossed. (Data of L. Outhwaite.)

to be pressed rigidly; but it seems reasonable. The bottom of the mound now being 18 feet below sea level, a subsidence of half a foot per century is indicated. The population may have averaged more than 100; but this would be rather a high figure for a native Californian village. It may have been augmented seasonally by visitors from the interior, but to compensate, its own inhabitants are likely to have spent five or six months of each year in the hills away from their mussels. However the question is approached, 3,500 years seems a conservative deduction.

A check has been attempted by another investigator. Fourteen per cent of Ellis Landing mound, according to a number of analyzed samples, is ash—a weight of over 7,000 tons. Assuming 3,500 years, we have a production of 11 pounds daily. The woods available in the vicinity yield less than 1 per cent of ash. Hence more than 1,200 pounds of wood were burned daily, or, on the previous estimate of population, about 80 pounds per family of 7 persons.

As a woman can carry this bulk in one load, the figure appears conservative. In other words, a test of the factors assumed in the first calculation yields a credible result.

Of course, many mounds are smaller, less or not at all depressed below sea level, and evidently more recent and shorter lived. But again, Ellis Landing may be by no means the most ancient. It seems extremely probable, therefore, that a minimum duration of 3,000 years must be allowed for the shell mound period on San Francisco Bay.

COMPOSITION OF SHELL MOUNDS.

The constituents that go to make up the coast mounds are classified in Table 14. Charcoal never amounts to more than a fraction of 1 per cent of the weight of the total bulk and has been counted as ash. Fish, bird, and mammal bones compose from 1 part in 400 down to mere traces. Soil includes rock, sand and gravel. The proportion of this varies noticeably, but is usually explained by topographical considerations. Gunther Island is sand and peat, Sausalito a rocky site, Castro several miles from the shore, Half Moon Bay on a slide from a hillside, Point Loma on a narrow shelf along the side of the headland. In the other mounds the inorganic material is less abundant, and does not fall below a sixth or rise above a third in weight of the whole mass.

TABLE 14. PERCENTAGE COMPOSITION OF CALIFORNIA SHELL MOUNDS.

	Shell.	Ash.	Soil.
Humboldt Bay—Gunther Island	16	2	82
San Francisco Bay:			
Emeryville	60	14	26
West Berkeley	53	24	23
Ellis Landing	70	14	16
Carquinez	55	27	18
San Rafael	54	25	21
Greenbrae	65	13	22
Sausalito	55	4	41
San Francisco (Presidio)	57	16	27
San Mateo Point	59	6	35
San Mateo	59	11	30
Castro	26	10	64
Coast south of San Francisco—Half Moon Bay	57	4	39
San Diego Bay—Point Loma	29	5	66

The ratio of shell to ash varies more, but its fluctuations are also partly intelligible. It is highest, about 14:1, at Half Moon Bay, an exposed spot more suited for occasional camping than continuous residence, and at Sausalito, where shelter, wood, and water are available but where abundance of clams may seasonally have drawn people from some distance about. The average proportion, 4 or 5:1, is found at Emeryville, Ellis Landing, Greenbrae, and San Mateo (on three sides of San Francisco Bay), and is only slightly exceeded on San Diego and Humboldt Bays. The ratio is low, between 2:1 and 3:1, at Carquinez, which is well up on brackish water; at San Rafael, an essentially inland site; Castro, also away from tidewater; and West Berkeley, where wealth of net sinkers indicates a fishing village rather than a mollusk-gathering station.

On San Francisco Bay the commonest shell in the mounds is the mussel, *Mytilus edulis*. This is regularly the prevailing mollusk. Next common, but far more irregularly distributed, is the common soft-shell clam, *Macoma nasuta*. The small local oyster, *Ostrea lurida*, is abundant at San Mateo, where the modern cultivated beds of introduced oysters are located, at West Berkeley, and at Emeryville, but scarce elsewhere. All three of these species are still regularly on the American market. The large ocean mussel, *Mytilus californianus*, is of importance, in examined mounds, only in those on the outlet to the bay, namely San Francisco and Sausalito. Barnacles constitute from 1 to 6 per cent of the total weight of shell. Their occurrence is such as to indicate that they were collected with the other mollusks or with driftwood to which they adhered. Haliotis is everywhere sparsely represented.

TABLE 15.- MOLLUSKAN PROPORTIONS (BY WEIGHT) IN SHELL MOUNDS.

	Mussel.	Clam.	Oyster.	Ocean mussel.	Barnacles.	Dust and unidentifiable fragments.
Emeryville................	35	18	8	(1)	2	34
West Berkeley....	41	4	19	(1)	2	32
Ellis Landing....	35	36	(1)	....	1	25
Carquinez...	68	(1)	(1)	....	1	29
San Rafael.............	44	(1)	(1)	(1)	5	48
Greenbrae.	47	1	1	(1)	3	46
Sausalito.	24	23	(1)	2	3	41
San Francisco..........	19	12	(1)	18	6	39
San Mateo Point.........	34	....	22	....	5	37
San Mateo...............	33	(1)	31	(1)	3	31

1 Less than 1 per cent.

Castro, whose location makes it abnormal in other ways, contains only traces of mussel and clam, and a small proportion of oyster. The dominant species is the horn shell, *Cerithidea californica*, a variety available at other mound sites, but usually neglected there in favor of more palatable foods. Next in abundance at Castro is *Pholas pacificus*, which is rare elsewhere. Crab carapaces are also far more conspicuous at Castro than at any other explored site of the region.

It is quite apparent that the molluskan fauna of San Francisco Bay has not changed appreciably even in its local distribution since the shell mounds were inhabited; and the topography and hydrography of the district are also likely to have remained substantially constant during the elapsed period of occupation.

On the open ocean at Half Moon Bay the native sea foods possessed a quite different range. *Tegula funebralis* was secured in greatest quantity, the *californianus* mussel came next, and *Paphia staminea* was obtained occasionally. The bay species are scarcely represented.

In the north, along the steep coast beyond Trinidad, the large ocean mussel seems to be the chief shell constituent of the refuse left by villages. The only quantitative determinations are from the sandy and marshy shores of Humboldt Bay, where the Gunther Island mound yielded *Schizothaerus nuttallii*, 23 per cent; *Macoma nasuta* (clam), 17; *Cardium corbis* (scallop), 14; *Paphia staminea*, 12; *Paphia tenerrima*, 1; *Saxidomus gigantea*, 1; *Mytilus edulis* and barnacles, trace; unidentifiable, 28. These are probably fairly representative proportions for the district. Yet a camp site on Freshwater slough, near Eureka, had about 58 per cent of its shell *edulis* mussel, with 34 per cent unidentifiable. On the other hand a coast site near Cape Mendocino showed the large mussel, *californianus*, predominant; " clam " and " cockle " next; and a sea snail, a conical shell, and haliotis frequent. The species recovered at the spot are *Mytilus californianus; Purpura crispata* and *saxicola; Acmaea pelta, spectrum*, and *mitra; Tapes staminea; Pholas californica; Fissurella aspera; Chrysodomus dirus; Haliotis rufescens; Chlorostoma] funebrale* and *brunneum;* and *Helix Townsendiana.*

ANCIENT CULTURE PROVINCES.

Exploration of prehistoric sites anywhere in the State rarely reveals anything of moment that is not apparent in the life of the recent natives of the same locality. This rule applies even to limited districts. The consequence is that until now the archaeology of

California has but rarely added anything to the determinations of ethnology beyond a dim vista of time, and some vague hints toward a recognition of the development of culture. But as regards endeavor in this direction, practically nothing has yet been achieved.

Nor do the local varieties of culture seem to have advanced or receded or replaced one another to any extent. Objects of Santa Barbara type are found only in the Santa Barbara district and practically never about San Francisco Bay. Humboldt Bay yields some variant types, but these are again peculiar to the locality. How ancient these may be, can not yet be stated, but they are certainly not mere recent types. Moreover, there is no indication whatever that the San Francisco Bay culture ever prevailed at Humboldt Bay, and it is certain that the characteristics of the culture of the latter district never penetrated far enough south to be even partly represented in the former region.

In other words, the upshot of the correlation of the findings of archaeology and ethnology is that not only the general Californian culture area, but even its subdivisions or provinces, were determined a long time ago and have ever since maintained themselves with relatively little change.

PURELY PREHISTORIC IMPLEMENTS.

In regard to a few utensils, we do know that customs have changed. Prominent among these are the mortar and metate. The mortar is found practically everywhere in California, and in most localities is rather frequent underground. But over a considerable part of the State, comprising roughly its northern half, it was not used by the historic tribes, at least not in portable form or for the purpose of grinding acorns. In this area it either consists of an excavation in bedrock, or is a small instrument used for crushing tobacco or meat, or is made of a basketry hopper set on a slab. It is therefore probable that at some time in the past, more or less remote, a change came over northern California which led to the abandonment of the large movable acorn mortar of stone in favor of these other devices. Even in the southern half of the State this mortar was not so extensively used in recent times as the frequency of the type among prehistoric remains has led to being generally believed.

The metate or grinding slab seems to have come in about as the mortar went out of use. The evidence is less complete, but it is significant that there are no metates in the San Francisco shell mounds, although a slab mortar is now and then to be found. It is possible that the historic but little known Costanoans and Coast Miwok of San Francisco Bay followed their ancestors or predecessors on the spot in going without the metate; but it would be rather surprising if they had done so, in view of the fact that modern interior tribes in the same latitude, such as the Miwok and Maidu, and even those farther north, grind on the metate, and that all the coast tribes from San Francisco Bay north uniformly employ the pounding slab. The latter may be a modification of the mortar under the influence of the metate in regions influenced by the metate culture but into which the metate proper did not penetrate. This rather intricate point has been discussed more fully in the chapters on the Maidu, Chumash, Luiseño, and Cahuilla.

In prehistoric deposits on Humboldt Bay, and at several interior points in extreme northern California, have been found examples of an ornamental stone object which can hardly have been anything but a club. It is of animal shape, the head fairly defined, the tail serving as handle, and the legs projecting somewhat as if they were spikes. This is a type with affiliations in Oregon and on the Columbia River, and was not used by any historic tribe in California. These animal-shaped clubs are almost certainly to be connected with the simpler edged fighting club of stone used by the recent Indians of northwestern California.

DEVELOPMENT OF CIVILIZATION ON SAN FRANCISCO BAY.

Enough mounds have been systematically excavated in the San Francisco Bay region to make possible a fairly accurate comparison of the culture represented by the deep, early strata with that partially preserved in the upper, late layers.

A number of difficulties must be mentioned. The mounds are highest at the center and slope toward the edges. The periphery is generally later than the middle of the base. A reckoning from the ground level upward would therefore be misleading. On the other hand, measurements of depth from the surface are not quite accurate because the mounds usually built up fastest in their central portions. A foot of mound material near the periphery may therefore stand for a period considerably longer—or sometimes less—than that required for a like thickness to accumulate in the middle. Theoretically, the correct procedure would accordingly be to follow lines of deposition in instituting comparisons; but this is not practical, stratification being confined to limited areas and often wholly imperceptible. In spite of some variation of age for the several parts of each mound, depths have therefore had to be calculated by absolute measurement from the modern surfaces.

In most cases, much more material was removed from the upper than from the lower levels of mounds. But the proportion varies according to the circumstances of excavation at each site. Absolute frequency of the various classes of implements, therefore, proves nothing. The number of objects of the several types has accordingly been expressed in percentage of the total number of artifacts discovered in each level.

Still other factors disturb. The mounds are very unequal in bulk and in height, and the excavations have removed quite different volumes. Collectors also preserve and classify their finds in somewhat divergent manners.

All these circumstances render any exactly reliable comparisons impossible at present. It is, however, fortunate that enough data are on record to allow of any inferences at all; and, with due heed to the considerations mentioned, the evidence may therefore be proceeded with.

Table 16 shows the relative frequency, as compared with all recovered articles of manufacture, of tools of obsidian, a material found only at some distance—some 25 to 50 miles—from the bay shores, and therefore a valuable index of tribal intercommunication; of mortars, pestles, and awls, three implements that are basic in the industrial life of all aboriginal Californians; and of a special class of well-finished objects of plummet-like shape, the so-called "charm stones," which presumably bore associations of magic and religion. In the mounds of medium height, which go down to a depth of 8 to 12 feet, all three of these classes of objects, except charm stones, are found quite generally down to the lowest levels. They occur in the same ratio in the higher and in general presumably more ancient mounds whose thickness extends to 20 and 30 feet. In fact in both of those from which data are available, at Emeryville and Ellis Landing, even charm stones are still relatively abundant at a greater depth than is attained by the six other mounds. This fact renders it likely that the absence of charm stones in the lowest 2 to 4 feet of the moderate deposits is due either to accident or to the low probability that objects of such comparative rarity as charm stones would normally occur in the small total number of artifacts that is characteristic of the bottom-most levels of all the bay shell heaps.

TABLE 16.—PERCENTAGES OF TOTAL ARTIFACTS CONSTITUTED BY CERTAIN IMPLE-
MENTS ACCORDING TO DEPTH IN SHELL MOUNDS.

CHIPPED IMPLEMENTS OF OBSIDIAN.

Mounds.	Depth in 2-foot and 4-foot intervals.									
	2	4	6	8	10	12	14	18	22	26
San Rafael................	0	0	23	100	.....	.....	.....	.....	.....	.....
Greenbrae.................	37	5	27	0	17	33	.....	.....	.....	.....
Sausalito..................	14	5	0	0	17	0	.....	.....	.....	.....
Ellis Landing [1]...........	0	0	1	0	42	0	0	0	29	8
Emeryville [2]..............	0	0	0	50	0	0	0	0	0	0
Visitacion (Bay Shore)....	0	0	3	0	0	.....	.....	.....	.....	.....
San Mateo................	0	12	0	0	.....	.....	.....	.....	.....	.....
Castro....................	6	0	0	6	.....	.....	.....	.....	.....	.....

MORTARS AND PESTLES.

	2	4	6	8	10	12	14	18	22	26
San Rafael................	25	0	18	0	.....	.....	.....	.....	.....	.....
Greenbrae.................	37	26	7	33	33	17	.....	.....	.....	.....
Sausalito..................	43	10	14	7	17	25	.....	.....	.....	.....
Ellis Landing	25	17	32	18	0	56	50	22	7	25
Emeryville................	56		0	10	33	0	0	45	18	40
Visitacion.................	14	27	6	0	0	.....	.....	.....	.....	.....
San Mateo................	22	19	33	29	.....	.....	.....	.....	.....	.....
Castro....................	37	22	23	33	.....	.....	.....	.....	.....	.....

BONE AWLS.

	2	4	6	8	10	12	14	18	22	26
San Rafael................	8	22	0	0	.....	.....	.....	.....	.....	.....
Greenbrae.................	12	37	27	0	17	17	.....	.....	.....	.....
Sausalito..................	0	30	14	0	8	12	.....	.....	.....	.....
Ellis Landing..............	9	30	6	13	0	0	0	0	7	0
Emeryville................	0	0	0	30	33	50	25	18	0	0
Visitacion.................	14	36	14	0	0	.....	.....	.....	.....	.....
San Mateo................	11	0	0	29	.....	.....	.....	.....	.....	.....
Castro....................	0	0	23	17	.....	.....	.....	.....	.....	.....

CHARM STONES.

	2	4	6	8	10	12	14	18	22	26
San Rafael................	8	0	6	0	.....	.....	.....	.....	.....	.....
Greenbrae.................	0	0	7	0	0	0	.....	.....	.....	.....
Sausalito..................	0	0	0	20	0	0	.....	.....	.....	.....
Ellis Landing..............	14	17	14	18	8	9	17	0	0	0
Emeryville................	0	0	25	0	0	0	25	6	0	0
Visitacion.................	0	9	9	0	0	.....	.....	.....	.....	.....
San Mateo................	22	0	22	0	.....	.....	.....	.....	.....	.....
Castro....................	0	3	6	0	.....	.....	.....	.....	.....	.....

[1] Excavation of 1907–1908.   [2] Excavation of 1906.

In short, then, all the classes of objects in question occur at the bottom, middle, and top of the mounds, and the table shows that they occur with substantially the same frequency. In other words, the natives of the San Francisco Bay region traded the same materials from the same localities one or two or three thousand years ago as when they were discovered at the end of the eighteenth century. They ate the same food, in nearly the same proportions (only mammalian bones became more abundant in higher levels), prepared it in substantially the same manner, and sewed skins, rush mats, and coiled baskets similarly to their recent descendants. Even their religion was conservative, since the identical charms seem to have been regarded potent. In a word, the basis of culture remained identical during the whole of the shell-mound period.

When it is remembered that the best authority—estimating, indeed, but using as exact data as possible and proceeding with scientific care—puts the beginning of this period at more than 3,000 years ago, it is clear that we are here confronted by a historical fact of extraordinary importance. It means that at the time when Troy was besieged and Solomon was building the temple, at a period when even Greek civilization had not yet taken on the traits that we regard as characteristic, when only a few scattering foundations of specific modern culture were being laid and our own northern ancestors dwelled in unmitigated barbarism, the native Californian already lived in all essentials like his descendant of to-day. In Europe and Asia, change succeeded change of the profoundest type. On this far shore of the Pacific, civilization, such as it was, remained immutable in all fundamentals. Even as some measure of progress shall be determined by continued investigation, it is probable that this will prove to have been unusually slow and slight. There are few parts of the world, even those inhabited by dark-skinned savages, where such a condition can be regarded as established. The permanence of Californian culture, therefore, is of far more than local interest. It is a fact of significance in the history of civilization.

If it be objected that the period dealt with is after all conjectural rather than established, the import of our inference may be diminished; but it is not destroyed. Cut the estimate of 3,500 years in half, or even to one-third: we are still carried back to the time of Charlemagne. The elapsed millennium has witnessed momentous alterations in Europe, in India, in Japan; even the Mohammedan countries, China, Central Asia, and Malaysia, have changed deeply in civilization, while our part of America has stood still.

PARALLEL CONDITIONS ELSEWHERE.

No similar computations can yet be made for ancient remains in other parts of California, because the débris deposits elsewhere have indeed been ransacked for finds, but no accurate record of the precise depth of each specimen has been preserved. Yet the fact that no site shows objects appearing to belong to two types of culture, except for some potsherds close to the surface about San Diego; that the finds at various sites over whole districts are uniform, and even the districts usually merge into each other—all these circumstances indicate that relatively little transformation and but slight succession of civilizations occurred in prehistoric California.

It may be added that in a review of the archaeology of the continent Doctor Dixon has found the Californian conditions to be typical of the entire Pacific coast, whereas in the Atlantic region and Mississippi Valley exact inquiry has often brought to light decisive evidence of two or several types of culture in each region. Types must, of course, be interpreted as periods; and Doctor Dixon connects the comparatively rapid succession of these in the East with a much greater tendency toward movements of population, as known in the historic period and supported by tradition for earlier times. Instability of population may not have been the only, perhaps not even the principal, cause of eastern instability of culture; but it is a fact that there is scarcely any record or even legend of migrations in California.

In the Southwest changes in the types of prehistoric remains are striking, and a definite sequence of ceramic wares, and behind these of civilizations, is being determined. Southwestern influences are so numerous in southern California that something of the tendency toward change may be expected to be discovered there as soon as sufficiently painstaking search is undertaken at ancient sites. This is the more likely because southern California differs from the remainder of the State in revealing some evidence of shifts of population.

LOCAL UNIFORMITY OF THE SAN FRANCISCO BAY DISTRICT.

The averaging constancy of the figures in Table 16 rests upon a very conspicuous irregularity in detail. But this wavering is indicative only of the limitation of data. Not over a couple of dozen charm stones or obsidian pieces of provenience of known depth are available from any one mound, and the total number of artifacts recovered from the largest excavations at single sites is only a few hundred. By the time these are distributed among several layers the numbers are so small that chance must vary their distribution considerably. With successive levels, particularly at the lower and comparatively barren depths, yielding, say, one, two, and no objects of a given class, the corresponding percentages can easily be 5, 33, and zero. Burials, which occur scatteringly, contain pockets of specimens and add further to the irregularity of distribution over small sections of mounds. The variation in frequencies from layer to layer, therefore, allows of no inferences; it is the absence of drift in cultural direction, from bottom to top of any mound as a whole, that is significant.

The tendency toward uniformity is almost as great for locality as for time. Table 17 gathers the data on this point. It is notable that the variations in frequency of many classes of objects is about as great between successive excavations in the same mound as between distinct sites. Thus Emeryville in 1902 yielded 9 per cent of mortars and pestles and about 30 per cent of awls; in 1906 the respective results were 26 and 12. In short, variations must again be ascribed largely to chance.

TABLE 17.—PERCENTAGES OF CLASSES OF ARTIFACTS ACCORDING TO LOCALITY OF SHELL MOUNDS.

Mound.	Total specimen depth.	Total specimens obtained.	Percentages.							
			Obsidian.	Mortars and pestles.	Sinkers.	Charm stones.	Ornaments of beads or bone or shell.	Awls.	Wedges	All others.
	Feet.									
San Rafael..........	7	42	19	14	0	5	2	7	2	51
Greenbrae..........	12	60	17	22	0	1	8	22	2	28
Sausalito............	12	84	5	15	12	5	19	13	0	31
Ellis Landing, 1906..	13	92	9	11	1	11	5	10	0	53
Ellis Landing, 1907–8	25	260	4	24	10	13	11	12	1	25
West Berkeley, 1902.	....	314	4	5	44	3	2	4	0	38
Emeryville, 1902....	[1] 25	[2] 340	[1] 7	9	1	3	[1] 7	[1] 30	4	39
Emeryville, 1906....	24	65	8	26	0	5	3	12	0	46
Visitacion (Bay Shore)............	9	75	1	12	1	7	19	19	0	41
San Mateo..........	8	41	4	24	0	10	10	7	5	40
Castro	8	87	2	27	0	5	21	8	1	36

[1] Approximate.

[2] The total number is about 600, but this includes waste chips, broken bones, and similar pieces which have not been counted from the other mounds. That the correction to 340 makes the total comparable to the other totals is indicated by the figure 39 in the last column, which is also the average of the 10 other figures in that column.

There are a few exceptions. The two highest frequencies for charm stones are both furnished by Ellis Landing. The probable inference is that the settlement here was a center of some particular shamanistic or ceremonial activity. Such a development would be most likely in a large town, and this the size of the mound indicates the place to have been. It is illustrative of the lack of flow pervading Californian culture that the flowering of this religious manifestation was not a transient phase, but something that endured for many centuries, as evidenced by the comparative regularity of the high proportion of charm stones at this site.

West Berkeley, on the other hand, was mainly a fishing settlement. Nearly half of its discovered artifacts are sinkers—flattish pebbles nicked on two sides for the string that bound them to the lower edge of the seine net. That it was more than a camp is clear from the extent and depth of the deposits, as well as the burials and ceremonial and ornamental pieces which they contain. The spot may have been unusually favorable for taking fish. Yet Ellis Landing and West Berkeley, but a few miles on either side, contain only the usual low percentage of sinkers; and however much the aboriginal West Berkeleyans fished, the little mountain of shells they left behind them proves them not to have neglected mollusks as a food supply.

Obsidian comes from Clear Lake and the head of Napa Valley, occasionally also in small lumps from upper Sonoma Valley. One should expect it to follow two routes in its distribution around San Francisco Bay—along the north and west border of San Pablo Bay to the Golden Gate, or across Carquinez Straits and southward along the eastern shore of San Francisco Bay proper. By either route the peninsular district of San Mateo and San Francisco would be the last to be reached. Analysis of the finds exactly tallies with these inferences from geography. San Rafael and Greenbrae, most northerly and nearest the source of supply, actually show much the heaviest proportion of obsidian implements; Visitacion, San Mateo, and Castro, the most southerly mounds and on the peninsula, the smallest frequency.

THE LOWER SAN JOAQUIN VALLEY.

In the delta region of the great interior valley, particularly in the vicinity of Stockton, several special objects have been found in sufficient numbers to insure their being characteristic of the region. These include narrow cylindrical jars or vases of steatite; clay balls, either plain or incised, perhaps slung shots for water fowl or substitutes for cooking stones in the alluvial region; neatly worked obsidian blades of about a finger's length and crescentically shaped; and thin ornaments of either haliotis or mussel shell cut into forms ranging from that of a human outline to more conventionalized figures, which, if they were of civilized origin, would suggest the form of a stringed musical instrument. The distribution of these types is so well localized as to give a first impression of a specific ancient subculture. But the area is one from which the historic tribes were early drained into the missions, so that historic data which would enable a comparison on the basis of ethnology are practically nil.

It is therefore quite possible that we are confronted by the usual phenomenon of a culture proceeding undisturbed from prehistoric times until its elimination by the Caucasian; with merely the peculiarity that its modern phase disappeared before being observed. This solution is indicated by the fact that investigations among the Miwok have developed that the so-called " Stockton curves " of obsidian were known to these Indians, the blades being attached to the fingers in imitation of bear claws by dancers who impersonated the animal. It seems rather likely that if the northern valley Yokuts survived in condition to depict the culture of their great-grandfathers, they would be able to explain most of the other types, which now appear isolated or peculiar, as something familiar in the region when the Spaniards came.

THE UPPER SAN JOAQUIN VALLEY.

A rather remarkable discovery of burials near the shores of Buena Vista Lake at the head of the San Joaquin Valley, in a territory that was historically Yokuts, seems at first sight to reveal a stronger influence of southern California, and even of the Southwest, than is discernible among the modern Indians of this region. (Pls. 41, 63, 72, 81.) A carefully preserved eagle skull with eyes of haliotis, for instance, suggested a definite connection with the Luiseño and Diegueño eagle-killing ceremony, until it became known that the modern Yokuts also practiced a mourning rite over eagles. But a specimen of a wooden club of the " potato-masher " type standard in southern California and the Southwest—unfortunately not preserved, but of definite description—does point to the conclusion indicated.

The same may be said of a number of bags twined in basketry technique but of soft string materials. (Pl. 63.) These are similar to the bags or wallets made by the Diegueño and Mohave, and bear an especial likeness, at any rate superficially, to utensils of the so-called " basket makers " who once lived at Grand Gulch, in southern Utah.

Another point is of interest. The hair preserved with some of the Buena Vista Lake skulls is wound or contained in typical central Californian head nets, but the hair itself is plastered in the long pencil-shaped masses which in the historic period the Colorado River tribes, and so far as known no others, followed as their fashion. (Pl. 72.) Yet the remains are those of natives of the region. So many of the objects preserved with them are articles of household use, and the interment of the dead is so precise, that there can be no suspicion of a party of raiding warriors having been slain and buried far from home.

Perhaps of greatest interest in this collection is an unornamented cotton blanket unquestionably made among one of the settled tribes of New Mexico or Arizona. This is one of the few authentic instances of long distance trade of any manufactured article either into or out of California. It is, however, suggestive that the last wearer of this blanket was certainly not following the style customary among the people who wove it. He had roughly cut into it two ragged holes for his arms, so that he could put it about himself somewhat as a coat. (Pl. 72.) Had the maker intended the blanket to be worn in this fashion, he might have woven it in one piece, but would have trimmed and seamed the holes.

Unfortunately there is no indication whatever of the age of this very unusual find. It represents a series of burials uncovered by natural causes and detached from the village to which they belonged. At any rate, if the latter stood in the vicinity, it left no evidences of refuse or other accumulation. The state of preservation of many of the articles is such as to suggest comparative recency. But as against this is to be set the high aridity of the district. The interments may not be more than a few centuries old; but they are certainly pre-Spanish.

THE SANTA BARBARA REGION.

The Santa Barbara Islands and mainland contain in their ancient graves the greatest number of unique forms and specialized types to be found in California. Unfortunately the historical culture of the Chumash and island Shoshoneans has been so completely wiped out that in the majority of instances it is quite impossible to say whether the peculiar objects dug out of graves were or were not in use by the Indians of 150 years ago. So far as seems safe, they have been tentatively connected with the technological and religious practices of these Indians, in the chapter on the Chumash. It does not seem possible to interpret them more decisively, or worth while to speculate upon them at greater length, until either additional historical information becomes accessible upon this group, or systematic excavations enable the characterization of the several periods and types of culture that may be represented in the prehistoric deposits of the region.

A word may be added about two types of implements in regard to which there has been some controversy: a stone ring or perforated disk, and a pear or plummet shaped object. It has been affirmed that the former was a club head, or again a net sinker. But the holed disk is most common in the Chumash region, and the surviving Chumash unanimously declare that it was slipped as a weight over the root-digging sticks of their women. The size and shape and all evidences of wear on the pieces confirm this interpretation. That now and then such a stone may have been used for a hammer or for cracking acorns is entirely natural, but marks indicative of such occasional secondary utilization can not be stretched into a basis for theories. The net sinker of California was a beach pebble, nicked or notched on opposite edges, or sometimes grooved. Anything more finished or ornate would have been a sheer waste of labor, which would not have appealed to so practical minded a people as the Californians; at any rate not in an occupation in which religion did not directly enter. The only exception that must be made to the interpretation of the round perforated stone as a digging stone weight is provided by a few specimens found slenderly hafted and feathered in a cave that contained several hundred other clearly ceremonial objects.

The plummet-shaped stone, which is often very symmetrically ground and well polished, and sometimes made of attractively colored or banded rock, is without doubt a ceremonial object. At least, every interpretation obtained from recent Indians is to the effect that stones of this type were amulets or fetishes for luck in hunting and fishing. They may possibly also have been used by rain-making shamans. The fact that traces of asphalt show some of these pieces to have been suspended is, of course, no proof of their having been used as sinkers, true plummets, or weaving weights. In fact, one such charm stone was actually found, only a few years ago, suspended from a string over a fishing place near an Indian settlement in the San Joaquin Valley. Whether these stones, which are most common in central California but are also known from Chumash territory, were originally made as charms, or whether they served some other purpose and were only put to magical use when they were discovered by later generations of natives, it is impossible to decide with certainty; but the positive knowledge as to their recent employment should weigh more heavily in the student's mind than any conjecture, no matter how appealing, as to what their still earlier use may have been.

PICTURED ROCKS.

About 50 sites with carved or painted rocks have become known in California. These range from bowlders bearing a few scratches to walls of caves or overhanging cliffs covered with a long assemblage of figures in red, yellow, black, and white. Their distribution (Fig. 78) is by no means uniform. About half occur in territory occupied in the historic period by Shoshoneans. Nearly all the remainder are in areas immediately adjacent to Shoshonean tracts. Other parts of California are practically devoid of such monuments of the past.

This distribution can not be accounted for by environment. It is true that the open plains of the great valley and the heavy redwood belt would furnish few exposed stones suitable for inscribing. But the half-forested broken country north and south of San Francisco and the foothills of the Sierra offer abundant opportunities which the inhabitants of these regions availed themselves of most sparsely.

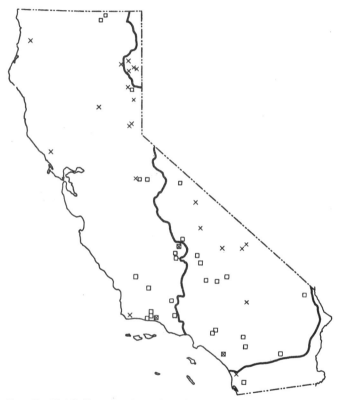

Fig. 78.—Distribution of petrographs. Squares, carved; crosses, painted; crossed squares, carved and painted. The lines are the limits of recent Shoshonean territory.

On the other hand, petrographs are common throughout the Great Basin, which was solidly tenanted by Shoshoneans. The inference is therefore strong that these people are mainly responsible for the painted and carved rocks of California, in part through the work of their ancestors' hands and partly by their influence on their neighbors. (Pl. 82.)

The most remarkable pictographs are those in the Chumash country, beginning with the famous Corral Rock in the Carrizo

Plains, the largest and most notable group in the State (Pl. 83);
stretching to the vicinity of Santa Barbara; and extending thence
easterly into Gabrielino land in the Sierra Madre and northeasterly
among the Yokuts in the southern Sierra Nevada. These pictographs
are almost all painted in several colors, protected from the weather
and well preserved except for defacings by civilized vandals, and inclined to the representation of recognizable figures—men, animals,
suns, and the like. Outside of this area carvings preponderate.
Although sometimes extensive, these are simpler, circles, spirals,
zigzags, rows of triangles, and other geometric designs prevailing,
usually in quite irregular arrangement.

It is true that the distinction between paintings and incised stones
must be made with caution. Stone is so much slower to work than
pigment that an equal effort would lead to much less elaborate results; and many of the carvings may originally have been over-
painted, the color quickly washing out in exposed locations, such as
granite outcrops. Yet caves and smooth overhangs occur in many
regions outside the district of the Chumash, Gabrielino, and southern Yokuts, and there can be little doubt that had the inhabitants
of the remoter regions felt impelled to produce complicated or life-
like pictures, they would have found the opportunity to make them,
and that their handiwork would have been more frequently preserved than is the case. The cave paintings of the south, therefore,
represent a particular art, a localized style or cult. This can be
connected, in all probability, with the technological art of the
Chumash and island Shoshoneans, as manifest in the occasional
carvings of whales, quadrupeds, and the like in steatite. Since these
paintings farther fall well within the region of the toalache religion,
in fact their distribution coincides fairly closely with the area in
which this religion was strongest, and since its cult was in certain
tracts worked out in visible symbols such as the sand painting, an
association with this religion is also to be considered, although
nothing positive is known in the matter.

Two questions are always asked about pictographs: What do
they mean? and How old are they? Neither can be answered.
The modern Indians are always familiar with them as landmarks,
but can give as little information as the visitor, except to say that
they have always been there. No connected story can be deciphered
from any of the groups of symbols, and many are so obviously
nonrepresentative as to leave even a speculative imagination baffled
for a clew. Many of the pictures may have been made by shamans;
but again there is no specific evidence pointing in this direction,
and it is quite possible that medicine men were not connected with
the making of any. Luiseño girls paint granite bowlders at the

conclusion of their adolescence rites. But this seems a local custom, and the paintings made in accordance with it are of different character from those found in caves farther north. They would in any case wash off in a generation or two. It has sometimes been conjectured that the symbols served as boundary marks, direction signs, or for some analogous practical purpose. Yet this interpretation fits neither their character, their location, nor the habits of native life. The Indian knew the limits of his territory and his way around in it; and as for strangers, his impulse would have been to obscure their path rather than blazon it.

The uncertainty is equal as regards age. Many of the pictures need not be more than two or three hundred years old, since all evidence goes to show that nothing survived in California tradition for even half a dozen lifetimes, except possibly in a garb wholly altered into myth. On the other hand, the sheltered paintings, and some of the deeper cut rocks, may well be several times as ancient. The only hope of a partial solution of this question seems to lie in an examination by mineralogists and geologists entitled to an opinion as to the resistance of stones, severity of exposure, and the rate of surface disintegration under given climatic conditions.

PRONUNCIATION OF NATIVE WORDS.

Many an Indian language contains more different sounds than the Roman alphabet has letters. If, according to a basic rule of philology, a distinct character were to be employed for each distinct sound, an alphabet of several hundred characters would have had to be devised for this book, since there are nearly a hundred native dialects in California of which some record has been made, and the vast majority of these contain sounds that are not identical. Such a scheme of orthography is both impracticable and unnecessary for anything but purely linguistic studies. On the other hand, the writing of Indian words with the current English values of the letters—sometimes falsely called "phonetic"—was out of the question, because words written in this way can often be read in two or three ways. If anyone can correctly pronounce a foreign word written by the English method, it is not because he can read it, but because his tongue remembers the pronunciation. It is impossible to convey to others a fixed pronunciation of alien terms rendered in English orthography.

The system of spelling followed in this work employs only letters of the Roman alphabet and three or four diacritical marks. In general, the vowel signs have the sound of the letters in the languages of the continent of Europe, the consonant signs the sound of the English letters. This system does not permit of any one of the Indian languages referred to being pronounced with absolute correctness. On the other hand, if the description of the sound or sounds denoted by each letter is carefully observed, this spelling will permit of the pronunciation of the native terms in this book with sufficient accuracy for an Indian to recognize all the words quoted from his dialect.

a   as in *father*, sometimes as in *what;* in Yurok only, sometimes as in *bad*.

b   usually a little more difficult to distinguish from p than in English.

c   not employed; s or k has been written instead.

ch   as in English, or nearly so.

d   somewhat as in English; but its quality is like that of b, its tongue position like t.

dh   in Mohave and Luiseño only, like th in English *the*.

dj   as in English, but with some approach to ch quality (compare b, d, g).

e   as in *met, there;* sometimes like a in *mate*.

f   rare; the upper lip touches the lower lip, not the teeth.

g   as in *go*, but harder to distinguish from k than in English; in Yurok, always a "fricative," that is, like g in Spanish *gente* or colloquial German *wagen*; in Pomo, and occasionally in other languages, both values of g occur, but are designated by the one letter.

h   sometimes as in English; occasionally fainter; sometimes more harshly made with constriction at the back of the mouth, producing a sound equal, or nearly so, to Spanish j or German ch. H must always be sounded, even at the end of words.

hl   a "surd" 1, made without vibration of the vocal cords.

hw   a "surd" w, much like wh in English *which*.

i   as in *pin*, long or short, or as in *machine*, long or short.

j   not used, except in dj.

940

k in languages which possess g, is as in English; in those which do not, it is usually somewhat nearer g than is English k, at least at the beginning and in the middle of words. Indian k is often pronounced much farther back in the mouth than English k.

l never quite the same as in English, but near enough in sound to be unmistakable.

m substantially as in English.

n substantially as in English.

ng as in English *singing*, not as in *finger*.

o as in *come*, *ore;* when long, sometimes like o in *note*, more frequently like aw in *law*.

p as in English, but with a tendency of approach toward b like that of k toward g.

q not used; kw has been written instead.

r much as in German, French, Spanish, or Irish brogue; only in Yurok it is "soft" as in American English. Yurok er is a vowel.

s is a sound of the same type as English s, though rarely quite identical. In languages like Yana and Mohave, in which sh has not been written, s is usually as similar in effect to English sh as to English s.

sh much as in English, but probably never quite the same.

t tends to approach d as k does g. Pomo, Yuki, Costanoan, Yokuts, Luiseño, Diegueño, Mohave, and perhaps other languages, possess one t made with the tip of the tongue against the teeth, and another against the front palate, the latter sounding almost like English tr; but the two sounds have been represented by one letter.

th in Mohave only, like English th in *thin*.

tl an "affricative surd" l, much like tl in English *little*.

u as in *rule*, long or short; or as in *full*, long or short; never as in *unit*.

ü in Shoshonean, Chumash, Yokuts, Miwok, Maidu, is spoken with the tongue in position for u, the lips formed as if for i or e. It is almost the "opposite" in articulation from German ü or French u.

v in Shoshonean, Mohave, and Karok; the lower lip touches the upper, not the teeth.

w as in English, or nearly so.

x not used. The sound of English x is represented by ks; the "fricative palatal" sound usually denoted by x in works on American Indian languages is here represented by h.

y as in English.

z as in English zebra.

zh rare; like s in *pleasure* or z in *azure*.

' the so-called glottal stop; a contraction of the larynx or Adam's apple, closing the breath passage; a cessation of sound, or pause, and therefore inaudible except sometimes as a faint click or catch. When written after p, t, k, ch, ts, tl, the closing of the larynx is usually simultaneous with the first part of the consonant, while the last portion of the sound is reenforced and has to the ear something of the quality of a smack or crack.

   denotes the accented or most loudly spoken vowel of the word. Accent is generally less marked in the Californian Indian languages than in English, and its designation has been omitted in all but a few instances.

   when used, denotes a long vowel; but as a rule, length and shortness of vowels have not been distinguished. Lengthened consonants are represented by being written twice. This device does not indicate shortness of the preceding vowel as in English.

BIBLIOGRAPHY.

A classification by numbers according to subject will be found at the end of the alphabetic bibliography.

1. ABBOTT, C. C. Chipped stone implements. Mortars and pestles. Steatite cooking pots. Articles made of wood. Smoking pipes of stone. Miscellaneous objects made of stone. Musical instruments. In [Putnam, F. W.] Rept. U. S. Geog. Surv. west of the 100th Meridian [Wheeler Surv. Rept.], vol. VII, Archaeology, pp. 49–69, 70–92, 93–116, 122–124, 125–134, 190–217, 234–238, Washington, 1879.

2. ALARCON, FERNANDO. Relation, 1540. Hakluyt, Voyages, vol. III, London, 1600; repr. 1810: Ternaux-Compans, Voyages, vol. IX Paris, 1838.

3. ANDERSON, R. A. Fighting the Mill Creeks. Chico, 1909
   [The title indicates the nature of this booklet. The Mill Creeks are the Yahi.]

4. ANGEL, MYRON. La piedra pintada. The painted rock of California. A Legend. Los Angeles, 1910.

5. ARROYO DE LA CUESTA, FELIPE. Grammar of the Mutsun language. Shea's Library of American Linguistics, vol. IV, New York, 1861.

6. ————. Vocabulary of the Mutsun language. Ibid., vol. VIII, 1862
   [A valuable collection by a competent Franciscan missionary. See Mason, J Alden.]

7. BAEGERT, JACOB. Nachrichten von der Amerikanischen Halbinsel Californien. Mannheim, 1772. Partly translated by Charles Rau Smithsonian Reports for 1863 and 1864, Washington, 1864, 1865.
   [Very valuable for Baja California, especially the extinct tribes of the southern half of the peninsula. The little book is probably the most spiritedly abusive description of a primitive people ever written by a priest, and certainly one of the most picturesque.]

8. BAER, K. E. VON, and HELMERSEN, G. VON. Beiträge zur Kentniss des Russischen Reiches. St. Petersburg, 1839.

9. BANCROFT, H. H. The native races of the Pacific states. The works of H. H. Bancroft, vols. I–V, San Francisco, 1883.
   [These five volumes on the aborigines are a fair sample of the thirty nine that comprise the entire remarkable collection. They contain much that is based on manuscript material, or, if in print, is otherwise accessible with difficulty. Nothing that bears on the subject is omitted. Most of the volumes are excellently written. All the material is externally organized Yet the series remains an immense drifting miscellany, without real plan, inner unity or definite point of view but extremely valuable for the numerous important items that it embodies.]

10. BARRETT, S. A. Basket designs of the Pomo Indians. Amer. Anthrop. n. s. vol. VII, pp. 648–653, 1905.

11. ————. Ceremonies of the Pomo Indians. Univ. Cal Publs Amer Archaeol. and Ethnol., vol. XII, pp. 397–441, 1917.

12. ————. A composite myth of the Pomo Indians. Jour Amer Folk-lore, vol XIX, pp. 37–51, 1906.

13 BARRETT, S. A. The ethno-geography of the Pomo and neighboring Indians. Univ. Cal. Publs. Amer. Archaeol. and Ethnol., vol. VI, pp. 1–332, 1908.
[A mine of data. Pages 28–36 reprint the account of Drake's landing in California.]

14. ——. The geography and dialects of the Miwok Indians. Ibid., vol. VI, pp. 333–368, 1908.

15. ——. Indian opinions of the earthquake of 1906. Jour. Amer. Folk-lore, vol. XIX. p. 324, 1906.

16. ——. The material culture of the Klamath Lake and Modoc Indians. Univ. Cal. Publs. Amer. Archaeol. and Ethnol., vol. V, pp. 239–292, 1910.

17. ——. Myths of the Southern Sierra Miwok. Ibid., vol. XVI, pp. 1–28, 1919.

18. ——. A new Moquelumnan territory in California. Amer. Anthrop., n. s. vol. V, p. 730, 1903.

19. ——. Pomo Bear doctors. Univ. Cal. Publs. Amer. Archaeol. and Ethnol., vol. XII, pp. 443–465, 1917.

20. ——. Pomo buildings. Holmes Anniversary Volume, pp. 1–17, Washington, 1916.

21. ——. Pomo Indian basketry. Univ. Cal. Publs. Amer. Archaeol. and Ethnol., vol. VII, pp. 133–306, 1908.
[Perhaps the fullest description ever written of the basket art of any one native people.]

22. ——. The Pomo in the Sacramento valley of California. Amer. Anthrop., n. s. vol. VI, 189–190, 1904.

23. ——. Totemism among the Miwok Indians. Journ. Amer. Folk-lore, vol. XXI. p. 237. 1908.

24. ——. The Washo Indians. Bull. Public Mus. of Milwaukee, vol. II, no. 1, pp. 1–52, 1917.
[Mainly a description of implements, but about all there is on the Washo.]

25. ——. The Wintun Hesi ceremony. Univ. Cal. Publs. Amer. Archaeol. and Ethnol., vol. XIV. pp. 437–488, 1919.
[A Kuksu ritual influenced by the ghost-dance.]

26. BARRINGTON, DAINES. Journal of a Spanish voyage in 1775 by Don Antonio Maurelle. Miscellanies, pp. 471–534, London, 1781.

27. BARROWS, DAVID PRESCOTT. The ethno-botany of the Coahuilla Indians of southern California. Univ. of Chicago, 1900.
[A spirited little book. Perhaps the best introduction to a study of the southern California Indians. The ethno-botany is excellent, and the author manages to present much of the culture along with it. One of the most human doctor's dissertations ever written.]

28. BARTLETT, J. R. Personal Narrative of explorations and incidents . . . connected with the United States and Mexican Boundary Commission, 1850–53. Vols. I–II. New York, 1854.
[An excellent book, with some valuable data on the tribes of southern California.]

29. BEACH, WM. W. The Indian miscellany. Albany, 1877.

30. BEECHEY, FREDERIC W. Narrative of a voyage to the Pacific and Berings strait, to cooperate with the Polar expeditions. Vols. I–II, London, 1831.

31. BLEDSOE, A. J. Indian wars of the Northwest. San Francisco, 1885.
[Written from the settler's point of view and without interest in the Indian as such, but contains some glimpses of ethnology.]

32. Boas, Franz. Anthropometrical observations on the Mission Indians of Southern California. Proc. Amer. Asso. Adv. Sci., vol. XLIV, pp. 261–269, 1895.
[All that there is on the racial type of this group.]

33. ———. Anthropometry of Central California. Bull. Amer. Mus. Nat. Hist., vol. XVII, pt. 4, pp. 347–380, 1905.
[Maidu, Wintun, Achomawi, Pomo, Yuki, Wailaki.]

34. ———. Notes on the Tillamook. Univ. Cal. Publs. Amer. Archaeol. and Ethnol., vol. XX, no. 1 (in press, 1923).
[Of comparative value for northwestern California.]

35. ———. Traditions of the Tillamook Indians. Journ. Amer. Folk-lore, vol. XI, pp. 23–38, 133–150, 1898.
[Some California allusions.]

36. ———. Zur Anthropologie der Nordamerikanischen Indianer. Verhandlungen der Berliner Anthropologischen Gesellschaft, pp. 367–411, May, 1895.
[Among the mass of summarized data are bodily measurements of several Californian groups.]

37. Bodega y Quadra. Primero viage, 1775. Anuario de la Direccion de Hidrografia, Año III, 1864, Madrid, 1865.

38. Bolton, H. E., ed. Expedition to San Francisco Bay in 1770. Diary of Pedro Fagés. Univ. Cal., Acad. Pac. Coast Hist., Publs., vol. II, no. 3, pp. [141]–[159], 1911.

39. ———. Father Escobar's relation of the Oñate expedition to California. Catholic Historical Review, vol. V, pp. 19–41, 1919.

40. ———. Kino's Historical Memoir of Pimería Alta. Cleveland, 1919.

41. ———. Spanish exploration in the Southwest, 1542–1706. New York, 1916.
[Contains authoritative translations of the Relation of Cabrillo, the Diary of Vizcaino, and the Journey of Oñate.]

42. Boscana, Geronimo. Chinigchinich. English translation in Robinson, Alfred, Life in California, New York, 1846. (The Spanish original is probably lost. Alexander Taylor reprinted the English version in the California Farmer, vol. XIII. The Robinson book has also been reprinted, but without the Chinigchinich.)
[This account of the religion and social customs of the Juaneño is by far the most valuable document on the California Indians preserved from the pen of any of the Franciscan missionaries. It is written in a spirited style, is based on unusually full knowledge, and is done with understanding. The ethnologist with local interest is at times puzzled how much of it to assign to Juaneño and how much to Gabrielino sources.]

43. Bourke, J. G. Notes on the cosmogony and theogony of the Mojave Indians. Journ. Amer. Folk-lore, vol. II, pp. 169–189, 1889.
[Excellent material somewhat confused.]

44. Bowers, Stephen. Santa Rosa Island. Rept. Smithson. Inst. for 1877, pp. 316–320, Washington, 1878.

45. Brinton, Daniel G. The American Race. New York, 1891.

46. Browne, J. Ross. The Indian reservations of California. Harper's Magazine, August, 1861. Reprinted in Beach, Indian Miscellany, pp. 303–322, Albany, 1877.
[Vigorous and to the point, but overdrawn.]

47. BUCHANAN, R. C.   Number, characteristics, etc., of the Indians of California, Oregon, and Washington. H. R. Ex. Doc. No. 76 (Serial no. 906), 34th Cong., 3d sess., Washington, 1857.

48. BURNS, L. M.   Digger Indian legends.   Land of Sunshine, vol. XIV, pp. 130–134, 223–226, 310–314, 397–402, 1901.
     [Shasta coyote tales.]

49. BUSCHMANN, J.   Die Sprachen Kizh und Netela von Neu Californien. Abhandlungen der Königlichen Akademie der Wissenschaften zu Berlin, 1855, pp. 499–531, 1856.
     [Gabrielino and Juaneño.]

50. ———.   Die Spuren der Aztekischen Sprache im nördlichen Mexico und höheren amerikanischen Norden.   Ibid., 1854, 2d suppl. vol., pp. 1–819, 1859.
     [A monumentally painstaking analysis of the linguistic materials available at the time from northern Mexico, the Southwest, and California.]

51. CABALLERIA [Y COLLELL, JUAN].   History of the city of Santa Barbara. Santa Barbara, 1892.
     [Contains a chapter on a Chumash dialect.]

52. CABALLERIA, JUAN.   History of San Bernardino valley.   San Bernardino, 1902.

   CABRILLO, JUAN RODRIGUEZ.   See Ferrel, B.

53. CARR, LUCIEN.   Measurements of crania from California.   Twelfth Ann. Rept. Peabody Museum, pp. 497–505, 1880.
     [Skulls from the Santa Barbara region.]

54. ———.   Observations on the crania from the Santa Barbara Islands. Rept. U. S. Geog. Surv. west of the 100th Meridian [Wheeler Surv. Rept.], vol. VII, Archaeology, pp. 277–292, Washington, 1879.

55. CHAMISSO, ADELBERT VON.   Reise um die Welt, 1815–1818.   Hildburghausen, 1869.

56. CHAPMAN, C. E., ed.   Expedition on the Sacramento and San Joaquin rivers in 1817.   Diary of Fray Narciso Duran.   Univ. Cal., Acad. Pacific Coast History, Publs., vol. II, no. 5, pp. [329]–[349], 1911.

57. CHESNUT, V. K.   Plants used by the Indians of Mendocino county, California.   Cont. U. S. National Herbarium, vol. VII, no. 3, Washington, 1902.

58. CHEVER, E. E.   The Indians of California.   Amer. Naturalist, vol. IV, pp. 129–148, 1870.
     [A pioneer's notes on the Maidu.]

59. CHORIS, L.   Voyage pittoresque autour du Monde.   Paris, 1822.   (Includes sections by Cuvier, Chamisso, Gall.)

60. CLARK, GALEN.   Indians of the Yosemite Valley and vicinity, their history, customs, and traditions.   Yosemite, 1904.

61. CLAVIGERO, F. X.   Storia della California.   Vols. I–II.   Venice, 1789.   Spanish translation, Historia de la Antigua ó Baja California.   Mexico, 1852.

   COSTANSÓ MIGUEL.   See Hemert-Engert, Adolph van, and Teggart, Frederick J.

62. COUES, ELLIOTT, ed.   On the trail of a Spanish pioneer.   The diary and itinerary of Francisco Garcés, 1775–76.   Vols. I–II.   New York, 1900.
     [A well translated and splendidly annotated version of the diary of an intrepid explorer and priest, rich in data of the greatest value.   The ethnological comments are by F. W. Hodge.]

63. COVILLE, FREDERICK V. Notes on the plants used by the Klamath Indians of Oregon. Cont. U S. Nat. Herbarium, vol. v, no. 2, Washington, 1897.

64. ———. The Panamint Indians of California. Amer. Anthrop., vol. v, pp. 351–361, 1892. ⊙
    [Brief but good, and there is little else on these people.]

65. ———. Wokas, a primitive food of the Klamath Indians. Rept. U. S. Nat. Mus. for 1902, pp. 727–739, Washington, 1904.
    [Model scientific report—clear, concise, exhaustive, and interesting. It shows the possibilities that lie in intelligent ethno-botanical studies.]

66. CULIN, STEWART. Games of the North American Indians. Twenty-fourth Rept. Bur. Amer. Ethn., Washington, 1907.
    [California is well represented in this exhaustive monograph.]

67. CURTIN, JEREMIAH. Achomawi myths. Edited by Roland B. Dixon. Journ. Amer. Folk-lore, vol. XXII, pp. 283–287, 1909.

68. ———. Creation myths of primitive America. Boston, 1898.
    [9 Wintun and 13 Yana myths, told at length with the stylistic peculiarities and comments characteristic of the author.]

69. ———. Myths of the Modocs. Boston, 1912.

70. DALTON, O. M. Notes on an ethnographical collection. Intern. Achiv für Ethnog., B. x, pp. 225–245, 1897.

71. DAVIS, EDWARD H. The Diegueño ceremony of the death images. Contr. Mus. Am. Indian Heye Found., vol. v, no. 2, pp. 7–33, 1919.

72. ———. Early cremation ceremonies of the Luiseño and Diegueño Indians of Southern California. Indian Notes and Monographs, vol. VII, no. 3, pp. 87–110, 1921.

73. DIXON, ROLAND B. Achomawi and Atsugewi tales. Journ. Amer. Folk-lore, vol. XXI, pp. 159–177, 1908.

74. ———. Basketry designs of the Maidu Indians of California. Amer. Anthrop., n. s. vol. II, pp. 266–276, 1900.

75. ———. Basketry designs of the Indians of Northern California. Bull. Amer. Mus. Nat. Hist., vol. XVII, pp. 1–32, 1902.

76. ———. The Chimariko Indians and language. Univ. Cal. Publs. Amer. Archaeol. and Ethnol., vol. v, pp. 293–380, 1910.
    [The results of a study undertaken just prior to the extinction of this tribe.]

77. ———. Linguistic relationships within the Shasta-Achomawi stock. International Congress of Americanists, XVth sess., vol. II, pp. 255–263, Quebec, 1907.

78. ———. Maidu: an illustrative sketch. Bull. 40, Bur. Amer. Ethn. (Handbook of American Indian Languages), pt. 1, pp. 683–734, Washington, 1911.
    [A rather complete account of Maidu grammar.]

79. ———. Maidu myths. Bull. Amer. Mus. Nat. Hist., vol. XVII, pp. 33–118, 1902.
    [Perhaps the most generally interesting collection of native traditions ever made in California.]

80. ———. Maidu texts. Publs. Amer. Ethnol. Soc., vol. IV, 1912.
    [The only considerable body of texts published in any Californian language except Athabascan, Yana, and Klamath-Modoc.]

81. ———. The mythology of the Shasta-Achomawi. Amer. Anthrop., n. s. vol. VII, pp. 607–612, 1905.

82. DIXON, ROLAND B.   The Northern Maidu.   Bull. Amer. Mus. Nat. Hist., vol. XVII, pp. 119–346, 1905.
   [Easily the most comprehensive and valuable ethnological study of any one group of California Indians.]

83. ———.   Notes on the Achomawi and Atsugewi of northern California.   Amer. Anthrop., n. s. vol. X, pp. 208–220, 1908.
   [Brief, but the best there is on these people.]

84. ———.   Outlines of Wintun grammar.   Putnam Anniversary Volume, pp. 461–476, New York, 1909.
   [All that is known of the structure of this important tongue.]

85. ———.   The pronominal dual in the languages of California.   Boas Anniversary Volume, pp. 80–84, New York, 1906.

86. ———.   The Shasta.   Bull. Amer. Mus. Nat. Hist., vol. XVII, pp. 381–498, 1907.
   [Second only to the author's "Northern Maidu" in value.]

87. ———.   The Shasta-Achomawi: a new linguistic stock with four new dialects.   Amer. Anthrop., n. s. vol. VII, pp. 213–217, 1905.

88. ———.   Shasta myths.   Journ. Amer. Folk-lore, vol. XXIII, pp. 8–37, 364–370, 1910.

89. ———.   Some coyote stories from the Maidu Indians of California.   Ibid., vol. XIII, pp. 267–270, 1900.

90. ———.   Some shamans of northern California.   Ibid., vol. XVII, pp. 23–27, 1904.

91. ———.   System and sequence in Maidu mythology.   Ibid., vol. XVI, pp. 32–36, 1903.

92. DIXON, ROLAND B., *and* KROEBER, A. L.   Linguistic families in California.   Univ. Cal. Publs. Amer. Archaeol. and Ethnol., vol XVI, pp. 47–118, 1919.

93. ———.   The native languages of California.   Amer. Anthrop., n. s. vol. V, pp. 1–26, 1903.
   [A classification of stocks according to types.]

94. ———.   New linguistic families in California.   Ibid., n. s. vol. XV, pp. 647–655, 1913.

95. ———.   Numerical systems of the languages of California.   Ibid., n. s. vol. IX, 663–690, 1907.

96. ———.   Relationship of the Indian languages of California.   Science, n. s. vol. XXXVII, p. 225, 1913.

97. DORSEY, GEORGE A.   Certain gambling games of the Klamath Indians.   Amer. Anthrop., n. s. vol. III, pp. 14–27, 1901.

98. ———.   Indians of the Southwest.   1903.
   [This exceedingly useful handbook, issued by the Atchison, Topeka, and Santa Fe Railway System, contains notes on Mohave, Chemehuevi, Yuma, Yokuts, Mono, and Miwok on pp. 193–216.]

99. DORSEY, J. OWEN.   The Gentile system of the Siletz tribes.   Journ. Amer. Folk-lore, vol. III, pp. 227–237. 1890.
   [The "gentes" are villages.   The Californian Tolowa are included.]

   DRAKE, SIR FRANCIS.   *See* Early English Voyages; *and* Barrett, S. A., the ethno-geography of the Pomo and neighboring Indians.

100. DUBOIS, CONSTANCE GODDARD.   Diegueño mortuary ollas.   Amer. Anthrop., n. s. vol. IX, pp. 484–486, 1907.

101. DuBois, Constance Goddard. Diegueño myths and their connections with the Mohave. International Congress of Americanists, XVth sess., 1906, vol. II, pp. 129–134, Quebec, 1907.

102. ———. The mythology of the Diegueños. Jour. Amer. Folk-lore, vol. XIV, pp. 181–185, 1901.

103. ———. The mythology of the Diegueños. International Congress of Americanists, XIIIth sess., New York, 1902, pp. 101–106, 1905.

104. ———. Mythology of the Mission Indians. Journ. Amer. Folk-lore, vol. XVII, pp. 185–188, 1904.

105. ———. The religion of the Luiseño and Diegueño Indians of Southern California. Univ. Cal. Publs. Amer. Archaeol. and Ethnol., vol. VIII, pp. 69–186, 1908.
    [An unusually sympathetic portrayal of a remarkable native religion.]

106. ———. Religious ceremonies and myths of the Mission Indians. Amer. Anthrop., n. s. vol. VII, pp. 620–629, 1905.

107. ———. The story of the Chaup: a myth of the Diegueños. Journ. Amer. Folk-lore, vol. XVII, pp. 217–242, 1904.
    [Valuable.]

108. ———. Two types or styles of Diegueño religious dancing. International Congress of Americanists, XVth sess., 1906, vol. II, pp. 135–138, Quebec, 1907.

109. Duflot de Mofras, Eugène. Exploration du Territoire de l'Oregon, des Californies, et de la Mer Vermeille. Vols. I–II. Paris, 1844.

Duran, Narciso. See Chapman, C. E.

110. Dutcher, B. H. Piñon gathering among the Panamint Indians. Amer. Anthrop., vol. VI, pp. 377–380, 1893.

111. Early English voyages to the Pacific coast of America. (From their own, and contemporary English, accounts.) Sir Francis Drake.—III. Out West, vol. XVIII, no. 1, pp. 73–80, Jan. 1903. See also Barrett, S. A.
    [Perhaps the most readily accessible republication of the passages descriptive of native life in the principal account of Drake's landing in Nova Albion.]

112. Early Western history. From documents never before published in English. Diary of Junipero Serra; Loreto to San Diego, March 28–June 30, 1769. Out West, vol. XVI, pp. 293–296, 399–406, 513–518, 635–642, 1902; vol. XVII, pp. 69–76, 1902.
    [Mostly Baja California, but there is some mention of the people later called Diegueño.]

113. Eisen, Gustav. An Account of the Indians of the Santa Barbara Islands in California. Sitzungsberichte der Königlichen Boehmischen Gesellschaft der Wissenschaften, II Klasse, Prag, 1904.
    [A compilation done with intelligence.]

114. Elliott, W. W., and Company, publishers, History of Humboldt County, California. San Francisco, 1881.

115. Emory, W. H. Notes of a military reconnaissance from Fort Leavenworth in Missouri to San Diego in California, made in 1846–47. Washington, 1848.

116. ———. United States and Mexican Boundary Survey. Report. Vol. I. Washington, 1857. (H. R. Ex. Doc. 135, 34th Cong., 1st sess.)

117. ENGELHARDT, ZEPHRYIN. Franciscans in California. Harbor Springs, Michigan, 1897.

　　　[A considerable number of facts about the Indians, mostly from sources otherwise accessible with difficulty, are included in this story of the missions and missionaries.]

118. ——. The missions and missionaries of California. Vols. I–IV. San Francisco, 1908–1914.

　　　[An important history, containing many passages of ethnological moment.]

　　EWBANK, THOMAS. See Whipple, A. W., Ewbank and Turner.

　　FAGÉS, PEDRO. See Bolton, H. E.; Priestley, H. I.; Ternaux-Compans, Henri.

119. FARRAND, LIVINGSTON. Notes on the Alsea Indians of Oregon. Amer. Anthrop., n. s. vol. III, pp. 239–247, 1901.

　　　[Of service for comparisons with the tribes of northwestern California.]

120. ——. Shasta and Athapascan myths from Oregon. Edited by L. J. Frachtenberg. Journ. Amer. Folk-lore, vol. XXVIII, pp. 207–242, 1915.

　　FASSIN, A. G. See Tassin.

121. FAYE, PAUL-LOUIS. Notes on the Southern Maidu. Univ. Cal. Publs. Amer. Archaeol. and Ethnol., vol. XX, no. 3 (in press, 1923).

122. FERREL, B. Relation or diary of the voyage which Rodriguez Cabrillo made. Translation with notes by H. W. Henshaw. Rept. U. S. Geog. Surv. west of the 100th Meridian [Wheeler Surv. Rept.], vol. VII, Archaeology, pp. 293–314, Washington, 1879. Transl. in Bolton, Spanish exploration in the Southwest, pp. 13–39, New York, 1916.

　　FONT, PEDRO. See Teggert, Frederick J., ed.

123. FORBES, ALEXANDER. A history of lower and upper California. London, 1839.

124. FREDERICK, M. C. Some Indian paintings. Land of Sunshine, vol. XV, no. 4, pp. 223–227, 1901.

　　　[Pictographs near Santa Barbara.]

125. FREELAND, L. S. Pomo doctors and poisoners. Univ. Cal. Publs. Amer. Archaeol. and Ethnol., vol. XX, no 4 (in press, 1923).

126. FRÉMONT, J. C. The exploring expedition to the Rocky Mountains, Oregon and California. Auburn and Buffalo, 1854.

127. ——. Geographical memoir upon Upper California. Washington, 1848.

128. ——. Report of an exploring expedition to Oregon and northern California. Washington, 1845.

129. FRIEDERICI, GEORG. Die Schiffahrt der Indianer. Stuttgart, 1907.

130. FRY, WINIFRED S. Humboldt Indians. Out West, vol. XXI, pp. 503–514, 1904.

131. GALIANO, D. A. Relacion del viage hecho por las goletas Sutil y Mexicana. Madrid, 1802.

132. GALLATIN, ALBERT. Hale's Indians of Northwest America. Trans. Amer. Ethn. Soc., vol. II, pp. xxiii–clxxxviii, 1–130, New York, 1848.

　　　[Includes Californian groups.]

133. ——. A synopsis of the Indian tribes in North America. Trans. Amer. Antiq. Soc. (Archaeologia Americana), vol. II, 1836.

　　GARCÉS, FRANCISCO. See Coues, Elliott, ed.

134. GATSCHET, ALBERT S. Analytical report upon Indian dialects spoken in southern California. U. S. Geog. Surv. west of the 100th Meridian, Ann. Rept. [of the Chief of Engineers] for 1876, Appendix JJ, pp. 550–563, Washington, 1876.

135. ———. Classification into seven linguistic stocks of western Indian dialects contained in forty vocabularies. Rept. U. S. Geog. Surv. west of the 100th Meridian [Wheeler Surv. Rept.], vol. VII, Archaeology, pp. 403–485, 1879.

136. ———. Indian languages of the Pacific states and territories. Magazine of Amer. Hist., March, 1877.

137. ———. The Klamath Indians of southwestern Oregon. Cont. N. Amer. Ethnol., vol. II, pts. 1 and 2, Washington, 1890.
[An enormous and carefully done monograph, mainly texts, grammar, and dictionary, also an ethnographic sketch. The Modoc are included with the Klamath.]

138. ———. Songs of the Modoc Indians. Amer. Anthrop., vol. VII, pp. 26–31, 1894.

139. ———. Specimen of the Chúmëto language. American Antiquarian, vol. V, pp. 71–73, 173–180, 1883.
[Sketch of the Southern Miwok dialect.]

140. ———. Der Yuma-Sprachstamm. Zeitschrift für Ethnologie, B. IX, pp. 341–350, 366–418, 1877; B. XV, pp. 123–147, 1883; B. XVIII, pp. 97–122, 1886.
[Scholarly work on crude materials. The contribution should by now be long out of date, but investigations of this stock have been neglected, and the work remains of value.]

141. ———. Zwölf Sprachen aus dem Südwesten Nord-Amerikas. Weimar, 1876.

142. GIBBS, GEORGE. Journal of the Expedition of Colonel Redick M'Kee . . . through Northwestern California . . . in 1851. In Schoolcraft, Indian Tribes, vol. III, pp. 99–177, Phila., 1853.
[A valuable report.]

143. ———. Observations on some of the Indian dialects of Northern California. Ibid., pp. 420–423. Continued under the title " Vocabularies of Indian languages in Northwest California." Ibid., pp. 428–445.

144. ———. Tribes of western Washington and northwestern Oregon. Cont. N. Amer. Ethnol., vol. I, pp. 157–241, Washington, 1877.
[Contains some allusions to California and is important for comparisons of the Indians of California with those farther north.]

145. GIFFORD, EDWARD WINSLOW. California kinship terminologies. Univ. Cal. Publs. Amer. Archaeol. and Ethnol., vol. XVIII, pp. 1–285, 1922.
[The fullest study of the kind attempted for any area.]

146. ———. Clans and moieties in Southern California. Ibid., vol. XIV, pp. 155–219, 1918.

147. ———. Composition of California shellmounds. Ibid., vol. XII, pp. 1–29, 1916.
[Bears on questions of fauna, topographic change, age, etc.]

148. ———. Dichotomous social organization in south central California. Ibid., vol. XI, pp. 291–296, 1916.

149. ———. Miwok moieties. Ibid., vol. XII, pp. 139–194, 1916.
[A thorough account of the organization of society.]

150. ———. Miwok myths. Ibid., vol. XII, pp. 283–338, 1917.

151. GIFFORD, EDWARD WINSLOW. Pomo lands on Clear Lake. Ibid., vol. xx, no. 5 (in press, 1923).

152. ———. Tübatulabal and Kawaiisu kinship terms. Ibid., vol. xII, pp. 219–248, 1917.

153. GODDARD, PLINY EARLE. Athapascan (Hupa). Bull. 40, Bur. Amer. Ethn. (Hankbook of American Indian Languages), pt. 1, pp. 85–158, Washington, 1911.

154. -———. Chilula texts. Univ. Cal. Publs. Amer. Archaeol. and Ethnol., vol. x, pp. 289–379, 1914.

155. ———. Elements of the Kato language. Ibid., vol. xI, pp. 1–176, 1912.

156. ———. Habitat of the Wailaki. Ibid., vol. xx, no. 6 (in press, 1923).

157. ———. Hupa texts. Ibid., vol. I, pp. 89–368, 1904.
    [The first of a valuable series of collections of texts from the Athabascan languages of California by this author.]

158. ——. The Kato Pomo not Pomo. Amer. Anthrop., n. s. vol. v, pp. 375–376, 1903.

159. ———. Kato texts. Univ. Cal. Publs. Amer. Archaeol. and Ethnol., vol. v, pp. 65–238, 1909.

160. ———. Lassik tales. Journ. Amer. Folk-lore, vol. xIx, pp. 133–140, 1906.

161. ———. Life and culture of the Hupa. Univ. Cal. Publs. Amer. Archaeol. and Ethnol., vol. I, pp. 1–88, 1903.
    [The best written general monograph on a California tribe, and the first coherent picture of the culture of northwestern California. The only defect of the work is its brevity.]

162. ———. The morphology of the Hupa language. Ibid., vol III, 1905.
    [An exhaustive grammar.]

163. ———. Notes on the Chilula Indians of northwestern California. Ibid., vol. x, pp. 265–288, 1914.
    [Sums up what is known.]

164. ———. The phonology of the Hupa language. Ibid., vol. v, pp. 1–20, 1907.

165. ———. Wayside shrines in northwestern California. Amer. Anthrop., n. s., vol., xv, pp. 702–703, 1913.

166. HALDEMAN, S. S. Beads. Rept. U. S. Geog. Surv. west of the 100th meridian [Wheeler Surv. Rept.], vol. vII, Archaeology, pp. 263–271, 1879.

167. HALE, HORATIO. Ethnology and philology. U. S. Exploring Expedition during the years 1838–1842, under the command of Charles Wilkes, U. S. N. Vol. vI. Phila., 1846.

168. HALL, SHARLOT M. The burning of a Mojave chief. Out West, vol. xvIII, pp. 60–65, 1903.

169. HARDACRE, EMMA C. Eighteen years alone. Scribner's Monthly, pp. 657–664, September, 1880.
    [The story of the lone woman of San Nicolas Island, the last of her people.]

170. HARRINGTON, JOHN PEABODY. A Yuma account of origins. Journ. Amer. Folk-lore, vol. xxI, pp. 324–348, 1908.
    [An important scholarly presentation.]

HELMERSEN, G. VON. *See* Baer, K. E. von, and Helmersen.

171. HEMERT–ENGERT, ADOLPH VAN, *and* TEGGART, FREDERICK J., *eds.* The narrative of the Portolá expedition of 1769–1770, by Miguel Costanso. Univ. Cal. Acad. Pac. Coast Hist., Publs. vol. I, no. 4, pp. [91]–[159], 1910.

172. HENLY, THOMAS J. California Indians. In Schoolcraft, Indian Tribes, vol. VI, Table XXXV, pp. 715–718, Phila., 1857.

173. HENSHAW, H. W. The aboriginal relics called "Sinkers" or "Plummets." Amer. Journ. Archaeol., vol. I, pp. 105–114, 1885.

174. ————. A new linguistic family in California. Amer. Anthrop., vol. III, pp. 45–49. 1890.
       [Esselen.]

175. ————. Perforated stones from California. Bull. 2, Bur. Amer. Ethn., Washington, 1887.
       [Concise, definite, and convincing.]

176. HEYE, GEORGE G. Certain aboriginal pottery from Southern California. Indian Notes and Monographs, vol. VII, no. 1, pp. [1]–[46]. 1919.

177. ————. Certain artifacts from San Miguel Island, California. Ibid., no. 4, pp. [1]–[211]. 1921.

178. HISTORY OF MENDOCINO COUNTY, CALIFORNIA. [Lyman L. Palmer, historian. Sometimes cited as by Alley Bowen and Company, the publishers.] San Francisco, 1880.

179. HISTORY OF NAPA AND LAKE COUNTIES, CALIFORNIA. [Lyman L. Palmer, historian. Sometimes cited under Slocum, Bowen and Company, the publishers.] San Francisco, 1880.

180. HITTELL, THEODORE H. History of California. Vols. I–IV. San Francisco, 1885–1897.

181. HODGE, F. W., ed. Handbook of American Indians North of Mexico. Bull. 30, Bur. Amer. Ethn., pts. 1–2, Washington, 1907–1910.
       HODGE, F. W. See Coues, Elliott, ed.

182. HOFFMAN, W. T. Hugo Reid's account of the Indians of Los Angeles county, California. Bull. Essex Institute, vol. XVII, 1885. [See Reid, Hugo.]

183. ————. Miscellaneous ethnographic observations on Indians inhabiting Nevada, California, and Arizona. Tenth Ann. Rept. U. S. Geol. and Geog. Surv. [Hayden Survey], Washington, 1878.

184. ————. Remarks on aboriginal art in California and Queen Charlotte's Island. Proc. Davenport Acad. Nat. Sci., vol. IV, pp. 105–122, 1884.
       [Petroglyphs.]

185. HOLDER, C. F. The ancient islanders of California. Pop. Sci. Mo., pp. 658–662, March, 1896.

186. HOLMES, WILLIAM H. Anthropological studies in California. Rept. U. S. Nat. Mus. for 1900, pp. 155–188, Washington, 1902.
       [A traveler's observations on various groups of Indians from the Maidu to the Diegueño, incidental to studies of the antiquity of man, done with a master hand. The paper is as exact as it is readable.]

187. ————. Preliminary revision of the evidence relating to auriferous gravel man in California. Amer. Anthrop., n. s. vol. I, pp. 107–121, 614–645, 1899. Reprinted in Smithsonian Report for 1899, pp. 419–472, Washington, 1901.
       [The findings are negative, but in the best manner of this lucid and brilliant master.]

188. HOOPER, LUCILE. The Cahuilla Indians. Univ. Cal. Publs. Amer. Archaeol. and Ethnol., vol. XVI, pp. 315–380, 1920.

189. HOUGH, WALTER. Primitive American armor. Rept. U. S. Nat. Mus. for 1893, pp. 625–651, Washington, 1895.

190. HRDLIČKA, ALEŠ. Contribution to the physical anthropology of California. Univ. Cal. Publs. Amer. Archaeol. and Ethnol., vol. IV, pp. 49–64, 1906.
    [A careful study of skulls from central California.]

191. ———. Skeletal remains suggesting or attributed to early man in North America. Bull. 33, Bur. Amer. Ethn., Washington, 1907.

192. ———. Stature of Indians of the Southwest and of northern Mexico. Putnam Anniversary Volume, pp. 405–426, New York, 1909.
    [Includes the lower Colorado tribes.]

193. HUDSON, J. W. An Indian myth of the San Joaquin Basin. Journ. Amer. Folk-lore, vol. XV, pp. 104–106, 1902.

194. ———. Pomo basket makers. Overland Monthly, 2d ser., vol. XXI, pp. 561–578, 1893.

195. ———. Pomo wampum makers. Ibid., vol. XXX, pp. 101–108, 1897.

196. HUMBOLDT, F. H. ALEXANDER DE. Essai politique sur le Royaume de la Nouvelle-Espagne. Vols. I–V, Paris, 1811. Translated by John Black, vols. I–IV, London, 1811.

197. INDIAN AFFAIRS (U. S.). Office of Indian Affairs (War Department). Reports, 1825–1848. Report of the Commissioner (Department of the Interior), 1849–1917.

198. JACKSON, HELEN M. H., and KINNEY, ABBOT. Report on the condition and needs of the Mission Indians of California. Washington, 1883.

199. JAMES, GEORGE WHARTON. Indian basketry. New York, 1904.

200. ———. The legend of Tauquitch and Algoot. Journ. Amer. Folk-lore, vol. XVI, pp. 153–159, 1903.

201. ———. A Saboba origin-myth. Journ. Amer. Folk-lore, vol. XV, pp. 36–39, 1902.

202. JOHNSTON, ADAM. The California Indians—their manners, customs, and history. In Schoolcraft, Indian Tribes, vol. IV, pp. 221–226, Phila., 1854.

203. JOHNS[T]ON, ADAM. Indian tribes, or bands, of the Sacramento Valley, California. In Schoolcraft, Indian Tribes, vol. VI, Table XXIX, p. 710, Phila., 1857.

204. ———. Languages of California. Ibid., vol. IV, pp. 406–415, Phila., 1854.

205. JOHNSTON, ADAM. [Report on the Indians of the Sacramento river and the Sierra Nevada.] Report of the Commissioner of Indian Affairs for 1850, pp. 122–125. (Sen. Ex. Docs. vol. I, 31st Cong., 2d sess.)

206. JONES, PHILIP MILLS. Mound Excavations near Stockton. Univ. Cal. Pub. Amer. Archaeol. and Ethnol., vol. XX, no. 7 (in press, 1923).

207. KELSEY, C. E. Report of the Special Agent for California Indians. Carlisle, Pa., 1906.

208. KERN, E. M. Indian customs of California. In Schoolcraft, Indian Tribes, vol. V, pp. 649-650, Phila., 1855.

    KINNEY, ABBOT. See Jackson, Helen M. H., and Kinney.

    KINO, FATHER. See Bolton, H. E.

    KOSTROMITONOW. See Baer, K. E. von.

209. KOTZEBUE, OTTO VON. Voyage of discovery into the South Sea and Behring's Strait, 1815–1818. Translated by H. F. Lloyd. Vols. I–III. London, 1821.

210. KRAUSE, FRITZ. Die kultur der kalifornischen Indianer in ihrer bedeutung für die ethnologie und die nordamerikanische völkerkunde. Institut für Völkerkunde, erste Reihe, Bd. 4, pp. 1–98, Leipzig, 1921.
   [A scholarly interpretation.]

211. KROEBER, A. L. The anthropology of California. Science, n. s. vol. XXVII, pp. 281–290, 1908.

212. ———. The archaeology of California. Putnam Anniversary Volume, pp. 1–42, New York, 1909.

213. ———. Basket designs of the Indians of northwestern California. Univ. Cal. Publs. Amer. Archaeol. and Ethnol., vol. II, pp. 104–164, 1905.

214. ———. Basket designs of the Mission Indians of California. Anthrop. Pap. Amer. Mus. Nat. Hist., vol. XX, pp. 147–183, 1922.

215. ———. At the bedrock of history. Sunset [Magazine], vol. XXV, pp. 255–260, 1910.
   [An archeological discovery in the San Joaquin valley.]

216. ———. California basketry and the Pomo. Amer. Anthrop., n. s., vol. XI, pp. 233–249, 1909.

217. ———. California culture provinces. Univ. Cal. Publs. Amer. Archaeol. and Ethnol., vol. XVII, pp. 151–169, 1920.

218. ———. California kinship systems. Ibid., vol. XII, pp. 339–396, 1917.

219. ———. California place names of Indian origin. Ibid., vol. XII, pp. 31–69, 1916.

220. ———. The Chumash and Costanoan languages. Ibid., vol. IX, pp. 237–271, 1910.

221. ———. The coast Yuki of California. Amer. Anthrop., n. s. vol. V, pp. 729–730, 1903.

222. ———. The dialectic divisions of the Moquelumnan family. Ibid., n. s. vol. VIII, pp. 652–663, 1906.

223. ———. Elements of culture in native California. Univ. Cal. Publs. Amer. Archaeol. and Ethnol., vol. XIII, pp. 259–328, 1922.

224. ———. Ethnography of the Cahuilla Indians. Ibid., vol. VIII, pp. 29–68, 1908.

225. ———. On the evidences of the occupation of certain regions by the Miwok Indians. Ibid., vol. VI, pp. 369–380, 1908.

226. ———. A Ghost dance in California. Journ. Amer. Folk-lore, vol. XVII, pp. 32–35, 1904.

227. ———. The history of native culture in California. Univ. Cal. Publs. Amer. Archaeol. and Ethnol., vol. XX, no. 8 (in press, 1923).

228. ———. Indian myths from south central California. Ibid., vol. IV, pp. 167–250, 1907.
   [Mainly Yokuts, but also Miwok and Costanoan tales, and comparisons.]

229. ———. Ishi, the last aborigine. World's Work, pp. 304–308, July, 1912.

230. ———. The languages of the coast of California north of San Francisco. Univ. Cal. Publs. Amer. Archaeol. and Ethnol., vol. IX, pp. 273–435, 1911.
   [Miwok, Pomo, Yuki, Wiyot, Yurok, Karok.]

231. ———. The languages of the coast of California south of San Francisco. Ibid., vol. II, pp. 29–80, 1904.
   [Chumash, Salinan, Esselen, Costanoan.]

232. KROEBER, A. L.   A Mission record of the California Indians.   Ibid., vol. VIII, pp. 1–27, 1908.

233. ———.   Notes on Shoshonean dialects of southern California.   Ibid., vol. VIII, pp. 235–269, 1909.

234. ———.   Origin tradition of the Chemehuevi Indians.   Journ. Amer. Folklore, vol. XXI, pp. 240–242, 1908.

235. ———.   Phonetic constituents of the native languages of California.   Univ. Cal. Publs. Amer. Archaeol. and Ethnol., vol. X, pp. 1–12, 1911.

236. ———.   Phonetic elements of the Mohave language.   Ibid., pp. 45–96.

237. ———.   Preliminary sketch of the Mohave Indians.   Amer. Anthrop., n. s. vol. IV, pp. 276–285, 1902.

238. ———.   The religion of the Indians of California.   Univ. Cal. Publs. Amer. Archaeol. and Ethnol., vol. IV, pp. 319–356, 1907.

239. ———.   Serian, Tequistlatecan, and Hokan.   Ibid., vol. XI, pp. 279–290, 1915.

240. ———.   Shoshonean dialects of California.   Ibid., vol. IV, pp. 65–166, 1907.
     [Contains considerable ethno-geography and a tribal classification.]

241. ———.   Two myths of the Mission Indians of California.   Journ. Amer. Folk-lore, vol. XIX, pp. 309–321, 1906.

242. ———.   Types of Indian culture in California.   Univ. Cal. Publs. Amer. Archaeol. and Ethnol., vol. II, pp. 81–103, 1904.

243. ———.   The Washo language of east central California and Nevada. Ibid., vol. IV, pp. 251–317, 1907.

244. ———.   Wishosk myths.   Journ. Amer. Folk-lore, vol. XVIII, pp. 85–107, 1905.
     [Wiyot.]

245. ———.   Wiyot folk-lore.   Ibid., vol. XXI, pp. 37–39, 1908.

246. ———.   The Yokuts and Yuki languages.   Boas Anniversary Volume, pp. 64–79, New York, 1906.

247. ———.   The Yokuts language of south central California.   Univ. Cal. Publs. Amer. Archaeol. and Ethnol., vol. II, pp. 165–377, 1907.
     [Contains a classification of tribes.]

248. ———.   Yokuts names.   Journ. Amer. Folk-lore, vol. XIX, pp. 142–143, 1906.

249 ———.   Yuman tribes of the Lower Colorado.   Univ. Cal. Publs. Amer. Archaeol. and Ethnol., vol. XVI, pp. 475–485, 1920.

     ———.   See Dixon, Roland B., and Kroeber.

250. KROEBER, HENRIETTE ROTHSCHILD.   Wappo myths.   Journ. Amer. Folk-lore, vol. XXI, pp. 321–323, 1908.

251. LANGSDORFF, G. H. VON.   Voyages and travels, 1803–1807.   Vols. I–II.   London, 1813–14.   Translation of: Bemerkungen auf einer Reise um die Welt.   Frankfurt, 1812.

252. LATHAM, R. G.   On the languages of New California.   Proc. Philol. Soc. London, 1852–53, vol. VI, pp. 72–86, London, 1854.

253. ———.   On the languages of northern, western, and central America. Trans. Philol. Soc. London, 1856, pp. 57–118, London, 1857.

254. ———.   Opuscula.   Essays chiefly philological and ethnographical.   London, 1860.

255. LEWIS, ALBERT BUELL. Tribes of the Columbia valley and the coast of Washington and Oregon. Memoirs of the Amer. Anthrop. Asso., vol. I, pt. 2, pp. 147–209, 1906.
[Important for the study of the relations of the cultures of California to those of the north.]

256. LOEFFELHOLZ, K. VON. Die Zoreisch-Indianer der Trinidad-Bai (Californien). Mitth. Anthrop. Ges. Wien, vol. XXIII, pp. 101–123, 1893.
[Yurok of Tsurau in 1857.]

257. LOEW, OSCAR. Notes upon the ethnology of southern California and adjacent regions. U. S. Geog. Surv. of Terr. west of the 100th Meridian, Ann. Rept. [Chief of Engineers] for 1876, Appendix JJ, Washington, 1876.

258. LOUD, LLEWELLYN L. Ethnogeography and archaeology of the Wiyot territory. Univ. Cal. Publs. Amer. Archaeol. and Ethnol., vol. XIV, pp. 221–436, 1918.
[The first detailed report of archaeological exploration in the north of California.]

259. LOWIE, ROBERT H. Culture connection of California and Plateau Shoshonean tribes. Ibid., vol. XX, no. 9 (in press, 1923).

260. LUMMIS, CHAS. F. The exiles of Cupa. Out West, vol. XVI, pp. 465–479; [continued under the title of] Two days at Mesa Grande, pp. 602–612, 1902.

261. LYON, C. How the Indians made stone arrow-heads. Historical Magazine, vol. III, p. 214, 1859.

262. MALLERY, GARRICK. Pictographs of the North American Indians. Fourth Rept. Bur. Ethn., pp. 3–256, Washington, 1886.
[Pp. 30–33 relate to California.]

263. ———. Picture writing of the American Indians. Tenth Rept. Bur. Ethn., Washington, 1893.
[There are some California data.]

264. MCKEE, REDICK. California Coast Tribes north of San Francisco, 1851. In Schoolcraft, Indian Tribes, vol. VI, Table XXX, p. 711, Phila., 1857.

265. ———. Report of expedition leaving Sonoma August 9, 1851 . . . to the Klamath. Sen. Ex. Doc. No. 4 (Serial no. 688), 33d Cong., Special sess., Washington, 1853.
———. See M'Kee, Redick.

266. MCKERN, W. C. Functional families of the Patwin. Univ. Cal. Publs. Amer. Archaeol. and Ethnol., vol. XIII, pp. 235–258, 1922.

267. ———. Patwin houses. Ibid., vol. XX, no. 10 (in press, 1923).
MCLEAN, JOHN J. See Rau. Charles.

268. MASON, J. ALDEN. The ethnology of the Salinan Indians. Univ. Cal. Publs. Amer. Archaeol. and Ethnol., vol. X, pp. 97–240, 1912.
[A careful comparative study of the broken data available on this group.]

269. ———. The language of the Salinan Indians. Ibid., vol. XIV, pp. 1–154, 1918.

270. ———. The Mutsun dialect of Costanoan, based on the vocabulary of [Arroyo] De la Cuesta. Ibid., vol. XI, pp. 399–472, 1916.
[The author has drawn a grammar and classified list of stems from a disordered phrase-book.]

271. MASON, OTIS T. Aboriginal American basketry. Rept. U. S. Nat. Mus. for 1902, pp. 171–548, Washington, 1904.
[The classic work on the subject, beautifully illustrated. California receives its due share of treatment.]

272. ———. Cradles of the American aborigines. Rept. U. S. Nat. Mus. for 1897, pp. 161–212, Washington, 1889.
[Pp. 178–184 refer to California.]

273. ———. The Ray collection from Hupa Reservation. Ann. Rept. Smithsonian Institution for 1886, pt. 1, pp. 205–239, Washington, 1889.
[The first accurate description of utensils typical of the culture of northwestern California. A few implements from Round Valley and northeastern California have got mixed in: Figures 20–25, 30–31, 35, 38–40, 56, 61–65, 68–69, 111–114.]

274. ———. The throwing-stick in California. Amer. Anthrop., vol. v, p. 66, 1892.

275. MATIEGKA, H. Ueber Schädel und Skelette von Santa Rosa [Island]. Sitzungsberichte der Königlichen Gesellschaft der Wissenschaften, Jahrgang 1904, pp. 1–121, Prag, 1905.
[An exhaustive anthropometric report on new material.]

MAURELLE, ANTONIO. See Barrington, Daines.

276. MENEFEE, C. A. Historical and descriptive sketch book of Napa, Sonoma, Lake, and Mendocino. Napa City, 1873.

277. MEREDITH, H. C. Archaeology of California: Central and Northern California. In Moorehead, W. K., Prehistoric implements, Section ix, pp. 258–294, Cincinnati, [1900].

278. MERRIAM, C. HART. The dawn of the world: myths and weird tales told by the Mewan Indians of California. Cleveland, 1910.
[Prepared for the general public, but contains some priceless fragments of the traditions of perished groups.]

279. ———. Distribution and classification of the Mewan stock of California. Amer. Anthrop., n. s. vol. ix, pp. 338–357, 1907.
[Full of important data on the ethno-geography of the Miwok and their valley neighbors.]

280. ———. Distribution of Indian tribes in the southern Sierra and adjacent parts of the San Joaquin valley, California. Science, n. s. vol. xix, pp. 912–917, 1914.
[An attempt to conform the distribution of Indians to biological life zones. The ethnic data are valuable.]

281. ———. The Indian population of California. Amer. Anthrop., n. s. vol. vii, pp. 594–606, 1905.
[The only serious attempt to approach this subject critically.]

282 ———. Indian village and camp sites in Yosemite Valley. Sierra Club Bulletin, vol. x, pp. 202–209, San Francisco, 1917.

283. ———. Some little-known basket materials. Science, n. s. vol. xvii, p. 826, 1903.

284. ———. Totemism in California. Amer. Anthrop., n. s. vol. x, pp. 558–562, 1908.

285. MERRIAM, JOHN C. Recent cave exploration in California. Amer. Anthrop., n. s. vol. viii, pp. 221–228, 1906.

286. ———. Recent cave exploration in California. International Congress of Americanists, XVth sess., 1906, vol. ii, pp. 139–146, Quebec, 1907.

287. MERRILL, RUTH EARL. Plants used in basketry by the California Indians. Univ. Cal. Publs. Amer. Archaeol. and Ethnol., vol. xx, no. 13 (in press. 1923).

288. MICHELSON, TRUMAN H. Two alleged Algonquian languages of California. Amer. Anthrop., n. s. vol. xvi, pp. 361–367, 1914.
    [Wiyot and Yurok.]

289. MILLER, JOAQUIN. Life amongst the Modocs. London, 1873.

290. MILLER, M. L. The so-called California Diggers. Popular Science Monthly, vol. L, pp. 201–214, 1897.

291. ———. Der Untergang der Maidu oder Diggerindianer in Kalifornien. Globus, B. LXXII, pp. 111–113, Braunschweig, 1897.

292. M'KEE, REDICK. Indian population of Northwestern California. In Schoolcraft, Indian Tribes, vol. III, p. 634, Phila., 1853.
    ———. See McKee, Redick.

293. MÖLLHAUSEN, B. Diary of a journey from the Mississippi to the coasts of the Pacific with a U. S. exploring expedition. Vols. I–II. London. 1860.

294. ———. Wanderungen durch die Prairien und Wüsten des westlichen Nord-amerika. Leipzig, 1860.

295. MOONEY, JAMES. The Ghost-dance religion. Fourteenth Rept. Bur. Ethn., pt. 2, Washington, 1896.
    [This monumental and unique work contains brief notices of the Northern Paiute and Washo.]

296. ———. Notes on the Cosumnes tribes of California. Amer. Anthrop., vol. III, pp. 259–262, 1890.
    [Data from Col. Z. A. Rice, who "recollects" stone axes, scaffold burial, boiling in clay-lined pits, and terrapin rattles worn on the knee!]

MOOREHEAD, W. K. See Yates, L. G. ; Meredith, H. C.

MOURELLE, F. A. See Maurelle.

297. NELSON, E. W. The Panamint and Saline Valley Indians. Amer. Anthrop., vol. IV, pp. 371–372, 1891.

298. NELSON, N. C. The Ellis Landing shellmound. Univ. Cal. Publs. Amer. Archaeol. and Ethnol., vol. VII, pp. 357–426, 1910.
    [This and the monograph by Uhle are the only scientific accounts dealing at any length with particular California shellmounds.]

299. ———. Flint working by Ishi. Holmes Anniversary Volume, pp. 397–402, Washington, 1916.

300. ———. Shellmounds of the San Francisco bay region. Univ. Cal. Publs. Amer. Archaeol. and Ethnol., vol. VII, pp. 309–356, 1909.
    [The classic paper on the subject. Its only fault is that it leaves off before discussing culture in detail.]

301. O'KEEFE, J. J. The buildings and churches of the Mission of Santa Barbara. Santa Barbara, 1886.

302. OETTEKING, BRUNO. Morphological and metrical variation in skulls from San Miguel Island, California. I, The sutura nasofrontalis. Indian Notes and Monographs, vol. VII, no. 2, pp. [47]–[85], 1920.

OÑATE. See Zárate-Salmerón.

303. PALMER, EDWARD. Plants used by the Indians of the United States. Amer. Nat., vol. XII, pp. 593–606, 646–655, 1878.
    [The flora of southern California figures largely in this paper.]

304. PALMER, FRANK M. Nucleus of Southwestern Museum. Out West, vol. XXII, pp. 23–34, 1905.
[Partial description of the Palmer-Campbell collection of southern California archæology.]

305. PALOU, F. Noticias de la Nueva California. Vols. I–IV. San Francisco, 1874.

306. ———. Noticias de las Californias. Documentos para la Historia de Mexico, ser. IV, vols. VI–VII, 1857.

307. ———. Relacion Historica de la vida . . . de . . . Fray Junípero Serra. Mexico, 1787. (Same, English trans. by Rev. J. Adam, San Francisco, 1884.)

308. PÉROUSE, J. F. G. DE LA. Voyage autour du monde. Vols. I–IV. Paris, 1797.

309. POPE, SAXTON T. The medical history of Ishi. Univ. Cal. Publs. Amer. Archaeol. and Ethnol., vol. XIII, pp. 175–213, 1920.

310. ———. Yahi archery. Ibid., pp. 103–152, 1918.

PORTOLÁ, G. DE. See Teggart, F. J., ed.; Smith, Donald E., and Teggart.

311. POWELL, J. W. Indian linguistic families of America north of Mexico. Seventh Rept. Bur. Amer. Ethn., pp. 1–142, Washington, 1891.

312. POWERS, STEPHEN. Aborigines of California: an Indo-Chinese study. Atlantic Monthly, pp. 313–323, March, 1874.
[A wild little speculation.]

313. ———. Tribes of California [and variant titles]. Overland Monthly, 1st ser., vols. VIII–XIV, passim, 1872–75.
[The basis of the following.]

314. ———. Tribes of California. Cont. N. Am. Ethn., vol. III, Washington, 1877. (Includes Appendix: Linguistics, by J. W. Powell.)
[The value of this remarkable work has been discussed in the preface. It is fundamental.]

315. PRIESTLEY, HERBERT I., ed. The Colorado River campaign, 1781–1782. Diary of Pedro Fagés. Univ. Cal., Acad. Pac. Coast Hist. Publs., vol. III, no. 2, pp. [133]–[233], 1913.

316. PURDY, CARL. Pomo Indian baskets and their makers. Out West, vol. XV, no. 6, pp. 438–449, December, 1901; vol. XVI, no. 1, pp. 8–19; no. 2, pp. 151–158; no. 3, pp. 262–273, 1902.
[Useful.]

317. PUTNAM, F. W. Evidence of the work of man on objects from Quaternary caves in California. Amer. Anthrop., n. s. vol. VIII, pp. 229–235, 1906.

318. ———, and others. Reports upon archaeological and ethnological collections from vicinity of Santa Barbara. Rept. U. S. Geog. Surv. west of the 100th Meridian [Wheeler Surv. Rept.], vol. VII, Archaeology, Washington, 1879.
[This comprehensive volume on the region of the archipelago is still the fundamental work on the archaeology of California. It contains sections by C. C. Abbott, Lucien Carr, A. S. Gatschet, S. S. Haldeman, H. W. Henshaw, Paul Schumacher, H. C. Yarrow, which are separately cited.]

319. PUTNAM, G. R. A Yuma cremation. Amer. Anthrop., vol. VIII, pp. 264–267, 1895.

320. RADIN, PAUL. Wappo Texts. First Series. Univ. Cal. Publs. Amer. Archaeol. and Ethnol. (in press, 1923).
[One of the few large collections of native texts from California.]

321. RAU, CHARLES. Prehistoric fishing in Europe and North America. Smithson. Cont. Knowledge, vol. xxv, Washington, 1884.
[Pages 254–256 refer to California shell mounds, especially a site near Cape Mendocino examined by John J. McLean.]

322. READ, CHARLES H. An account of a collection of ethnographical specimens formed during Vancouver's voyage. Journ. Anthrop. Inst. Great Britain and Ireland, vol. xxi, pp. 99–108, 1892.
[Chumash spear thrower, harpoon, etc.]

323. REID, [or RIED] HUGO. The Indians of Los Angeles County. Los Angeles Star, 1852. Republished by Alexander S. Taylor in the California Farmer, vol. xiv, Jan 11–Feb. 8, 1861. [See W. J. Hoffman.]
[The fullest data on the Gabrielino.]

324. RILEY, J. H. Vocabulary of the Kah-we'yah and Kah-so'-wah Indians. Historical Magazine, 2d ser., vol. iii, pp. 238–240, 1868.
[The tribes are Yokuts, the vocabulary is Miwok.]

325. RIVET, PAUL. Recherches anthropologiques sur la Basse Californie. Jour. Soc. Americ., n. s., vol. vi. pp. 147–253, 1909.

326. ROYCE, CHARLES C. Indian land cessions in the United States. Eighteenth Rept. Bur. Amer. Ethn., pt. 2, pp. 521–694, Washington, 1899.
[A useful work. California is of course represented.]

327. RUSSELL, FRANK. The Pima Indians. Twenty-sixth Rept. Bur. Amer. Ethn., pp. 3–389, Washington, 1908.
[An extremely valuable work, describing a tribe usually reckoned as Southwestern but presenting innumerable resemblances to those of the lower Colorado river.]

328. RUST, HORATIO N. A cache of stone bowls in California. Amer. Anthrop., n. s. vol. viii, pp. 686–687, 1906.

329. ———. The obsidian blades of California. Amer. Anthrop., n. s. vol. vii, pp. 688–695, 1905.

330. ———. A puberty ceremony of the Mission Indians. Amer. Anthrop., n. s. vol. viii, pp. 28–32, 1906.

331. SANCHEZ, NELLIE VAN DE GRIFT. Spanish and Indian place names of California. San Francisco, 1914.
[The best general work on the subject.]

332. SAPIR, EDWARD. The fundamental elements of Northern Yana. Univ. Calif. Publs. Amer. Archaeol. and Ethnol., vol. xiii, pp. 215–234, 1922.

333. ———. Luck-stones among the Yana. Journ. Amer. Folk-lore, vol. xxi, p. 42, 1908.

334. ———. Notes on the Takelma Indians of southwestern Oregon. Amer. Anthrop., n. s. vol. ix, pp. 251–275, 1907.
[An invaluable little paper dealing with a region on which practically nothing else is available. The data are only fragments of memories, but the author presents them with such discriminating precision that they picture the culture accurately.]

335. ———. The position of Yana in the Hokan stock. Univ. Cal. Publs. Amer. Archaeol. and Ethnol., vol. xiii, pp. 1–34, 1917.

336. ———. Religious ideas of the Takelma Indians of southwestern Oregon. Journ. Amer. Folk-lore, vol. xx, pp. 33–49, 1907.

337. ———. Song recitative in Paiute mythology. Ibid., vol. xxiii, pp. 455–472, 1910.

338. ———. Terms of relationship and the levirate. Amer. Anthrop., n. s. vol. xviii, pp. 327–337, 1916.
[Largely Yahi.]

339. SAPIR, EDWARD. Text analyses of three Yana dialects. Univ. Cal. Publs. Amer. Archaeol. and Ethnol., vol. xx, no. 15 (in press, 1923).

340. ———. Wiyot and Yurok, Algonkin languages of California. Amer. Anthrop., n. s. vol. xv, pp. 617–646, 1913.

341. ———. Yana terms of relationship. Univ. Cal. Publs. Amer. Archaeol. and Ethnol., vol. XIII, pp. 153–173, 1918.

342. ———. Yana texts. Ibid., vol. IX, pp. 1–235, 1910.
[A scholarly work, as important ethnologically as philologically.]

343. SCHMIDT, W. Die Altstämme Nordamerikas. Festschrift Eduard Seler, pp. 471–502, Stuttgart, 1922.
[Mostly on the tribes of California. A reconstructive historical interpretation of their culture.]

344. SCHOOLCRAFT, HENRY R. Historical and statistical information, respecting the history, condition and prospects of the Indian tribes of the United States. Vols. I–VI. Philadelphia, 1851–57. Same, printed under the title "Archives of Aboriginal Knowledge," vols. I–VI, Philadelphia, 1860.
[See Gibbs, Henly, Johnson, Kern. M'Kee. There is a California passage by Schoolcraft himself in vol. v, pp. 214–217.]

345. SCHUMACHER, PAUL. Ancient graves and shell-heaps of California. Ann. Rept. Smithson. Inst. for 1874, pp. 335–350, Washington, 1875.
[Careful work in the little explored coast region of San Luis Obispo.]

346. ———. Die anfertigung der angelhaken aus muschelschalen bei den früheren bewohnern der inseln im Santa Barbara Canal. Arch. für Anthrop., vol. VIII, pp. 223–224, 1875.

347. ———. The method of manufacture of several articles by the former Indians of southern California. [Eleventh] Ann. Rept. Peabody Mus., vol. II, pp. 258–268, 1878.
[Stone pots, mortars, digging stick weights, pipes.]

348. ———. The method of manufacture of soapstone pots. Rept. U. S. Geog. Surv. west of the 100th meridian [Wheeler Surv. Rept.], vol. VII, Archaeology, pp. 117–121, 1879.

349. ———. The methods of manufacturing pottery and baskets among the Indians of Southern California. [Twelfth] Ann. Rept. Peabody Mus., vol. II, pp. 521–525, 1880.

350. ———. Remarks on the kjökken-möddings on the northwest coast of America. Ann. Rept. Smithson. Inst. for 1873, pp. 354–362, Washington, 1874.
[Southern Oregon coast.]

351. ———. Researches in the kjökkenmöddings and graves of a former population of the Santa Barbara Islands and the adjacent mainland. Bull. U. S. Geol. Surv., vol. III, pp. 37–56, Washington, 1877.
[Useful.]

352. SCOULER, JOHN. Observations on the indigenous tribes of the N. W. coast of America. Journ. Royal Geog. Soc., vol. XI, pp. 215–249, London, 1841.
[Includes the Coulter vocabularies.]

SERRA, JUNÍPERO. See Early Western history.

353. SINCLAIR, W. J. Recent investigations bearing upon the question of the occurrence of Neocene man in the auriferous gravels of California. Univ. Cal. Publs. Amer. Archaeol. and Ethnol., vol. VII, pp. 107–130, 1908.

354. SITJAR, BONAVENTURE. Vocabulary of the language of San Antonio Mission, California. Shea's library of Amer. Linguistics, vol. VII, New York, 1861.

SLOCUM, BOWEN AND COMPANY. *See* History of Napa and Lake Counties, California.

355. SMITH, DONALD E., *and* TEGGART, FREDERICK J., *eds.* Diary of Gaspar de Portolá during the California expedition of 1769–1770. Univ. Cal., Acad. Pacific Coast History, Pubs., vol. I, no. 3, pp. [31]–[89], 1909.

356. SMITH, WAYLAND H. The relief of Campo. Out West, vol. XXII, pp. 13–22, 1905.

357. SPARKMAN, PHILIP STEDMAN. The culture of the Luiseño Indians. Univ. Cal. Publs. Amer. Archaeol. and Ethnol., vol. VIII, pp. 187–234, 1908.
    [Compact. Fullest on the material side of the civilization.]

358. ———. A Luiseño tale. Journ. Amer. Folk-lore, vol. XXI, pp. 35–36, 1908.

359. ———. Sketch of the grammar of the Luiseño language. Amer. Anthrop., n. s. vol. VII, pp. 656–662, 1905.

360. SPENCER, D. L. Notes on the Maidu Indians of Butte County. Journ. Amer. Folk-lore, vol. XXI, pp. 242–245, 1908.

361. SPIER, LESLIE. Southern Diegueño customs. Univ. Cal. Publs. Amer. Archaeol. and Ethnol., vol. XX, no. 16 (in press, 1923).

362. SPINDEN, H. J. The Nez Percé Indians. Mem. Amer. Anthrop. Asso., vol. II, pp. 171–274, 1908.
    [The best account of a group having many affinities with the Klamath and Modoc.]

363. STEARNS, ROBERT E. C. On certain aboriginal implements from Napa County, California. Amer. Nat., vol. XVI, pp. 203–209, 1882.

364. ———. Ethno-conchology. Rept. U. S. Nat. Mus. for 1887, pp. 297–334, 1889.
    [Useful.]

365. ———. On the Nishinam game of " Ha " and the Boston game of " Props." Amer. Anthrop., vol. III, pp. 353–358, 1890.

366. ———. Shell-money. Amer. Nat., vol. III, pp. 1–5, 1869.

367. STEWART, GEORGE W. Two Yokuts traditions. Journ. Amer. Folk-lore, vol. XXI, pp. 237–239, 1908.

368. ———. A Yokuts creation myth. Ibid., vol. XIX, p. 322, 1906.

369. STRATTON, R. B. Captivity of the Oatman girls. New York, 1857.
    [Tries hard to be lurid, but a few facts on the Mohave have crept in.]

370. TASSIN [or " FASSIN "], A. G. The Concow Indians. Overland Monthly, 2d ser., vol. IV, pp. 7–14, 1884.

371. ———. Un-koi-to ; the Savior. A legend of the Concow Indians. Ibid., pp. 141–150, 1884.

372. TAYLOR, ALEXANDER S. Bibliografa Californica, 1510–1865. Sacramento Union, June 25, 1863–March 13, 1866.

373. ———. Indianology of California. California Farmer and Journal of Useful Sciences, vols. XIII–XX, San Francisco, Feb. 22, 1860, to Oct. 30, 1863.
    [A very miscellaneous but famous and valuable collection of data on every aspect of the Indian history of the state. The author was untrained as a scholar, indefatigable in his inquiries, and a most industrious compiler. He obtained access to many rare publications and to a number of manuscript sources no longer available, and omitted nothing that he could publish or republish. Very few files of the California Farmer are extant and a republication of the Indianology, with annotations and corrections of typographical errors, is greatly to be desired.]

374. TEGGART, FREDERICK J., *ed.* The Anza expedition of 1775–1776. Diary of Pedro Font. Univ. Cal., Acad. Pac. Coast Hist., Pubs., vol. III, no. 1, pp. [1]–[131], 1913.

375. ———. The official account of the Portolá expedition of 1769–1770. Ibid., vol. I, no. 2, pp. [15]–[29], 1909.
   [The first of a series of important editions and translations of documents bearing on the Spanish exploration of California.]

376. ———. The Portolá expedition of 1769–1770. Diary of Miguel Costansó. Ibid., vol. II, no. 4, pp. [161]–[327], 1911.

   TEGGART, FREDERICK J. *See* Smith, Donald E., and Teggart.

377. TEN KATE, H. Materiaux pour servir à l'anthropologie de la presqu'île californienne. Bull. Soc. d'Anthrop., pp. 551–569, 1884.

378. TERNAUX-COMPANS, HENRI, *tr.* Voyage en Californie, par D. Pedro Fagés. Nouvelles Annales des Voyages, vol. CI, pp. 145–182, 311–347, Paris, 1844.
   [The Spanish text, with English translation by H. I. Priestley, is in press in Univ. Cal., Acad. Pac. Coast Hist. Publ., under the title, Pedro Fagés, Noticias de Monterey.]

379. THOMPSON, LUCY. To the American Indian. Eureka, California, 1916.
   [Written by a Yurok on the Yurok. Valuable.]

   TURNER, W. W. *See* Whipple, A. W., Ewbank, and Turner.

380. UHLE, MAX. The Emeryville shellmound. Univ. Cal. Publs. Amer. Archaeol. and Ethnol., vol. VII, pp. 1–106, 1907.
   [An exhaustive description and interpretation by an investigator of wide comparative experience.]

381. UNITED STATES DEPARTMENT OF COMMERCE. Bureau of the Census. Indian population in the United States and Alaska, 1910. Washington, 1915.
   [The results of the first effort of the Bureau to obtain particular statistics on the Indian, and the only census worth anything as regards the Indians of California. Sections on Number, Tribes, Sex, Age, Fecundity, and Vitality by R. B. Dixon.]

382. U. S. GEOGRAPHICAL SURVEYS OF THE TERRITORY OF THE U. S. WEST OF THE 100TH MERIDIAN, in charge of First Lieut. Geo. M. Wheeler. Reports. Vol. VII, Archaeology, Washington, 1879. (*See* Putnam, F. W.)

383. VANCOUVER, GEORGE. Voyage of discovery to the North Pacific Ocean, and round the world, 1790–95. Vols. I–III. London, 1798.

   VAN HEMERT ENGERT, ADOLPH. *See* Hemert-Engert, Adolph van.

384. VENEGAS, MIGUEL. Noticia de la California, y de su conquista temporal y espiritual hasta el tiempo presente. Vols. I–III. Madrid, 1757. *Same,* English trans., vols. I–II, London, 1759; *Same,* French trans., vols. I–III, Paris, 1767.

385. VIZCAINO, SEBASTIAN. Diary of Sebastian Vizcaino, 1602–1603. Transl. in Bolton, Spanish exploration in the Southwest, pp. 52–103, New York, 1916.

   VON BAER, K. E. *See* Baer, K. E. von.

   VON HELMERSEN, G. *See* Baer, K. E. von, and Helmersen.

386. WARDLE, H. NEWELL. Stone implements of surgery (?) from San Miguel Island, California. Amer. Anthrop., n. s. vol. XV, pp. 656–660, 1913.

387. WASHINGTON, F. B. Customs of the Indians of western Tehama county. Journ. Amer. Folk-lore, vol. XIX, p. 144, 1906.

388. WATERMAN, T. T. Analysis of the Mission Indian creation story. Amer. Anthrop., n. s. vol. XI, 41–55, 1909.

389. WATERMAN, T. T.   Diegueño identification of color with the cardinal points. Journ. Amer. Folk-lore, vol. xxi, pp. 40–42, 1908.

390. ———.   The last wild tribe of California.   Pop. Sci. Mo., pp. 233–244, March, 1915.
     [Story of the extinction of the Yahi.]

391. ———.   Native musical instruments of California, and some others.   Out West, vol. xxviii, pp. 276–286, 1908.

392. ———.   The phonetic elements of the Northern Paiute language.   Univ. Cal. Publs. Amer. Archaeol. and Ethnol., vol. x, pp. 13–44, 1911.

393. ———.   The religious practices of the Diegueño Indians.   Ibid., vol. viii, pp. 271–358, 1910.
     [A vivid and accurate portrayal.]

394. ———.   The Yana Indians.   Ibid., vol. xiii, pp. 35–102, 1918.

395. ———.   Yurok affixes.   Ibid., vol. xx, no. 18 (in press, 1923).

396. ———.   Yurok geography.   Ibid., vol. xvi, pp. 177–314, 1920.
     [An exhaustive study of the ethnogeographical basis of a culture, with many references to the culture.]

     WHEELER, GEORGE M.   See U. S. Geographical Survey West of the 100th Meridian.

397. WHIPPLE, A. W., EWBANK, THOMAS, and TURNER, WM. W.   Report upon the Indian tribes.   U. S. War Dept. Repts. of Explorations and Surveys . . . for a Railroad from the Mississippi River to the Pacific Ocean, 1853–4, vol. iii, Washington, 1855.
     [Some useful data on the Mohave and Chemehuevi.]

398. WILKES, CHARLES.   Western America, including California and Oregon. Philadelphia, 1849.

     ———.   See Hale, Horatio.

399. WILLOUGHBY, CHARLES C.   Feather mantles of California.   Amer. Anthrop., n. s. vol. xxiv, pp. 432–437, 1922.

400. WOOD, L. K.   The discovery of Humboldt bay.   Humboldt Times (Eureka, California), 1856.
     [Probably most accessible in W. W. Elliott and Co.'s History of Humboldt County, 1881, one of the innumerable anonymous compilations, avowed only by their publishers, of which H. H. Bancroft's " Works " is the most ambitious and glorified example. Many of the county histories contain data that are not available elsewhere.]

401. WOODRUFF, CHARLES E.   Dances of the Hupa Indians.   Amer. Anthrop., vol. v, pp. 53–61, 1892.

402. WOODS, ETHEL B.   La Piedra Pintada de la Carrisa.
     [Privately printed, San Luis Obispo, California.]

403. WOOSLEY, DAVID J.   Cahuilla tales.   Journ. Amer. Folk-lore, vol. xxi, pp. 239–240, 1908.

404. WOZENCRAFT, O. M.   [Report on the Indians of California.]   Rept. Com. Ind. Aff. for 1851, pp. 224–231, 242–249, Washington, 1851.   (Sen. Ex. Docs. vol. iii, 32d Cong., 1st sess.)

405. WRANGELL, FERDINAND VON.   Observations recueillies par l'Amiral Wrangell sur les habitants des côtes nord-ouest de l'Amérique; extraites du Russe par M. le prince Emanuel Galitzin.   Nouvelles Annales des Voyages, tome i, Paris, 1853.

406. YARROW, H. C.   Report of the operations of a special party for making ethnological researches in the vicinity of Santa Barbara. Rept. U. S. Geog. Surv. west of the 100th Meridian [Wheeler Surv. Rept.], vol. VII, Archaeology, pp. 32–46, Washington, 1879.

407. YATES, L. G.   Aboriginal weapons of California.   Overland Monthly, 2d ser., vol. XXVII, pp. 337–342, 1896.

408. ———.   Archaeology of California : Southern California.   In Moorehead, W. K., Prehistoric Implements, Section VII, pp. 230–252, Cincinnati, [1900].

409. ———.   Charmstones or " plummets " from California.   Ann. Rept. Smithson. Inst. for 1886, pp. 296–305, Washington, 1889.

410. ———.   The deserted homes of a lost people.   Overland Monthly, 2d ser., vol. XXVII, pp. 538–544, 1896.
        [The Chumash islanders.]

411. ———.   Fragments of the history of a lost tribe.   Amer. Anthrop., vol. IV, pp. 373–376, 1891.

412. ———.   Indian medicine men.   Overland Monthly, 2d ser., vol. XXVIII, pp. 171–182, 1896.
        [A little on California is included.]

413. ———.   Indian petroglyphs in California.   Overland Monthly, 2d ser., vol. XXVIII, pp. 657–661, 1896.

414. ———.   Prehistoric man in California.   Santa Barbara, 1887.

415. ZÁRATE-SALMERÓN.   Relacion.   Translated in Land of Sunshine, vol. XI, no. 6; vol. XII, nos. 1 and 2, Nov., 1899, to Jan., 1900.   Transl. in Bolton, Spanish exploration in the Southwest, pp. 268–280, New York, 1916.
        [Oñate's trip from New Mexico to California in 1604–05. The last section is of the greatest importance for the Yuman tribes of the Colorado.]

CLASSIFICATION OF TITLES BY SUBJECT.

ARCHAEOLOGY.

General or comparative: 173, 175, 187, 212, 227, 285, 286, 317, 353, 364, 409.

Northern coast: 258, 321, 350.

Pictographs: 4, 124, 184, 262, 263, 402, 413.

San Francisco Bay: 147, 277, 298, 300, 363, 380.

San Joaquin Valley: 186, 206, 215, 277.

Southern California: 1, 44, 113, 166, 177, 185, 186, 304, 318, 328, 329, 345–349, 351, 382, 386, 406–411.

ETHNOLOGY—TOPICAL.

Basketry: 10, 21, 74, 75, 194, 199, 213, 214, 216, 271, 283, 287, 316.

Ethnobotany: 27, 57, 63, 240, 283, 287, 303.

Ethnogeography: 13, 14, 18, 22, 151, 156, 158, 219, 225, 247, 249, 258, 279, 280–282, 292, 311, 323, 326, 331, 381, 394, 396, 415.

Material culture: 16, 20, 24, 60, 64, 66, 70, 76, 82, 86, 97, 161, 169, 176, 186, 189, 195, 210, 224, 261, 267, 272, 274, 299, 310, 322, 323, 357, 361, 364–366, 391, 399.

Myths and beliefs: 12, 15, 17, 43, 48, 67, 68, 69, 73, 76, 79, 81, 88, 89, 101–107, 120, 137, 150, 154, 157, 159, 160, 170, 193, 228, 234, 241, 244, 245, 250, 278, 320, 337, 342, 358, 361, 367, 368, 371, 388, 403.

Religion: 11, 19, 25, 42, 71, 72, 82, 86, 90, 91, 100, 104–106, 108, 125, 138, 165, 226, 238, 295, 323, 333, 361, 379, 393, 412.

Social institutions: 23, 82, 86, 145, 146, 148, 149, 152, 210, 218, 248, 266, 284, 338, 361, 379.

ETHNOLOGY—TRIBAL.

General or comparative: 9, 75, 90, 118, 145, 146, 180, 181, 210, 211, 217, 218, 223, 227, 238, 242, 259, 268, 281, 287, 313, 314, 334, 343, 344, 355, 373, 375, 378, 398.

Achomawi and Atsugewi: 67, 73, 81, 83.

Baja California: 7, 61, 112, 384.

Cahuilla and Cupeño: 27, 146, 188, 224, 260, 403.

Chemehuevi: 98, 234, 397.

Chilula: 31, 154, 163.

Chimariko: 76.

Chumash: 41, 51, 70, 113, 122, 129, 171, 177, 274, 318, 322, 383, 385, 410.

Costanoan: 55, 59, 109, 131, 228.

Diegueño: 71, 72, 100–108, 112, 176, 356, 361, 389, 398.

Gabrielino: 42, 169, 182, 323.

Hupa: 157, 161, 273, 401.

Juaneño: 42.

Karok: 142, 213, 292.

Kato: 158, 159.

Koso: 64, 110, 297.

Luiseño: 72, 146, 200, 201, 241, 357, 358.

Maidu: 58, 74, 75, 79, 82, 89, 90, 91, 121, 186, 203, 290, 291, 360, 370, 371, 399.
Miwok (Interior): 14, 17, 23, 75, 98, 149, 150, 225, 228, 278–280, 284, 296.
Miwok (Coast): 13, 14, 18, 60, 111, 282.
· Modoc and Klamath: 16, 63, 65, 69, 97, 137, 138, 289.
Mohave: 41, 43, 62, 98, 101, 168, 237, 369, 397, 414.
Mono: 98, 148.
Oregon: 34, 35, 99, 119, 120, 144, 217, 255, 271, 334, 336, 362.
Pomo: 10, 11, 12, 13, 19, 20, 21, 22, 57, 125, 151, 178, 179, 186, 194, 195, 216, 265, 276, 316.
Salinan: 268.
Serrano groups: 62, 146.
Shasta: 48, 86, 88, 120, 292.
Southern California: 146, 183, 186, 198, 214, 232, 257, 293, 294, 303, 330, 384, 388, 397.
Tolowa: 99.
Wailaki: 57, 156.
Wappo: 179, 250, 320.
Washo: 24, 295.
Wintun and Patwin: 13, 25, 68, 75, 266, 267, 387.
Wiyot: 114, 244, 245, 258, 400.
Yana and Yahi: 3, 69, 75, 229, 299, 309, 310, 333, 338, 342, 390, 394.
Yokuts: 62, 98, 148, 193, 228, 248, 367, 368.
Yuki: 13, 57, 221.
Yuma and Yuman tribes: 2, 28, 41, 62, 98, 146, 170, 249, 315, 319, 415.
Yurok: 130, 142, 213, 256, 265, 292, 379, 396.

LANGUAGES.

Comparative: 85, 92, 93, 94, 95, 96, 134–136, 141, 143, 204, 230, 235, 252–254, 288, 311, 314, 335, 341, 352, 373.
Athabascan: 153–155, 157, 159, 162, 166.
Chimariko: 76.
Chumash: 220, 231.
Costanoan: 5, 6, 220, 231, 270.
Esselen: 174, 231.
Karok: 230.
Lutuami: 137, 138.
Maidu: 78, 80.
Miwok: 13, 14, 139, 222, 230, 279, 324.
Pomo: 13, 230.
Salinan: 231, 268, 354.
Shastan: 77, 87.
Shoshonean: 49, 50, 134, 233, 240, 359, 392.
Washo: 243.
Wintun: 13, 84.
Wiyot: 230, 288, 340.
Yana: 332, 335, 339, 342.
Yokuts: 246, 247.
Yukian: 13, 230, 246, 320.
Yuman: 140, 236, 239.
Yurok: 230, 288, 340, 395.

PHYSICAL TYPES.

Living: 32, 33, 36, 192.
Skeletal: 53, 54, 190, 191, 275, 302, 325, 377.

CLASSIFIED SUBJECT INDEX

A. TANGIBLE CULTURE

BODY AND DRESS:

Body garments, 76, 173, 240, 276, 283, 292, 310, 317, 326, 405, 467, 519, 572, 597, 634, 651, 654, 721, 804.

Robes, capes, 76, 173, 276, 327, 406, 416, 467, 519, 546, 615, 634, 654, 805, 935.

Hats and caps, 76, 92, 155, 173, 311, 327, 332, 467, 532, 548, 561, 591, 597, 654, 698, 700, 807, 808; pl. 2, 53, 55, 71, 73.

Hair nets, 156, 173, 276, 293, 405, 416, 808, 934; pl. 55, 72.

Footgear, 76, 144, 240, 283, 292, 311, 317, 323, 327, 405, 519, 597, 654, 721, 805, 807; pl. 62.

Snowshoe, 76, 295, 327, 405, 410, 807.

Coiffure, 77, 293, 299, 406, 519, 598, 633, 721, 729, 803, 934; pl. 57, 64, 72.

Comb, 327, 406, 519.

Ornaments, 240, 406, 739.

Paint, 56, 186, 729, 730, 732, 733, 765; pl. 61.

Tattoo, 77, 146, 173, 215, 293, 311, 357, 406, 467, 519, 520, 521, 641, 651, 675, 721, 729, 808.

Deformation, mutilations, 77, 240, 311, 326, 406, 519; pl. 65.

Postures, 520, 728.

SUBSISTENCE:

Foods, 40, 84, 144, 174, 238, 309, 323, 358, 409, 467, 523–527, 547, 591, 615, 631, 694, 814.

Food preferences, 88, 293, 411, 649.

Foods, rejected, 84, 111, 216, 310, 409, 526, 547, 631, 652, 737, 814.

Insects, worms, etc., 84, 111, 409, 525, 527, 592, 652; pl. 61.

Fish, mollusks, 84, 409, 467, 525, 722, 737, 920, 922–925, 933.

Nets, weirs, fish traps, 58, 85, 93, 132, 148, 174, 213, 214, 246, 294, 309, 325, 359, 410, 415, 529, 652, 737, 815, 816, 933; pl. 4, 6, 7, 33, 59, 67.

Fishhooks, 326, 564, 652, 815.

Fish poison, 529, 652, 817.

Snaring, trapping, 86, 213, 294, 309, 326, 528, 530, 615, 652, 817; pl. 46.

Surrounding, 144, 409, 528, 817.

Decoys, 86, 342, 359, 410, 528, 652, 817; pl. 8.

Other hunting methods, 144, 174, 294, 295, 326, 395, 410, 530, 572, 652, 817.

Ethnobotany, 649, 694–696.

Digging stick, 563, 736, 935.

Seed beater, 91, 172, 291, 332, 415, 701, 814; pl. 24, 29.

Mortar, pestle, hopper, metate, grinding slab, 87, 91, 148, 153, 172, 214, 284, 291, 323, 358, 411, 448, 527–528, 548, 562, 572, 592, 631, 653, 695–698, 700, 722, 736, 737, 814, 926–930, 932; pl. 16, 24, 44, 45, 60, 66.

Pulverized food, 293, 294, 323, 409, 528, 572, 592, 649, 652, 695, 736, 814.

SUBSISTENCE—Continued.

Storage, 85, 91, 242, 294, 309, 410, 447, 548, 561, 592, 598, 618, 699, 828; pl. 38, 54, 60.

Leaching, 88, 293, 467, 524, 527, 649, 814; pl. 14.

Cooking, 87, 156, 527, 592, 652, 654, 695, 722, 737, 814; pl. 23.

Stirrers, 87, 172, 291, 310, 411, 446, 447, 527, 572, 737, 829; pl. 17, 44.

Spoons, 93, 147, 174, 205, 284, 290, 310, 411; pl. 20.

Salt, 84, 174, 256, 294, 310, 340, 363, 467, 530, 546, 747, 762.

Agriculture, 597, 722, 735, 797, 803, 815; pl. 67.

HOUSES:

Earth house, 175, 276, 290, 312, 317, 327, 340, 358, 365, 407, 447, 572, 654, 704, 721, 731, 809, 811; pl. 56.

Plank house, 12, 18, 39, 78, 140, 289, 809; pl. 9, 10, 12.

Bark house, 111, 140, 141, 144, 146, 175, 213, 240, 284, 311, 317, 358, 407, 447, 468, 522, 572, 809.

Thatch or mat house, 241, 328, 340, 407, 468, 521, 522, 557, 572, 598, 608, 612, 618, 628, 634, 650, 703, 809; pl. 46.

Sweat house and dance house, 12, 41, 80, 140, 141, 144, 147, 156, 175, 189, 205, 213, 241, 284, 290, 312, 317, 328, 358, 365, 375, 387, 446, 447, 468, 522, 557, 572, 591, 608, 618, 628, 655, 703, 704, 722, 735, 793, 810; pl. 10, 13, 14, 56, 60.

Menstrual house, 80, 150, 254, 290, 299, 329, 358, 402, 409, 810.

Camps, shades, 140, 176, 241, 290, 311, 327, 358, 482, 506, 522, 655, 704, 765.

Partitions, beds, 79, 81, 290, 358, 409, 521, 557, 612.

Furniture, 79, 80, 93, 558; pl. 9, 10, 19.

TRANSPORTATION:

Boats, 83, 111, 126, 147, 155, 214, 243, 277, 291, 310, 329, 416, 558, 630, 634, 652, 654, 723, 812–813; pl. 3, 5, 13, 15.

Balsa and raft, 243, 277, 329, 359, 416, 468, 531, 608, 630, 652, 654, 723, 739, 813.

Paddles, 83, 330, 468, 559, 723, 813; pl. 67.

Ferrying, 35, 83, 174, 739, 813.

Carrying basket or frame, 91, 153, 172, 247, 291, 532, 571, 591, 597, 698, 699, 738, 814, 828; pl. 23, 24, 54, 73.

Carrying net, 173, 240, 247, 416, 467, 533, 592, 698, 699, 704, 722, 828.

Water basket (bottle), 533, 561, 571, 591, 597, 605, 628, 634, 701; pl. 53, 55.

Cradle, baby carrier, 92, 248, 291, 323, 327, 358, 534–537, 571, 704, 738, 829; pl. 35, 39, 40.

WEAPONS:

Bow and arrow, 89, 214, 277, 310, 332, 417, 530, 545, 559, 572, 591, 597, 632, 650, 652, 704, 751, 817–818; pl. 18, 78.

Quiver, 90, 323, 417, 752.

Arrow release, 417, 652, 818; pl. 18, 78.

969

GENERAL INDEX